Selected Plays

A Note on the Translations

This collection includes new translations of *Master Olof,
The Father, Creditors, The Stronger, Playing with Fire,* and
The Dance of Death (I). All other translations have previous-
ly appeared as follows:

August Strindberg, *Miss Julie*, trans. Evert Sprinchorn
(San Francisco: Chandler, 1961).

August Strindberg, *The Ghost Sonata* and *The Pelican,* in
The Chamber Plays, trans. Evert Sprinchorn (New York: E.
P. Dutton, 1962); paperback 2d revised edition (Minnea-
polis: University of Minnesota Press, 1981).

August Strindberg, *To Damascus* (I) and *Crimes and
Crimes*, trans. Evert Sprinchorn, in *The Genius of the Scandinavian Theater* (New York: The New American Library,
1964).

A Note on Stage Directions

The stage directions in these translations follow the
nineteenth-century Scandinavian custom of indicating left
and right from the point of view of the audience, not the
actor.

"We are poor lost souls — all of us!"
A Dream Play

Everyone should have some
Strindberg in their collection.

Rob, 1997

Selected Plays

August Strindberg

Translated and Introduced by Evert Sprinchorn

University of Minnesota Press □ Minneapolis

Published by the University of Minnesota Press
2037 University Avenue Southeast, Minneapolis MN 55414.
Published simultaneously in Canada
by Fitzhenry & Whiteside Limited, Markham.
Printed in the United States of America.

Library of Congress Cataloging-in-Publication Data

Strindberg, August, 1849–1912.
  Selected plays.

  Bibliography: p.
  1. Strindberg, August, 1849–1912 — Translations, English. I. Title.
PT9811.A3S635 1986b   839.7'26   86-4290
ISBN 0-8166-1506-3

The University of Minnesota
is an equal-opportunity
educator and employer.

With two actors I could create
a little world; and with three,
move it.

August Strindberg

Contents

Introduction

Strindberg's dramatic writings are as remarkable for their variety as for their quantity. The plays in this collection are meant to serve as an introduction to them by representing the different phases in Strindberg's career and the different styles and forms he either adopted or invented.

Although Strindberg began his creative career as a dramatist, he achieved his first unqualified success with the public and critics as a novelist when he published *The Red Room* in 1879. In his native Sweden, Strindberg is equally esteemed as novelist and dramatist. He is also Sweden's greatest social satirist. He differs from all the other truly great dramatists in that he was productive in nearly every form and genre of literature. In addition to his fifty or sixty plays (the number varies depending on whether one includes uncompleted works and how one counts double dramas and trilogies) and four novels, his collected works consist of two volumes of poetry, nine volumes of short stories, three volumes of cultural history, ten volumes of autobiography, and fifteen volumes of articles, essays, and sketches on every conceivable subject. If these writings are regrouped and arranged strictly in the order in which he wrote them, a significant pattern emerges: in each of the four major phases of his career the drama became the vehicle for his deepest thought and most daring techniques.

In the first phase, spanning the 1870s, Strindberg appears as a social critic rebelling against the establishment. In the 1880s the social rebel immerses himself in psychological studies. In his third phase, which links the nineteenth and twentieth centuries, the psychologist plunges into the depths of the soul and there discovers forces larger than social or psychological ones. A few years later the mystic attempts to describe and analyze the great comprehensive design formed out of individual destinies. In passing through these phases the young romantic writer becomes successively a realist, a symbolist, an expressionist, and a surrealist.

This dazzling variety has blinded many students, critics, and casual readers to Strindberg's accomplishments as a spokesman for his time and as a thinker for the ages, while many critics who are willing to accept him as a remarkable chronicler reprobate him for being the spokesman for reactionary and unsavory ideas.

An eminent professor of literature at one of America's larger universities once opined at a cocktail party that Strindberg could not be placed among the truly great creative artists because there was too much hatred in him. Pressed for evidence of this, the professor admitted he had read only *The Father* and *Miss Julie*, and those long ago. His point was that Strindberg's reputation reposed mainly on these plays and that they were filled with a venomous hatred of women. The young students who had formed an adoring circle around their mentor were left to infer how different Strindberg was from Ibsen and Shakespeare in his attitude toward women. Shakespeare had given us such adorable creatures as Juliet, Mariana, Desdemona, Beatrice, and Portia; and Ibsen had spearheaded the feminist movement in the latter half of the nineteenth century by writing *A Doll's House*. Nothing was said about Lady Macbeth as the incarnation of evil, or about Lear's anathemas denouncing the female sex, or about the revulsion against womankind expressed in the sonnets. No one noted the number of times that Ibsen allows women to offer up themselves on the altar of male genius. No one pointed out that the woman in one of Ibsen's earlier plays who calmly accepts the fact that her lot in life is to love, to sacrifice all, and then be forgotten is only one of many such women in the plays of the Norwegian "feminist." No one remarked that Ibsen himself disclaimed the honor of having worked for women's rights and that he was quite unclear about what those rights were. He was very clear, however, concerning women's function in the advancement of civilization: they were to be mothers, first of all, entrusted with the task of breeding and rearing, educating and disciplining children.

Except for the emphasis on discipline, Strindberg agreed with Ibsen that a woman's primary role in society was to be a mother. Coming from Strindberg, however, the thought always seemed antifeminist. Yet it was Strindberg, not Ibsen, who drew up a platform of women's rights (in his preface to a collection of short stories, *Getting Married*) in which he advocated that boys and girls should be allowed to mix more freely in school, that women should be given the franchise as soon as possible, and that separate bedrooms should be the rule in marriages to ensure women the right to possess their own bodies. Ibsen prudently left the idea of women's independence as a vague concept and won the adoration of the feminists. Strindberg was explicit and won their hatred.

Why? One answer can be found in Strindberg's short story "A Doll's House," a riposte to Ibsen's play. Strindberg regarded Ibsen's Nora with all her talk about miracles and sacrifices as a hysterical type, an unnatural woman who disliked physical sex. To Strindberg she was the product of a social class that was overcultured, and consequently she was of interest only to others of her class.

Strindberg himself said that his misogyny was largely theoretical, by which he meant that it was his contribution to the feminist question, a heatedly debated issue in the 1880s, just as it was to be three-quarters of a century later in America. (To the student of social history the feminist movement in the 1960s and 1970s seems like a repetition of events in Scandinavia.) His stand on the subject was intended to complement what he considered to be the narrow views of Ibsen.

Refusing to be identified with the feminist movement, Ibsen averred that his task had been the description of humanity. Strindberg would have said the same about himself. He would never have prosecuted the women's rights movement if he had not been passionately interested in the behavior of human beings. He first approached the matter as a sociologist might, but when he was drawn into a bitter conflict with the feminists, he began to see the whole question in the light of psychology, a subject that was coming into its own during those years. The feminist question provided the means by which he could enter certain unexplored areas of the human soul. Out of these investigations came, among other things, a five-volume autobiography and the penetrating psychological dramas *The Father* and *Miss Julie*.

He called his autobiography *The Son of a Servant* and gave it the subtitle "The Story of the Evolution of a Human Soul." The title indicated that his political sympathies were with the lower classes, and the subtitle suggested that he had aligned himself with the French naturalists, who believed that creative writers should adopt the experimental method of scientists, discounting the ideal and concerning themselves exclusively with physical reality. Writing as a scientist who had shed all social and religious prejudices and preconceptions and who believed he was studying the world objectively, Strindberg argued that parents were inevitably tyrannical, that the family was a prison, that children should be allowed to escape from it as soon as possible, that the natural instincts should be given full expression, and that masturbation would not lead to nervous debility but that sexual abstinence might. For espousing these advanced ideas, which only during the height of the Victorian age were deemed particularly dangerous, Strindberg was disowned by the young liberals and ostracized by virtually everybody. By the late 1880s Strindberg, who thought of himself as a great emancipator, was the most hated man in Sweden.

He closed his shop in Stockholm, moved to Berlin and then to Paris, where he occupied himself with alchemical experiments, hoping to prove that the so-called elements could be reduced further and that they could be transmuted one into another. For about five years the investigating scientist usurped the place of the creative writer. When he returned to writing, it became apparent that those years of scientific research had indeed effected a transmutation – not of the elements, however, but of Strindberg himself. The political agitator who had given currency to the term "the lower classes," the aggressive polemicist, the social satirist who had lampooned well-known and recognizable figures and institutions, the atheistic naturalist who had portrayed human beings as animals driven by their instincts, had been transformed into a religious thinker for whom the only reality was that of the spirit. To most of his countrymen the emergence of this new Strindberg was as deplorable an event as the appearance of the first Strindberg had been, but it confirmed them in their view that Strindberg had been quite mad all along. The dangerous radical who had overreached himself in his endeavors to undermine society had now suffered the just consequences: social and mental alienation.

Strindberg's active participation in political and sexual controversies was and still is an impediment to a proper appreciation and understanding of his accomplishments as a creative artist. To most critics he remains a rather unpleasant eccentric at best, a misogynistic madman at worst, an antifeminist pamphleteer with some genuine insight into human behavior, and a mentally unbalanced artist capable of some strokes of genius. It should be apparent now, so many years after his death, that he was a consummate artist, a comprehensive chronicler of the times in which he lived, a perceptive analyst of human nature, and, like all great writers, a profound moral philosopher.

His more severe critics always judged him from their own moral and political positions, which was how Strindberg wanted it. If it was difficult at times to see the artist's technical mastery because politics obscured the view, it was never difficult to see where Strindberg stood on the major social issues. The conflict between those who were for Strindberg and those who were against him embroiled the whole of Sweden near the end of his life, when he deliberately sought a confrontation, challenging his critics to come out of their aesthetic lairs. The resulting public debate, known as the Strindberg controversy, revealed that the judgments pronounced on the moral and artistic value of his works and the diagnoses made of his mental health had been made primarily on social and political grounds. At the time of the controversy the combatants were most readily identified as either pro- or anti-Strindberg, which meant pro- or anti-establishment, pro- or anti-militarism. If the battle had lasted longer, and in a very real sense it did, other labels would have been applied. Not surprisingly, those who ranged themselves against Strindberg in 1910 and who lived on into the 1920s and 1930s revealed themselves with amazing consistency as Fascists and Nazis, while those who had sided with Strindberg came out as supporters of the democracies and the free world.

A late and instructive example of the sort of thinking that characterized the anti-Strindbergian forces is provided by the English critic F. L. Lucas, who in his book *Ibsen and Strindberg* (1962) writes perspicaciously on the former and obtusely on the latter. He sees Strindberg, like Dostoyevsky, as embodying "the assault of chaos and madness on all that is most valuable in western civilization" and finds that the climax of Strindberg's novelette *Chandala* is "worthy, indeed, of a Nazi imagination." But, unable to change his spots, Lucas says elsewhere in the same book that the characters in Tennessee Williams's *Cat on a Hot Tin Roof* "make me feel only that the best thing for the lot of them would be a humane and efficient gas-chamber."

If class conflicts and sexual politics do not get in the reader's way, Strindberg's theatrical techniques probably do. With most dramatists the word carries nearly the entire burden of the play, and even when dramatists such as Shakespeare and Ibsen make exciting use of the stage medium, readers of their plays feel that the message lies exclusively in the words. Strindberg's plays—this is especially true of those he wrote after 1897—exist on the page as unfinished works that have to be brought to completion by directors and designers. In this sense many of Strindberg's plays resemble movie scripts, and in plays like *To Damascus, A Dream Play*, and *The Ghost Sonata* what one sees is sometimes more significant than what one hears. Strindberg had an actor's personality and a painter's eye. He knew that the theater was a collaborative art. He expected actors and designers to embellish his scripts, which he never considered sacrosanct. Readers who have not worked in the theater do not expect to be called on to add "business" to a scene when they peruse a playscript, or to construct sets out of the scanty descriptions Strindberg gives. Those who do work in the theater, however, enjoy the offer Strindberg extends to them to participate in a creative enterprise.

Strindberg theatricalized the theater, drawing on all its resources and trying to discover new ones when he felt he had exhausted the means of expression offered by the realistic drama. Like Ibsen, he was compelled by the theatrical standards of his time to write plays that were supposed to produce a photographic likeness on stage of the streets and parlors and people that could be seen outside the theater. Both Ibsen and Strindberg chafed under the severe restrictions of the realistic theater, not because they found it difficult to give a convincing representation of real life using the cardboard conventions of the theater (that is what troubled the Goncourt brothers, masters of the realistic novel) but because the reality that they became increasingly interested in lay not in the streets and parlors outside the theater but within people. They wanted to portray the life of the soul. Ibsen accommodated himself to the realistic theater by filling it with symbols. Strindberg felt he had to go even further. He broke up the form of the realistic play and converted form into symbol. Conventional ideas could be expressed in the conventional form, but Strindberg's investigations of the subconscious or unconscious life of the human being demanded new forms. The idea determined the form, and for each new idea came a new form. To readers familiar with the standard play of the time, the well-made play, Strindberg's experiments with form were bewildering. It was as if he asked them to put aside *David Copperfield* and turn to *Ulysses*. And, as with Joyce's novel, readers are likely to lose their way unless they have a guide.

Another obstacle to a full appreciation of Strindberg's genius is the difficulty of rendering his prose in another language and another time. During his lifetime he was praised even by his most implacable enemies as a master stylist. He energized the Swedish language, modernized it, and gave it a flexibility that no one had thought it capable of. Now, however, much of Strindberg's prose seems old-fashioned and obscure, since the Swedish language has changed almost as much in the last eighty years as the English language did between Shakespeare and Dryden. To convey the original excitement of Strindberg's prose, a translator would have to reinvent his or her own language.

Strindberg's style is characterized by its spontaneity, by a strong, irresistible rhythmic drive, by the introduction of new words, usually drawn from the sciences, by frequent glances at familiar sayings and old adages, by allusions to the Bible (which everyone read in Strindberg's time), and by the use of submerged metaphors, as in Shakespeare. All this makes Strindberg more difficult to translate and to understand than the Ibsen who wrote realistic plays. Ibsen's dialogue transmits a vast amount of information, and as long as the translation conveys that information, the play makes sense, even though subtleties of characterization and emotional shadings may be lost. Strindberg's dialogue, in contrast, often conveys a good deal of background information that may have only a slight basis in fact, material that the characters invent or embroider because it suits them to do so. As in real life, the way something is said becomes much more significant than what is said.

Adding to the difficulty is the poverty of stage directions in Strindberg's plays. Playwrights generally wrote for actors, not readers. Ibsen was the first dramatist in modern times who created a large reading public for plays, and he made it possible for dramatists like Shaw and O'Neill to publish plays with detailed character sketches that one usually finds in novels and with elaborate instructions that actors often ignore. Strindberg expected his actors to find the right tone and inflection as they worked with one another and to adjust lines if a change was needed to build rhythm, to cover a movement, or to get someone on or off stage. Strindberg's scripts are not novels in the form of dialogues.

Selected Plays

Introduction
to
Master Olof

Strindberg's first efforts as a fledgling playwright reflect his religious upbringing, his growing skepticism, his desire to commit himself to a life in art, and his alienation from his businessman-father. Away from home, as a student at the University of Uppsala, Strindberg came upon the writings of Søren Kierkegaard and read the impassioned speeches of Ibsen's Brand. Coming just then, when Strindberg was trying to resolve his own conflicts and to chart his course through life, they made a tremendous impact. Both believed that the pure heart of the solitary individual weighed more in the scales of salvation than the daily experience and common sense of the multitude. Both made absolute commitment to an ideal or a cause the highest purpose of human existence. "All or nothing" was Brand's motto, and for the sake of his calling he sacrificed his child, his wife, his earthly happiness, only to find at the end of his struggles that he stood alone, scorned by his former followers, apparently having accomplished nothing by way of reforming the paltering, equivocating, and materialistic society in which he lived. Yet he had no regrets. If he could have lived his life over, he would still have pursued the unattainable ideal.

The combined voices of Kierkegaard and Ibsen proved irresistible to the young Strindberg. In the summer of 1872, when he was twenty-three, he went to an island in the Stockholm archipelago, populated only by fishermen, where nothing would disturb his concentration. Within two months he wrote *Master Olof*. Ostensibly it was a chronicle play about the efforts of a Lutheran churchman to introduce the Reformation into Sweden and presented the inevitable clash of religion and politics, of priest and king, at a time when nations were contesting the power of the Catholic church.

Strindberg's chief model was Shakespeare, especially *Henry IV*. Having read an essay by the Danish critic Georg Brandes on how the English dramatist blended homely and insignificant details of character with mighty actions, Strindberg determined to do the same, to show his historical figures both at home and on public display, to lift them from the dead pages of the history books and make them as real and vivid as possible, even if that meant that they would be speaking like nineteenth-century Swedes. Shakespeare employed both prose and verse, which allowed him to move easily from tavern to court. Strindberg stuck to prose, thereby violating a principal rule of the conventional history play of his time. But he gave his characters two kinds of prose to speak: one, common and everyday, the other, exalted and biblical.

As far as theme was concerned, Strindberg intended his play as a reply to the vague and ethereal idealism of Ibsen's *Brand*. Although Brand built himself a church, it is never made clear what the dogmas and tenets of his church are, apart from the paradoxical exhortation that anything worth living for is worth sacrificing one's life for. By giving his hero a specific program and by setting his play in a time when there was a radical transformation of thought in Europe, Strindberg could raise some questions about the moral validity of Brand's teachings. The English historian Henry Thomas Buckle had treated political and social ideals not as eternally true but as ever-changing. He tried to describe the social process of making ideas in the same way that Darwin had described the process of evolution in the realm of biology. "What is truth?" Pontius Pilate had asked, without staying for an answer. Strindberg thought of using Pilate's skeptical question as the title for his play. Why sacrifice one's happiness and that of others for the sake of some truth when there is no truth but only a succession of illusory ideals? Why devote one's life to a cause if today's "ism" is destined to be tomorrow's "wasm." Better to seize the day and its pleasures. Yet when Strindberg wrote *Master Olof*, he temporarily resolved all doubts by choosing the side of total commitment if the cause was a worthy one. For the uncommitted life was not worth living, and only the committed life was worth examining.

Ibsen's *Brand* is a landmark in the history of ideas, not simply in the history of drama, because it was the first literary work to present the existential doctrine that individuals create their own systems of values. Even Kierkegaard had kept the Christian God as final arbiter in matters of the spirit, as Maker Unmade. Ibsen took the final step and made the heroic individual God the

Creator. In writing *Master Olof*, Strindberg turned from philosophy to politics. If the new element in Ibsen's epic drama was existential thought, the new element in Strindberg's historical drama was socialism. Although most of the major events in *Master Olof* are drawn from the historical record, Strindberg invented the character of Gert the Printer, who becomes the pivotal figure in the play. *Master Olof* was composed shortly after the rise and fall of the Paris Commune had exhilarated the political radicals throughout Europe and had alarmed the conservatives. The rousing speeches of Gert, the introduction of the revolutionary Anabaptists into Stockholm against the historical record, and the repeated references to Pentecost, a day that had special meaning to political radicals since it was on that day (May 28, 1871) that the French government soldiers massacred thousands of the Communards, all suggest that the play should be read as a study of the intrusion of the third force into the political life of Europe.

Strindberg's youthful and revolutionary ardor imbue the play with dramatic life, and that is what has kept it alive. The theater in Sweden, not surprisingly, would not stage it at first. Twice Strindberg rewrote it entirely in an effort to make it conform with the dramatic conventions and political attitudes of the established theater. However, the dictum that good plays are not written but rewritten does not hold true for *Master Olof*. Interesting as the other two versions are as a record of Strindberg's five-year struggle to come to terms with everything he was fighting against, the first version, in spite of its unwieldiness, its over-long speeches, and its romantic pathos, is the one that still holds the stage.

Master Olof

(1872 version)

A Play in Five Acts

CHARACTERS

MASTER OLOF
GERT THE PRINTER
GUSTAV VASA, King of Sweden
HANS BRASK, Bishop of Linköping
MAGNUS SOMMAR, Bishop of Strängnäs
NATIONAL MARSHAL OF SWEDEN, Lars Siggeson, Lord
High Constable
LARS ANDERSSON, Archdeacon in Strängnäs, later Chancellor
to King Gustav
LARS PEDERSSON, Olof's younger brother
HANS WINDRANK, sea captain
THE FARMER FROM SMÅLAND
THE GERMAN
THE DANE
FRIAR MARTIN, a Dominican
FRIAR NILS, a Dominican
THE INNKEEPER
WILLIAM, a student at the abbey school
PETER, another student
THE SEXTON (Bengt) of the Great Church in Stockholm
CATHERINE, the sexton's wife
OLOF'S MOTHER
CHRISTINA, Gert's daughter
THE PROSTITUTE
A NOBLEMAN, young
CITIZEN OF STRÄNGNÄS
CITIZEN'S WIFE
THE SERVANT at Gustav's court, elderly
FOREMAN OF THE WORK CREW
THE DRAYMAN, a young man
MINOR CHARACTERS

The play takes place in Sweden in the first half of the sixteenth
century.

ACT I

In Strängnäs, a town some forty miles from Stockholm.

The arcade of the monastery; behind it, the cloister garth with tree-shaded walks. The side chapel in the distance. To the right, the main portal of the cathedral. At the back, a low wall over the top of which fruit trees in bloom are visible. It is late afternoon.

Master Olof is sitting on a stone bench, listening to two students, William and Peter, who are reciting their parts from "The Comedy of Tobias," a play that Olof has written.

PETER:
"Are we children of Israel never to be free?
Must we abide in Babylon in captivity?"

WILLIAM:
"Alas, dear brother, why raise your voice to complain?
In this foreign land we must forever remain.
Our foe has taken all we had: our flocks, our land.
This is now home, this vale of tears where we stand.
Did I not long ago prophesy our lot?
The covenant of Abraham is long forgot."

LARS ANDERSSON (*has entered during the last speech. He is about twenty-five years older than Olof*): What are you doing?

OLOF: Playing.

LARS ANDERSSON: Playing!!

OLOF: Yes. A little play about the children of Israel and the Babylonian captivity. I wrote it, and now we are—

LARS ANDERSSON: Have you nothing better to do? Great deeds need doing, and you're the man to do them.

OLOF: No, I'm not. I'm too young.

9

LARS ANDERSSON: Too young! Say not you're too young.

OLOF: It's true, I shouldn't. Too many use that excuse.

LARS ANDERSSON: (*produces a scroll, unrolls it, stares hard at Olof, and then reads from it*): "Then the word of the Lord came unto me"—Jeremiah—"saying, 'Before I formed thee in the belly I knew thee; and before thou camest forth out of the womb I sanctified thee, and I ordained thee a prophet unto the nations.'

"Then said I, 'Ah, Lord God! behold, I cannot speak: *for I am a child.'*

"But the Lord said unto me, 'Say not, *I am a child:* for thou shalt go to all that I shall send thee, and whatsoever I command thee thou shalt speak. . . . '

"'For, behold, I have made thee this day a defenced city, and an iron pillar, and brasen walls against the whole land, against the kings of Judah, against the princes thereof, against the priests thereof, and against the people of the land.'

"'And they shall fight against thee; but they shall not prevail against thee; for I am with thee,' said the Lord, 'to deliver thee.'"

OLOF (*jumping to his feet*): Did the Lord say that?

LARS ANDERSSON (*reading on*): "'Thou therefore gird up thy loins, and arise, and speak unto them all that I command thee.'"

OLOF: You're a coward.

LARS ANDERSSON: Perhaps. I don't have the strength to be a hero. You do. Now may God give you the faith!

OLOF: Oh, indeed, indeed. There was a time I had the faith, and its fire burned brightly. But a brigade of monks came and doused it with their holy water. They wanted to exorcise the devil from my body.

LARS ANDERSSON: That was only a fire in a haystack. It was meant to fizzle out. Now the Lord will build you a real fire, a fire of great logs, that will burn and consume the Philistines, even to their seed. . . . What do you want out of life?

OLOF: I don't know. I only know that I feel I am suffocating when I think of our poor people, whose souls are gasping for freedom. They're crying out for water, the living water, but no one has any to give.

LARS ANDERSSON: Tear down that rotten old building, Olof. That's the first thing. You can do it. The Lord Himself will build them a new one.

OLOF: They would have no roof over their heads, not for a long while.

LARS ANDERSSON: At least they would have fresh air.

OLOF: To take away the faith from a whole people – they would be driven to despair.

LARS ANDERSSON: Exactly: they would be *driven* to despair.

OLOF: They will revile me, call down curses on me, and drag me before the authorities.

LARS ANDERSSON: Are you afraid?

OLOF: No, it's just that I'd die provoking – instead of –

LARS ANDERSSON: Olof, you were born to be a provocation. You were born to fight. Somebody will get hurt, but the Lord will heal.

OLOF: I can feel the current drawing me. I still have hold of the gate of the dam. If I let go, I'll be swept away.

LARS ANDERSSON: Let go of it, Olof. Others will hold the gate.

OLOF: Will you reach out to me if I get caught in the maelstrom?

LARS ANDERSSON: That isn't in my power. You have to go into the maelstrom even if you perish.

OLOF: You've stirred up a storm in my soul. There I sat in the shade of the tree and played. It was the eve of Pentecost. It was spring, and I was at peace. And now –? Why aren't the trees shaking in the storm; why aren't the heavens dark? Put your hand on my forehead. Can't you feel my blood beating, my pulse pounding? Don't leave me, Lars. I can see an angel coming toward me, with a chalice. She's walking on the rays of the setting sun; her path is blood red; and she's carrying a cross in her hands. —No, Lars, I cannot do it. I'm going back to my peaceful valley. Let others fight; I'll watch. . . . No, I'll follow the troops and heal the wounded. I'll whisper "Peace be with you" in the ears of the dying. Peace. . . . No, not that either. I want to join in the fighting. . . . But I'll take my place in the last ranks. Why should I be in the front?

LARS ANDERSSON: Because you are the boldest.

OLOF: Not the strongest?

LARS ANDERSSON: The strong will be behind you. And the strongest of all will be at your side. He is the one who exhorts you to do battle.

OLOF: Oh, God in heaven, help me! . . . Very well. I'll do it.

LARS ANDERSSON: Amen.

OLOF: And you'll go with me?

LARS ANDERSSON: You must go alone—with God.

OLOF: Why do you draw back?

LARS ANDERSSON: I wasn't born to fight. But I'll make your armor. The pure words of God shall be your weapons. But I'll fashion them, and you'll put them in the hands of the people. The door to the pope's armory has been broken in, and now everyone who calls himself a human being shall fight for the freedom of his own soul.

OLOF: Fight against whom? I'm lusting to do battle, but I don't see my enemies.

LARS ANDERSSON: You won't have to issue a challenge. They'll come. Godspeed, Olof. Begin whenever you feel like it. God go with you!

OLOF: Don't go! I need to talk to you.

LARS ANDERSSON: Here comes the vanguard. Arm yourself! (*He leaves.*)

> *A group of citizens, men, women, and children, approach the church on the right. They stop in front of the door, take off their hats, and cross themselves.*

Among the group is Gert the Printer, who has disguised himself as one of the citizens.

GERT: They haven't rung the bells for vespers. And this is the eve of Pentecost. Most unusual!

CITIZEN: The door is shut. The church is closed! Could the priest be sick?

GERT: Perhaps he hasn't risen yet.

CITIZEN: What is that supposed to mean?

GERT: I mean he's sick, that's all.

CITIZEN: I don't understand it. He's got plenty of acolytes. One of them could conduct Mass.

GERT: All busy, obviously.

CITIZEN: Doing what, I'd like to know.

GERT: Wouldn't we all!

CITIZEN: Take care, my good man. None of that Luther talk. I happen to know that Bishop Brask—he's the bishop in Linköping—is in town. And so is the king himself.

GERT: Bishop Brask here?

CITIZEN: As God is my word. —Shouldn't we try that door again?

GERT (*runs up the steps of the church and pounds on the door*): The house of the Lord is closed this Saturday, this eve of Pentecost. The reverend priests will not grant you an audience with God this evening. You praiseworthy citizens will have to go home and to bed without your evening mass. Look, good people, look at this door! A wooden door, a simple wooden door. But lined with copper. Look at it! If I tell you that God dwells within—it is, after all, His house—if I tell you that the bishop's *diaconus* or *secretarius* or *canonicus* (you can't be a man of God unless you have a Latin title)—if I tell you that such a man with a Latin title has the key to his door hanging on a nail in his bedroom, I do not mean to imply thereby that that man has locked us out from God and hung the key on a nail in his bedroom; I merely mean to say that we who have gathered here cannot enter the church this evening to hold divine service—we who have slaved for six days, making shoes, weaving cloth, we who have brewed the ale, baked the bread, and dressed the flesh for six days for these worshipful priests in order that on the seventh day they might have the strength to hold divine service for us. No, I do not reproach the right reverend canons or blame the bishop, for they are but mere men, like us, and it was only God who could work for six days and rest on the seventh.

CITIZEN: Blasphemy! You blaspheme against God!

GERT: No need to worry. He can't hear me. The door is closed.

WOMAN IN THE CROWD: Holy Mother of God! An antichrist!

GERT (*pounding on the door*): Hear how hollow it sounds. The veil of the temple separated men from the Holy of Holies. But when Christ was crucified the veil was rent in twain from top to bottom. This must be true because it's in the Bible. But whether the priests sewed the veil together again, the Bible does not say. And what the Bible does not say is not necessarily a lie.

> *The crowd of townspeople surge toward Gert. The children cry out in fear.*

CITIZEN: A Lutherist! Woe unto you! A Lutherist! We have sinned! That is why the Lord has closed to us the door of His house. Can't you hear how the children cry at the very sight of you, as at the sight of an evil spirit!

GERT: You are trampling them beneath your feet, my friends!

WOMAN IN THE CROWD: Don't you dare go near him! He has the devil in him!

CITIZEN: Down with him! Down with him!

GERT: Touch me not! This is God's sanctuary! This place is sanctified!

CITIZEN: God does not shield Lucifer! Lucifer was cast out!

GERT: Perhaps God does not, but the Holy Church does! And I stand within its consecrated walls.

CITIZEN: Take him! Drag him outside the walls!

GERT: If ye have no fear of God, ye should at least have fear of thy Holy Father who will rebuke thee.

WOMAN IN THE CROWD: Drag him from the door! It is his evil spirit that has bewitched the church!

CITIZEN: True! True! God does not open his house to the devil!

> *They are about to set upon Gert when the Bishop's Secretary enters, preceded by a deacon, who calls for silence.*

SECRETARY (*reading from a proclamation*): "Inasmuch as the people of this diocese have not fulfilled their obligations and paid their tithes to the bishop's see, and inasmuch as the people of Strängnäs have continued to neglect these obligations, the cathedral chapter, in conformity with its rights and with the full approbation of the consistory, has deemed it necessary to close the doors of this church and to cease the holding of mass and the offering of oblations until the aforementioned grievances have been corrected. Let it be published and made known that whosoever does not fulfill his obligations will incur the extreme disfavor of the chapter. *Datum vigilia assumptionis Mariae.* Strängnäs Chapter." (*He leaves.*)

GERT: Now what do you have to say, my good people?

CITIZEN: No mass on the eve of Pentecost! It's scandalous!

GERT: Take care! Speak not ill of the priests. They are not to blame.

CITIZEN: Then who is?

GERT: The church. The invisible, all-powerful church. The institution. It is *the* Church that has closed *this* church.

> *Murmurs of displeasure from the crowd.*
>
> *Olof has come forward, and now he takes hold of a rope hanging down from the tower and rings the vesper bell.*

OLOF: If the services mean so much to you, I shall celebrate mass with you.

CITIZEN: We thank you, Master Olof. But we don't wish to get you in trouble. Do you realize what they might do to you?

OLOF: It is better to fear God than to fear men.

> *The people kneel.*

OLOF: Dear friends, brothers and sisters in Jesus Christ, we are gathered here—

CITIZEN: Master Olof.

OLOF: Yes?

CITIZEN: We want to have a proper mass. Nothing newfangled.

GERT: Yes, Master Olof. It has to be in Latin. If it isn't in Latin how can we poor Swedes understand what you're saying?

CITIZEN: It has to be in the holy language. Otherwise anyone could say mass.

OLOF: Very true, my good friend. That is exactly how it should be. Every man a church unto himself and with God.

> *Protests from the crowd: "Lutherist!" "Go back to Germany!" "We don't need your sort here!"*

CITIZEN: I see, Master Olof, I see. You are young and hot-headed. You've been infected by that German devil. Now I'm an old man and I know the world. I wish you well, Master Olof; and I say to you: turn back while you're still young. . . . And now, Master Olof, give us what we wish to have: the mass we're accustomed to.

OLOF: No! It's time to put an end to that farce. —In truth should ye worship, in the spirit should ye pray, and not in words ye do not understand.

CITIZEN: My young friend, do you not suppose that our Lord understands Latin?

GERT: Of course. Only Swedish is beyond His comprehension!

CITIZEN: Master Olof, are you going to let these people walk away from here without the words that their souls crave? Do you not see how they thirst for God? Offer up your sinful obstinacy for their sake, and let them not wander as sheep without their shepherd.

OLOF: My obstinacy? Sinful?

CITIZEN: You are a hard man.

OLOF: Am I? A hard man? Do you know what it has cost me to ring this bell?

CITIZEN: Your pride.

GERT: And your peace! That bell was the tocsin calling all men to arms. This is it! The war begins! The bells in Stockholm will soon answer, and then the blood of Huss, of Zizka, the blood of all those thousands of peasants who died in Germany and Bohemia will be upon the heads of the princes and the papists!

WOMAN IN THE CROWD: Oh, my God! He's a lunatic!

CITIZEN: Do you know this man, Master Olof?

OLOF: No.

GERT: Olof! Not know me? Deny me not, Olof! Are you afraid of these poor wretched souls who don't know what's best for them? Who have never heard the word "Freedom"?

OLOF: Who are you?

GERT: If I were to tell you, you would tremble! Yes, and why not? Ye must tremble lest ye never waken from your sleep. I am the fallen angel, who will rise again ten thousand times. I am the liberator who came before his time. I am called Satan because I loved you more than life itself. I have been called Luther; I have been called Huss; and now I am called Anabaptist!

> *The people in the crowd huddle together in fear, crossing themselves and muttering, "Anabaptist!"*
>
> *Gert removes his disguise. Without it, he looks much older.*

GERT: Do you know me now, Olof?

OLOF: Father Gert!

CITIZEN: He calls him "Father"!

> *The people draw back, repeating, "Anabaptist! Anabaptist!"*

WOMAN IN THE CROWD: Do you see who that is? He's the man they excommunicated, it's—

CITIZEN: Yes. Gert the Printer. The printer for Bishop Brask.

MAN IN THE CROWD: He printed Luther!

WOMAN IN THE CROWD: God have mercy on us and on our town! Alas for our priests when they make friends with the antichrist.

CITIZEN: He denies baptism!

WOMAN IN THE CROWD: He denies God.

> *The crowd breaks up and disperses.*

OLOF: Well, Father Gert, that was quite a speech. And very dangerous.

GERT: Dangerous, do you think, Olof? God bless you for that.

OLOF: I meant dangerous for you.

GERT: And for no one else?

OLOF: Let's hope not.

GERT: You knew Luther, didn't you?

OLOF: Yes. And now I want to do his work in my land.

GERT: That's all?

OLOF: What do you mean?

GERT: I mean it's not enough. Luther is dead. He made a beginning. We have to carry on where he left off.

OLOF: Whither wilt thou lead me, Father?

GERT: Far, Olof. Far.

OLOF: You make me fear you, Father.

GERT: Good, good. I shall make you sore afraid. I want to set
you upon a very high mountain where you can look out over the
world. This is the feast of Pentecost, Olof. It was then that the
Holy Spirit descended and poured itself over the apostles—nay,
over all flesh. You can receive the Holy Spirit, Olof, just as I
received it, because I believed in it. The spirit of God descended
unto me, I feel that. And that is why they locked me up as a madman. But now I am free; now I shall speak the word because—
don't you see, Olof?—because now we stand on that high mountain.
Look at those people crawling on their knees. Crawling toward
those two men sitting on thrones. The bigger one holds two keys
in his right hand and a thunderbolt in the other. That is the pope.
When the pope raises the thunderbolt, a thousand souls are forever
sent to perdition. And the ones who are not kiss his foot and sing
Gloria Deo. And the man on the throne turns his head and smiles.
Now look at the other one. He holds a sword and a scepter. Bow
down before his scepter, or his sword will smite you. He frowns
and glowers, and all the people tremble. He turns his head toward
his friend on the other throne, and now they both smile. Two idols
of Baal. But there's a rumbling in the air. Like the murmuring
of a crowd. "Why that clamour?" roars the pope, and he shakes
his thunderbolt. "Who is grumbling?" And the emperor shakes
his sword. No one answers. But there is still a rumbling in the air
and a rustling, and the sound forms a word and that word is
"Think!" The pope is startled, and the emperor turns pale with
rage and demands to know who spoke. "Who said, 'Think!' Bring
him before me, and I shall have his head." And the pope roars,
"Bring him before me, and I shall take his soul!" But there is no
one to be brought forward. No one spoke. It was the wind in the
trees. But the voice grows louder, and the wind becomes a storm
sweeping across the Alps, roaring through Bavaria, churning the
Baltic Sea, echoing against the shore. And then, multiplied a
thousand times, the cry goes out over the world: "Freedom!
Freedom!" And the pope throws his keys into the ocean, and the
emperor puts his sword back into its sheath. What can they do
against the word? —Olof, you want to strike down the pope, but
you forget the emperor. The emperor who murders untold num-

bers of his subjects because they moan when they are trampled underfoot. You want to strike down the pope in Rome, but, like Luther, you want to give them a new pope: Holy Scripture. Olof, listen to me! Don't put any bonds whatsoever on the human spirit. Do not forget the great day of Pentecost and what it means: the descent of the Holy Spirit. Don't forget what your goal must be: a life of the spirit and the freedom of the spirit. Close your ears to those deadly words: "All that is, is good." Because if you do, the millennium will never come and man will never enter the kingdom of the free. That kingdom beckons us now.

> *Olof is silent.*

Does the thought make your head reel?

OLOF: You go too far, Gert.

GERT: Too far! The day will come when I shall be called a papist! He shoots higher who shoots at the moon than he who aims at the tree.

OLOF: Turn back, Gert. You will bring ruin to yourself and to the kingdom. The land is still shaking from the wounds and fever of the last war. And now you want to sow the seeds of civil war. That's ungodly.

GERT: Once the surgeon's knife is in the flesh, he must cut that the body may live.

OLOF: I'll report you as a traitor.

GERT: You! You have set yourself irreversibly against the church today. There's no going back. . . . Moreover . . .

OLOF: Well, what is it? You look like Satan himself.

GERT: I'll let you in on a secret. Make of it what you will. The king travels to Malmö today, and the day after tomorrow, or thereabouts, Stockholm will be in revolt.

OLOF: How do you know?

GERT: Have you heard of Rink and Knipperdollink?

OLOF (*startled*): The Anabaptists!

GERT: Why so amazed? Two middle-class clods fighting the wrong battles. Up in arms against infant baptism because it can have no meaning, since an infant has no soul. And in their innocence devoting their energies to abolishing the oath of confirmation because it is nothing more than premeditated perjury extorted from an unthinking adolescent. Who the hell cares?

OLOF: There must be more to Rink and Knipperdollink than that.

GERT: What might that be?

OLOF: They are possessed.

GERT: Yes! Possessed of the spirit! The mighty wind that will sweep us into the future howls through their souls. Take care if you are caught in its path.

OLOF: It must be stopped. I shall go to the king.

GERT: Wait, Olof! We should be friends, you and I. . . . Your mother lives in Stockholm, doesn't she?

OLOF: You know she does.

GERT: But do you know that my daughter Christina is living with your mother?

OLOF: Christina?

GERT: Yes, for the time being. You see, if we win, my daughter will stand as surety for your mother. And if the Catholics win, well, then my daughter will be safe because of your mother's presence. And you do care about Christina?

OLOF: Gert! Gert! Where did you learn to be so clever and calculating?

GERT: In the madhouse.

OLOF: Get thee from me! You want to make my life miserable. You want to deprive me of my happiness.

GERT: Yes! if to be miserable is to be deprived of all earthly happiness, to suffer poverty, to be clapped in jail, to be mocked and reviled, all for the sake of the truth. If that's what you mean by a miserable existence, you don't deserve it. I thought you of all people would understand me. I counted on you, because you have a soul of fire. But I see now that the world tempts you. Go; swim with the current. And be happy.

OLOF: No one man can remake his time.

GERT: Luther did.

OLOF: One man alone cannot turn the current.

GERT: You fool! Lead the current. What is the current? It is we, the multitude, the people. The old ones are stagnant pools; you won't have to struggle against them. But don't let them dry up and turn to muck. Cut a channel for them, and they too will be swept up.

OLOF: I do understand you! You have spawned a thought in my soul, and if I do not strangle it at birth, it will be the death of me.

GERT: Believe me, you shall become a Daniel, who will show the truth to the kings. And they will seek thy life, but the Lord will be thy shield. — Now I can leave; now I am confident. Thine eyes are as lamps of fire, and the cloven tongues of fire flicker above thy head. Happy Pentecost, Master Olof! (*He starts to leave; then turns back.*) Here comes the Prince of Flies. Don't let him speck your immaculate soul.

OLOF: Lord Jesus, stand by me now.

> *Enter Hans Brask, Bishop of Linköping, and Magnus Sommar, Bishop of Strängnäs. Magnus approaches Olof; Brask stands to one side, looking the place over.*

MAGNUS: *Canonicus!* Who rang the vesper bell?

OLOF (*quietly but firmly*): I did.

MAGNUS: Were you not aware of the injunction?

OLOF: That it was prohibited I was well aware.

MAGNUS: And you deliberately defied it!

OLOF: Yes. When I saw the people milling around like sheep without their shepherd, I thought I should gather them.

MAGNUS: So you think to reproach us for the action we have taken. The truth is you are an impudent young man.

OLOF: The truth is always impudent.

MAGNUS: I do believe our young hero wants to play the apostle of truth. You will win no plaudits for that.

OLOF: No, I expect to be hissed.

MAGNUS: Well, don't peddle your ideas here. There's no market for them.

OLOF (*passionately*): Advice worthy of the Father of Lies! (*Humbly.*) I'm sorry. Forgive me.

MAGNUS: Do you know whom you are talking to?

OLOF (*heatedly*): To Magnus Sommar, bishop, *servus servi servorum*, the servant of all those who serve.

BISHOP BRASK (*coming forward*): Who is this man?

MAGNUS: One of the assistants at this church.

BRASK: What is his name?

MAGNUS: Olof Pedersson, also known as Olaus Petri.

BRASK: (*taking a long look at Olof*): So you are Master Olof!

Olof bows and looks at Brask.

BRASK: Young man, I like you. Will you serve as my secretary?

OLOF: I thank you, Your Grace. But I'm afraid I don't have the proper references.

BRASK: Bishop Magnus, what do you make of him?

MAGNUS: I believe he was highly praised by Martin Luther.

BRASK: So I have heard. A hot-headed youth — that's what we have here. We shall take him in hand and educate him.

OLOF: I'm afraid it's too late for that.

BRASK: A twig can be bent.

MAGNUS: This young branch already inclines strongly toward heresy. This very day he dared to defy our orders.

BRASK: Is that so?

MAGNUS: The celebration of mass was interdicted on entirely legal grounds. Yet he dared to hold mass. What's worse, a Lutheran mass; and by doing so, he stirred up the people. Your Grace should not take asps to his bosom.

BRASK: Take care, young man. As you well know, the penalty for preaching Lutheranism is excommunication.

OLOF: Yes. But I fear no other god than God.

BRASK: Weigh your words before you speak. I wish you well, and you repulse me.

OLOF: I have a cure for your sick faith. You want to buy it. And here I am impudently refusing to sell it to you.

BRASK: By Saint George, I swear you are utterly out of your mind!

OLOF: If I am, don't cure me as you would cure Gert the Printer. You put him in an asylum. It made him very clever, I'm afraid.

BRASK (*to Magnus*): You know this Gert fellow, don't you?

MAGNUS: No, your Grace.

BRASK: A madman. He worked for me – trained as a typesetter. When I gave him anti-Lutheran documents to print, he used my presses to print pro-Lutheran pamphlets. A fanatic, raving about the apocalypse and the millennium. (*To Olof.*) Have you seen him?

OLOF: He was just here. And little good can you expect from him.

BRASK: He's loose again, is he?

OLOF: He will soon be in Stockholm, where I am sure he will make his presence known. A warning, my Lord Bishop.

BRASK: Ah ha. Nothing to fear for a while.

OLOF: No? There are Anabaptists in Stockholm.

BRASK: What?

OLOF: The Anabaptists. They are in Stockholm.

BRASK: The Anabaptists!

King Gustav Vasa enters hastily.

GUSTAV: What the hell is going on?! The whole town is in an uproar. People storming up and down the streets demanding mass. What's behind all this?

BRASK: Mischief, Your Majesty, mischief.

GUSTAV: Bishop Magnus!

MAGNUS: Strängnäs has not paid its tithes, Your Majesty.

GUSTAV: And because of that you refuse to hold services!! 'Sdeath!

BRASK: Your Majesty would do well to bear in mind that—

GUSTAV: Bishop Magnus! I want an answer.

MAGNUS: Your Majesty would do well to bear in mind that matters of this kind, which come under the jurisdiction of the church, should—

GUSTAV: Yes, and I'm ordering you to stick to your business and do your job.

BRASK: Must I remind you, Sire, that the bishops in the kingdom of Sweden take their orders only from the highest authority: the pope and the canon law.

GUSTAV (*subdued*): I know. I know. But the pope can't always keep his eye on you.

BRASK: That is our affair.

GUSTAV (*flaring up, but controlling himself*): You are right, Brask. It shall be your affair.

BRASK: To change the subject, I hear that Stockholm is about to break out into rebellion.

GUSTAV: Where have you heard that?

MAGNUS: From our *canonicus* here.

GUSTAV: Your schoolmaster? Where is he? (*Turning in the*

direction indicated by Magnus.) You're the *canonicus*? What's your name?

OLOF: Olof Pedersson.

GUSTAV: Ah! Master Olof. So you're the heretic. Plotting against the Holy Church, hm? A dangerous undertaking.

BRASK: Today he found the occasion for unmasking himself. He openly violated the chapter's prohibition against holding mass. Consequently, we request Your Majesty's consent to what may be the appropriate and condign punishment.

GUSTAV: That's a matter for the chapter to settle. It's none of my business. (*To Olof.*) Now what's this about a rebellion in Stockholm?

OLOF: The Anabaptists are there.

GUSTAV: Is that all?

BRASK: Sire, you surely know what trouble these mad fanatics have caused in Germany. We would suggest that Your Majesty return to Stockholm with his troops.

GUSTAV: That is a matter that you must leave to my discretion.

BRASK: But civil war, Your Majesty!

GUSTAV: That is my affair. —Master Olof, I am appointing you secretary in chief of the city council in Stockholm. You will proceed immediately. Once there you will speak to the people. I am counting on you, Olof.

BRASK: Sire, for the sake of the fatherland I beg you to bear in mind how foolish it is to reason with fools.

GUSTAV: One doesn't bend the spirit with the sword. Bear that in mind, my lords.

BRASK: The church has never attempted—

GUSTAV: No, nor with keys either. (*To Olof.*) Go to my chancellor. He'll give you the necessary papers.

BRASK: One moment! I would advise our canon to think the matter over.

GUSTAV: He is our secretary. Our orders take precedence over yours.

BRASK: The church must first exact its claims on him. —Olaus Petri—

GUSTAV (*correcting him*): Secretary Olof Pedersson.

BRASK: Secretary Olof Pedersson: you are not free to leave Strängnäs until the chapter has pronounced sentence on you.

GUSTAV: The chapter does not pronounce sentence until it has tried the case.

BRASK: That is our affair!

GUSTAV: It is not your affair. Your diocese is Linköping. A canon in Strängnäs cannot be judged by a bishop of Linköping. Am I right, Bishop Magnus?

MAGNUS (*hemming and hawing*): I . . . in the light of what has occurred, I . . . would be inclined to think that . . .

BRASK: That further explanations should be unnecessary!

GUSTAV: Or that Bishop Brask should not involve himself. —Or that he should withdraw while I talk privately with Bishop Magnus. —Privately, I said.

Bishop Brask steps to one side.

Now what have you to say, Lord Magnus?

MAGNUS: I see no alternative . . . other than . . . since Bishop Brask . . .

GUSTAV: We are talking about Master Olof now. —I'm sure that your lordships can postpone the inquiry. Now if your lordships might take your leave of us—

Brask and Magnus leave.

GUSTAV (*turning to Olof*): Will you join with me?

OLOF: As Your Grace's secretary?

GUSTAV: No: as my right hand. On condition that for the time being the left hand doesn't know what the right hand is doing. Go to Stockholm.

OLOF: The cathedral chapter here will demand my return and excommunicate me.

GUSTAV: Before they go that far, I shall let you lay the blame on me. But until then you will be your own man, as far as possible.

OLOF: What does Your Grace want of me?

GUSTAV: I want you to talk to those fanatics in Stockholm.

OLOF: And then what?

GUSTAV: I don't dare think that far ahead. . . . Let the Anabaptists preach. Our people are apathetic and half-asleep. It can't hurt them to hear some new ideas, even if they are crazy ones. But I won't tolerate any violence! If violence breaks out, the sword will come into play. Fare thee well, Olof. (*He leaves.*)

OLOF (*alone*): Interesting! The emperor would prefer not to shake hands with the pope.

> *The students William and Peter, who have been waiting in one of the tree-lined walks, come forward.*

WILLIAM: Should we go on with the play, Master Olof?

OLOF: Playtime is over, children.

WILLIAM: You're not going to leave us, are you?

OLOF: Yes, I'm afraid so. And I probably won't be coming back.

WILLIAM: Why can't you stay through Pentecost? Then we could put on our play.

PETER: And I can be the angel Gabriel!

WILLIAM: Please don't go, Master Olof. You were the only one who was nice to us. You didn't make us fast all the time.

PETER: Please, Master Olof. Don't leave us!

OLOF: Oh, my children, ye know not what ye ask. The day shall come when you will thank God that I went away from you. —No, no, no! May that day never come! . . . Well, let's not waste any time saying goodbye. (*He embraces them, and they kiss his hand.*) Goodbye, Peter. Goodbye, William.

> *Lars Andersson has entered and observed the leave-taking.*

WILLIAM: Aren't you ever coming back, Master Olof?

LARS ANDERSSON (*coming forward*): Are you ready?

OLOF: No, I am never coming back.

PETER (*leaving*): Goodbye.

WILLIAM (*leaving*): Don't forget us!

> *Olof follows them with his eyes as they depart.*

LARS ANDERSSON: I have spoken with the king.

OLOF (*absentmindedly*): You have?

LARS ANDERSSON: Do you know what he said?

OLOF: No.

LARS ANDERSSON: He said, "Well, I've got myself a hunting dog that will raise the game. But I wonder if he'll come when I whistle."

OLOF: Look at them! Playing among the gravestones, playing and picking flowers, and singing Pentecostal hymns.

LARS ANDERSSON (*taking him by the arm*): You child!

OLOF (*startled*): What?

LARS ANDERSSON: I thought that today you had put your hand to the plow. No man, having done so, and looking back, is fit for the kingdom of God.

> *Olof waves at the students.*

LARS ANDERSSON: Still dreaming?

OLOF: A last lovely morning dream before we go to work. Forgive me. Now I'm awake.

> *They go toward the right. Reaching the wings, Olof turns to take one last look at the students. But at this moment the Dominican friars Martin and Nils, wearing their long black mantles, appear just where the students exited.*
>
> *Olof gasps in astonishment, and his hand flies to his forehead.*
>
> *Lars leads him off.*

CURTAIN

ACT II

Scene I

*Stockholm. A tavern in the wall of the Great Church.
At back a counter with tankards, mugs, steins. To the
right of the counter is a table, and behind it an iron door
that leads to the interior of the church. The monks
Martin and Nils, clad like ordinary townspeople, are
seated at this table, drinking beer. Farmers, sailors, and
German soldiers are seated and standing around the
other tables. The door to the street is at the right. Sitting
on a barrel is a musician, fiddle in hand. The soldiers
are throwing dice. All those in the room are in various
stages of drunkenness and talking noisily.*

*Gathered around one of the tables are a Farmer from the
province of Småland (at this time under the Danish
crown), a Dane, a German, and Hans Windrank, a sea
captain.*

THE GERMAN (*addressing The Dane*): You mean to sit there
and defend that bloody king of yours, that tyrant King Christian!

THE DANE: God preserve us, he's a man like the rest of us!

THE GERMAN: He's a monster! A bloody butcher! A
cowardly, sneaking, lying Dane! How many Swedes didn't he kill
when he marched into Stockholm and had himself crowned king
of Sweden! One hundred Swedes in one day! The massacre of
Stockholm.

THE DANE: Holy Jesus! Look who's talking about blood! What
about those murders — not a mile from here — in 1389 — when you
Germans dragged the Swedes out of Parliament, locked them in
a shed, and burned them!! On Corpus Christi Day!!

WINDRANK: Gentlemen, gentlemen! We're supposed to be

31

enjoying ourselves. Now let me tell you about America. Now there's—

THE GERMAN (*to The Dane*): Why blame me? I'm not German. I'm from Lübeck.

THE DANE: For God's sake, all I'm saying is that the Germans are just—

WINDRANK: What's the point of arguing! (*Shouts at The Innkeeper.*): Schnapps here! Four! —Now let's settle down and have a good time. America—now there's a place! The last time I was there, let me tell you—

The Innkeeper serves the liquor.

THE GERMAN (*tasting it*): *Wunderbar!* Just think, gentlemen, what progress we have made! Today the grain is growing in the field and—

WINDRANK: And tomorrow it will be made into whiskey. I wonder, just who was the man who made that discovery.

THE GERMAN: Begging your pardon—it's a German *invention.* I say invention. One *discovers* America.

WINDRANK: Yes. And the Germans never *discover* anything!

THE GERMAN: *Verdammt!*

WINDRANK: What's the matter? You're not German. You're from Lübeck.

THE DANE (*to The German*): All right. Here's one for you. Who invented the story that the Germans made Gustav Vasa king of Sweden?

General laughter.

THE GERMAN: Ah, ha! We did. It was us. We Lübeckians made Gustav king of Sweden when the country was on the verge of collapse.

WINDRANK (*raising his cup*): To the king! Skoal!

THE DANE: To Lübeck! Skoal!

THE GERMAN (*flattered*): That's very kind. I don't know how to express—

WINDRANK: Hell, you're not the king!

THE GERMAN: Begging your pardon, it was my Danish friend's toast—

THE DANE: Hell, you're not a Lübecker! What are you doing here? You're a Stockholmer!

WINDRANK (*turning to The Farmer from Småland*): You're not saying much. Why aren't you drinking?

THE FARMER: I don't mind drinking your schnapps, but as for your toast, this is what I think of it!

> *He crushes the tin cup and throws it on the floor. Windrank reaches for his knife.*

WINDRANK: You refuse to drink to our King!?

THE FARMER: I've drunk from his cup so long I ain't got no desire to drink his health. Like hell I'll drink to him!

WINDRANK: 'Sblood!

THE GERMAN (*suddenly interested in The Farmer*): Shut up! Let's hear what he's got to say.

THE DANE (*also involved*): Yes, for God's sake, let him talk.

THE FARMER: Lord help me when I get home. (*He seems to be on the verge of tears.*)

WINDRANK (*moved*): What the hell's the matter, old boy? You look like you lost your last friend. Money? Is that it? Look! (*He takes out his purse.*) There. Help yourself. Half my pay's there. —Come on, what's the matter?

THE FARMER: I don't want to talk about it. More schnapps! (*Signals to The Innkeeper.*) Schnapps! —Money? I got money. Look! (*He puts a small purse on the table.*)

> *The Innkeeper brings the liquor.*

Trouble is, it's not mine. What the hell! I'm going to drink it all up – every damn cent of it! And if you're my friends, you're going to help me.

WINDRANK: That's not your money? What's going on?

THE GERMAN: Oh, somebody's done you in, huh? I can tell. Something awful?

THE FARMER: I'm ruined. Lost everything. I come up from Småland to sell two hundred head of cattle. Borrowed money to get them. When I get here to Stockholm, the king's bailiff steps in and says I have to sell at the price the king decides. No higher. It's the king who sets the prices, not us farmers. It's the king who's ruined me.

THE GERMAN: I don't believe it!

THE FARMER: There's a lot more you won't believe. He's going to take the monks and the priests away from us. That's what I heard. You know why? To make the nobles richer. Take from the church, give to the lords.

THE DANE: To the lords and landowners! God!

THE FARMER: It's true, every word. That bloody king of yours, that King Christian, he should be here right now to lop off a few more Swedish heads. God bless him!

WINDRANK: Well, I'll be swiggered! King Gustav setting that course! For the nobles! I thought he was sitting on them.

THE FARMER: Sitting on them! Ha! He's letting them hatch and run wild. They'd be cutting the oak trees on my land – if I had any land left. Oh, I had a parcel of land – once. Then along comes a high-and-mighty lord and he says my great-grandmother had it on loan from his great-grandfather. And he grabbed it – my land!

THE GERMAN: Is that what the king is up to! I had absolutely no idea.

THE FARMER: Ha! The lords even let their kids run around in our woods with their guns, killing deer just for the hell of it! But if one of us was dying of starvation and knocked off a deer, he wouldn't die of starvation, let me tell you! He'd be hung from

a tree. And not an oak tree! God forbid! That would be a disgrace
to the oak. The oak is the royal tree. Because its branches form
a crown, you see. But the pine tree isn't meant to have a crown.
So it isn't royal. Like the song says:

> "The peasants rose and burned the crops;
> The land was red with blood and fire.
> Then came the lords and raised them higher,
> Strung them up in the pine tree tops."

See! Pine tree tops; no crowns.

THE GERMAN: But the pine tree stands straight and tall.

THE FARMER: Right, right. Come on, slug it down! Here's to
you! I mean it.

They drink.

Oh, that's good. Kill you or cure you. . . . It's the wife and
kids, you know. If I didn't have them−. Oh, what the
hell! . . . Oh, there are things I could tell you. Such things. But
I ain't opening my mouth.

WINDRANK: What sort of things?

THE GERMAN: Something funny, I'll bet.

THE FARMER: Yeah, something funny. Like: if you counted
them all up, there'd be a lot more pines than oaks.

THE GERMAN: Is that right?

WINDRANK: Now wait. I don't like this. You say only bad
things about the king. I don't know what he's up to, and it's none
of my business. But I know one thing for sure: he's building up
the merchant fleet. Who outfitted those ships for the Spanish
trade? King Gustav. Who made me a captain? King Gustav. So
I damn well ain't got nothing to complain about.

THE GERMAN: Yes, but why? Out of spite! To hurt the
Lübeck shippers. But it's Lübeck money that's kept him going.
And this is how he repays them. Pure spite, I tell you!

THE FARMER: He'll get his! You can castrate a bull, but he's still got horns. — Thanks, fellows, for your company. I've got to be going.

THE GERMAN: Oh, come on. Just one more. We've got a lot of talking to do.

THE FARMER: No, thanks. You've been good. But I don't dare. I've got a wife and kids at home waiting for me, and I've got to go and tell them that we've lost — everything. I can't face it. . . . All right, Deutschman, I'll take you up on that. Let's have another.

THE GERMAN: Now you're talking!

> *They drink.*
>
> *The Farmer empties his cup, then jumps up.*

THE FARMER: Oh, God! Hell and damnation! What the devil's in it? Bitter. (*He stumbles out of the tavern, obviously sick.*)

THE GERMAN (*to The Dane*): I wouldn't want to be in his shoes when he sobers up.

> *The Dane nods.*
>
> *The din in the tavern has gotten worse. The fiddler plays louder and faster. And then the sound of the church organ is heard over the din.*

WINDRANK: I still say it's strange that the king allows a beer tavern within the church wall.

THE GERMAN: Don't tell me you're particular, Captain. The king doesn't know about this.

WINDRANK: Maybe. Still, it doesn't sound right — church music and this kind of singing. I've always been a god-fearing man, you see. Brought up that way.

THE GERMAN (*ironically*): Lucky you! No doubt your mother — your dear mother —

WINDRANK (*sentimentally*): My mother!

THE GERMAN: Tucked you into bed every night and told you

to say, "Now I lay me down to sleep; I pray the Lord . . . "

WINDRANK: She did, she did.

THE GERMAN: What a good, kind woman.

WINDRANK (*becoming maudlin*): Oh, if you only knew!

THE GERMAN: God has heard her prayers. You're crying. . . . You really are a good man.

THE DANE: God almighty, yes.

THE GERMAN: Oh, if your mother could only see you now! With those tears in your eyes!

WINDRANK: I'm just a poor sinner, I know that. But one thing I know: I've got a heart. God damn me if I don't. If some wretch told me he needed a bite to eat, I'd give him the shirt off my back.

THE GERMAN: Good for you! Let's have another round.

WINDRANK: No, no. No, I don't think so.

> *A few loud blows are heard on the iron door leading to the church. Commotion in the tavern.*

WINDRANK (*frightened*): Oh, my God!

THE GERMAN: No cause for alarm. It's not Peter, and it's not the gate to heaven.

WINDRANK: I'll never take another drink. I swear to God!

THE GERMAN (*to The Dane*): Nothing like liquor. A blessed drink. It can transform a rascal like this into a Bible thumper. Worse. It's made him a teetotaler. Nothing but liquor can do that!

THE DANE: Right, right! There's nothing like it!

THE GERMAN: It swells the heart and shrinks the head. That's how it makes good people out of us. Because to be good means to have a lot of heart and little brains.

THE DANE: Right. But that ain't all. It makes us religious because it stop us from thinking. And reason blocks the way to the soul.

THE GERMAN: Oh, it's a holy thing, liquor, a holy thing! Strange that no one—

THE DANE: Enough said.

> *More pounding on the iron door.*
>
> *Windrank has dropped off, but the pounding wakes him with a start.*

WINDRANK: Help! Help! I'm dying!

THE GERMAN: Pity! Such a sweet soul, too.

> *The iron door is thrown open, and as it swings, it knocks over the table at which the monks Nils and Martin are sitting. Mugs and steins crash to the floor.*
>
> *A woman wearing a black and red skirt—the required dress of a prostitute—and with a nun's veil over her face is virtually thrust into the room. Momentarily Gert can be glimpsed behind the door, which is quickly slammed shut.*

THE PROSTITUTE (*looking about, stunned and afraid*): Please help me! They want to kill me!

A GERMAN SOLDIER: A whore—in a nun's veil! Ha! (*He laughs, and others join in.*)

MARTIN (*crossing himself*): A whore! Who brought her in here? This is a respectable place. —Innkeeper, take her out. You want to ruin your reputation and stain the sanctity of the church?

THE PROSTITUTE: Please! Won't someone help me?

> *The Innkeeper has grabbed her arm and is pulling her toward the street door.*

THE PROSTITUTE: Please! Don't turn me over to that mob out there! All I wanted was to slip into the house of the Lord. All I wanted was a bit of His mercy. And the monks drove me back. They set the people on me. They would have killed me, but Father Gert saved me. Brought me here.

MARTIN: Do you hear that? She has profaned the sanctity of the church. Look at her! Trying to conceal the skirt of shame with the veil of holiness!

THE GERMAN: Only the veil wasn't long enough!

MARTIN: Off with the mask! Let's see you for what you are – an abomination! (*He goes to her and tears the veil from her face. He gasps in surprise.*)

THE PROSTITUTE: You! Martin! – Murderer!

THE GERMAN: What do you know – old acquaintances!

MARTIN: A dirty lie! I've never seen her before. I'm Friar Martin, a Dominican, and Brother Nils here is my witness!

NILS (*drunk and slobbering*): 'S true. I can vouch for that. Brother Martin's never seen this woman.

THE PROSTITUTE: Nils, how can you? You yourself showed me Martin's letter of absolution. I was cast out of the cloister, but they gave Martin absolution.

NILS: 'S true! Can't deny it.

MARTIN (*in a rage, grabs Nils and shakes him*): You lie! (*Turning to the crowd.*) You can see he's drunk!

THE GERMAN: My good friends, I can vouch that this holy man is drunk – and therefore is lying.

> *Noises of displeasure and indignation from the crowd. "A drunken priest." "A Dominican, and drunk!"*

THE GERMAN: Ah, well! Liquor absolves the liar. Isn't that so, Father Martin?

THE INNKEEPER: Quiet! Quiet! I can't have any disturbances here. I'd lose my customers. I might get brought before the church chapter. Now will you please remove this wretched person from the premises? She's the cause of all this trouble.

MARTIN: Get her out of here, or I'll see to it that you're excommunicated. Don't you realize that we are within the walls of the holy church? The chapter has set aside this part of it for travelers—for their bodily refreshment.

THE GERMAN: Good people, don't you see?! This is a holy room. Look about you! Isn't this God's dwelling place?

> *The crowd forcibly drags The Prostitute toward the street door.*

THE PROSTITUTE: Jesus, help me! Please, help me, Jesus!

> *Master Olof stands in the doorway. He pushes his way through the people, takes The Prostitute by the hand and draws her away from the mob.*

OLOF: Who is this woman? Answer me!

MARTIN: This is no woman.

OLOF: What do you mean?

MARTIN: Not a man, either—although she is disguised.

OLOF: You said "she"; so she is a woman.

MARTIN: A whore!

OLOF (*shocked, lets go of her hand*): A whore?

THE GERMAN: Don't let go of her, Master Olof. She'll run away.

OLOF: Why are you laying hands on her? What has she done?

THE GERMAN: She went into the church.

OLOF: I see. (*Looking around.*)

MARTIN: What are you looking for?

OLOF (*taking note of him*): A priest?

MARTIN: I am a Blackfriar.

OLOF: Yes, I thought so. So you're the one who roused the mob against her.

MARTIN: It was I who protected the church from this slime,

who sought to keep the church free from vice. This woman has been excommunicated. She commits usury of the flesh. She sells her body, which should be the temple of God.

She falls on her knees before Olof.

OLOF (*taking her by the hand*): A Blackfriar, are you? I am taking this woman by the hand and setting her up against you. She has sold her body, you say. How many souls have *you* bought? . . . I too am a priest. No, merely a human being, and not so presumptuous as to lock the door of God's house. Being a sinful creature, I reach my hand to a fellow creature, who cannot be without sin. Come forward, he that is without sin among you. Let him first cast a stone at her. . . . Come forward, Brother Martin, you angel of light. You have dressed yourself in the black robes of austerity, and you have shaved your head so that no one can see that you have grown grey with sin. What? You have no stone to throw? Alas, what have you done with them, all those stones you were to give to the people when they ask for bread? Have you already given them away? . . . Come forward, you respectable citizen.

Olof addresses Captain Windrank, who in his drunken stupor has slipped off his chair and is lying asleep on the floor.

You who sleep like a beast, why don't you wake up and hurl your knife at her? Do you see how red he is? Red from shame at finding himself in this doubtful company, or red from debauchery?

The people in the tavern murmur resentfully.

Why do you grumble? Are you embarrassed by my words or ashamed of yourselves? Why do ye not cast stones? Ah, of course, ye have none. Well, open the door. Call up the people, let them run her down. If you fear that fifty men could not tear her to pieces, be assured that five hundred women would. . . . Still silent? . . . Woman, stand up. They do not condemn you. Go, and sin no more. But don't show yourself to the priests. They will throw you to the women.

During this speech Martin has repeatedly tried to interrupt Olof but has been prevented from doing so by The German. Now he has his way and produces a paper.

MARTIN: Listen to me! This man is a heretic. I don't have to tell you that. His words make it clear enough. A heretic! And he has been excommunicated!! It's in this paper. See for yourselves! (*He takes a candle from one of the tables and throws it in the middle of the floor.*) "As this light is extinguished, which we here cast down, so shall all joy and contentment be extinguished in him, along with all good he might have from God!"

The people cross themselves and shrink back from Olof. He stands alone with The Prostitute in the middle of the floor. The people mutter, "Anathema!"

MARTIN (*to The Prostitute*): You see! What good is Master Olof's absolution now?

Olof has been stung and silenced by Martin's words.

OLOF: Woman! Do you fear to put your trust in me? Do you dare to put your faith in my words? Don't you hear the lightning bolts of excommunication striking over our heads? Why don't you join those twenty righteous men who stand within the shadow of the holy church? . . . Answer me! Do you believe God has cast me out, as these have done?

THE PROSTITUTE: No!

OLOF (*taking the broadsheet containing the order of excommunication*): Very well. The great bishop in that little town of Linköping has sold my soul to Satan for life—no more, because his power reaches no farther than that. And this he has done to me because I invited the people to seek God—at the wrong time. Here is the contract. Just as the church through this has bound me to hell, so I free myself from it— (*He tears the sheet to pieces.*) —and from the excommunication! May God help me! Amen.

The people howl, "Anathema!"

MARTIN: Grab him! Strike him down! He is excommunicate.

OLOF (*places himself in front of The Prostitute*): Listen to the devils howling for their victim! — Touch me not!

MARTIN: Come on! Down with him!

> *One of the soldiers raises his weapon to strike at Olof. At that moment the iron door is flung open, and a group of Anabaptists, led by Knipperdollink, storm in, shouting and carrying broken crucifixes, fragments of statues of saints, and shredded ecclesiastical vestments.*

KNIPPERDOLLINK (*starts speaking as soon as the door is opened*): What do we have here! Look at this! One more house of holiness. What does this signify? A beer tavern in the temple itself. It means, look you, that the abomination has grown so great that the sanctuary itself is defiled. But I shall cleanse it with fire. The church into the flames! The saints onto the bonfire!

> *The people in the tavern have thronged toward the street door.*
>
> *Olof steps forward.*

OLOF: Be sure you know what you are doing!

KNIPPERDOLLINK: Do you fear that the beer barrels will burst from the heat, you Belial? Are you the pope's tavernkeeper that you think nothing of building a chapel of vice in the walls of the church?

OLOF: I am secretary of the town council. In the name of the king and by virtue of the authority invested in me, I order you to keep the peace!

KNIPPERDOLLINK: Ah ha! You are the man the king sent to defeat our sacred cause. Forward, you men of god! Seize him! Seize him first. Time enough later to rid the Lord's house of this idolatry.

MARTIN: Lay hold of him! He is a heretic! He is excommunicate!

KNIPPERDOLLINK: Heretic? Not a Catholic?

OLOF: Hardly, since I've been excommunicated.

KNIPPERDOLLINK: Then you are one of ours!

Olof is silent.

KNIPPERDOLLINK: Answer! Are you for us or against us?

MARTIN: He is Olof Pedersson, the king's man.

KNIPPERDOLLINK: Olof Pedersson, are you?

OLOF: Yes.

KNIPPERDOLLINK: But you are a heretic?

OLOF: I am proud to say I am.

KNIPPERDOLLINK: A heretic—in the king's service?

OLOF: Yes.

> *The Anabaptists shout and surround Olof.*
>
> *The iron door opens, and Gert the Printer enters quickly.*

GERT: Stop! What are you doing?

KNIPPERDOLLINK: Gert! —You can tell us. Who is this man?

GERT: One of ours. Let him go, my friends. —There, there stand the devil's emissaries!

> *He points at Martin and Nils. The Anabaptists assault them. Martin and Nils run out through the street door, pursued by the Anabaptists.*
>
> *Gert has followed as far as the door. He turns and faces Olof.*
>
> *The tavern is quiet. The Prostitute has crept into a corner. Captain Windrank is still asleep under the table. Olof, deep in thought, stands in the middle of the room. Gert throws himself down on one of the benches, exhausted.*

GERT: It's hard work, Olof.

OLOF: What have you done?

GERT: Done? We've done with the church. Cleaned it out. That's a beginning.

OLOF: That will cost you dearly.

GERT: We still have the upper hand. The whole town is in an uproar. Right now Rink is at work in St. George's chapel. — Tell me, did the king pick you to fight us?

OLOF: Yes.

GERT: Very wise.

OLOF: Tomorrow I am to preach. In the new pulpit.

GERT: New pulpit?

OLOF: Yes. I designed it. After the ones in Germany.

GERT: Indeed! This royal mission — how are you handling that? Here you stand with your arms across your chest, doing nothing.

OLOF: Come to church tomorrow. Bring your Anabaptist friends.

GERT: To hear a Catholic sermon? Or what?

OLOF: I was excommunicated today.

GERT (*leaps up to embrace Olof*): God bless you, Olof! This is truly a rebaptism. Now you are reborn.

OLOF: I still cannot understand you. Why do you carry on like wild animals? You defile all that is sacred.

GERT (*picking up a piece of one of the broken wood statues*): Is this sacred? This? A St. Nicholas, I believe. Jesus came in vain to dwell among us if we still worship sticks of wood. Do you call that a god: a stick I can break? Like this!

OLOF: But he is sacred — to the people.

GERT: So was the golden calf. So was Zeus. And Thor and Odin. And yet they were struck down. (*He notices The Prostitute.*) What woman is that? Oh, I see. The one I pushed in here for you to save. . . . Olof: tell me something. Has the king bought you?

OLOF: Go away, Gert. I abhor you.

GERT (*seeing Windrank*): Who is that pig sleeping on the floor?

OLOF: Don't you see? When I face you, I shrivel up. Please leave me alone. I want to do my work, not yours.

GERT: Now listen—

OLOF: You want to weave the fabric of your life into mine.

GERT: Now listen to me—

OLOF: No. You have spun an invisible web around me. You have proclaimed me an Anabaptist. How will I explain that to the king?

GERT: Which king?

OLOF: King Gustav.

GERT: Oh, that king. . . . Goodbye, Olof. . . . Preaching tomorrow, are you? . . . (*Pointing to The Prostitute.*) Why does she hang around here? . . . Goodbye. (*He leaves.*)

OLOF: God's errand boy, or Satan's?

THE PROSTITUTE (*approaches Olof and kneels before him*): Let me thank you.

OLOF: Give your thanks to God alone, who saved your soul. And do not go from here believing your sins have been atoned for. You must find strength to know yourself as damned and cursed for all your life. God has forgiven you. Human beings never will.

> *Olof takes her by the hand and starts to lead her toward the street door. The iron door opens, and Friar Martin steps into the room, followed by Olof's Mother and Christina, Gert's daughter.*

MARTIN: We must have come the wrong way.

> *Olof's Mother catches sight of Olof holding the hand of The Prostitute.*

MOTHER (*beside herself*): Olof! Olof!

CHRISTINA: Who is that? That woman, she looks so sad.

MARTIN: What a horrible place. Let us get out of here!

Olof turns and runs to the iron door, which Martin slams shut.

OLOF: Mother! Mother!

He rushes out through the other door.

The stage grows dark.

INTERLUDE

Once again the door to the church opens, slowly this time. Bengt, the Sexton, who serves as organ blower and general caretaker of the Great Church, steps cautiously into the room. He is accompanied by his wife, Catherine.

SEXTON: Catherine, sweet! Hold the lantern while I put the padlock on the door.

CATHERINE: Bengt, dear, let's have a look round at this mess first. I had no idea the tavern was so close. Why, this is terrible. Look at these huge barrels of beer.

SEXTON: And there's aquavit and liquor. What a smell! It's giving me a headache. Let's get out of here.

CATHERINE: God's mercy, what ungodly things must have gone on here.

SEXTON: Katey, my sweet.

CATHERINE: Yes, love?

SEXTON: I don't think I'm feeling very good. It's so cold and clammy down here.

CATHERINE: Maybe we'd better go home.

SEXTON: I think I'd better sit down and rest for a moment on this bench.

CATHERINE: You shouldn't be sitting in the damp and cold. Let's go back into the church.

SEXTON: I don't know. I think it was colder in there.

CATHERINE: Don't have a fever, do you?

SEXTON: I think maybe I do. I'm burning.

CATHERINE: Would you like something to drink?

SEXTON: There's an idea. Might help.

CATHERINE: I'll see if I can find some water.

SEXTON: Water? You wouldn't find water in a hole like this.

CATHERINE: Well, you can't drink beer when you've got a fever.

SEXTON: To tell the truth, the fever's gone. I've got a terrible chill, that's what.

CATHERINE: I'll find some small beer for you.

SEXTON: I don't think it will do any good. Won't have any effect unless it's strong. There's some. That butt: Rostock, number 4, marked A.W.

CATHERINE (*searching*): I don't see it. . . . Here's an Amsterdam, number 3.

SEXTON: Try the fourth shelf up and toward the right.

> *Catherine looks.*

SEXTON: The spigot's there to the left, right next to the funnel.

CATHERINE: Don't see it.

SEXTON: I ought to know.

CATHERINE: Found it! Here it is.

> *As the Sexton gets up to help her, he stumbles over Captain Windrank.*

WINDRANK (*waking up slowly, and mumbling*): Oh, oh. Jesus Christ. . . . Saints Peter and Paul . . . and Ferdinand and Isabella . . . and St. George and the dragon and whatever else . . . in came . . . Judgment of God . . . Hocus-pocus . . . the Big Dipper wrongside up . . . spills out . . . don't cry over it. . . . And the cow jumped over the moon. . . . Now I lay me down to sleep. . . . Four angels to my bed, Gabriel stands at the head. . . . Avast! Who's stepping on my stomach?

SEXTON (*frightened*): Would you, sir, deign to tell me what or who you are?

WINDRANK: A dog, usually; tonight, a pig.

SEXTON: A dog? What sort, may I ask?

WINDRANK: A sea dog. I sail with the wind. But that is no reason why you, good sir, should take the wind out of me by stepping on my bellows.

SEXTON. Good sir, I make my living by stepping on bellows— for the organ here in the Great Church.

WINDRANK: Ah ha, the organ blower. I'm honored.

SEXTON: Sexton, really. I also run a little clothing shop, within the church wall.

WINDRANK: So you are organ blower, church sexton, and clothes pedlar—

SEXTON: Three in one. "Conjoined without confusion and without change."

WINDRANK: A most respectable trinity!

SEXTON: One shouldn't joke about such things.

WINDRANK (*yelling*): Oh, oh! I'm drowning! Help!

SEXTON: What in the name of the Lord is going on?

WINDRANK: Look at this flood! Foh!

SEXTON: Katey, my sweet! Where are you, angel? (*Rushing about.*) Oh, Jesus, you've scared the wits out of my wife. She's run out of here and taken the spigot with her, and all the beer's running out of the cask. Get up, good sir, get up! Let's leave this ungodly doghole.

WINDRANK: Leave? My good friend, I have just come into my element. I'm for staying.

SEXTON: Whatever you say, but the clock is striking twelve. The witching hour!

WINDRANK (*getting to his feet hurriedly*): You've changed my mind!

The Sexton starts to lead Windrank out.

WINDRANK: Sexton, I'm being assailed by strong doubts about the trinity.

SEXTON: What's that you say? Dear me!

WINDRANK: I mean *your* trinity.

SEXTON: What do you mean, Captain?

WINDRANK: There are four of you, or you can hang me from the yardarm.

SEXTON: Four? Which four?

WINDRANK: What about the beer tapster? Ha, ha! Have to include him, hm?

SEXTON: Sh! Sh! He's included only at night.

They both fall over the broken statue of St. Nicholas.

WINDRANK: Oh! Oh! Spooks! Holy Mother of God!

SEXTON (*getting to his feet and picking up the statue*): It's enough to make your hair stand on end. St. Nicholas, smashed to bits and swimming in beer. Things have come to a pretty pass when holy things are dragged into the dirt like this. The world can't last long. "If they do these things in a green tree, what shall be done in a dry?"

WINDRANK (*has picked himself up*): Wet, don't you mean?

SEXTON: Captain, you blaspheme. St. Nicholas is my patron saint. I was born on his day.

WINDRANK: That must be why both of you like beer so much.

SEXTON: It's all the fashion now to be a heretic.

WINDRANK: Yes, it must be in the air. Usually I'm a very God-fearing man. But don't you cry. I'll glue the pieces of your St. Nicholas together.

SEXTON (*yelling into the church through the iron door*): Katey! Catherine!

WINDRANK: Sh! Sh! Hell, man, you'll raise the devil's dam!

SEXTON: That's not nice! I have to live with her!

They leave.

TABLEAU CURTAIN

Scene 2

The sacristy of the Great Church. A large door is visible, and a smaller one leading to the pulpit. Chasubles and copes are hanging on the walls. Prayer stools and some small chests. The sun is shining in through a window.

Bells are ringing. From behind the left wall can be heard the monotonous sound of a voice intoning prayers.

The Sexton and his wife, Catherine, enter through the large door, stop, and say a silent prayer.

SEXTON: That's that. Well, get a move on, sweet, and do a little dusting.

CATHERINE: Well, there's no need to be particular. It's only Master Olof who's preaching today. And I don't understand why the chapter allows it.

SEXTON: He has the support of the king, that's why.

CATHERINE: Yes, yes, I know.

SEXTON: The ambo isn't good enough for him. He's built himself a special speaking place, up in the air. A pulpit, he calls it. A basket, that's what it is. Crazy, newfangled notions. Luther! Luther!

CATHERINE: I suppose it will be the same shambles today as yesterday. I thought they would tear down the whole church.

SEXTON (*as he takes a cup of water up to the pulpit*): I suspect he'll be needing to wet his whistle today, poor fool.

CATHERINE (*while the Sexton is in the pulpit*): It's all the same to me.

SEXTON (*from the pulpit*): Catherine! Master Olof's coming!

CATHERINE: He can't be! How awful! They haven't rung the sermon bell yet. Well, I suppose they wouldn't bother ringing it for someone like him.

> *Olof enters, looking solemn and serious. He goes to the prayer stool and kneels.*
>
> *The Sexton has come down from the pulpit. He takes a robe and holds it for Olof.*

OLOF (*standing up*): God's peace.

> *Catherine curtsies and leaves.*
>
> *The Sexton offers to put the robe on Olof.*

OLOF: Hang it up again.

SEXTON: Master Olof, you have got to wear your robe.

OLOF: No.

SEXTON: But it's always done. The napkin?

OLOF: Not necessary.

SEXTON: Well, I must say!

OLOF: If you don't mind, please leave me, my friend.

SEXTON: You want me to go? I've always—

OLOF: Yes, if you don't mind.

SEXTON: Oh, I see. Yes. Well, I've put the missal to the right as you come up, and I've stuck a spill in to mark the place, and

I've put the water next to it. And don't forget to turn the hour-glass, otherwise things just might go on too long, you know—

OLOF: Have no fear. Many out there will tell me when to stop.

SEXTON: Oh, yes, Lord help us. Beg your pardon. But we do have our customs, don't you know.

OLOF: What's that mournful mumbling I hear?

SEXTON: A pious brother reading prayers for some lost soul. (*He leaves.*)

OLOF: "Thou therefore gird up thy loins, and arise, and speak unto them all that I command thee." . . . God help me. (*He kneels at a prie-dieu and finds a piece of paper on it. Reads.*) "Do not go into the pulpit today. They seek your life." —Words of the tempter! (*He tears the paper to bits.*)

Olof's Mother comes in.

MOTHER: You've gone astray, my son.

OLOF: Who's to say?

MOTHER: *I* am. Your mother. And I am still here. I reach out to you. Turn back!

OLOF: Where would you lead me?

MOTHER: To the path of virtue and to the fear of God.

OLOF: If the decrees of the pope's chancery stand for virtue and the fear of God, I'm afraid you've come too late.

MOTHER: It's not just what you teach; it's the way you live.

OLOF: You say that because of the woman you saw me with last night. I'm too proud to answer you. What good would it do, anyway?

MOTHER: So this is how I'm repaid for all I had to sacrifice that you might see the world and receive a good education.

OLOF: Mother, I swear your sacrifices shall not be wasted. It is to you that I owe my thanks for this day, when at long last I can come forward and openly speak the truth as I see it.

MOTHER: You talk of the truth! You who have made yourself the prophet of lies!

OLOF: Harsh words, Mother.

MOTHER: Did I and all my people before me live a lie? Believe in and die for a lie?

OLOF: It *was* not a lie; it has *become* a lie. When you were young, Mother, you were right. When I grow old, perhaps I'll be in the wrong. One doesn't grow with the times.

MOTHER: I don't understand you.

OLOF: I know. That is the single greatest sorrow of my life: that everything I say and do, however pure my intentions, strikes you as wrongdoing, as godlessness.

MOTHER: Olof, I know that you've made your decision and I know that you are confused. I can't do anything about that, since you know so much more than I do. And I trust God that he will bring you back into the fold. But, Olof, I beg you, don't risk your life today; don't hurl yourself into hell. Don't throw your life away!

OLOF: What do you mean? They won't kill me while I'm in the pulpit.

MOTHER: Haven't you heard that Bishop Brask is negotiating with the pope to bring to Sweden the law that condemns heretics to the stake?

OLOF: The Inquisition?

MOTHER: Yes! The Inquisition!

OLOF: That's enough, Mother! I must speak to the people today; I must go into the pulpit.

MOTHER: I won't let you go!

OLOF: Nothing can stop me.

MOTHER: I have prayed to God to change your heart. I will tell you something, but you must never mention it to anyone. Old as I am—my legs could hardly carry me—I sought out a servant of the Lord and pleaded with him, who stood closer to God, to say

mass for your soul. He denied me because you were excommunicated. . . . Oh, I did a terrible thing. God forgive me for
it. I bribed him, yes, fouled his soul with gold, the devil's gold,
all to save your soul.

OLOF: No, Mother, no! I don't believe it.

> *Olof's Mother takes him by the hand and leads him
> toward the wall at the left.*

MOTHER: Listen! . . . Listen. . . . He is praying for you
now in the chapel.

OLOF: So that was the mumbling I heard. Who is it?

MOTHER: A Blackfriar. You know him: Martin.

OLOF: You've got Satan himself saying prayers for me. Forgive
me, Mother, I know you mean well, but—

MOTHER (*crying and kneeling*): Olof! Olof!

OLOF: Don't! Don't! A mother's prayers can tempt angels to fall.
They have finished the hymn. I have to go into the pulpit.
They're waiting.

MOTHER: You are driving me to my grave, Olof.

OLOF (*violently*): The Lord will raise you! (*Kisses her hand.*)
Don't say anything more. I don't know what I'm saying.

MOTHER: Listen! Listen to that muttering.

OLOF: I'm going. I'm going. That God who held His hand over
Daniel in the lions' den shall protect me. (*Olof goes up into the
pulpit.*)

> *During the following scene, Olof's voice can be heard, a
> strong orator's voice, delivering the sermon, but the
> words cannot be made out. A few moments into the
> sermon, murmurs of discontent can be heard, which
> grow into a roar, punctuated by shouts of disapproval.*
>
> *Christina, Gert's daughter, enters.*

CHRISTINA: Did you see him?

MOTHER: You here, child? I told you to stay home.

CHRISTINA: Why am I not allowed to enter the house of the Lord? You're hiding something from me.

MOTHER: Go home, Christina.

CHRISTINA: I can't hear Olof preach? Why not? If it is the word of God —. It is, isn't it?

Olof's Mother is silent.

CHRISTINA: Why don't you answer, Mother? What is going on? Doesn't he have permission to preach? The people out there looked as if they were hiding something. They were muttering when I walked in.

MOTHER: Don't ask, child. Go back home and thank God for your ignorance.

CHRISTINA: You treat me like a child. You don't dare tell me —

MOTHER: Your soul is like the living water. Don't let it be muddied. You have no part in this quarrel.

CHRISTINA: Quarrel! I thought as much.

MOTHER: Yes, the battle is raging. Keep clear of it. You know what our lot is when men wage war.

CHRISTINA: At least let me know what it's all about. I can't stand being left in ignorance. I see darkness all around me, and shadows that move. Give me light that I may know where I am. Perhaps I know who these ghosts are.

MOTHER: You will tremble when you recognize them.

CHRISTINA: I would rather tremble than be tormented by this horrible calm.

MOTHER: Don't call down the lightning. It will destroy you.

CHRISTINA: If you mean to frighten me, you have succeeded. But I still want to know the truth. If you don't tell me, I'll find someone who will.

MOTHER: You said you had decided to become a nun and enter a convent. Is that your firm decision?

CHRISTINA: My father wishes it.

MOTHER: That means *you* have doubts.

Christina is silent.

MOTHER: Something is holding you back?

CHRISTINA: You know there is.

MOTHER: Yes, I do; and you must break that bond.

CHRISTINA: That will soon be impossible.

MOTHER: I can help you, my child. You can be saved. I shall offer unto the Lord the greatest sacrifice I can make if that will save one soul from damnation: my son.

CHRISTINA: Olof!

MOTHER: He is lost. It's true. That his own mother should have to say it!

CHRISTINA: Lost?

MOTHER: He is a prophet of lies. The devil has seized his soul.

CHRISTINA (*passionately*): It's not true!

MOTHER: I wish to God it weren't.

CHRISTINA: Why did you wait till now to tell me? Why? —Of course, because it's a lie; that's why! (*She goes to the door and opens it slightly.*) Look at him there in the pulpit! Is that the evil spirit speaking through his mouth? Is that the fire of hell burning in his eyes? Can a lie be uttered by lips that tremble with conviction? Can the darkness send light? Don't you see the glow around his head? No, you are wrong. I know it! I don't know what ideas he preaches. I don't know what ideas he denies. Whatever they are, he is right. He is right, and God is with him!

MOTHER: How little you know the world and the cunning of the devil. Take care. (*She pulls Christina away from the door.*) You mustn't listen to him! Your spirit is weak. He is an apostle of Antichrist!

CHRISTINA: Who is Antichrist?

MOTHER: Those who believe in Luther.

CHRISTINA: You have never told me who Luther is. But if Olof is his apostle, then Luther must be a great man.

MOTHER: Luther is possessed by the devil.

CHRISTINA: No one told me this before. Why not? I don't believe it now.

MOTHER: I am telling you now. Forgive me; I wanted to keep you untouched by the evil in this world, so I kept you in ignorance.

CHRISTINA: I don't believe you! Let go of me! I must see him, I must hear him. He doesn't talk like the others.

MOTHER: Oh, Jesus, my Savior! You too are possessed by unclean spirits.

CHRISTINA (*at the door*): Listen! "Ye shall not bind the souls of men." That's what he is saying to them. . . . "Ye are free, for God has made you free!" They tremble at his words. Some are standing. Some are protesting. . . . "If ye do not wish to be free, then woe unto you! That is a sin against the Holy Ghost!"

SEXTON (*as he enters*): I don't think it's advisable for you ladies to remain here. The people are up in arms. Oh, dear, I'm afraid this won't end well for Master Olof.

MOTHER: Oh, Holy Mother of God, what are you saying?

CHRISTINA: Don't be afraid. The spirit of God is with him!

SEXTON: I don't know about that, but I never heard a sermon like that one. Even an old sinner like me couldn't help crying as I sat up there in the organ loft. I don't understand it—how a heretic and an Antichrist can talk like that! Well, I must say, that Luther!

Cries and yells are heard from within the church.

SEXTON: What did I tell you! There's going to be a terrible row. Why did King Gustav have to be out of town just now?

MOTHER: We had better go. If God is with him, they cannot harm him. And if it is the devil—well, Lord God, let Thy will be done. But pray forgive him.

> *More yelling is heard from within the church. Christina and Olof's Mother leave.*
>
> *The stage is empty for a moment. Olof's voice can be heard, louder than before. Catcalls and the sound of stones hitting the pulpit door.*
>
> *Christina returns, closes the door behind her, and throws herself down on one of the hassocks.*
>
> *Sound of stones striking the pulpit door and of tumult within the church. It grows quiet, and Olof comes in from the pulpit, looking wan and defeated, blood on his forehead. Not seeing Christina, he flings himself into a chair.*

OLOF: All for nothing! They don't care. I loosen his bonds, and the captive strikes me. I tell him he is free, and he doesn't believe me. Is that little word so big that the mind of man can't take it in? If only there were one person who believed. But to be all alone—a fool, whom no one understands.

CHRISTINA: I believe in you, Olof.

OLOF: Christina!

CHRISTINA: *You* are right.

OLOF: How do you know that I am?

CHRISTINA: I don't know how. I only believe it. I was listening.

OLOF: And you don't curse me?

CHRISTINA: Aren't you preaching the word of God?

OLOF: Yes.

CHRISTINA: Why haven't we heard these things before? Why do they speak a language we don't understand?

OLOF: Young woman, someone has been putting words in your mouth. Who?

CHRISTINA: I don't know. I never thought about it.

OLOF: Your father?

CHRISTINA: He wants me to enter a convent.

OLOF: Has it come to that? What do you want?

CHRISTINA (*noticing Olof's injury*): You've been hurt, Olof. Oh, my God! Let me put a bandage on it.

OLOF (*sitting down*): Have I undermined your faith?

CHRISTINA (*takes Olof's napkin—left behind when he went into the pulpit—tears it into strips and binds his forehead during the following*): My faith? I don't understand. . . . Tell me, who is Luther?

OLOF: I mustn't tell you.

CHRISTINA: That's what you all say. It's what my father says, it's what your mother says, it's what you say. Does no one dare to tell me the truth? Is the truth so dangerous?

OLOF: It is! Look! (*He points to his forehead.*)

CHRISTINA: So you want to see me shut up in a nun's cell, living in ignorance—not living at all, really.

> *Olof says nothing.*

CHRISTINA: You want to see me weeping away my life, my young years, saying my prayers endlessly until my soul sinks into sleep. Well, I don't want it. I've been awakened. People are fighting. They're suffering, they're in despair. I've seen it, but I'm not to be allowed a part, not even allowed to look, not even to know what it's all about. You treat me like a stupefied animal. Don't you suppose I have a soul, a soul that cannot be nourished on bread or the stale prayers that you put in my mouth. "Ye cannot bind the souls of men"—that is what you said. Oh, if you only knew how those words struck me. The light dawned for me, and those words struck me. The light dawned for me, and those wild yells out there sounded to me like the singing of birds at daybreak.

OLOF: Christina, you're a woman. You were not born to fight.

CHRISTINA: All right. Then for God's sake let me at least suffer. Anything is better than to sleep my life away. Don't you see? God awakened me after all. You wqould never have dared to tell me who the Antichrist is, never let me know who Luther is. When your mother frightened me by saying you were another Luther, I called down a blessing on him. Whether he's a heretic or a believer, I don't know. I don't care. Because neither Luther nor the pope nor the Antichrist can give me peace of soul if I do not have faith in the everlasting God.

OLOF: Oh, Christina! Will you help me? Be at my side in the battle? You could be all things to me. For me, there is no one but you.

CHRISTINA: Yes, Olof! Yes, with all my heart! I know what I want. I don't have to run to Father and ask him. I feel free. Because I am free!

OLOF: Do you know what you're doing? – what sort of life you're asking for?

CHRISTINA: I do now. Don't worry. You won't have to destroy any illusions. They're gone. . . . Although I admit I have dreamed of a knight in armor who would come to offer me a kingdom and who would speak of love and flowers. . . . Olof, I want to be your wife. Here is my hand. But there is one thing you should know. You were never that shining knight of my dreams. Thank God he never came. He would have vanished as all dreams do.

OLOF: Yes, you shall be mine, Christina, and you shall be happy. I promise you. You were always in my mind when despair seized me and the devil tempted me. Now you shall be at my side. You were always the fair maid of my dreams, held captive in a tower by the lord of the castle. Now you are mine.

CHRISTINA: Beware of dreams, Olof.

Knocking at the door.

OLOF: Who is it?

GERT (*from outside*): Gert.

OLOF: What will he say now? I promised him!

CHRISTINA: Afraid? Let me open the door.

Olof opens the door.

GERT (*startled*): Christina! —Olof? —You have broken your promise!

OLOF: No!

GERT: Liar! You have stolen my child, my life's consolation.

CHRISTINA: Olof isn't lying.

GERT: You have been to church, Christina?

CHRISTINA: I have heard what you didn't want me to hear.

GERT: Lord, You have begrudged me my one joy!

OLOF: Open the floodgates, you said. Let the torrent rage, you said. Well, it claims whatever stands in its way.

GERT: You have stolen my child from me.

OLOF: Then give her to me, Father Gert!

GERT: Never!

OLOF: Isn't she free to make up her own mind?

GERT: She is my child!

OLOF: So much for the freedom you preach! No, she is mine. God has given her to me, and you cannot take her back.

GERT: You are, Olof—and God be praised for it—a priest!

OLOF *and* CHRISTINA: A priest!

GERT: And therefore prohibited from marrying.

OLOF: And if I marry anyway?

GERT: You wouldn't dare.

OLOF: Yes, I would.

GERT: Would you want a husband who is excommunicate, Christina?

CHRISTINA: I don't even know what that means.

OLOF: You see, Gert, you see!

GERT: Oh, Lord, you have chastened me sore.

OLOF: Truth is not partial.

GERT: Your love is greater than mine. Mine was a selfish love. God bless you both. Now I stand alone. (*Embraces them.*) There! Go home, Christina, and set their minds at ease. I want to talk to Olof.

    Christina leaves.

GERT (*to Olof*): Now you are mine.

OLOF: What do you mean?

GERT: My kinsman. —Did you get my note?

OLOF: So it was you that warned me not to go into the pulpit.

GERT: Quite the contrary, Olof. It's just that I expressed myself in a roundabout way.

OLOF: I don't understand.

GERT: Of course not. You're still too young. That's why you have need of providence. To a man like you one says "don't do it" when one wants it done.

OLOF: Why weren't you in church with your friends?

GERT: Only the sick need doctors, Olof. We were at work elsewhere. You've done a good job today, and I see that you got paid for it. Today I made you a free man, Olof.

OLOF: You?

GERT: The king ordered you to calm the rebellious spirits. And look at what you have done!

OLOF: I begin to understand you, Gert.

GERT: I'm delighted! Yes, indeed, you set a fire under the sluggards.

OLOF: I did indeed.

GERT: Now what do you suppose the king will say to that?

OLOF: I'll take responsibility.

GERT: Good!

OLOF: The king will approve of what I have done. He wants a reformation, only he's afraid of carrying it out himself.

GERT: You've got it wrong, boy.

OLOF: I know what you want: to set me against the king.

GERT: Tell me, how many masters do you think you can serve?

Olof says nothing.

GERT: The king is back in town.

OLOF: What?

GERT: He just returned.

OLOF: And the Anabaptists?

GERT: Imprisoned, of course.

OLOF: And you stand here doing nothing.

GERT: I'm getting on in years. I once carried on as you do now, but it only exhausted me. Rink and Knipperdollink have formed my advance guard. They had to fall, that was obvious. Now I begin my work.

Drums are heard in the street outside.

OLOF: What's that?

GERT: The royal drums marching the captives to prison. Take a look.

OLOF (*stands on a bench and looks out through the window*): Women and children! Dragged off by soldiers!

GERT: They threw stones at the king's guard. That was naughty.

OLOF: Next they'll be putting the mad and the sick in prison.

GERT: There are two kinds of madmen: one kind gets prison, pills, and cold baths. The other kind gets his head lopped off. A radical cure—but then the disease *is* dangerous, wouldn't you say?

OLOF: I'm going to see the king. He won't allow these atrocities.

GERT: Watch out for your head, Olof.

OLOF: Watch out yourself, Father Gert.

GERT: I'm in no danger. I've been certified mad.

OLOF: I can't bear to see this. I'm going to the king even if it costs me my life. (*Goes toward the door.*)

GERT: It's not a matter that the king can settle. You should appeal to the law.

OLOF: The king is the law.

GERT: Yes, unfortunately. (*He looks out the window.*) Stupid horses. If they knew their strength, you couldn't harness them. When a horse does wise up, it runs away. They call that a crazy horse. . . . Let's pray to God for the sanity of these poor wretches.

CURTAIN

ACT III

Scene 1

A large room in the castle in Stockholm. At back, a gallery, which will later be closed off by a curtain.

An old Servant is pacing his round in the gallery.

Olof enters.

OLOF: Is the king receiving today?

SERVANT: Yes.

OLOF: Can you tell me why I've been kept waiting for four days?

SERVANT: I'm sure I wouldn't know.

OLOF: It seems very strange that I haven't been admitted.

SERVANT: What is your business?

OLOF: No concern of yours.

SERVANT: No, no, of course not. I merely thought that I might provide some information.

OLOF: Are you customarily in charge of the king's audiences?

SERVANT: No, no, nothing like that. But anyone who gets to hear as much as I do picks up things here and there.

Pause.

OLOF: How long will it be?

The Servant pretends not to hear.

OLOF: I say, do you know if the king will be here soon?

SERVANT (*with his back to Olof, slighting him*): Beg pardon, what —?

OLOF: Do you know whom you're talking to?

SERVANT: Have no idea, sorry.

OLOF: I am the king's secretary in the council.

SERVANT: Bless me, Master Olof is it! I knew your father, Peter the blacksmith. You see, I'm from Örebro, too.

OLOF: That's hardly an excuse for poor manners.

SERVANT: True, my boy. When one rises in the world, the poor relations are forgot. Sad but true, my dear boy.

OLOF: It's possible my father honored you with his acquaintance, but I'm sure that when he died, he didn't make you my father. So if you don't mind—

SERVANT: My, my, we are touchy! Pity your poor mother. (*He moves off to the left.*)

> *A moment's silence. Olof is alone. Then Lars Siggeson, National Marshal and Lord High Constable, enters from the right.*
>
> *Without really looking at Olof, the Marshal casually tosses his coat to him.*

MARSHAL: Will the king be here soon?

> *Olof drops the coat on the floor.*

OLOF: I wouldn't know.

MARSHAL: Bring me a chair.

OLOF: That's not one of my duties.

MARSHAL: I am not provided with a list of the doorman's duties!

OLOF: I am not a doorman!

MARSHAL: I don't care what you are. I don't have a list of servants with me, either. It's your duty to be polite.

> *Olof says nothing.*

MARSHAL: Don't stand there! What the devil's got into you?

OLOF: I beg your pardon. As secretary of the council, I am not obliged to wait on people.

MARSHAL: What! —Ah, it's Master Olof! So it amuses you to stand by the door and play the servant in order to reveal yourself as God Almighty. And I thought you had some pride! (*During this, he has picked up his coat and placed it on a bench.*)

OLOF: Lord Marshal—

MARSHAL: Never mind! You're a vain upstart. No need to stand lurking there. Come, sit here, Mr. Secretary. (*Shows him a place, and then goes into a side room.*)

> *Olof sits down.*

> *A young Nobleman enters and greets Olof from the gallery.*

NOBLEMAN: Good morning, Mr. Secretary! Good morning! Anyone arrive yet? How are things here in Stockholm? I've come directly from Malmö.

OLOF: Deplorable!

NOBLEMAN: So I have heard. As usual, the mob blusters when the king has his back turned. And the priests—what a stupid lot they are! Oh, forgive me! But you are a freethinker, are you not, Mr. Secretary?

OLOF: I'm afraid I don't quite follow.

NOBLEMAN: Don't be embarrassed on my account. I was educated in Paris. You see? Francis the First, oh *Saint-Sauveur*! That man will go far. Do you know what he said to me at a *bal masque*—only recently in carnival time?

> *Olof lets the question hang.*

NOBLEMAN: *"Monsieur,"* he said, *"la religion est morte, est morte."* That's what he said. That doesn't prevent him from attending mass, however.

OLOF: Really?

NOBLEMAN: And do you know what he said when I asked him why he went to mass? "*Poésie*," he said, "*poésie.*" Isn't he divine?

OLOF: And what did you say?

NOBLEMAN: "Your Majesty," I said—in French, of course— "happy the land that is ruled by a king who sees so far beyond the limited horizons of his time that he can comprehend the tenor of things to come without compelling the sleeping masses to embrace those higher ideals for which they will not be ready until centuries have passed." Well said, don't you think?

OLOF: Absolutely. Though it lost something in the translation. Some things have to be said in French.

NOBLEMAN (*momentarily disconcerted*): Perfectly right, of course, indeed you are. Dear fellow, you could *faire fortune*, you're so far ahead of the times.

OLOF: Not so far, I'm afraid. Unfortunately, my education was somewhat scanted. I went to Germany for it, as you know, and the Germans have not got beyond religion.

NOBLEMAN: How true, how absolutely true! Can you tell me why they are making such a fuss over that reformation in Germany? Oh, Luther is an enlightened man, I know that; I am sure of it. But why can't he keep it to himself?—the reformation, I mean. Why throw brilliant ideas out to the masses? Pearls before swine. Anyone who looks out over the wide world, anyone who is part of the great intellectual movements, can see the cause of that imbalance, that loss of equilibrium, which is apparent in all the cultured lands. I speak not of Sweden, which has no culture. Do you know what that center of gravity is? That center any disturbance of which turns the world upside down? That center of gravity is—the nobility. The aristocracy, the intelligentsia! Feudalism has had its day—*hoc est* the way of the world! Civilization is collapsing, culture is dying. I see you don't believe it. But a mere glance at history proves me right. Had there been no aristocracy there would have been no crusades! Without the nobility —none of this, none of that. Why is Germany torn to pieces? Because the peasants have risen in revolt against the nobility. They're cutting off their own head. Why does France—*la France*

—stand firm and solid? Because France *is* the aristocracy, and the aristocracy is France. They are one and the same, an identity. And—to put another question—why is Sweden today shaken to its very foundations? Because the nobility has been crushed. Now Christian the Second, there was a genius! He knew how to conquer a land. He didn't saw off a leg or an arm; he cut off the head. Ah, well! Sweden shall be saved. King Gustav knows how. The nobility shall be restored and the church crushed.—What do you say to that?

OLOF (*getting to his feet*): Nothing.

A moment's silence.

OLOF: You're a freethinker?

NOBLEMAN: But of course!

OLOF: And therefore you don't believe that Balaam's ass could talk?

NOBLEMAN: My God, no!

OLOF: I do.

NOBLEMAN: Extraordinary!

LARS ANDERSSON (*coming in*): God's peace, Olof.

OLOF (*embracing him*): Welcome, Lars.

NOBLEMAN (*as he leaves*): *Racaille!*

LARS ANDERSSON: Does your new job agree with you? How do you like it here in Stockholm?

OLOF: It's too stuffy.

LARS ANDERSSON: I'm sure.

OLOF: And the ceilings are too low.

LARS ANDERSSON: He must stoop who has a low door.

OLOF: In just ten minutes here I've become so much the courtier that I've learned to hold my tongue when an ass brays.

LARS ANDERSSON: No harm in that.

OLOF: What's the king up to?

LARS ANDERSSON: He keeps his own counsel.

> *In the meantime several people have come into the room and are waiting to see the king.*

OLOF: How does he look?

LARS ANDERSSON: Like a question mark followed by several exclamation points.

> *Bishop Brask enters. Everyone makes way for him.*
>
> *Lars Siggeson, the National Marshal, already on the scene, approaches him and greets him.*
>
> *Thereupon Olof greets him. Brask is amazed.*

BRASK (*to The Marshal*): Are these the clerks' quarters?

MARSHAL: They shouldn't be, but our king is infintely obliging.

BRASK: Patronizing, is more like it.

MARSHAL: Quite.

BRASK: Rather large attendance today, I see.

MARSHAL: Yes. Mostly social calls, congratulating His Majesty on his safe return.

BRASK: I shall find it a pleasure, my Lord Constable, to inform His Majesty that I am in complete sympathy with his felicitous solution to a difficult problem.

MARSHAL: My Lord Bishop is most gracious to put himself to so much trouble. It's a long journey from Linköping, especially for a man of your years.

BRASK: Yes, it is. More so, since my health isn't too reliable.

MARSHAL: Indeed. I'm sorry to hear that my Lord's health isn't what it should be. It's always depressing not to be in full vigor, and especially so when one occupies a high position with all its responsibilities.

BRASK: I must say you look in good shape.

MARSHAL: Yes, thank God.

The conversation dies for a moment.

BRASK (*sitting down*): Do you feel a draft, my Lord Marshal?

MARSHAL: Yes, it's possible I do. Perhaps we should have them close the door?

BRASK: No, thank you. I don't think that is necessary.

Again the conversation dies.

MARSHAL: The king seems to be taking his time.

BRASK: Yes.

MARSHAL: Perhaps there is no point in waiting for him.

BRASK: Perhaps not.

MARSHAL: If you wish, I could call your servants.

BRASK: Having waited this long, I suppose I can wait a while longer.

Silence. Then the Servant announces the arrival of King Gustav.

SERVANT: His Majesty!

GUSTAV: Welcome, my lords. (*He sits down at a table.*) If my lords will be good enough to step out into the antechamber, I shall receive you one at a time.

Everyone except Bishop Brask starts to withdraw.

GUSTAV: Our National Marshal may stay.

BRASK: But Your Majesty—!

GUSTAV (*raising his voice*): Lars Siggeson!

> *Lars Siggeson, the National Marshal, turns and approaches Gustav. Bishop Brask leaves.*
>
> *Silence.*

GUSTAV: Well, speak up! What should I do?

MARSHAL: Your Majesty: the situation is clear. The state is tottering because it has lost its main support. Its existence is in peril because it has acquired an enemy stronger than itself. Strengthen the main support, the nobility, and crush the enemy, the church.

GUSTAV: I dare not.

MARSHAL: Sire, you have no choice.

GUSTAV: No choice! No choice!

MARSHAL: Begging your leave, Sire, no. Bishop Brask is negotiating right now with the pope to bring the Inquisition here. Lübeck is becoming more insistent in its exorbitant demands for the repayment of our debts, and is even threatening war. The national treasury is empty; there are insurrections in every part of the country —

GUSTAV: Enough, enough! . . . What matters is that I have the people behind me.

MARSHAL: Have you? Forgive me, Your Majesty, but take the Dalesmen, for example. A spoiled tribe, who dispute the Lübeckers the honor of having provided Sweden with a king, who stand ready to revolt at the first opportunity, and who issue demands such as — (*He reads from a slip of paper.*) "No foreign styles in clothes, such as slashed and pouched apparel and brocaded fabric, which have recently been introduced at court, shall be countenanced."

GUSTAV: Damnation!

MARSHAL: "Anyone who eats meat on Fridays or Saturdays is to be burned at the stake or otherwise deprived of his life." Or this: "No new faith or creed or Lutheran doctrine is to be imposed on us." — I tell you, a faithless and insolent people!

GUSTAV: Still, they were real men once, when I stood alone and had need of them.

MARSHAL: Real men? When their houses were on fire, they carried water. Who wouldn't? Real men? How many times haven't they broken their word? For words mean nothing to them—except of course words of praise. And those they have heard so often that they now actually believe that their crude insolence is good old Swedish bluntness.

GUSTAV: You belong to the nobility.

MARSHAL: I do. And I am convinced that the yeoman has played out his part: the exercise of brute muscle power to drive the enemy out of Sweden. . . . Your Majesty: eliminate the church, which keeps the people in chains; use the wealth of the church to pay off the nation's debts; and return to the prostrate nobility the gold that the church cheated them of.

GUSTAV: Call in Brask!

MARSHAL: But Your Majesty—

GUSTAV: Bishop Brask, I said!

> *The Marshal leaves.*
>
> *Bishop Brask enters.*

GUSTAV: Now, Bishop Brask, let me hear what you have to say.

BRASK: May I offer our warmest wishes for your—

GUSTAV: Thank you, my Lord Bishop. To business.

BRASK: Regrettably, there have been rumors of complaints from various parts of the kingdom concerning Your Majesty's unpaid loans from the church. I refer to the silver tribute levied by Your Majesty.

GUSTAV: And you have come to demand payment. Does the church actually use all those chalices for communion?

BRASK: Yes, Your Majesty.

GUSTAV: Let them drink out of tin mugs.

BRASK: Your Majesty!

GUSTAV: Any other business?

BRASK: The most serious of all: heresy.

GUSTAV: That doesn't concern me. I am not the pope.

BRASK: I am bound to inform Your Majesty that the church will insist upon its rights even at the risk of running into conflict. . . .

GUSTAV: With whom?

BRASK: With the state.

GUSTAV: Your church can go to the devil! Is that clear enough?

BRASK: It was clear enough before.

GUSTAV: And you only wanted to hear it from my own lips?

BRASK: Yes.

GUSTAV: Take care! You travel with two hundred men in your retinue and dine off silver while the people eat the bark off trees.

BRASK: Your Majesty takes too narrow a view of the matter.

GUSTAV: And you are a broad-minded, enlightened man? What about Luther? How do you account for that phenomenon? What about the movements now sweeping through Europe?

BRASK: Reaching forward but stepping backward. Luther's role is simply to provide the purgative fire for what is centuries old, tried and true, in order that, through strife, it may prove itself victorious.

GUSTAV: I'm not interested in your sophistries.

BRASK: But Your Majesty harbors criminals and encroaches on the rights of the church. Your Master Olof has grievously offended the church.

GUSTAV: Excommunicate him.

BRASK: That has been done. Yet he is still in Your Majesty's service.

GUSTAV: What more do you want to do to him? . . . Well?

Pause.

BRASK: Furthermore, there seems to be no stopping him. I have learned that he has secretly married in direct violation of canonical law.

GUSTAV: Well, well! He does move fast.

BRASK: Your Majesty can turn his back on that, of course. Suppose, however, he rouses the people?

GUSTAV: Then I shall take the matter into my hands. — Is there anything else?

BRASK (*waits before speaking*): I beg you, Sire, for heaven's sake, do not drive the country into wrack and ruin again. It is not ready for a new religion. We are frail reeds that can bend. But the church? No! The faith? No, never!

GUSTAV (*extending his hand*): Perhaps you are right. Let us be avowed enemies, Hans, old Hans, rather than false friends.

BRASK: Fair enough. But do not do anything you might regret. Every stone you take from the wall of the church the people will cast at you.

GUSTAV: Do not drive me to extremes, Bishop. We do not want the horrible spectacles that Germany has witnessed. For the last time: will you make concessions if the welfare of the country is at stake?

BRASK: The church . . . never . . .

GUSTAV: The church first, yes. Very well. God be with you.

Brask leaves.

The Marshal enters.

GUSTAV: Bishop Brask confirmed what you said. That was precisely the idea. Now we need masons, not for building but for demolishing. The walls may stand; the cross may remain on the roof and the bells in the tower. But I shall leave the cellars in ruins. Begin with the foundations, always.

MARSHAL: The people think that we are depriving them of their faith. They will have to be taught otherwise.

GUSTAV: We shall have Master Olof preach to them.

MARSHAL: A very dangerous fellow.

GUSTAV: And the very man we need now.

MARSHAL: He has been acting like an Anabaptist instead of fighting against them.

GUSTAV: I know. That will come later. Send him in.

MARSHAL: Chancellor Lars would be better.

GUSTAV: Have them both come in.

MARSHAL: Or Olof's brother, Lars Pedersson.

GUSTAV: Won't do just now. He's too tender-hearted. His time will come, too.

> *The Marshal brings in Olof and Chancellor Lars Andersson.*

GUSTAV (*addressing Lars Andersson*): I need your help, Lars.

LARS ANDERSSON: As regards the church?

GUSTAV: Yes. It must be demolished.

LARS ANDERSSON: I'm not your man. Perhaps Your Majesty should ask Master Olof.

GUSTAV: You mean you won't help?

LARS ANDERSSON: I mean I cannot. But I can provide you with a weapon.

> *He hands to Gustav the Swedish translation of the Bible. Gustav opens it and turns a few pages.*

GUSTAV: It's done. A Swedish translation of the Holy Scriptures. A job well done, Lars! A good weapon. Will you make use of it, Olof?

OLOF: Yes, with God's help.

Gustav signals to Lars Andersson to leave.

GUSTAV: Have you calmed down yet, Olof?

Olof doesn't reply.

I gave you four days to think things over. How did you fare with the assignment I gave you?

OLOF (*brusquely*): I have spoken to the people—

GUSTAV: Yes. Which left you as hot-headed as ever. You intend to defend those crazy fools, the ones they call Anabaptists?

OLOF (*boldly*): Yes!

GUSTAV: Calm yourself. . . . I hear you got married in all haste.

OLOF: Yes.

GUSTAV: And you have been excommunicated?

OLOF: Yes.

GUSTAV: And you're still as brash as ever. Now suppose that as a troublemaker in the realm you accompanied the others to the gallows—what would you say to that?

OLOF: I would regret that I had been unable to complete my work—and thank God for what little I was able to accomplish.

GUSTAV: Good, very good. Would you dare to go to Uppsala, that old owl's nest, and tell those doting professors that the pope is not God and that he has nothing to do with Sweden?

OLOF: Is that all?

GUSTAV: Will you tell them that God's word is to be found only in the Bible?

OLOF: Is that all you want of me?

GUSTAV: One thing more: you are not to mention Luther's name.

OLOF (*thinks about it for a moment*): No. I can't agree to that.

GUSTAV: Would you prefer to die with the others?

OLOF: No. But I think my king has need of me.

GUSTAV: It isn't very magnanimous of you to take advantage of my situation. — Very well, say what you want to say. However, you will have to forgive me if I make some revisions later on.

OLOF: One doesn't haggle over the truth.

GUSTAV: Damnation! (*Abruptly changing his tone.*) Do as you wish.

OLOF (*on his knees*): I am allowed to say exactly what I want said?

GUSTAV: Yes.

OLOF: Then my life won't be wasted — not if I cast a spark of doubt into these complacent souls. There shall be a reformation, after all.

GUSTAV (*taking time to reply*): Yes.

Pause.

OLOF (*worried*): What will become of the Anabaptists?

GUSTAV: Why ask? To the gallows, that's what.

OLOF: Will Your Majesty allow me a question?

GUSTAV: Tell me, what do these crazy fools want?

OLOF: The trouble is that they don't really know themselves. If I might —

GUSTAV: Yes? Speak out.

Gert the Printer enters in haste, acting insane.

GUSTAV: How dare you burst in here! Who are you?

GERT: Sire, I most humbly petition Your Majesty to attest to the correctness of this certificate.

GUSTAV: Wait until you are called.

GERT: Oh, *I* can wait, Sire. But the guards won't wait for me. I fled, you see, from the prison. It wasn't the place for me.

GUSTAV: Were you with the Anabaptists?

GERT: Yes, I got mixed up with them. But I have a certificate that I belong in the asylum. Division number three—for incurables, that is. Cell number seven.

GUSTAV (*to Olof*): Call the guards.

GERT: That isn't necessary, Sire. All I'm asking for is justice, and the guards aren't in charge of that.

GUSTAV (*staring at him*): Didn't you take part in the sacrileges committed against the churches here?

GERT: That would follow. Would a sane man do such crazy things? We had in mind to make only a few changes—stylistic ones. The ceilings were too low, in our opinion.

GUSTAV: What did you really accomplish?

GERT: Oh, so much, so much, and still only half of it done. So much and so quickly that our thoughts can't keep up. They are always a little behind. Oh, yes, refurbish the walls in the church, that's what we wanted. And the windows removed to get rid of the musty smell. Some other things, too, but that should do for now.

GUSTAV (*to Olof*): A fearful illness. Can't be anything else.

OLOF: Who knows?

GUSTAV: I'm tired. You have two weeks to get ready. Give me your hand and your promise that you will help me.

OLOF: I shall do my part.

GUSTAV: Give orders for the removal of Rink and Knipperdollink to Malmö.

OLOF: Then what?

GUSTAV: They can escape—to Germany. And this idiot you can send back to the asylum. Fare thee well.

Gustav leaves.

Gert shakes his fist at Gustav's back.

GERT: Shall we go?

OLOF: Where?

GERT: Home.

Olof is silent.

GERT: You wouldn't put your father-in-law in the madhouse, would you, Olof?

OLOF: Wouldn't I? My duty!

GERT: Are there no higher duties than obeying orders?

OLOF: Don't start that again.

GERT: What would Christina say if you left her father among the mad folk?

OLOF: Don't tempt me.

GERT: You see how hard it is to serve the king.

Olof is silent.

GERT: Dear boy, I won't cause you any distress. Here is absolution for your conscience. (*He shows Olof a piece of paper.*)

OLOF: What is it?

GERT: A bill of health. A release from the asylum. You see, you have to be mad among the sane, and sane among the mad.

OLOF: How did you get this?

GERT: You sound as if I don't deserve it.

OLOF: I wonder.

GERT: Of course. You're still afraid.

The Servant enters.

SERVANT: I'll have to ask you to leave. The room has to be swept.

GERT: And aired out?

SERVANT: You can be sure of it.

GERT: Don't forget to open the windows.

SERVANT: Never fear. It needs it. We're not used to this kind of company.

GERT: Oh, by the way, old boy, I have greetings from your old man.

SERVANT: Oh?

GERT: You do know your father?

SERVANT: What's that to you?

GERT: You know what he said?

SERVANT: No.

GERT: He said, "He that blows into the dust fills his eyes with it."

SERVANT: I don't see the point.

GERT: We all have excuses. (*He leaves.*)

SERVANT: Riffraff!

TABLEAU CURTAIN

Scene 2

Olof's study. Windows at the back with the sun shining through them. Trees outside. Christina is standing at one of the windows, watering flowers and talking to songbirds in a cage. Olof is at his desk, writing. From time to time he looks up from his work and glances impatiently at Christina. This is repeated several times until Christina knocks down a flower pot. Olof stamps the floor in irritation.

CHRISTINA: Oh, my poor, dear flower. Look, Olof, four buds broke off.

OLOF: Yes, yes, I'm not blind.

CHRISTINA: You're not even looking. Come here and see.

OLOF: Dearest, I haven't time.

CHRISTINA: You haven't even looked at the goldfinches I bought for you this morning. Don't you think they sing beautifully?

OLOF: Like a bird.

CHRISTINA: Like a bird?

OLOF: Frankly, it's hard to work with that screeching.

CHRISTINA: They don't screech, Olof. You're just partial to screeching at night. The owl doesn't bother you. What does that owl mean that you have on your signet ring?

OLOF: The owl is an ancient symbol of wisdom.

CHRISTINA: That's silly. A wise man wouldn't like the dark.

OLOF: A wise man hates the dark, he hates the night. But he turns night into day with his keen vision.

CHRISTINA: You always have the right answer, Olof. I wonder why?

OLOF: Because, my sweet, I know you enjoy letting me be right.

CHRISTINA: Right again! —What are you working on?

OLOF: I'm translating.

CHRISTINA: Read some of it to me.

OLOF: Oh, I don't think you would understand this.

CHRISTINA: Isn't it Swedish?

OLOF: Yes, but it's very abstract.

CHRISTINA: Abstract? What does that mean?

OLOF: I can't explain it. Let me put it this way: if you don't understand what I read, then you'll know what abstract means.

CHRISTINA (*taking up her knitting*): You read, and I'll knit.

OLOF: Listen carefully now, and don't blame me if I bore you.

CHRISTINA: I'll understand. I'm determined to.

OLOF (*reading*): "Matter, conceived as an abstraction from form, is completely without predicates, undefined and undifferentiated. Because not from pure non-being but only from the non-being of reality, that is, from being as potentiality, can anything originate. Potential being is no more non-being than reality. Every existence is therefore a realized possibility. Matter is thus for Aristotle a more positive substratum than it is for Plato, who explained it as pure non-being. From this it is possible to understand how Aristotle could conceive of matter in contrast to form as a positive negativity."

CHRISTINA (*throwing aside her knitting*): Oh, stop! I don't understand a word! Why? Why? I'm ashamed of myself, Olof. I must make a pretty poor wife, who can't understand what her husband is saying. I'd best stick to my knitting. I'll clean your study and dust your books. At least I'll learn to understand the looks in your eyes. Oh, Olof, I'm not worthy of you. Why did you take me as your wife? You overrated me, because you were momentarily infatuated with me. You'll come to regret it, and we'll both be unhappy.

OLOF: Christina, calm yourself. Now sit down here, darling, beside me. (*He picks up the knitting.*) Would you believe me if I told you that it is absolutely impossible for me to do work like this? Absolutely impossible. I could never manage it. So you must be more skillful than I am, and I must be less than you.

CHRISTINA: Why can't you do it?

OLOF: For the same reason that you didn't understand me just now: I haven't learned. Will it make you happy if I tell you that you can learn to understand this book—which is not mine: be sure you understand that—while I, on the other hand, can never learn how to do your work?

CHRISTINA: Why not?

OLOF: Because I'm not made that way. And because I don't want to.

CHRISTINA: But if you did want to?

OLOF: That, darling, is my weak point. I could never make myself want to. Believe me, you are stronger than I am. You are the master of your will; I'm the slave of mine.

CHRISTINA: Do you really think I could learn to understand that book of yours?

OLOF: I'm convinced of it. But you mustn't.

CHRISTINA: I must always be kept in ignorance, is that what you want?

OLOF: No, no, it's not that. But suppose you understood everything I understand. You wouldn't look up to me.

CHRISTINA: As a god?

OLOF: Whatever. Believe me, you would lose what makes you greater than me: the strength to curb your will. Then you would be less than me, and I couldn't look up to you. You see what I mean? We're happy because we overrate each other. Let's hold on to our delusions.

CHRISTINA: Now I don't understand you at all. Still, I have to believe you, Olof. I'm sure you're right.

OLOF: I need to be alone, Christina. Do you mind? Please.

CHRISTINA: Am I disturbing you?

OLOF: Christina, I have serious business to attend to. Today is decisive. The king has abdicated because Parliament wouldn't accept his proposals. Today I'll either reach my goal or start from scratch again.

CHRISTINA: I want to be happy today. It's Midsummer Eve, Olof.

OLOF: Why should you be especially happy today?

CHRISTINA: Why shouldn't I be? I was a captive. I've become your wife.

OLOF: I hope you will forgive me if I find it difficult to share all your joy. I've paid for my bliss: it cost me a mother.

CHRISTINA: I know what it cost you. I feel it deeply, too. When she learns of our marriage, your mother will forgive you, but she will curse me. Who will have the harder time of it? I don't mind—it's for your sake. I understand that. I know that enormous struggles lie ahead, that daring ideas are fermenting in your brain. Know that I can never take part in the struggle, never help with advice, never defend you against abuse and smears. Have to see it happening and still live in my small world, doing all the little things that I don't believe you appreciate but that you'd miss if I didn't do them. Since we can't cry together, Olof, maybe we could laugh together. That would make things easier for me. Come down from the heights where I can't reach you. Come home once in a while from those battles you fight in the mountains. If I can't climb up to you, can't you come down to me for a moment? Forgive me for talking like a child, Olof. You are sent by God; I know that. I have felt the blessing of your words. But you are also a man; you are my husband, or at least you should be. You won't lower yourself too much if you would drop the solemn talk and just for once let me see the sun on your face rather than the clouds. Are you so great that you can't look at a flower or listen to the birds sing? I put the flowers on your desk, Olof, to give your eyes something restful to look at; you had the girl take them away because they gave you a headache. I wanted to relieve the lonely silence of your work with the song of birds; you called it screeching. I asked you to come to dinner a while ago; you didn't have time. I want to talk with you now; you haven't got the time. Although you despise this little world of mine, you tell me to live in it. If you don't want to lift me up to your world, at least have the kindness not to trample on mine. I'll take away everything that disturbs your precious thoughts. You'll be rid of me and all my rubbish. (*She throws the flowers out the window, takes the birdcage, and starts to leave.*)

OLOF: Christina, dearest, I'm sorry. Forgive me. You just don't understand.

CHRISTINA: That's all you ever say: "You don't understand." It comes to me now—that moment in the sacristy with you. I grew up so fast that I became old in an instant. A different person.

OLOF: Christina, come. I'll look at your birds; I'll talk to your flowers.

CHRISTINA (*carrying the birdcage away*): No. No more baby talk. We'll be serious. Don't be afraid of my noise and laughter. It was all for you, but since it doesn't suit you or your great calling—(*She bursts into tears.*)

OLOF (*taking her in his arms and kissing her*): Christina, Christina, dearest. You're quite right. I'm sorry.

CHRISTINA: Olof, that gift you gave me, the gift of freedom—it was too much. I don't know what to do with it. I have to have someone I can obey.

OLOF: I think we'll find someone. But let's not talk about that now. Off to dinner! I'm really quite hungry.

CHRISTINA (*happily*): I don't believe it! You hungry? (*She happens to look out the window and is startled by what she sees.*) Why don't you go in, Olof, and I'll come right away. I want to straighten up here a little.

OLOF (*as he leaves*): Don't make me wait as long as you had to wait for me!

> *Christina clasps her hands in prayer and stands waiting for someone to enter through the street door.*
>
> *Pause.*
>
> *Olof's Mother enters and walks past Christina without deigning to look at her.*

MOTHER: Is Master Olof home?

> *Christina has approached her in a friendly way, but struck by the woman's snub and by her tone of voice, she adopts the same tone.*

CHRISTINA: No, he isn't. If you care to wait, he'll be here soon.

MOTHER: Thank you. (*She takes a seat.*)

Pause.

MOTHER: Give me a glass of water.

Christina serves her.

MOTHER: Now leave me.

CHRISTINA: As the wife in the house, I'm obliged to keep you company.

MOTHER: And since when does a priest's housekeeper call herself his wife?

CHRISTINA: I am Master Olof's wife in the sight of God. Don't you know that we are married?

MOTHER: You are a harlot! That I know.

CHRISTINA: I don't know what that means.

MOTHER: That woman Olof spoke to in the tavern that night—she was a harlot.

CHRISTINA: She looked so miserable. It's true, I'm not happy.

MOTHER: I can well believe it. Get out of my sight! Your presence here is an insult to me.

CHRISTINA (*on her knees*): For the sake of your son, don't treat me as if I were some shameless creature.

MOTHER: As his mother, I order you out of his house, whose threshold you have desecrated.

CHRISTINA: As his wife and as mistress of the house, I'll open the door to anyone I please. I would have shut it on you, if I had known what you had to say.

MOTHER: Mighty fine talk! I order you to leave this house!

CHRISTINA: What gives you the right to force your way in here and drive me out of my own house? You bore a child, yes, brought him up: that was your purpose in life; and you can thank God that you fulfilled it so well. Not everyone is so fortunate. Now you stand on the brink of the grave. Don't stand in his way any longer. Let him stand on his own two feet before you come to the end of your journey. Or did you bring up your son so badly that like a child he still has to hold your hand? If it's gratitude you want, you won't get it that way. Do you think that one's purpose in life is to sacrifice oneself to one's parents out of gratitude? A voice is calling him to forge ahead. Your voice calls him back. "Come here, you thankless child!" Is he to stray from his true path in life, sacrifice his strength and talent, which belong to the world, to humanity itself, merely to satisfy the petty wishes of one selfish mother? Do you think that bearing and rearing a child earns you its everlasting gratitude? Didn't that child provide you with an aim and a purpose? Shouldn't you be grateful to God for having given meaning to your life? Or did you do it all in order to be repaid bit by bit till your dying day? Don't you realize that that one word "gratitude" destroys all you have done? And what gives you rights over me? You seem to think that by marrying I mortgaged myself and my free will to whomever nature selected as the mother and father of my husband, who unfortunately wouldn't be here but for the two of them. You are not my mother. I never swore to be true to you when I took Olof as my husband. And I have enough respect for my husband not to let anyone insult him without hearing from me—not even his mother! That's why you're hearing from me!

MOTHER: Now I see the fruits of the doctrines my son is spreading.

CHRISTINA: If you insist on insulting your son, you'll have to do it to his face! (*She goes to the door and calls.*) Olof!

MOTHER: Already the sly one, aren't you?

CHRISTINA: Already? Wasn't I always? I just didn't know I was sly until I needed to be.

OLOF (*entering*): Mother! Welcome.

MOTHER: Thank you. And goodbye!

OLOF: Goodbye? Why? I want to talk to you.

MOTHER: That won't be necessary. She has said everything. You won't have to show me the door.

OLOF: What in the name of God are you talking about? Christina, what's going on?

MOTHER (*starts to go*): Goodbye, Olof. I will never forgive you for this. Never!

OLOF (*standing in her way*): Wait! At least explain to me.

MOTHER: You ought to be ashamed. You send her out to tell me that you owe me nothing, that I'm no longer of any use to you. That's hard. (*She leaves.*)

OLOF: What did you say to her, Christina?

CHRISTINA: I don't remember. A whole lot of things. I don't know where the words came from. I said things I didn't even dare think about before. Things I must have dreamed about all the years my father kept me under his thumb.

OLOF: Christina, you're so different. I hardly recognize you.

CHRISTINA: I'm not surprised. I'm beginning to wonder myself who I am.

OLOF: You must have been very unkind to Mother.

CHRISTINA: Yes, I suppose I was. Don't you think I've become hard? Olof?

OLOF: Did you tell her to leave?

CHRISTINA: I'm sorry, Olof. I didn't behave properly. —I—

OLOF: For my sake at least, you might have shown her more consideration. Why didn't you call me right away?

CHRISTINA: I wanted to see if I could take care of myself. —Olof, are you going to take her side against me when she asks you to?

OLOF: I'd have to think about that.

CHRISTINA: I can answer for you. You don't mind giving in to your mother voluntarily because you're strong. It amuses you. It's different with me. I'd be mortified, because I'm weak. I'll never give in to her.

OLOF: Not even if I beg you?

CHRISTINA: You can't ask that of me. Not unless you want me to hate her. . . . Tell me, Olof, what is a harlot?

OLOF: You do ask the strangest questions.

CHRISTINA: Don't you think I deserve an answer?

OLOF: Will you forgive me if I don't answer?

CHRISTINA: Always the same. No answers. Am I never to be told anything? Am I supposed to remain a child? Then put me in the nursery; dandle me on your knees!

OLOF: It means an unfortunate woman, a fallen woman.

CHRISTINA: No, there's more to it than that.

OLOF: Has anyone dared to call you that?

CHRISTINA (*hesitates*): No.

OLOF: You're not being straight with me, Christina.

CHRISTINA: No. . . . Since yesterday I've become wicked.

OLOF: Something happened then that you're keeping from me.

CHRISTINA: Yes. I thought I could deal with it, but I can't. I can't.

OLOF: Tell me, please.

CHRISTINA: Don't say I'm weak. . . . A crowd of people pursued me right to the door, calling me this name. "Harlot! Harlot!" And I didn't know what they could mean. "Harlot." One doesn't laugh at an "unfortunate" woman.

OLOF: Yes, my dear, that's exactly what they do.

CHRISTINA: I didn't understand what they were saying, but their gestures made everything clear enough. And since then I've been full of hate.

OLOF: And in spite of all that, you've been so kind to me. Forgive me for being so hard on you. — "Whore" — that's what brutes call their victims. You'll be hearing more about what it means. But I warn you: never defend one of these "unfortunate" women. You'll be dragged into the dirt.

Enter a Messenger with a letter.

OLOF: At last! (*He reads the letter hastily.*) Read it to me, Christina. I want to hear the good news from your lips.

CHRISTINA (*reading*): "Victory is yours, young man. I, who fought against you, want to be the first to tell you this. I do not write to you in humiliation. You wielded the weapons of the spirit when you spoke for the new faith. Whether you are right or not, I do not know, but I believe you are entitled to the counsel of an old man. Go no further, now that your enemies have fled the field. Do not grapple with shadows. They will cripple your arm, and you will wither and die. Neither rely on the princes of the realm. This is the advice of a once-powerful man, who now steps aside and commits to the hands of the Lord the fate of His ruined church." Signed "Johannes Brask." — Olof, you have won!

OLOF (*ecstatic*): Oh, God, I thank thee for this moment! (*Pause.*) No — I'm afraid, Christina! It's wrong. It's too much. I'm too young to have reached my goal. Nothing more to accomplish — what a terrible thought. Not to fight anymore, not to struggle — that's death.

CHRISTINA: Rest awhile, and be thankful it's over.

OLOF: Can it ever be over? Can such a beginning have an end? No, no! I want to begin all over again. It wasn't victory I wanted but the battle itself.

CHRISTINA: Don't tempt God, Olof. I feel it's far from over, far.

The Nobleman enters.

NOBLEMAN: Good day, Mr. Secretary. Wonderful news!

Christina excuses herself and leaves.

OLOF: Good day to you, sir! I've already heard some of it.

NOBLEMAN: My thanks to you—and my congratulations—for that remarkable defense you made in the debate at Uppsala University against that—that—professor of theology—what's his name? —Galle. A stupid man, really. You cooked his goose, I must say. Overdid it perhaps. Too much heat. A dash of malice in the sauce would have been more subtle.

OLOF: You have some news from the king?

NOBLEMAN: Oh, I do indeed; indeed I do! Here are the enactments of the estates, in sum. (*He takes out a paper and consults it.*) First. Mutual agreement to resist and punish all rebels.

OLOF: Go on.

NOBLEMAN: Second: the right of the king to take possession of the castles and strongholds of the bishops, to determine their revenues, and—

OLOF (*interrupting*): Third.

NOBLEMAN: Yes. Now comes the best part, the kernel of the whole enterprise. Third: the right of the nobility to reclaim those estates that they possessed in fee simple and that fell to the churches and monasteries as a result of the perquisitions of King Charles VIII in 1454, provided—

OLOF: Yes, yes! Fourth.

NOBLEMAN: —provided that the claimant upon the sworn oaths of twelve men can confirm his birthright before the judicial assembly. (*He folds up the paper.*)

OLOF: Is that all?

NOBLEMAN: Isn't it superb?

OLOF: There's nothing more?

NOBLEMAN: Oh, some minor points. Nothing of significance.

OLOF: Could I hear them?

NOBLEMAN (*unfolding the paper and looking at it*): There's a fifth item about the right of preachers to promulgate the Gospel. But they had that before, didn't they?

OLOF: And nothing else?

NOBLEMAN: Well, there's the decree itself. "The incomes of bishops, dioceses, and canons shall be recorded, and the king shall have the right to determine—"

OLOF: That's irrelevant.

NOBLEMAN: —"how much of this income they may retain and how much shall be given him for the needs of the crown." . . . "That priestly offices"—yes, this ought to interest you—"that priestly offices, lower as well as higher, shall henceforth be filled only with the crown's approval, so that—"

OLOF: The point about the faith, about God's word, please read that to me.

NOBLEMAN: The word? . . . The faith? . . . There's nothing about that. Ah, yes, here it is. "The Bible shall from this day forward be studied in all schools."

OLOF: That's all?

NOBLEMAN: That's all. —No, I almost forgot. I have special orders—very sensible, I must say—from the king to you, that as long as the people are unsettled by these changes, you are not in any way to disturb the old traditions—not to do away with the mass, or holy water, or other rites. Nor are you to attempt any radical changes whatsoever. For the king, you see, is not going to close his eyes to your actions as he did before when he was powerless to do anything else.

OLOF: I do see. And the new faith that he told me I could preach—what about that?

NOBLEMAN: It is to ripen slowly. It will come, it will come.

OLOF: Anything else?

NOBLEMAN (*rising to his feet*): No. Be calm and patient, young man, and you'll go far. —Oh, the best news! It almost slipped my mind. Rector Pedersson, may I offer you my compliments! Here is your letter of appointment. Rector of the Great Church of Stockholm, with three thousand dalers a year—and at your age! My word, now you can settle down and enjoy life—even if you never rise any higher. . . . Isn't it wonderful to have attained your goal at such an early age! My congratulations! (*He leaves.*)

OLOF (*throwing the letter of appointment on the floor*): An appointment! I fought and suffered for this? A royal appointment! I served Belial instead of God! Woe to you, false king, who sold out your Lord and your God! Woe to me, who sold my life and my life's work to Mammon! God in heaven, forgive me! (*He collapses on a bench, crying.*)

> *Christina and Gert enter, Christina coming forward, Gert remaining in the background.*
>
> *Christina picks up the letter of appointment, reads it, and then goes to Olof with a happy expression on her face.*

CHRISTINA: Olof! I'm so happy for you. Congratulations!

> *She starts to embrace and kiss him. He stands up and thrusts her away.*

OLOF: Get away from me! You, too!

GERT (*coming forward*): Well, Olof. How stands it with you and your faith?

OLOF: With me and the faithless, you mean!

GERT: Come, look at it this way. We've taken care of the pope. Shall we have a go at the king now?

OLOF: Yes. We began at the wrong end.

GERT: Ah! At last!

OLOF: You were right, Gert. Now I'm your man. Let there be war. But fair and square.

GERT: You've been living in a dreamworld, like a child, until today.

OLOF: I know. Now comes the flood. Now let it come! Woe to them and to us!

CHRISTINA: Olof, you can't! For heaven's sake, stop!

OLOF: Go, Christina, go away. You'll drown here. Or you'll draw me under with you.

GERT: He's right, my girl. What can you do out in the storm?

> *She leaves.*
>
> *The ringing of bells, shouts of joy, music and drums are heard.*
>
> *Olof goes to the window and looks out.*

OLOF: What's all the shouting for?

GERT: The king is treating the people to a Maypole and music outside North Gate.

OLOF: And they don't realize that in place of the rod he has given them the sword.

GERT: If only they did realize! If only they did!

OLOF: Poor souls! They dance to his pipes, and to the beat of his drums they march to their deaths. Are all to die that one may live?

GERT: No. One shall die that all may live!

> *Olof recoils, stunned.*

CURTAIN

ACT IV

A room in the house of Olof's Mother. To the right, a four-poster bed, Olof's Mother, ill, asleep in it. Christina is dozing in a chair. Lars Pedersson, Olof's younger brother, fills the night lamp with oil and turns the hourglass.

LARS (*talking to himself*): Midnight. . . . A decision has to be made. (*He goes over to his Mother's bed and listens.*)

> *Christina moans in her sleep. Lars goes to her and wakes her up.*

LARS: Christina!

> *She wakes with a start.*

LARS: Go to bed, Christina. I'll keep watch.

CHRISTINA: No, I want to be here. I have to talk to her before she dies. . . . Olof will be here soon, I know.

LARS: You're sitting here for Olof's sake, aren't you?

CHRISTINA: Yes. You won't tell him I fell asleep, will you?

LARS: Dear Christina! . . . You're not very happy.

CHRISTINA: Did anyone say we are supposed to be happy?

LARS: Does Olof know you're here?

CHRISTINA: No, he would never allow it. He sees me as a saint, a statue on a shelf. The smaller and weaker I become in his eyes, the more he enjoys laying his strength at my feet.

MOTHER (*stirring*): Lars!

> *Christina holds Lars back and goes to the bed.*

97

MOTHER: Who is that? Who is here?

CHRISTINA: Your nurse.

MOTHER: Christina!

CHRISTINA: Can I get you anything?

MOTHER: I want nothing from you.

CHRISTINA: Please let me help.

MOTHER: You can help by leaving. Don't embitter my last moments. Leave this house!

LARS (*coming to the bed*): What do you want, Mother?

MOTHER: Take this woman away from here. Bring my father confessor before I die.

LARS: Don't you think your own son should hear your last confession? Isn't he worthy of your trust?

MOTHER: He's done nothing to make himself worthy of it. —Has Martin come yet?

LARS: Martin!—that disreputable monk!

MOTHER: God, Thy punishment is too great for me. My own children put themselves between Thee and me. Am I to die without the consolations of my faith? You have been the death of me, isn't that enough? Now do you want to send my soul to perdition—your mother's soul? (*She sinks back in a faint.*)

LARS: You heard that, Christina. What should we do? Which is it to be? Either she dies swindled by that wretched Friar Martin—and maybe thanks us for it—or else in her last prayer she will curse us. No. No. Let them give the last rites. Who do you think, Christina?

CHRISTINA: I don't dare think anything.

LARS (*goes out to fetch the monks in. Returns almost immediately*): It's dreadful! They are drunk and asleep. They've been sitting out there throwing dice and drinking. And they're supposed to purge my mother's soul before she dies!

CHRISTINA: You've got to tell her the truth.

LARS: She wouldn't believe it. To her it would be one more lie to be held against us.

MOTHER: Lars! It is the last thing I shall ask of you. Don't deny me.

LARS (*going out*): God forgive me!

CHRISTINA: Olof would never have done it.

> *Lars accompanies the friars Martin and Nils into the room, then leaves, taking Christina with him.*
>
> *Martin goes to the bed.*

MARTIN: She's sleeping.

> *Nils has carried in with him a chest, which he places on the floor, and draws from it holy water, censers, ampullas, palm branches, and candles.*

NILS: So we can't go to work yet.

MARTIN: If we've waited this long, we can wait a little longer. As long as that devil of a priest doesn't show up.

NILS: Master Olof, you mean. . . . Say, you don't think he saw anything out there, do you?

MARTIN: So what if he did! As long as the old lady forks out the money, I'm not worried.

NILS: You really are a son-of-a-bitch, aren't you.

MARTIN: Maybe. But I'm getting tired of all this. I need some peace and quiet. Do you know what life is?

NILS: No.

MARTIN: It's pleasure. The flesh is God. Says so somewhere, doesn't it?

NILS: "The Word was made flesh" – that's what you're thinking of.

MARTIN: Is that what it says? Oh, well.

NILS: You could really have amounted to something—with a mind like yours.

MARTIN: You are right. I could have become somebody. That's what they were afraid of. I had too much spirit. So they beat it out of me in the monastery. I had a soul then. Now I'm just body. And the body wants to make up for the harm done.

NILS: They must have whipped the conscience out of you at the same time.

MARTIN: Pretty much. . . . What about that recipe for mulled Rochelle you were telling me about, before we fell asleep out there?

NILS: Did I say Rochelle? I meant claret. Hell, it doesn't make any difference. Here's what you do. You take half a gallon wine, half a pound cardamom, well husked—

MARTIN: Shut up, damn it! She's stirring. Get the book out!

During the following, Nils recites softly:

NILS:

> *Aufer immensam, Deus aufer iram;*
> *Et cruentatum cohibe flagellum:*
> *Nec scelus nostrum proferes ad aequam*
>   *Pendere lancem.**

MOTHER: Is that you, Martin?

MARTIN: It's Brother Nils supplicating the Holy Virgin.

While he recites, Nils lights the censer.

MOTHER: What a great comfort it is to hear the Lord's word in the holy tongue.

MARTIN: No offering is so pleasing to the Lord as are the prayers of pious souls.

* "Put aside, Lord, put aside Your boundless wrath, and stay Your bloodied scourge. Drag forth not our sins to be weighed on the scales." From a hymn by Georg Thymus.

MOTHER: Like incense my heart is kindled by holy devotion.

MARTIN (*sprinkles her with the aspergillum*): From the filth of thy sins God washes thee clean.

MOTHER: Amen. . . . Martin, I am going hence. The ungodliness of King Gustav forbids me to give earthly gifts to the Holy Church that they may strengthen its power to save souls. So I ask you, Martin, as a man of God, to receive my possessions and to pray for my children. Pray to the Almighty that they shall turn their hearts away from the lie and that one day we shall meet in heaven.

MARTIN (*accepting a money bag from her*): Madam, your gift is pleasing to the Lord, and for your sake God will hear my prayers.

MOTHER: Now I want to sleep awhile. To gather my strength for the last sacrament.

MARTIN: No one will disturb your last moments. I shall see to it. Not even those who once were your children.

MOTHER: It is a hard thing, Father Martin, but it is God's will. (*She sleeps.*)

> *Martin and Nils move away from the bed. Martin opens the money bag and kisses the gold coins.*

MARTIN: Ah, what a treasure! How many hours of voluptuous delights lie hidden in these cold, hard coins. Ah!

NILS: Should we leave now?

MARTIN: I could do that, certainly, having performed the service. But it's a shame to let the old girl die unblessed.

NILS: Unblessed?

MARTIN: Yes.

NILS: You don't believe that?

MARTIN: It's hard to know what to believe right now. Some enter the kingdom of heaven this way, some that way. Everyone claims to have found *the* way.

NILS: What if you were to die now, Martin?

MARTIN: Not possible.

NILS: I said "if."

MARTIN: Oh, I'd go to heaven like everybody else. Only I'd have a little score to settle with Master Olof first. You see, Brother Nils, there is one pleasure sweeter than all the rest. Revenge.

NILS: What's he done to you?

MARTIN: He has seen through me. Ripped off my mask. Read my thoughts. Damn!

NILS: And for that you hate him?

MARTIN: Could there be a better reason?

> *Knocking at the street door.*

MARTIN: Somebody's at the door! Read, damn it!

> *Nils rattles off the Latin verses.*
>
> *Sound of a key being inserted into the lock of the door, which is then opened from the outside. Olof enters, looking distracted and perturbed.*

MOTHER (*wakes up and calls*): Father Martin!

OLOF (*going to her bed*): It's Olof, Mother! I'm here. Why didn't you let me know you were ill?

MOTHER: Goodbye, Olof. I'll forgive you, Olof, the hurt you've given me if you will leave me alone while I prepare myself for heaven. —Father Martin! Give me extreme unction that I may die in peace.

OLOF: So this is why you did not send for me! (*He catches sight of the money purse that Martin had neglected to conceal and snatches it from him.*) You're trading in souls! And this is the price! Get out of this house! Leave this deathbed! This is my place, not yours.

MARTIN: You can't keep us from carrying out our duties.

OLOF: I'm telling you to get out!

MARTIN: Our office here is by authority not of the pope but of the king, as long as we have not been suspended.

OLOF: I shall cleanse the house of the Lord, even if the pope and the king will not have it so.

MOTHER: Olof! Would you have me cast into the fire? Would you have me die with a curse on my lips?

OLOF: Be calm, Mother. You shall not die trusting in a lie. Seek God yourself, in your prayers. He is nearer than you think.

MARTIN: Only a disciple of the devil would not want to spare his own mother the throes and torments of purgatory.

MOTHER: Jesus, come! Succor my soul!

OLOF (*to the monks*): Get out of here before I throw you out! And take this superstitious nonsense with you! (*He kicks the sacramentals.*)

MARTIN: Hand over the money your mother gave to the church. Then I'll go.

MOTHER: Is that why you came, Olof? For my gold? Give it to him, Martin. Olof, you can have it all, all. Just leave me in peace. You shall have more. Everything!

OLOF: In the name of God, take the money and go! I beg you!

Martin snaps up the purse and starts to leave with Nils.

MARTIN: Madam, where the devil walks, our power ceases. (*To Olof.*)—As a heretic, you are damned for all eternity. As a lawbreaker, you will receive your punishment here in this life. Beware the king.

They leave.

Olof kneels by his Mother's bed.

OLOF: Listen to me, Mother! Hear me before you die!

She is half-unconscious.

OLOF: Mother, please. Mother, if you can still hear me, talk to me. Forgive me. I cannot do otherwise. I know you have suffered all your life for my sake. You have prayed to God that I should do His bidding. And the Lord has heard your prayers. Do you want me to confound all that you have done? Do you want me to break what you have built, what has cost you so much effort and so many tears, by doing your bidding now? Forgive me!

MOTHER: Olof, my spirit no longer belongs to this world. I am speaking to you from the hereafter. Turn back, Olof, loosen the unclean bond that your body has made. Receive again the faith I gave you; and I shall forgive you.

OLOF (*with tears of despair*): Mother! Mother!

MOTHER: Swear to me that you will!

OLOF (*is silent, then*): No!

MOTHER: You are under the curse of God. I can see Him. I see God in His wrath! Help me, Holy Mother of God!

OLOF: Isn't God love? That isn't the God you see.

MOTHER: No, He is the God of vengeance! It is you who have offended Him. It is you who cast me into the fire of his fury. —Cursed be the hour I gave you birth! (*She dies.*)

OLOF: Mother! Mother! (*He takes her hand.*) She's dead. Without forgiving me. . . . Oh, Mother, if your spirit dwelleth in this place, look down upon your son. I shall do thy will; what is sacred to you shall be sacred to me. (*He lights the tall wax candles left by the friars and places them around the bed.*) You shall have the consecrated tapers to light you on your way—(*He places a palm branch in her hand.*)—and with the palm of peace you shall forget your last struggle with earthly matters. Mother, if you see me now, I know you will forgive me!

> *The sun has begun to rise and it lights up the window curtains with a reddish glow.*

OLOF (*springing to his feet*): Morning sun, you put my candles to shame. There is more loving-kindness in you than in me. (*He goes to the window and opens it.*)

Lars enters quietly. He is astonished to see Olof.

LARS: Olof!

OLOF (*embracing him*): Dear brother! It's all over.

LARS (*goes to the bed, kneels, and rises*): She is dead. (*He says a silent prayer.*) You were alone here.

OLOF: You were the one who let in the monks.

LARS: You drove them out!

OLOF: Yes. It's what you should have done.

LARS: She didn't forgive you, did she?

OLOF: She died cursing me.

Silence.

LARS (*pointing to the candles*): Who arranged the ceremony?

Pause.

OLOF (*nettled and embarrassed*): A moment of weakness.

LARS: You are human, after all. I'm glad to see it.

OLOF: Are you sneering at me because I was weak?

LARS: No, I'm admiring you for it.

OLOF: And I hate myself for it. God in heaven, am I not right?

LARS: No, you're not.

CHRISTINA (*has just entered*): You are so right it hurts.

OLOF: Christina! What are you doing here?

CHRISTINA: I couldn't stand it at home – so quiet and lonely.

OLOF: I asked you not to come here.

CHRISTINA: I thought I might be of some help, but I see I'm not. Next time I'll stay home.

OLOF: You've been up all night.

CHRISTINA: It was no hardship. I'll go if you want me to.

OLOF: Go in the other room and rest. I want to talk to Lars.

Lost in her thoughts, Christina puts out the candles.

OLOF: What are you doing, Christina?

CHRISTINA: It's broad daylight.

Lars looks at Olof.

OLOF: My mother is dead, Christina.

Tender but restrained, Christina goes to Olof to be kissed on the forehead.

CHRISTINA: You have my sympathy, Olof. (*She leaves.*)

Pause. Lars and Olof follow Christina with their eyes, and then look at each other.

LARS: As your brother, Olof, and as your friend, I beg you not to carry on as you have.

OLOF: You never change, do you, Lars? Harping always on the same string. But the ax is now laid unto the root of the tree, and one doesn't stop chopping until the tree falls. The king has abandoned our cause; now it lies in my hands.

LARS: The king is no fool.

OLOF: He's a greedy muckworm, that's what he is—a traitor who licks the boots of the nobility. First he treated me like a dog; now he kicks me away.

LARS: He has more insight than you. If you went out and spoke to three million people and said to them, "Your faith is a false one; trust me!" do you really believe that on an impulse they would rid themselves of those deep convictions and beliefs that have sustained them year in and year out, in sorrow and in joy? Never! The human soul would be a sorry mess if it were that easy to throw overboard all that's tried and true.

OLOF: It isn't like that at all! The whole nation is torn by doubt. There is scarcely one priest who knows what to believe in—that is, if he has any beliefs at all. Everything points to a change. And the blame rests with you, you who are weak of heart, who dare not take it on your consciences to cast out doubt when the only faith is a frail and wavering one.

LARS: Take care, Olof! You want to play God.

OLOF: Someone has to. Haven't you heard? God no longer comes down to us His miracles to perform.

LARS: But you only tear down, Olof. Soon there will be nothing but emptiness. What are you going to put in place of the old? Not that, you say. And not that. Then what? You never answer.

OLOF: What presumption! Do you think faith is something one gives? Has Luther given us anything new? No. He has simply torn down the screens that shut out the light. The new idea that I represent is distrust of the old—not because it is old but because it is rotten.

Lars gestures toward their Mother.

OLOF: I know what you mean. But the truth is she was too old, and I thank God that she died. Now I am free, now for the first time in my life! It was God's will!

LARS: You are out of your mind—or else you are inhuman.

OLOF: You mustn't reproach me. I value her memory as much as you do. But if she had not died now, I don't know how much longer I could have gone on compromising my principles. . . . In the spring the dead leaves cover the ground and smother the young plants that want to grow. What do they do? They shove the dry leaves to one side, or they push right straight through them. Because they *have* to grow.

LARS: You're not entirely wrong, Olof; I admit that. . . . The laws you broke were broken during a time of trouble and strife in the church. But what was forgivable then must now be punished. Don't compel the king to show himself worse than he is. Don't force him to punish your infractions when he knows how much he owes you. You cannot do whatever you like.

OLOF: Doing whatever he likes is how he rules. He must learn to tolerate it in others. . . . You're in service with the king. You'll be working against me, won't you?

LARS: Yes.

OLOF: So we are enemies. Good, I need them, since the old ones are gone.

LARS: Olof, the blood tells.

OLOF: Not to me. Except at its source: the heart.

LARS: You wept for Mother.

OLOF: Frailty. Perhaps devotion and gratitude. But not blood. What is blood, anyway?

LARS: You look dog-tired, Olof.

OLOF: I'm exhausted. I've been up all night.

LARS: You came so late.

OLOF: I wasn't at home.

LARS: Your work shuns the light of day.

OLOF: The light of day shuns my work.

LARS: Beware, Olof, the false apostles of freedom.

OLOF (*fighting against sleep and exhaustion*): A contradiction in terms. No more talking, if you don't mind. I'm done in. I've spoken so much at our meetings. —I forgot: you wouldn't know about our secret meetings. . . . *Concordia res parvae crescunt.* . . . Sallust. . . . "Concord makes small enterprises succeed; discord destroys the great ones." . . . We're going to pursue the reformation to its end. . . . Gert is a far-sighted man. I'm nothing next to him, I'm nothing. . . . Goodnight, Lars. (*He falls asleep in a chair.*)

LARS (*looking at him with sympathy*): My dear brother. God protect you.

Loud knocking on the outside door.

LARS: Who can that be? (*He looks out the window.*)

GERT (*from outside*): Open up, for God's sake!

LARS (*going out*): It can't be that important, Father Gert.

GERT (*still outside*): For the love of heaven, let me in!

> *Christina comes into the room, carrying a blanket.*

CHRISTINA: Olof, why do they keep knocking? — He's asleep. (*She covers Olof with the blanket.*) I wish I were Morpheus; then you would come to my arms when you are weary of the battle.

> *The rumbling of a heavy cart in the street outside can be heard. It comes to a stop.*

OLOF (*wakes up suddenly*): Five o'clock already?

CHRISTINA: It's only three, Olof.

OLOF: I thought I heard the baker's cart.

CHRISTINA: I don't think it is. It wouldn't sound so heavy. (*She looks out the window.*) Look, Olof. What is that?

OLOF (*at the window*): The hangman's wagon! —No, it isn't. What—?

CHRISTINA: It's a cart for the dead!

LARS (*entering, followed by Gert*): The plague!

OLOF *and* CHRISTINA: The plague!

GERT: Yes, it's broken out! Christina, my child, you must leave this house. The angel of death has placed his mark on the door.

OLOF: Who sent that cart to this house?

GERT: Whoever put that black cross on the door. The bodies of the dead have to be carted away immediately.

OLOF: Friar Martin—he's your angel of death. The whole thing is a fabrication.

GERT: No. Look out the window. The cart is filled with corpses.

Pounding on the door.

GERT: Do you hear? They're waiting.

OLOF: Without proper burial! Never!

LARS: What price ceremonies, Olof?

GERT: Come, Christina, you must leave with me. This is a pesthouse. I'll take you out of town to some safer place.

CHRISTINA: My place is with Olof. If you had loved me a little less, Father, you would have done less harm.

GERT: Olof, she will listen to you. Tell her to come with me.

OLOF: I took her out of your hands once. You wanted her all to yourself. She will never go back.

GERT: Christina, at least leave this house.

CHRISTINA: Not a step until Olof orders me out.

OLOF: I don't order you to do anything, Christina. Remember that.

Two Draymen enter.

FIRST DRAYMAN: Was told to pick up a body here. Got to hurry.

OLOF: Get out of here!

FIRST DRAYMAN: King's orders.

LARS: Olof, don't be rash. It's the law.

GERT: It won't do to delay. The people are going crazy. They're up in arms against you, Olof. Yours was the first house to be marked with the cross. "The vengeance of the Lord—upon the heretic!" That's their hue and cry.

OLOF (*on his knees beside the bed*): Forgive me, Mother. (*Stands up.*) Do what you must.

The Draymen go to the bed and begin lifting it with ropes.

GERT (*aside to Olof*): "The vengeance of the Lord—upon the King!" That's *our* hue and cry.

CURTAIN

ACT V

Scene 1

The churchyard of the Convent of Saint Clara in Stock-
holm. At the back, a half-razed convent building, from
which workmen are carrying old timber and debris. To
the left, a burial chapel, candlelight shining through its
windows. When the door to the chapel is opened later on,
a strongly lighted statue of Christ can be seen within,
above a sarcophagus.

In the yard some graves lie open. The moon is rising
above the ruins. Captain Windrank is sitting on watch
at the chapel door. From within the chapel singing can
be heard.

Friar Nils enters and goes up to Windrank.

NILS: Good evening, Captain Windrank.

WINDRANK: Please. Don't talk to me.

NILS: Now what's the matter?

WINDRANK: Are you deaf?

NILS: Ah ha! So that dishonorable discharge from your ship has
done you in, eh? Made you renounce the world.

WINDRANK: Fifty-two, fifty-three, fifty-four, fifty-five, fifty-
six, fifty-seven —

NILS: Have you gone out of your mind?

WINDRANK: Fifty-eight, fifty-nine, sixty. For God's sake, will
you get out!

NILS: Not until you've had a little nightcap with me.

WINDRANK: Sixty-four, sixty-five. I might have known. Go

away, tempter. I'm never touching the stuff again. . . . Not until the day after tomorrow.

NILS: It's medicine—against the plague. The air in a place like this is very dangerous to your health.

WINDRANK: Seventy. —It really works against the plague?

NILS: Like nothing else.

WINDRANK (*taking a drink*): Just a drop.

NILS: Just a drop. —Have you got dizzy spells? Why are you counting to a hundred? Does it work?

WINDRANK: Shhh! Shhhh! A new era!

NILS: What? A new era?

WINDRANK: Yes. Begins day after tomorrow.

NILS: That's why you're counting?

WINDRANK: No. I'm counting so I'll keep my mouth shut. (*Slapping himself.*) Shut up, damn it! —Get out of here before I ruin everything. Seventy-one, seventy-two, seventy-three.

NILS: Who's in there?

WINDRANK (*firmly*): Seventy-four, seventy-five—

NILS: A burial? Whose?

WINDRANK: Seventy-six, seventy-seven. —Why don't you go to hell!

NILS: One little shot more, eh? Makes the counting easier.

WINDRANK: One little one. What the hell! (*He drinks.*)

Singing is heard.

NILS: It's the nuns of Saint Clara, coming to celebrate her memory for the last time.

WINDRANK: What a hoax! In these enlightened times!

NILS: The king gave them permission. The plague broke out in the parish of Saint Clara. So they blame it on the sacrilegious tearing down of her convent.

WINDRANK: So now they expect to use songs to drive the plague away? That devil of a plague can't have an ear for music. On the other hand, I'd be surprised if he didn't flee from this caterwauling.

NILS: Tell me, who's profaning this last sanctuary? The bones of Saint Clara are to be buried here before they tear it down.

WINDRANK: There's going to be a brawl, for sure.

> *The singing has grown louder, and now a procession of Dominican monks, in black, and Franciscan nuns or Poor Clares, in gray, enter, Friar Martin leading the way. They stop but continue to sing. The laborers are all the while noisily at work in the back.*

THE MONKS *and* NUNS:

> *Cur super vermes luteos furorem*
> *sumis, o magni fabricator orbis!*
> *Quid sumus quam fex putris, umbra, pulvis*
> *glebaque terrae!**

MARTIN (*to the Abbess*): You see, sister, how they have laid waste the dwelling place of the Lord.

ABBESS: The Lord who has delivered us into the hands of the Egyptians will redeem us out of Egypt when he sees fit.

MARTIN (*to the workmen*): You there! We are here to do reverence to a saint, and you are disrupting and interfering with our ceremonies.

---

* "Why do you rage against the worms in the mud, You the creator of the wide world? What are we other than putrefying slime, shadows, dust, lumps of turf?" From the hymn by George Thymus quoted in Act IV.

FOREMAN: We are under orders to work round the clock till this place is leveled to the ground.

ABBESS: I see that impiety has infected even the lowest level of people.

MARTIN (*to the Foreman*): May I remind you that the king has authorized our presence here. We have his permission to bless the memory of Saint Clara.

FOREMAN: Don't let me stop you.

MARTIN: On his authority I demand that you stop what you're doing. I shall take it up with your workers. You have forced them into this nefarious undertaking. I shall appeal directly to them. We shall see if they have any respect for what is holy and sacred.

FOREMAN: I wouldn't, if I were you. I give the orders around here. Let me tell you something. They're happy to be getting rid of this wasp's nest. They're the ones who had to pay for it. Besides, they're thankful to be getting some work and pay during this famine. (*He walks upstage.*)

MARTIN: Sister, let us put aside the wickedness and tumult of this world, and let us enter the sanctuary to pray for them.

ABBESS: Lord God, Thy holy cities are a wilderness; Zion is a wilderness; Jerusalem a desolation.

WINDRANK (*barring Martin and the Abbess from the chapel*): One hundred! No one goes in!

> *From within the chapel voices raised in unison can be heard: "We swear!"*

MARTIN: Who is in there? Who has profaned the chapel?

WINDRANK: What chapel? It's the king's storehouse.

> *The door to the chapel is flung open. Enter the conspirators: Olof, Lars Andersson, Gert, The German, The Dane, The Farmer from Småland, and others.*

OLOF (*seeing the nuns and monks; heatedly*): What sort of tomfoolery is this?

MARTIN: Make room for the dedicated servants of the holy Saint Clara!

OLOF: Do you think that your idols can dispel the plague—which the one true God has sent to punish you? Do you suppose that the Lord is so pleased by those bits of bones that you are carrying in that reliquary that He will forgive your grievous sins? Away with the abomination! (*He snatches the chest from the Abbess and throws it into one of the open graves.*) Dust thou art and unto dust shalt thou return—even if you are Sancta Clara da Spoleto and ate only three slices of bread a day and slept with the pigs at night.

> *The nuns shriek.*

MARTIN: If you fear not your Lord in heaven, perhaps you will fear your lord on earth. He, at least, has so much respect for the divine that he fears the wrath of the saints. (*He hands Olof an offical-looking document.*)

OLOF: You know what the Lord did to the king of Assyria when he endorsed idolatry. He slew him *and* his people. For when the king is wrong, the righteous suffer with the unrighteous. In the name of the one Almighty God I hereby abolish this adoration of Baal, even though all the kings of earth countenance it. The pope wanted to sell my soul to Satan, but, as you may remember, I tore that contract to pieces. Why should I now fear a king who will sell his people to the Baalim? (*Olof tears the order to pieces.*)

MARTIN (*to the nuns and monks*): You are my witnesses that he defames the king!

OLOF (*to the conspirators*): You are my witnesses before God that I have turned His people away from an impious king.

MARTIN: Hear me, you true believers, it is because of this heretic that the Lord has struck us with the plague. And the punishment of the Lord descended first on his mother!

OLOF: Hear me, you papist infidels! The Lord punished me because I served Sennacherib against Judah. Now I shall atone for my sins. I shall lead Judah against the kings of Assyria and Egypt!

*The rising moon has turned red and a reddish glow fills
the stage. The people are frightened. Olof steps up on a
grave mound.*

OLOF: You see, Heaven itself weeps blood for your sins, for
your idolatries! Punishment shall happen. It shall fall upon us
because of those who rule and have the power. It is they who
have offended! Do you not see how the very graves gape, awaiting
the victims?

*Gert grabs Olof's arm, whispers to him, and brings him
down.*

The people mill about, frightened.

ABBESS: Give us back our reliquary and allow us to quit this
desolate place.

MARTIN: Sister, better that the saint's bones should rest in this
holy ground than that they should be desecrated by the hands of
heretics.

OLOF: Cowards! It is the plague you fear! Where now is your
faith in the power of sacred bones?

Again Gert whispers to Olof.

*By this time most of the crowd has dispersed. Only a few
people remain on stage.*

OLOF (*to Martin*): Are you quite satisfied now, you hypocrite?
Why don't you tell your earthly master that a silver casket is
buried here? He'll rip it out of the earth with his fingernails. Go
tell your lord and master that the silver moon has turned to gold.
Then for once in his life he'll raise his eyes from earth to heaven.
Tell him that you have succeeded, by means of this blasphemous
trumpery, in arousing the indignation of a true man of principle.
Tell him—

*Martin and the rest of the procession have left the stage
by this time.*

GERT: That's enough, Olof. (*To the conspirators, except for Olof and Lars Andersson.*) Leave us.

> *The conspirators whisper and mutter among themselves and leave.*

GERT (*to Olof and Lars*): It's too late to turn back. You know that.

OLOF: What's on your mind, Gert? Speak out.

GERT (*takes out a manuscript*): To you two servants of God, a whole nation—(*He taps the manuscript.*)—comes forward to make a confession. Do you acknowledge your oath?

OLOF *and* LARS: We have sworn.

GERT: This book is the fruit of my silent labors. Each page— each line—each word is a cry from a people who in their blindness believed it was God's will that they were oppressed. To them it was a sacred duty not to believe in their deliverance.

> *Olof reads here and there in the manuscript.*

GERT: From those pages you will hear cries of distress rise up from the most remote villages of the Norrland to the seaports on the Sound. Cries that come to this: out of the debris of the church the nobility builds castles for itself and prisons for the people. You shall read how the king traffics in justice and barters with the law, letting even murderers escape punishment if only they will work for him in the salt furnaces. You shall learn how he profits from sin, making prostitutes pay taxes to his coffers. Yea, the very fish in the rivers, the salt ocean itself pays tribute to him. But that's over now. The eyes of the people have been opened. The times are seething, the pot is coming to a boil. The oppressors shall be overwhelmed; the people shall be made free!

OLOF: Who has written this?

GERT: A whole people! Call them folksongs. This is what they sing when they plod along with yokes on their necks. I have gone from street to street, from town to town. I have asked, "Are you

happy?" And here are the answers. I have held inquests, and here
the findings are set down. Olof, do you think that the millions
are meant to be ruled by one person? Do you believe that God
bestowed this land, this wealth, these human beings, on one
person to do with as he wishes? Or do you not rather believe that
that one person should do the will of all? . . . You do not
answer. Of course. You tremble at the thought that it can be, that
one can put an end to it. . . . Now let me make confession to
you. Tomorrow the oppressor is to die, and you shall all be free.

OLOF *and* LARS: What?!

GERT: Have you understood nothing of what I said at our
meetings?

OLOF: You have tricked us into this!

GERT: Not at all. You are free to do as you wish. Two voices
less make no difference. Everything is prepared.

LARS: Have you thought of the consequences?

GERT: Idiot! It was for the sake of the consequences that I have
done this.

OLOF: Can you be right? What do you say, Lars?

LARS: I was not born to lead the way.

OLOF: Everyone is born to lead, but not everyone wants to lay
down his life.

GERT: Only the man who has the courage to be laughed at and
scoffed at marches in the vanguard. Hatred is nothing; it is ridicule that kills.

OLOF: If the plan should fail—?

GERT: A risk worth taking. You don't seem to know that
Thomas Münzer has set up in Mühlhausen a spiritual kingdom
where the means of life are owned in common. You don't seem
to realize that the whole of Europe is in revolt. Here in Sweden,
when Dacke led the rebellion of the people of Småland against
King Gustav, who was he if not a defender of the downtrodden?
Why did the Dalesmen north of here rise up if not to defend their

freedom against a king who had broken faith and violated his promise? And he goes unpunished. But when the people defend themselves, they are called faithless traitors and rebels!

OLOF: So this is the point to which you have been leading me all this time?

GERT: No, it was the current that carried you here. You didn't dare act out your wishes. Tomorrow in the Great Church the mine explodes: the signal for the people to rise up and choose a ruler after their own hearts.

OLOF (*flipping the pages of the manuscript*): If everyone wants it, then nothing can stop it. Gert, let me take this book to the king, and let him hear the people speak. Then he must do them justice.

GERT: What an innocent you are! He might be frightened for a moment—even give back a silver stoup to some church. But a moment later he would point to heaven and say, "It is not my will that causes me to sit here and be unjust to you; it is God's will."

OLOF: Very well. Let God's will be done!

GERT: How?

OLOF: All right. Let him die that all may live. —Murderer, ungrateful wretch, traitor—that's what they will call me. So be it. I have sacrificed everything else—my honor, my conscience, my faith. There is only one thing left for me to give to these poor souls who cry for deliverance. —Come, let us go, before I have regrets.

GERT: Wouldn't matter. It's too late for regrets. That Friar Martin is one of the king's spies—or didn't you know? Sentence is probably even now being pronounced on the man who instigated the rebellion.

OLOF: No matter. I shall have no regrets. Why should I? I am executing the decree of God! Onward, in the name of the Lord!

> *They leave.*
>
> *The Prostitute has come in and knelt at one of the graves. She strews it with flowers.*

PROSTITUTE: Have I not been struck often enough? Am I now not worthy of Thy forgiveness?

CHRISTINA (*entering in great haste*): Please, good woman, have you seen Master Olof?

PROSTITUTE: Are you a friend of his, or an enemy?

CHRISTINA: That's insulting!

PROSTITUTE: Sorry. I haven't seen him since the last time I said my prayers.

CHRISTINA: You look done in. . . . I recognize you now. You were the woman Olof talked to that night in the Great Church.

PROSTITUTE: You shouldn't be seen talking to me. Don't you know what I am?

CHRISTINA: Yes, I do.

PROSTITUTE: You mean they told you? Who?

CHRISTINA: Olof told me.

PROSTITUTE: God! And you don't disdain me?

CHRISTINA: An unfortunate, unhappy woman, Olof said. Trampled on. Why should I disdain unhappiness?

PROSTITUTE: You would, unless you are unhappy yourself.

CHRISTINA: Yes. We have something in common.

PROSTITUTE: So I've got company. You fell in love with some scamp who wasn't worth it.

CHRISTINA: Wasn't worth it?

PROSTITUTE: Sorry. If he makes us love, he's worth it. Who was it?

CHRISTINA: Do you know Master Olof?

PROSTITUTE: Not Master Olof! It can't be true. Don't take away my faith in him. It is all I have left—since God took my child from me.

CHRISTINA: At least you have had a child. You have known some happiness.

PROSTITUTE: Happiness? I thank God for never letting my child know how unworthy of him I was.

CHRISTINA: Your sin cannot be that terrible.

PROSTITUTE: It is. I buried it here not long ago.

CHRISTINA: Your baby? I don't believe it. Every day I pray to God that he will give me a child, one child, for me to love.

PROSTITUTE: You poor girl! God keep you.

CHRISTINA: I don't understand. What are you trying to say, my good woman?

PROSTITUTE: Don't call me that. You know what I am.

CHRISTINA: We all hope to be something better. One prays in church for those who hope.

PROSTITUTE: Not for the likes of us.

CHRISTINA: "Likes of us?"

PROSTITUTE: You pray for the other sort. You damn our kind.

CHRISTINA: "Other sort?"—What do you mean?

PROSTITUTE: Do you know Master Olof's wife?

CHRISTINA: I am Master Olof's wife.

PROSTITUTE: You! Of course. Forgive me. I shouldn't have said those things. You and him—you wouldn't know sin if you saw it. —Leave me. You're an innocent child. You don't know how evil the world is. You mustn't talk to me anymore. God bless you. Goodbye. (*She prepares to leave.*)

CHRISTINA: No, don't leave me. Whoever you are, stay, please, for God's sake! They've broken into my house. My husband has disappeared. Take me with you—to your place—anywhere. You're a good woman. I know you're not a criminal.

PROSTITUTE: (*interrupting*): Stop that! Whatever they say or do to you, the mob can't hurt you half as much as keeping company with me would. You'll thank me if I go now.

CHRISTINA: What have you done?

PROSTITUTE: Done, I'm damned, that's all. The curse that God pronounced on woman at the Fall has come true in me. Don't ask any more questions. If I answered, you'd damn me some more, and I'd have to defend myself, and that would be even more damnable. —Here comes someone who might be a gentleman and take care of you, that is, if you give him your honor and your reputation and your eternal peace of mind in return for his trouble. That's all he wants for offering his protection to young girls late at night. —I'm sorry. I'm bitter, but it has nothing to do with you.

WINDRANK (*enters, drunk*): Damn it! Can't a man be alone even among the corpses? Listen, ladies, please don't ask me anything. I can't be responsible—for my responses. Until day after tomorrow, when I'll tell all. Because it'll be too late. . . . Ladies, you're not from a nunnery, are you? And without a place to lay your heads? Ha, ha! Your ladyships—ships of the night?—Well, well, I don't presume to have the right to be ungentlemanly. Even though the sun has set. There's an old law: no one can be nabbed after sunset. But the law is a scoundrel. In spite of which he's gentleman enough not to force himself upon women. —Shut up, shut up. My tongue keeps on rattling like a spinning wheel. It's that damned liquor. . . . I mean, why me? Why drag me into it? Huh? . . . They're paying me, that's why? I'll be well off. Don't get me wrong; I'm not doing it for the money. . . . Anyway, it's done. . . . But I don't want it, no part of it. I want to sleep in peace. No ghosts haunting me. . . . Maybe I could go and tell them. No, they'd nab me. —Someone else could go and tell 'em. One of you nuns, maybe. Would you?

Christina confers with The Prostitute.

CHRISTINA: If this is something weighing on your conscience, yes, tell us.

WINDRANK: Tell you? That's what I'm trying not to do! It's

awful. I can't take any more. I'll do it! —But why me? Why me? I don't want it, no part of it!

CHRISTINA: If you're thinking of committing—

WINDRANK: Murder! Who said so? —You know, huh? Thank God. Go, go and tell them. Right away. Otherwise I'll have no peace, never, for all eternity.

CHRISTINA (*astonished at first; controls herself*): Why—why murder him?

WINDRANK: Lots of reasons. Look how he's tearing down your monasteries!

CHRISTINA: The king?

WINDRANK: He's the one. Father of his country. Liberator of Sweden. Of course he's a pest and a plague. But you don't kill someone for that.

CHRISTINA: When?

WINDRANK: Tomorrow, that's it. In the Great Church. Right in the church itself.

At a sign from Christina, The Prostitute leaves.

CHRISTINA: Why did they choose you to do such a thing?

WINDRANK: Well, I've got some connections with the servants in the church. Besides, I'm poor. Got no work. Need the money. —Anyhow, doesn't make any difference who fires the gun. All depends on somebody clever to aim it. Besides, we've got other plans up our sleeve. Although I'm the one who starts it. I open fire. —Aren't you going to tell 'em?

CHRISTINA: It's already taken care of.

WINDRANK: Thanks be to God. —Goodbye money, riches, wealth.

CHRISTINA: Who is in this with you?

WINDRANK: Oh, no! You won't get that out of me.

Friar Nils, soldiers, and others pass across the stage.

CHRISTINA: They're already looking for you.

WINDRANK: I wash my hands of it!

NILS (*approaches Windrank without seeing Christina*): Have you seen Olaus Petri?

WINDRANK: Why?

NILS: He's being sought after.

WINDRANK: No, I haven't seen him. Anybody else they're looking for?

NILS: Oh, yes, quite a few.

WINDRANK: No, I haven't seen a soul.

NILS: We'll get to you soon enough. (*Leaves.*)

CHRISTINA: Were they looking for the conspirators?

WINDRANK: Yes. What a business! I've got to get away. Goodbye.

CHRISTINA: Before you go, tell me—

WINDRANK: No time to lose!

CHRISTINA: Was Master Olof one of them?

WINDRANK: Of course.

> *Christina falls senseless on one of the graves.*
>
> *Windrank suddenly sobers up and is deeply touched.*

WINDRANK: Oh, my God! It must be his wife. (*He goes to her.*) I think I've killed her! Oh, Hans, Hans! Now you can go and hang yourself. What business had you with your betters. —Hey, over here. Help this woman!

> *Olof is led in, surrounded by soldiers carrying torches. He breaks free of them, rushes to Christina, and falls on his knees by her side.*

OLOF: Christina!

CHRISTINA: Olof! You're alive! Thank God. Take me home with you.

OLOF (*crushed*): It's too late.

TABLEAU CURTAIN

Scene 2

A portion of the Great Church in Stockholm, near the west portal. The door to the sacristy is at the left. Pillories are to the right of the portal. A stool of repentance is next to the pillory.

Olof and Gert, in prison clothes, are in the stocks. The church organ is playing; bells are ringing. The service has ended, and the congregation is leaving.

The Sexton Bengt and his wife, Catherine, are standing to one side, downstage.

SEXTON: Chancellor Lars was pardoned, but not Master Olof.

CATHERINE: The Chancellor was always a peaceable man. Never did make much of a fuss. I simply don't understand how he could let himself become part of such awful goings-on.

SEXTON: Always a bit peculiar, I thought. Never said much. And now he's pardoned by the king. But it cost him every penny he owned. Still, I can't help feeling sorry for Master Olof. I always did like him, even though he was difficult a lot of the time.

CATHERINE: Why would they make such a young boy rector of the church, anyway?

SEXTON: Yes, he was pretty young. Bad mistake on his part. But give him time, he'll correct it.

CATHERINE: No he won't. He's going to his death today.

SEXTON: My God! I almost forgot. It's so hard to believe.

CATHERINE: Has he repented yet, do you know?

SEXTON: I doubt it. I'm sure he's as stiff-necked as ever.

CATHERINE: He'll turn to putty when he sees his students. He won't be confirming them this year.

SEXTON: I don't mind saying it: the king is pretty ruthless when he sets his mind to it. I can't get over it: making the rector suffer his punishment on the very day that his students are to be confirmed. Almost as disgusting as that time he made Dean George drink a toast to the public executioner. Or the time he made the prelates take off their mitres and ride through town with birch-bark baskets on their heads.

CATHERINE: The worst of it is that he's forcing Olof's own brother to make Olof ready for death.

SEXTON: Look! Here they come. All the students. How sad they look. Can't say I blame 'em. I think I'm going to cry.

> *Carrying bunches of flowers, the confirmands, boys and girls, pass by Olof. They look sad and depressed, their eyes downcast. The older people follow behind them. Some point their fingers at Olof, others reprimand them for doing so.*
>
> *The student William comes last. He stands shyly in front of Olof, kneels and places his flowers at Olof's feet. Olof has his cowl over his face and does not notice. Some of the people murmur disapprovingly, others express their approval. Friar Martin approaches Olof to remove the flowers, but some of the people thrust him back.*
>
> *Soldiers make way for Olof's brother, Lars Pedersson, who is dressed in full pontificals. The crowd slowly disperses, leaving Lars, Olof, and Gert alone.*
>
> *The organ stops playing, but the pealing of the bells continues.*

LARS (*to Olof*): Olof. The citizens of Stockholm presented a formal petition for your pardon to King Gustav. He has rejected it. . . . Have you made yourself ready for death?

OLOF: I can't think that far ahead.

LARS: I am here by order of the king. I have come to prepare you.

OLOF: You have your work cut out for you. I am far from ready. The blood still seethes in my veins.

LARS: Have you repented?

OLOF: No!

LARS: Would you enter the life eternal with an intransigent heart?

OLOF: Forget the formulary or I won't listen to you. I don't think I can die right now. There's too much left in me.

LARS: I agree. And that's why I can tell you that I am here to prepare you—for a new life in this world.

OLOF: You mean I am to live?

LARS: Yes. On condition you confess that your past life was in error and provided you retract your remarks about the king.

OLOF: How can I? That truly would be death to me.

LARS: I have given you the conditions. The decision is yours.

OLOF: Principles aren't negotiable.

LARS: Even a delusion can become a principle. Think it over, Olof. (*Lars goes out.*)

GERT: This was not the time to reap the harvest. Much snow will have to fall if the autumn seed is to rise and prosper. Civilizations will rise and fall before even the first seed sprouts. The conspirators have been caught. That's what they say, and offer thanks to God. But they are mistaken. The conspirators are all around us: in the king's rooms, in the churches, in the city squares. Only they don't dare as we have dared. Not yet. But they will, one day. . . . Farewell, Olof. You ought to live on; you're young, Olof. I'm perfectly happy to die now. Another martyr, a new name for a battle cry for a new pack of conspirators. Lies never fire the human spirit—never believe that. Never lose your faith in those emotions that shook you to the core when you saw violence, physical or spiritual, inflicted on a human being. Even if the whole world says you're wrong, believe what your heart tells you, if you have the courage to do so. The day you deny your own soul you are truly dead. And eternal damnation shall seem a tender mercy for those who have sinned against the Holy Ghost.

OLOF: You talk as if my release were a certainty.

GERT: The citizens of Stockholm have offered five hundred ducats for your ransom. Since it only cost two thousand ducats to have Birgitta declared a saint, I should think five hundred would be enough to have you declared innocent. The king doesn't dare take your life.

> *The Marshal, Lars Siggeson, enters with the executioner and several soldiers.*

MARSHAL: Take Gert the Printer! Away with him!

GERT (*as he is led out*): Farewell, Olof. Take care of my daughter. And, Olof, never forget the great day of Pentecost!

MARSHAL: Master Olof. You are a young man, and, being young, you were easily led astray. The king pardons you because of your youth. But as surety he demands that you publicly apologize for exceeding your authority and for acting contrary to the orders of the king.

OLOF: So the king still has need of me.

MARSHAL: There are many who have need of you. You must not, however, count on clemency until you have satisfied these conditions. I hold here the king's pardon. Your chains can be removed in an instant, if you wish it. On the other hand, this paper can be torn to shreds in an instant.

OLOF: Anyone who is satisfied with five hundred ducats is not going to trouble himself about a recantation.

MARSHAL: You are in error. The executioner is waiting for you also. . . . I beg you to listen to a few words from an old man. I was once young like you, and I too was driven by strong passions and high ideals. That's part of being young, and those passions are meant to be overcome. I was very much like you. Went about telling the truth to all and sundry, and all I got was ingratitude—at best, a laugh. I, too, wanted to build a little heaven here on earth—(*With emphasis.*) naturally on foundations other than yours. But I soon learned to listen to the voice of reason and I banished idle dreams. . . . I certainly don't believe that you are the kind that seeks to win fame by making trouble; I won't say that. You have good intentions, but your good intentions do a great deal of harm. You have hot blood in your veins. It rushes to your head and blinds you. You lash out at the world, heedless of consequences. You preach freedom, yet you drive thousands into the slavery of their passions. Turn back. Atone for your transgressions; rebuild what you have torn down. For this the people will bless you.

OLOF (*shaken and troubled*): It's true, what you say. I can tell it is. Where did you learn all this?

MARSHAL: Experience taught me. That's what you lack.

OLOF: Have I lived and fought for a lie? Must I profess that my youth and the best years of my manhood have been wasted—pointless—thrown away? No, let me rather die with my illusions.

MARSHAL: You are here because you have held on to them too long. . . . Now calm yourself. Your life is still ahead of you. The past has been an education—a hard one, admittedly, but all the sounder for that. Up to now you have followed your whims. You have indulged in folly. You have neglected the demands of reality. . . . Outside this door stand the people of Stockholm. They have claims on you. This pardon that I hold in my hand represents their investment in you. The clergy of the new church have a lien on you: they want you to live in order that you may complete the work you so brilliantly began. The citizens have their claim: they want you as secretary of the town council. The congregation wants its pastor; the students, their teacher. These are your legal claimants. But there is still someone else out there, perhaps the one to whom you owe the most, although she makes no claim on you: your young wife. You took her from her father, and now you're driving her out into the storm. You rooted out

her childhood faith, and sowed dread in her heart. Because of
your foolish actions an enraged mob has hunted her out of her
home. Yet she does not ask in repayment that you should love
her, only that she may live out her life sharing your sufferings
with you. . . . You call us selfish, but you can see that we too
concern ourselves with our fellow men. . . . Now let me open
this door for you, the door that will lead you back into the world.
Bend your spirit while it is still young and supple, and thank God
for giving you the years that lie ahead in which to serve mankind.

OLOF (*sobbing*): I am lost!

> *The Marshal signals the executioner who releases Olof
> from the pillory and removes his prison attire. The
> Marshal then opens the door to the sacristy, and dele-
> gates representing the city council, the clergy, and the
> citizens of Stockholm enter.*

MARSHAL: Olaus Petri, lately Dean of the Great Church of
Stockholm, do you hereby plead guilty and ask the king's grace
and pardon for your infractions against the royal mandates? Do
you recant those statements made in excess of the authority
granted you by the king? Do you abjure those of your actions
taken contrary to the king's orders? And do you swear fealty to
the king of Sweden, avowing and affirming that you will serve
him faithfully?

> *Olof remains silent.*
>
> *Lars and Christina go to him. Gesturing, the delegates
> implore him to accept the terms of the king's pardon.*

OLOF (*coldly, decisively*): Yes.

MARSHAL: In the name of the king, I now declare you a free
man.

> *Olof and Christina embrace. The delegates gather
> around Olof, shake his hand, and wish him well.*

OLOF (*tonelessly*): Before I leave this place, let me have a moment alone with my God. I have need of it. It was here that not so long ago I struck my first blow. It was here—

LARS: It was here that you won your greatest victory. Today.

Everyone leaves, except Olof. He falls on his knees.

The student William comes into the church, quietly, hesitatingly. He is astonished to see that Olof is alone and out of the pillory.

WILLIAM: Master Olof. I've come to say goodbye to you, before you enter the life to come.

OLOF (*standing up*): William, my dear boy. You were always steadfast. Never gave up on me. . . . I feel like crying with you when I think of the happy moments of my youth.

WILLIAM: Before you die I want to thank you, Master Olof, for all that you have done for us. These flowers—I gave them to you—but you didn't see them. They're trampled on, I see. I wanted them to be a souvenir of that time we played under the linden trees in the garden at the monastery in Strängnäs. You said when you left that we would thank God if you never came back. I thought you might be happy to know that we never did thank God for that. We never forgot you. You stopped the cruel punishments. You opened those heavy monastery doors and let us out. You made us feel free. We saw how blue the sky was and how happy life could be. Why you should be made to die—we don't understand that. For us, you could only do right. They say you are dying because you helped some people who were oppressed. If that is so, then your death cannot be painful, even if it hurts us deeply, very deeply. You told us about how they burned Huss at the stake, because he dared to tell the truth to the high and mighty. You described how he stepped onto the pyre and with joy commended his soul to God, and how he prophesied that a swan would one day come to sing songs hailing a new age of freedom. That's how I've seen you going to meet your death, your head high, your eyes raised to heaven, while the people shout, "Like this, dies a witness to the truth!"

As if struck, Olof slumps down on the stool of repentance.

GERT (*his voice resounding from far within the church*): Renegade!

Olof collapses on the pillory, utterly crushed.

CURTAIN

Introduction

to

The Father

In 1871, not long before Strindberg conceived *Master Olof*, Georg Brandes, lecturing at the University of Copenhagen on the main currents in nineteenth-century literature, declared that Scandinavia was a stagnant pool unaffected by these currents. The reason for this state of affairs was that serious Scandinavian literature concerned itself almost exclusively with religious ideals and not with contemporary issues. If Scandinavian writers were to join the mainstream of development, said Brandes, they would have to follow the French example and "submit problems to debate."

Taking his cue from Brandes, Ibsen did just that. So did Strindberg, and together they made Scandinavia the fountainhead of modern drama. *A Doll's House*, published at the end of 1879, inaugurated a whole series of plays dealing with the problem of women's rights. Strindberg thought Ibsen's presentation of the feminist question was biased against normal couples who found pleasure in sex and was consequently of interest only to a small segment of the population, which Shaw would later call the "neurotic classes." In essays, short stories, and plays, Strindberg chafed, ridiculed, and assailed the Norwegian dramatist and his "bluestocking" followers. One of these plays, which after several rewritings was published under the title *Comrades*, ws a parody of *A Doll's House*. The husband is the doll in Strindberg's play, tyrannized by a woman who is a marauder, invading the male labor market. In place of Ibsen's famous tarantella scene, in which Nora dances as if she were sacrificing her life for her husband's honor, Strindberg has the husband almost persuaded to dress up in drag as a Spanish dancer for a costume ball. It is he who makes the sacrifice to save the marriage by switching numbers on his and his wife's paintings so that she can win a prize and thus feel equal or superior to her comrade-husband. The *raisonneur*, in one version of the play, twits Ibsen for his uncompromising and gloomy view of life in a speech that ticks off all the famous slogans and catchwords in Ibsen's plays.

Oh, give us back the joy we knew, you who preach
the joy of life. Give us the cheering spirit of compromise and send the troll kings home. They came down
from misty moors with mountainous demands and
bills for ideal expenses and made life dark and
unpleasant. Give us the sun again, just a little bit of
sunshine, enough for us to see that the old planet still
possesses a bit of the old heavens.

If Strindberg could have sustained the mood of this speech,
Comrades might have been a light-hearted romp through the
fields of feminism. Unfortunately Strindberg could not involve
himself in the women's rights question without becoming
increasingly acrimonious. He did not mind that his views were
attacked and ridiculed as long as he was allowed to reply, but he
was rightly infuriated when the feminists tried to silence him by
bringing him to court (not for writing against the feminists,
which was not a criminal offense, but for blasphemy against the
state church, which was).

Furthermore, his marriage to a career woman, an actress,
brought the feminist controversy into his own home, and he
began to magnify the importance of the women's rights movement. What at first had seemed to him a social question of secondary importance now became an issue that would fundamen-
tally affect the civilization of Europe. It was, in Strindberg's
view, no longer a matter of career spouses dueling with each
other or of a few neurotic women of ambiguous sexuality; it was
a conflict that pitted all women against all men in a struggle to
decide who would rule at home, in the courts, and in the councils
of state. He found his fearful intimations spelled out in an article
by the Marxist sociologist Paul Lafargue, "Le Matriarcat. Etude
sur les origines de la famille," printed in the 15 March 1886 issue
of *La Nouvelle Revue*. Lafargue believed that the pioneering
studies of such cultural historians as Bachofen, L. H. Morgan,
and Friedrich Engels offered unmistakable evidence that present
male-dominated society had been preceded in prehistorical times
by a society in which women were dominant by virtue of the fact
that it was only through the mother that indubitable parental
links could be established. The patriarchal family was, he said,
a comparatively new form, whose "development was marked by

as many crimes as we can probably expect in the event society should seek to return to the matriarchal form."

This ominous forecast, which Strindberg quoted in the preface to the second volume of his collection of stories *Getting Married*, came as a revelation. Lafargue explained why the women's rights question had assumed such alarming proportions and why the feminist hordes had descended on Strindberg when he tried to talk sensibly on the subject. He thought it was the beginning of a world revolution in which women would triumph over men through a series of crimes, a revolution without crimes being a logical impossibility.

What a subject for a drama! Not a trifling lampoon like *Comrades*, but a searching drama about the coming of a new order in society, a new order of morality. Lafargue had explained that the trial of Orestes at the end of Aeschylus's trilogy the *Oresteia*, in which the male principle replaces the female principle and fathers become more important in the social structure than mothers, encapsulated the revolution in communal life that had occurred before writing had been invented. Strindberg now conceived of a drama, the first in a proposed trilogy, that would reveal the vast wheel of history turning backward, with women fighting to gain ascendancy over men.

But what crimes could they commit if they were the weaker sex and the vassals of men? The crime of destroying man's faith in himself, of sowing the seeds of doubt in the one area that was essential to the patriarchy: fatherhood. Once this much was fixed in Strindberg's mind, his knowledge of abnormal psychology, a subject in which he was particularly well-read, provided the mechanism that would set the wheel turning.

The result was *The Father*, a play in which the protagonist, a man of science and of arms, representing the accomplishments and power of patriarchal society, finds himself in a house of women, women of all sorts and ages, forming a matriarchal society. One reason for the captain's defeat is that he is committed to a moral code developed by patriarchal society, whereas his wife can consider herself not subject to it. Hence she appears in the play as immoral, driven only by her instincts.

Once moral considerations have been put aside, the conflict becomes basically one of wills. The outer action seems erratic, spasmodic, illogical. But as Robert Brustein has remarked, *The*

Father possesses "a kind of internal logic, which makes all its external contradictions seem rather minor; and it maintains this dreamlike logic right up to its shattering climax. For it assumes total warfare between men and women, in which unconscious thoughts are as blameworthy as explicit actions."

The bitter conflict forces the unconscious thoughts to come to the surface, and in doing so it reveals that man has sown the seeds of his own destruction. Patriarchal society created the Christian religion and along with it evolved an ideal image of woman. Man became a slave to the image of the madonna, worshiping her purity while seeking sexual satisfaction from her. Torn by his irreconcilable longings for both the mother and the prostitute, the saint and the sinner, the captain destroys himself, using his wife as instrument. Not only does *The Father* suggest that a Nietzschean transvaluation of values is about to occur in European civilization; it adumbrates in the climactic scene at the end of Act II certain ideas that were to form the cornerstone of the new psychology of the unconscious.

The present translation of *The Father* is based on the latest scholarly edition, prepared by Gunnar Ollén and printed in *August Strindbergs Samlade Verk*, vol. 27 (Uppsala, 1984), as well as on Strindberg's own French translation, *Père* (Helsingborg, 1888). I have also consulted the Danish translation by Peter Nansen, *Faderen* (Copenhagen, 1888).

The Father

(Fadren)

A Tragedy in Three Acts

CHARACTERS

CAPTAIN, in the cavalry (Adolf)
LAURA, his wife
BERTHA, their daughter, about 14 years old
DR. EASTLAND
PASTOR, Protestant, Laura's brother (Jonas)
MARGARET, a maid, the Captain's old nurse
HAPPY, a corporal in the cavalry
ORDERLY, the Captain's

The action takes place in Sweden in a December in the 1880s.

ACT I

The parlor of the Captain's house. A door in the rear wall, to the right, leads to the entrance hall. In the middle of the room, a large round table, with newspapers, magazines, and scientific journals on it. To the right, a leather sofa with a table in front of it. To the far right, a wallpapered jib door, of the sort common in nineteenth-century Swedish homes. To the left, a secretary; a pendulum clock above it. Also to the left, the door to the inner rooms. Weapons of various sorts, hunting rifles and game-bags, hanging on the walls. Near the rear door, a clothes tree with military coats hanging on it. A lamp is burning on the center table.

[1]

The Captain and the Pastor are sitting on the leather sofa. The Captain is in undress uniform except for his boots and spurs. The Pastor is dressed in black and white neck-cloth but without clerical collar. He is smoking a pipe.

The Captain rings.

ORDERLY: Sir?

CAPTAIN: Is Happy out there?

ORDERLY: Waiting your orders, sir, in the kitchen.

CAPTAIN: In the kitchen again! Damn! Get him in here right away!

ORDERLY: Yes, sir! (*Exits.*)

CAPTAIN: That son-of-a-gun has been too familiar with the help. Got the kitchen maid pregnant. A hot little devil, isn't he?

PASTOR: You mean Happy? He was in trouble last year! Same thing!

CAPTAIN: Ah, you remember. Why don't you help the cavalry out and talk to him—friendly. Might set him right. I've bawled him out, sworn at him, even thrashed him. Nothing makes an impression.

PASTOR: And you want me to read a sermon to him? What impression do you think God's word makes on a cavalry trooper?

CAPTAIN: Well, as my brother-in-law you know it makes no impression on me.

PASTOR: I do indeed.

CAPTAIN: However, it might on him. Give it a try, hm?

[2]

Happy enters.

CAPTAIN: All right, Happy, out with it!

HAPPY: With your permission, sir, I can't talk about it—I mean with the pastor here.

PASTOR: Don't be embarrassed on my account, my lad.

CAPTAIN: Come on now, let's have it, the whole story. It's that or punishment duty.

HAPPY: Well, you see—well—we went to dance at Gabriel's house, and then—well, then Louis said that—

CAPTAIN: What's Louis got to do with it? Don't go making up stories.

HAPPY: Well, you see, after a while Emma said let's go to the barn.

CAPTAIN: I see. It was Emma who seduced you!

HAPPY: Not exactly, but that ain't far wrong. Let me tell you, if the girl doesn't want to, nothing happens.

CAPTAIN: We're wasting time. Are you or are you not the father of this baby?

HAPPY: How should I know?

CAPTAIN: What! If you don't know, who does?

HAPPY: Well, sir, how can you ever know?

CAPTAIN: You mean you weren't the only one?

HAPPY: Oh, sure, that time I was; but you still can't be certain you're the only one. I mean—

CAPTAIN: Are you trying to implicate Louis in this? Is that your game?

HAPPY: It's hard to know who's at fault.

CAPTAIN: Now just a minute. You told Emma that you wanted to marry her.

HAPPY: Well, you always gotta say that—

CAPTAIN (*to the Pastor*): My God, what's the world coming to?

PASTOR: The same old refrain. —But tell me, Happy, you must be man enough to know if you're the father.

HAPPY: Well, sure I know I got it off with her. But Pastor, you know yourself that don't necessarily mean anything comes of it.

PASTOR: Listen, young man, we are talking about you!—Surely you can't leave the girl to take care of the child by herself. You cannot be forced to marry her, perhaps, but you certainly must help care for the child. I'll see to that.

HAPPY: Then Louis has got to go in with it too!

CAPTAIN: All right! We'll have to let the courts settle it. I can't untangle this mess. I find it rather tedious. That's all. Dismissed.

PASTOR: Happy! Just a second. . . . Don't you think it's a bit unfair to toss the poor girl out into the street like that, with her baby? Don't you? You must realize that conduct like that can only . . . well . . .

HAPPY: Naturally, if I really knew I was the father, but, well, how can you ever know that? Go slaving through life for somebody else's child—I ain't cut out for that. Pastor, you and the captain, sir, you can understand what I mean.

CAPTAIN: Dismissed!

HAPPY: Yes, sir! (*Exits.*)

CAPTAIN: Not that way! Stay out of the kitchen!

[3]

CAPTAIN: Why didn't you whale the daylights out of him?

PASTOR: What do you mean? I thought I really let him have it.

CAPTAIN: Ha! You just sat there sputtering.

PASTOR: Frankly, I don't know what to say. I feel sorry for the girl. And I feel sorry for the boy. Suppose he isn't the father? The girl can put the baby in a maternity hospital, nurse it for four months, and the child is taken care of thereafter. Not the boy—he can't wet-nurse it. The girl can get a good place afterward in some decent home, but the boy's whole future might be ruined— dishonorable discharge and all that.

CAPTAIN: I damn well wouldn't want to sit on the bench and pass judgment in this case. The lad isn't exactly blameless. How can one tell? One thing is certain; the girl is guilty to some extent —if there's any guilt at all.

PASTOR: Yes, that's true. I don't presume to judge any- one. . . . What were we talking about before we got involved in this damned mess? —Bertha and her confirmation.

CAPTAIN: More than her confirmation; it was the question of her whole upbringing. This house is filled with women, and every one of them wants to bring up my little girl. Your step- mother wants her to be a spiritualist; Laura hopes to make an artist out of her; the governess wants her to be a Methodist; old Margaret steers her to the Baptists; and the kitchen help want her to join the Salvation Army. You can't pull a person in several different directions at once without their coming apart. The trouble is that I, who have the primary responsibility for develop- ing her mind and talents, am constantly thwarted. I've got to get her out of this house.

PASTOR: The trouble is you have too many women running things.

CAPTAIN: You can say that again. I live in a cage filled with tigers. If I didn't hold an iron red-hot under their noses, they would tear me to pieces. —All right, laugh, you bastard. It wasn't bad enough that I married your sister; you had to foist your old stepmother on me too.

PASTOR: For heaven's sake, a man can't have his stepmother living in the same house with him.

CAPTAIN: No, you prefer a mother-in-law as a boarder—in somebody else's house.

PASTOR: Yes, well, everyone has his lot in life.

CAPTAIN: Maybe. But I've got a lot too much to bear. I've still got my old nurse, from the time I was a child, and she treats me as if I were still wearing a bib. Oh, she's very kind, Lord knows, but she just doesn't belong here.

PASTOR: You've got to learn to keep the womenfolk in line. You let them run things too much.

CAPTAIN: All right, you old horse, would you be so good as to enlighten me on how women are supposed to be kept in line?

PASTOR: To tell the truth, Laura was always—. She's my own sister, but she certainly could be quarrelsome.

CAPTAIN: Laura? Oh, she can be difficult, but she's not the worst. I can handle her.

PASTOR: Come on, get if off your chest. I know what she's like.

CAPTAIN: She was brought up like a sentimental schoolgirl and she's having a little difficulty getting adjusted. That's all. After all, she's my wife—

PASTOR: And therefore she can do no wrong? No, you don't fool me; she's the one who's putting the screws on you.

CAPTAIN: Anyway, the point is that now the whole house is in an uproar. Laura won't let our child leave, while I can't let her stay in this nuthouse.

PASTOR: Ah, ha, just as I thought: Laura *won't*. In that case, I fear the worst. When she was a child she would lie stiff and still, playing dead, until she got what she wanted. And when she got it, she gave it back, saying it wasn't the thing that she wanted so much, she just wanted to have her own way.

CAPTAIN: Really. Already like that! . . . You know, she gets herself into such a state sometimes, she scares me. I think something's the matter with her.

PASTOR: Now what is it that you and Laura want for Bertha that is so impossible to agree on? Can't you reach a compromise?

CAPTAIN: Don't get the idea that I want to make her into a *Wunderkind* or a prodigy or remake her in my own image. And I don't want to be a matchmaker to my own daughter, bringing her up just so she can get married. If you do that, and things don't work out, she'll turn into a sour old maid. On the other hand, I don't want her to pursue a man's profession, which would take years of study. And all that education would be absolutely wasted if she decided to get married.

PASTOR: So what do you want?

CAPTAIN: I want her to be a teacher. If she doesn't get married, she can still support herself and won't be any worse off than those poor teachers who have to share their salaries with their families. If she gets married, she can use what she's learned to educate her own children. Now what's wrong with that?

PASTOR: Nothing. Nothing's wrong with it. On the other hand, could it be that she has shown such a talent for painting that it would be a crime not to encourage it?

CAPTAIN: No, not at all! I showed some samples of her work to a well-known painter who said it was ordinary, uninspired stuff, the kind of thing one learns in art classes. But then last summer some young whippersnapper, with all the answers—you know the type—comes along and says Bertha has a colossal talent. And that closed the case in favor of Laura.

PASTOR: I suppose he had a crush on Bertha?

CAPTAIN: Of course, what else!

PASTOR: Well then, old boy, God help you. You're going to need His help. Really sad—I mean, Laura has her own faction— in there. (*Pointing to the inner rooms.*)

CAPTAIN: You can bet on that! The whole house is ready to explode. And just between you and me, it isn't exactly what I'd call a fair fight that's being fought on that side.

PASTOR (*rising*): You think I don't know?

CAPTAIN: You know, eh?

PASTOR: Who'd know better?

CAPTAIN: The worst of it is, it seems to me that Bertha's career is being decided in there on the basis of some pretty vile reasons. "This will teach the men." – "Women can do this and women can do that." Man against woman – that's all I hear, all day long. – You're not leaving, are you? No, no, stay for supper. I don't know what we've got in the house; we'll find something. The new doctor is going to drop in. I told you I was waiting for him. Have you seen him?

PASTOR: I caught a glimpse of him as I rode by. Looked like a proper and sensible sort.

CAPTAIN: Good, that's something. Do you think I can find an ally in him?

PASTOR: Who knows? All depends on how long he has lived with women.

CAPTAIN: Oh, come on now, won't you stay?

PASTOR: No, thanks very much, old friend. I promised I'd be home for supper – and the old lady gets so worried if I'm late.

CAPTAIN: Worried? Furious, you mean. Well, as you wish. Here, let me help you with your overcoat.

PASTOR: Must be awfully cold tonight. Ah, thank you, thank you. You should look after yourself, Adolf. You seem so tense and nervous.

CAPTAIN: Do I act nervous?

PASTOR: Well, a little. Are you sure you're feeling all right?

CAPTAIN: What's Laura been telling you? For twenty years now she's been treating me as if I had one foot in the grave.

PASTOR: Laura? No, no, no. It's just that you worry me. Take care of yourself; a bit of free advice. Goodnight, you old horse. —Wait, I thought you wanted to talk about Bertha's confirmation?

CAPTAIN: Not at all. Let me tell you, I'm not going to interfere with the public conscience. Let it run its appointed course. I'm neither a proselytizer nor a martyr. We're beyond all that, right? Say hello to those at home.

PASTOR: Goodnight, Adolf. Say hello to Laura.

[4]

CAPTAIN (*opens the leaf of the secretary and sits down to do the accounts*): Thirty-four, -nine, forty-three, -seven, -eight, fifty-six.

LAURA (*enters through the door at left*): Would you mind telling me —

CAPTAIN: Just a second. —Sixty-six, seventy-one, eighty-four, eighty-nine, ninety-two, one hundred. What did you want?

LAURA: Maybe I'm bothering you.

CAPTAIN: Not at all. The household money, I suppose?

LAURA: That's right. The household money.

CAPTAIN: Put the bills there, and I'll go through them.

LAURA: Bills?

CAPTAIN: Yes.

LAURA: What's this about bills?

CAPTAIN: I've got to have the receipts, obviously. Our financial position isn't too good, and in case of an audit, you've got to produce the bills and receipts; otherwise our creditors could accuse us of negligence.

LAURA: If our finances are that bad, it isn't my fault.

CAPTAIN: That's exactly what we'll find out by going through the accounts.

LAURA: Listen, if that tenant farmer of ours doesn't pay up, it's not my fault.

CAPTAIN: And who gave that tenant farmer the highest recommendation? You did! And why did you recommend this – this – shall we say, wastrel?

LAURA: And why did you give this – this – wastrel a lease?

CAPTAIN: Because you wouldn't let me eat in peace, sleep in peace, or work in peace until you got him here. You wanted him here because your brother wanted to get rid of him. Your mother wanted him because I *didn't* want him. The governess wanted him because he was a Bible-reading pietist. And old Margaret wanted him because she knew his grandmother when they were children. That's why he was hired. And if I hadn't taken him on, by now I'd be raving in the madhouse or pushing up daisies. – Anyway, here's the budget money and your allowance. You can give me the bills and receipts later.

LAURA (*curtseying*): Thank you so much! . . . What about you? – Do you keep track of what you spend apart from housekeeping expenses?

CAPTAIN: I don't think that's any of your business.

LAURA: No, apparently not – just as little as my child's education is. I see the House and Senate met this evening. What did you and my brother decide?

CAPTAIN: I had already reached my decision, and therefore I had merely to convey it to the only friend I and the rest of my family have in common. Bertha is going to live in town. She will be leaving in two weeks.

LAURA: And where will she be living – if I may ask?

CAPTAIN: She'll be boarding with the Savbergs, the judge advocate.

LAURA: That atheist!

CAPTAIN: A child is to brought up in the faith of its father – that's the law.

LAURA: And the mother has nothing to say about it?

CAPTAIN: Nothing at all. She sold her birthrights in a legal exchange, relinquishing her rights in return for the husband's support of her and her children.

LAURA: So the mother has no rights over her child?

CAPTAIN: None whatsoever. Once you've sold something, you can't take it back and keep the money.

LAURA: What if the father and the mother should come to an agreement . . . ?

CAPTAIN: An agreement?! I want her to live in town, you want her to live out here. Averaging it out arithmetically, she'd move into the railway station, halfway between here and the town. It's a problem without a solution. Do you understand?

LAURA: Then we'll have to invent one, won't we? . . . What did Happy want with you just now?

CAPTAIN: That's a military secret.

LAURA: And the talk of the whole kitchen.

CAPTAIN: Then you must know all about it!

LAURA: I most certainly do!

CAPTAIN: And no doubt you have already handed down your decision.

LAURA: It's in the law books!

CAPTAIN: The law books don't tell who the father of the child is.

LAURA: One usually knows.

CAPTAIN: People with any sense say one can never really know.

LAURA: Isn't that remarkable! You mean you can't know who the father is?

CAPTAIN: So they say.

LAURA: Really remarkable! Then tell me, how can the father have rights over the mother's child?

CAPTAIN: He has them only if he takes on certain responsibilities—or has them forced on him. Besides, in marriage there's no question about who the father is.

LAURA: No question?

CAPTAIN: I should hope not.

LAURA: Not even when the wife has been unfaithful?

CAPTAIN: That doesn't have any application in the present case. Anything else you want to ask?

LAURA: Not a thing.

CAPTAIN: Good. Then I'm going up to my room, and maybe you'll be good enough to inform me when the doctor comes. (*Closes the secretary and stands up.*)

LAURA: Yes, sir, my captain!

CAPTAIN (*opening the wallpapered door at the right*): As soon as he comes, mind you. I don't want to seem rude to him. Understand? (*Exits.*)

LAURA: I understand. Perfectly.

[5]

Laura looks at the money she is holding in her hand.

VOICE OF THE MOTHER-IN-LAW (*from within*): Laura!

LAURA: Yes, what is it?

VOICE OF THE MOTHER-IN-LAW: Where's my tea?

LAURA (*in the doorway to the inner rooms*): Coming—in a moment.

> *Laura is going to the entrance door at the rear when the door is opened, and the Orderly enters, followed by Dr. Eastland.*

ORDERLY: Doctor Eastland.

DR. EASTLAND: How do you do?

LAURA (*going to meet him and offering her hand*): How good of you to come, Doctor. Welcome to our house. The captain is out just now, I'm afraid, but he'll be back soon.

DR. EASTLAND: I beg your pardon for coming so late, but I have already had to make a house call.

LAURA: Please sit down, won't you?

DR. EASTLAND: Thank you.

LAURA: Yes, there seems to be quite a lot of illness in this area right now, but I do hope you'll find everything to your liking here. You know, for us who are rather isolated here in the country it's very important to find a doctor who takes a genuine interest in his patients. I've heard so many good things about you, Doctor. I do hope we shall get along well together.

DR. EASTLAND: Very kind of you, madam. Let me say on my part that I hope my calls here will be social ones and not professional ones. Your family is quite healthy and—

LAURA: Yes, fortunately we haven't had any severe illnesses. Still, things aren't the way they should be.

DR. EASTLAND: Really?

LAURA: Yes, things aren't as good as we might wish.

DR. EASTLAND: I'm sorry to hear that.

LAURA: There are certain situations in family life that, for the sake of propriety and one's conscience, one is compelled to conceal from the world.

DR. EASTLAND: Not from one's doctor, I trust.

LAURA: True. That is why I feel it is my painful duty to let you know right from the start what the true situation is.

DR. EASTLAND: I see. I wonder if we should not put off this discussion until I've met your husband?

LAURA: No! No, you must hear me out *before* you see him.

DR. EASTLAND: So the matter concerns him?

LAURA: Yes, him—my dearly beloved husband.

DR. EASTLAND: How distressing. I assure you, you have my sympathy.

LAURA (*taking out a handkerchief*): My husband is mentally ill. . . . There, I've said it. Now you can judge for yourself.

DR. EASTLAND: I can't believe it! I've read the captain's papers on mineralogy. I've admired them; they reveal a very clear and penetrating intellect.

LAURA: Indeed! You don't know how happy it would make all of us here in the family if we were mistaken.

DR. EASTLAND: Of course it may be that his mind is disturbed in other areas. Perhaps you could tell me—?

LAURA: That's exactly what we fear! You see, sometimes he gets the strangest ideas. He's entitled to them, I suppose—as a scientist, I mean, if only they didn't affect the well-being of the whole family. For instance, he has an absolute mania for buying all sorts of things.

DR. EASTLAND: Oh? What sort of things?

LAURA: Books! Boxes and boxes of them—which he never reads.

DR. EASTLAND: Well, scientists do buy books; that doesn't seem so strange.

LAURA: You don't believe me?

DR. EASTLAND: Madam, I'm convinced that you believe what you say.

LAURA: Then tell me, is it reasonable to think that you can see in a microscope what happens on another planet?

DR. EASTLAND: He says he can do that?

LAURA: That's what he says.

DR. EASTLAND: In a microscope?

LAURA: Yes, in a microscope!

DR. EASTLAND: I must admit that doesn't sound good, if it's true.

LAURA: If it's true! I see you have no confidence in me, Doctor. And here I sit confiding the family secrets to you.

DR. EASTLAND: Now, now, now, madam, what you say will go no further. I'm gratified you feel you can trust me. But as a doctor I have to examine – I have to test things before I can make a diagnosis. Has the captain shown any symptoms of instability, of extreme vacillation?

LAURA: Oh, the stories I could tell you! We've been married for twenty years, and he's never once made up his mind without changing it.

DR. EASTLAND: Is he obstinate? Rigid and difficult to reason with?

LAURA: He always wants his own way, in everything. And once he gets it, he shrugs it off and tells *me* to make the decision.

DR. EASTLAND: Does give one pause, I must say. Perhaps this does need looking into. You see, madam, it's volition, the will, the ability to make decisions, that constitutes the backbone of the psyche; and if that is weakened, the whole mind may collapse.

LAURA: Oh, God knows what I've had to put up with during all these trying years, forcing myself to agree to everything he says. If you only knew how I've struggled with him to keep things going. If you only knew!

DR. EASTLAND: Madam, your misfortune touches me deeply. I assure you I shall do whatever can be done. You have my heart-felt sympathies. I beg you to rely completely on me. From what you tell me there's one thing that I would like to suggest. Avoid bringing up any thoughts with strong emotional associations. In a weak mind they spread like wildfire and turn into obsessions and manias. I think you know what I mean.

LAURA: Yes. You mean anything that would arouse his suspicions.

DR. EASTLAND: Precisely. A sick man can convince himself of anything; he's so susceptible.

LAURA: Yes, of course. . . . Yes, I understand. . . . Yes.

A bell rings from within.

Excuse me, my mother is ringing for me. Could you wait just a moment, please? — Oh, why here's Adolf now —

Laura leaves.

[6]

The Captain enters through the jib door.

CAPTAIN: What, are you already here, Doctor? Welcome, welcome.

DR. EASTLAND: Captain. It's a great pleasure for me to make the acquaintance of such a well-known scientist.

CAPTAIN: Oh, please, please. My military duties don't allow me much time for deep research. Still, I think I may be on the track of an important discovery.

DR. EASTLAND: Really!

CAPTAIN: Yes, yes! I've been subjecting meteor stones to spectroscopy, and I've found carbon, in other words, vestiges of organic life! What do you say to that?

DR. EASTLAND: You can see that in a microscope?

CAPTAIN: No, damnation, man, in the spectroscope!

DR. EASTLAND: Ah, spectroscope! Excuse me, of course, of course. Pretty soon I suppose you'll be telling us what's happening on Jupiter.

CAPTAIN: Not what's happening, but what has happened. If only that damned bookseller in Paris would send me the books. I think all the bookdealers of the world are in a plot against me. For two months I have not had a single reply from any one of them. Imagine, no answers to my orders, my letters, my abusive telegrams, nothing! It's driving me out of my mind. I don't know what's behind it.

DR. EASTLAND: Oh, it's probably just plain ordinary carelessness. You shouldn't get yourself so worked up over that.

CAPTAIN: But, devil take it, I won't be able to get my paper ready in time. And I know that right now in Berlin they're working along the same lines. —But we're not supposed to be talking about this. Forgive me. Now let's get at *your* problem. If you want to live here, we can offer the small flat in the wing of the house. Or do you want to live in the old servants' quarters?

DR. EASTLAND: Just as you wish. Makes no difference to me.

CAPTAIN: No, it's up to you. Take your pick.

DR. EASTLAND: No, I'll let you decide that.

CAPTAIN: No. I'll decide nothing of the sort. It's up to you to say what you want. I have no preference, none at all.

DR. EASTLAND: Well, I can't decide—

CAPTAIN: For Christ's sake man, just say what you want! I don't care. I have no preference, no wish in this matter. What are you, a milksop? Come, come, make up your mind. Infuriating!

DR. EASTLAND: Well, if it's up to me—all right, I'll move in here.

CAPTAIN: Good! That's more like it. Thank you. —I'm sorry, Doctor, but there's nothing that irks me so much as hearing someone say "makes no difference to me." (*He rings.*)

The nurse Margaret enters.

CAPTAIN: Oh, so it's you, Margaret. Say, do you know if the apartment in the wing is ready for the doctor?

MARGARET: Yes, Captain. It's all ready.

CAPTAIN: Good. Then I won't detain you, Doctor. You must be tired. Goodnight. Make yourself at home. I'll see you in the morning, I hope.

DR. EASTLAND: Good evening, Captain.

CAPTAIN: I trust my wife has made things clear to you—given you the lay of the land, as it were.

DR. EASTLAND: Yes, your splendid wife has given me some

pointers that it might be good for an outsider to know. Well, goodnight, Captain.

[7]

CAPTAIN: Ah, dear old Margaret! Now what can I do for you?

MARGARET: My big boy Adolf! Could I speak to you for a moment?

CAPTAIN: My dear old nurse, you go right ahead and say whatever's on your mind. You're the only one I can listen to around here without climbing the walls.

MARGARET: Now Adolf, don't you think you could meet Laura halfway and work out something with her about your child? After all, she's the mother and—

CAPTAIN: After all, I'm the father, Margaret.

MARGARET: Yes, yes, yes. But a father has other things to think about; the mother has only her child.

CAPTAIN: That's exactly it. She's only got one burden to carry, while I have three. And what she carries I also have to carry. Don't you think I would have been something other than an old soldier by now if I didn't have a wife and child?

MARGARET: Well, that isn't what I mean.

CAPTAIN: No, I'm sure it isn't. You're just trying to put me in the wrong.

MARGARET: Oh, Adolf, my boy, don't you believe that I want only the best for you?

CAPTAIN: Of course, I believe it, you dear old girl. But you don't know what is best for me. You see, it isn't enough for me just to have given life to a child; I also want to give it my mind and soul.

MARGARET: Well, I wouldn't know about things like that. I just think that people should make an effort to get along together.

CAPTAIN: You're not my old friend, are you, Margaret?

MARGARET: Me? What are you saying, Adolf? Do you think I can forget you were my baby boy when you were a little tyke?

CAPTAIN: No, old girl. Do you think I can forget? You've been like a mother to me. You've given me aid and comfort – up to now – when everyone else was against me. But now when the chips are down, you betray me and join the enemy.

MARGARET: Enemy?

CAPTAIN: Yes, enemy! You know how things stand in this house. You've seen it all, from beginning to end.

MARGARET: Yes, I've seen – more than enough. For heaven's sake, why should two people torture each other like this – two good people so kind to everybody else? Laura is never like that to me or to the others.

CAPTAIN: No, only to me. I know. But let me tell you, Margaret, if you abandon me now, you'll be doing a bad thing. They're spinning a web around me. And that doctor is no friend of mine.

MARGARET: Oh, Adolf, Adolf, you think the worst of everybody. You know why? Adolf, it's because you don't have the true faith. That's why, Adolf.

CAPTAIN: But you and the Baptists have found the one and only true faith. How fortunate you are.

MARGARET: I am not as unfortunate as you, Adolf, let me tell you. If you would humble your heart you would see that God would make you happy. Thou shalt love thy neighbor.

CAPTAIN: It's remarkable; you just so much as talk of God and love and your voice gets as hard as iron and your eyes glint like steel. No, no, Margaret, you certainly haven't found the true faith.

MARGARET: All right, you be proud and almighty with your books and learning. You'll see how far that gets you when it really counts.

CAPTAIN: How haughtily speak the humble at heart! Of course learning doesn't mean much to cows like you!

MARGARET: You ought to be ashamed! . . . But I still love my boy, my big, silly boy, and he'll come back to his old nurse, like a poor runaway boy, when the winds begin to howl.

CAPTAIN: Margaret! I'm sorry . . . Margaret, you've got to believe me, no one here wants to help me—no one but you. Help me. I know something is going to happen. I don't know what, but whatever it is, it's all wrong.

A sharp cry from within.

What's that? Who's screaming?

[8]

Bertha enters from the right.

BERTHA: Papa, Papa! Help, help! Save me!

CAPTAIN: There, there, my dear child! There, there. What's the matter?

BERTHA: Oh, Daddy, help me! She wants to hurt me!

CAPTAIN: Now, now, who wants to hurt you? Hm? Tell me. Come on now, tell me.

BERTHA: Grandma does. —But it was my fault. I tricked her.

CAPTAIN: All right, now you tell me just what happened.

BERTHA: You've got to promise not to tell. Promise? Promise?

CAPTAIN: Yes, yes. Now what is this all about?

Margaret exits.

BERTHA: It happens at night. Grandma comes in, and turns the lamp down low, and then she sets me down at the table with a pen in my hand over a piece of paper. And then she says the spirits will write.

CAPTAIN: What kind of nonsense—! And you haven't told me about this before?

BERTHA: I'm sorry. I didn't dare. Grandma said the spirits would get back at me if I told on them. And then the pen begins to write, and I don't know if I'm doing it or not. And sometimes it writes a lot, and sometimes nothing comes. But it has to come, she says, it has to. And tonight I thought I was doing good, and then Grandma says it was from Shakespeare, and that I had tricked her. And then she got awfully mad.

CAPTAIN: Do you think there are spirits?

BERTHA: I don't know.

CAPTAIN: But I know that there aren't any.

BERTHA: Grandma says that you don't understand such things, and that you have much worse things that can see what's going on on other planets.

CAPTAIN: Is that what she says? What else does she say?

BERTHA: She says that you really can't do any conjuring.

CAPTAIN: I never said I could. You know what meteor stones are? Stones that have fallen from other heavenly bodies. Well, I can examine them and find out if they contain the same elements as our earth. That's all that I can see.

BERTHA: Grandma says that there are things that she can see but that you can't see.

CAPTAIN: Well, Bertha, that's not true.

BERTHA: Grandma wouldn't tell a lie.

CAPTAIN: Why not?

BERTHA: Then Mama is lying too.

CAPTAIN: Uh huh.

BERTHA: If you say Mama is lying, I'll never believe you again.

CAPTAIN: I haven't said that. And that's why you must believe me when I say that it's best for you, best for your future, that you get away from this house. Do you want to do that? Do you want to go and live in town and learn something practical?

BERTHA: Oh, Daddy, how I want to live in town! Get away

from here, anywhere! As long as I could still see you now and then. Often. Everything here is so gloomy—dark like a long winter night. But when you come home, Daddy, it's like a spring morning.

CAPTAIN: You dear little chatterbox! My dearest little girl!

BERTHA: But, Daddy, if only you could be nice to Mommy, you know. She cries a lot.

CAPTAIN (*murmurs noncommittally, and then says*): So you want to live in town?

BERTHA: Yes, I do, I do!

CAPTAIN: Suppose Mama doesn't want you to?

BERTHA: But she has to want me to!

CAPTAIN: Just suppose she doesn't?

BERTHA: Then I don't know what to do. She has to want me to, she has to!

CAPTAIN: Will you ask her if you can go?

BERTHA: No, you ask her, ask her nice and sweet. She doesn't pay any mind to me.

CAPTAIN: Hmmm. . . . Well now, if you want to go, and I want you to go, and she *doesn't* want you to go, what do we do then?

BERTHA: Oh, no. Then the bickering will start again. Why can't you both—?

[9]

Laura enters.

LAURA: Ah, so this is where you are, Bertha! This seems to be a good time for hearing what she thinks. We've got to settle the question of her future sooner or later.

CAPTAIN: The child can scarcely have any sound opinion about her future. She doesn't know what lies ahead for a young girl. We on the other hand have a pretty good idea. We've seen a lot of girls grow up and go through life.

LAURA: But since we don't see eye to eye, why not let Bertha's opinion tip the scales?

CAPTAIN: No! I won't allow anyone to usurp my rights, neither women nor children. Bertha, leave us.

Bertha leaves.

LAURA: You were afraid of what she would say. You knew she would come around to me.

CAPTAIN: I know that she herself wants to get away from home. I also know that you have the power to change her mind any way you wish.

LAURA: Really. Am I so strong?

CAPTAIN: You've got the strength of the devil in getting your own way. So has anyone who has no scruples about the means he uses. For example, how did you get rid of Doctor Norling, and how did you get the new doctor out here?

LAURA: Yes, how *did* I manage that?

CAPTAIN: You kept insulting Norling until he left in disgust, and you got your brother to "arrange" the appointment of the new one.

LAURA: What was wrong with that? Very simple and perfectly legal. Is Bertha leaving soon?

CAPTAIN: Yes, in two weeks she'll move into town.

LAURA: That is your decision?

CAPTAIN: Yes!

LAURA: Have you spoken to Bertha about it?

CAPTAIN: Yes.

LAURA: Then I guess I shall have to try to put a stop to it.

CAPTAIN: You can't!

LAURA: Oh, no? Do you suppose a real mother will allow her daughter to go and live with trash and to have the child learn that everything she has implanted in her mind is stupid, so that for the rest of her life she'll be despised by her own daughter?

CAPTAIN: Do you suppose that a real father will allow ignorant superstitious women to teach his daughter that he is a charlatan?

LAURA: It doesn't mean as much in the case of the father.

CAPTAIN: Why not?

LAURA: Because the mother is closer to the child. It's a fact that no one can really know who the father of a child is.

CAPTAIN: I don't see the application in the present case.

LAURA: You don't know if you are Bertha's father.

CAPTAIN: I don't know?

LAURA: Since no one knows, how can you?

CAPTAIN: This is a poor joke.

LAURA: Who's joking? I'm only making use of your teachings. Besides, how do you know I haven't been unfaithful?

CAPTAIN: I can believe you capable of almost anything, but not that. And you wouldn't talk about it if it were true.

LAURA: Suppose I were willing to endure anything, to be shunned, despised, anything to hold on to my child and bring her up as I see fit, and suppose I am sincere when I declare: "Bertha is my child but not yours." Suppose—

CAPTAIN: That's enough!

LAURA: Just suppose. Then your power would be at an end.

CAPTAIN: That is, if you could prove that I was not the father.

LAURA: That shouldn't be difficult. Would you like me to try?

CAPTAIN: I said that's enough!

LAURA: All I would have to do is reveal the name of the real father, specify the time and place. For example—when was Bertha born?—three years after we got married—

CAPTAIN: For the last time I'm telling you—!

LAURA: Telling me what? —You're right, we've had enough. But be very careful what you do and what you decide. And above all, don't make yourself ridiculous.

CAPTAIN: Ridiculous? I think it's tragic.

LAURA: The more you think so, the more comical you become.

CAPTAIN: I get the laughs and you get the tears. Is that it?

LAURA: Yes. Aren't we women clever?

CAPTAIN: That's why we can't fight against you.

LAURA: Then why do you get yourself involved in a fight with a superior enemy?

CAPTAIN: Superior?

LAURA: Yes. It's strange, but I could never look at a man without feeling superior.

CAPTAIN: Well, you'll soon learn who your master is. And you won't forget it.

LAURA: That should be interesting.

MARGARET (*entering*): The table's set. Would you like to have something to eat now?

LAURA: Yes, Margaret, thank you.

> *The Captain hesitates. Sits in the armchair near the table in front of the divan.*

LAURA: Aren't you going to have supper?

CAPTAIN: No thanks. I don't care for anything.

LAURA: What's the matter? Depressed?

CAPTAIN: No, just not hungry.

LAURA: Come, otherwise they'll start asking questions, unnecessary questions. . . . You can have the decency—. . . . All right, if you won't, then sit there! (*She leaves.*)

MARGARET: Adolf, now what's going on here?

CAPTAIN: I don't know what's going on. Can you tell me how you women can handle a grown man as if he were a child?

MARGARET: I don't know. I suppose it's because you are all born of women, all of you, big and small . . .

CAPTAIN: And no woman is born of man. But I've got to be Bertha's father. Tell me, Margaret, you believe that, don't you? You believe it?

MARGARET: Heavens, but you're silly! Of course you're your own child's father. Come on now and get something to eat. Don't sit there putting a face on. There, there. Come on now.

CAPTAIN (*standing up*): Get out of here, you old woman! To hell with all you witches! (*At the door to the hallway.*) Corporal! Orderly!

ORDERLY (*entering*): Yes, sir!

CAPTAIN: Harness up the one-horse sleigh. Immediately!

MARGARET: Adolf! Don't do anything–!

CAPTAIN: Get out, woman! –At once, do you hear!

MARGARET: Lord help us, what are you up to?

CAPTAIN (*putting on his military cap and great coat, etc.*): Don't expect me home. Not before midnight. (*Leaves.*)

MARGARET: God have mercy! Now what's he up to?

ACT II

Same set as first act. The kerosene lamp is burning on the table. Night.

[1]

Dr. Eastland and Laura are in conversation.

DR. EASTLAND: According to what I gathered from our conversation, I'm still not convinced about his condition. In the first place, you were mistaken in saying he had arrived at some astonishing conclusions about the other planets by looking through a microscope. Now that I've found out that it was a spectroscope, I would say that not only is he sane but that he merits the highest praise for his work as a scientist.

LAURA: But, Doctor, I never said anything of the kind!

DR. EASTLAND: Madam, I took notes on our conversation, and I distinctly recall that I asked about this crucial point, fearing that I had not heard you correctly. One has to be extremely scrupulous in making accusations that could lead to a man's being certified and committed.

LAURA: Certified?

DR. EASTLAND: You surely know that a person who is declared insane loses his civil and domestic rights.

LAURA: No, I wasn't aware of that.

DR. EASTLAND: And there's another point that strikes me as questionable. He mentioned that his letters to the booksellers had gone unanswered. Forgive me for asking, but I must know whether you—with the best intentions in the world—have interfered with his correspondence?

LAURA: Yes, I have. I felt it was my duty to look after the best interests of the family. I could not let him ruin us all without doing something.

DR. EASTLAND: Forgive me for saying this, but I don't believe you have seriously considered the possible consequences of your actions. If he finds out that you have been secretly meddling in his affairs, there is no telling what will happen. One confirmed suspicion can set off an avalanche of doubts. Or to put it another way: interfering in his business is like putting a spoke in a wheel, the worst thing for his nervous condition. I'm sure you yourself know how the mind is fretted and torn when your deepest wishes are thwarted, your will paralyzed.

LAURA: Yes, I certainly do.

DR. EASTLAND: Then you know what he must have felt.

LAURA (*rising*): It's midnight and he's still not home. We can fear the worst now.

DR. EASTLAND: Madam, I beg of you to tell me what happened tonight after I left. I must know.

LAURA: He let his imagination run away with him. He had the craziest notions. He was seized with the idea that he was not the father of his own child.

DR. EASTLAND: Strange. Very strange. What brought that up?

LAURA: I can't imagine—unless—well, he was questioning one of his troopers about the parentage of some child, and when I defended the girl in the case, he got all excited and said no one could tell who was the father of a child. God knows I did everything I could to quiet him, but now I think the whole thing's hopeless. (*Cries.*)

DR. EASTLAND: This can't be allowed to continue. Something has to be done—without arousing his suspicions, of course. I wonder if you could tell me if the captain has had such odd notions before?

LAURA: Six years ago there was a similar situation. That time he admitted—in his own letter to his doctor—that he feared for his sanity.

DR. EASTLAND: I see, I see. A case with roots deep in the past. And the sanctity of the family—and now this—I can't pry into everything; I must keep to what meets the eye. What's done can't be undone, unfortunately, and the treatment should have begun at that time. . . . Where do you think he is now?

LAURA: I don't have the slightest notion. I only know he gets the wildest ideas.

DR. EASTLAND: Do you want me to wait up for him? To avoid arousing his suspicions I could say that I was making a call on your mother—some complaint or ailment.

LAURA: Yes, that's excellent. And, Doctor, please don't leave us. If you only knew how upset I am. I wonder, wouldn't it be better if we told him right out what you think of his condition?

DR. EASTLAND: That's something one never tells the mentally disturbed before they themselves bring it up, and only then in exceptional cases. It all depends on how things develop. But we shouldn't be sitting here. Perhaps I should slip into the next room; things would look more natural.

LAURA: Yes, that would be better. And Margaret can sit in here. She always waits up for him. She's the only one who knows how to handle him. (*Goes to the door at left.*) Margaret! Margaret!

MARGARET: Yes, is there something you want? Has the captain come home?

LAURA: No, I want you to sit here and wait for him. And when he comes, you're to tell him that my mother is ill, and that's why the doctor is here.

MARGARET: Yes, yes. All right, I'll tend to it.

LAURA (*opens the door to the inner rooms*): Doctor, would you mind stepping this way?

> *Dr. Eastland leaves with Laura.*

[2]

MARGARET (*sitting at the table. Produces a hymnbook and a pair of spectacles*): Ah, yes, yes. Yes, yes. (*Reading half to herself.*)

"A vale of tears, dark and drear,
Is this our life, and short its span.
Death's angel is ever near
Warning every living man:
        All are mortal, all is vain."

All mortal. If that isn't the truth.

"Yea, all that lives on earth must die
And to the scythe of death succumb.
Only sorrow stays to sigh
And etch with tears the silent tomb:
        All are mortal, all is vain."*

Etch with tears, yes. Yes.

During this Bertha has entered, carrying a tray with a coffee pot and a piece of embroidery on it.

BERTHA (*softly*): Margaret, can I sit here with you? It's so gloomy upstairs.

MARGARET: God in Heaven, are you still up?

BERTHA: I have to work on Daddy's Christmas present. And here's coffee for you.

MARGARET: Ah, you're a sweet child, but this just won't do. You have to get up in the morning, and it's after midnight.

BERTHA: What difference does that make? I don't dare sit alone upstairs. There are ghosts up there, I'm sure there are.

MARGARET: I knew it, I knew it, just what I said! Mark my words, there's no good fairy watching over this house. What did you hear, Bertha?

BERTHA: I—I heard someone singing in the attic.

MARGARET: In the attic! At this time of night!

BERTHA: Such a moaning, mournful song, the most mournful song I've ever heard. And it sounded like it came from the storage

* A hymn by J. O. Wallin, the most prolific of Swedish hymnists.

room up in the attic, where the cradle is, you know, the room to the left —

MARGARET: Hooo, hooo! . . . And Lord what weather tonight!

> "Alas, what is this life we lead on earth?
> Unending toil and pain, and nothing worth.
> Even on the best of days we found
> Cares and tribulations did abound."*

Yes, dear child, may God grant us a happy Christmas.

BERTHA: Margaret, is it true that Daddy is sick?

MARGARET: Yes, I'm afraid he is.

BERTHA: Then we won't be allowed to celebrate Christmas. Why isn't he in bed if he's sick?

MARGARET: Well, Bertha, he has the kind of an illness where he can be up and about. — Shhh! There's someone out in the hall. Now, you be a good girl and go to bed. And take the coffee pot with you; otherwise your daddy will be mad.

BERTHA (*goes out with the serving tray*): Goodnight, Margaret.

MARGARET: Goodnight, child. God bless you.

[3]

CAPTAIN (*enters, covered with snow. Takes off his overcoat*): You still up? Go to bed.

MARGARET: I was only waiting for . . .

> *The Captain lights a candle. Opens the leaf of the secretary. Sits down and takes some letters and newspapers from his pocket.*

MARGARET: Adolf—?

CAPTAIN: What do you want?

---

* From a hymn by J. Rosenthal.

MARGARET: Laura's mother is sick. And the doctor is here.

CAPTAIN: Anything serious?

MARGARET: No, I don't think so. Only a cold.

CAPTAIN (*standing up*): Who was the father of your child, Margaret?

MARGARET: I've told you the whole story so many times. It was that good-for-nothing Johnson.

CAPTAIN: Are you certain it was him?

MARGARET: Don't be silly – of course I'm certain, since he was the only one.

CAPTAIN: Yes – but was *he* certain he was the only one? No, he couldn't be certain, but you could. There's the difference.

MARGARET: I don't see any difference.

CAPTAIN: No, you can't see it; but it's there all the same. (*He leafs through a photograph album on the table.*) Do you think Bertha looks like me? (*Contemplates a portrait in the album.*)

MARGARET: Why, you're as like as two peas in a pod.

CAPTAIN: Did Johnson admit he was the father?

MARGARET: He had to – what else could he do?

CAPTAIN: Awful! Incredible.

[4]

Dr. Eastland enters.

CAPTAIN: Good evening, Doctor. How is my mother-in-law feeling?

DR. EASTLAND: Oh, it's nothing serious. She sprained her left ankle slightly.

CAPTAIN: I thought I heard Margaret say it was a cold. There seems to be a slight difference of opinion. Go to bed, Margaret.

Margaret exits.

Pause.

CAPTAIN: Sit down, won't you? Sit down, Doctor.

DR. EASTLAND (*seating himself*): Thank you.

CAPTAIN: Is it true that if you cross a zebra with a mare, the foal is striped?

DR. EASTLAND (*taken aback*): Quite true! Absolutely.

CAPTAIN: And is it true that if you continue the breeding with a studhorse, the succeeding foals will also be striped?

DR. EASTLAND: Yes, that's also true.

CAPTAIN: So: under certain conditions a studhorse can be the sire of striped foals, and under other conditions, not.

DR. EASTLAND: Yes, so it would seem.

CAPTAIN: In other words, similarity between offspring and father proves nothing.

DR. EASTLAND: I, ah —

CAPTAIN: In other words, fatherhood cannot be proved.

DR. EASTLAND: Ah, ha . . .

CAPTAIN: You're a widower, aren't you? And have had children?

DR. EASTLAND: Yes, I —

CAPTAIN: Didn't you feel ridiculous at times? Being a father, I mean. I don't know anything so comical as seeing a father parading his children down the street. Or hearing a father talk about *his* children. "My wife's children" — that's what he should say. Didn't you ever sense how false your position was? — Never any little stabs of doubt? — I won't say suspicions; as a gentleman, I presume your wife was above suspicion.

DR. EASTLAND: No, I never had that. But, Captain, you have to accept the parentage of your children in good faith. As Goethe says. I believe it was Goethe.

CAPTAIN: Good faith where a woman is involved? That's taking a big risk, isn't it?

DR. EASTLAND: Well, Captain, there are all kinds of women.

CAPTAIN: No, Doctor! Only three kinds—and only one genus. The latest research has made that clear. When I was young and strong and—let me boast—handsome—I recall now two fleeting impressions that since then have left me apprehensive. I was traveling one time by steamboat. I sat in the forward salon, some friends and I. The young woman who ran the restaurant came and sat down opposite me, sat down sobbing, and told us her fiancé had gone down with his ship. We offered our sympathies, and I ordered champagne. After the second glass, I touched her foot; after the fourth, her knee; and by morning I had completely consoled her.

DR. EASTLAND: We all have our failings and weaknesses. There are spots even on the sun.

CAPTAIN: Yes, and on the leopard, too. You know what they say about them. . . . My second example: I was at a resort, and there was a young wife there who had her children with her while her husband was in town on business. Very religious woman, with the strictest principles, always preaching to me, and utterly honorable, I'm sure. A very plain woman, physically unattractive. I avoided her. I fled from her. But she, on the pretext of borrowing books from me, dogged my heels. I loaned her a book—two books—and when she was about to move, she—strangely enough—returned the books. Have you heard of such a thing! Three months later I found in these selfsame books a visiting card with a sufficiently clear declaration of her feelings. Quite innocent—as innocent as any avowal of love from a married woman to a strange man who has never made any advances to her can be.

DR. EASTLAND: A vulgar, scheming woman, obviously.

CAPTAIN: No, not at all, no! No! She was sincere in her religious beliefs, sincere in her morality, sincere in her marital fidelity. The proof: she actually confided in her husband that she was infatuated with me. You see, therein lies the great peril. This is what fills me with apprehension. They are utterly unconscious of their instinctive deceitfulness. Such is the genus "woman."

DR. EASTLAND: You must not let these morbid thoughts get the better of you, Captain. You'll end up a sick man.

CAPTAIN: Sick? Such an imprecise word for a doctor to use. All steam boilers explode when the manometer goes past one hundred. But one hundred doesn't represent the same pressure on different boilers. Understand? Besides, are you not here to watch over me? If I were not a man, I would have the right to present my case — or to make a case, slyly, out of insinuations. I might in fact provide you with a complete diagnosis, a clinical account of my illness. Alas, and unfortunately, I am only a man, and can do nothing but fold my arms on my chest like an ancient Roman and hold my breath until I die. Goodnight.

DR. EASTLAND: Captain! . . . If you are ill or deeply distrubed, it would do no offense to your honor as a man to tell me all there is to tell. I want to hear the other side of the story, too.

CAPTAIN: Hearing one side of this story is enough, I should think.

DR. EASTLAND: No, Captain. When I saw *Ghosts* and heard Mrs. Alving giving us a postmortem on her husband, I said to myself, "Damned shame the dead can't speak."

CAPTAIN: Do you think he would speak if he were alive? And if *any* dead husband rose up and spoke, do you think he'd be believed? Goodnight, Doctor. You can see I am quite calm. You can go to bed. Go home.

DR. EASTLAND: Very well, Captain, goodnight. I have done all I can do.

CAPTAIN: Do we part as enemies?

DR. EASTLAND: Not at all. I very much regret that we can't be friends. Goodnight. (*Exits.*)

> *The Captain follows Dr. Eastland to the door at rear.*
> *Then he goes to the door at left and opens it halfway.*

CAPTAIN: Come in; let's have a talk. I knew you were eavesdropping.

[5]

*Laura enters, somewhat abashed. The Captain sits
down at the secretary, the leaf of which is still down.*

CAPTAIN: I know it's late, but we've got to have this out. Sit
down. (*Pause.*) I went to the post office tonight and picked up
some letters. From them I learn that you have held back both my
incoming and outgoing mail. The immediate consequence of this
is that, because of the loss of time, others shall rush ahead of me
in my research, and I shall fall into the shade.

LAURA: I did what I did for your own good. You were neglecting your military duties for this other work.

CAPTAIN: My good? No! You were quite certain that one day
I'd win more honor with my scientific work than with my military duties. And your primary aim was to see to it that I didn't
win any honors, because that would emphasize your insignificance. But there's more: I've intercepted some letters addressed
to you.

LAURA: What a gentleman you are!

CAPTAIN: From which it appears you have special plans for
me. For a long time now you have been gathering my former
friends against me by spreading rumors about my mental condition. And you have succeeded in your efforts to the extent that
from the colonel down to the cook, there is scarcely anyone who
believes I'm not mad. Now as far as my illness is concerned, these
are the facts. My mind is clear, as you know, so that I can carry
out my duties and my responsibilities as a father. My emotions
are still pretty much within my control and will be as long as my
willpower remains in working order. But you have gnawed and
chewed on it so that the cogs are worn smooth, and soon the gear
wheels will slip and the whole mechanism will spin backward
and fly to pieces. I won't appeal to your feelings—since you lack

them: therein lies your strength. I do, however, appeal to your best interests.

LAURA: What does that mean?

CAPTAIN: Your behavior has succeeded in arousing my suspicions to the point where my acumen is blunted and my thoughts run wild—the onset of madness—what you have been waiting for, and which might come at any moment. Now I put this question to you: is it in your better interest that I am of sound or unsound mind? Think about it. If I collapse, I lose my position in the army, and where would you be? If I die, you get my insurance. However, if I should take my own life, you would receive nothing. So you see, it is in your interest that I live my life out.

LAURA: Is this supposed to be a trap?

CAPTAIN: Of course! It's up to you to set your foot in it or go around it.

LAURA: You say you'll kill yourself. You won't!

CAPTAIN: Can you be sure? Do you think a man can live when he has nothing and no one to live for?

LAURA: So you capitulate?

CAPTAIN: No, I'm suggesting an armistice.

LAURA: On what conditions?

CAPTAIN: That I retain my reason and sanity. Rid me of my suspicions and I lay down my arms.

LAURA: What suspicions?

CAPTAIN: Concerning Bertha's parentage.

LAURA: Are there any suspicions about that?

CAPTAIN: With me there are. Suspicions you have fed and nourished.

LAURA: I? How?

CAPTAIN: You have dropped them like hebona in the porches of my ear, and circumstances have made them doubly poisonous.

Free me from uncertainty. Tell me plainly I'm right, and I shall forgive you in advance.

LAURA: You don't expect me to assume a guilt that's not mine!

CAPTAIN: What difference does that make, since you can be certain that I won't reveal it. A man doesn't go around trumpeting his shame.

LAURA: If I say your suspicions are wrong, you can't be certain; but if I say they are right, then you can be certain. So you want your suspicions to be right.

CAPTAIN: Fantastic, but true. The first instance cannot be proved, you see; only the second.

LAURA: Have you any grounds for these suspicions?

CAPTAIN: Yes and no.

LAURA: I know what you are up to. You want me to admit my guilt so you can get rid of me and keep the child entirely to yourself. No, you won't catch me in that trap.

CAPTAIN: Do you think I'd want to bring up somebody else's child if I were certain of your guilt?

LAURA: I'm confident you wouldn't. And that's why I realize you were lying a moment ago when you said you'd forgive me in advance.

CAPTAIN (*rising*): Laura, save me and my reason. You don't understand what I'm trying to say. If the child isn't mine, I have no rights over it, and want none. Isn't that exactly what you want? Do you want more? What else? You want power over the child, with me on hand to support both her and you? Is that it?

LAURA: Yes, power. What is this whole life-and-death struggle but a struggle for power?

CAPTAIN: For me, since I do not believe in a life in the hereafter, my child was my life in the future. It was my form of immortality, the only form of it that has any basis in reality. Take that from me, and you cut the thread of life.

LAURA: Why didn't we separate before?

CAPTAIN: Because the child held us together. But the child became a chain. How did it happen? How? How? . . . I never thought about it before, but now I remember something that happened—a memory that implicates and condemns you. We had been married two years and had no children—you best know why. I fell ill and lay near death. One time when the fever left me, I heard voices in the sitting room. You and the lawyer talking about the money I possessed—at that time. He explained that you couldn't inherit any of it since we didn't have any children, and he asked if you were pregnant. What you said I couldn't hear. I recovered—and we had a child. Who is the father?

LAURA: You!

CAPTAIN: No, not me, not me! There's a crime buried in the past, a crime now coming to light. And what a devilish crime! Your tender consciences made you free the black slaves, but you held on to the white. I have worked and slaved for you, for your child, your mother, your maids. I have sacrificed my career and promotion; I've been whipped from pillar to post, gone without sleep, worried myself sick about taking care of you until my hair has turned gray—gone through hell in order that you might enjoy a trouble-free life and spend your old age enjoying life again through your child. I've endured it all without complaining because I thought I was father of this child. This is the lowest form of theft, the most brutal slavery. I've suffered seventeen years at hard labor as an innocent man; how can you repay me for that?

LAURA: Now you are mad!

CAPTAIN (*sitting down*): That's what you want, isn't it? I've seen how you've worked to conceal your crime. I took pity on you because I didn't understand what was troubling you. I often lulled your troubled conscience, thinking I was chasing away a nightmare. I have heard you cry out in your sleep. I didn't want to listen. I remember now—the other night—the night before Bertha's birthday. Between two and three in the morning, I was still up, reading. You shrieked as if someone were choking you. "Go away, go away—or I'll tell!" I pounded on the wall—I—didn't want to hear more. I've harbored my suspicions a long time, afraid to hear them confirmed. This I have suffered for you; what will you do for me?

LAURA: What can I do? I swear by God and everything that's holy that you are Bertha's father.

CAPTAIN: What good does that do when you've already said that a mother may and should commit any crime for the sake of her child? I beg you, by the memory of all that's past—I beg you like a wounded man asking for the *coup de grace*—tell me all. Don't you see I am as helpless as a child; can't you hear I have come to cry to you as to my mother; can't you forget that I am a man, a soldier commanding man and beast? I ask only for the pity you would show a dying man; I surrender the tokens of my power; I beseech you, have mercy on me. (*He is on his knees.*)

LAURA (*puts her hand on his head*): What! You're crying. A man like you crying!

CAPTAIN: Yes, I am crying. A man and crying. Hath not a man eyes? Hath not a man hands, organs, senses, affections, passions? Is he not fed with the same food, hurt with the same weapons, warmed and cooled by the same summer and winter as a woman is? If you prick us, do we not bleed? If you tickle us, do we not laugh? If you poison us, do we not die? Why should not a man be allowed to wail, a soldier to cry? Because it is unmanly? Why is it unmanly?

LAURA: Cry, cry, my boy, and your mother will comfort you, as she did before. Remember? It was as your second mother that I came into your life. Your big, strong body was a bundle of nerves. You were a giant child who had come into the world too early, or perhaps had come unwanted.

CAPTAIN: It's true. My mother and father did not want me, and so I was born without strength of will. I hoped that I could make myself whole by becoming one with you. And so I let you take charge. I who in the field, who before the troops gave the orders, became with you the one who obeyed. I couldn't do without you. I looked up to you as a higher, more intelligent being, listening to your every word like a stupid child.

LAURA: It's true, it was like that. And I loved you for the child in you. But—oh, you saw it well enough, every time your nature changed and you came to me as my lover, I blushed with shame, and your lovemaking was a joy followed by the anguish of incest. The mother became her boy's lover—. Disgusting!

CAPTAIN: Yes, I felt your disgust but I didn't understand the cause of it. When I saw in you what I thought was your contempt for my unmanliness, I sought to win the woman in you by being a man.

LAURA: That was the mistake. The mother in me was your friend, you see. The woman was your enemy, and love between the sexes is war. And don't think I gave myself. I didn't give, I took—what I wanted. But you had the upper hand, and I always felt it, and longed for the day it would be mine.

CAPTAIN: You always had the upper hand. You could hypnotize me blind and deaf, so that I neither saw nor heard, only obeyed. You could hand me a raw potato and make me believe it was a peach. You could convince me that your silly whims were flashes of genius. You could have induced me to commit a crime —to do the cheapest, most contemptible things. How? Why? Because you didn't think, you didn't reason, you didn't listen to me; you did whatever came into your head. But when I woke from your spell, reflected on what had happened, I saw that my honor was stained, my reputation tarnished. I wanted to restore it by doing something grand—a daring exploit, a great discovery, at least a face-saving suicide. I wanted to fight in the field; I was denied my request. So I turned to science, made it my life. And now when I am about to reach out and pluck the fruit of my endeavors, you hack off my arm. Now I have no honor, and my life is at an end; for a man cannot live without honor.

LAURA: And a woman?

CAPTAIN: Yes. She has her children; but he doesn't. —What are you getting at? Feminism, women's emancipation, Ibsenism? . . . We—all of us—lived our little lives, unconscious as children, full of ideals, illusions, delusions. And then we woke up. Right enough, but we woke up all turned round, with our feet on the pillow, and he who woke us was himself walking in his sleep. When women grow old and cease to be women, they grow beards; I wonder what happens to men when they grow old and cease to be men? Those emanicapators who crowed to make the sun rise were no longer cocks but capons, and those who answered the cockcrow were sexless hens, so that when the sun was to rise we found it was nothing but moonshine, and we were still sitting among ruins, just as in the good old days. It had all been nothing but a little morning nap, a crazy dream, and no waking up at all.

LAURA: You know, you should have been a writer.

CAPTAIN: Who knows?

LAURA: Well, I'm sleepy. If you have any more fantasies, save them for morning.

CAPTAIN: Just one word more about realities. Do you hate me?

LAURA: Yes, sometimes. When you act the man.

CAPTAIN: It's like race hate. If it's true that we are descended from the apes, it must have been from two different species. We're not like each other, are we?

LAURA: What are you getting at?

CAPTAIN: I feel that in this struggle one of us has to go under.

LAURA: Which one?

CAPTAIN: The weaker, naturally.

LAURA: And the stronger is in the right?

CAPTAIN: Always, since he has the power.

LAURA: Then I am in the right.

CAPTAIN: You mean you are already in power?

LAURA: Yes—and legally! As of tomorrow morning when you'll be declared incapable of managing your affairs.

CAPTAIN: Certified?

LAURA: That's right. And I'll be free to bring up my child without having to put up with your wild ideas.

CAPTAIN: And who'll pay for this upbringing when I'm no longer around?

LAURA: Your army pension.

CAPTAIN (*goes toward her threateningly*): How can you have me put under guardianship?

LAURA (*taking out a letter*): With this letter, a certified copy of which is now in the hands of the court.

CAPTAIN: What letter?

LAURA (*moving backward toward the door at the left*): Yours! Your declaration to your doctor that you are insane!

> *The Captain stares at her dumbly.*

LAURA: You have fulfilled your function as an unfortunately indispensable father and family provider. Now you're no longer needed. You're dismissed. You can go. Go—now that you see my mind is as strong as my will. I'm sure you won't want to stay and face up to that!

> *The Captain crosses to the table; takes the burning lamp and throws it at Laura, who has exited backward toward the door.*

ACT III

The same set. A different lamp is on the table. The jib door is barricaded with a chair.

[1]

Laura and Margaret on stage.

LAURA: Did he give you the keys?

MARGARET: Give! No, Lord help me, I took them from the captain's clothes when Happy was brushing them outside.

LAURA: So Happy is on duty today.

MARGARET: Yes, that he is.

LAURA: Give me the keys.

MARGARET: All right, but it's no better than stealing. Listen to him walking up there—back and forth, back and forth.

LAURA: Are you sure he can't get in through that door?

MARGARET: Locked, bolted, barricaded—and Happy on guard outside.

LAURA (*opening the secretary and seating herself at it*): Control yourself, Margaret. We've got to be calm if we want to save ourselves.

A knocking at the hall door.

Who is that?

MARGARET (*opening the door to the hall*): It's Happy.

LAURA: Let him in.

HAPPY (*entering*): A dispatch from the colonel.

LAURA: Give it here. (*Reads it.*) I see. . . . Happy, have you removed all the cartridge from all the guns and all the hunting bags?

HAPPY: I did exactly as you ordered.

LAURA: Wait outside until I've answered the colonel's letter.

Happy exits. Laura sits down to write.

MARGARET: Listen! Do you hear that? What do you suppose he's doing up there now?

LAURA: Quiet! Can't you see I'm writing?

The sound of someone sawing can be heard.

MARGARET (*half aloud, to herself*): God have mercy. . . . Where's it all going to end?

LAURA: There. Give this to Happy. And don't breathe a word of this to my mother. Do you hear?

Margaret goes to the door. Laura opens the drawers of the secretary and takes out some papers.

[2]

The Pastor enters and takes a chair. Sits down next to Laura at the secretary.

PASTOR: Good evening, Laura. I've been gone the whole day and just now got back. It's been a bad day for you, hasn't it?

LAURA: The worst night and day I've ever been through.

PASTOR: Well, I see you weren't harmed, in any event.

LAURA: No, thank God. But just think what might have happened.

PASTOR: Tell me, what started it all? I've heard so many different stories.

LAURA: It started with his crazy idea that he wasn't Bertha's father and ended with his throwing a lighted lamp right in my face.

PASTOR: That's appalling! He's completely insane. What are you going to do now?

LAURA: We have to prevent further outbreaks of violence. The doctor has sent for a straitjacket from the hospital. In the meantime I've sent word to the colonel, and I'm trying to familiarize myself with the household finances, which he has completely mismanaged.

PASTOR: What a wretched affair. I can't say I'm surprised though. Fire – water – pressure. Explosion! What have you got in that box?

Laura has taken a drawer from the secretary.

LAURA: Look at this! Here's where he's kept everything.

PASTOR (*going through the contents*): Dear God. . . . He's kept your little doll . . . and here's your christening cap – and Bertha's rattle . . . and all your letters . . . and your locket. . . . (*Drying his eyes.*) He must have held you very dear, Laura, sister. I haven't kept mementos like that.

LAURA: He may have held me dear once upon a time. But time – time brings so many changes.

PASTOR: What's that large piece of paper? – The deed to a cemetery plot. Yes, rather the cemetery than the asylum. Laura – tell me: are you quite blameless in all this?

LAURA: Me? Why blame me because somebody goes insane?

PASTOR: Yes. . . . Well, I shan't say anything. Blood is still thicker than water.

LAURA: Exactly what are you insinuating?

PASTOR (*confronting her*): Listen to me.

LAURA: Well?

PASTOR: You certainly can't deny that this fits in perfectly with your plans to bring up Bertha on your own terms.

LAURA: I don't understand.

PASTOR: I really admire you, Laura.

LAURA: Me? Huh!

PASTOR: I'll be appointed guardian to that atheist! Fact is, I've always regarded him as a weed in our garden.

LAURA (*gives a short laugh, quickly stifled; abruptly serious*): You dare to say this to me, his wife!

PASTOR: God, but you're strong, Laura! Unbelievably strong! Like a fox in a trap, you'd rather bite off your own leg than be caught. Like a master thief—no accomplices, not even your own conscience. —Look at yourself in the mirror. You wouldn't dare.

LAURA: I never use a mirror.

PASTOR: No, you don't dare! —Let me look at your hands. —Not a spot of incriminating blood, not a trace of the secret poison. A little innocent murder, beyond the law's reach. An unconscious crime! Unconscious? Marvelous invention! —Listen to him sawing away up there. —Watch out! If he gets loose, he'll saw you in half.

LAURA: Talk, talk, talk—as if your conscience bothered you. If you think I'm guilty, accuse me—if you can.

PASTOR: I cannot.

LAURA: You see? You cannot. Therefore I am innocent. Now you take charge of your ward, and I'll tend to mine. —Ah, the doctor.

[3]

Dr. Eastland enters.

LAURA (*getting up*): Hello, my dear Doctor. You will help, won't you? Though I'm afraid there isn't much that can be done. Do you hear how he's carrying on upstairs? Are you convinced now?

DR. EASTLAND: I am convinced that an act of violence was

committed. The question is, should this act be regarded as due to an outburst of rage or of insanity?

PASTOR: Putting aside the outburst, you have to admit he was obsessed with certain fixed ideas.

DR. EASTLAND: In my view, Pastor, your ideas are even more fixed. Are they obsessions?

PASTOR: I have definite views regarding higher spiritual matters. They are not —

DR. EASTLAND: Shall we leave our views out of this? . . . Madam, the decision is up to you whether you want to see your husband fined and imprisoned or sent to the asylum. How do you judge his behavior?

LAURA: I can't answer that now.

DR. EASTLAND: In other words, you have no definite views regarding the best interests of the family? Is that right, Pastor?

PASTOR: Either way there will be a scandal. . . . It's difficult to say.

LAURA: If he's only fined for assault and battery, he might become violent again.

DR. EASTLAND: And if he's sent to jail, he'll soon be out again. I take it we're agreed: it's best for all concerned that he be treated as insane. — Where's his old nurse?

LAURA: Why?

DR. EASTLAND: She will have to put the straitjacket on him, after I've spoken to him and given the order. But not before! I have the — the garment out here. (*Goes out into the hall and returns with a large parcel.*) Would you please ask Miss Margaret to step in here?

Laura rings.

PASTOR: I don't like this one bit. "It is a fearful thing to fall into the hands of the living God."

Margaret enters.

DR. EASTLAND (*unwrapping the straitjacket*): Now listen to me carefully. You must slip this jacket on the captain from behind, if and when I think the need should arise, to prevent any violence on his part. As you can see, it's got these unusually long arms, designed to restrain any movement. These arms are to be tied behind his back. Now these two straps go through these buckles and are then fastened to a chair or the sofa, or whatever is convenient. That's all there's to it. Are you willing to do it?

MARGARET: No, Doctor, I can't. Oh, I couldn't, I couldn't.

LAURA: Why don't you do it yourself, Doctor?

DR. EASTLAND: Because he mistrusts me, Madam. You, of course, would be the obvious choice, but I'm afraid he mistrusts you too.

Laura gives him a sharp look, then turns away.

DR. EASTLAND: Perhaps you, Pastor—?

PASTOR: No, I'm afraid I must decline.

[4]

Happy enters.

LAURA: Have you already delivered the message?

HAPPY: As you ordered.

DR. EASTLAND: Ah, my lad. You know the situation here, don't you? The captain is mentally ill, and you've got to help us with him.

HAPPY: Anything I can do to help the captain, sir, I'll be glad to do.

DR. EASTLAND: You've got to get him into this straitjacket—

MARGARET: No. No, he mustn't touch him. I don't want the captain hurt. I'd rather do it myself, gently, very gently. But you can stand outside, Happy, in case I need help. Now that's the way it has to be.

A pounding on the wallpapered door.

DR. EASTLAND: That's him! Hide the straitjacket under your shawl on the chair, and all of you go out—the pastor and I will receive him—that door won't last much longer. Out, out!

MARGARET (*exiting to the left*): Lord help us!

> *Laura closes the secretary and exits to the left. Happy exits at the rear.*

[5]

> *The door is broken in. The lock is torn from its seat, and the chair blocking the door is hurled out into the room. The Captain, wearing a wool shirt, enters with several books under one arm, a saw in one hand, his hair rumpled, a wild expression on his face.*

CAPTAIN (*placing the books on the table*): The same thing in every book! And that proves it—I'm not crazy! The *Odyssey*, first book, line 215. Telemachus talking to Athena: "My mother calls me the son of the man"—meaning Odysseus—"but I myself do not know. No one has ever been certain of his father." And this is the suspicion entertained by Telemachus of Penelope, the most virtuous of all women! Beautiful, eh? Beautiful! . . . And here we have the prophet Ezekiel: "The fool says: Lo here is my father, but who can know whose loins have engendered him?" What could be clearer? —And what have I here? History of Russian literature by Merzlyakov. Alexander Pushkin, Russia's greatest poet, tormented to death by the widespread rumors of his wife's unfaithfulness. That was more the cause of his death than the bullet fired into his chest during a duel. On his deathbed he swore that she was innocent. What an ass! Ass! How could he swear to that? You see I've been doing my homework. —Ah, Jonas, so you are here! And the good doctor, naturally. Have you heard how I replied to an English lady who complained that Irish husbands threw lighted kerosene lamps right in the faces of their wives? "My God, what women!" I said. "W-w-women?" she stammered. "Of course," said I. "When things have gone so far that a man, a man who has loved and adored his woman, takes a lighted lamp and throws it in her face—then you can be sure!"

PASTOR: Sure of what?

CAPTAIN: Nothing. One can't be sure of anything, one can only have faith. Right, Jonas? Believe and you'll be saved. That's the way, isn't it Jonas? No! One is damned for believing! I know that for a fact.

DR. EASTLAND: Captain—!

CAPTAIN: Quiet! I don't wish to talk to you. The human telephone transmitting what they tell you in there. In there! (*Indicates the inner rooms.*) You know. You know. —Tell me, Jonas, do you think you are the father of your children? I seem to remember that you once employed a tutor in your house— pretty face, dimpled cheeks—people talked about him. Oh, yes.

PASTOR: Adolf, that's enough!

CAPTAIN: Feel under your wig and see if there aren't two bumps there. Upon my soul, I do believe he's turning pale. Come, come, it's only tittle-tattle. —But, my God, they tattle so much! Ain't we a lovely bunch of ridiculous rascals, we husbands? Right, Doctor? Right? By the way, how were things in your marriage bed? Wasn't there a lieutenant staying in the house—hmm? Just a minute now, his name—his name was— (*Whispers in Dr. Eastland's ear.*) Look at that! He's turning pale, too. Oh, don't look so upset. She's dead and buried, and what's done cannot be undone. However, I did know the fellow and can tell you that he is now—look at me, Doctor—no, no, right in my eyes—a major in the dragoons! My God, I swear you've got horns, too!

DR. EASTLAND (*irritated*): Captain can't you find something else to talk about?

CAPTAIN: Now look at that! Right away he wants to talk about something else when I want to talk about horns.

PASTOR: Adolf . . . you know that you are mentally ill.

CAPTAIN: I know that well enough. And could I treat your antlered brains some space of time, I would soon have you locked up too. Crazy I may be, but what made me crazy? That doesn't concern you; it doesn't concern anyone. Now let us talk of other things. (*Takes the photograph album from the table.*) My God, there she is! —My child. My? That we cannot know. You know what we should do in order that we might know? First, get married for appearance's sake, get divorced soon after, become lovers, and then adopt the child. That way you can at least be certain that it is your adopted child. Isn't that logical? What good does it do me now—now that you have taken my kind of immortality from me? What good is philosophy and science when I have nothing to live for? What does life mean to me when honor is gone? I grafted my right arm, half my brain, half my spinal cord on another stem. I thought they would grow together, entwine to form a single, more nearly perfect tree. And then someone comes with a knife and cuts just under the graft, leaving me as a mere half-tree. But the other shoots up with my right arm and half my brain, while I wither and die, for those were the best parts of me that I gave away. Now I want to die. Do with me what you will. I no longer exist.

> *Dr. Eastland and the Pastor whisper together. They go into the inner rooms off left. Shortly thereafter Bertha enters.*

[6]

> *The Captain is sitting at the table, hunched over.*

BERTHA (*approaching him*): Are you sick, Daddy?

CAPTAIN (*looking up dully*): I?

BERTHA: You know what you have done? Don't you know that you threw the lamp at Mommy?

CAPTAIN: Did I?

BERTHA: Yes, you did. Suppose she had been hurt?

CAPTAIN: What difference would that make?

BERTHA: You can't be my father if you talk like that!

CAPTAIN: What? Not your father? How do you know? Who told you? And who is your father? Who?

BERTHA: Well, certainly not you!

CAPTAIN: Still not me? Then who? You appear to be well informed. Who informed you? That I should live to see the day when my child comes to me and tells me to my face that I am not her father! Don't you realize that you disgrace your mother when you say this? Don't you understand that if it's true, your mother is shamed?

BERTHA: Don't say anything bad about Mother! I won't have it!

CAPTAIN: No, you all stick together, all against me. And you've done it from the very start!

BERTHA: Daddy!

CAPTAIN: Don't ever use that word again!

BERTHA: Daddy, Daddy!

CAPTAIN (*holding her close*): Bertha, my dearest own child, you are my child! Yes, yes, it's true. It can't be any other way. The rest was only a sick thought brought by the wind like fever or the plague. Look at me so that I may see my soul in your eyes. . . . But I see her soul, too! You have two souls, and you love me with the one and hate me with the other. You must love only me! You must have only one soul, otherwise you will never have peace, nor shall I. You must have only one mind, the child of my mind; you must have only one will, which is my will.

BERTHA: No, I don't want that! I want to be myself.

CAPTAIN: That you may not be! You see, I am a cannibal and I want to eat you. Your mother wanted to eat me, but she couldn't. I am Saturn who ate his own children because it had been prophesied that they would eat him. Eat or be eaten — that is the question! If I don't eat you, you will eat me — and you've already bared your teeth. Don't be afraid now, my dearest girl, I'm not going to hurt you. (*Goes over to the wall where the weapons hang and takes a revolver.*)

BERTHA (*trying to get away, going toward the door*): Help, Mommy! Mommy, help, help! He'll kill me!

MARGARET (*entering*): Adolf, what is going on here?

CAPTAIN (*examining the revolver*): Did you remove the cartridges?

MARGARET: Yes, I've put them away. But if you just sit nice and still here, I'll bring them out again.

> *Takes the Captain by the arm and seats him in the chair, where he remains seated, dull and apathetic. She picks up the straitjacket and stands behind the chair. Bertha slips out to the left.*

MARGARET: Adolf, do you remember when you were my dear little boy, and I tucked you into bed at night, and we would say, "Now I lay me down to sleep"? Remember how I would get up at night and give you a glass of water? Remember how I would light the candle and tell you lovely fairy tales when you had bad dreams and couldn't sleep. Remember?

CAPTAIN: Go on talking, Margaret; it soothes my head and feels so good. When I was a child and you were my nanny . . .

MARGARET: All right, but you must listen. . . . Remember the time you took the big kitchen knife to carve boats and how I had to trick you into giving it to me. You were being very difficult, and so I had to trick you, because you didn't believe it was for your own good. . . . "Give me that snake," I said, "before it bites you!" And then you let me have the knife. (*Takes the revolver from the Captain's hand.*) And then there were the times you were to get dressed and didn't want to. I had to coax and wheedle and say you were going to have a golden coat and be dressed like a prince. And then I took the little undershirt, which was only green wool, and held it in front of you and said, "Pop in your arms, both arms." And then I would say, "Now you just sit still while I button up the back." (*She has the straitjacket on him by this time.*) And then I would say, "Now stand up and let's see how it looks. Walk across the floor so we can see how it fits." (*She leads him to the sofa.*) And then I would say, "Now it's time to go to bed."

CAPTAIN: Bed? Go to bed when you've just dressed me? —Damn! Damn! What have you done to me! (*Struggles to get loose.*) Oh, you damned deceitful woman! Who would have thought you could be so clever! (*Lying down on the sofa.*) Captured, shorn, outwitted, and not even allowed to die!

MARGARET: Forgive me, Adolf, forgive me, but I couldn't let you kill the child.

CAPTAIN: Why did you not let me kill the child? Life on earth is hell and death is the kingdom of heaven, and the children belong to heaven.

MARGARET: What can you know of what comes after death?

CAPTAIN: That's all we do know. Of life we know nothing. Oh, if we had only known that from the beginning.

MARGARET: Adolf, bow your head, humble your proud heart, and call on God for mercy. It is still not too late. It was not too late for the thief on the cross when the Redeemer said, "Today shalt thou be with me in Paradise!"

CAPTAIN: What, croaking over the corpse already, you old crow!

Margaret takes her hymnbook from her apron pocket.

CAPTAIN (*calling*): Happy! Are you there, Happy? Orderly!

Happy enters.

CAPTAIN: Throw this woman out of here! She wants to suffocate me in the fumes of her psalms. Throw her out the window or up the chimney, wherever you damn please!

HAPPY (*looking at Margaret*): Lord, help me, Captain, really, I mean—I just can't. Honestly, I can't. Six guys, sure, but not a woman.

CAPTAIN: Can't manage one woman, is that what you mean?

HAPPY: Sure I can, but they're something special. I mean, you don't want to do violence to them.

CAPTAIN: Something special? Haven't they done violence to me?

HAPPY: I can't, sir, I mean — well, I can't, sir. It's just like you asking me to hit the pastor here, sir. It's something inside, like religion. I can't.

[7]

Laura enters and signals Happy to leave.

CAPTAIN: Omphale! Omphale! You play with his club while Hercules spins your wool.

LAURA (*crosses to the sofa*): Adolf, look at me. Do you think I am your enemy?

CAPTAIN: Yes, I do believe that. I believe that you are all my enemies. My mother, who didn't want me to come into this world because my birth would cause her pain; she was my enemy. She deprived my first cells of nourishment, stunting and crippling me before I was born. My sister was my enemy when she taught me to be meek and sweet to her. The first woman I made love to was my enemy for she gave me ten years of disease in exchange for the love I gave her. My daughter became my enemy when she had to choose between you and me. And you, my wife, are my mortal enemy, for you would not leave me until I had been cast down lifeless.

LAURA: I don't know that I have ever thought about or intended any of the things you imagine. Perhaps some dim desire to remove you as an obstacle ruled my actions at times. If you see some design in them, it's possible it was there, though I wasn't aware of it. I never laid any plans. Things merely rolled along the rails you yourself laid out. And before God and my conscience I feel that I am innocent, even if I am not. Your presence was like a stone weighing on my breast, pressing and hurting until I had to shake off the burden. That's how it was, and if I have struck you, as a reflex action, I ask you to forgive me.

CAPTAIN: Sounds plausible enough. But what good does it do me? And where does the blame lie? In modern marriage, perhaps, the marriage of minds. One used to marry a wife; now one goes into partnership with a career woman, or sets up housekeeping with a friend. After which one either copulates with the business partner or rapes the friend. What happened to love? Good, sound, carnal love? Died in the process of incorporation. And what about the offspring in this marriage corporation where no one assumes responsibility and love dividends are periodically payable to the stockholder? Who owns the assets when the crash comes? Who is the physical father to the spiritual child?

LAURA: Your suspicions about the child, Adolf—they're completely groundless.

CAPTAIN: That's just what's so terrible. If only there were some grounds for them, there would be something to hang on to—to take hold of. Now there are only goblins hiding in the bushes, sticking their heads out to laugh. It's just shadowboxing, a sham battle fought with blanks. Against something real and deadly one can fight with brain and brawn. But now my thoughts dissolve into nothingness: the grist is gone and my brain grinds on stone until it catches fire. Put a pillow under my head. And throw something over me. I'm freezing. I'm freezing to death.

Laura takes her shawl and spreads it out over him.

Margaret goes out for a pillow.

LAURA: Give me your hand as a friend.

CAPTAIN: My hand! Which you tied behind me. . . . Omphale, Omphale! I feel your soft shawl against my mouth—as warm and soft as your arm. It smells like vanilla, as your hair did when you were young. Laura, when you were young, and we walked among the birch trees—cowslips and thrushes—beautiful, heavenly! How beautiful life was—and look at it now. You didn't want it to be like this; I didn't want it; and still it got to be like this. Who is it makes our lives?

LAURA: God, only God—

CAPTAIN: The god of war, then! Or goddess nowadays. Take away this cat on my chest! Take it away!

Margaret comes in with the pillow; removes the shawl.

CAPTAIN: Give me my army coat. Throw it over me.

Margaret takes his army overcoat from the clothes tree and spreads it over him.

CAPTAIN: Ah, my hard lion skin that you wanted to take from me, Omphale, Omphale! What a cunning woman — the peace lover who invented disarmament. Awaken, Hercules, before they take your club from you! You want to cheat us of our armor, too, and have us believe it is only for show. No, lady, it was iron before it became tassels and braids. The blacksmith used to make the tunic, now it's the seamstress. Omphale, Omphale! Brute strength has fallen before wily weakness. I spit on you, you devil of a woman! To hell with your whole damned sex! (*He raises himself up to spit at her but falls back on the sofa.*) What kind of a pillow have you given me, Margaret? So hard and cold, so cold. Come and sit here on the chair, next to me. Like that, yes. Let me lay my head in your lap. There! . . . That's better. So warm. Lean over me so I can feel your breast. . . . How soft and lovely it is to sleep on a woman's bosom, a mother's or a mistress's, but loveliest a mother's.

LAURA: Do you want to see your child, Adolf? . . . Adolf, do you?

CAPTAIN: My child? A man has no children; only women have children. That's why the future can be theirs, since we die childless. . . . Now I lay me down to sleep, I —

MARGARET: Listen, he's praying to God.

CAPTAIN: No, to you, to lull me to sleep. I'm tired, so tired. . . . Goodnight, Margaret, and blessed be thou among women. (*He raises himself up but falls with a cry back into Margaret's lap.*)

[8]

Crossing to the left, Laura calls in Dr. Eastland, who enters with the Pastor.

LAURA: Help us, Doctor, if it's not too late! He's not breathing.

DR. EASTLAND (*taking the Captain's pulse*): He's had a stroke.

PASTOR: Is he dead?

DR. EASTLAND: No, he may still come to life, but to which life one cannot say.

PASTOR: "Once to die, but after this the judgment."

DR. EASTLAND: No judgment. And no incriminations. You who believe that a god governs our destinies can take the matter up with Him.

MARGARET: Pastor, he prayed to God in his last moment.

PASTOR (*to Laura*): Is that true?

LAURA: Yes, it's true.

DR. EASTLAND: If it is—and I can no more judge of that than of his illness—then my skills can do no more for him. Now try yours, Pastor.

LAURA: Is that all you can find to say at a man's deathbed, Doctor?

DR. EASTLAND: Yes, that's all. I know no more. Let him who knows more speak.

BERTHA (*entering from the left, running to her mother's arms*): Mother, Mother!

LAURA: My child! My own child!

PASTOR: Amen.

Introduction

to

Miss Julie

Through his study of psychology, Strindberg had come to believe that life in the modern age was basically a struggle of minds. Laura in *The Father* is physically weaker than her military husband, but she has a stronger will, and through her strength of will she overcomes brute force and moral scruples.

In presenting this "battle of brains" on stage, the set was relatively unimportant. All that was really needed to stage *The Father* was a table, two chairs, a lamp, and a straitjacket. Strindberg was quite proud of the classic simplicity he had achieved in this modern *Agamemnon* and thought his drama would please Emile Zola, the leader of the naturalistic movement in France, where Strindberg, now the declared enemy of the establishment in Sweden, increasingly placed his literary hopes. Zola had called for a new drama that would be grand, true, and simple, uncluttered with meaningless intrigues meant only to build suspense. Strindberg sent *The Father* to Zola and explained to him that in this play he sought to present "the interior action, dispensing with theatrical tricks, reducing the set decor to a minimum, and preserving the unity of time as far as possible" (29 August 1887). To Strindberg's surprise and disappointment, Zola found *The Father* too simple. He wanted less abstract characters, more description, and more explanation.

In his next play Strindberg took great pains to answer Zola's strictures. Zola's naturalism was predicated on the idea that the methods of physical science and experimental medicine, which had produced miracles in the nineteenth century, should be applied to literature. In practice this meant that characters and their actions should be explained in terms of heredity and environment. In writing *Miss Julie*, Strindberg carefully built up the backgrounds of the two principal characters and placed them in a realistically detailed set. Moreover, he saw to it that the environment, the kitchen, determines what happens to Miss Julie.

Strindberg's theatrical methods, spelled out in his preface, were the result of the success of André Antoine's Théâtre-Libre, which had opened in Paris in March 1887. Antoine had established his theater to give uncommercial and unconventional plays a chance to be seen. Because he began his theater on a gas-clerk's salary, expenses had to be held to a minimum. The actors in his productions were not skilled professionals, the theater he hired was comparatively small, and the sets were often extremely realistic (a real side of beef cost less than a painted one). The very amateurishness of his theater made it the perfect showcase for naturalistic plays.

Reading about its success, Strindberg wrote *Miss Julie* with that kind of theater in mind, a theater that would not cater to the tastes of the general public, that would allow the treatment of unusual, perhaps unsavory, subjects, and that would encourage subtlety in acting. Strindberg's preface to *Miss Julie* reveals the extent to which he was influenced by the Théâtre-Libre.

The preface was written after the play, and although it is undoubtedly the most important manifesto of naturalistic theater, it is remarkable less for its originality than for its comprehensiveness. Strindberg managed to find a place in it for everything that was new or controversial, whether in theater (Antoine), literature (Zola), painting (the impressionists), biology (Darwin), psychology (Ribot, Bernheim), sociology (feminism), politics (the rise of the lower classes), or philosophy (Nietzsche). Fundamental to the play is the Darwinian theory of evolution, which had become the central concern of nineteenth-century intellectual life because it undermined religious faith and pointed to ethical relativism and a world without values. The outcome of the struggle between servant and mistress in the play is an instance of the survival of the fittest. In both the sexual conflict and the class conflict the servant comes out on top.

To keep the plot simple, Strindberg had to find a substitute for the complications that furnished action and suspense in conventional drama. He built his play out of symbols and parallelisms. The songbird and the dog that has got itself pregnant obviously represent aspects of Miss Julie, and the ever-present boots stand for her father. Jean's dream counterbalances Julie's, and Jean's story of how he was caught in the gentry's privy when he was a child becomes the paradigm for Julie's situation in the play itself. She is trapped in the servant's quarters, and also trapped by her own uncontrollable desires. Jean as a child had been forced to crawl through excrement; now the trapped Julie begs Jean to "lift me out of this awful filth I'm sinking in." By such means Strindberg imposes meaning and order on the naturalistic details.

The ending has given actresses and audiences a great deal of trouble, more than it gave Strindberg, who had an actual case in mind. It was clear that Julie had to die, and the manner of her death was determined by what happened to a woman writer who, like Julie, was unhappy in love.

There are motives enough for Julie's suicide. She is bound by the aristocratic code of honor, and she is extremely wrought up by the events of the day. More important, she is filled with shame and self-loathing and knows that she will repeat the episode, knows that, if not today, then tomorrow, she will again seek to degrade herself. By taking her own life, she regains some dignity and claims our sympathy.

The precise manner of her suicide was suggested to Strindberg by the death of the Swedish writer Victoria Benedictsson, a married woman who wrote under the pseudonym Ernst Ahlgren. She was trying to win a place for herself among Scandinavian writers with her realistic short stories, and she had hoped to form an alliance, literary and sexual, with the famous critic Georg Brandes. Strindberg had gotten to know her when he stayed at her hotel in the winter of 1887-88. In January, Victoria, despondent about her career and convinced that Brandes neither respected her as a writer nor loved her as a person, feeling that she was "only a little planet that had come too close to a bigger one," decided to kill herself by taking an overdose of morphine. She confided in her comrade Axel Lundegård, who had collaborated with Strindberg on a play called *Comrades*. Lundegård watched Victoria take the morphine and then, told to leave, he went to Strindberg's room, woke him up, and confided in him. He would always remember Strindberg's response. "He listened," said Lundegård, "with an expression of implacable, cannibal-like interest without the slightest trace of human compassion." Perhaps his interest was not purely that of the objective artist; his own desperate position had often led him to think of killing himself, how seriously it is hard to say, given as he was to self-dramatization.

Victoria Benedictsson did not die on that night. Months later, in July 1888, she made another attempt, this time using a razor. Only after slashing her throat several times did she succeed. Shortly after he heard the news, Strindberg started to write *Miss Julie*. In the meantime, he had learned more about Victoria Benedictsson. Julie blames her neurotic disposition and her unhealthy and self-destructive sexual desires on her upbringing. Victoria's childhood had been much like Julie's.*

The present translation follows the latest scholarly edition of *Fröken Julie*, edited by Gunnar Ollén and printed in *August Strindbergs Samlade Verk*, vol. 27 (Uppsala, 1984). I have also consulted the excellent commentary and critical apparatus in Carl Reinhold Smedmark's edition, *August Strindbergs dramer*, vol. 3 (Stockholm, 1964).

* For more on Victoria Benedictsson, see Evert Sprinchorn, "Ibsen and the Immoralists," in *Comparative Literature Studies*, vol. 9, no. 1 (March 1972), pp. 58–79.

Miss Julie

(Fröken Julie)

A Naturalistic Tragedy

with a preface by the author

Preface

Like the arts in general, the theater has for a long time seemed to me a *Biblia Pauperum*, a picture Bible for those who cannot read, and the playwright merely a lay preacher who hawks the latest ideals in popular form, so popular that the middle classes—the bulk of the audiences—can grasp them without racking their brains too much. That explains why the theater has always been an elementary school for youngsters and the half-educated, and for women, who still retain a primitive capacity for deceiving themselves and for letting themselves be deceived, that is, for succumbing to illusions and responding hypnotically to the suggestions of the author. Consequently, now that the rudimentary and undeveloped mental processes that operate in the realm of fantasy appear to be evolving to the level of reflection, research, and experimentation, I believe that the theater, like religion, is about to be replaced as a dying institution for whose enjoyment we lack the necessary qualifications. Support for my view is provided by the theater crisis through which all of Europe is now passing, and still more by the fact that in those highly cultured lands which have produced the finest minds of our time—England and Germany—the drama is dead, as for the most part are the other fine arts.

Other countries, however, have thought to create a new drama by filling the old forms with new contents. But since there has not been enough time to popularize the new ideas, the public cannot understand them. And in the second place, controversy has so stirred up the public that they can no longer look on with a pure and dispassionate interest, especially when they see their most cherished ideals assailed or hear an applauding or booing majority openly exercise its tyrannical power, as can happen in the theater. And in the third place, since the new forms for the new ideas have not been created, the new wine has burst the old bottles.

In the play that follows I have not tried to accomplish anything new—that is impossible. I have only tried to modernize the

204

form to satisfy what I believe up-to-date people expect and demand of this art. And with that in mind I have seized upon – or let myself be seized by – a theme that may be said to lie outside current party strife, since the question of being on the way up or on the way down the social ladder, of being on the top or on the bottom, superior or inferior, man or woman, is, has been, and will be of perennial interest. When I took this theme from real life – I heard about it a few years ago and it made a deep impression on me – I thought it would be a suitable subject for a tragedy, since it still strikes us as tragic to see a happily favored individual go down in defeat, and even more so to see an entire family line die out. But perhaps a time will come when we shall be so highly developed and so enlightened that we can look with indifference upon the brutal, cynical, and heartless spectacle that life offers us, a time when we shall have laid aside those inferior and unreliable mechanical apparatuses called emotions, which will become superfluous and even harmful as our mental organs develop. The fact that my heroine wins sympathy is due entirely to the fact that we are still too weak to overcome the fear that the same fate might overtake us. The extremely sensitive viewer will of course not be satisfied with mere expressions of sympathy, and the man who believes in progress will demand that certain positive actions be taken for getting rid of the evil, a kind of program, in other words. But in the first place absolute evil does not exist. The decline of one family is the making of another, which now gets its chance to rise. This alternate rising and falling provides one of life's greatest pleasures, for happiness is, after all, relative. As for the man who has a program for changing the disagreeable circumstance that the hawk eats the chicken and that lice eat up the hawk, I should like to ask him why it should be changed. Life is not prearranged with such idiotic mathematical precision that only the larger gets to eat the smaller. Just as frequently the bee destroys the lion (in Aesop's fable) – or at least drives him wild.

If my tragedy makes most people feel sad, that is their fault. When we get to be as strong as the first French Revolutionists were, we shall be perfectly content and happy to watch the forests being cleared of rotting, superannuated trees that have stood too long in the way of others with just as much right to grow and flourish for a while – as content as we are when we see an incurably ill man finally die.

Recently my tragedy *The Father* was censured for being too unpleasant—as if one wanted merry tragedies. "The joy of life" is now the slogan of the day. Theater managers send out orders for nothing but farces, as if the joy of living lay in behaving like a clown and in depicting people as if they were afflicted with St. Vitus's dance or congenital idiocy. I find the joy of living in the fierce and ruthless battles of life, and my pleasure comes from learning something, from being taught something. That is why I have chosen for my play an unusual but instructive case, an exception, in other words—but an important exception of the kind that proves the rule—a choice of subject that I know will offend all lovers of the conventional. The next thing that will bother simple minds is that the motivation for the action is not simple and that the point of view is not single. Usually an event in life—and this is a fairly new discovery—is the result of a whole series of more or less deep-rooted causes. The spectator, however, generally chooses the one that puts the least strain on his mind or reflects most credit on his insight. Consider a case of suicide. "Business failure," says the merchant. "Unhappy love," say the women. "Physical illness," says the sick man. "Lost hopes," says the down-and-out. But it may be that the reason lay in all of these or in none of them, and that the suicide hid his real reason behind a completely different one that would reflect greater glory on his memory.

I have motivated the tragic fate of Miss Julie with an abundance of circumstances: her mother's basic instincts, her father's improper bringing-up of the girl, her own inborn nature, and her fiancé's sway over her weak and degenerate mind. Further and more immediately: the festive atmosphere of Midsummer Eve, her father's absence, her period, her preoccupation with animals, the erotic excitement of the dance, the long summer twilight, the highly aphrodisiac influence of flowers, and finally chance itself, which drives two people together in an out-of-the-way room, plus the boldness of the aroused man.

As one can see, I have not been entirely the physiologist, not been obsessively psychological, not traced everything to her mother's heredity, not found the sole cause in her period, not attributed everything to our "immoral times," and not simply preached a moral lesson. Lacking a priest, I have let the cook handle that.

I am proud to say that this complicated way of looking at things is in tune with the times. And if others have anticipated me in this, I am proud that I am not alone in my paradoxes, as all new discoveries are called. And no one can say this time that I am being one-sided.

As far as the drawing of characters is concerned, I have made the people in my play fairly "characterless" for the following reasons. In the course of time the word *character* has acquired many meanings. Originally it probably meant the dominant and fundamental trait in the soul complex and was confused with temperament. Later the middle class used it to mean an automaton. An individual who once for all had found his own true nature or adapted himself to a certain role in life, who in fact had ceased to grow, was called a man of character, while the man who was constantly developing, who, like a skillful sailor on the currents of life, did not sail with close-tied sheets but who fell off before the wind in order to luff again, was called a man of no character—derogatorily of course, since he was so difficult to keep track of, to pin down and pigeonhole. This middle-class conception of a fixed character was transferred to the stage, where the middle class has always ruled. A character there came to mean someone who was always one and the same, always drunk, always joking, always melancholy, and who needed to be characterized only by some physical defect such as a club foot, a wooden leg, or a red nose, or by the repetition of some such phrase as, "That's capital," or "Barkis is willin'." This uncomplicated way of viewing people is still to be found in the great Molière. Harpagon is nothing but a miser, although Harpagon could have been both a miser and an exceptional financier, a fine father, and a good citizen. Worse still, his "defect" is extremely advantageous to his son-in-law and his daughter who will be his heirs and who therefore should not find fault with him, even if they do have to wait a while to jump into bed together. So I do not believe in simple stage characters. And the summary judgments that writers pass on people—he is stupid, this one is brutal, that one is jealous, this one is stingy, and so on—should not pass unchallenged by the naturalists who know how complicated the soul is and who realize that vice has a reverse side very much like virtue.

Since the persons in my play are modern characters, living in

a transitional era more hectic and hysterical than the previous
one at least, I have depicted them as more unstable, as torn and
divided, a mixture of the old and the new. Nor does it seem
improbable to me that modern ideas might also have seeped
down through newspapers and kitchen talk to the level of the
servants. Consequently the valet may belch forth from his
inherited slave soul certain modern ideas. And if there are those
who find it wrong to allow people in a modern drama to talk
Darwin and who recommend the practice of Shakepeare to our
attention, may I remind them that the gravedigger in *Hamlet*
talks the then fashionable philosophy of Giordano Bruno
(Bacon's philosophy), which is even more improbable, seeing that
the means of spreading ideas were fewer then than now. And
besides, the fact of the matter is that Darwinism has always
existed, ever since Moses' history of creation from the lower
animals up to man, but it was not until recently that we discovered it and formulized it.

My souls — or characters — are conglomerations from various
stages of culture, past and present, walking scrapbooks, shreds of
human lives, tatters torn from old rags that were once Sunday
best — hodgepodges just like the human soul. I have even supplied
a little source history into the bargain by letting the weaker steal
and repeat words of the stronger, letting them get ideas (suggestions as they are called) from one another, from the environment
(the songbird's blood), and from objects (the razor). I have also
arranged for *Gedankenübertragung** through an inanimate
medium to take place (the count's boots, the servant's bell). And
I have even made use of "waking suggestions" (a variation of hypnotic suggestion), which have by now been so popularized that
they cannot arouse ridicule or skepticism as they would have
done in Mesmer's time.

I say Miss Julie is a modern character not because the man-
hating half-woman has not always existed but because she has
now been brought out into the open, has taken the stage, and is
making a noise about herself. Victim of a superstition (one that
has seized even stronger minds) that woman, that stunted form
of human being, standing with man, the lord of creation, the
creator of culture, is meant to be the equal of man or could ever

* Telepathy

possibly be, she involves herself in an absurd struggle with him in which she falls. Absurd because a stunted form, subject to the laws of propagation, will always be born stunted and can never catch up with the one who has the lead. As follows: A (the man) and B (the woman) start from the same point C, A with a speed of let us say 100 and B with a speed of 60. When will B overtake A? Answer: never. Neither with the help of equal education or equal voting rights – nor by universal disarmament and temperance societies – any more than two parallel lines can ever meet. The half-woman is a type that forces itself on others, selling itself for power, medals, recognition, diplomas, as formerly it sold itself for money. It represents degeneration. It is not a strong species for it does not maintain itself, but unfortunately it propagates its misery in the following generation. Degenerate men unconsciously select their mates from among these half-women, so that they breed and spread, producing creatures of indeterminate sex to whom life is a torture, but who fortunately are overcome eventually either by a hostile reality, or by the uncontrolled breaking loose of their repressed instincts, or else by their frustration in not being able to compete with the male sex. It is a tragic type, offering us the spectacle of a desperate fight against nature; a tragic legacy of romanticism, which is now being dissipated by naturalism – a movement that seeks only happiness, and for that strong and healthy species are required.

Miss Julie, however, is also a vestige of the old warrior nobility that is now being superseded by a new nobility of nerve and brain. She is a victim of the disorder produced within a family by a mother's "crime," of the mistakes of a whole generation gone wrong, of circumstances, of her own defective constitution – all of which put together is equivalent to the fate or universal law of the ancients. The naturalists have banished guilt along with God, but the consequences of an act – punishment, imprisonment, or the fear of it – cannot be banished for the simple reason that they remain whether or not the naturalist dismisses the case from his court. Those sitting on the sidelines can easily afford to be lenient; but what of the injured parties? And even if her father were compelled to forgo taking his revenge, Miss Julie would take vengeance on herself, as she does in the play, because of that inherited or acquired sense of honor that has been transmitted to the upper classes from – well, where does it come from? From the

age of barbarism, from the first Aryans, from the chivalry of the
Middle Ages. And a very fine code it was, but now inimical to
the survival of the race. It is the aristocrat's form of hara-kiri, a
law of conscience that bids the Japanese to slice his own stomach
when someone else dishonors him. The same sort of thing sur-
vives, slightly modified, in that exclusive prerogative of the aristocracy, the duel. (Example: the husband challenges his wife's
lover to a duel; the lover shoots the husband and runs off with
the wife. Result: the husband has saved his *honor* but lost his
wife.) Hence the servant Jean lives on; but not Miss Julie, who
cannot live without honor. The advantage that the slave has over
his master is that he has not committed himself to this defeatist
principle. In all of us Aryans there is enough of the nobleman,
or of the Don Quixote, to make us sympathize with the man who
takes his own life after having dishonored himself by shameful
deeds. And we are all of us aristocrats enough to be distressed at
the sight of a great man lying like a dead hulk ready for the scrap
pile, even, I suppose, if he were to raise himself up again and
redeem himself by honorable deeds.

The servant Jean is the beginning of a new species in which
noticeable differentiation has already taken place. He began as a
child of a poor worker and is now evolving through self-
education into a future gentleman of the upper classes. He is
quick to learn, has highly developed senses (smell, taste, sight),
and a keen appreciation of beauty. He has already come up in the
world, for he is strong enough not to hesitate to make use of other
people. He is already a stranger to his old friends, whom he
despises as reminders of past stages in his development, and
whom he fears and avoids because they know his secrets, guess
his intentions, look with envy on his rise and with joyful expec-
tation toward his fall. Hence his character is unformed and
divided. He wavers between an admiration of high positions and
a hatred of the men who occupy them. He is an aristocrat—he
says so himself—familiar with the ins and outs of good society.
He is polished on the outside, but coarse underneath. He wears
his frock coat with elegance but offers no guarantee that he keeps
his body clean.

Although he respects Miss Julie, he is afraid of Christine,
because she knows his innermost secrets. Yet he is sufficiently
hard-hearted not to let the events of the night upset his plans for

the future. Possessing both the coarseness of the slave and the toughmindedness of the born ruler, he can look at blood without fainting, shake off bad luck like water, and take calamity by the horns. Consequently he will escape from the battle unwounded, probably ending up as proprietor of a hotel. And if he himself does not get to be a Rumanian count, his son will doubtless go to college and possibly end up as a government official.

Now his observations about life as the lower classes see it, from below, are well worth listening to—that is, they are whenever he is telling the truth, which is not too often, because he is more likely to say what is advantageous to him than what is true. When Miss Julie supposes that everyone in the lower classes must feel greatly oppressed by the weight of the classes above, Jean naturally agrees with her since he wants to win her sympathy. But he promptly takes it all back when he finds it expedient to separate himself from the mob.

Apart from the fact that Jean is coming up in the world, he is also superior to Miss Julie in that he is a man. In the sexual sphere, he is the aristocrat. He has the strength of the male, more highly developed senses, and the ability to take the initiative. His inferiority is merely the result of his social environment, which is only temporary and which he will probably slough off along with his livery.

His slave nature expresses itself in his awe of the count (the boots) and his religious superstitions. But he is awed by the count mainly because the count occupies the place he wants most in life; and this awe is still there even after he has won the daughter of the house and seen how empty that beautiful shell was.

I do not believe that any love in the "higher" sense can be born from the union of two such different souls; so I have let Miss Julie's love be refashioned in her imagination as a love that protects and purifies, and I have let Jean imagine that even his love might have a chance to grow under other social circumstances. For I suppose love is very much like the hyacinth that must strike roots deep in the dark earth *before* it can produce a vigorous blossom. Here it shoots up, bursts into bloom, and turns to seed all at once. Such plants can only be short-lived.

Christine—finally to get to her—is a female slave, spineless and phlegmatic after years spent at the kitchen stove, bovinely unconscious of her own hypocrisy, and with a full quota of moral and religious notions that serve as scapegoats and cloaks for her sins—which a stronger soul does not require since he is able either to carry the burden of his own sins or to rationalize them out of existence. She attends church regularly where she deftly unloads unto Jesus her household thefts and picks up from him another load of innocence. She is only a secondary character, and I have deliberately done no more than sketch her in—just as I treated the country doctor and parish priest in *The Father* where I only wanted to draw ordinary everyday people such as most country doctors and parsons are. That some have found my minor characters one-dimensional is due to the fact that ordinary people while at work are to a certain extent one-dimensional and do lack an independent existence, showing only one side of themselves in the performance of their duties. And as long as the audience does not feel it needs to see them from different angles, my abstract sketches will pass muster.

Now as far as the dialogue is concerned, I have broken somewhat with tradition in refusing to make my characters into interlocutors who ask stupid questions to elicit witty answers. I have avoided the symmetrical and mathematical design of the artfully constructed French dialogue and have let minds work as irregularly as they do in real life, where no subject is quite exhausted before another mind engages at random some cog in the conversation and governs it for a while. My dialogue wanders here and there, gathers material in the first scenes which is later picked up, repeated, reworked, developed, and expanded like the theme in a piece of music.

The action of the play poses no problem. Since it really involves only two people, I have limited myself to these two, introducing only one minor character, the cook, and keeping the unhappy spirit of the father brooding over the action as a whole. I have chosen this course because I have noticed that what interests people most nowadays is the psychological action. Our inveterately curious souls are no longer content to see a thing happen; we want to see how it happens. We want to see the strings, look at the machinery, examine the double-bottom drawer, put on the magic ring to find the hidden seam, look in the deck for the marked cards.

In treating the subject this way I have had in mind the case-history novels of the Goncourt brothers, which appeal to me more than anything else in modern literature.

As far as play construction is concerned, I have made a stab at getting rid of act divisions. I was afraid that the spectator's declining susceptibility to illusion might not carry him through the intermission, when he would have time to think about what he has seen and to escape the suggestive influence of the author-hypnotist. I figure my play lasts about ninety minutes. Since one can listen to a lecture, a sermon, or a political debate for that long or even longer, I have convinced myself that a play should not exhaust an audience in that length of time. As early as 1872 in one of my first attempts at the drama, *The Outlaw*, I tried out this concentrated form, although with little success. I had finished the work in five acts when I noticed the disjointed and disturbing effect it produced. I burned it, and from the ashes there arose a single, complete reworked act of fifty pages that would run for less than an hour. Although this play form is not completely new, it seems to be my special property and has a good chance of gaining favor with the public when tastes change. My hope is to educate a public to sit through a full evening's show in one act. But this whole question must first be probed more deeply. In the meantime, in order to establish resting places for the audience and the actors without destroying the illusion, I have made use of three arts that belong to the drama: the monologue, the pantomime, and the ballet, all of which were part of classic tragedy, the monody having become the monologue and the choral dance, the ballet.

The realists have banished the monologue from the stage as implausible. But if I can motivate it, I make it plausible, and I can then use it to my advantage. Now it is certainly plausible for a speaker to pace the floor and read his speech aloud to himself. It is plausible for an actor to practice his part aloud, for a child to talk to her cat, a mother to babble to her baby, an old lady to chatter to her parrot, and a sleeping man to talk in his sleep. And in order to give the actor a chance to work on his own for once and for a moment not be obliged to follow the author's directions, I have not written out the monologues in detail but simply outlined them. Since it makes very little difference what is said while asleep, or to the parrot or the cat, inasmuch as it does not affect the main action, a gifted player who is in the midst of the situation and mood of the play can probably improvise the monologue better than the author, who cannot estimate ahead of time how much may be said and for how long before the illusion is broken.

Some theaters in Italy have, as we know, returned to the art of improvisation and have thereby trained actors who are truly inventive—without, however, violating the intentions of the author. This seems to be a step in the right direction and possibly the beginning of a new, fertile form of art that will be genuinely *creative*.

In places where the monologue cannot be properly motivated, I have resorted to pantomime. Here I have given the actor even more freedom to be creative and win honor on his own. Nevertheless, not to try the audience beyond its limits, I have relied on music—well motivated by the Midsummer Eve dance—to exercise its hypnotic powers during the pantomime scene. I beg the music director to select his tunes with great care, so that associations foreign to the mood of the play will not be produced by reminders of popular operettas or current dance numbers or by folk music of interest only to ethnologists.

The ballet that I have introduced cannot be replaced by a so-called crowd scene. Such scenes are always badly acted, with a pack of babbling fools taking advantage of the occasion to "gag it up," thereby destroying the illusion. Inasmuch as country people do not improvise their taunts but make use of material already to hand by giving it a double meaning, I have not composed an original lampoon but have made use of a little known round dance that I noted down in the Stockholm district. The words do not fit the situation exactly, which is what I intended, since the slave in his cunning (that is, weakness) never attacks directly. At any rate, let us have no comedians in this serious story and no obscene smirking over an affair that nails the lid on a family coffin.

As far as the scenery is concerned, I have borrowed from impressionistic painting the idea of asymmetrical and open composition, and I believe that I have thereby gained something in the way of greater illusion. Because the audience cannot see the whole room and all the furniture, they will have to surmise what's missing; that is, their imagination will be stimulated to fill in the rest of the picture. I have gained something else by this: I have avoided those tiresome exits through doors. Stage doors are made of canvas and rock at the slightest touch. They cannot even be used to indicate the wrath of an angry father who storms out of the house after a bad dinner, slamming the door behind him "so that the whole house shakes." (In the theater it sways and billows.) Furthermore, I have confined the action to one set, both to give the characters a chance to become part and parcel of their environment and to cut down on scenic extravagance. If there is only one set, one has a right to expect it to be as realistic as possible. Yet nothing is more difficult than to make a room look like a room, however easy it may be for the scene painter to create waterfalls and erupting volcanos. I suppose we shall have to put up with walls made of canvas, but isn't it about time that we stopped painting shelves and pots and pans on the canvas? There are so many other conventions in the theater that we are told to accept in good faith that we should be spared the strain of believing in painted saucepans.

I have placed the backdrop and the table at an angle to force the actors to play face to face or in half profile when they are seated opposite each other at the table. In a production of *Aida* I saw a flat placed at such an angle, which led the eye out in an unfamiliar perspective. Nor did it look as if it had been set that way simply to be different or to avoid those monotonous right angles.

Another desirable innovation would be the removal of the footlights. I understand that the purpose of lighting from below is to make the actors look more full in the face. But may I ask why all actors should have full faces? Doesn't this kind of lighting wipe out many of the finer features in the lower part of the face, especially around the jaws? Doesn't it distort the shape of the nose and throw false shadows above the eyes? If not, it certainly does something else: it hurts the actor's eyes. The footlights hit the retina at an angle from which it is usually shielded (except in sailors who must look at the sunlight reflected in the water), and the result is the loss of any effective play of the eyes. All one ever sees on stage are goggle-eyed glances sideways at the boxes or upward at the balcony, with only the whites of the eyes being visible in the latter case. And this probably also accounts for that tiresome fluttering of the eyelashes that the female performers are particularly guilty of. If an actor nowadays wants to express something with his eyes, he can only do it looking right at the audience, in which case he makes direct contact with someone outside the proscenium arch—a bad habit known, justifiably or not, as "saying hello to friends."*

I should think that the use of sufficiently strong side lights (through the use of reflectors or something like them) would provide the actor with a new asset: an increased range of expression made possible by the play of the eyes, the most expressive part of the face.

I have scarcely any illusions about getting actors to play for the audience and not directly at them, although this should be the goal. Nor do I dream of ever seeing an actor play through all of an important scene with his back to the audience. But is it too much to hope that crucial scenes could be played where the author indicated and not in front of the prompter's box as if they were duets demanding applause? I am not calling for a revolution, only for some small changes. I am well aware that transforming the stage into a real room with the fourth wall missing and with some of the furniture placed with backs to the auditorium would only upset the audience, at least for the present.

If I bring up the subject of make-up, it is not because I dare hope to be heeded by the ladies, who would rather be beautiful than truthful. But the male actor might do well to consider if it is an advantage to paint his face with character lines that remain there like a mask. Let us imagine an actor who pencils in with soot a few lines between his eyes to indicate great anger, and let us suppose that in that permanently enraged state he finds he has to smile on a certain line. Imagine the horrible grimace! And how can the old character actor wrinkle his brows in anger when his false bald pate is as smooth as a billiard ball?

In a modern psychological drama, in which every tremor of the soul should be reflected more by facial expressions than by gestures and grunts, it would probably be most sensible to experiment with strong side lighting on a small stage, using actors without any make-up or a minimum of it.

And then, if we could get rid of the visible orchestra with its disturbing lights and the faces turned toward the public; if the auditorium floor could be raised so that the spectator's eyes are

* "Counting the house" would be the equivalent in American theater slang.—Trans.

not level with the actor's knees; if we could get rid of the proscenium boxes and their occupants, arriving giggling and drunk from their dinners; and if we could have it dark in the auditorium during the performance; and if, above everything else, we could have a *small* stage and an *intimate* auditorium — then possibly a new drama might arise and at least one theater become a refuge for cultured audiences. While we are waiting for such a theater, we shall have to write for the dramatic stockpile and prepare the repertory that one day shall come.

Here is my attempt. If I have failed, there is still time to try again!

CHARACTERS

MISS JULIE,* twenty-five years old
JEAN, valet, thirty years old
CHRISTINE, cook, thirty-five years old
THE CHORUS, a party of country folk

The scene is a country estate in Sweden.

The time: A Midsummer Night in the 1880s. The hours after midnight, June 24, St. John the Baptist's Day.

---

* Julie is not a countess; she is the daughter of a count. Her title "fröken" corresponds to the German "Fräulein" and the French "mademoiselle."

THE SET

The scene is the kitchen of the estate belonging to the count, Miss Julie's father. It is a large kitchen, situated along with the servants' quarters in the basement of the manor house. The side walls and the ceiling of the kitchen are masked by the tormentors and borders of the set. The rear wall runs obliquely upstage from the left. On this wall to the left are two shelves with pots and pans of copper, iron, and pewter. The shelves are decorated with goffered paper. A little to the right can be seen three-fourths of a deep arched entry with two glass doors, and through them can be seen a fountain with a statue of a cupid, lilac bushes in bloom, and the tops of some Lombardy poplars.

From the left of the stage the corner of a large, Dutch-tile kitchen stove protrudes with part of the hood showing.

Projecting from the right side of the stage is one end of the servants' dining table of white pine, with a few chairs around it.

The stove is decorated with branches of birch leaves; the floor is strewn with juniper twigs.

On the end of the table is a large Japanese spice jar filled with lilacs.

An icebox, a sink, a washbasin.

Over the door a big old-fashioned bell; and to the left of the door the gaping mouth of a speaking tube.

* * *

Christine is standing at the stove, frying something in a pan. She is wearing a light-colored cotton dress and an apron.

Jean enters, dressed in livery and carrying a pair of high-top boots with spurs. He sets them where they are clearly visible.

JEAN: What a night! She's wild again! Miss Julie's absolutely wild!

CHRISTINE: You sure took your time getting back!

JEAN: I took the count down to the station, and on my way back, I passed the barn and went in for a dance. And there was Miss Julie leading the dance with the game warden. Then she noticed me. And she ran right into my arms and chose me for the ladies' waltz. And she's been dancing ever since like – like I don't know what. Wild, I tell you, absolutely wild!

CHRISTINE: That's nothing new. But she's been worse than ever during the last two weeks, ever since her engagement was broken off.

JEAN: Yes. I never did hear all there was to that. He was a good man, too, even if he wasn't rich. Well, they've got such crazy ideas. (*He sits down at the end of the table.*) Tell me, isn't it strange that a young girl like her – all right, young woman – prefers to stay home here with the servants rather than go with her father to visit her relatives?

CHRISTINE: I suppose she's ashamed to face them after that fiasco with her young man.

JEAN: No doubt. He wouldn't take any nonsense from her. Do you know what happened, Christine? I saw the whole thing. Of course, I didn't let on.

CHRISTINE: You were there? I don't believe it.

JEAN: Well, I was. They were in the stable yard one evening – and she was training him, that's what she called it. Do you know what? She was making him jump over her riding whip – training him like a dog. He jumped over twice, and she whipped him both times. But the third time, he grabbed the whip from her, [scratched her face with it – long scratch on her left cheek;]* then broke it in a thousand pieces – and walked off.

*The passage in brackets was deleted in Strindberg's manuscript, probably by Strindberg himself.

CHRISTINE: I don't believe it! What do you know!

JEAN: Yes, that put an end to that affair. —What have you got for me that's really good, Christine?

CHRISTINE (*serving him from the frying pan*): Just a little bit of kidney. Cut it from the veal roast.

JEAN (*smelling it*): Wonderful! One my special *délices*! (*Feeling the plate.*) Hey, you didn't warm the plate!

CHRISTINE: You're more fussy than the count himself when you set your mind to it. (*She rumples his hair affectionately.*)

JEAN (*irritated*): Cut it out! Don't muss up my hair. You know how particular I am!

CHRISTINE: Oh, don't get mad. Can I help it if I like you?

Jean eats. Christine gets out a bottle of beer.

JEAN: Beer on Midsummer Eve! No thank you! I've got something much better than that. (*He opens a drawer in the table and takes out a bottle of red wine with a gold seal.*) Do you see that? Gold Seal. Now give me a glass.

She hands him a tumbler.

—No, a wineglass of course. This has to be drunk properly. No water.

CHRISTINE (*goes back to the stove and puts on a small saucepan*): Lord help the woman who gets you for a husband. You're an old fussbudget!

JEAN: Talk, talk! You'd consider yourself lucky if you got yourself a man as good as me. It hasn't done you any harm to have people think I'm your fiancé. (*He tastes the wine.*) Very good. Excellent. But warmed just a little too little. (*Warming the glass in his hands.*) We bought this in Dijon. Four francs a liter, unbottled—and the tax on top of that. . . . What on earth are you cooking? It stinks like hell!

CHRISTINE: Some damn mess that Miss Julie wants for her Diana, that damn dog of hers.

JEAN: You should watch your language, Christine. . . . Why do you have to stand in front of the stove on a holiday, cooking for that mutt? Is it sick?

CHRISTINE: Oh, she's sick, all right! She sneaked out to the gatekeeper's pug and — got herself in a fix. And you know Miss Julie, she can't stand anything like that.

JEAN: She's too stuck-up in some ways and not proud enough in others. Just like her mother. The countess felt right at home in the kitchen or down in the barn with the cows, but when she went driving, one horse wasn't enough for her, she had to have a pair. Her sleeves were always dirty, but her buttons had the royal crown on them. As for Miss Julie, she doesn't give a hoot in hell how she looks and acts. I mean, she's not really refined, not really. Just now, down at the barn, she grabbed the game warden right from under Anna's eyes and asked him to dance. You wouldn't see anybody in our class behaving like that. But that's what happens when the gentry try to act like the common people — they become common! . . . However, I'll say one thing for her: she *is* beautiful! Statuesque! Ah, those shoulders — those — and so forth, and so forth!

CHRISTINE: Oh, don't exaggerate. Clara tells me all about her, and Clara dresses her.

JEAN: Clara, pooh! You women are always jealous of each other. I've been out riding with her. . . . And how she can dance . . . !

CHRISTINE: Listen, Jean, you *are* going to dance with me, aren't you, when I'm finished here?

JEAN: Certainly! Of course I am.

CHRISTINE: Promise?

JEAN: Promise! Listen if I say I'm going to do a thing, I do it. . . . Christine, I thank you for a delicious meal. Superb! (*He shoves the cork back into the bottle.*)

> *Miss Julie appears in the entry, talking to someone outside.*

MISS JULIE: I'll be right back. Don't wait for me.

> *Jean slips the bottle into the table drawer quickly and rises respectfully. Miss Julie comes in and crosses over to Christine, who is at the stove.*

MISS JULIE: Did you get it ready?

> *Christine signals that Jean is present.*

JEAN (*polite and charming*): Are you ladies sharing secrets?

MISS JULIE (*flipping her handkerchief in his face*): Don't be nosy!

JEAN: Oh, that smells good! Violets.

MISS JULIE (*flirting with him*): Don't be impudent! And don't tell me you're an expert on perfumes, too. I love the way you dance! – No, mustn't look! Go away!

JEAN (*cocky but pleasant*): What are the ladies cooking up? A witches' brew for Midsummer Eve? So they can tell the future? Read what's in the cards for them, and see who they'll marry?

MISS JULIE (*curtly*): You'd have to have good eyes to see that. (*To Christine.*) Pour it into a small bottle, and seal it tight. . . . Jean, come and dance a schottische with me.

JEAN (*hesitating*): I hope you don't think I'm being rude, but I've already promised this dance to Christine.

MISS JULIE: She can always find someone. Isn't that so, Christine? You don't mind if I borrow Jean for a minute, do you?

CHRISTINE: It ain't up to me. If Miss Julie is gracious enough to invite you, it ain't right for you to say no, Jean. You go on, and thank her for the honor.

JEAN: Frankly, Miss Julie, I don't want to hurt your feelings, but I wonder if it's wise – I mean for you to dance twice in a row with the same partner. Especially since the people around here love to talk.

MISS JULIE (*bridling*): What do you mean? What kind of talk? What are you trying to say?

JEAN (*retreating*): I wish you wouldn't misunderstand me, Miss Julie. It just doesn't look right for you to prefer one of your servants to the others who are hoping for the same unusual honor.

MISS JULIE: Prefer! What an idea! I'm really surprised. I, the mistress of the house, am good enough to come to their dance, and when I feel like dancing, I want to dance with someone who knows how to lead. After all I don't want to look ridiculous.

JEAN: As you wish, Miss Julie. I am at your orders.

MISS JULIE (*gently*): Don't take it as an order. Tonight we're all just having a good time. There's no question of rank. Now give me your arm. —Don't worry, Christine. I won't run off with your boyfriend.

Jean gives her his arm and leads her out.

★ ★ ★

PANTOMIME SCENE

This should be played as if the actress were actually alone. She turns her back on the audience when she feels like it; she does not look out into the auditorium; she does not rush through the scene as if afraid the audience will grow impatient.

Christine alone. In the distance the sound of the violins playing the schottische. Christine, humming in time with the music, cleans up after Jean, washes the dishes, dries them, and puts them away in a cupboard. Then she takes off her apron, takes a little mirror from one of the table drawers, and leans it against the jar of lilacs on the table. She lights a tallow candle, heats a curling iron, and curls the bangs on her forehead. Then she goes to the doorway and stands listening to the music. She comes back to the table and finds the handkerchief that Miss Julie left behind. She smells it, spreads it out, and then, as if lost in thought, stretches it, smooths it out, and folds it in four.

* * *

Jean enters alone.

JEAN: Wild! I told you she was wild! You should have seen the way she was dancing. Everyone was peeking at her from behind the doors and laughing at her. What's the matter with her, Christine?

CHRISTINE: You might know it's her monthlies, Jean. She always acts peculiar then. . . . Well, are you going to dance with me?

JEAN: You're not mad at me because I broke my promise?

CHRISTINE: Of course not. Not for a little thing like that, you know that. I know my place.

JEAN (*grabs her around the waist*): You're a sensible girl, Christine. You're going to make somebody a good wife—

Miss Julie, coming in, sees them together. She is unpleasantly surprised.

MISS JULIE (*with forced gaiety*): Well, aren't you the gallant beau—running away from your partner!

JEAN: On the contrary, Miss Julie. As you can see, I've hurried back to the partner I deserted.

MISS JULIE (*changing tack*): You know, you're the best dancer I've met. —Why are you wearing livery on a holiday? Take it off at once.

JEAN: I'd have to ask you to leave for a minute. My black coat is hanging right here—(*He moves to the right and points.*)

MISS JULIE: You're not embarrassed because I'm here, are you? Just to change your coat? Go in your room and come right back again. Or else stay here and I'll turn my back.

JEAN: If you'll excuse me, Miss Julie. (*He goes off to the right. His arm can be seen as he changes his coat.*)

MISS JULIE (*to Christine*): Tell me something, Christine. Is Jean your fiancé? He acts so familiar with you.

CHRISTINE: Fiancé? I suppose so. At least we say we are.

MISS JULIE: What do you mean?

CHRISTINE: Well, Miss Julie, you have had fiancés yourself, and you know—

MISS JULIE: But we were properly engaged—!

CHRISTINE: I know, but did anything come of it?

> *Jean comes back, wearing a black cutaway coat and derby.*

MISS JULIE: *Très gentil, monsieur Jean! Très gentil!*

JEAN: *Vous voulez plaisanter, madame.*

MISS JULIE: *Et vous voulez parler français!* Where did you learn to speak French?

JEAN: In Switzerland. I was *sommelier* in one of the biggest hotels in Lucerne.

MISS JULIE: My! but you look quite the gentleman in that coat! *Charmant!* (*She sits down at the table.*)

JEAN: Flatterer!

MISS JULIE (*stiffening*): Who said I was flattering you?

JEAN: My natural modesty would not allow me to presume that you were paying sincere compliments to someone like me, and therefore I could only assume that you were exaggerating, which, in this case, means flattering me.

MISS JULIE: You certainly have a way with words. Where did you learn to talk like that? Seeing plays?

JEAN: And other places. You don't think I stayed in the house for six years when I was a valet in Stockholm, do you?

MISS JULIE: I thought you were born in this district. Weren't you?

JEAN: My father worked as a farmhand on the district attorney's estate, next door to yours. I used to see you when you were little. Of course you didn't notice me.

MISS JULIE: Did you really?

JEAN: Yes. I remember one time in particular –. But I can't tell you about that!

MISS JULIE: Of course you can. . . . Oh, come on. Just this once – for me.

JEAN: No. No, I really couldn't. Not now. Some other time maybe.

MISS JULIE: Some other time? That means never. What's the harm in telling me now?

JEAN: There's no harm. I just don't feel like it. – Look at her.

> *He nods at Christine, who has fallen asleep in a chair by the stove.*

MISS JULIE: Won't she make somebody a pretty wife! I'll bet she snores, too.

JEAN: No, she doesn't. But she talks in her sleep.

MISS JULIE (*archly*): Now how could you know she talks in her sleep?

JEAN (*coolly*): I've heard her . . .

> *Pause. They look at each other.*

MISS JULIE: Why don't you sit down?

JEAN: I wouldn't take the liberty in your presence.

MISS JULIE: Not even if I ordered you?

JEAN: Of course I'd obey.

MISS JULIE: Well then: sit down. — Wait a minute. Could you get me something to drink?

JEAN: I don't know what there is in the icebox. Only beer, I suppose.

MISS JULIE: Only beer?! I have simple tastes. I prefer beer to wine.

> *Jean takes a bottle of beer from the icebox and opens it. He looks in the cupboard for a glass and a plate, and serves her.*

JEAN: At your service, *mademoiselle*.

MISS JULIE: Thank you. What about you?

JEAN: I'm not much of a beer-drinker, thank you, but if it's your wish —

MISS JULIE: My wish! I should think a gentleman would want to keep his lady company.

JEAN: A point well taken! (*He opens another bottle and takes a glass.*)

MISS JULIE: Now drink a toast to me!

> *Jean hesitates.*

You're not shy, are you? A big, strong man like you?

> *Playfully, Jean kneels and raises his glass in mock gallantry.*

JEAN: To my lady's health!

MISS JULIE: Bravo! Now you have to kiss my shoe, too. Then you will have hit it off perfectly.

> *Jean hesitates, then boldly grasps her foot and touches it lightly with his lips.*

Superb! You should have been an actor.

JEAN (*rising*): This has got to stop, Miss Julie! Someone might come in and see us.

MISS JULIE: So what?

JEAN: People would talk, that's what! If you knew how their tongues were wagging out there just a few minutes ago!

MISS JULIE: What did they say? Tell me. Sit down and tell me.

JEAN. I don't want to hurt your feelings. . . . They used expressions that — that hinted at certain — you know what I mean. You're not a child. And when they see a woman drinking, alone with a man — and a servant at that — in the middle of the night — well . . .

MISS JULIE: Well what?! Besides, we're not alone. Christine is here.

JEAN: Sleeping!

MISS JULIE: I'll wake her up. (*She goes over to Christine.*) Christine! Are you asleep? (*Christine babbles in her sleep.*) Christine! —My, how sound she sleeps!

CHRISTINE (*talking in her sleep*): Count's boots are brushed . . . put on the coffee . . . right away, right away, right . . . mm—mm . . . poofff . . .

Miss Julie shakes Christine.

MISS JULIE: Wake up, will you!

JEAN (*sternly*): Let her alone! Let her sleep!

MISS JULIE (*sharply*): What?

JEAN: She's been standing over the stove all day. She's worn out when night comes. Anyone asleep is entitled to some consideration.

MISS JULIE (*changing her tone*): That's a very kind thought. It does you credit, Jean. You're right, of course. (*She offers Jean her hand.*) Now come on out and pick some lilacs for me.

During the following, Christine wakes up and, drunk

*with sleep, shuffles off to the right to go to bed. A polka
can be heard in the distance.*

JEAN: With you, Miss Julie?

MISS JULIE: Yes, with me.

JEAN: That's no good. Absolutely not.

MISS JULIE: I don't know what you're thinking. Aren't you
letting your imagination run away with you?

JEAN: No. Other people are.

MISS JULIE: How? Imagining that I'm — *verliebt* with a servant?

JEAN: I'm not conceited, but it's been known to happen. And to
these people nothing's sacred.

MISS JULIE: "These people!" Why, I do believe you're an aristocrat!

JEAN: Yes, I am.

MISS JULIE: I'm climbing down —

JEAN: Don't climb down, Miss Julie! Take my advice. No one
will believe that you climbed down deliberately. They'll say you
fell.

MISS JULIE: I have a higher opinion of these people than you
do. Let's see who's right! Come on! (*She gives him a long, steady
look.*)

JEAN: You know, you're very strange.

MISS JULIE: Perhaps. But then so are you. . . . Besides,
everything is strange. Life, people, everything. It's all scum,
drifting and drifting on the water until it sinks — drowns. There's
a dream I have every now and then. It's coming back to me now.
I'm sitting on top of a pillar. I've climbed up it somehow and I
don't know how to get back down. When I look down I get dizzy.
I have to get down but I don't have the courage to jump. I can't
hold on much longer and I want to fall; but I don't fall. I know
I won't have any peace until I get down; no rest until I get down,
down on the ground. And if I ever got down on the ground, I'd

want to go farther down, right down into the earth. . . . Have you ever felt anything like that?

JEAN: Never! I used to dream that I'm lying under a tall tree in a dark woods. I want to get up, up to the very top, to look out over the bright landscape with the sun shining on it, to rob the bird's nest up there with the golden eggs in it. And I climb and I climb, but the trunk is so thick, and so smooth, and it's such a long way to that first branch. But I know that if I could just reach that first branch, I'd go right to the top as if on a ladder. I've never reached it yet, but someday I will—even if only in my dreams.

MISS JULIE: Here I am talking about dreams with you. Come out with me. Only into the park a way. (*She offers him her arm, and they start to go.*)

JEAN: Let's sleep on nine midsummer flowers, Miss Julie, and then our dreams will come true!*

> *Miss Julie and Jean suddenly turn around in the doorway. Jean is holding his hand over one eye.*

MISS JULIE: You've caught something in your eye. Let me see.

JEAN: It's nothing. Just a bit of dust. It'll go away.

MISS JULIE: The sleeve of my dress must have grazed your eye. Sit down and I'll help you. (*She takes him by the arm and sits him down. She takes his head and leans it back. With the corner of her handkerchief she tries to get out the bit of dust.*) Now sit still, absolutely still. (*She slaps his hand.*) Do as you're told. Why, I believe you're trembling—a big, strong man like you. (*She feels his biceps.*) With such big arms!

JEAN (*warningly*): Miss Julie!

MISS JULIE: Yes, *Monsieur Jean?*

---

* A girl would pick in silence on Midsummer Eve nine different sorts of flowers, make a bouquet of them, and place them under her pillow. The man who appeared in her dreams would be the man she would marry.

JEAN: *Attention! Je ne suis qu'un homme!*

MISS JULIE: Sit still, I tell you! . . . There now! It's out. Kiss my hand and thank me!

JEAN (*rising to his feet*): Listen to me, Miss Julie—Christine has gone to bed!—Listen to me, I tell you!

MISS JULIE: Kiss my hand first!

JEAN: Listen to me!

MISS JULIE: Kiss my hand first!

JEAN: All right. But you'll have no one to blame but yourself.

MISS JULIE: For what?

JEAN: For what! Are you twenty-five years old and still a child? Don't you know it's dangerous to play with fire?

MISS JULIE: Not for me, I'm insured!

JEAN (*boldly*): Oh, no, you're not! And even if you are, there's inflammable stuff next door.

MISS JULIE: Meaning you?

JEAN: Yes. Not just because it's me, but because I'm young and—

MISS JULIE: And irresistibly handsome? What incredible conceit! A Don Juan, maybe! Or a Joseph! Yes, bless my soul, that's it: you're a Joseph!

JEAN: You think so?!

MISS JULIE: I'm almost afraid so!

> *Jean boldly steps up to her, grabs her around the waist, tries to kiss her. She slaps his face.*

None of that!

JEAN: More games? Or are you serious?

MISS JULIE: I'm serious.

JEAN: Then you must have been serious a moment ago, too!

You take your games too seriously; that's dangerous. Well, I'm tired of your games, and if you'll excuse me, I'll return to my work. (*Takes up the boots and starts to brush them.*) The count will be wanting his boots on time, and it's long past midnight.

MISS JULIE: Put those boots down.

JEAN: No! This is my job. It's what I'm here for. I never undertook to be your playmate. That's something I could never be. I consider myself too good for that.

MISS JULIE: You are proud.

JEAN: In some ways. Not in others.

MISS JULIE: Have you ever been in love?

JEAN: We don't use that word around here. But I've hankered after some girls, if that's what you mean. . . . I even got sick once because I couldn't have the one I wanted—really sick, like the princes in the Arabian Nights—who couldn't eat or drink for love.

MISS JULIE: Who was she?

Jean does not reply.

Who was the girl?

JEAN: You can't get that out of me.

MISS JULIE: Even if I ask you as an equal—ask you—as a friend? . . . Who was she?

JEAN: You.

MISS JULIE (*sitting down*): How—amusing . . .

JEAN: Yes, maybe so. Ridiculous. . . . That's why I didn't want to tell you about it before. Want to hear the whole story? . . . Have you any idea what you and your people look like from down below? Of course not. Like hawks or eagles, that's what: you hardly ever see their backs because they're always soaring so high up. I lived with seven brothers and sisters—and a pig—out on the wasteland where there wasn't even a tree growing. But from my window I could see the wall of the count's

garden with the apple trees sticking up over it. That was the
Garden of Eden for me, and there were many angry angels with
flaming swords standing guard over it. But in spite of them, I and
the other boys found a way to the Tree of Life. . . . How contemptible, that's what you're thinking.

MISS JULIE: For stealing apples? All boys do that.

JEAN: That's what you say now. All the same, you think me contemptible. Never mind. One day I went with my mother into this
paradise to weed the onion beds. Next to the vegetable garden
stood a Turkish pavilion, shaded by jasmine and hung all over
with honeysuckle. I couldn't imagine what it was used for; I only
knew I had never seen such a beautiful building. People went in,
and came out again. And then one day the door was left open.
I sneaked in. The walls were covered with portraits of kings and
emperors, and the windows had red curtains with tassels on
them. —Recognize it? Yes, the count's private privy. . . . I—
(*He breaks off a lilac and holds it under Miss Julie's nose.*) I had
never been inside a castle, never seen anything besides the
church. This was more beautiful. And no matter what I tried to
think about, my thoughts always came back—to that little
pavilion. And little by little there arose in me a desire to experience just for once the whole pleasure of—. *Enfin*, I sneaked in,
looked about, and marveled. And just then I heard someone
coming! There was only one way out—for the upper-class people.
But for me there was one more—a lower one. And I had no other
choice but to take it. (*Miss Julie, who has taken the lilac from Jean,
lets it fall to the table.*) Then I began to run like mad, plunging
through the raspberry bushes, ploughing through the strawberry
patches, and came up on the rose terrace. And there I caught
sight of a pink dress and a pair of white stockings. You! I crawled
under—well, you can imagine what it was like—under thistles
that pricked me and wet dirt that stank to high heaven. And all
the while I could see you walking among the roses. I said to
myself, "If it's true that a thief can enter heaven and be with the
angels, isn't it strange that a poor man's child here on God's green
earth can't enter the count's park and play with the count's
daughter."

MISS JULIE (*sentimentally*): Do you think all poor children have
felt that way?

JEAN (*hesitatingly at first, then with mounting conviction*): If all poor ch–? Yes–yes, naturally. Of course!

MISS JULIE: It must be terrible to be poor.

JEAN (*with exaggerated intensity*): Oh, Miss Julie! You don't know! A dog can lie on the sofa with its mistress; a horse can have its nose stroked by the hand of a countess; but a servant–! (*Changing his tone.*) Of course, now and then you meet somebody with guts enough to work his way up in the world, but how often? –Anyway, you know what I did afterward? I threw myself into the millstream with all my clothes on. Got fished out and spanked. But the following Sunday, when Pa and everybody else in the house went to visit Grandma, I arranged things so I'd be left behind. Then I washed myself all over with soap and warm water, put on my best clothes, and went off to church–just to see you there once more. I saw you, and then I went home determined to die. But I wanted to die beautifully and comfortably, without pain. I remembered some stories I had heard about how fatal it was to sleep under an elderberry bush. And we had a big one that had just blossomed out. I stripped it of every leaf and blossom it had and made a bed of them in a bin of oats. Have you ever noticed how smooth oats are? As smooth to the touch as human skin. . . . So I pulled the lid of the bin shut and closed my eyes. Fell asleep. And when they woke me I was really very sick. However, I didn't die, as you can see. –What was I trying to prove? I don't know. There was no hope of winning you. It was just that you were a symbol of the absolute hopelessness of my ever getting out of the class I was born in.

MISS JULIE: You know, you have a real gift for telling stories. Did you go to school?

JEAN: A little. But I've read a lot of novels and gone to the theater. And I've also listened to educated people talk. That way I learned the most.

MISS JULIE: You mean to tell me you stand around listening to what we're saying!

JEAN: Certainly! And I've heard an awful lot, I can tell you– sitting on the coachman's seat or rowing the boat. One time I heard you and a girlfriend talking–

MISS JULIE: Really? . . . And just what did you hear?

JEAN: Well, now, I don't know if I can repeat it. I can tell you I was a little amazed. I couldn't imagine where you had learned such words. Maybe at bottom there isn't such a big difference as you might think, between people and people.

MISS JULIE: How vulgar! At least people in my class don't behave like you when we're engaged.

JEAN (*looking her in the eye*): Are you sure? —Come on now, it's no use playing the innocent with me.

MISS JULIE: He was a beast. The man I offered my love was a beast.

JEAN: That's what you all say—afterward.

MISS JULIE: All?

JEAN: I'd say so. I've heard the same expression used several times before in similar circumstances.

MISS JULIE: What kind of circumstances?

JEAN: The kind we're talking about. I remember the last time I—

MISS JULIE (*rising*): That's enough! I don't want to hear any more.

JEAN: How strange! Neither did she! . . . Well, now if you'll excuse me, I'll go to bed.

MISS JULIE (*softly*): Go to bed on Midsummer Eve?

JEAN: That's right. Dancing with that crowd up there really doesn't amuse me.

MISS JULIE: Jean, get the key to the boathouse and row me out on the lake. I want to see the sun come up.

JEAN: Do you think that's wise?

MISS JULIE: You sound as if you were worried about your reputation.

JEAN: Why not? I don't particularly care to be made ridiculous, or to be kicked out without a recommendation just when I'm trying to establish myself. Besides, I have a certain obligation to Christine.

MISS JULIE: Oh, I see. It's Christine now.

JEAN: Yes, but I'm thinking of you, too. Take my advice, Miss Julie. Go up to your room.

MISS JULIE: When did you start giving me orders?

JEAN: Just this once. For your own sake! Please! It's very late. You're so tired, you're drunk; you don't know what you're doing. Go to bed, Miss Julie. —Besides, if my ears aren't deceiving me, they're coming this way, looking for me. If they find us here together, you're done for!

THE CHORUS (*is heard coming nearer, singing*):

> Said Jill to Jack, "Soil needs a tilling."
> Tri-di-ri-di-ralla, tri-di-ri-di-ra.
> Said Jack to Jill, "Time's a-spilling."
> Tri-di-ri-di-ralla-la.
> Said Jill to Jack, "Gold's a-hoarding."
> Tri-di-ri-di-ralla, tri-di-ri-di-ra.
> Said Jack to Jill, "Tell not my lording."
> Tri-di-ri-di-ralla-la.
> Said Jill to Jack, "Hair is for plaiting."
> Tri-di-ri-di-ralla, tri-di-ri-di-ra.
> "But Jill for Jack is not waiting."
> Tri-di-ri-di-ralla-la!*

MISS JULIE: I know these people. I love them just as they love me. Let them come. You'll see.

JEAN: Oh, no, Miss Julie, they don't love you! They take the food you give them, but they spit on it as soon as your back is turned. Believe me! Just listen to them. Listen to what they're singing. —No, you'd better not listen.

MISS JULIE (*listening*): What are they singing?

JEAN: A nasty song—about you and me!

*The Swedish original of this song appears on p. 238.

BONDFOLKETS DANSVISA

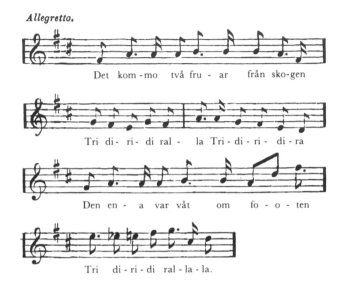

Allegretto.

Det kom-mo två fru - ar   från sko-gen

Tri di- ri- di ral -   la Tri - di - ri - di - ra

Den en - a var våt   om   fo - o - ten

Tri   di - ri - di ral - la - la.

De talte om hundra riksdaler
Tri (etc.)
Men ägde knappast en daler
Tri (etc.)

Och kransen jag dig skänker
Tri (etc.)
En annan jag påtänker
Tri (etc.)

The melody of the peasants' song was not printed in the first Swedish edition, but it did appear in Charles de Casanove's French translation of the play in 1893.

MISS JULIE: How disgusting! Oh, what cowardly, sneaking—

JEAN: That's what the mob always is—cowards! You can't fight them; you can only run away.

MISS JULIE: Run away? Where? There's no way out of here. And we can't go in to Christine.

JEAN: What about my room? What do you say? Rules don't count in a situation like this. You can trust me. —You said, let's be friends. Remember? Well, I'm your friend—your true, devoted, respectful friend.

MISS JULIE: But suppose—suppose they looked for you there?

JEAN: I'll bolt the door. If they try to break it down, I'll shoot. Come, Miss Julie! (*On his knees.*) Please, Miss Julie!

MISS JULIE (*meaningfully*): You promise me that you won't—

JEAN: I swear to you!

> *Miss Julie goes out quickly to the right. Jean follows her impetuously.*

★ ★ ★

THE BALLET

> *The country people enter in festive costumes, with flowers in their hats. The fiddler is in the lead. A keg of small beer and a little keg of liquor, decorated with greenery, are set up on the table. Glasses are brought out. They all drink. Then they form a circle and sing "Said Jill to Jack," dancing the round dance as they sing. At the end of the dance, they all leave singing.*

★ ★ ★

> *Miss Julie comes in alone; looks at the devastated kitchen; clasps her hands together; then takes out a powder puff and powders her face. Jean enters. He is in high spirits.*

JEAN: You see! You heard them, didn't you? You've got to admit it's impossible to stay here.

MISS JULIE: No, I don't. But even if I did, what could we do?

JEAN: Go away, travel, get away from here!

MISS JULIE: Travel? Yes—but where?

JEAN: Switzerland, the Italian lakes. You've never been there?

MISS JULIE: No. Is it beautiful?

JEAN: Eternal summer, oranges, laurel trees, ah . . . !

MISS JULIE: What do we do when we get there?

JEAN: I'll set up a hotel—a first-class hotel with a first-class clientele.

MISS JULIE: Hotel?

JEAN: I tell you that's the life! Always new faces, new languages. Not a minute to think about yourself or worry about your nerves. No looking for something to do. The work keeps you busy. Day and night the bells ring, the trains whistle, the buses come and go. And all the while the money comes rolling in. I tell you it's the life!

MISS JULIE: Yes, that's the life. But what about me?

JEAN: The mistress of the whole place, the star of the establishment! With your looks—and your personality—it can't fail. It's perfect! You'll sit in the office like a queen, setting your slaves in motion by pressing an electric button. The guests will file before your throne and timidly lay their treasures on your table. You can't imagine how people tremble when you shove a bill in their face! I'll salt the bills and you'll sugar them with your prettiest smile. Come on, let's get away from here—(*He takes a timetable from his pocket.*)—right away—the next train! We'll be in Malmö at six-thirty, Hamburg eight-forty in the morning; Frankfurt to Basle in one day, and to Como by way of the Gotthard tunnel in—let me see—three days! Three days!

MISS JULIE: You make it sound so wonderful. But, Jean, you have to give me strength. Tell me you love me. Come and put your arms around me.

JEAN (*hesitates*): I want to . . . but I don't dare. Not anymore, not in this house. I do love you – without a shadow of a doubt. How can you doubt that, Miss Julie?

MISS JULIE (*shyly, very becomingly*): You don't have to be formal with me, Jean. You can call me Julie. There aren't any barriers between us now. Call me Julie.

JEAN (*agonized*): I can't! There are still barriers between us, Miss Julie, as long as we stay in this house! There's the past, there's the count. I've never met anyone I feel so much respect for. I've only got to see his gloves lying on a table and I shrivel up. I only have to hear that bell ring and I shy like a frightened horse. I only have to look at his boots standing there so stiff and proud and I feel my spine bending. (*He kicks the boots.*) Superstitions, prejudices that they've drilled into us since we were children! But they can be forgotten just as easily! Just we get to another country where they have a republic! They'll crawl on their hands and knees when they see my uniform. On their hands and knees, I tell you! But not me! Oh, no. I'm not made for crawling. I've got guts, backbone. And once I grab that first branch, you just watch me climb. I may be a valet now, but next year I'll be owning property; in ten years, I'll be living off my investments. Then I'll go to Rumania, get myself some decorations, and maybe – notice I only say maybe – end up as a count!

MISS JULIE: How wonderful, wonderful.

JEAN: Listen, in Rumania you can buy titles. You'll be a countess after all. My countess.

MISS JULIE: But I'm not interested in that. I'm leaving all that behind. Tell me you love me, Jean, or else – or else what difference does it make what I am?

JEAN: I'll tell you a thousand times – but later! Not now. And not here. Above all, let's keep our feelings out of this or we'll make a mess of everything. We have to look at this thing calmly and coolly, like sensible people. (*He takes out a cigar, clips the end, and lights it.*) Now you sit there and I'll sit here, and we'll talk as if nothing had happened.

MISS JULIE (*in anguish*): My God, what are you? Don't you have any feelings?

JEAN: Feelings? Nobody's got more feelings than I have. But I've learned to control them.

MISS JULIE: A few minutes ago you were kissing my shoe – and now – !

JEAN (*harshly*): That was a few minutes ago. We've got other things to think about now!

MISS JULIE: Don't speak to me like that, Jean!

JEAN: I'm just trying to be sensible. We've been stupid once; let's not be stupid again. Your father might be back at any moment, and we've got to decide our future before then. – Now what do you think about my plans? Do you approve or don't you?

MISS JULIE: I don't see anything wrong with them. Except one thing. For a big undertaking like that, you'd need a lot of capital. Have you got it?

JEAN (*chewing on his cigar*): Have I got it? Of course I have. I've got my knowledge of the business, my vast experience, my familiarity with languages. That's capital that counts for something, let me tell you.

MISS JULIE: You can't even buy the railway tickets with it.

JEAN: That's true. That's why I need a backer – someone to put up the money.

MISS JULIE: Where can you find him on a moment's notice?

JEAN: You'll find him – if you want to be my partner.

MISS JULIE: I can't. And I don't have a penny to my name.

> *Pause.*

JEAN: Then you can forget the whole thing.

MISS JULIE: Forget – ?

JEAN: And things will stay just the way they are.

MISS JULIE: Do you think I'm going to live under the same roof with you as your mistress? Do you think I'm going to have people sneering at me behind my back? How do you think I'll ever be able to look my father in the face after this? No, no! Take me away from here, Jean—the shame, the humiliation. . . . What have I done? Oh, my God, my God! What have I done! (*She bursts into tears.*)

JEAN: Now don't start singing that tune. It won't work. What have you done that's so awful? You're not the first.

MISS JULIE (*crying hysterically*): Now you think me contemptible—I'm falling, falling!

JEAN: Fall down to me, and I'll lift you up again!

MISS JULIE: What awful hold did you have over me? What drove me to you? The weak to the strong? The falling to the rising! Or maybe it was love? Love? This? You don't know what love is!

JEAN: Want to bet? Did you think I was a virgin?

MISS JULIE: You're coarse—vulgar! The things you say, the things you think!

JEAN: That's the way I was brought up. It's the way I am! Now don't get hysterical. And don't play the fine lady with me. We're eating off the same platter now. . . . That's better. Come over here and be a good girl and I'll treat you to something special. (*He opens the table drawer and takes out the wine bottle. He pours the wine into two used glasses.*)

MISS JULIE: Where did you get that wine?

JEAN: From the wine cellar.

MISS JULIE: My father's burgundy!

JEAN: Should be good enough for his son-in-law.

MISS JULIE: I was drinking beer and you—!

JEAN: Shows I have better taste than you.

MISS JULIE: Thief!

JEAN: You going to squeal on me?

MISS JULIE: Oh, God! Partner in crime with a petty house thief! I must have been drunk; I must have been walking in my sleep. Midsummer Night! Night of innocent games—

JEAN: Yes, very innocent!

MISS JULIE (*pacing up and down*): Is there anyone here on earth as miserable as I am?

JEAN: Why be miserable? Look at the conquest you've made! Think of poor Christine in there. Don't you think she's got any feelings?

MISS JULIE: I thought so a while ago; I don't now. A servant's a servant—

JEAN: And a whore's a whore!

MISS JULIE (*falls to her knees and clasps her hands together*): Oh, God in heaven, put an end to my worthless life! Lift me out of this awful filth I'm sinking in! Save me! Save me!

JEAN: I feel sorry for you, I have to admit it. When I was lying in the onion beds, looking up at you on the rose terrace, I—I'm telling you the truth now—I had the same dirty thoughts that all boys have.

MISS JULIE: And you said you wanted to die for me!

JEAN: In the oat bin? That was only a story.

MISS JULIE: A lie, you mean.

JEAN (*getting sleepy*): Practically. I think I read it in a paper about a chimney sweep who curled up in a wood-bin with some lilacs because they were going to arrest him for nonsupport of his child.

MISS JULIE: Now I see you as you really are.

JEAN: What did you expect me to do? It's always the fancy talk that gets the women.

MISS JULIE: You dog!

JEAN: You bitch!

MISS JULIE: Well, now you've seen the eagle's back—

JEAN: Wasn't exactly its back—!

MISS JULIE: I was going to be the window dressing for your hotel—!

JEAN: And I the hotel—!

MISS JULIE: Sitting at the desk, attracting your customers, padding your bills—!

JEAN: I could manage that myself—!

MISS JULIE: How can a human soul be so dirty and filthy?

JEAN: Then why don't you clean it up?

MISS JULIE: You lackey! You shoeshine boy! Stand up when I talk to you!

JEAN: You lackey lover! You bootblack's tramp! Shut your mouth and get out of here! Who do you think you are telling me I'm coarse? I've never seen anybody in my class behave as crudely as you did tonight. Have you ever seen any of the girls around here grab at a man like you did? Do you think any of the girls of my class would throw themselves at a man like that? I've never seen the like of it except in animals and prostitutes!

MISS JULIE (*crushed*): That's right! Hit me! Walk all over me! It's all I deserve. I'm rotten. But help me! Help me to get out of this—if there is any way out for me!

JEAN (*less harsh*): I'd be doing myself an injustice if I didn't admit that part of the credit for this seduction belongs to me. But do you think a person in my position would have dared to look twice at you if you hadn't asked for it? I'm still amazed—

MISS JULIE: And still proud.

JEAN: Why not? But I've got to confess the victory was a little too easy to give me any real thrill.

MISS JULIE: Go on, hit me again!

JEAN (*standing up*): No. . . . I'm sorry I said that. I never hit a person who's down, especially a woman. I can't deny that, in one way, it was good to find out that what I saw glittering up above was only fool's gold, to see that the eagle's back was as gray

as its belly, that the smooth cheek was just powder, and that there
could be dirt under the manicured nails, that the handkerchief
was soiled even though it smelled of perfume. But, in another
way, it hurts to find that everything I was striving for wasn't very
high above me after all, wasn't even real. It hurts me to see you
sink far lower than your own cook. Hurts, like seeing the last
flowers cut to pieces by the autumn rains and turned to muck.

MISS JULIE: You talk as if you already stood high above me.

JEAN: Well, don't I? Don't forget I could make you a countess
but you can never make me a count.

MISS JULIE: I have a father for a count. You can never have
that!

JEAN: True. But I might father my own counts—that is, if—

MISS JULIE: You're a thief! I'm not!

JEAN: There are worse things than being a thief. A lot worse.
And besides, when I take a position in a house, I consider myself
a member of the family—in a way, like a child in the house. It's
no crime for a child to steal a few ripe cherries when they're falling off the trees, is it? (*He begins to feel passionate again.*) Miss
Julie, you're a beautiful woman, much too good for the likes of
me. You got carried away by your emotions and now you want
to cover up your mistake by telling yourself that you love me.
You don't love me. Maybe you were attracted by my looks—in
which case your kind of love is no better than mine. But I could
never be satisfied to be just an animal for you, and I could never
make you love me.

MISS JULIE: How do you know that for sure?

JEAN: You mean there's a chance? I could love you, there's no
doubt about that. You're beautiful, you're refined—(*He goes up to
her and takes her hand.*)—educated, lovable when you want to be,
and once you set a man's heart on fire, I'll bet it burns forever.
(*He puts his arm around her waist.*) You're like hot wine with
strong spices. One of your kisses is enough to—

>   *He attempts to lead her out, but she rather reluctantly
>   breaks away from him.*

MISS JULIE: Let me go. You don't get me that way.

JEAN: Then how? Not by petting you and not with pretty words, not by planning for the future, not by saving you from humiliation! Then how, tell me how?

MISS JULIE: How? How? I don't know how! I don't know at all! —I hate you like I hate rats, but I can't get away from you.

JEAN: Then come away with me!

MISS JULIE (*pulling herself together*): Away? Yes, we'll go away! —But I'm so tired. Pour me a glass of wine, will you?

Jean pours the wine, Miss Julie looks at her watch.

Let's talk first. We still have a little time. (*She empties the glass of wine and holds it out for more*)

JEAN: Don't overdo it. You'll get drunk.

MISS JULIE: What difference does it make?

JEAN: What difference? It looks cheap. —What did you want to say to me?

MISS JULIE: We're going to run away together, right? But we'll talk first—that is, I'll talk. So far you've done all the talking. You've told me your life, now I'll tell you mine. That way we'll know each other through and through before we become . . . traveling companions.

JEAN: Wait a minute. Are you sure you won't regret this afterward—surrendering your secrets to me?

MISS JULIE: I thought you were my friend.

JEAN: I am—sometimes. Just don't count on it.

MISS JULIE: You don't mean that. Anyway, everybody knows my secrets. —My mother's parents were very ordinary people, just commoners. She was brought up, according to the theories of her time, to believe in equality, the independence of women, and all that. And she had a strong aversion to marriage. When my father proposed to her, she swore she would never become his wife but that she might possibly consent to become his mistress. So he told her he didn't want to see the woman he loved enjoy less respect than he did. But she said she didn't care what the world thought—and he, believing that he couldn't live without her, accepted her conditions. That did it. From then on he was cut off from his old circle of friends and left without anything to do in the house, which couldn't have kept him occupied anyway. Then I came into the world—against my mother's wishes, as far as I can make out. My mother decided to bring me up as a nature child. And on top of that I had to learn everything a boy learns, so I could be living proof that women were just as good as men. I had to wear boy's clothes, learn to handle horses—but not to milk the cows! Girls did that! I was made to groom the horses and harness them, and learn farming and go hunting—I even had to learn how to slaughter the animals. It was disgusting. Awful! And on the estate all the men were set to doing women's chores, and the women to doing men's work—with the result that the whole place fell to pieces, and we became the local laughing-stock. Finally, my father must have come out of his trance. He rebelled, and everything was changed according to his wishes. They got married—very quietly. Then my mother got sick. I don't know what kind of sickness it was, but she often had convulsions, and she would hide herself in the attic or in the garden, and sometimes she would stay out all night. Then there occurred that big fire you've heard about. The house, the stables, the cowsheds, all burned down—and under very peculiar circumstances that led one to suspect arson. You see, the accident occurred the day after the insurance expired, and the premiums on the new policy, which my father had sent in, were delayed through the messenger's carelessness, and didn't arrive in time. (*She refills her glass and drinks.*)

JEAN: You've had enough.

MISS JULIE: Who cares! —We were left without a penny to our name. We had to sleep in the carriages. My father didn't know where to turn for money to rebuild the house. Then Mother suggested to him that he might try to borrow money from an old friend of hers, who owned a brick factory not far from here. Father took out a loan, but there wasn't any interest charged, which surprised him. So the place was rebuilt. (*She drinks some more.*) Do you know who set fire to the place?

JEAN: Your honorable mother!

MISS JULIE: Do you know who the brick manufacturer was?

JEAN: Your mother's lover?

MISS JULIE: Do you know whose money it was?

JEAN: Let me think a minute. . . . No, I give up.

MISS JULIE: It was my mother's!

JEAN: The count's, you mean. Or was there a marriage settlement?

MISS JULIE: There wasn't a settlement. My mother had a little money of her own which she didn't want under my father's control, so she invested it with her – friend.

JEAN: Who pinched it!

MISS JULIE: Right! He kept it for himself. Well, my father found out what happened. But he couldn't go to court, couldn't pay his wife's lover, couldn't prove that it was his wife's money. That was how my mother got her revenge because he had taken control of the house. He was on the verge of shooting himself. There was even a rumor that he tried and failed. But somehow he took a new lease on life and he forced my mother to pay for her mistakes. Can you imagine what those five years were like for me? I loved my father, but I took my mother's side because I didn't know the whole story. She had taught me to hate all men – I'm sure you've heard how she hated men – and I swore to her that I'd never be slave to any man.

JEAN: You got engaged to the attorney, didn't you?

MISS JULIE: Only to make him my slave.

JEAN: I guess he didn't go for that, did he?

MISS JULIE: Oh, he wanted to well enough. I didn't give him the chance. I got bored with him.

JEAN: Yes, so I noticed – in the stable yard.

MISS JULIE: What did you notice?

JEAN: I saw how he—. [Still see it on your cheek.

MISS JULIE: What!

JEAN: The stripe on your cheek.]* He broke it off.

MISS JULIE: It's a lie! I broke it off! Did he tell you that? He's beneath contempt!

JEAN: Come on now, as bad as that? So you hate men, hm?

MISS JULIE: Yes, I do. . . . Most of the time. But sometimes, when I can't help myself—oh . . . (*She shudders in disgust.*)

JEAN: Then you hate me, too?

MISS JULIE: You have no idea how much! I'd like to see you killed like an animal—

JEAN: Like when you're caught having sex with an animal: you get two years at hard labor and the animal is killed. Right?

MISS JULIE: Right.

JEAN: But there's no one to catch us—and *no animal!*—So what are we going to do?

MISS JULIE: Go away from here.

JEAN: To torture ourselves to death?

MISS JULIE: No. To enjoy ourselves for a day or two, or a week, for as long as can—and then—to die—

JEAN: Die? That's stupid! I've got a better idea: start a hotel!

MISS JULIE (*continuing without hearing Jean*): —on the shores of Lake Como, where the sun is always shining, where the laurels bloom at Christmas, and the golden oranges glow on the trees.

JEAN: Lake Como is a stinking wet hole, and the only oranges I saw there were on the fruit stands. But it's a good tourist spot with a lot of villas and cottages that are rented out to lovers. Now there's a profitable business. You know why? They rent the villa for the whole season, but they leave after three weeks.

* The passage in brackets was deleted in Strindberg's manuscript, probably by Strindberg himself.

MISS JULIE (*naively*): Why after only three weeks?

JEAN: Because that's about as long as they can stand each other. Why else? But they still have to pay the rent. You see? Then you rent it out again to another couple, and so on. There's no shortage of love—even if it doesn't last very long.

MISS JULIE: Then you don't want to die with me?

JEAN: I don't want to die at all! I enjoy life too much. And moreover, I consider taking your own life a sin against the Providence that gave us life.

MISS JULIE: You believe in God? You?

JEAN: Yes, certainly I do! I go to church every other Sunday—. Honestly, I've had enough of this talk. I'm going to bed.

MISS JULIE: Really? You think you're going to get off that easy? Don't you know that a man owes something to the woman he's dishonored?

JEAN (*takes out his purse and throws a silver coin on the table*): There you are. I don't want to owe anybody anything.

MISS JULIE (*pretending not to notice*): Do you know what the law says—?

JEAN: Lucky for you the law says nothing about women who seduce men!

MISS JULIE (*as before*): What else can we do but go away from here, get married, and get divorced?

JEAN: Suppose I refuse to enter into this *mésalliance*?

MISS JULIE: *Mésalliance*?

JEAN: For me! I've got better ancestors than you. I don't have a female arsonist in my family.

MISS JULIE: You can't prove that.

JEAN: You can't prove the opposite—because we don't have any family records—except in the police files. But I've read the whole history of your family in that peerage book in the drawing room. Do you know who the founder of your family line was? A miller—who let his wife sleep with the king one night during the

Danish war. I don't have any ancestors like that. I don't have any ancestors at all! But I can become an ancestor myself.

MISS JULIE: This is what I get for baring my heart and soul to someone too low to understand, for sacrificing the honor of my family—

JEAN: Dishonor! —I warned you, remember? Drinking makes one talk, and talking's bad.

MISS JULIE: Oh, how sorry I am! . . . If only it had never happened! . . . If only you at least loved me!

JEAN: For the last time—what do you want me to do? Cry? Jump over your whip? Kiss you? Lure you to Lake Como for three weeks and then—? What am I supposed to do? What do you want? I've had more than I can take. This is what I get for involving myself with women. . . . Miss Julie, I can see that you're unhappy; I know that you're suffering; but I simply cannot understand you. My people don't behave like this. We don't hate each other. We make love for the fun of it, when we can get any time off from our work. But we don't have time for it all day and all night like you do. If you ask me, you're sick, Miss Julie. Your mother's mind was affected, you know. There are whole counties affected with pietism. That was your mother's trouble—pietism. It's spreading like the plague.

MISS JULIE: You can be understanding, Jean. You're talking to me like a human being now.

JEAN: Well, be human yourself. You spit on me, but you don't let me wipe it off—on you.

MISS JULIE: Help me, Jean. Help me. Tell me what I should do, that's all—which way to go.

JEAN: For Christ's sake, if only I knew myself!

MISS JULIE: I've been crazy—I've been out of my mind—but does that mean there's no way out for me?

JEAN: Stay here as if nothing had happened. Nobody knows anything.

MISS JULIE: Impossible! Everybody who works here knows. Christine knows.

JEAN: They don't know a thing. Anyhow they'd never believe it.

MISS JULIE (*slowly, significantly*): But . . . it might happen again.

JEAN: That's true!

MISS JULIE: And one time there might be . . . consequences.

JEAN (*stunned*): Consequences!! What on earth have I been thinking of! You're right. There's only one thing to do: get away from here! Immediately! I can't go with you—that would give the whole game away. You'll have to go by yourself. Somewhere—I don't care where!

MISS JULIE: By myself? Where? —Oh, no, Jean, I can't. I can't!

JEAN: You've got to! Before the count comes back. You know as well as I do what will happen if you stay here. After one mistake, you figure you might as well go on—the damage is already done. Then you get more and more careless until—finally you're exposed. I tell you, you've got to get out of the country. Afterward you can write to the count and tell him everything—leaving me out, of course. He'd never figure it was me. He wouldn't even let himself think it was me.

MISS JULIE: I'll go—if you'll come with me!

JEAN: Lady, are you out of your mind? "Miss Julie elopes with her footman." The day after tomorrow it would be in all the papers. The count would never live it down.

MISS JULIE: I can't go away. I can't stay. Help me. I'm so tired, so awfully tired. . . . Tell me what to do. Order me. Start me going. I can't think anymore, can't move anymore . . .

JEAN: Now do you realize how weak you all are? What gives you the right to go strutting around with your noses in the air as if you owned the world? All right, I'll give you your orders. Go up and get dressed. Get some traveling money. And come back down here.

MISS JULIE (*almost in a whisper*): Come up with me!

JEAN: To your room? . . . You're going crazy again! (*He hesitates a moment.*) No! No! Go! Right now! (*He takes her hand and leads her out.*)

MISS JULIE (*as she is leaving*): Don't be so harsh, Jean.

JEAN: Orders always sound harsh. You've never had to take them.

> *Jean, left alone, heaves a sigh of relief and sits down at the table. He takes out a notebook and a pencil and begins to calculate, counting aloud now and then. The pantomime continues until Christine enters, dressed for church, and carrying Jean's white tie and shirtfront in her hand.*

CHRISTINE: Lord in Heaven, what a mess! What on earth have you been doing?

JEAN: It was Miss Julie. She dragged the whole crowd in here. You must have been sleeping awfully sound if you didn't hear anything.

CHRISTINE: I slept like a log.

JEAN: You already dressed for church?

CHRISTINE: Yes, indeed. Don't you remember you promised to go to communion with me today?

JEAN: Oh, yes. Of course, I remember. I see you've brought my things. All right. Come on, put it on me. (*He sits down, and Christine starts to put the white tie and shirtfront on him. Pause.*)

JEAN (*yawning*): What's the lesson for today?

CHRISTINE: The beheading of John the Baptist, what else? It's Midsummer. It's his feast day.

JEAN: My God, that will go on forever. —Hey, you're choking me! . . . Oh, I'm so sleepy, so sleepy.

CHRISTINE: What were you doing up all night? You look green in the face.

JEAN: I've been sitting here talking with Miss Julie.

CHRISTINE: That girl! She doesn't know how to behave herself!

Pause.

JEAN: Tell me something, Christine . . .

CHRISTINE: Well, what?

JEAN: Isn't it strange when you think about it? Her, I mean.

CHRISTINE: What's so strange?

JEAN: Everything!

> *Pause. Christine looks at the half-empty glasses on the table.*

CHRISTINE: Have you been drinking with her?

JEAN: Yes!

CHRISTINE: Shame on you! —Look me in the eyes! You haven't . . . ?

JEAN: Yes!

CHRISTINE: Is it possible? Is it really possible?

JEAN (*thinking about it*): Yes. It is.

CHRISTINE: Oh, how disgusting! I could never have believed anything like this would happen! No. No. This is too much!

JEAN: Don't tell me you're jealous of her?

CHRISTINE: No, not of her. If it had been Clara—or Sophie—I would have scratched your eyes out! But her—? That's different. I don't know why. . . . But it's still disgusting!

JEAN: You're not mad at her?

CHRISTINE: No. Mad at you. You were mean and cruel to do a thing like that, very mean. The poor girl! . . . Let me tell you, I'm not going to stay in this house a moment longer, not when I can't have any respect for my employers.

JEAN: Why do you want to respect them?

CHRISTINE: Don't try to be smart. You don't want to work for people who behave like pigs, do you? Well, do you? If you ask me, you'd be lowering yourself by doing that.

JEAN: Oh, I don't know. I think it's rather comforting to find out that they're not one damn bit better than we are.

CHRISTINE: Well, I don't. If they're not any better, there's no point in us trying to be like them. — And think of the count. Think of all the sorrows he's been through in his time. My God! I won't stay in this house any longer. . . . Imagine! You, of all people! If it had been the attorney fellow; if it had been somebody respectable —

JEAN: Now just a minute —!

CHRISTINE: Oh, you're all right in your own way. But there's a big difference between one class and another. You can't deny that. — No, this is something I can never get over. She was so proud, and so sarcastic about men, you'd never believe she'd go and throw herself at one. And at someone like you! And she was going to have Diana shot because the poor thing ran after the gatekeeper's mongrel! — Well, I tell you, I've had enough! I'm not going to stay here any longer. When my term's up, I'm leaving.

JEAN: Then what'll you do?

CHRISTINE: Well, since you brought it up, it's about time that you got yourself a decent place, if we're going to get married.

JEAN: Why should I go looking for another place? I could never get a job like this if I'm married.

CHRISTINE: Well, I know that! But you could get a job as a porter, or maybe try to get a government job as a caretaker somewhere. A square deal and a square meal, that's what you get from the government — and a pension for the wife and children.

JEAN (*wryly*): Fine, fine! But I'm not the kind of guy who thinks about dying for his wife and children this early in the game. Let me tell you, I've got slightly bigger plans than that.

CHRISTINE: Plans! Ha! What about your obligations? You'd better start giving them a little thought!

JEAN: Don't start nagging me about obligations! I know what I have to do without you telling me. (*He hears a sound upstairs.*)

Anyhow, we'll have plenty of chance to talk about this later. You just go and get yourself ready, and we'll be off to church.

CHRISTINE: Who is that walking around up there?

JEAN: I don't know. Clara, I suppose. Who else?

CHRISTINE (*starting to leave*): It can't be the count, can it? Could he have come back without anybody hearing him?

JEAN (*frightened*): The count? No, it can't be. He would have rung.

CHRISTINE (*leaving*): God help us! I've never heard the like of this.

> *The sun has now risen and strikes the tops of the trees in the park. As the scene progresses, the light shifts gradually until it is shining very obliquely through the windows. Jean goes to the door and signals. Miss Julie enters, dressed for travel, and carrying a small birdcage, covered with a towel. She sets the cage down on a chair.*

MISS JULIE: I'm ready now.

JEAN: Shh! Christine's awake.

MISS JULIE (*extremely tense and nervous during the following*): Did she suspect anything?

JEAN: She doesn't know a thing. —My God, what happened to you?

MISS JULIE: What do you mean? Do I look so strange?

JEAN: You're white as a ghost, and you've—excuse me—you've got dirt on your face.

MISS JULIE: Let me wash it off. (*She goes over to the washbasin and washes her face and hands.*) There! Do you have a towel? . . . Oh, look, the sun's coming up!

JEAN: That breaks the magic spell!

MISS JULIE: Yes, we were spellbound last night, weren't we? Midsummer madness . . . Jean, listen to me! Come with me. I've got the money!

JEAN (*suspiciously*): Enough?

MISS JULIE: Enough for a start. Come with me, Jean. I can't travel alone today. Midsummer Day on a stifling hot train, packed in with crowds of people, all staring at me—stopping at every station when I want to be flying. I can't, Jean, I can't! . . . And everything will remind me of the past. Midsummer Day when I was a child and the church was decorated with leaves—birch leaves and lilacs . . . the table spread for dinner with friends and relatives . . . and after dinner, dancing in the park, with flowers and games. Oh, no matter how far you travel, the memories tag right along in the baggage car . . . and the regrets and the remorse.

JEAN: All right, I'll go with you! But it's got to be now—before it's too late! This very instant!

MISS JULIE: Hurry and get dressed! (*She picks up the birdcage.*)

JEAN: No baggage! It would give us away.

MISS JULIE: Nothing. Only what we can take to our seats.

JEAN (*as he gets his hat*): What in the devil have you got there? What is that?

MISS JULIE: It's only my canary. I can't leave it behind.

JEAN: A canary! My God, do you expect us to carry a birdcage around with us? You're crazy. Put that cage down!

MISS JULIE: It's the only thing I'm taking with me from my home—the only living thing who loves me since Diana was unfaithful to me! Don't be cruel, Jean. Let me take it with me.

JEAN: I told you to put that cage down! —And don't talk so loud. Christine can hear us.

MISS JULIE: No, I won't leave it with a stranger. I won't. I'd rather have you kill it.

JEAN: Give it here, the little pest. I'll wring its neck.

MISS JULIE: Oh, don't hurt it. Don't—. No, I can't do it!

JEAN: Don't worry, I can. Give it here.

Miss Julie takes the bird out of the cage and kisses it.

MISS JULIE: Oh, my little Serena, must you die and leave your mistress?

JEAN: You don't have to make a scene of it. It's a question of your whole life and future. You're wasting time!

> *Jean grabs the canary from her, carries it to the chopping block, and picks up a meat cleaver. Miss Julie turns away.*

You should have learned how to kill chickens instead of shooting revolvers—(*He brings the cleaver down.*)—then a drop of blood wouldn't make you faint.

MISS JULIE (*screaming*): Kill me too! Kill me! You can kill an innocent creature without turning a hair—then kill me. Oh, how I hate you! I loathe you! There's blood between us. I curse the moment I first laid eyes on you! I curse the moment I was conceived in my mother's womb.

JEAN: What good does your cursing do? Let's get out of here!

MISS JULIE (*approaches the chopping block, drawn to it against her will*): No, I don't want to go yet. I can't. —I have to see. —Shh! (*She listens but keeps her eyes fastened on the chopping block and cleaver.*) You don't think I can stand the sight of blood, do you? You think I'm so weak, don't you? Oh, how I'd love to see your blood, your brains on that chopping block. I'd love to see the whole of your sex swimming in a sea of blood just like that. I could drink blood out of your skull. Use your chest as a foot bath, dip my toes in your guts! I could eat your heart roasted whole! —You think I'm weak! You think I loved you because my womb hungered for your semen. You think I want to carry your brood under my heart and feed it with my blood? Bear your child and take your name? —Come to think of it, what is your name? I've never even heard your last name. I'll bet you don't have one. I'd be Mrs. Doorman or Madame Garbageman. You dog with *my* name on your collar—you lackey with *my* initials on your buttons! Do you think I'm going to share you with my cook and fight

over you with my maid?! Ohh! —You think I'm a coward who's
going to run away! No, I'm going to stay—come hell or high
water. My father will come home—find his desk broken into—his
money gone. He'll ring—on that bell—two rings for the valet.
And then he'll send for the sheriff—and I'll tell him everything.
Everything! Oh, what a relief it'll be to have it all over . . . over
and done with . . . if only it will be over. . . . He'll have a
stroke and die . . . and there'll be an end to all of us. There'll
be peace . . . and quiet . . . forever. . . . The coat of arms
will be broken on his coffin; the count's line will be extinct—
while the valet's breed will continue in an orphanage, win
triumphs in the gutter, and end in jail!

> *Christine enters, dressed for church and with a hymn-*
> *book in her hand. Miss Julie rushes over to her and*
> *throws herself into her arms as if seeking protection.*

MISS JULIE: Help me, Christine! Protect me against this man!

CHRISTINE (*cold and unmoved*): This is a fine way to behave
on a holy day! (*She sees the chopping block.*) Just look at the mess
you've made there! How do you explain that? And what's all this
shouting and screaming about?

MISS JULIE: Christine, you're a woman, you're my friend! I
warn you, watch out for this—this monster!

JEAN (*feeling awkward*): If you ladies are going to talk, you won't
want me around. I think I'll go and shave. (*He slips out to the*
right.)

MISS JULIE: You've got to understand, Christine! You've got
to listen to me!

CHRISTINE: No, I don't. I don't understand this kind of she-
nanigans at all. Where do you think you're going dressed like
that? And Jean with his hat on? —Well? —Well?

MISS JULIE: Listen to me, Christine! If you'll just listen to me,
I'll tell you everything.

CHRISTINE: I don't want to know anything.

MISS JULIE: You've got to listen to me—!

CHRISTINE: What about? About your stupid behavior with Jean? I tell you that doesn't bother me at all, because it's none of my business. But if you have any silly idea about talking him into skipping out with you, I'll soon put a stop to that.

MISS JULIE (*extremely tense*): Christine, please don't get upset. Listen to me. I can't stay here, and Jean can't stay here. So you see, we have to go away.

CHRISTINE: Hm, hm, hm.

MISS JULIE (*suddenly brightening up*): Wait! I've got an idea! Why couldn't all three of us go away together?—out of the country—to Switzerland—and start a hotel? I've got the money, you see. Jean and I would be responsible for the whole affair—and Christine, you could run the kitchen, I thought. Doesn't that sound wonderful! Say you'll come, Christine, then everything will be settled. Say you will! Please! (*She throws her arms around Christine and pats her.*)

CHRISTINE (*remaining aloof and unmoved*): Hm. Hm.

MISS JULIE (*presto tempo*): You've never been traveling, Christine. You have to get out and see the world. You can't imagine how wonderful it is to travel by train—constantly new faces, new countries. We'll go to Hamburg, and stop over to look at the zoo—it's famous, has everything—you'll love that. And we'll go to the theater and the opera. And then when we get to Munich, we'll go to the museums, Christine. They have Rubenses and Raphaels there—those great painters, you know. Of course you've heard about Munich where King Ludwig lived—you know, the king who went mad. And then we can go and see his castles—they're just like the ones you read about in fairy tales. And from there it's just a short trip to Switzerland—with the Alps. Think of the Alps, Christine, covered with snow in the middle of summer. And oranges grow there, and laurel trees that are green the whole year round—

> *Jean can be seen in the wings at the right, sharpening his straight razor on a strop held between his teeth and his left hand. He listens to Miss Julie with a satisfied expression on his face, now and then nodding approvingly. Miss Julie continues tempo prestissimo.*

—and that's where we'll get a hotel. I'll sit at the desk while Jean stands at the door and receives the guests, goes out shopping, writes the letters. What a life that will be! The train whistle blowing, then the bus arriving, then a bell ringing upstairs, then the bell in the restaurant rings—and I'll be making out the bills—and I know just how much to salt them—you can't imagine how timid tourists are when you shove a bill in their face! —And you, Christine, you'll run the whole kitchen—there'll be not standing at the stove for you—of course not. If you're going to talk to the people, you'll have to dress. And with your looks—I'm not trying to flatter you, Christine—you'll run off with some man one fine day—a rich Englishman, that's who it'll be, they're so easy to—(*Slowing down*)—to catch. —Then we'll all be rich. —We'll build a villa on Lake Como. —Maybe it does rain there sometimes, but—(*More and more lifelessly.*)—the sun has to shine sometimes, too—even if it looks cloudy. —And—then . . . or else we can always travel some more—and come back . . . (*Pause.*)—here . . . or somewhere else . . .

CHRISTINE: Do you really believe a word of that yourself, Miss Julie?

MISS JULIE (*completely beaten*): Do I believe a word of it myself?

CHRISTINE: Do you?

MISS JULIE (*exhausted*): I don't know. I don't believe anything anymore. (*She sinks down on the bench and lays her head between her arms on the table.*) Nothing. Nothing at all.

CHRISTINE (*turns to the right and faces Jean*): So! You were planning to run away, were you?

JEAN (*taken aback, lays his razor down on the table*): We weren't exactly going to run away! Don't exaggerate. You heard Miss Julie's plans. Even if she's tired now after being up all night, her plans are perfectly practical.

CHRISTINE: Well, just listen to you! Did you really think you could get me to cook for that little—!

JEAN (*sharply*): You keep a respectful tongue in your mouth when you talk to your mistress! Understand?

CHRISTINE: Mistress!

JEAN: Yes, mistress!

CHRISTINE: Well of all the—! I don't have to listen—

JEAN: Yes, you do! You need to listen more and blabber less. Miss Julie is your mistress. Don't you forget that! And if you're going to despise her for what she did, you ought to despise yourself for the same reason.

CHRISTINE: I've always held myself high enough to—

JEAN: High enough to make you look down on others!

CHRISTINE: —enough to keep from lowering myself beneath my station. Don't you dare say that the count's cook has ever had anything to do with the stable groom or the swineherd. Don't you dare!

JEAN: Yes, you got yourself a decent man. Lucky you!

CHRISTINE: What kind of a decent man is it who sells the oats from the count's stables?

JEAN: Listen to who's talking! You get the gravy on the groceries and take bribes from the butcher!

CHRISTINE: How dare you say a thing like that!

JEAN: And you say you can't respect your employers. You of all people! You!

CHRISTINE: Are you going to church or aren't you? You need a good sermon after your great exploits.

JEAN: No, I'm not going to church! Go yourself. Go tell God how bad you are.

CHRISTINE: Yes, I'll do just that. And I'll come back with enough forgiveness for your sins, too. Our Redeemer suffered and died on the cross for all our sins, and if we come to Him in faith and with a penitent heart, He will take all our sins upon Himself.

JEAN: Rake-offs included?

MISS JULIE: Do you really believe that, Christine?

CHRISTINE: With all my heart, as sure as I'm standing here. It was the faith I was born into, and I've held on to it since I was a little girl, Miss Julie. Where sin aboundeth, there grace aboundeth also.

MISS JULIE: If I had your faith, Christine, if only—

CHRISTINE: But you see, that's something you can't have without God's special grace. And it is not granted to everyone to receive it.

MISS JULIE: Then who receives it?

CHRISTINE: That's the secret of the workings of grace, Miss Julie, and God is no respecter of persons. With Him the last shall be first—

MISS JULIE: In that case, he does have respect for the last, doesn't he?

CHRISTINE (*continuing*): —and it is easier for a camel to go through the eye of a needle than for a rich man to enter the kingdom of God. That's how things are, Miss Julie. I'm going to leave now—alone. And on my way out I'm going to tell the stable boy not to let any horses out, in case anyone has any ideas about leaving before the count comes home. Goodbye. (*She leaves*)

JEAN: She's a devil in skirts! —All because of a canary!

MISS JULIE (*listlessly*): Never mind the canary. . . . Do you see any way out of this, any end to it?

JEAN (*after thinking for a moment*): No.

MISS JULIE: What would you do if you were in my place?

JEAN: In your place? Let me think. . . . An aristocrat, a woman, and—fallen. . . . I don't know. —Or maybe I do.

MISS JULIE (*picks up the razor and makes a gesture with it*): Like this?

JEAN: Yes. But I wouldn't do it, you understand. That's the difference between us.

MISS JULIE: Because you're a man and I'm a woman? What difference does that make?

JEAN: Just the difference that there is—between a man and a woman.

MISS JULIE (*holding the razor in her hand*): I want to! But I can't do it. My father couldn't do it either, that time when he should have.

JEAN: No, he was right not to. He had to get his revenge first.

MISS JULIE: And now my mother is getting her revenge again through me.

JEAN: Didn't you ever love your father, Miss Julie?

MISS JULIE: Yes, enormously. But I must have hated him too. I must have hated him without knowing it. It was he who brought me up to despise my own sex, to be half woman and half man. Who's to blame for what has happened? My father, my mother, myself? Myself? I don't have a self that's my own. I don't have a single thought I didn't get from my father, not an emotion I didn't get from my mother. And that last idea—about all people being equal—I got that from him, my fiancé. That's why I say he's beneath contempt. How can it be my own fault? Put the blame on Jesus, like Christine does? I'm too proud to do that—and too intelligent, thanks to what my father taught me. . . . A rich man can't get into heaven? That's a lie. But at least Christine, who's got money in the savings bank, won't get in. . . . Who's to blame? What difference does it make who's to blame? I'm still the one who has to bear the guilt, suffer the consequences—

JEAN: Yes, but—

> The bell rings sharply twice. Miss Julie jumps up. Jean changes his coat.

JEAN: The count's back! What if Christine—(*He goes to the speaking tube, taps on it, and listens.*)

MISS JULIE: Has he looked in his desk yet?

JEAN: This is Jean, sir! (*Listens. The audience cannot hear what the count says.*) Yes, sir! (*Listens.*) Yes, sir! Yes, as soon as I can.

(*Listens.*) Yes, at once, sir! (*Listens.*) Very good, sir! In half an hour.

MISS JULIE (*trembling with anxiety*): What did he say? For God's sake, what did he say?

JEAN: He ordered his boots and his coffee in half an hour.

MISS JULIE: Half an hour then! . . . Oh, I'm so tired. I can't bring myself to do anything. Can't repent, can't run away, can't stay, can't live . . . can't die. Help me, Jean. Command me, and I'll obey like a dog. Do me this last favor. Save my honor, save his name. You know what I ought to do but can't force myself to do. Let me use your willpower. You command me and I'll obey.

JEAN: I don't know—. I can't either, not now. I don't know why. It's as if this coat made me—I can't give you orders in this. And now, after the count has spoken to me, I—I can't really explain it—but—I've got the backbone of a damned lackey! If the count came down here now and ordered me to cut my throat, I'd do it on the spot.

MISS JULIE: Then pretend you're him. Pretend I'm you. You were such a good actor just a while ago, when you were kneeling before me. You were the aristocrat then. Or else—have you been to the theater and seen a hypnotist?

> *Jean nods.*

He says to his subject, "Take this broom!" and he takes it. He says, "Now sweep!" and he sweeps.

JEAN: The person has to be asleep!

MISS JULIE (*ecstatic, transported*): I'm already asleep. The whole room has turned to smoke. You seem like an iron stove, a stove that looks like a man in black with a high hat. Your eyes are glowing like fading coals in a dying fire. Your face is a white smudge, like ashes.

> *The sun is now shining in on the floor and falls on Jean.*

It's so good and warm—(*She rubs her hands together as if warming them at a fire.*)—and so bright—and so peaceful.

JEAN (*takes the razor and puts it in her hand*): There's the broom. Go now, when the sun is up—out into the barn—and—(*He whispers in her ear.*)

MISS JULIE (*waking up*): Thanks! I'm going to get my rest. But tell me one thing. Tell me that the first can also receive the gift of grace. Tell me that, even if you don't believe it.

JEAN: The first? I can't tell you that. —Wait a moment, Miss Julie. I know what I can tell you. You're no longer one of the first. You're one of—the last.

MISS JULIE: That's true! I'm one of the last. I am the very last! —Oh! —Now I can't go! Tell me just once more, tell me to go!

JEAN: Now I can't either. I can't!

MISS JULIE: And the first shall be the last . . .

JEAN: Don't think—don't think! You're taking all my strength from me. You're making me a coward. . . . What?! I thought I saw the bell move. No. . . . Let me stuff some paper in it. —Afraid of a bell! But it isn't just a bell. There's somebody behind it. A hand that makes it move. And there's something that makes the hand move. —Stop your ears, that's it, stop your ears! But it only rings louder. Rings louder and louder until you answer it. And then it's too late. Then the sheriff comes—and then—(*There are two sharp rings on the bell. Jean gives a start, then straightens himself up.*) It's horrible! But there's no other way for it to end. —Go!

Miss Julie walks resolutely out through the door.

Introduction
to
Creditors

There are indications that *Miss Julie* first took shape in Strindberg's mind as a three-act drama, like *The Father*. But he probably soon realized that he could enhance the effectiveness of his naturalistic, Darwinian tragedy if he imitated the form of ancient Greek drama. All the plays of the Greek tragedians conformed to the same pattern: no more than three actors, a playing time of ninety minutes, and the use of music, of song and dance. The element of intrigue was kept to a minimum, with the stage action centering on one crucial event. By adhering to this formula, which had withstood the test of time, Strindberg was able to fashion a drama that was a mixture of the very old and the very new, a drama that compressed into a ninety-minute span the whole course of sexual love, from the initial sexual attraction, through the game-playing, the sexual teasing, the adopting of roles, through the sex act itself, and on to the falling out of love, the sexual disgust of the woman, and her death—the whole process shown step by step, with every step explained and motivated. No other play in the history of drama had ever done that.

At this time in his career, Strindberg was obsessed and fascinated by the power of drama to concentrate action and ideas. He wanted to surpass the Greeks in this respect. He explained to Georg Brandes that

> in every play there is one real scene. That's the one I want. Why should I bother with the left-overs and give six or eight actors the trouble learning that stuff?
>
> In France I always ordered five mutton chops, to the astonishment of the autochthons. A mutton chop has 1/2 pound of bone and 2 inches of fat. Within was a ball—*la noix*—the nut that I ate. "Give me the nut"—that's what I tell playwrights.
>
> (Letter of 29 November 1888.)

Creditors, written immediately after *Miss Julie*, carries the process of concentration a step further and relies even more on the power of suggestion. In it, Strindberg eliminated the dance that provided a respite in *Miss Julie* and examined the lives and psychological constitutions of three people, not just two, in the same ninety-minute span of time. The result, he said, was "better than *Miss Julie*, with three persons, one table, two chairs, and no sunrise." (Letter of 21 August 1888.)

The most difficult of the three roles is Adolph's. If he is made too weak and pathetic, there will be no tension in his scenes with Gustav. Like Miss Julie, he is, in Strindberg's eyes, a neurotic and unhealthy type. Although he surely put a great deal of himself into the character, he also drew the type from the medical books and psychological studies that he read voraciously. In Henry Maudsley's standard text, *The Pathology of Mind* (London, 1879), there are descriptions of cases similar to Adolph's, people who have convulsions, an unsteady walk, and great artistic talent. Whereas Julie was sexually abnormal, partly because of her upbringing and education, Adolph suffers from what Maudsley refers to as a "morbid hereditary taint." Sexual excess has also taken its toll on Adolph and made him a nervous wreck, and in this weakened condition he quickly falls under the spell of the strong-willed, purposeful creditor Gustav, who has come to claim restitution for his lost honor.

In *Miss Julie*, the heroine lets herself succumb to the stronger will of Jean. She goes to her death in a hypnotic trance. The death of Adoph in *Creditors* is the result of a psychic shock administered by Gustav, who has made the hysterical and epileptic Adolph subservient to his will through the power of suggestion. At the time the play was written, the most hotly debated question in psychology concerned the part that suggestion and hypnotism played in patients suffering from hysteria. In the 1880s, nearly 800 books and articles dealing with hypnosis were published. The most eminent investigator of hysteria, Dr. Charcot in Paris, had demonstrated to his own satisfaction that hypnosis was a form of hysterical or neurotic behavior that could be divided into three phases: catalepsy, lethargy, somnambulism. In Nancy, Dr. Bernheim challenged this idea, arguing that the three phases were induced in the patients by the doctors. The patients went through the three phases because they knew subconsciously what was expected of them. Furthermore, Dr. Bernheim amassed a great deal of evidence showing that suggestibility operated not only on those who were under hypnosis but often also on those who were wide awake. Far from being a purely pathological symptom, suggestibility was a phenomenon of everyday life. "The study of suggestibility," wrote Bernheim in his book *De la suggestion* (1888), "opens new horizons in the fields of medicine, psychology, and sociology. The impoverished human imagination is open to all sorts of impressions, good and bad, salutary and pernicious."

As the author of *The Father*, in which suggestibility plays an important role, Strindberg was entranced by these new horizons, and he broadened them by arguing that suggestibiliy was continually at work in every sphere of life. "All political, religious, and literary conflicts appear to me," he wrote, "as deriving from the struggles of individuals and parties to transmit suggestions, that is, to form opinions, which is nothing more than the struggle for power, at present a battle of brains, since the battle of brawn has gone out of style." ("The Battle of Brains," 1888.)

Gustav, in *Creditors*, is able to undo Adolph simply through the power of suggestion. Tekla is, however, not so suggestible, and Gustav must use cunning and deceit to avenge himself on her.

Although the manner of Adolph's death may seem absurd to modern readers, it, like everything else in the play, was grounded in the scientific and medical knowledge of the time. Hysteria and epilepsy were thought to be basically similar illnesses, and some doctors described intense sexual orgasm as being a genuine epileptiform seizure. Even the extravagant idea mentioned in the play that a child born to a woman who has taken a second husband or lover would quite likely resemble her first sexual partner was accepted by learned men. It was expounded by the eminent historian Jules Michelet in his widely read moral tract, *l'Amour*, and the factually minded Emile Zola made it central to the plot of his novel *Madeleine Férat*.

Like *Miss Julie*, *Creditors* is a naturalistic play, but its tone is different, so different that Strindberg called it a tragicomedy. In Paris there had sprung up a type of play known as *comédie rosse*, brutal, rough, cynical, and often sexually frank—not unlike the *film noir* of more recent times. Still hopeful that Paris would prove more hospitable than Stockholm to his examinations of the psychology of sex, Strindberg meant *Creditors* to be his contribution to the new genre.

In giving advice on how the play should be performed, Strindberg suggested (in a letter to his second wife, September 1896) that it should be acted in the manner of French boulevard comedy: delicately, softly, elegantly; that the inner life be brought to light; that Tekla be portrayed as acting out of her unconscious, not as a fury destroying her man but as a bewitching coquette who destroys without knowing what she is doing; that Gustav carry out his assassination of Adolph with a tender hand, acting out of a complex of intentions, calculations, impulses, and chance; and that above all a sense of Greek fate should hover over the action, so that the poor human creatures play their parts as puppets, criminal in their deeds but still guiltless. He also gave some special advice to an actor about to undertake the role of Gustav, telling him to portray Gustav as "playful and good-natured, which he as the superior person can afford to be. He plays with Adolph as cat with mouse. Never gets angry, never moralizes, never preaches." (Letter of 3 March 1889.) This is perfectly in keeping with Strindberg's conception of Gustav as a Darwinian evolutionist and Nietzschean superman, for whom morality is an invention of the ruling order and emotions merely instincts that must be subordinated to intellect.

Creditors

(Fordringsägare)

A Tragicomedy

CHARACTERS

TEKLA, a novelist
ADOLPH, her husband, a painter
GUSTAV, her first husband, a teacher at a university, traveling
  under an alias

Non-speaking parts:
TWO LADIES
WAITER

The parlor or common room in a small hotel at a seaside resort. At the rear a door opens onto a veranda with a view of the land and water. Just right of center, a table with newspapers on it. A chair to the left of the table, a sofa to the right. At right a door leads to another room.

Adolph and Gustav are at the table, right. Adolph is sculpting a wax figure on a small stand. Propped up near him are his crutches.

ADOLPH: —and for all this I have you to thank.

GUSTAV (*puffing on a cigar*): Nonsense.

ADOLPH: No, it's true. During those first few days when my wife was away, I lay on a sofa, helpless, longing for her. I couldn't move. It was as if she had taken my crutches with her. All I could do was sleep. But after a few days I woke up, pulled myself together. My fever-maddened head cooled off. Old projects, ideas I'd nearly forgotten, popped back into my head. I felt like working, felt the itch to create again. Once again I had vision. Could see the shapes hidden in things. And then you showed up.

GUSTAV: Yes, you were in rotten shape—hobbling on your crutches—no denying that. But that doesn't mean it was my presence that brought you back to health. You needed a rest, obviously. In fact, what you really needed was some masculine company.

ADOLPH: I think you've hit it. You're always right, you know. I had men friends before, of course; but when I got married, they seemed superfluous. I had my dearly beloved; and she was all I needed. Oh, I hung around with other people, got to know a lot of them. But my wife was jealous of them. Wanted me all to herself. Worse than that, she wanted my friends, too—all to herself. Which left me all alone and feeling jealous.

GUSTAV: Well, Adolph, face the fact: you have a jealous constitution.

ADOLPH: I was afraid of losing her and I tried to circumvent it. What normal man wouldn't do the same? I never feared she was being unfaithful to me, you understand—

GUSTAV: No, the doting husband never does.

ADOLPH: No. Remarkable, isn't it? What I really feared was that her friends would influence her, her mind, her tastes; and in that way indirectly exercise a power over me. That's what I couldn't stand.

GUSTAV: Simply put: you and your wife had a difference of opinion.

ADOLPH: Maybe. I've told you so much already, you might as well hear the rest. . . . My wife likes to be independent. —What are you smiling at?

GUSTAV: Don't mind me. She "likes to be independent" . . .

ADOLPH: Yes, so independent that she wouldn't accept anything I had to offer.

GUSTAV: Only what others had to offer!

ADOLPH (*mulling that over*): Y-e-s. . . . How to explain it? She abhorred my ideas not because they were so screwy but because they were mine. I mean, she would grab one of my old ideas and push it as one of hers. Had to be hers, see? Even if she got it from one of my friends who had got it from me. She got a kick out of that. She got a kick out of everything, except what came from me.

GUSTAV: I gather from this that you aren't too happy.

ADOLPH: I wouldn't say that. . . . No, I'm happy. I married the woman I loved, and I've never wanted anyone else.

GUSTAV: Never wanted to be a free man?

ADOLPH: No, I can't say I have. Of course I've sometimes imagined how peaceful things would be if I were single again. But whenever she left me, I felt how much I needed her, like I need my arms, legs. I know it's strange, but sometimes I think of her not as somebody else but as a part of me. She's my heart and guts. In her is my will to live and my lust for life. It's as if I had deposited in her all my gray matter, what the anatomy books call the cerebral cortex.

GUSTAV: That may be pretty close to the truth, when all is said and done.

ADOLPH: No, that doesn't make any sense. After all, she's an independent person with lots of ideas of her own. And when I met her, I was nothing—a painter in diapers—and she brought me up, educated me.

GUSTAV: However, you subsequently developed her mind, didn't you, and brought her up?

ADOLPH: No, she just stopped growing, and I shot up past her.

GUSTAV: Yes, it's a remarkable fact that she never wrote anything better than her first book. Of course, that time she had a good subject. Rumor has it that she put her first husband into that book. Did you ever know him? An absolute idiot, from what I hear.

ADOLPH: I never knew him. He had left Tekla six months before I met her. But it did sound like he was a horse's ass. That is, from Tekla's description of him. (*Pause.*) And her description was right on the mark, you can be sure of that.

GUSTAV: Oh, I am, I am. . . . Odd. What possible reason could she have had for marrying him, I wonder?

ADOLPH: A good reason: she didn't know what he was like. You never get to know each other until afterward.

GUSTAV: For which reason one shouldn't get married until—afterward. He must have been a bully, that's obvious.

ADOLPH: Why is that obvious?

GUSTAV: All husbands are. (*Feeling his way.*) You're no exception, you know.

ADOLPH: Me?! I let my wife come and go as she pleases.

GUSTAV: That's not saying much. After all, you can't keep her under lock and key, now can you? —Does it bother you if she stays out all night, runs around with other men?

ADOLPH: Of course it does.

GUSTAV: See what I mean? (*Suddenly changing his tone.*) Frankly speaking, it only makes you look ridiculous.

ADOLPH: Ridiculous? How can I look ridiculous if I show everybody that I trust my wife?

GUSTAV: Well, you can. In fact, you do. Look ridiculous. Like a horse's ass.

ADOLPH (*exploding convulsively*): Me? Ridiculous?! I won't have it! There'll be some changes made! God, will there not!

GUSTAV: Easy, easy! You'll have another one of your attacks.

ADOLPH: I don't get it. Why doesn't she look like a fool if I stay out all night and carry on?

GUSTAV: Who knows? That's beside the point. It just happens to be a fact. And while you're trying to figure it out, disaster strikes!

ADOLPH: What disaster?

GUSTAV: As I was saying: her husband was a bully, but she married him to be independent and live her own life. Now how can that be? you ask. Simple: how does a girl get to be free and independent? Answer: by having a cover—a blind. Then she can go anywhere. And who is the cover? Her husband.

ADOLPH: Exactly.

GUSTAV: And now you're the cover, aren't you?

ADOLPH: Me?

GUSTAV: Well, you are her husband.

> *Adolph is lost in thought.*

GUSTAV: Am I right, or am I right?

ADOLPH (*troubled*): I don't know. . . . You live with a woman for years, never thinking too much about her, or about your life together. And then something happens—you begin to reflect— and that's the beginning of the end. . . . Gustav, you're my friend. The only man I can call a friend. You've given me a new lease on life this past week. It's as if your personality galvanized me. You've been my repairman. You took this clockwork brain of mine, fixed the mainspring, and set it going again. Can't you see how I'm thinking more clearly, talking more logically? I even think my voice has recovered its timbre.

GUSTAV: I think so too. How do you explain that?

ADOLPH: A man talks more softly to a woman. After a while, it gets to be a habit. Tekla always bawled me out for yelling at her.

GUSTAV: So you made your voice small and let her wear the pants in the family.

ADOLPH: That's not how it was! (*After a moment's thought.*) It was worse. . . . Let's not talk about that now. —Where was I? Oh, yes. You arrived on the scene; you showed me what was wrong with my painting. For a long time I had been losing interest in painting. It didn't offer me the scope I needed. I couldn't express what I had to say. And you understood why that was. You explained why a painter today couldn't be the artistic conscience of our times. That was an eye-opener for me. I saw that from here on I could not possibly produce anything worthwhile in oils and colors on a flat surface.

GUSTAV: And are you certain now that you can't paint anymore? Certain that you won't fall back into the old ways?

ADOLPH: Absolutely! I've already put it to the test. That evening after our long chat, when I lay in bed, I went over your argument point by point. I could tell it was right. However, after a good night's sleep and waking up with a clear head, it struck me like a bolt of lightning that you might be wrong. So I ran to my easel, took brushes and palette in hand and—you know what? Nothing. No sense of illusion. Nothing but daubs of pigments. It made me sick to think that I could make myself believe—make others believe—that that painted canvas was anything more than painted canvas. The veil had dropped from my eyes, and I could no more go back to painting than I could become a newborn child again.

GUSTAV: That's when you came to understand that if realism

is the tendency of our times, then the only way to achieve the true illusion of reality—its palpableness, its concreteness—is through sculpture—the physical body, the filling of space in all three dimensions.

ADOLPH (*faltering*): The three dimensions . . . yes . . . the body, the physical body.

GUSTAV: And so you became a sculptor. Which is to say, you had always been one, but you had lost your way, and all you needed was a guide to steer you in the right direction. . . . Tell me, Adolph, do you feel that lust for life now when you're at work?

ADOLPH: It's the only time I really feel alive.

GUSTAV: Let me look at it. Do you mind?

ADOLPH: A female nude.

GUSTAV: And no model? Striking! So alive!

ADOLPH (*dully, his mind drifting*): Yes. And so much like her. That woman lives in my body, just as I do in hers. It's strange.

GUSTAV: The latter isn't strange at all. Do you know what a transfusion is?

ADOLPH: Blood transfusion? Yes.

GUSTAV: Well, you've given too much of yours. Looking at this statue, I understand a lot that I only suspected before. You've loved her deeply, madly.

ADOLPH: So madly I couldn't tell whether she was I or I was she. When she smiles, I smile; when she cries, I cry. And when— I swear it's true—when she gave birth to our child, I felt the labor pains.

GUSTAV (*shaking his head*): You are in a bad way, my dear fellow. But I'm not surprised. I'm sorry to tell you this, but you're already displaying the symptoms of a nervous breakdown, of convulsive epilepsy.

ADOLPH (*shaken*): I am? How can you tell?

GUSTAV: I know them. Emotional explosions, flying off the handle, convulsions, and worse. I know what they are and what brings them on. Saw them in my younger brother. His problem was sex. Addicted to it.

ADOLPH: What were they like—the symptoms?

> *Gustav gives a vivid demonstration. Adolph observes intently and involuntarily begins to imitate Gustav's gestures and grimaces.*

GUSTAV: I tell you it was horrible to see. If you feel the least bit weak, I won't torture you with a description.

ADOLPH (*in anguish, but fascinated*): No, no, no, don't stop. Don't stop.

GUSTAV: All right. My little brother got himself married to a sweet little thing—bangs on her forehead, the eyes of a dove, the face of a child, the soul of an angel. Nonetheless, she contrived to arrogate to herself the prerogative of the male.

ADOLPH: The prerogative of the male? You mean—?

GUSTAV: The sexual initiative. What else? She made the advances. And the result was that the insatiable little angel nearly succeeded in sending my innocent little brother to heaven. First, however, he had to be crucified. Nailed to the cross. God, it was horrible!

ADOLPH (*hanging on every word*): Yes, horrible. What happened?

GUSTAV (*slowly, deliberately*): We might be sitting and talking, just he and I—and after I had been talking awhile, his face would become white—like chalk. His arms and legs grew stiff. And his thumbs would turn inward like this.

> *Gestures, and Adolph imitates him.*

Then his eyes became bloodshot, and he began working his jaws, like this.

> *Chews. Adolph imitates him.*

The saliva rattled in his throat. His chest contracted, as if in a vise. His pupils flickered, like the flames in a gas lamp. His tongue whipped the saliva into a froth. He began to slip down . . . slowly . . . backward . . . in his chair. As if he were drowning. The next thing —

ADOLPH (*in a hoarse whisper*): Stop, that's enough!

GUSTAV: The next thing —. Something the matter? Not feeling well?

ADOLPH: No.

GUSTAV (*fetches a glass of water*): Here, drink this. We'll talk about something else

ADOLPH (*weakly*): Thanks. . . . Let me hear the rest.

GUSTAV: You sure you want to? When he came to, he didn't remember anything that had happened. He had completely lost consciousness. Ever had that experience?

ADOLPH: Yes, I've had fainting spells sometimes. The doctor says it's because I'm anemic.

GUSTAV: Of course. That's how it begins. But, believe me or not, it turns into epilepsy if you don't take care of yourself.

ADOLPH: What should I do?

GUSTAV: Stop having sex. That's the first thing.

ADOLPH: For how long?

GUSTAV: Half a year. At least.

ADOLPH: I couldn't! What kind of married life would that be?

GUSTAV: Then it's curtains for you, I'm afraid.

ADOLPH (*as he drapes the cloth over the wax figure*): I couldn't, not possibly.

GUSTAV: Not even to save your life? . . . Very well. . . . I was wondering — since you have put me so much in your confidence — if there might not be some other sore spot in your life, something that secretly troubles you. Life is so complicated — there are so many causes of misunderstandings — it's very rare for there to be only one source of friction. There must be some skeleton in the closet that only you know about. That child you mentioned, for instance. Why isn't the child here with you?

ADOLPH: My wife wanted it that way. Didn't want it around.

GUSTAV: There must have been a reason. . . . Come on, let's hear it.

ADOLPH: Reason? Because the child, when it got to be three years old, began to look like him—the first husband.

GUSTAV: Indeed! . . . Have you ever seen him—the first husband?

ADOLPH: No, never have. Once I cast a glance at a portrait of him, a poor picture. I couldn't see any resemblance.

GUSTAV: Portraits always lie. Besides, he might have changed a lot. Anyway, you couldn't have any reason to be suspicious, now could you?

ADOLPH: Absolutely not. Our child was born a full year after we were married. And her first husband was traveling abroad when I met Tekla here. This is where I met her, you know, at this resort. This very house. That's why we come here every summer.

GUSTAV: So there weren't any grounds for suspecting any hanky-panky. Not even the resemblance. The child of a widow who remarries often resembles the dead husband. It's a fact, annoying but true. That's why in India they burn the widows. —Tell me honestly, haven't you ever been jealous of him, of her memory of him? Suppose you and Tekla met him on the street. Wouldn't it make you feel sick to hear him say, with his eyes on her, "we" instead of "I"? Not "I"—"We."

ADOLPH: The thought has occurred to me. Often. I can't deny it.

GUSTAV: You see! It will haunt you forever. It'll become an obsession, a discord that you can't resolve, a jarring note always ringing in your ears. All you can do is stuff cotton in them, and work. Work; grow older and wiser; gather experiences, lots of new experiences to pile on top of the coffin and lay to rest the ghost that haunts you.

ADOLPH: It's funny—forgive me for interrupting—it's remarkable how much you resemble Tekla at times. When you talk, you have the habit of squinting one eye, as if taking aim. And you look at me just as she does sometimes. Hypnotically.

GUSTAV: Not really.

ADOLPH: There! You even said "Not really" with that same nonchalant tone. She's always saying "Not really" like that.

GUSTAV: Perhaps we're distantly related. Everybody is, one way or another. Still it is odd. It might be amusing to meet your wife and see for myself.

ADOLPH: You know, she never picks up anything from me. No, she carefully avoids my vocabulary, and I've never seen her use one of my gestures. Married couples are supposed to take after each other, to have telltale habits; that's how you know they're married.

GUSTAV: Yes, I'm sure. —Now let me tell you something. That woman has never loved you.

ADOLPH: What?

GUSTAV: Forgive me, but it's true. Listen: a woman in love is a receptacle. She takes. And if she doesn't take from a man, she doesn't love him. I tell you, she has never loved you.

ADOLPH: You don't think it's possible for her to fall in love a second time?

GUSTAV: No. You only allow yourself to be cheated once. After that, you keep your eyes peeled. Your trouble is that you've never been cheated. Watch out for those who have. They're dangerous, very dangerous.

ADOLPH: Your words are like knives; I feel I'm being slashed. But I can't do anything about it. In fact, I need it. It's like boils that have to be lanced because they would never ripen and burst by themselves. . . . Never loved me? —Then why did she take me? Why?

GUSTAV: You tell me first *how* she came to take you. And did she take you, or did you take her?

ADOLPH: God knows! I don't. – How it happened? It didn't happen all at once.

GUSTAV: With a little guesswork I can work out how it happened. Let me have a stab at it.

ADOLPH: A waste of time. You can't even imagine.

GUSTAV: My dear fellow, with what you've told me about your wife, I can reconstruct the whole episode. Listen, my child, and you shall hear. (*Factually, almost as if telling a funny story.*) The husband is away doing research, and his wife is left alone. At first she feels happy, being free. Then comes the emptiness. I think I can assume she did feel rather empty – two weeks without a husband. Now, enter the other man, and gradually the emptiness is filled up. In comparison, the absent husband fades into insignificance – simply because he is so far away. You know, the law of sexual attraction: inversely proportional to the square of the distance. But now their passions flare up, and they begin to feel queasy about themselves, their consciences, and about him. They want to conceal their embarrassment – with fig leaves; they play at being brother and sister. And the more physical their relationship becomes, the more spiritual they pretend it is.

ADOLPH: Brother and sister! How do you know that?

GUSTAV: A hunch. Little children play husband and wife; when they're bigger, they play brother and sister – to hide what has to be hidden. . . . So now they take a solemn vow of chastity, which means they play "I spy" with each other. Until one day, neither one wants to be "it," and they both hide in a dark corner where they are certain no one can see them. (*Putting on a severe air.*) However, they know in their hearts that someone, someone in particular, sees them even in the dark. And that frightens them. And in their fear, the absent one begins to haunt them, looms up before their eyes, becomes a bogeyman, a nightmare disturbing their nights of love. A creditor, knocking at the door, come to collect. In bed, about to pluck the fruit of paradise, they see his black hand on it. They hear his piercing voice stabbing the quiet of the night, which should be throbbing with the beating of their blood. Maybe he can't stop them from having each other, but he can make them miserable. And when they feel his invisible presence destroying their happiness, when they finally run away—ah, but run away in vain—can't escape the memories that pursue them, the debts they can't pay, the public opinion that unnerves them. —And since they haven't the strength to assume the responsibility for what they've done, a scapegoat has to be found and slaughtered. Oh, they are free-thinking, liberated people, but they haven't the courage to go to him and tell him frankly, "We love each other." No, they are cowards. And therefore the tyrant has to be got rid of, done away with, disposed of. —How am I doing?

ADOLPH: Fine. But you forgot something. She taught me, inspired me, fed me new ideas.

GUSTAV: I didn't forget. Now you tell me, how was it that she couldn't teach her first husband also, couldn't inspire him—make him a freethinker?

ADOLPH: That's easy. He was an idiot.

GUSTAV: Of course! I had forgotten: he was an idiot. Still, what's an idiot? A rather imprecise term. In that novel she wrote, her husband is supposed to be an idiot because he couldn't under-stand her. Forgive me for asking, but is your wife really so pro-found? I haven't discovered any great depths in her novels. Have you?

ADOLPH: No. —In fact, I have to admit that I don't find it easy to understand her either. It's as if the cogs and wheels in my brain don't mesh with hers. When I try to grasp her meaning, the wheels just spin madly.

GUSTAV: Oh, dear! It couldn't be that you're an idiot, too?

ADOLPH: No. At least, I don't think so. In fact, I almost always think she's wrong. Look at this letter; you'll see what I mean. It came today. (*He takes a letter from his wallet.*)

GUSTAV (*scanning the letter*): Hmm. It's a hand that I think I've seen before.

ADOLPH: A man's handwriting, wouldn't you say?

GUSTAV: I might. I know of one man, at least, who has a similar hand. —She calls you "Brother." Are you still playing games, the two of you? Still wearing fig leaves?—albeit a little withered. —"Brother?" Aren't you on a first-name basis? No pet names?

ADOLPH: I don't like pet names. We respect each other.

GUSTAV: Is that so? You mean that she wins your respect by calling herself your sister?

ADOLPH: I respect her as being above me. I want her to be my better self.

GUSTAV: Come off it! Be your own better self. More of a bother, admittedly, than letting somebody else be it. —You really want to be inferior to your wife? I don't believe it!

ADOLPH: That's exactly what I want. I enjoy being a little less clever than she is. Look: I taught her how to swim, and now I think it's fun to hear her brag that she's better at it than I am—faster—takes more chances. At first I pretended I couldn't keep up with her, said I was afraid, just to give her courage. And then, somehow, one day I actually was less strong, more afraid. It struck me that she had taken my courage and made it hers—literally.

GUSTAV: What else, I wonder, have you taught her?

ADOLPH: Well—strictly between ourselves I taught her how to write. She couldn't spell worth a damn. And you know what happened? After I taught her, she took charge of all the correspondence; I didn't have to write at all. So for years I didn't keep in practice, and—well you can imagine. Now I've even forgotten my grammar. But do you suppose she remembers who it was that taught her how to write? Not a bit! Now *I'm* the idiot, naturally.

GUSTAV: Ah ha! You're the idiot, so soon!

ADOLPH: That's a joke, you understand.

GUSTAV: Of course I understand. —It's cannibalism, wouldn't you say? I mean, savages eat their enemies to acquire their outstanding qualities. She has eaten you, this woman—your heart, your courage, your knowledge—

ADOLPH: —My belief in myself. . . . I was the one who encouraged her to write her first book.

GUSTAV (*making a wry face*): Did you now?

ADOLPH: I was the one who praised her writing to the skies, even when I thought it was pretty shabby stuff. It was I who introduced her into literary circles, so she could buzz around and gather honey from all the beautiful people. It was I who spoke to the critics and asked them to go easy on her. And when she lost inspiration, I gave it to her. But in inspiring her, I expired. I gave and gave and gave for her sake—until there was nothing left of me to give. —Here I am, baring my soul to you, but so what! You know, right now it seems to me—oh, the ways of the soul are strange!—when my success as a painter threatened to overwhelm her success and overshadow her reputation, I attempted to enhearten her by reducing my own significance, telling her my art was inferior to hers. I told her so often that painting was a relatively unimportant art, and invented so many reasons to convince her, that I ended up believing it myself. My faith in painting was only a house of cards, Gustav. All you had to do was blow on it.

GUSTAV: Forgive me, but I must remind you that at the beginning of our little chat you said she never takes anything from you.

ADOLPH: It's true. She doesn't. Not now. There's nothing left for her to take.

GUSTAV: The python is sated. Now it regurgitates.

ADOLPH: Perhaps she has taken more from me—things I don't know about.

GUSTAV: That you can be sure of. She took when you weren't looking. I call that theft.

ADOLPH: Maybe I never learned anything from her.

GUSTAV: And she everything from you? In all probability. But she was clever enough to make you think the opposite. Let me ask you: how did she go about teaching you?

ADOLPH: Well, in the beginning . . . (*Hesitates.*)

GUSTAV: Yes? In the beginning—?

ADOLPH: Well—well, I—I—

GUSTAV: No. *She—she.*

ADOLPH: I don't want to talk about it now.

GUSTAV: Ah, ha, you see!

ADOLPH: Well, it's just that—. My faith in myself, my work— she had eaten that, too. I went into a decline, until you came and gave me something I could throw myself into, heart and soul.

GUSTAV (*smiling*): Sculpture?

ADOLPH (*unsure of himself*): Well . . . yes.

GUSTAV: And you put your heart in that! An abstract, out- moded form of art? Sculpture dates back to primitive times, when people were like children. You don't really believe that pure form—in three dimensions, no less—can mean anything to people nowadays, who want realism—that you can create realism without color? Good heavens! Without color! You don't really—

ADOLPH (*crushed*): No, I don't.

GUSTAV: Nor do I.

ADOLPH: Then why did you tell me you did?

GUSTAV: I felt sorry for you.

ADOLPH: I feel sorry for myself. And well I may! I'm finished, bankrupt, done for! Nothing's left. Not even her.

GUSTAV: What on earth do you want her for?

ADOLPH: Some people have God. I had her. What God was to me before I became an atheist, she was to me: something to worship. She was the object of my veneration.

GUSTAV: Bury your idol, and let something better grow out of it. Like good, healthy contempt.

ADOLPH: I can't live without something to look up to—

GUSTAV: Slave!

ADOLPH: A woman whom I can adore, revere.

GUSTAV: Jesus Christ! Go back to God! Better Him than her if you have a need to cross yourself and genuflect. An atheist who still believes in the feminine mystique! A freethinker who thinks what you're told to think about the dames. What's so profound, so sphinxlike, so unfathomable about that wife of yours? You know what she really is? Stupid. Dumb. Look! (*Points to the letter.*) She can't even tell the difference between i-e and e-i. She doesn't know whether she's coming or going. She's all mixed up. She's like a cheap watch: the case looks expensive, but it can't give you the right time. . . . It's all in the skirts, my boy. Put a pair of pants on her; take a piece of burnt cork and draw a moustache under her nose. Then lend a sober ear to her prattle; you'll hear the real sound of her. A phonograph, that's all, playing back your words—or somebody else's—just a little tinnier. . . . Have you ever seen a naked woman? Sorry! Of course you have. A teenager with tits, an undeveloped man, a kid who shot up and stopped short. A chronic anemic, who spews blood like clockwork thirteen times a year. —What can such a creature possibly amount to?

ADOLPH: All right, suppose I accept all that, for the sake of argument—then what is it that makes me believe she's my equal?

GUSTAV: It's a hallucination. I told you: it's all in the skirts; they've bewitched you. —Or—who knows?—maybe you have become equal. Like water seeking its own level. Her capillary tubes have sucked up your manhood, and now you're both on the same level. —Listen, old boy (*Taking out his watch.*), we've been talking for six hours. Your wife should be back any minute now. Haven't we had enough? You should get some sleep.

ADOLPH: No, no, don't go away. I don't dare to be left alone.

GUSTAV: Buck up; it's only for a short while. She'll soon be here.

ADOLPH: Yes, she'll be here. . . . It's strange. Although I yearn for her, I'm afraid of her. She fondles me, she's tender; but there's something in her kisses that suffocates me, sucks my strength, paralyzes me. Reminds me of the child who works in the circus. The clown pinches him offstage so his cheeks look pink and rosy for the public.

GUSTAV: My friend, I'm truly sorry for you. I don't have to be a doctor to see that you're ill, a dying man. You only have to look at your last paintings. It's all there.

ADOLPH: What do you mean, it's all there?

GUSTAV: The colors! Pale, washed out. You can see the canvas through them—yellow like a corpse. When I look at them, I see your hollow, clay-colored cheeks showing through.

ADOLPH: All right! Enough!

GUSTAV: It's not just my opinion, you know. Have you read this morning's paper?

ADOLPH (*startled*): No!

GUSTAV: It's right here on the table.

ADOLPH (*reaches for the paper, but dares not take it*): It's in the paper?

GUSTAV: Go ahead. Or should I?

ADOLPH: No . . .

GUSTAV: I'll go, if you want me to.

ADOLPH: No, no, no. —I don't know what I—. I think I'm beginning to hate you but still can't let you go. I'm drowning; you haul me up, and when I'm up, you hit me on the head and dunk me again. As long as I kept my secrets to myself, I had some guts. Now I'm empty. There's a painting by an Italian master—a scene of torture. There's a saint, and his intestines are being pulled out and wound on a windlass. The martyr lies there, looking at what's happening to him. He's getting thinner and thinner, and the roll on the wheel is getting thicker and thicker. I can see how much bigger you've grown since you began digging into my life; and when you leave me, you'll take my innards with you and leave behind an empty shell.

GUSTAV: You do have an imagination, Adolph. Anyway, your wife will be bringing your heart back to you, won't she?

ADOLPH: Oh, no. Not now. You put the torch to her. You've turned everything to ashes—my art, my love, my hope, my faith.

GUSTAV: Somebody else had already done that—and done it well.

ADOLPH: Maybe. But there was still time to save something. Now it's too late. Arsonist!

GUSTAV: Come on, we've only scorched the ground a little. Now we'll sow seeds in the fertile ashes.

ADOLPH: I detest you! Damn you!

GUSTAV: A good sign. There's still some spunk left in you. And now I'm going to haul you up again. Listen to me. . . . Will you listen to me? And will you do as I tell you?

ADOLPH: Do with me as you wish. I'll obey.

GUSTAV (*standing up*): Look at me.

ADOLPH (*fastening his eyes on Gustav*): Now you're looking at me again with those eerie eyes that draw me to you.

GUSTAV: Now listen to me.

ADOLPH: All right, I'm listening. But talk about yourself. Not about me. I'm one big open wound, and I can't bear being touched.

GUSTAV: Myself? There's nothing to talk about. I'm a classicist, a teacher of dead languages; and a widower. That's the whole of it. —Now take my hand.

ADOLPH (*takes his hand*): What terrible power you must have! It's like plugging into a socket.

GUSTAV: Then consider: I was once as weak as you. —Get up!

ADOLPH (*stands up; starts to fall; grabs Gustav by the neck*): I'm like a baby. My bones haven't grown together yet, and my brains are slipping through them.

GUSTAV: Take a few steps. Cross the floor.

ADOLPH: I can't.

GUSTAV: You can't?! I'll slap your face!

ADOLPH (*rears up*): What!

GUSTAV: I'll slap your silly face!

ADOLPH (*jumps back, furious*): You'll what?

GUSTAV: Ah, ha! You see! Now the blood rose to your head. Some of the old confidence came back, didn't it? Now I'll give you another jolt of electricity. —Where's your wife?

ADOLPH: Where's my wife?

GUSTAV: Yes. Where is your wife?

ADOLPH: She's at a—at a meeting.

GUSTAV: You're sure?

ADOLPH: Absolutely.

GUSTAV: What kind of meeting?

ADOLPH: Trustees' meeting for an orphanage.

GUSTAV: When she went off to the meeting, it was a friendly parting?

ADOLPH (*hesitating*): Not exactly.

GUSTAV: In other words you'd had a tiff. —What did you say that riled her?

ADOLPH: You're terrible. You really scare me. How could you know?

GUSTAV: I have three known quantities. It's simple to calculate the unknown one. —Now what did you say to her?

ADOLPH: I said—. They were just three words. They were awful words. I regret them, oh, how I regret them!

GUSTAV: You shouldn't. Now what were they?

ADOLPH: I said: "You old whore."

GUSTAV: That's all?

ADOLPH: Not a word more.

GUSTAV: Yes, you did. Only you've forgotten it—because you don't dare remember. You've tucked it away in a secret drawer in that brain of yours, and now it's time to open it.

ADOLPH: I tell you I can't bring it to mind.

GUSTAV: But I can. What you said was this: "You ought to be ashamed. Flirting at your age, when you're too old to attract a lover."

ADOLPH: Is that what I said? I must have. —But how could you know?

GUSTAV: She told the whole story on the steamship that I took coming here. That's how I heard it—overheard it.

ADOLPH: Told it to whom?

GUSTAV: To four young men she was keeping company with. She's already infatuated with innocent young boys, just like—

ADOLPH: There's nothing wrong in that.

GUSTAV: No, of course not. It's like playing sister and brother when you're really mommy and daddy.

ADOLPH: So you've seen her, actually seen her?

GUSTAV: Yes, I have. Which you never have. Seen her when you weren't looking at her. I mean, when you weren't present. And that's why a man can't possibly get to know his wife. —Do you have a photograph of her?

> *Adolph takes a photograph from his wallet; wonders what Gustav is up to.*

GUSTAV: You weren't there when this picture was taken?

ADOLPH: No.

GUSTAV: Look at it. Is it like the portrait you painted? No. The features are the same, but the expression is different. You can't see that because you superimpose on it your own image of her. Now try to look at it as a painter, without thinking of the original. . . . Who is the person in that picture? All I can see is a flirt, with lots of makeup, and a saucy wink in her eye. Look at that brazen smile. *You* never get to see that. Look at the way her eyes are prowling for some man. And it isn't you. Look at the low cut of her dress—the hair done up differently—her sleeves pushed up, the bared arms. Do you see?

ADOLPH: Yes. I see. Now.

GUSTAV: Take care, my friend. Watch out!

ADOLPH: For what?

GUSTAV: Revenge! — You have hit her where it hurts, don't forget that. You told her she couldn't attract a man. Now if you had said that what she writes in her books is crap, she would only have laughed at your lack of taste and discrimination. But now — believe me — if she hasn't already gotten even with you, it isn't for want of trying.

ADOLPH: I've got to know.

GUSTAV: That's right. You've got to find out.

ADOLPH: Yes. Find out.

GUSTAV: See to it. Now. I can help if you want me to.

ADOLPH: Why not? I'm going to die anyway. As well now as later. What do you have in mind?

GUSTAV: First, some information. Doesn't your wife have a single vulnerable spot?

ADOLPH: Hardly. She's got nine lives like a cat.

A steamship's whistle is heard.

GUSTAV: That's the steamer coming in to dock. She'll be here soon.

ADOLPH: I have to go to the dock to meet her!

GUSTAV: No! You're going to stay right here. You're going to be rude and impolite. No currying. If her conscience is clear, you'll get a bawling out that will make your ears ring. However, if she's feeling guilty, she'll be sweetness itself, and coo and cuddle up to you.

ADOLPH: You're sure this will really work?

GUSTAV: Not really. Rabbits sometimes double back and run rings around the dogs. Not to worry, old boy, I'll take care of it. — My room is next to this one. (*Points to the door at right, behind the chair.*) I'll post myself there and keep an eye on you while you play games with her in here. And when you've had your fun, we'll change places. I'll go into the lion cage, and you'll be at the keyhole. Afterward we'll meet in the park and compare notes. But hold your ground. If I see you weakening, I'll pound twice on the floor with a chair.

ADOLPH: Agreed! But don't abandon me. I've got to know that you're in that room.

GUSTAV: Rest assured. —A warning, however: don't get sick when you see me dissecting a human soul and laying the pieces out on this table. An autopsy is a horrible experience for the novice. But nobody who's seen one regrets it. —Oh, one thing more. Not a word about meeting me. You never met anybody while she was away. Not anybody, understand? —And leave it to me to find her Achilles' heel. —Quiet! She's already here. She's in her room. I can hear her humming to herself. That means she's mad as a hornet. —All right! Straighten up! Shoulders back! Sit down in your chair—there, so she'll have to sit in mine. That way I can see you both at once.

ADOLPH: It's an hour till dinnertime. I haven't heard the desk bell ring, and that means no new guests have arrived. So we're alone. Unfortunately.

GUSTAV: Feeling weak?

ADOLPH: Feeling nothing. —No, I'm afraid of what's going to happen. But I can't stop it from happening. The stone has started to roll. Wasn't the last drop of water that set it going, and not the first. It was all of them together.

GUSTAV: So let it roll! You won't have any peace until it does. —I'll see you soon. (*He exits.*)

> *Adolph nods. Looks at the photograph in his hands. He tears it to pieces and throws them under the table. Sits down in his chair, fusses with his tie, runs his fingers through his hair, nervously adjusts the lapels on his coat, and so on.*
>
> *Tekla enters. Goes straight to him and kisses him. She is friendly, frank, cheerful, and charming.*

TEKLA: Hello, Adolph! How's my little brother?

ADOLPH (*succumbing to her charm in spite of himself; resistingly, jokingly*): What have you been up to that entitles me to a kiss?

TEKLA: What do you think? I've been spending money like mad!

ADOLPH: Have any fun doing it?

TEKLA: A lot! But certainly not at that awful foundling home! What a lot of shit!—if you'll pardon my French. —Now tell me what Little Brother has been up to while Pussycat was away. (*She looks around the room, trying to find some clue to what has been going on.*)

ADOLPH: Boring myself to death.

TEKLA: No company?

ADOLPH: No. All alone.

> *Tekla scrutinizes him. Sits in the sofa.*

TEKLA: Who's been sitting here?

ADOLPH: Sitting there? No one.

TEKLA: How odd! The seat's still warm. And there's a depression here in the arm made by somebody's elbow. Oh ho! I do believe Little Brother has been entertaining a lady.

ADOLPH: Me?! You don't believe that at all.

TEKLA: You're blushing! Don't tell me Little Brother is trying to play games with me. Come over here and tell Pussycat all about it. Little Brother has something on his conscience, hasn't he?

> *She pulls him toward her. He sinks down and puts his head in her lap.*

ADOLPH (*smiling*): You're a little devil; you know that, don't you?

TEKLA: No. I don't know a thing about myself.

ADOLPH: You mean you never think about yourself?

TEKLA (*looks around, suspecting something, still trying to find a clue*): I think only *of* myself. I'm a frightful egotist. —My! haven't you become analytical!

ADOLPH: Put your hand on my forehead.

TEKLA (*babytalking*): Has my little boy got bugsy-wugsy in his head? Shall I make them go away? Hmm? Hmm? (*She kisses his forehead.*) There now! Isn't that better?

ADOLPH: Yes. Much better.

    Pause.

TEKLA: Now my little boy is going to tell me what he's been doing while I've been away, isn't he? Has he been painting?

ADOLPH: No. I've had it with painting. I'm through.

TEKLA: What? Through painting?

ADOLPH: Finished! Don't bawl me out! It's not my fault that I can't paint anymore.

TEKLA: What on earth are you going to do with yourself?

ADOLPH: I'm taking up sculpture.

TEKLA: Oh, God! Always something new!

ADOLPH: I said, don't start bawling me out! I mean it. —Take a look at what I've done.

TEKLA (*removes the cloth from the wax figure*): Well, I declare! Who is it supposed to be?

ADOLPH: Guess!

TEKLA (*breezily*): Is that supposed to be your Pussycat? Have you no shame?

ADOLPH: It's like you, isn't it?

TEKLA: How should I know? It's got no face.

ADOLPH: It's got a lot else —(*Indicating her breasts.*) those big brown eyes here—another bunch of delicacies there . . .

TEKLA (*playfully slapping his face*): Shut your mouth—or I'll close it for you—with a kiss.

ADOLPH (*avoiding her*): Cut it out! Someone might come in!

TEKLA: What do I care! Isn't a wife allowed to kiss her husband? I want to exercise my legal rights.

ADOLPH: Fine, fine! Except that here at the hotel they don't believe we're married: we're always kissing each other. And our little spats don't convince them otherwise. Lovers' quarrels, that's what they think.

TEKLA: Then let's not quarrel. Why can't you always be as sweet as you are now? Why? . . . Don't you—? Don't you want us to be happy together? Hm?

ADOLPH: If you only knew how much! But—but . . .

TEKLA: Now what's the matter with you? . . . Whoever told you you should give up painting?

ADOLPH: Why should it be anybody? You're always suspecting somebody behind what I do and what I think. As if I couldn't act on my own. —You know what? You're jealous!

TEKLA: Of course I am, you silly! I'm afraid somebody will come and take Little Brother away from me.

ADOLPH: How can you be? You know that no woman on earth could take your place. I can't live without you.

TEKLA: It's not the women I'm afraid of. It's your male friends—the ones who put crazy ideas into your head.

ADOLPH (*studying her closely*): You *are* afraid. Afraid of what?

TEKLA (*standing up*): Someone has been here, I know it. Who was it?

ADOLPH: Why can't you look me in the eye?

TEKLA: Not like that. You never used to look at me like that.

ADOLPH: I'm just looking into your eyes.

TEKLA: No, your eyes are veiled. You're looking through your eyelids.

ADOLPH: Through yours, you mean. I want to see what's going on behind them.

TEKLA: Go ahead; take a good look! I've got nothing to hide. . . . There's something funny going on. You're talking different — using expressions. . . . (*Searchingly.*) Analyzing. . . . What's going on? (*Advancing on him threateningly.*) I want to know who's been here!

ADOLPH: No one — except my doctor.

TEKLA: Your doctor! You don't have a doctor here.

ADOLPH: My doctor from Rivertown.

TEKLA: What's his name?

ADOLPH: Seaberg.

TEKLA: What did he have to say?

ADOLPH: He said . . . he said a lot of things. . . . He said . . . that I was in danger of having an epileptic attack.

TEKLA: A lot of things? What else?

ADOLPH: Something pretty . . . distressing.

TEKLA: Well, out with it!

ADOLPH: He forbade us to have sex together for a while.

TEKLA: Forbade —! I knew it! Oh, I knew that was coming! They want to separate us. I've seen that coming for a long time.

ADOLPH: You couldn't possibly have seen it coming. It's never once happened!

TEKLA: I tell you I've seen it coming!

ADOLPH: You couldn't see what wasn't there — unless you were afraid. Your imagination made you see what never existed. What are you afraid of? That I would get to see you with someone else's eyes? See you for what you are — and not for what I took you to be?

TEKLA: Don't let your imagination run away with you, Adolph. Imagination is the monster that dwells in man's soul, Adolph.

ADOLPH: Oh, God! Where on earth did you hear that? From the innocent adolescents on the steamboat? —Right?

TEKLA (*unflustered, without skipping a beat*): That's right. Even the young have something to teach us.

ADOLPH: My, my! I do believe you've fallen in love with youth. Already!

TEKLA: Haven't I always? Why do you think I loved you? What have you got against youth?

ADOLPH: Nothing. I just prefer to be loved alone, and not as part of a group.

TEKLA (*babytalking playfully*): Pussycat has a great big heart. Little Brother knows what a big heart she has. There's room in it for many besides him.

ADOLPH: Maybe Little Brother doesn't want any brothers.

TEKLA: Come here to Big Sister. What you need is a spanking. It isn't good to be jealous. No, you're envious; that's what you are. Tut, tut.

> *The sound of two raps with the chair in Gustav's room are heard.*

ADOLPH: Cut it out! I'm not in the mood for games. I want a serious talk.

TEKLA (*as if to a child*): Heaven's to betsy! Does the little man want a serious talk? Gracious, hasn't he become the somber one! (*She takes his head in her hands and kisses him.*) Now let me see a little smile. A little chuckle.

ADOLPH (*smiling in spite of himself*): You damned witch! You can charm the pants off a man!

TEKLA: There, there. Of course I can. You know I can. That's why you shouldn't quarrel. Because I'll charm you right out of your skin.

ADOLPH (*getting to his feet*): Tekla! Sit there with your profile toward me. I want to put a face on my statue.

TEKLA: Happy to oblige. (*Poses.*) How's that?

ADOLPH (*studies her; pretends to model*): Good. Now put me out of your thoughts. Think of someone else.

TEKLA: All right. My most recent conquest. Will that do?

ADOLPH: The innocent young boy?

TEKLA: Yes, exactly. Oh, he had such a darling little moustache, and his cheeks were all peaches and cream. So soft and tender, I wanted to bite into them.

ADOLPH (*frowning*): That's it! That expression around your mouth—hold it!

TEKLA: Which expression?

ADOLPH: Cynical, brazen. An expression I've never seen on you before.

TEKLA (*making a face*): You mean this one?

ADOLPH: Precisely. (*Stands up.*) Do you know how Bret Harte describes an adulteress?

TEKLA (*smiling*): His name's Harte and he writes about women? How quaint. Never read him.

ADOLPH: He says an adulteress is a pale woman who can never blush.

TEKLA: Never? Oh, come on, when she meets her lover, I'm sure she blushes. Only her husband—or Mr. Harte—isn't there to see it.

ADOLPH: Are you sure?

TEKLA (*sweetly*): Yes. The husband isn't man enough to make the blood rush to her head, so he never gets to see that enchanting sight.

ADOLPH (*furious*): Damn you!

TEKLA: Silly nincompoop!

ADOLPH: Tekla!

TEKLA: Little Brother should call me Poodycat, and I'll blush—all over—just for you. You want me to? Do you?

ADOLPH (*defenseless*): I'm so mad at you, you monster, I could bite you!

TEKLA (*playfully*): Come on! Come and bite me! Come!

> *She stretches out her arms to him. Adolph embraces her and kisses her.*

ADOLPH: I'll bite and bite until you die.

TEKLA (*teasingly, recalling his earlier words*): Careful! Someone might come in!

ADOLPH: What the hell do I care! I don't give a damn about anything as long as I have you!

TEKLA: And when you don't have me—?

ADOLPH: I'll die.

TEKLA: No fear of that, is there? Since I'm so old no one wants me.

ADOLPH: Oh, Tekla, you can't forget I said that, can you? I'm sorry. I take back those words.

TEKLA: You're so jealous, and at the same time so cocksure of yourself. How do you explain that?

ADOLPH: I can't explain anything. Possibly the thought that someone else has possessed you, maybe that thought lies and rankles in me. Sometimes I think that our love is an act of self-defense, a story we've had to invent to save our self-respect, an affair of the heart that has become a point of honor. Because I know that nothing torments me more than the thought that *he* might see I'm unhappy. Oh, God, I've never seen him, but the mere idea that there is someone out there who is praying I'll be miserable, who every day calls down curses on my head, who will laugh himself sick when I fall—just that thought is like an incubus riding me, compulsively driving me into your arms, obsessing me, paralyzing me.

TEKLA: Do you suppose I'd give him that pleasure? Do you think I'd want to make his dreams come true?

ADOLPH: I don't want to believe it, no.

TEKLA: Then why can't you settle down and forget about it?

ADOLPH: How can I when you carry on like a flirt? Why do you play your idiotic little games?

TEKLA: They're not games. I want to be liked and admired, that's all.

ADOLPH: Yes, but only by men.

TEKLA: Naturally. Women don't like each other; they envy each other.

ADOLPH: Tell me something. . . . Have you heard—from him—recently?

TEKLA: Not for half a year.

ADOLPH: Don't you ever think of him?

TEKLA: No. Since our child died, there's been no connection between us.

ADOLPH: You've never bumped into him—on the street?

TEKLA: No. He's living somewhere on the west coast. Why do you worry yourself about that?

ADOLPH: I don't know. These last few days, when I've been alone here, I couldn't help wondering how he must have felt when he found himself all alone, when you left him.

TEKLA: Dear me? Don't tell me your conscience is bothering you.

ADOLPH: Well, it is.

TEKLA: You feel like a thief, don't you?

ADOLPH: Something like that.

TEKLA: That's lovely! What does that make me? You think you can steal women like you steal chickens or kidnap children? You think I'm his personal property—chattel goods? Thanks a lot!

ADOLPH: No. I think of you as his wife. That's not the same as a piece of furniture. You can't buy another one.

TEKLA: Of course you can! Let me tell you, if you heard he had married again, you wouldn't have these silly quirks. —Look, you've replaced him for me, haven't you?

ADOLPH: Is that what I've done? Didn't you ever love him?

TEKLA: I most certainly did!

ADOLPH: And what happened?

TEKLA: I got bored with him.

ADOLPH: Suppose you got bored with me?

TEKLA: I won't. I won't.

ADOLPH: If someone else came along, someone who had what you're looking for — *now* — in a man — I say *suppose* — you'd toss me aside.

TEKLA: Never!

ADOLPH: Even if he fascinated you? — swept you off your feet? — so you couldn't live without him — of course you'd live without me.

TEKLA: No. That doesn't follow.

ADOLPH: You don't mean you could love two at once?

TEKLA: Sure. Why not?

ADOLPH: That's beyond me.

TEKLA: There are things in heaven and earth, darling, that are not dreamt of in your philosophy. All people are not created alike.

ADOLPH: I think I'm beginning to understand.

TEKLA: Not really.

ADOLPH (*imitating her inflection*): "Not really." (*Adolph tries to remember something but cannot quite bring it into focus.*) Tekla, your frankness is beginning to give me a pain.

TEKLA: Frankness is the highest virtue. That's what you used to preach.

ADOLPH: I know I did. But now I have the distinct impression that you're hiding out in the open.

TEKLA: The latest thing in camouflage. Didn't you know?

ADOLPH: No, I didn't. I only know that it's getting to be unpleasant here. What do you say we leave for home — tonight!

TEKLA: Now what are you up to? I just arrived! I have no desire to leave.

ADOLPH: Well, I want us to.

TEKLA: All right, it's a free country. Go on, leave, if that's what you want.

ADOLPH: I'm telling you to leave with me on the next boat.

TEKLA: Telling me! Who do you think you are?!

ADOLPH: I'll have you know that you are my wife!

TEKLA: I'll have you know that you are my husband!

ADOLPH: Exactly! And there's a difference between those two things.

TEKLA: Ah ha! So you've sunk to that level! . . . I knew you never loved me.

ADOLPH: Never loved you?!

TEKLA: No. Because to love means to give.

ADOLPH: To love like a man means to give. To love like a woman means to take. And, God knows, I have given — *given — given*!

TEKLA: Pooh! What have you given?

ADOLPH: Everything!

TEKLA: A hell of a lot that was! — Even if it's true, I was good enough to accept it. Are you going to send me bills for your gifts? If I took what you gave, it proves I loved you. A woman only accepts gifts from her lover.

ADOLPH: Lover! That's it! That's the truth. I've been your lover, never your husband.

TEKLA: How convenient for you. You never had to be a cover for me. —However, if you're not content to be a lover, off you go! I certainly don't need a husband hanging around.

ADOLPH: So I've noticed. These past few months when I saw how you wanted to sneak away like a thief in the night, saw how you sought out your own kind, with whom you could parade around in borrowed feathers—my feathers—and sparkle with my brilliant wit, that's when I tried to remind you of what you owed me. And in an instant I was transformed into the troublesome creditor, who wouldn't go away. You wanted to tear up the IOU's. And to avoid going deeper into debt, you stopped dipping into my wallet: you went to others. I became your husband— without wanting to. And as soon as I played the husband, you hated me. But now I'm going to *be* your husband, whether you like it or not since I can't be your lover.

TEKLA (*playfully*): You're talking nonsense, you know that, you darling idiot!

ADOLPH: A word of advice, Tekla. It's dangerous to go around thinking everyone's an idiot except yourself.

TEKLA: Doesn't everybody?

ADOLPH: I'm beginning to suspect that possibly he—your first husband—wasn't an idiot.

TEKLA: Heaven help us! Don't tell me you're beginning to feel sorry for him!

ADOLPH: What if I am?

TEKLA: Well, what *do* you know! You want to meet him— perhaps pour out your heart to him. What a pretty picture that would make. —Funnily enough, even I'm beginning to feel attracted to him, now that I've gotten bored being your nurse-maid. At least he was a real man. The only thing wrong with him was that he was mine.

ADOLPH: I knew it. —For God's sake, don't talk so loud! We can be overheard.

TEKLA: So what! They'd only take us for a married couple.

ADOLPH: So you've got a hankering for real he-men—and for pure young men—both at the same time.

TEKLA: My hankerings have no limit. It's simple. I open my heart to all, for all—the short and the tall, the pretty and the plain, what's old, what's new. I love the whole world.

ADOLPH: You know what that means?

TEKLA: I don't know what anything means. I only feel.

ADOLPH: It means you're getting old.

TEKLA: Harping on that again? Watch out, sonny!

ADOLPH: You watch out!

TEKLA: What for?

ADOLPH: The knife!

TEKLA (*babytalking*): Little Brother shouldn't play with such things. He might hurt himself.

ADOLPH: Who says I'm playing?

TEKLA: You want to be serious? Dead serious? All right, I'll show you what a mistake you're making. But you'll never know what I'll do to you, never really know. The whole world will be in on it—everybody except you. You'll suspect it, sense it always, and you'll never have a moment's peace. You'll feel in your bones what a fool you are, how I'm being unfaithful to you, but you'll never get your hands on a shred of evidence. The husband never does. Oh, I'm going to make you pay!

ADOLPH: You really hate me, don't you?

TEKLA: No, I don't hate you. I won't ever come to hate you. How could I? You're such a child.

ADOLPH: *Now* I am, yes. But what about the time when we had it rough. You cried like a baby in diapers. You sat in my lap, and I had to kiss your eyes until you fell asleep. I was your nurse then. Had to comb your hair and straighten you up so you wouldn't go out looking a mess. Get your shoes repaired. Cook something on the stove. I had to sit by your side for hours, holding your hand. You were afraid, afraid of the whole world. Didn't have a friend. The critics, the public, everybody was against you. You were crushed, and I had to give you the courage to go on, talking to you through the night until my tongue withered and cracked, and my head ached. I had to convince myself that I was strong—force myself to believe that tomorrow would be better. And finally I succeeded in breathing life into you, when you lay as if dead. I astonished you then, and you admired me. Then I was the man, the real man, not that sexual athlete you had left but a man with a strength of spirit—the hypnotist who stroked his energy into your slack muscles and recharged your empty brain with his electricity. I rehabilitated you. Made friends for you. Provided you with a little court of admirers who, out of friendship to me, let themselves be talked into fawning over you. I set you above myself and my home. I portrayed you in my most beautiful paintings—in rose and azure against a gilt background; and there wasn't an exhibition in which you didn't occupy the best spot. Sometimes you were St. Cecelia, or you might be Mary Stuart, or Maria Walewska. I advertised you, made you the focus of attention. I got the whole braying mob of asses to see you through my adoring eyes. I drilled your personality into their lives, forced you down their throats. Finally everybody knew who you were, liked you. You were a celebrity. Then you were on your own. . . . But it was I who made you, and, having made you, I had no strength left. The effort had been too much for me. In making you, I had undone myself. I was in the dumps and you were riding high. I became ill, and my illness embarrassed you. Sometimes I felt that what was behind it was a desire to get rid of me, the creditor, the man who knew too much about you. Your love for me changed. You became the grown-up sister, always acting uppity. I didn't have much choice. I learned my new part: Little Brother. You were so tender—even more so than before. But all that sweetness had a thin coating of pity, and that pity contained a large amount of disrespect, and that disrespect grew into contempt as my talent withered on the vine while yours blossomed in the sun. . . . But then something happened. Unforeseen. Your well of inspiration seemed to go dry when I wasn't there to replenish it. Or rather, when you tried to prove that you didn't have to dip into it. The result was that we both dried up. And now you want someone to blame. Somebody new. Because you're weak. Because you can never blame yourself or pay your own debts. I became the scapegoat to be sacrificed. You cut me up. But you didn't realize that when you cut my tendons, you crippled yourself—because by then we had grown together like Siamese twins. I was the plant and you were the shoot taken from me, but you tried to grow on your own before you had taken root. You couldn't survive—and the plant couldn't live without its main branch. So we both died.

TEKLA: What you're trying to say is that *you* wrote *my* books!

ADOLPH: That's what you want me to say—to make me out a liar. I carefully avoided expressing myself as coarsely as that. I've been talking for five minutes because I wanted to render all the nuances, all the shadings, all the modulations. You keep harping on one note. I'm an orchestra and you're a tin whistle.

TEKLA: Talk, talk! In one word, you're saying you wrote my books!

ADOLPH: No! I'm saying that you can't put what I'm saying into one word. You can't break up a chord of music and play it as one note. You can't reduce a lifetime of experiences to one number. I never said anything so stupid as that I wrote your books.

TEKLA: It's what you meant!

ADOLPH (*furious*): It's not what I meant!

TEKLA: It was the sum total of what you said, the bottom line!

ADOLPH (*in a wild rage*): There can't be a bottom line if you don't add! You get a quotient, a long quotient with an endless number of decimal places when you divide and it doesn't come out even. I tell you I wasn't adding!

TEKLA: No? Well, I was!

ADOLPH: I just bet you were! But I wasn't!

TEKLA: But you wanted to! Didn't you? Didn't you?

ADOLPH (*giving up; closing his eyes*): No, no, no, I tell you. . . . Don't talk to me. You're giving me convulsions. Just shut up and go away. You're prying my brain apart with that crowbar tongue of yours. . . . Your nails claw into my thoughts and tear them to shreds. (*He seems to fall into a stupor. Stares vacantly, rolls his thumbs inward against his palms.*)

TEKLA (*solicitously*): What's the matter? Adolph—are you ill? Adolph?

Adolph waves her away.

TEKLA: Adolph!

Adolph shakes his head.

TEKLA: Adolph?

ADOLPH: What?

TEKLA: Now do you admit you were unfair?

ADOLPH: Yes, yes, yes. I admit it.

TEKLA: And are you going to ask my forgiveness?

ADOLPH: Yes, yes, yes. I beg you to forgive me. Just stop talking to me!

TEKLA: Now give me a kiss.

Adolph kisses her.

TEKLA: Kiss my hand.

ADOLPH (*kisses her hand*): There. I kiss your hand. Just stop talking to me.

TEKLA: Now go outside and get some fresh air before dinner.

ADOLPH: I certainly need it. Then we'll pack our bags and leave.

TEKLA: We'll do nothing of the sort!

ADOLPH (*rising to his feet*): Why not? You must have a good reason.

TEKLA: My good reason is that I have promised to partake in the *soirée* this evening.

ADOLPH: So that's it! I knew it!

TEKLA: Yes, that's it. I promised I'd be there.

ADOLPH: No you didn't. You said you'd think about it. That's not going to prevent you from saying you've thought about it and decided not to go.

TEKLA: That's how you might act. I stick to my word.

ADOLPH: A person sticks to his promises, but he doesn't have to stick to every word he says. Did you *promise* anyone that you'd go?

TEKLA: Yes.

ADOLPH: All right. Then you can be released from your promise. You can tell them that your husband is not feeling good.

TEKLA: I'll do nothing of the sort! Besides, you're not so sick you can't come too.

ADOLPH: Why do you always want me tagging along? Does my presence make you more comfortable?

TEKLA: I don't know what you mean.

ADOLPH: That's what you always say when you know exactly what I mean and don't like what I mean.

TEKLA: Is that so? And just what is it that I don't like?

ADOLPH: Enough, enough! Don't let's start again. —Go on, goodbye. —Only for God's sake, think what you're doing. (*He leaves by the door at rear and turns right.*)

> *Tekla is alone for a few moments.*
>
> *Gustav enters. He goes directly to the table and picks up a newspaper, pretending not to see Tekla.*
>
> *Seeing him, she is visibly shaken. Gets control of herself.*

TEKLA: I don't believe it!

GUSTAV (*recognizing her*): I'm afraid it's true. Sorry.

TEKLA: How did you get here?

GUSTAV: By land. —Don't fret. I won't be staying here, since—you—

TEKLA: Don't let that stop you. . . . Well, well, it's been a long time, hasn't it?

GUSTAV: Yes, a long time.

TEKLA: You've changed a lot.

GUSTAV: And you're just as lovely and charming as ever. Even more youthful. I'm sorry to break in on you like this. Don't worry; I don't intend to sour your happiness by hanging around. If I had known you were here, I would never have—

TEKLA: Stay, by all means—that is, if you don't find it too awkward. Please.

GUSTAV: For my part, there's no reason why I shouldn't. However, I was thinking of—. Oh, dear, whatever I say, it's going to hurt someone.

TEKLA: Sit down for a while. You won't hurt me. You have that rare gift, Gustav—you've always had it—of being tactful and discreet.

GUSTAV: You're too kind, Tekla. Nevertheless, whatever you may say, your husband isn't likely to regard my qualities as indulgently as you do.

TEKLA: On the contrary. Just now he was telling me how much sympathy he had for you.

GUSTAV: Is that so? Well, we all grow and change. Like initials carved on a tree. Not even dislike can make a permanent place for itself in our hearts.

TEKLA: How could he feel dislike for you when he's never seen you? . . . As far as I'm concerned, I've always entertained a dream—seeing the two of you for a moment as friends—or at least seeing you meet in my presence—greeting each other as friends—and then going your separate ways.

GUSTAV: I, too . . . have had a secret desire . . . of seeing you—whom I have loved more than life itself—of seeing you in good hands, well cared for. I've heard nothing but good things about him, and I've kept up with his work. However, before I grow old, I'd like to clasp his hand in mine, look him in the eye, and ask him to guard well that treasure that providence left in his possession. By that very act I would also be ridding myself of the hatred that one instinctively and inevitably feels, here inside. I'd find the peace of mind I need, the humility of spirit, that would enable me to live out the rest of my sad days.

TEKLA: My very thoughts. You've understood me perfectly. Thank you, Gustav.

GUSTAV: Dear me, I cut such a poor figure, I'm so insignificant, I could never stand in your light. My simple, monotonous daily routine, my dull work, my small circle of friends could never have satisfied you. You wanted freedom, broad horizons, fast company. I admit it now. But you must understand – you've studied human nature enough – how difficult it has been for me to face up to it.

TEKLA: It's noble of you, Gustav; it shows a magnanimous soul to be able to admit one's failings. Not everyone is capable of it. (*Sighs.*) However, you were always honest, loyal, and dependable. That's what I valued in you. But –

GUSTAV: No, no. I wasn't that at all. Not *then*. But suffering purifies and sorrow ennobles. And *I* have suffered.

TEKLA: My poor Gustav. Can you ever forgive me? Can you? . . . Say you can, Gustav.

GUSTAV: Forgive you? What kind of talk is that? It is I who beg forgiveness of you.

TEKLA (*suddenly warm and intimate*): I think we're both about to cry. A couple of sentimental old fools.

GUSTAV (*adjusting to her changed tone, but warily*): Old? *I* am, but not you. You grow younger with each passing day.

> *Unobtrusively, he sits down on the chair, right; whereupon Tekla seats herself on the sofa.*

TEKLA: How sweet of you.

GUSTAV: And you know how to dress.

TEKLA: You taught me how. Remember? You showed me what colors were most becoming to me.

GUSTAV: No.

TEKLA: Of course you do. Don't you remember? You even got mad at me whenever I didn't wear something poppy-red.

GUSTAV: Come, come. Not mad. I never got mad at you.

TEKLA: Yes, you did—when you tried to teach me to think logically. Remember? I couldn't think at all.

GUSTAV: Of course you could. Everybody can think. Look at you now—you've got a sharp mind. At least when you write.

TEKLA (*rushing ahead, unhappy with this turn in the conversation*): Well, dear Gustav, it is delightful to see you again—and in such quiet circumstances too.

GUSTAV: You really can't accuse me of kicking up a row, you know. Things were rather quiet when you were with me.

TEKLA: Yes, a little too quiet.

GUSTAV: Indeed! Odd, I thought that's how you wanted me— quiet. That's the impression I got when we were engaged.

TEKLA: Who knows what they want when they're engaged? As Momma told me: to get a man a girl has to make a bit of an ass of herself.

GUSTAV: Now look at you! Always on the go, riding the merry-go-round of success. Never a dull moment in the life of an artist, and I gather your husband isn't the retiring sort.

TEKLA: Sometimes you can have too much of a good thing.

GUSTAV (*suddenly taking note of her earrings*): Look at that! You're still wearing the earrings I bought you.

TEKLA (*embarrassed*): Why shouldn't I wear them? We've never been enemies, you and I. Besides, I thought I should wear them as a kind of symbol—as a memento, I mean, since we always got along. Anyway, you can't buy this kind anymore, you know that? (*She takes off one of the earrings.*)

GUSTAV: None of my business, of course. But what does your husband think of it?

TEKLA: Why should I care what he thinks?

GUSTAV: You don't care, maybe, but what about him? Puts him in a bad light. Makes him look like a fool.

TEKLA (*curtly, as though to herself*): He was that to begin with.

> *She has been having trouble putting the earring back on. Gustav goes over to help her.*

GUSTAV: Mind if I lend a helping hand?

TEKLA: Thanks.

GUSTAV (*pinches her ear*): That sweet, lovely ear. . . . Suppose the man of the house saw us like this!

TEKLA: He'd bawl like a baby.

GUSTAV: Jealous, is he?

TEKLA: That man jealous? Ha! You can't imagine.

> *A noise in the room offstage right.*

GUSTAV: Who's in there?

TEKLA: I don't know. . . . Why don't you tell me about yourself? How things are—what you're working on.

GUSTAV: You tell me how things are with you.

> *Tekla is preoccupied and troubled. Moves about and absentmindedly removes the cloth from the figure on the stand.*

GUSTAV: My, my! Who is it? —What do you know, it's you!

TEKLA: Not very likely.

GUSTAV: Oh, but very like you.

TEKLA (*impudently*): How would you know?

GUSTAV: Reminds me of the old joke. Two men skinny-dipping. They come out of the water; see two ladies walking toward them. They put their towels over their heads so they won't be recognized. One lady says to the other, "That looks like Horace."

TEKLA (*guffaws*): You're too much! —Do you know any new jokes?

GUSTAV: No. But I bet you do.

TEKLA: Afraid not. Nowadays I never get to hear anything funny.

GUSTAV: Bashful, is he?

TEKLA: You might say—when he talks.

GUSTAV: Not otherwise?

TEKLA: Well, he's sick now.

GUSTAV: Oh, the poor thing. Well, Little Brother shouldn't go sticking his nose into somebody else's honey pot.

TEKLA (*laughing*): You're too awful, you really are!

GUSTAV: How about that time when we were just married? And we lived in this very room. It wasn't the lounge then, and it was furnished differently. There was a washbasin, wasn't there?—over there, between the windows. And—over there—was the bed . . .

TEKLA: Better stop now.

GUSTAV: Look at me.

TEKLA: All right, I'm looking at you. So . . . ?

They look intensely at each other.

GUSTAV: You don't really think I can forget? Forget the things that affected me most?

TEKLA: No. Memories have a terrible power. Especially the memories of our youth.

GUSTAV: Remember when I first met you? You were a small, lovable child. Your mind was pure and simple, like one of those little slates that children write on. There was nothing on it except some scribblings by your parents and your nanny. I wiped the slate clean and wrote my own words on it, and kept on writing until you felt there wasn't room for more. That's the real reason, you know, why I wouldn't want to be in your husband's shoes. However, that's his affair. It's also the reason why it's such a joy to see you again. Our thoughts dovetail, always have. When I sit here like this, talking to you, it's as if I were opening a bottle of my favorite wine, from my own vineyard. My own wine comes back to me, only improved with age. And now, when I'm thinking about getting married again, I have deliberately chosen a young girl whom I can raise to suit myself. Woman is supposed to be the child of man, you know; and if she isn't, *he* becomes *her* child; and that turns the world upside down.

TEKLA: You're going to get married again?

GUSTAV: Yes; tempting fortune once again. This time, however, I'm going to hold the reins tight. No running wild.

TEKLA: Is she pretty?

GUSTAV: To me she is. Maybe I'm getting old. The strange thing is that now—when chance has brought me close to you again—now I have my doubts about it—about playing the hand over again.

TEKLA: Meaning what?

GUSTAV: My roots are still imbedded in you. I feel it. I'm part of you, and the old wounds are opening up again. You're a dangerous woman, Tekla.

TEKLA: Am I now? How nice! And my young fellow says I'm past the age of making any more conquests.

GUSTAV: That means he no longer loves you.

TEKLA: What he means by love—that's what I don't understand.

GUSTAV: Your trouble is that the two of you have been playing hide-and-seek too long without finding each other. Happens sometimes. You had to pretend to be innocent—remote and pure—to please yourself—and consequently he could never be brash and bold. Oh, yes, changing the game creates problems. It does create problems.

TEKLA: You reproach me—

GUSTAV: Not at all. Whatever happens happens out of some kind of necessity. If that hadn't happened, something else would have. This happened to us, and it happened to turn out this way.

TEKLA: That's what I like about you, Gustav. You're broad-minded and understanding. I can't talk intelligently with anyone else the way I can with you. No sermons, no exhortations. You don't make demands on people. I feel free and relaxed in your company. You know, I think I'm beginning to feel jealous of your wife-to-be.

GUSTAV: You know, I feel jealous of your husband.

TEKLA (*getting up*): And now we must part. Forever.

GUSTAV: Yes, we must part. But not without a fond farewell. What do you say?

TEKLA (*uneasy*): No.

GUSTAV (*pursuing her across the floor*): I say yes! A fond fare-well, a last fling! We'll drown the past in drink. We'll get so drunk that when we wake, all our memories will have vanished. It's possible, you know: a binge to end all binges. (*Puts his arm around her waist.*) You've caught some disease from that sick soul. He's infected you with spiritual anemia. Let me breathe new life into you. Perhaps it is autumn for us, but I'll make your talent burst into bloom again—like a remontant rose. I'll—

> *Two ladies pass by outside on the veranda. Catching sight of Gustav and Tekla, they look surprised. Point their fingers, giggle, and move on.*

TEKLA (*freeing herself from Gustav's embrace*): Who was that?

GUSTAV (*indifferently*): A couple of tourists.

TEKLA: Get away from me. You scare me.

GUSTAV: How so?

TEKLA: You're taking my heart and soul.

GUSTAV: And giving you mine in their place. — What do you mean, your soul? You don't have any. It's a mirage.

TEKLA: You have a wonderful way of saying unkind things without making me mad.

GUSTAV: That's because you owe me. I hold the first mortgage on you. — Now tell me: when? And where?

TEKLA: I can't. I feel too sorry for him. He still loves me, I'm sure. I don't want to hurt him anymore.

GUSTAV: He doesn't love you. Want me to prove it? Do you want evidence?

TEKLA: How can you give me evidence?

> *Gustav picks up the pieces of the torn photograph from the floor.*

GUSTAV: Here it is! See for yourself.

TEKLA: Oh! It's scandalous! Outrageous!

GUSTAV: What more proof do you want? — So . . . when? And where?

TEKLA: The dirty little cheat!

GUSTAV: When?

TEKLA: He's sailing tonight on the eight o'clock boat.

GUSTAV: So—?

TEKLA: Nine. All right?

> *Noise is heard offstage in the room to the right.*

Who the devil is making all that noise? Who's in there?

GUSTAV (*goes to the door and peeps through the keyhole*): Let's take a look. . . . There's an end table that's been knocked over. . . . And a broken water carafe. That's all. Maybe they locked in a dog. —All right. Nine o'clock. Agreed.

TEKLA: Agreed. He's got no one to blame but himself. —What a cunning little wretch. He was always preaching frankness and honesty. Always telling me to be above board. —Now, wait a minute! There's something strange about this. . . . Let me think. . . . He didn't greet me the way he used to. Wasn't very friendly. Didn't come down to the dock. And . . . he said something about the boys on the steamboat, which I pretended not to understand. How could he have known about that? Now just a minute—he began to talk about women—analyzing them. . . . Then—he couldn't stop talking about you, thinking about you. . . . Said something about taking up sculpture because that was the art form of the modern age. Carried on about art exactly as you used to do.

GUSTAV: Not really!

TEKLA: "Not really!" —Ah, ha! I get it! I see it now. Oh, what an awful bastard you are! —You were here. You tore him into little pieces. It was you who had been sitting on that sofa. You got him to believe that he had epilepsy. You told him he had to— to—abstain from sex. Told him he should act like a man and rise up in revolt against his wife. You—you—it was you! —How long have you been here?

GUSTAV: A week.

TEKLA: So it was you I saw on the steamboat!

GUSTAV: I'm afraid it was.

TEKLA: And you really thought you could trap me?

GUSTAV: I already have.

TEKLA: Not yet, you haven't!

GUSTAV: Oh, yes, my dear, I have.

TEKLA: The big bad wolf sneaking up on my little lamb. Coming here with some dastardly plot to destroy my happiness—and you even put it in operation. Until I caught on to what you were up to, and put a spoke in your wheels.

GUSTAV: You haven't got it quite right. Let me fill in the details. . . . Of course I wanted to see you fall flat on your face. That was the wish I nourished secretly in my heart. However, I didn't really believe I would have to take any action. I was pretty sure things would go wrong without my intervention. Besides, I had so many other things that demanded my attention, there was no time left over for laying elaborate plots. But one day when I went out for a stroll, and by chance saw you with the boys on the boat, I thought the time was ripe for me to drop in on you. . . . I came here, and your little lambkin immediately threw himself into the arms of the big bad wolf. I won his sympathy because we were rather like mirrors reflecting each other. I'm afraid it would be very rude of me to explain. At first it was I who couldn't help sympathizing with him. After all, he was now in the same predicament I had once been in. Then, alas, he had to go and pick the scab off my old sores: the book you wrote about me, "the idiot," all that. That's when I could not resist the temptation to knock Humpty-Dumpty off the wall and make sure no one could ever put him together again. And it worked—thanks to you who had so conscientiously done all the preliminary work. . . . That left you. You were the mainspring in the works. All I had to do was wind you up till the spring broke, and all the wheels started spinning and whirring. . . . When I came to you here, I honestly didn't know what I was going to say. I suppose I had a number of alternatives in mind, like a good chess player; but it was your moves that determined my strategy. One thing led to another; Lady Luck played her part; and at last you were trapped, finished, kaput.

TEKLA: I am not kaput.

GUSTAV: Oh, but you are! What you least wanted has happened. The world—represented in this instance by two tourists (I assure you I never arranged it; I don't connive with others)—the world has seen you, the famous novelist, reconciled with your former husband—seen you, the repentant wife, crawling back into his ever faithful arms. What more could I wish for?

TEKLA: Nothing, if revenge is what you want. But then tell me—if you're so enlightened and fair-minded—how it happens that you, who believe that everything happens out of necessity, and that all our actions are predetermined—

GUSTAV (*correcting her*): *To a certain extent* predetermined.

TEKLA: It's the same thing.

GUSTAV: No, it isn't!

TEKLA: —How can it be that you, who regard me as innocent—and you have to, since it was my temperament and circumstances that compelled me to act the way I did—how can you imagine that you have the right to take revenge?

GUSTAV: On the same basis that you've argued—the basis being that my *temperament* and *my* circumstances compelled me to seek revenge. . . . Same rules for both sides. The two of you happened to draw the low cards. And do you know why?

Tekla sneers.

GUSTAV: —Why the two of you were so easy to fool? Because I was stronger than either of you, and cleverer. You, Tekla, you were the idiot. So was he. Understand? A person isn't an idiot just because he doesn't write novels or paint pictures. Keep that in mind for next time.

TEKLA: You are utterly devoid of feeling, aren't you?

GUSTAV: Utterly. That's why nothing gets in the way of my brains. Which means I can think—you knew that from before. And act—as you've just found out.

TEKLA: And all this merely because I hurt your little ego!

GUSTAV: Not the only reason. And why hurt other people's egos? It's their most sensitive spot.

TEKLA: Vengeful bastard! You disgust me!

GUSTAV: Frivolous bitch! You nauseate me!

TEKLA: It's my nature to be a frivolous bitch. Like it or lump it.

GUSTAV: It's my nature to be a vengeful bastard. Where does that leave us? You don't give a damn about other natures as long as your nature can take its course. But somebody gets hurt that way. Then comes judgment day and a wailing and a gnashing of teeth.

TEKLA: You can never forgive what was –

GUSTAV: Yes, I can. I've forgiven you, haven't I?

TEKLA: Forgiven me?

GUSTAV: Certainly. Have I ever raised my hand against you in all these years? Not once. All I did was come here to have a look at the two of you. One look and you split apart like a ship on the rocks. Have I ever reproached you, or lectured you, ever judged you? No. All I did was have a little fun with your spouse. That's all it took to make him crumble. – What am I doing? Why am I defending myself? I'm the plaintiff, not you. Tekla: have you nothing to reproach yourself with?

TEKLA: Nothing, nothing whatsoever! It's providence that determines our actions; that's what Christians say. Others call it fate. Either way, it makes us innocent.

GUSTAV: You think that fits all the facts, covers everything. It doesn't. Something more is needed – for the seams. You need some extra material for them – for our debts, which have to be forgiven. Sooner or later the bill collectors show up. Innocent? Yes, before God – who no longer exists. But still responsible to oneself and to one's fellow creatures.

TEKLA: So you've come to collect.

GUSTAV: I've come to take back what you stole, not what I gave you as a gift. You stole my honor, my reputation. How could I get it back without taking yours? Wasn't I right?

TEKLA: Honor! Ha! – Are you satisfied now?

GUSTAV: Yes! Now I'm satisfied.

He rings for a Waiter.

TEKLA: Running off to your girlfriend? Your fiancée?

GUSTAV: I haven't got one; and will never have one. And not running home. Because I haven't got a home; and don't want one.

The Waiter enters.

GUSTAV: Could you let me have my bill, please? I'm taking the eight o'clock boat.

The Waiter bows and leaves.

TEKLA: No reconciliation?

GUSTAV: Reconciliation? Your vocabulary is full of words that no longer have any meaning. How can we be reconciled? Should we arrange a cozy little threesome? You're the one who should reconcile us by making up for the harm you've done. But that you cannot do. Because you have only taken, and what you've taken, you've consumed, so there's nothing left to give back. . . . Would it satisfy you if I said: forgive me for allowing you to tear my heart and soul to pieces? Forgive me that you dishonored me. Forgive me for being made fun of by my students every day for seven years. Forgive me for liberating you from the tyranny of your parents, for educating you and freeing your mind from old superstitions and silly old ideas. For making you mistress of my house, for giving you friends and a social position. For making the child I first met into a woman. Forgive me my debts as I forgive you yours! —All right? I tear up all the IOU's; cancel all our debts. Now you settle your account with the other man.

TEKLA: What have you done with him? My God! You've done something, haven't you? Something terrible.

GUSTAV: With him? Do you still love him?

TEKLA: Yes.

GUSTAV: And a moment ago you said you loved me. Didn't you mean that?

TEKLA: I meant it, yes!

GUSTAV: You know what that makes you?

TEKLA: You despise me?

GUSTAV: I feel sorry for you. —Loving as you do—I don't say it's wrong, simply disadvantageous. It leads to the wrong things. —Poor Tekla! I almost regret what I've done, although I'm innocent. Like you. Perhaps you can learn something from going through what I had to go through. — Do you know where your husband is?

TEKLA: I . . . think I do. He's there—in the next room, isn't he? He's heard everything, hasn't he? And seen everything. And the man who sees his own double, he dies.

> *Adolph appears at the veranda door, deathly pale, a streak of blood on his cheek. His eyes are blank and expressionless, and he is frothing at the mouth.*

GUSTAV (*recoils at the sight of him*): No, he's here! —Settle up with him. Let's see if he's as generous as I have been. —Goodbye, Tekla. (*He moves toward the door at the left, but stops.*)

> *Tekla approaches Adolph, her arms outstretched toward him.*

TEKLA: Adolph!

> *Adolph sinks to the floor against the doorjamb. Tekla throws herself on his body, caressing him.*

TEKLA: Adolph! My sweet child! Don't die, don't die! Speak to me, Adolph. Forgive Tekla who was so mean to you. Forgive me, forgive me! Forgive me. Little Brother mustn't be mean. He must answer when he's being spoken to, do you hear?! Oh, God, he doesn't hear me. He's dead. Oh, God in heaven, my dear God, help us, help us!

GUSTAV: She really does love him, too! Poor fool!*

---

* In Strindberg's original manuscript (1888) the last line reads simply, "She loves him!" Strindberg expanded it in the French translation that he prepared and in the printed Swedish text.

Introduction
to
The Stronger

The critical success of Antoine's Théâtre-Libre in Paris inspired Strindberg to organize his own experimental theater in Scandinavia. His wife, Siri, was to be the star, and three or four amateurs would be recruited to form the company. For economic reasons the plays had to have small casts and simple sets, if the company was to tour. *Miss Julie* and *Creditors* were to be the show pieces in the repertoire, and Strindberg would furnish new plays as the venture prospered. Regrettably and predictably, it proved to be a fiasco. The Experimental Theater was to open in Copenhagen with a performance of *Miss Julie*, but the Danish censor forbade the public performance of that shocking play, even though Siri appealed directly to him. A newspaper demanded that its scurrilous author be made to leave the country. *Creditors* had to be substituted at the last moment, and the first performance of *Miss Julie* took place five days later, on 14 March 1889, when Strindberg rented a hall and invited theatergoers to a "private" presentation. A few days later the Experimental Theater performed in southern Sweden, and that was the end of it. Strindberg's dreams of having his own theater were broken by bad notices, poor actors, and unyielding censors.

One of the plays Strindberg wrote with the touring company in mind was *The Stronger* (written December 1888–January 1889), which was probably intended to be performed with either *Miss Julie* or *Creditors* to make a full evening in the theater. The short, serious sketch, called *quart d'heure*, had just come into vogue in Paris at the Théâtre-Libre.

The unusual feature of Strindberg's sketch was that one of the two actresses remains silent throughout. It is a clever tour-de-force, popular in acting classes, and another example of Strindberg's ability to concentrate dramatic action.

Inevitably the question arises: who is the stronger: the married talkative actress or the silent single one? Strindberg's own remarks, with one possible exception, indicate that the married woman is stronger because she has learned to be adaptable. The exception is that Strindberg told a Danish newspaper that the heroine of the skit does not say a word. But what did he mean by heroine? A scholar who has gathered all the material, pro and con, that bears on the question has concluded that Strindberg has neatly balanced one role against the other.* In the theater the question is settled by the way in which the parts are cast.

Strindberg's advice (letter of March 1889) to his wife when she was about to take the role of the married actress is clear and sensible.

> Play the part
> (1) bearing in mind she's an actress; in other words, not your conventional proper family wife.
> (2) as the stronger, that is, the more pliant. The cataleptic one snaps, but the supple one bends under pressure – and rises again.
> (3) elegantly dressed – use your dress from *Miss Julie*, or get a new one.
> (4) If you get a new coat, beware of smooth surfaces, smooth pleats – and buy a new hat. Something in fur, bonnet shape, not English style.
> (5) Study the part awfully carefully, but play it simply – that is, not simply. Make 50% of it phoney profound, like Mrs. Hwasser [as Nora in *A Doll's House*] and Ibsen, and hint at deep profundities that don't exist.
> (6) Change phrases if they don't feel natural – and fix up your exit to get applause (but don't hiss at Y).

* Egil Törnqvist, *Strindbergian Drama* (Stockholm and Atlantic Highlands, N.J., 1982), pp. 64–70.

The Stronger

(Den starkare)

A Sketch

CHARACTERS

MRS. X, actress
MISS Y, actress
[A WAITRESS]

Time: 1888

*A ladies' café, only one corner of it visible. Two small wrought-iron bistro tables; a red shag sofa; some chairs.**

Mrs. X enters, wearing a hat and a winter overcoat, with a handsome Japanese basket on her arm.

Miss Y is sitting at one of the tables, a glass of beer, half-empty, in front of her, reading an illustrated magazine, which she exchanges for others as the scene progresses.

MRS. X: Well, hello, Amelia! Darling, what *are* you doing here —alone on Christmas Eve? Like some poor bachelor.

Miss Y looks up from her magazine, nods, and goes on reading.

Mrs. X takes off her coat. Her dress is tasteful and modish.

MRS. X: Oh, Amelia, dearest Amelia! This is distressing. You mustn't sit here all by yourself, alone on Christmas Eve, in a restaurant. I won't have it. Reminds me of when I was in Paris and saw a wedding party in a restaurant, and the bride sat there looking at the comics in a magazine, while the groom played billiards with the best man and the ushers. My God, I said to myself, if it's like this on the wedding night, how will it be in the morning, how will it all end? . . . Playing billiards on his wedding day!

* In a letter to Siri von Essen, March 1889, Strindberg suggested how the set could be quickly improvised. " 'Erect' onstage the corner of the café, a cave-like section, a booth . . . using flats from other plays in rehearsal. Hang up scenic vistas, travel posters, theater posters on the walls, so it looks like a café, with the counter and cases offstage. Set out an umbrella stand, coat rack, and so on."

—Well, she was reading the comics—that's what you're thinking. Not quite the same thing, though, is it?

> *The Waitress enters, brings in the cup of hot chocolate that Mrs. X had ordered, and exits.*

MRS. X: You know what, Amelia? Whatever I may have thought *then,* *now* I think you should have held on to him. I know I was the first to tell you to forgive and forget. You do remember that, don't you? Why, you'd be married now, and have a home for yourself. Remember last Christmas, how happy you felt out there on the farm, visiting your fiancé's parents? How you went on about the joys of family life—how you wanted to get away from the theater? . . . It's true, Amelia; having a home is still the best—after the theater. —And children, of course. Darling, you wouldn't understand that.

> *Miss Y gives her a contemptuous glance.*

> *Mrs. X takes a few sips of chocolate, using her teaspoon. Opens her basket and displays Christmas presents.*

MRS. X: Let me show you what I've bought for the kiddies. (*Shows a doll*). Isn't it cute? It's for Lisa. Look—it can roll its eyes, and its neck turns. What do you think, hmm? —And this is for Maia: a toy gun.

> *Mrs. X loads the popgun, aims it as Miss Y, and shoots. Miss Y gestures in fear.*

Mrs. X: Afraid?! You didn't really believe I'd shoot you, did you? Really! Bless my soul, I didn't think you'd harbor such nasty thoughts, darling. Now, if *you* had wanted to shoot *me,* that wouldn't surprise me. After all, I did get that part you had your heart set on, didn't I? You'll never get over it, I know. But I assure you I had absolutely nothing to do with it. You still believe, don't you, that I plotted to get you out of the City Theater. Well, I didn't. No matter what you believe, I didn't. . . . What's the use of talking. No matter what I say, you still believe I was behind it all. (*Takes out a pair of embroidered slippers.*) And here's what I got for the old man. Tulips! I embroidered them myself. I simply abominate tulips, really I do, but he has to have tulips on everything.

Miss Y raises her eyes from her magazine, suddenly interested, a sardonic expression on her face.

MRS. X (*putting a hand in each slipper*): He's got such tiny feet, Bob has. Don't you think? —And he walks so elegantly. Well, you've never seen him in his slippers, so you wouldn't know.

Miss Y laughs aloud.

MRS. X: Then when he gets mad—look—he stamps on the floor —like this. "That damned cook! Can't she ever learn how to make a decent cup of coffee?"—"Those aren't maids; they're cretins! They can't even trim a wick!" . . . Now there's a cold draft blowing across the floor, and his feet are cold. "Damn! It's freezing in here. Those blockheads, can't they keep a fire going in the stove?" (*She rubs the slippers together, the sole of one against the toe of the other.*)

Miss Y guffaws.

MRS. X: Now he's just come home, and he's looking for his slippers, which Marie has put under the bureau. . . . Oh, I shouldn't be making fun of him like this. He's such a sweet man, really, my dear little hubby. You should have one just like him, Amelia. Do you a world of good. —What are you laughing at? Hm? Hm? What's so funny? —Listen, darling, one thing I know for sure: that he's faithful, true to me. Absolutely. He's told me all about it. —Now what are you grinning at? —That time when I was touring the provinces and along came that disgusting ogress Frederika and tried to seduce him. Can you imagine anything quite so infamous? (*Pause.*) I would have scratched her pink little eyes out if she tried anything like that while I was home. I would have. (*Pause.*) Fortunately, Bob told me all about it, so I didn't have to hear it via the grapevine. (*Pause.*) Of course, Frederika wasn't the only one. Believe me, she wasn't! I don't know why, but the women go gaga over him. He's *my* husband, but they want him. Evidently they think he's got something to say about

their contracts because he works in the administration. . . . I
suppose you've been on the prowl after him, too. . . . I've never
really trusted you, but there's one thing I do know: he was never
interested in you. And you always bore him some sort of a
grudge. Well, that's how it struck me.

> *Pause. They glance at each other, both a little tense and*
> *edgy.*

MRS. X: Oh, come on, Amelia; spend Christmas Eve with us.
Just to show that you're not mad at us—not at me, at any rate.
I don't know why, but it's so unpleasant—our not being friends,
I mean. I don't mind the others, but you—. I suppose it's because
I got that part you wanted. (*Rallentando.*) Or because—. I haven't
the foggiest idea. . . . Why? . . . I mean, why?

> *Pause. Miss Y stares probingly at Mrs. X.*

MRS. X (*thoughtfully*): It was so odd—our friendship. When I
met you for the first time, I was afraid of you. So scared I didn't
dare let you out of my sight. No matter where I went, I always
found myself near you. I didn't dare have you for an enemy, so
I made friends with you. Still, there was a wall between us, even
when you visited us at home. I could see that Bob couldn't stand
you. I could tell that something was out of kilter, just wasn't
right. Like a dress that doesn't fit properly. I did everything I
could to make him like you. But no luck. Not until you got yourself engaged. Than all of a sudden you became great friends. It
was as if the two of you couldn't let down your defenses until *you*
had found some security. And then—? What *did* happen? I didn't
get jealous, no. . . . So strange! . . . I remember the christening, when you were there as godmother, and I made him kiss you.
And he did kiss you, and you got so flustered. Funny, I didn't
think of it then. Didn't think of it till later. Never thought about
it till—*this moment*! (*Stands up abruptly.*) Why don't you say
something? You haven't said a single word all this time. You've
just let me sit here prattling on and on. Sitting looking at me,
dragging out my thoughts. Like raveling out silk from the
cocoon, where they've been lying all this time. Sleeping thoughts.
Things I suspected but didn't dare—. Let me think. . . . Why

did you break off your engagement? Why did you never come to our house after that time? Why won't you come home to us tonight?

Miss Y looks as if she is about to speak.

MRS. X: No, don't say it! You don't have to say anything. I can see it all now. The whole thing. Why that was. −And that. −And that. Oh, yes. It all adds up. That's it, all right. −How disgusting! I refuse to sit at the same table with you.

She moves her things to the other table.

That was why I had to embroider tulips on his slippers. I detest tulips. It was you who liked tulips. That was why−

Throws the slippers on the floor.

we had to have our summer place up at Lake Mälar: because you simply couldn't stand the ocean. That was why my boy was named Eskil. Because that was your father's name. That was why I had to wear colors that suited you, read books you liked, eat your favorite dishes, drink your favorite drinks−hot chocolate, for instance. That was why−.

The enormity of the thought strikes her.

Oh, my God! Oh, God in heaven. How awful! How disgusting! Everything, even what we did when we made love−everything comes from you. . . . Your soul crept into mine like a worm into an apple, bored its way in, ate and burrowed until there was nothing left but the skin and some black crumbs. I wanted to get away from you, only I couldn't. You lay there like a serpent, your black eyes bewitching me. I wanted to run away from you but my feet were like lead. I felt like I had been thrown into the water with my legs tied together, and the more I struggled with my arms, the faster I sank. Down . . . down until I hit bottom. And there you were, lying in wait, like a gigantic crab, to catch me in your claws. That's where I am now. . . .

My God, how I hate you, detest you, abhor you! Let me look at you. You just sit there, silent, indifferent, not caring whether it's Christmas or New Year's, new moon or full moon, whether others are happy or sad. Incapable of loving or hating. Quiet and unmoving, like a cat at a rat hole. You don't know how to catch your prey on your own; you don't know how to hunt it down; all you can do is outwait it. So all you do is sit here in your favorite corner. By the way, darling, you know what they call it, don't you?—because of you—"The Crocodile's Den." Reading the papers to find out what show is floundering, who's been thrown overboard, so you can gobble up the part. The crocodile flicks her tail, figures out who'll sink, who'll swim, looks for victims and collects her tributes.

Poor, dear Amelia. You know, darling, I really feel sorry for you. I can't help it. Because I know you're unhappy. Unhappy because you've been hurt; and malicious because it does hurt so. —I can't even get mad at you. I want to, only I can't. Because you're such a little person. So small and helpless. All that hanky-panky with Bob—why should I bother about that? What's it got to do with me? If you hadn't taught me to like hot chocolate, somebody else would have. What difference does it make?

Sips a spoonful of chocolate. Assumes a know-it-all air.

Besides, chocolate is very good for one's health. —Maybe I did learn from you what sort of clothes to wear. So what? *Tant mieux.* Now he's more mine than ever before. Where you lost, I won. In fact, to judge by certain indications, I believe you've already lost him. —Of course, I know what you thought would happen: I'd leave him. That's what you thought. Because that's what *you* did. Now you're sitting here regretting it. But, Amelia dearest, I have no intention of leaving him. Now we mustn't be small-minded, right? And if nobody else wanted him, why would I want him?

Maybe after all is said and done, maybe at this moment I really am the stronger of us. You never got anything from me. You only gave things—ideas. I feel almost like a thief in the night. You woke up, and I had everything you'd lost.

How else can you explain it? Everything you touched became worthless. You had the touch of sterility. You couldn't keep his love — any man's love, for that matter — with your tulips and your lovemaking. But I could. You couldn't learn the art of living, not for all those books. But I did. You didn't have a baby you could name Eskil. You only had a father named Eskil.

And why do you never say anything? Always, eternally not saying anything? I thought it was your strength; I did. But I guess I was wrong. You just didn't have anything to say. Because you don't have a thought in your head.

Rises and picks up the slippers.

Well, I'm going home. And taking the tulips with me. *Your* tulips. . . . You couldn't learn from others; you couldn't bend and adapt. So you broke like a dry stick. Well, darling, I didn't!

Thanks, dear Amelia, for all your help, your how-to-do-it lessons. Thanks for teaching my husband how to be a good lover. — Now I'm going home, to love him.

Exits.

Introduction

to

Playing with Fire

In 1891 and 1892 when Strindberg was separated from his wife, Siri, and involved in divorce proceedings, he wrote a series of one-act plays that he later characterized as "scenes from the cynical life." The series concluded with two longish plays that Strindberg wanted published together: *Playing with Fire* and *The Bond*, the first about erotic passion, sex and marriage; the second about sexual hatred and divorce.

Strindberg wrote *Playing with Fire* in August 1892, when, like Axel in the play, he was waiting for his divorce to become final. The situation in the comedy reproduced a factual episode from the previous year, the characters in the play being so unmistakably identifiable that publishers hesitated to print the play. Axel, however, is only twenty-six years old, not forty-two as Strindberg was at the time, and it has been persuasively argued (by Hans-Görman Ekman) that Strindberg chose to dramatize this episode because it so closely resembled one that had occurred in the 1870s when the twenty-six-year-old Strindberg had met and fallen in love with Siri. At that time she was married to Baron Carl Gustaf Wrangel. The baron eased Strindberg into Siri's arms. The three of them played with fire and they eventually suffered the consequences. Thus, Strindberg's 1892 play is a cautionary tale.

Both in its subject matter and in its tone it lies midway between sprightly French boulevard comedy of the nineteenth century and Chekhov's richly atmospheric and understated drama, which was still to be written. As in French erotic comedy, the plot takes shape around a few contretemps and ill-timed intrusions. As in Chekhov's plays, there are long, meaningful pauses and silences; the characters seem to be obsessed by love and have all the time in the world to play at it.

In *Creditors*, Gustav says that the lovers did not have the courage to tell the husband that they love each other. In *Playing with Fire* the lovers do exactly that. *Creditors* ends tragically; *Playing with Fire* ends comically. But hardly with any great inevitability. Strindberg wrote three endings for the play. As first written, the play ended with Axel discovering that Kerstin is two months pregnant. For the German translation, Strindberg provided another ending in which Axel learns from a letter that his divorce is not final. In both these versions, external reasons prompt Axel's sudden departure. In the final version, printed in 1897, Strindberg avoided any last-minute revelations and let Axel himself realize how intolerable his situation is.

Playing with Fire

(Leka med elden)

A Comedy in One Act

CHARACTERS

THE FATHER, 60, of independent means
THE MOTHER, 58
KNUT, their son, 27, a painter
KERSTIN, his wife, 24
AXEL, Knut's friend, 26
ADELE, Knut's cousin, about 20

Time and place: a seaside resort on a summer morning in the 1890s.

The set: a glassed-in veranda used as a living room. Doors at both ends of the veranda, and a door at the back leading to the garden.

[1]

Knut is at his easel, painting.

His wife, Kerstin, enters, wearing a dressing gown.

KNUT: Has he gotten up yet?

KERSTIN: Axel? How would I know?

KNUT: I thought you had your eyes on him.

KERSTIN: Shame on you. If I didn't know you don't have a jealous bone in your body, I'd think the green-eyed monster had got you.

KNUT: And if I didn't know that you could never be unfaithful to me, I'd never let you out of my sight.

KERSTIN: What brought this on? And why now?

KNUT: You heard me say "if" – "if I didn't know." You know how I feel about Axel. He's our best friend and good to have around. I think it's wonderful that you share my sympathy for that poor troubled soul. It's fine with me.

KERSTIN: Yes, I can see he's unhappy. But I must say he does act strangely at times. Last summer, for instance. Dashing off in such a hurry, without even saying goodbye, and leaving all his stuff behind. Why?

KNUT: Bizarre, wasn't it? I thought he left because he was in love with cousin Adele.

KERSTIN: Oh, did you?

KNUT: I did; but not anymore. Mamma's theory is that he went back to his wife and child.

KERSTIN: How could he? Weren't they divorced?

KNUT: Not definitely. And still aren't. He's expecting the final papers any day now.

KERSTIN: So you thought he was in love with Adele, did you? Interesting. Funny you never said anything before. Not a bad idea, the two of them getting together. Not bad at all.

KNUT: I wonder. Adele is such a wet blanket.

KERSTIN: Adele! Ha! A lot you know.

KNUT: She may have a marvelous figure, but I'll bet she's about as passionate as a fish.

KERSTIN: What do you want to bet?

KNUT: What do you know about it?

KERSTIN: I know that if she ever lets down her hair—well!!!

KNUT: Really?

KERSTIN: You seem interested.

KNUT: In a way.

KERSTIN: Which way?

KNUT: She posed for me, you know. When I painted the swimmer coming out of the water.

KERSTIN: Yes, I know she posed for you. But who hasn't? —Which reminds me, Knut: you shouldn't show your sketches to every Tom, Dick, and Harry who comes along. —Ah, here's Mommykins!

[2]

The Mother enters, unkempt, frowsily dressed, a wide-brimmed, showy Japanese hat on her head, a wicker basket on her arm.

KNUT: Mama! You look like something the cat dragged in.

MOTHER: Such a sweet boy!

KERSTIN: Knut likes to be shocking. Find anything tempting in the shops this morning?

MOTHER: I saw these delicious flounder, and couldn't resist.

KNUT (*poking around in the basket*): What the hell! What are these? — Ducklings!

KERSTIN: Not very plump, are they? Feel the breasts.

KNUT: Oooh, I'd love to! May I?

KERSTIN: Naughty!

MOTHER: Well, he's back, isn't he? Your friend, Axel. I saw him come in last night.

KNUT: My friend! Ha! Kerstin's friend. She's nuts about him. They went for each other like lovers last night when he came through the door.

MOTHER: You shouldn't joke about it, Knut. You know what happens when you play with fire.

KNUT: I know, I know. But you can't teach an old dog. —Anyway, look at me. Why should such a handsome dog need to be jealous?

MOTHER: It's not what shows, Knut. Is it, Kerstin?

KERSTIN: I haven't the faintest idea what you mean.

MOTHER (*tapping her lightly on the cheek*): Don't overdo it, little girl.

KNUT: Kerstin is incredibly innocent—and an old hen like you shouldn't go around wising her up.

KERSTIN: You have a nasty way of joking. I can never tell whether you're serious or not.

KNUT: I'm always serious.

KERSTIN: It looks like it. You keep a straight face when you make your disgusting remarks.

MOTHER: I can see the two of you are just itching for a quarrel. Didn't you sleep well?

KNUT: We didn't sleep at all.

MOTHER (*clucking her tongue*): Shame on you. —Well, I can't waste the day standing here. Papa will be cursing a blue streak.

KNUT: Where is the old man? I haven't seen him.

MOTHER: I suppose he's out taking his constitutional with Adele.

KNUT: Aren't you jealous—a little bit?

MOTHER: Pooh!

KNUT: I am.

MOTHER: Jealous of whom?—if I may ask.

KNUT: Of the old man, of course.

MOTHER: Do you hear that, Kerstin? You see what a fine family you've married into.

KERSTIN: If I didn't know what Knut is really like—and if I hadn't known when I married him that artists are a tribe apart, I honestly wouldn't know what to make of you all.

KNUT: Just a minute! I'm the artist, the bohemian. Mom and Pop are philistines.

MOTHER (*no anger in her voice*): Nonsense. You're the philistine. Typical middle-class son, you are. You've never worked a day in your life—and how old are you now? And your father was no profiteering capitalist when he built this house for a good-for-nothing like you.

KNUT: Oh, it isn't easy to be the only son. It's hard, hard, hard. Come on, off you go. Otherwise the old man will be cursing you *here*—and I don't want to have my delicate ears singed. —I can see him. Hurry!

MOTHER: I'll slip out the other way. (*She exits.*)

KNUT: There's a hell of a draft in this house. Blows right through. Might as well be out in the open.

KERSTIN: Yes. Why can't your parents leave us alone a bit? Why do we have to eat at their table? Why can't we have our own maid?

KNUT: Why do you put crumbs on the windowsill for the birds? To have the pleasure of watching them eat.

KERSTIN (*listening to footsteps outside*): Shhh! Try to be a little more pleasant to your old man. I hate these morning tiffs.

KNUT: If only I could. It's not entirely my fault. He's never in the mood for my brilliant wit.

[3]

> *The Father enters, wearing a white vest and a black velvet jacket with a rose in the lapel.*
>
> *Cousin Adele comes in a little later. At first she walks around rather aimlessly, then begins to dust and clean.*

FATHER (*has kept his hat on*): It's chilly in the morning.

KNUT: So I see.

FATHER: Do I look cold?

KNUT: Evidently your head is freezing.

> *The Father looks at him disdainfully.*

KERSTIN: You shouldn't talk to your father like that, Knut.

FATHER: "A fool's mouth is his destruction" – "and the father of a fool has no joy."

KNUT: Without the Bible, you'd be tongue-tied.

KERSTIN (*to Adele*): The room's already been dusted, Adele.

FATHER: "Every wise woman buildeth her house: but the foolish plucketh it down with her hands." Proverbs 14.

KNUT: Did you hear that, Adele?

ADELE: Me?

KNUT: Yes. Here's another one for you: "A fair woman who is without discretion is like a gold ring in a swine's snout."

KERSTIN: That's enough, Knut!

FATHER: I see you had a visitor last night. Late.

KNUT: *Too* late, you mean.

FATHER: I don't mean anything. However . . . why can't a young man choose a more convenient time to drop in?

KNUT: So you do think it was late.

FATHER: Was he invited?

KNUT: What is this? The inquisition? Have you brought the thumbscrews?

FATHER: No, that's your department. —If I ask you the simplest question, you threaten to leave. I built this house for you so I could spend some time with you, at least in the summer. When you get to be my age, you have a desire to live for others.

KNUT: Come off it! You're not old. Look at you! You look like you've been courting. A rose in your lapel! Who's the lucky girl?

FATHER: There are limits, Knut—even for your jokes. Wouldn't you agree, Kerstin?

KERSTIN: Knut *is* dreadful. But he doesn't mean anything. If he did—!

FATHER: If he doesn't mean anything when he says something, he's an idiot. (*He studies the portrait of Axel, which Knut has started on.*)

FATHER: Who's that supposed to be?

KNUT: Don't you recognize him? My friend, Kerstin's friend, our friend in common.

FATHER: Looks common. A bad sort, if you ask me—in this portrait.

KNUT: Well, he's not.

FATHER: A man without religion is a bad sort. And a man who breaks his marriage vows is a bad sort. So say I.

KERSTIN: But he hasn't broken his marriage vows. He's letting the courts dissolve the marriage.

FATHER: There was a time when Knut did nothing but revile your friend. Now it seems he can do nothing wrong. What happened?

KNUT: I didn't know him before. I've learned what he's really like. —Are you going to take any more pot shots? Or have you used up your morning supply?

FATHER: How about another proverb. I don't believe you've heard this one.

KNUT: I've heard all your proverbs and all your stories.

FATHER: There's "a time to love—and a time to hate." Ecclesiastes 3:8. —Good morning. (*He leaves.*)

[4]

Adele has started to water the flowers.

KERSTIN: They've already been watered, dear girl.

ADELE: I'd prefer it if you didn't call me that. I'm not your dear girl. You hate me.

KERSTIN: I don't hate you. Perhaps I should. It's because of you there's all this quarreling in the family.

KNUT: And now the two of you are at it.

KERSTIN: Well, why does she always have to be dusting and cleaning and watering in *my* house? You think she's helping me out. She's not. It's her way of criticizing me and showing me up.

ADELE: You take it that way because you know you're neglecting your house and your child. But I don't have any designs on you. I do these chores because I want to be useful. That's all. I don't want to live on charity. But you! You! What do you do?

KNUT (*going to Adele and taking a long look at her*): So you've got a temper, have you? Hot and excitable, hmm? Hot and passionate, too? Hmm?

KERSTIN: Forget it, Knut. Her passions have nothing to do with you.

ADELE: That's true. I'm poor. I can't afford to have any moods, any opinions, any desires, any passions. But if you get yourself a rich man and marry him, then you can do what you like—be waited on at table, have your bed made for you, do just what you want — *even at night!*

KERSTIN: You watch your tongue!

ADELE: You watch it! I could say plenty. I've got a good pair of eyes in my head! And ears, too! (*She leaves.*)

[5]

KNUT: All hell is breaking loose.

KERSTIN: Not yet, but it will. The day isn't over. I'm warning you, Knut: watch out for that girl. . . . Do you realize what would happen if your mother should die?

KNUT: No. What would?

KERSTIN: Your father could remarry.

KNUT: Ah ha! Adele?

KERSTIN: Exactly!

KNUT: Damn! — But we could put a stop to that. (*Thinking out the situation.*) She'd become my stepmother, and her children would share in the inheritance.

KERSTIN: I've already heard rumors that your father has changed his will to include Adele.

KNUT: It's not serious, is it? How far have they gone?

KERSTIN: Nowhere — all the way — who knows? One thing is sure: he's very fond of her.

KNUT: Fond, yes. That's all.

KERSTIN: Over head and ears, I'd say. Even last year he was jealous of Axel.

KNUT: Good! Let's pair them off. If they married each other —

KERSTIN: Put a bridle on Axel?? Not so easy.

KNUT: Why not? He's always in heat — like all ex-husbands.

KERSTIN: I'm beginning to feel sorry for him. He's too good for that she-devil.

KNUT: For some reason, the air is getting awfully heavy in here. Feels like a storm coming on. Oh, to get away from it all—go abroad.

KERSTIN: On what? You haven't sold any of your paintings. And if we leave here, your father will cut off your allowance. . . . Let's talk to Axel—tell him the whole story. He's good at arranging other people's lives—even if he made a mess of his own.

KNUT: Do you think it's prudent to ask a stranger to wash our dirty linen?

KERSTIN: He's our only friend, you said so yourself. How can you call him a stranger?

KNUT: It still bothers me for some reason. Blood is thicker than water. . . . Anyway, I don't like it. . . . As the old man likes to say, quoting the Seven Sages, "Always treat friends like future enemies."

KERSTIN: Now he's got you quoting his aphorisms. He has another one, just as awful: "The one to fear is the one you love."

KNUT: Oh, he's a hard man when he puts his mind to it.

KERSTIN (*seeing Axel offstage*): Well, good morning! Rip van Winkle is finally awake! (*Going to meet him.*) Did you sleep well?

[6]

> Axel enters. He has on a light summer jacket, a blue necktie, and white tennis shoes.

KNUT: Top of the morning, Axel.

AXEL: Good morning, good morning! You haven't been waiting for me, I hope?

KERSTIN: We certainly have.

KNUT: Kerstin here has been worrying herself sick thinking you didn't get any sleep last night.

AXEL (*puzzled and embarrassed*): How so? Why wouldn't I?

KNUT (*to Kerstin*): Look at him! He's so bashful.

Kerstin studies Axel carefully, her curiosity aroused.

AXEL: Glorious morning, isn't it? What a delight to wake up in a house with happy people in it. Makes one feel that life is worth living.

KNUT: You think Kerstin and I are happy people?

AXEL: Of course! And your father is doubly happy. He's got his children and his grandchildren. With them around, he can live the best days of his life all over again. I tell you, fate allots few men such a happy old age.

KNUT: Never envy anyone!

AXEL: Oh, I don't. Quite the contrary. What makes me happy is seeing how beautiful life can be – for some people. Leads me to hope that life will smile on me sometime. Especially when I consider what your father has gone through: bankruptcy, ostracism, disowned by his parents . . .

KNUT: And now he has his own house – and property – a son well married. Or don't you think so?

AXEL: Of course I do. Absolutely.

KNUT: But what about last summer? Don't tell me you weren't in love with my wife?

AXEL: I wouldn't say that. Oh, I was mad about her for a while. . . . That's all over now.

KERSTIN: Aren't you the fickle one!

AXEL: Only when I'm infatuated. Fortunately – for me.

KNUT: So why did you run away last year? You dashed out of here as if the house were on fire. Was it because of another lady? . . . Or because of Adele?

AXEL (*embarrassed*): Now you're prying.

KNUT: Ah ha! It was Adele! I told you so, Kerstin.

KERSTIN: Why on earth would you be afraid of her? Unless you're afraid of girls.

AXEL: I'm not afraid of girls, only of my feelings for them.

KNUT: You're wriggling, Axel; and you're good at it. Never know where you're at.

AXEL: Why this particular interest in me?

KNUT: Do you know what my father said when he saw that portrait of you?

KERSTIN: Knut, don't!

KNUT: He said you looked like a bad sort.

AXEL: It must be a striking likeness. I am a bad sort—at least for the time being.

KERSTIN: You're always bragging about how bad you are.

AXEL: Maybe it's my way of hiding the fact that I am.

KERSTIN: You don't fool me. You're a good person, much better than you let on. But the way you act scares your friends away.

AXEL: Are you scared?

KERSTIN: Yes, sometimes—when I don't know what's going on in your head.

KNUT: You have to get married again. That's all there's to it.

AXEL: That's all, huh? And whom have you in mind for me?

KNUT: Ohhh . . . Adele, for example.

AXEL: Let's change the subject, if you don't mind.

KNUT: Ah ha! That's where the shoe pinches. You see, I was right all along. It's Adele.

AXEL: Enough of this chit-chat. I think it's time I changed. Into something darker.

KERSTIN: You'll do nothing of the sort. That outfit is perfectly charming. Adele will adore you in it.

KNUT: Listen to that, Axel! My wife thinks you're perfectly charming.

KERSTIN: What's so terrible about saying he looks nice?

KNUT: Women don't ordinarily go around publicly flattering the men they meet. Of course, we're not ordinary people, are we?

AXEL: After I've changed, perhaps you can help me find a room in town.

KERSTIN: What do you mean? You're staying here with us.

AXEL: No, I never intended to do that.

KNUT: Well how about that!

KERSTIN: Why won't you stay here with us? I want to know.

AXEL: I don't know. . . . Maybe you should be left alone. —Who knows, we might get bored with one another.

KERSTIN: Are you already bored with us? —Now, Axel, it just won't do, your staying in town. Tongues would start wagging.

AXEL: Wagging about what?

KERSTIN: Oh, come on, you know how people make up stories. You arrive one night, you move out the next day . . .

KNUT: It's settled: you're staying here. Let them talk all they want. If you stay here, they'll say you're my wife's lover—obviously. If you move into town, they'll say the lovers have split up—obviously. Or that I kicked you out. Given those alternatives, I think your reputation suffers less if you are taken to be my wife's lover. What say you?

AXEL: Phrased with admirable clarity. But if you don't mind, under the circumstances, I'd prefer to consider *your* reputation.

KERSTIN: There's something behind this—something you haven't told us.

AXEL: Quite frankly, I don't dare stay. . . . Listen, you know—. I mean . . . it's so easy to live someone else's life. . . . Enjoying their happiness. Your feelings merge with theirs. And after that, it's very difficult to separate.

KNUT: Why separate?! Now look, you're going to move in here with us. —Come on, give my wife your arm, and we'll go for a stroll.

Abashed and uneasy, Axel offers his arm to Kerstin.

KERSTIN: I think you're trembling. —Knut, the poor boy's shaking.

KNUT: You look so handsome, the two of you, arm in arm. —He really is all atremble. All right, stay here if you're shivering.

AXEL: Yes, if you don't mind, I'd prefer to sit here and read the paper.

KERSTIN: Of course, Axel, by all means. You do just what you like. And I'll send Adele in to keep you company. Knut and I will do a little shopping, won't we? (*Calling and waving offstage.*) Yoo-hoo, Adele! I've got something for you!

[7]

Adele enters.

AXEL: Would you mind keeping me company while Knut and Kerstin go shopping?

ADELE: Are you afraid of being alone?

AXEL: Terrified.

Knut and Kerstin leave.

AXEL (*checking to see that they are alone*): This may be my only chance to speak to you in confidence, as a member of the family. May I?

ADELE: Of course.

AXEL: You know how much I like Knut and Kerstin. —You're smiling. I know what you're thinking. It's more than a liking. It's true: Kerstin, being a young woman, exerts a certain attraction on me. But I assure you that, as far as her attractions are concerned, I keep my feelings reined in. Only for one moment was I afraid they had run away with me.

ADELE: Well, I am not surprised that you're a little taken with

Kerstin. She can be captivating, I know. What I don't understand is what you see in Knut. He seems to exercise some power over you. But he's a nonentity, far beneath you in talent and experience.

AXEL: A child, that's what you mean, a little boy. But that's what I like about him. After spending a whole winter among academics and intellectuals, I find his company gives me peace of mind.

ADELE: So can playing with children, but it's boring. Yet you never get bored with Knut. Explain that if you can.

AXEL: I haven't thought about it. However, I can see that you have. What's your explanation?

ADELE: I think that, without knowing it, you're in love with Kerstin.

AXEL: I don't think that's it. I like them best when they're together. Each one separately isn't as good company as the two of them together. If I saw them apart from each other, they'd both fade away. Anyway, even if what you say is true, if I were in love with Kerstin, what difference would that make, as long as I hide my feelings?

ADELE: The peculiar thing about feelings is that they spread — like fire.

AXEL: Possibly. I still don't see any danger in it. I've just gone through all the torments of a divorce. Rest assured I have no desire to see anyone else go through them — and much less would I want to be the cause of them. — Besides . . . Kerstin is in love with her husband.

ADELE: In love? She's never loved him. Unless you think being in love means having the same routines and habits. But Knut has very strong appetites. And one day he's going to get bored with the same old strawberries and sweet cream for dessert.

AXEL: Listen to you! You must have had a long engagement.

ADELE: Why do you say that?

AXEL: You seem so familiar with the territory. Let's go a bit deeper into it. I get the impression that there have been a lot of changes here since last year.

ADELE: For instance?

AXEL: There's a different atmosphere, a different way of talking, of thinking. —There's something that makes me uncomfortable.

ADELE: So you've noticed? Well, it is a strange family. The father hasn't done a thing for ten years except collect dividends. His son hasn't done a thing since the day he was born except clip coupons. They eat, they sleep, and await their going hence by passing their time on earth in the most agreeable fashion. Nothing to live for, no ambitions, no genuine passions. Just a general dismissive indifference to what's going on in the world. "He's a bad sort"—that fits everybody, explains everything. It's served up every day with our daily bread and a bit of the Bible, especially Ecclesiastes: "All is vanity."

AXEL: You're remarkably eloquent. And very penetrating.

ADELE: Like hate.

AXEL: Anyone who hates as you do must also be able to love.

ADELE: Pooh!

AXEL: Adele, now that we've thoroughly abused our friends, we have to be friends to each other, whether we want to or not.

ADELE: Whether we want to or not.

AXEL: Give me your hand on it. Promise not to hate—me. (*He offers his hand to her, and she takes it.*)

ADELE: My, but your hand is cold.

Kerstin can be seen in the doorway.

AXEL: Makes you seem all the warmer.

ADELE: Shh! There's Kerstin!

AXEL: We'll have to continue our little chat some other time.

[8]

Silence.

KERSTIN: So quiet all of a sudden. I hope I'm not intruding?

ADELE: Not at all. Perhaps I'm the intruder.

KERSTIN (*handing a letter to Axel*): This is for you. From a lady, I see.

> *Axel looks at it and turns noticeably paler.*

KERSTIN: You're white as a ghost. If you're still freezing, I can loan you my shawl. (*She takes off her shawl and puts it over Axel's shoulders.*)

AXEL: Thanks. At least that's warm.

ADELE: Perhaps you'd like a cushion under your feet?

KERSTIN: It might be better to have a fire laid in your room. After a couple of days of rain everything down here by the ocean gets so damp and clammy.

ADELE: Yes, that's very true.

AXEL: All this trouble for my sake. Please don't bother.

ADELE: Bother? It's no bother at all. (*She leaves.*)

[9]

> *Silence.*

AXEL: So quiet all of a sudden.

KERSTIN: Just like a moment ago. You two looked like you were exchanging secrets.

AXEL: I was getting a load off my chest. An old habit that I haven't outgrown.

KERSTIN: Unload some of it on me. . . . You're unhappy . . .

AXEL: Mainly because I can't seem to do any work.

KERSTIN: And you can't work because–?

AXEL: Yes? Because?

KERSTIN: Are you still clinging to your wife?

AXEL: Not to *her*—only to the memory of her.

KERSTIN: Then why not relive the memories?

AXEL: Not on your life!

KERSTIN: Was she the one you ran off to last summer?

AXEL: No, she wasn't. I ran to other women. Since you ask.

KERSTIN: I think that's disgusting.

AXEL: Maybe. But they say that if you've been stung badly, the best remedy is a roll in the mud. Toughens the skin.

KERSTIN: I think that's awful. You, of all people!

AXEL: Bear in mind: there's good clean mud—and there's dirty mud.

KERSTIN: What's that supposed to mean?

AXEL: You know. You're a married woman. And we're both past puberty. Within marriage is consecrated earth; outside marriage is profane earth. But it's all dirt, all of it.

KERSTIN: You don't mean to compare—!

AXEL: Oh, but I do mean to.

KERSTIN: What sort of woman was she, the one you married?

AXEL: A virtuous woman, from the best of families.

KERSTIN: And you loved her?

AXEL: Much too deeply.

KERSTIN: And what happened?

AXEL: We got to hate each other.

KERSTIN: But why? . . . Why?

AXEL: There are a lot of unanswered questions in life, and that's one of them.

KERSTIN: There has to be a reason.

AXEL: I thought so too. However, it turned out that the causes of our hate were actually the consequences of it. We just didn't get along. It wasn't our differences that caused the breakup. Our love did. When love ended, the breakup began. That's how it is. And that's why the so-called loveless marriages are the happiest.

KERSTIN (*innocently*): I guess Knut and I have never had any serious difficulties that way.

AXEL: Now you're being a little too candid, Kerstin.

KERSTIN: How so? What did I say?

AXEL: You said that you've never loved your husband.

KERSTIN: Loved? Yes, what does it mean to love?

AXEL (*rising*): What a question! And from a married woman. What is it to love? I'll tell you: it's something you do but can't explain.

KERSTIN: Was your wife pretty?

AXEL: I thought so. In a way she was much like you.

KERSTIN: Does that mean that you think I'm pretty?

AXEL: Yes.

KERSTIN: Knut didn't think I was, until you told him so. It's remarkable how attractive he finds me when you're around. You seem to light a fire under him. He becomes so passionate.

AXEL: Does he now? That explains why he's so eager to have me hanging around. What about you?

KERSTIN: Me?

AXEL: I guess we'd better call a halt—before we go too far.

KERSTIN (*bristling*): What do you mean? What do you take me for?

AXEL: Nothing bad, Kerstin. Nothing at all. Forgive me if I offended you.

KERSTIN: You offended terribly. Even though I know you have a low opinion of women.

AXEL: Not all women. For me you are—

KERSTIN: Yes, what am I?

AXEL: My friend's wife—and therefore—

KERSTIN: And if I weren't?

AXEL: Time again to stop. Kerstin, you strike me as a girl who isn't accustomed to being flattered by men and played up to.

KERSTIN: It's true, I'm not. That's why being liked by someone just a little means a lot to me. Just a little.

AXEL: Just a little? Lucky you! You can't help but be happy in this life if you expect so little from it.

KERSTIN: What do you know about my expectations?

AXEL: You're not ambitious. You don't want to remake the world, climb to the top, become *somebody*.

KERSTIN: No. None of that means much to me. But I can't stand this monotony—no work, no emotional excitement, every day the same. You know, I get so bored I think the most awful things. Anything, even a great sorrow, is better than nothing. Sometimes I find myself yearning for—an epidemic—or hoping the house will burn down— (*Whispers.*) or wishing that my child would die. —Or that I would die.

AXEL: You know what's behind this, don't you? Idleness. Too many of the good things the earth offers. . . . Perhaps something else.

KERSTIN: What?

AXEL: What you need is sex—and you need it bad.

KERSTIN: What did you say?

AXEL: I'd rather not repeat it. You heard it, and you know what I mean. —And I didn't mean anything ugly or demeaning, so don't say I offended you.

KERSTIN: I'll say one thing: I don't know anybody like you. You slap your friends in the face and they don't really feel it.

AXEL: Could be. I've heard tell of women who love to be struck.

KERSTIN: You sound dangerous.

AXEL: I am.

KERSTIN: Who are you anyway? What do you want? What are you really up to?

AXEL: Don't be too inquisitive, Kerstin. You'll get your nose bent.

KERSTIN: Another insult.

AXEL: No, just friendly advice. —Why are we always quarreling when your husband isn't around? Have you noticed? It's not a good sign.

KERSTIN: Of what?

AXEL: Of a lasting friendship. We need a third party—a lightning rod.

KERSTIN: There are times when I think I could hate you. This is one of them.

AXEL: Now there's a good sign. . . . Tell me, haven't you ever felt that you could love me?

KERSTIN: Yes, once in a while.

AXEL: For instance?

KERSTIN: You've been pretty frank with me. I feel like being equally frank.

AXEL: So? When do you feel you could?

KERSTIN: When I see you talking to Adele.

AXEL: You seem to have the same heating system as your husband. He gets hot and amorous when I'm around. Adele and I seem to have the same function: we turn on the heat.

KERSTIN (*laughs*): That sounds so funny I can't help laughing. I can't even get mad at you.

AXEL: You should never get mad. It becomes you even less than others. —To change the subject: where's the man of the house?

> *Axel rises, walks over to the window, and looks out. Kerstin follows and also looks out. She is upset by what she sees.*

AXEL: I'm sorry. I had no idea he was there in the garden with Adele.

KERSTIN: So what! It's not the first time I've seen him kissing Adele.

AXEL: Too bad that Adele can't poke up your husband's fire enough to make you glow too. Very unfortunate. You know, there's a lot going on in this house that bothers me this year. I'm sure there's something rotting beneath the floorboards.

KERSTIN: I haven't noticed. Anyway, it's only a game.

AXEL: A game! With lighted matches, hunting knives, sticks of dynamite? That's no game!

[10]

The Father comes in, wearing his hat.

FATHER: Is Knut here?

KERSTIN: No, he went out shopping. Did you want to speak to him?

FATHER: Why else would I ask for him? What about Adele? Have you seen her?

KERSTIN: Not for quite a while.

The Father notices Axel.

FATHER: I'm sorry. Didn't see you. How are you?

AXEL: Fine, thank you. And how are you, Mr. Anderson?

KERSTIN: Perhaps I can be of help.

FATHER: Yes, you might at that, thank you. But if this is an inconvenient moment, I can come back.

KERSTIN: Inconvenient? Of course not.

FATHER: I have a little problem. There are mosquitoes in my bedroom, and I was wondering if I might sleep in your attic room.

KERSTIN: How awkward! We've just arranged for Axel to stay there.

FATHER: Ah! So he has settled in here, has he? Well, of course, if I had known that, I would never have ventured to suggest—

AXEL: I would never have considered the invitation to stay here, sir, if I had known that you—

FATHER: Now, now, now. I don't want to get in the way. There's an old saying: Put not your hand between the bark and the tree. Or between a lover and his lass.

        Embarrassed silence.

Has Knut started painting?

KERSTIN: No, he doesn't feel inclined to.

FATHER: He has never felt inclined to work—now less than ever.

KERSTIN: Anything else you wanted?

FATHER: No, no. It doesn't matter. —Oh, yes: no need to speak to Knut about the room, if you don't mind.

KERSTIN: Mind? I'd be happy not to.

FATHER: Yes. No point in making a fuss if nothing can be done about it. Just embarrassing. If I could have had the room, that would be different. But if it's taken—! Well, see you later. (*He leaves.*)

[11]

AXEL: Excuse me, Kerstin. I'll be back in a minute or two.

KERSTIN: Where are you going in such a hurry?

AXEL: I'd . . . rather not say.

KERSTIN: You're going to look for a room in town, aren't you?

AXEL (*has his hat in his hand*): You can't think I'd want to stay here after being shown the door like that? I know when I'm not wanted.

KERSTIN (*attempting to take his hat from him*): No, you mustn't go! We didn't show you the door; he did. Besides —

[12]

Knut enters.

KNUT: What's this? Fighting? Or making love?

KERSTIN: Call it a lovers' tiff. Knut, can you imagine that this poor restless soul wants to leave us again and get himself a room in town? And all because Daddy came in and asked if he could have the attic room.

KNUT: Don't be silly. Why would he want the attic room? That was an excuse. He wanted to see what the two of you were up to. Don't tell me you wanted to go your way because of him! Axel! Axel! Down on your knees and beg Kerstin's pardon.

Axel kneels.

Now kiss her foot. She's got such beautiful feet, believe me.

Axel gives her shoe a fleeting kiss; then stands up.

AXEL: All right? I've begged forgiveness for going out to get a room. Satisfied? Goodbye for now. (*Exits hastily.*)

KERSTIN (*riled*): Axel! Axel!

[13]

KERSTIN: Why did the old man have to stick his nose in here like that? Absolutely indecent of him, if you ask me. Disturbing our domestic bliss! Now we'll never have a moment's peace — night or day.

KNUT: We'll have to make do somehow. I still think you could make a little effort to hide your true feelings. A wee little effort.

KERSTIN: What feelings? What *are* you talking about? Don't tell me you're . . . jealous?

KNUT: Jealous! Me? What's going on here! I was talking about your bad feelings toward my father.

KERSTIN (*suddenly sweet*): Knut, don't let's talk anymore about feelings. (*She takes a package from her purse and opens it.*) Here! Put on this necktie. It'll make you look more like a human being.

KNUT: What? Another tie! And blue again!

KERSTIN (*as she puts the tie on Knut and knots it*): We should do something about your clothes, too. You shouldn't go around looking so shabby. And you should comb your moustache.

KNUT: All right, Kerstin. Cut it out! You're so obvious. I can see right through you.

KERSTIN: What?

KNUT: Shouldn't I have a white linen jacket, too? And tennis shoes?

KERSTIN: Not a bad idea. It would suit you, now that you're getting a bit thick in the middle.

KNUT: And I should lose a little weight, too, hm? Look haggard and worn? Only one thing would be lacking: a divorce.

KERSTIN: Oh, my, Knut! Oh, my! Now you *are* jealous.

KNUT: I think you've gone the limit. Maybe. I don't know. It's strange. I'm in the grip of the green-eyed monster, but I don't feel envy or anger. I'm so fond of this guy that I can deny him nothing. I mean nothing.

KERSTIN: Nothing! Do you know what you're saying?

KNUT: Yes, I know what I'm saying. It's crazy, it's criminal, it's base, but if he asked me if he could sleep with you, I'd say, "Sure, go ahead."

KERSTIN: You're terrible! Talk about the limit! I've heard you say some awful things; I've taken a lot from you, but this—!

KNUT: It's not my fault. I can't do anything about it. You know, sometimes I'm haunted by a vision . . . when I'm awake . . . when I'm asleep. I seem to see the two of you together—I mean *together* . . . and I don't suffer any pain or anguish. Instead I sort of revel in it, as at the sight of something very beautiful.

KERSTIN: You really have gone the limit!

KNUT: An unusual case, perhaps. But, come on now, isn't it devilishly interesting?

KERSTIN: There are times, Knut, when I believe you want to get rid of me.

KNUT: You don't believe that for a moment.

KERSTIN: Yes, I do. Sometimes I have the distinct impression that you're nudging him, pushing him into my arms, so that you can make a case for a divorce.

KNUT: Hardly likely. Tell me, Kerstin, have the two of you ever made love?

KERSTIN: No, I swear it—on my mother's grave.

KNUT: Promise me, Kerstin, when it does happen, you'll be perfectly frank with me, and say, "It's happened."

KERSTIN: Knut, you're losing your mind.

KNUT: Yes. To prevent which I have to *know*. Either I give you up to him or I hold onto you and wonder if you're being unfaithful. I'd rather give you up and know where I stand.

KERSTIN: I've had just about enough of your soul-searchings. What about mine? What's going on between you and Adele?

KNUT: Nothing that you don't know and approve of.

KERSTIN: I have *never* approved of adultery!

KNUT: Ah ha! Changing your tune! It was harmless a moment ago. Now it's a crime.

KERSTIN: There's no change. A moment ago my relationship with Axel was perfectly harmless. It still is.

KNUT: Harmless and innocent today, but who knows what the morrow will bring?

KERSTIN: Wait till tomorrow and find out.

KNUT: Might be too late.

KERSTIN: Well, what *do* you want?

KNUT: I don't know. — Yes. An end to this business. If there is an end. We have woven our own net and trapped ourselves in it. God, how I hate him when he's out of my sight. But when I see him, and he looks at me with those big sad eyes, I love him like a brother, like a sister. . . . I can understand the effect he has on you. What I don't understand is what's going on with me. Evidently I've been living for such a long time alone with you and your skirts and petticoats that my senses have been infected — womanized — as if I had caught from you your affection for him. . . . Your love for him must be as wide as the ocean, although you don't know it.

KERSTIN: It's true. And now you're trying to put the blame on me! Of all the nerve!

KNUT: No, that's what you're trying to do!

KERSTIN: I am not! You are!

KNUT: You are! — I'm going stark raving mad!

KERSTIN: That's obvious.

KNUT: And you don't feel a bit of pity for me!

KERSTIN: Why should I pity *you* when you're torturing *me*!

KNUT: You have never loved me!

KERSTIN: You have never loved me!

KNUT: Here it is! The ultimate squabble — the one that will last till the day we die.

KERSTIN: Let's give it a rest — before it's too late. . . . Go take a swim. It will cool you off.

KNUT: I see. You want to be alone.

[14]

Axel enters, in high spirits.

AXEL: Well, I was in luck. Just as I was leaving I ran into Adele who had a room—

KERSTIN: Don't tell me that working girl rents rooms, too?

AXEL: She knew *of* a room.

KERSTIN: I'll just bet she did. She knows a lot, that girl.

AXEL (*taking out his cigarette case*): Cigarette?

KNUT (*pettishly*): No, thanks.

AXEL: That's a handsome tie. Who gave it to you?

KNUT: Like it? I'll bet you do!

AXEL: You've been saying nasty things about me in my absence. It's written all over you.

KNUT (*agitated*): Excuse me. I have to go for a swim. (*He leaves quickly.*)

[15]

AXEL: What's the matter with him?

KERSTIN: Jealousy.

AXEL: Really? But there's no reason for it.

KERSTIN: Knut believes there is. Where does Adele have that room you mentioned?

AXEL (*his thoughts elsewhere*): Room? Oh, over there, right across from the pilot's house.

KERSTIN: Isn't that cleverly arranged! From there you can look right into her room. What a little schemer she is!

AXEL: I don't think Addy ever gave it a thought.

KERSTIN: Addy! You call her Addy now? You must be very chummy with each other.

AXEL: Kerstin, you're making a mountain out of a molehill. You're letting your imagination run riot. Leave it alone, I say, or else—

KERSTIN: I know. Or else you'll run away, as usual. But this time I won't let you. You have no right to.

AXEL (*lighting a cigarette*): Maybe I have an obligation.

KERSTIN: If you're a true friend, Axel, you won't leave me here alone and unprotected. My honor is at stake, don't you see? In this house Knut is uncontrollable. His parents protect him. He can do whatever he feels like, no matter how indecent. You won't believe it. He even sank so low as to say he would, if he had to, give me up . . . to you.

AXEL: I thought you said he was jealous. I call that a most endearing form of jealousy. What was your response?

KERSTIN: How could I answer such a suggestion?

AXEL: Why ask me?

KERSTIN (*hysterically*): You're playing cat and mouse with me! I'm in your power. You see how I suffer, how I twist and turn to escape from this net you've trapped me in. Axel, look at me! Give me one pitying glance, but don't sit there like a stone statue, waiting for adoration and sacrifice. (*She goes to her knees before him.*) You're so strong; you can control your feelings. You're so proud, so honorable. Because you've never known what it is to love, to love as I love you!

AXEL: A lot you know about it! —Oh, for God's sake, get up, Kerstin! —Now go over there. —No, way over there! Sit in the easy chair. . . . That's better. . . . Now let me speak my piece. (*He remains sitting, smoking his cigarette.*) I have loved you—I guess that's the word for it—from the first moment I saw you. Remember an evening at sunset last year when we got to know each other? Your husband was at his easel, down in the dale, painting, when I happened to walk by. I was introduced to you, and we stood there talking to each other until we got tired standing. You sat down on the grass, asked me to join you. But there was a heavy evening dew, and I hesitated to sit on the wet grass. Then you unbuttoned your coat, spread out one of the tails, and offered it to me to sit on. You can't possibly imagine how I felt. It was as if you had opened your arms to me and asked me to lay my head in your lap. There I was, so unhappy, tired to death, all alone, and within that coat of yours was warmth, comfort, softness. I wanted to creep into it, physically, and hide myself in your young, virginal bosom. But I felt ashamed and ridiculous when I suddenly glimpsed in your innocent eyes a flickering smile. You were laughing at me, of course, seeing that a man like me could be overcome and flustered by your charms. . . . We saw each other time and again. Knut seemed to get some sort of pleasure out of the adoring attention I paid you. It was as if I discovered you for him. So I became your captive, and you played your little games with me. Knut felt no embarrassment in teasing me openly, even at parties. He was so cocksure, so confident, I felt insulted. Sometimes I could hardly resist the temptation to knock him right out of his shoes—and step into them. Remember that afternoon when I invited you both to celebrate my birthday? You told me you would arrive a little late. And after we had waited—for an hour—you made your entrance, dressed in a pansy-colored skirt and a bright, flowery bodice. And you had on a large straw hat, trimmed with yellow lawn, which filtered the light and showered your whole figure with golden rays. And when you handed me a bouquet of roses, with the shy impudence of a fourteen-year-old girl, I found you so overpoweringly beautiful that I lost my tongue, could say neither hello nor thanks. Tears welled up in my eyes, and I had to leave the room.

KERSTIN: I'll say one thing for you: you certainly know how to hide your feelings.

AXEL: Later that night, after the midnight supper, remember how for hours we talked, trading stories about our lives, letting our souls embrace? How Knut solemnly—and evidently with your consent—invited me to come live with you in town that winter? Do you remember what I replied?

KERSTIN: You replied—I remember the exact words—"I dare not."

AXEL: And the next morning I was gone.

KERSTIN: And I was in tears the whole day. So was Knut.

AXEL: Think how many tears there will be now!

KERSTIN: Now? —Now?

AXEL: Sit still!! —Now that everything is out in the open, nothing remains but for us to part.

KERSTIN: No, no! We mustn't part! Why can't things remain as they are? You're taking it calmly, and I'm not at all worried. What does Knut have to do with our feelings, as long as we control them? Look at us: we're sitting here, calm and collected, examining what has happened like an old married couple reminiscing about the time they fell in love.

AXEL: You're talking like a child. After you've said you love each other, you can never be just friends again. Don't you know that? If you don't, I wonder what sort of married life you've had. And me! I'm about as cool as a bursting boiler. As collected as a keg of dynamite with a lighted fuse! I—! I've agonized; I've fought against myself; but I can't answer for myself.

KERSTIN: I can. I can answer for myself.

AXEL: Yes, I'm sure you can. You can put out the fire as soon as it flares up. You've got a fireman in the house. But I live alone. —God, what an infernal idea! To live here after all that's been said! Feeding on crumbs from the rich man's table, filling my lungs with the air you breathe, drinking in the heady perfume of your flowers, my senses reeling, my blood boiling— and my mind burdened with a bad conscience.

KERSTIN: Why should you have a bad conscience? He doesn't make any bones about having a mistress whom he kisses in full view of everybody.

AXEL: Don't try that, Kerstin! Don't try shifting the blame. That shows how desperate you are. Dancing along the precipice, with nothing left but the final, fatal fall. Let's be different; let's be original for once. Let's show the world what it means to behave honorably. We'll make a clean breast of it. The instant he walks in we'll tell Knut, "This is it. We love each other. We want your advice. Tell us what we should do."

KERSTIN: Oh, Axel, Axel! That's magnificent! That's noble. Yes, that's what we must do. And whatever happens afterward, let it happen! And we can do this with our heads held high, because our hands are clean.

AXEL: And afterward? Of course, he'll tell me to leave.

KERSTIN: Or he might ask you to stay.

AXEL: On what conditions? That everything remains as it was? No, I couldn't accept that. Do you really think that after all this I could endure to see the two of you cuddling each other, hear the door to your bedroom close at night? No! There's no way out. Still, he has to be told, otherwise I could never look him in the eye again, never shake his hand. We have to tell him everything, and see what happens.

KERSTIN: Oh, how I wish the next hour were already over. Tell me you love me. I've got to hear it, otherwise I'll never have the courage to plunge the knife into his heart. Tell me you love me!

> *Both Axel and Kerstin stay seated, far apart from each other.*

AXEL: I love you body and soul. I love your little feet, peeping out from beneath the hem of your dress. I love your pretty white teeth—that mouth made for kisses—your ears—your sexy, inviting eyes. I love every bit of your lighter-than-air body. I want to throw it on my shoulders and carry if off to the woods. Once when I was young I met a girl in the street, lifted her in my arms, and carried her up four flights of stairs. I was a kid then; imagine what I could do now!

KERSTIN: Is that all you see in me—just a body? I've got a soul, too.

AXEL: I love that too. Because it's frailer than mine, combustible like mine, faithless like mine!

KERSTIN: Won't you let me get up now and come to you?

AXEL: No! Absolutely not!

KERSTIN: Knut is coming! I can hear his footsteps. I won't be able to say anything unless you let me kiss you . . . on the forehead.

AXEL: You hear him coming?

KERSTIN: Shhhh!

[16]

The Father enters, hat on head. He crosses directly to Axel, who, startled, stands up.

FATHER (*picking up a newspaper from a table behind Axel's chair*): Pardon the intrusion. I was looking for something to read. (*To Kerstin.*) Have you seen Adele?

KERSTIN: That's the fifth time you've asked after Adele.

FATHER: Didn't know you were counting. Aren't you going for a swim before lunch?

KERSTIN: No, not today.

FATHER: Not wise of you to neglect your daily swim, when your health is so delicate.

Silence.

The Father leaves.

[17]

AXEL: This is too much! I can't stay here a moment longer!

KERSTIN (*approaches him and looks at him passionately, her eyes like glowing coals*): Shall we run away?

AXEL: Not "we." *I* shall run away.

KERSTIN: Then I'll run away too! We can die together!

AXEL (*taking her in his arms and kissing her*): We're lost, you know. Why did I do this? Why? It's the end. The end of honor and faith. The end of friendship. The end of peace. Talk about the fires of hell! Here they are—burning and searing all that was green and blooming. Oh, God!

They separate, move off in opposite directions, and sit down.

[18]

Knut enters on the run. His Father has obviously spoken to him.

KNUT: Why are you continents apart from each other?

KERSTIN: Because we . . .

KNUT: Why these troubled looks?

KERSTIN: Because we . . . (*Long pause.*) love each other.

KNUT (*studying them both for a while. To Axel*): Is that true?

AXEL: It's true.

KNUT (*somewhat crushed, slumps into a chair*): Why did you have to tell me?

KERSTIN: This is the thanks we get for being upright and honest!

KNUT: It's very original, but it's also shameless.

KERSTIN: You said yourself that when the time came we—

KNUT: True, true! And the time has come. It strikes me that I've known all along what was going to happen. And yet it's so strange to me that I can't take it all in. Whose fault was it? No one's. Everyone's. —Well now what do we do? What's next?

AXEL: Do you have anything to reproach me with?

KNUT: No. You fled when you saw the danger. You rejected our invitation to come live with us. You concealed your true feelings so well that Kerstin thought you hated her. Still, why did you come back to us?

AXEL: Because I thought my feelings were dead.

KNUT: Very plausible. I believe you. In the meantime we have to deal with a situation that we neither asked for nor could put a stop to. We tried to avert the peril by being ever so sophisticated and frank—joked about it—and all the good that did was to bring the danger ever closer. And now we're in over our heads. . . . What should we do? . . . I suggest we have a calm

discussion and remain friends right through to the end. . . .
What do you say? . . . What do we do?

>   *Silence.*

No one answers. . . . Come, come, we can't just sit here while
the house is on fire. (*He gets to his feet.*) Let's begin by considering
the consequences.

AXEL: The most sensible thing would be for me to withdraw,
wouldn't it?

KNUT: I'm inclined to agree.

KERSTIN (*wildly*): No! No! You mustn't go! If you do, I'll
follow you!

KNUT: Is this your idea of a calm discussion?

KERSTIN: Love is not calm! (*She goes over to Axel.*)

KNUT: At least spare me the sight of your unbridled lust. Have
some consideration for my feelings. I am the innocent party—
comparatively—and I always end up suffering the most.

KERSTIN (*hanging on Axel's neck*): You mustn't go away, do you
hear! I won't have it!

>   *Knut takes Kerstin's arm and pulls her away from
>   Axel.*

KNUT: You might at least behave like decent people and wait
until I have left the premises. (*To Axel.*) Listen, old friend: we
have to come to some sort of arrangement, and as quickly as possible. They'll be calling us to lunch at any moment now. It's
obvious to me that you can't conquer your love for Kerstin, while
mine for her, on the other hand, can be vanquished—with a bit
of effort. Furthermore, for me to continue to live intimately with
a woman who loves someone else would always be unfulfilling.
It would always seem like polygamy to me. Consequently, I shall
depart. But—but not until I have some guarantee from you that
you will marry Kerstin.

AXEL: For some odd reason, your magnanimous offer is more

humiliating than any guilt I might have felt if I had stolen her from you.

KNUT: I can see that. I find it less humiliating to give a wife away than to be robbed of one. Now, you've got five minutes to make up your mind. I'll be right back. (*Knut leaves.*)

[19]

KERSTIN: Now what?

AXEL: Don't you see how ridiculous I've become?

KERSTIN: It isn't ridiculous to be honorable.

AXEL: Not always, maybe. But in this case it strikes me that the husband is less ridiculous. And one day you will despise me.

KERSTIN: Is that all you can say at a moment like this? Now, when nothing stands between us, and you can open your arms to me with a clear conscience, now you hesitate.

AXEL: Yes, I hesitate! Because I'm beginning to see my frank and honorable Kerstin for what she is. You don't hold anything back because you have no sense of decency. And you love to talk about honor because you have no heart.

KERSTIN: Well, of all the—!

AXEL: And that rotten smell I noticed in this house—I have a pretty good idea where it comes from.

KERSTIN: And so do I! It was you who seduced me! Pretending to be cold and indifferent, giving me those innocent little-boy looks, treating me brutally, getting me all excited, standing over me with a whip in your hands. Oooh! And now the clever seducer plays the virtuous prig! God!

AXEL: There's another version. It was you who—

KERSTIN: No! No! No! It was you! You! You! (*She throws herself full-length on the sofa and shrieks.*) Help me! Please help me! I'm dying! I'm dying!

Axel does not move.

Why don't you help me? Have you no pity, no compassion? You're a beast! Don't you see I'm sick? Help me, help me!

Axel still does not move.

Send for a doctor! You might at least do for me what any man would do for a stranger! —Call Adele!

Axel walks out.

[20]

Knut comes in.

KNUT: What's this? What's going on? (*To Kerstin.*) Don't tell me you didn't come to an agreement?

KERSTIN: Shut up! I don't want to hear one word from you!

KNUT: Why did he dash through the garden like that? Ran as if his pants were on fire. A human tornado uprooting bushes and trees!

[21]

The Mother and Adele enter.

MOTHER: Well, children, do you feel like a bit of lunch?

KNUT: Lovely idea! Just the thing!

MOTHER: Now where's Axel? Shall we wait for him, or not?

KNUT: We certainly won't wait for him. He has fled the field.

MOTHER: A bizarre fellow, I must say! Dear me! I fried the flounder for his sake.

The Father enters.

KNUT (*to his Father*): That attic room's available now, if you're still interested.

FATHER: No, thanks. I no longer have a need for it.

KNUT: You're remarkably changeable.

FATHER: Not the only one around here. However, "He that is slow to anger is better than the mighty; and he that ruleth his spirit than he that taketh a city." Proverbs 16:32.

KNUT: I have one for you. Say not to a friend, "Get thee hence and come again."

FATHER: Not bad. Where did you pick that up?

KNUT: I got that from Kerstin.

FATHER: Ah, Kerstin, my child! Have you had your swim yet?

KNUT: No, she hasn't. She settled for a cold shower.

The luncheon bell is heard.

MOTHER: There! Come to lunch!

KNUT (*to his Father*): You take Kerstin in, and I'll take Adele.

FATHER: Nothing doing, my boy! You keep Kerstin for yourself!

CURTAIN

Introduction

to

To Damascus

Much of the best work that Strindberg produced from 1886 to 1892 was part of what he called an "artistic-psychological" series (letter of 22 December 1887), in which he hoped to furnish "clues to the pathology of the soul" obtained by means of "all the resources of modern psychology." (*A Madman's Defense,* 1887-88.) Although he consulted medical books, scientific tomes, and learned journals, his chief source for these clues was his own life, especially married life. The psychological battle of brains that fascinated him was more often than not the battle of the sexes. When his first marriage came to an end, so did the artistic-psychological series. *Playing with Fire* and its companion piece, *The Bond,* both written in 1892, concluded the series by connecting its origin with its termination. Whereas the first play harks back to the time when he initially met the woman who was to become his wife, *The Bond* depicts the bitter and painful legal battles that took place at the time of their divorce.

In 1892, separated from his wife and children, and slighted by Swedish publishers and theater producers, Strindberg left his native country to begin a new life and another career. For the next five years he lived the life of a drifter, obeying the whim of the moment, yielding to impulse, moving erratically from Germany to Austria to France, changing his mailing address more often than the season changed, and living almost entirely off the generosity of friends and supporters. In 1893 he married an Austrian journalist, much younger than himself, but that union lasted only a few years.

He wrote no plays during this period. All his creative energies went into scientific pursuits and painting. Instead of continuing his studies in psychology, he investigated the physical world. He performed countless experiments in his makeshift, portable laboratory, attempting to demonstrate that the so-called chemical elements were not elemental and that the atom was not the basic building block of the physical universe. Flying in the face of orthodox scientific thinking, he dreamed of achieving a trans-

mutation of the elements, that old alchemical dream. The experiments failed of course, the only tangible result being damage to
his hands for which he had to be treated at a hospital in Paris.
Ironically, his stay in the hospital occurred just when he was
gaining some fame among Parisian intellectuals as a dramatist
and essayist.

His lack of success in the laboratory did not deter him from
formulating a new conception of the cosmos, radically different
from the one he had entertained in the 1880s when he had proclaimed himself a Darwinist, a naturalist, and an atheist. Then
life had appeared to him as a struggle for survival, a brutish
struggle, even if brains had replaced brawn, with no other purpose than the improvement of the species. In his naturalistic
plays he had made it clear that Darwinian evolution, scientific
determinism, and moral indifference were inseparable from one
another. In *Creditors*, Tekla's polyandrous nature was no more to
be condemned than Gustav's thirst for revenge.

Nevertheless, an ethical question kept asserting itself. In his
preface to *Miss Julie* he had written that "the naturalists have
banished guilt along with God, but the consequences of an act—
punishment, imprisonment, or the fear of it—cannot be banished." The idea of punishment, the need to adjust the punishment to the crime, seemed to introduce a moral element into the
naturalistic scheme. Moreover, Strindberg could never quite sub-
jugate the religious yearnings that had been inculcated on him
when he was a child. Even as an atheist, he had a nostalgia for
God. "I sometimes wish I still had God and heaven with me," he
wrote in 1886 (letter to Frölander, 18 February).

When his travels during those years of apparent drifting are
charted, they can be seen as leading to a definite goal. He had embarked on a journey to find what had been lost in the atheistic
eighties. His endless treks, his frustrating alchemical research, his
experimental painting freed his mind and opened up the unconscious, and there he found what he had been looking for. He might
have taken to heart the words of Novalis: "We dream of traveling
through the world. But isn't the world within us? We little know
the depths of our own minds. The mysterious road goes inwards."

In *The Father*, and in some of his other writings, Strindberg had ventured into the dark continent of the human soul, usually following but sometimes leading the clinical psychologists who were investigating the causes of neurosis and hysteria. In the 1890s he embarked on a solitary expedition that would take him into the interior of the dark continent, guided by dreams, impulses, and free-floating ideas. At almost the same time, Sigmund Freud set out on a similar journey, hoping to reveal those powerful mental processes that are hidden from consciousness.

In *To Damascus*, written in 1898, Strindberg represented his own discoveries in dramatic form by projecting his inner life on the outer, thus giving a shape and form to the intangible unconscious world. His restless wanderings became the physical counterpart of his spiritual struggles. In the course of his journey his whole life had been turned around, and the structure of the play represents this turnabout, the late scenes repeating the early scenes in reverse order. More difficult was the problem of putting onstage the peculiar topography of the unconscious. Strindberg resorted to symbols, colors, literary allusions, myths, legends, and all the resources of the theater. A table and two chairs would not suffice for this new supranaturalistic drama. He needed total theater in which a visual or aural effect could be more suggestive than words. In the second of the seaside scenes, the three unrigged masts of a foundered ship are an obvious reminder of Golgotha. But these crosses bear no thieves and no savior. Their emptiness becomes a vivid symbol of the hero's quest for a moral order that lies beyond Christianity and vicarious atonement. Here the significance of the symbol is obvious and underscored in the accompanying dialogue. Elsewhere the symbol is unexplained, the legend obscure, the allusion personal.

Although the story line of *To Damascus* is extremely simple, the inner action is extraordinarily complex. Everything that happens is seen from the protagonist's point of view as he tries to make sense of what is happening to him inwardly. The first step in this process is the fragmentation of his personality. The opening scene of the play shows this occurring step by step as the hero begins his descent into the unconscious. All the characters he meets have an existence in their social world; but the protagonist gives them specific roles to play that accord with fragments of his personality. The Doctor, for instance, represents the hero's conscience; and The Beggar, the skeptical ego of the artist who lives from hand to mouth.

To objectify the subjective, and to give a sense of the confusion in the hero's mind while simultaneously intimating that in all this confusion there is coherence and meaning, Strindberg used analogies, parallels, and extended metaphors. The hero's journey or pilgrimage provides the basic parallel, serving to remind the viewer of Saul's conversion on the way to Damascus. The hero's descent into his unconscious is also a descent into a hell of anguish and torment; hence the first nine scenes suggest the nine circles of Dante's inferno. At various times in the play the hero is compared to Cain, Lucifer, Jesus, and other figures of legend and myth. In design and form, *To Damascus* is a collage of myths and metaphors, allegories and allusions. Although Strindberg knew of the symbolic techniques employed in medieval religious drama and of its use of correspondences to link the spiritual realm to the physical and heaven to earth, *Damascus* puts all the elements together in an entirely new way, no different in principle from what artists like Picasso and Braque were to do a decade later and what Joyce was to achieve in that intricate construct he called *Ulysses*. Literary critics and historians have been slow to realize the truth of Maurice Valency's 1963 description of *Damascus*: "a quasi-medieval work that was to furnish the blueprint for the most advanced drama of the twentieth century, and perhaps for the Joycean novel as well; . . . astonishing as it may be, such seems to be the case."

It is likely that painters provided the inspiration for some of Strindberg's new literary and dramatic techniques. An innovative painter himself, he was aware of the new directions being taken by the Postimpressionists. He admired the allegorical canvases of Puvis de Chavannes, who was coming back into favor at this time. He was familiar with the paintings of the still virtually unknown Gauguin and closely acquainted with Edvard Munch, who was creating in oils, etchings, and lithographs indelible images of his inner torment. Gauguin had painted symbolic self-portraits in which he depicted himself as Christ in the Garden of Gethsemane and as Adam with halo, apple, and snake. Strindberg transferred to the stage the allegorical quality of Puvis, the ironic allusiveness of Gauguin, and the subjectivism of Munch, along with the conventional and overt symbolism of the Pre-Raphaelite painters. His development from *Miss Julie* to *To Damascus*, from naturalism to what he termed supernaturalism, closely paralleled the path from impressionism to neo-impressionism and symbolism taken by the experimental artists.

Because the subjective aspects of the chief character completely dominate the drama, *To Damascus* is usually seen as a precursor of expressionistic theater (which indeed it is), rather than as a symbolist drama.

Unfortunately, this association with the heaviness, somberness, and unpent emotionalism of expressionistic drama has led to a basic misunderstanding of the play. In spirit, *Damascus* is much closer to Joyce's novel. Like *Ulysses*, Strindberg's play is a kind of comedy. In both novel and play the intellect of the hero-author coolly analyzes what his troubled soul is suffering. The sudden shifts in tone, the unexpected parallels and correspondences, the juxtaposition of old myths and new ideas produce a distancing effect, allowing the readers or viewers to enjoy the cleverness of the author at the same time that they understand the deep emotion lying beneath the glittering surface. Even the resolution is brought about by means of a pun.

Staging *To Damascus*, Part I, as a portentous drama of madness is a common and lamentable mistake. The proper tone for the play is suggested in the first scene when The Stranger remarks that he does not know if he is joking or serious. One of those closest to Strindberg at the time *To Damascus* was written found that the key to the man lay in his peculiar and enigmatic smile, "half skeptical and self-mocking, half resigned and melancholy." Strindberg's humor is much like Hamlet's, and in the long run there is nothing that wears better. What keeps *To Damascus* fresh and satisfying, no matter how often it is read, is that strange Strindbergian mixture of humor and melancholy, of tragic anguish and comic frustration. And if it is not there when the play is staged, something very essential to the spirit of the whole will be lacking.

When it was produced for the first time, in 1900, Strindberg saw to it that the young actress who had enchanted him as Puck in *A Midsummer Night's Dream* was cast as The Lady. He fell in love with her, and she later became his third wife. On the day of the opening of the play, he sent her the following note along with some red roses.

Dear Miss Harriet Bosse,
Since I shan't put in an appearance at the
theater tonight I want to thank you now for
what I saw at the dress rehearsal. It was
great and beautiful, although I thought the
part should have been given in a lighter tone,
with some touches of roguishness, with less
reserve and more buoyance.

A little bit of Puck—that was my first
bit of advice to you, and will be my last!

A smile or two in the midst of misery
indicates there is still hope, and after all
the situation turns out not to be hopeless.

Anyway, good luck to you on your journey
over the stones and thistles. It's a rough
road. I can only strew it with a few flowers.

August Strindberg

To Damascus

(Till Damaskus)

Part I

CHARACTERS

THE STRANGER
THE LADY
THE BEGGAR
THE DOCTOR
THE SISTER
THE OLD MAN
THE MOTHER
THE ABBESS
THE CONFESSOR
MINOR CHARACTERS and PHANTOMS

SCENES*

ACT I: On the Street Corner
          At the Doctor's Home

ACT II: In the Hotel Room
          By the Sea
          On the Road
          In the Ravine
          In the Kitchen

ACT III: In the Rose Room
          The Asylum
          The Rose Room
          The Kitchen

ACT IV: In the Ravine
          On the Road
          By the Sea
          In the Hotel Room

ACT V: At the Doctor's Home
          The Street Corner

Time: 1898

---

* The act divisions given here were not followed when the play was first staged in 1900 at the Dramatic Theater in Stockholm. Strindberg wanted only one intermission—after the Asylum scene—and no curtains, except to mark the intermission and the end of the play. Grandinson, the director, went along with the idea of a single intermission but shifted it to the end of the first Rose Room scene. And, probably because of difficulties in making some of the scene changes, he also brought the curtain down briefly at the end of the first scene, at the end of the second Kitchen scene, and at the end of the second Hotel Room scene, thus providing a five-act division but different from the one given in the printed version of the play.

ACT I

On the Street Corner

A street corner in a small mid-European town. A bench under a tree. One can see the side portal of a small Gothic church. A post office, and a café with sidewalk tables. The post office and the café are closed.

The sound of a funeral march (Mendelssohn's "Songs without Words," Opus 62, No. 3) is heard drawing nearer and then fading away.

The Stranger is standing at the curb and seems to be wondering which way to go. The clock in a church tower strikes, first four strokes in a high tone, sounding the quarter, then three strokes in a lower tone.

The Lady enters. Greets The Stranger. She starts to go past him, but stops.

THE STRANGER: Ah, there you are. I knew you would come.

THE LADY: Then you did call for me. I might have guessed. I could feel it. —Why are you standing here on the street corner?

THE STRANGER: Have to stand somewhere while I'm waiting.

THE LADY: Waiting for what?

THE STRANGER: If only I knew. For forty years I've been waiting for something. Luck, I believe it's called. Or at least the end of bad luck. —There it comes again. That terrible music! Listen to it. Don't go, please don't go, I beg you. When you leave me, I'm all alone and frightened.

THE LADY: Now just a minute! Yesterday was the first time we met. It's true we talked for four hours—the two of us—and I admit you aroused my sympathy. But you shouldn't take advantage of it like this.

THE STRANGER: It's true, I shouldn't. But I implore you:

390

don't leave me all alone. I'm in a strange town – without a single true friend. And my few acquaintances are worse than strangers to me – more like enemies, I'd say.

THE LADY: Enemies wherever you go, lonesome all the time. Why on earth did you leave your wife and children?

THE STRANGER: I wish I knew. Above all, I wish I knew why I exist, why I'm standing here, which way I should turn, what I should do. – Do you believe that there are some people damned from the start?

THE LADY: No, I don't believe that.

THE STRANGER: Take a look at me.

THE LADY: Haven't you ever been happy?

THE STRANGER: No. Whatever I thought was happiness turned out to be a mirage to lure me into more misery. And whenever the golden fruit fell into my hands, it turned out to be poisoned or rotten inside.

THE LADY: What's your religion? – if you don't mind my asking.

THE STRANGER: Simple. When things get too tough, I'll go my way.

THE LADY: Go where?

THE STRANGER: Into the great nothingness. The fact that I have – death here within my grasp gives me an absolutely incredible sense of power.

THE LADY: My God! Playing with death!

THE STRANGER: Playing with life, you might say. I was a writer, a creator of fictions. In spite of my congenital melancholy, I have never been able to take anything really seriously, not even my own great sorrows. And there are moments when I doubt that life is any more real than my novels.

> *The funeral procession is heard, the choir chanting "De profundis."* *

* Psalm 130.

Here they come again. Why must they go parading around the streets like that?

THE LADY: Is that who you're afraid of?

THE STRANGER: Not afraid; just edgy. Makes me feel things are bewitched. . . . It's not death I'm afraid of, but being alone. In my loneliness I meet someone. I don't know whether it's myself or someone else. All I know is that in the midst of my loneliness I'm not alone. The air thickens, congeals. Certain presences begin to take shape, invisible but tangible, and possessing a life of their own.

THE LADY: How fascinating!

THE STRANGER: Yes. For some time now everything has struck me as remarkable. Before all I saw was objects and movements, forms and colors. Now I see meanings and connections. Life, which was all nonsense before, now begins to make a kind of sense. Where I formerly saw only chance and chaos I now see plan and purpose. —That's why, when I met you yesterday, I straightway got the notion that you were sent here either to save me or destroy me.

THE LADY: Silly! Why should I want to destroy you?

THE STRANGER: We each of us have our purpose in life—that was yours.

THE LADY: I haven't the faintest idea—. Now really, how could I? You know, I've never met a person like you, never in my whole life. Just to look at you makes me want to cry. . . . What's on your conscience? Something that hasn't been found out, something you haven't been punished for?

THE STRANGER: A good question. I'm sure I haven't more sins on my conscience than many who go around carefree and happy. —Oh yes, one: I couldn't abide being made a fool of—by Life, I mean.

THE LADY: It's impossible to live without being deceived or cheated to some extent.

THE STRANGER: Seems to be a law—one that I'd like to get

around. . . . Maybe there's some other secret in my life that I'm not aware of. . . . You know, there's a story in my family that I'm a changeling.

THE LADY: A what?

THE STRANGER: A changeling. A child whom the elves substituted for the human child that was born.

THE LADY: Do you believe that?

THE STRANGER: No, although I must admit it has something to be said for it—as a symbol, you understand. When I was a child, I cried all the time and felt as if I didn't belong anywhere. Hated my parents as much as they hated me. Couldn't stand orders, conventions, laws. I longed for the forest and the sea.

THE LADY: Have you ever had—visions?

THE STRANGER: Never! But I have often sensed that two different spirits were in control of my destiny. The one gives me everything I ask for while the other stands beside him and wipes filth on it, so that when the gift is handed to me, I don't even want to touch it. No, it's really true, I've had all I wished for in life—and have found it all worthless.

THE LADY: You've had everything and you're still not satisfied!

THE STRANGER: That's what I call damnation—God-damnation!

THE LADY: Don't. I don't like you taking the Lord's name in vain. —Why haven't you wished for something beyond this life, far beyond, where the dirt of life doesn't exist?

THE STRANGER: Because I doubted there was anything beyond this existence.

THE LADY: What about the elves?

THE STRANGER: A fairy tale. —Don't you think we might sit down here on the bench?

THE LADY: All right. But first tell me honestly what it is you're waiting for.

THE STRANGER: Honestly, I'm waiting for the post office to open. There's a letter in poste-restante waiting there for me. It's been forwarded and forwarded without catching up to me.

They sit down.

Now what about you? Tell me something about yourself?

The Lady crochets.

THE LADY: There's nothing to tell.

THE STRANGER: It's strange, but I like to think of you as impersonal and nameless. I don't even know your name. I'd like to christen you myself. What shall I call you? . . . I have it! I shall call you Eve. (*Making a gesture to the wings.*) A fanfare, if you please! (*The funeral march is heard.*) Oh, no, not again! That funeral march. —Now let me assign you an age, since I don't know how old you are either. . . . From here on you shall be thirty-four, and consequently born in 1864. —As for your character and disposition, since I don't know that either, I shall endow you with a very kind nature—your voice reminds me so much of my poor dead mother's. By mother I mean of course the abstract conception of mother, pronounced "mom." You see, my mother never fondled me in her lap or dandled me on her knee. I remember only how she whipped me. Reared and raised in hate, I was. Hate! Give as good as you get. Blow for blow! An eye for an eye! You see this scar on my forehead? I got that from an ax swung by my dear brother—whose front tooth I knocked out with a stone. My father threw me out of my sister's wedding—so I didn't bother going to *his* funeral. I was born, as they say, outside the bonds of matrimony, while the family was involved in bankruptcy proceedings and with everybody dressed in mourning after the suicide of my uncle. That's my family! The fruit doesn't fall far from the tree. I figure that altogether I have escaped by the skin of my teeth fourteen years punishment at hard labor and so I have every reason to be grateful to, if not exactly contented with—the elves.

THE LADY: I love to hear you talk, really I do. But please leave the elves out of it. That really bothers me, it really does.

THE STRANGER: Well, I really don't believe in them. However, that doesn't prevent them from cropping up all the time. Aren't elves unblessed souls who have never been redeemed? There you have my case. Bewitched! There was a time when I thought my redemption was at hand. Through a woman. Seventh heaven. What a delusion! It was the beginning of the seventh hell.

THE LADY: How you talk! Perhaps you are a lost soul now, but you don't have to be.

THE STRANGER: You mean peals of church bells and drops of holy water will lull me into peace? . . . I've tried that. It only made matters worse. Made me feel like the devil when he sees the sign of the cross. —Let's talk about you now.

THE LADY: Why bother? . . . Have you ever been accused of wasting your talents?

THE STRANGER: Of course. What haven't I been accused of? No one in my town was hated as much as I was, no one shunned as much. Left the house alone, came back home alone. If I went into a restaurant, everybody moved five yards away from me. When I wanted to rent rooms, they were always taken. Priests denounced me to their congregations, teachers to their classes, and parents to their children. And once the church council tried to take my children from me. That's when I forgot myself and raised my hand against—heaven.

THE LADY: Why did they hate you?

THE STRANGER: Ask them! —Oh, I know. You see I couldn't bear to see people suffer. So I told them to free themselves and promised I would help them. I said to the poor: don't let the rich suck you dry! And to the women: don't let the men oppress you! And I said—and this was the worst—I said to the children: don't obey your parents when they're unjust. The consequences? Utterly incomprehensible. They all ganged up on me—rich *and* poor, men *and* women, parents *and* children. And on top of that came illness and poverty, beggary and dishonor, divorce and lawsuits, exile, loneliness, and now finally—. Do you think I'm mad?

THE LADY: No, I don't think that.

THE STRANGER: You must be the only one. And all the dearer to me for that.

THE LADY (*rising*): Now I really have to leave . . .

THE STRANGER: You too? You see.

THE LADY: But you can't stay here.

THE STRANGER: Where would you suggest I go?

THE LADY: Home to your work.

THE STRANGER: I'm no worker, I'm a writer.

THE LADY: I don't want to hurt your feelings, but you said yourself that writing is a gift. It can be taken back. Don't forfeit it.

THE STRANGER: Where are you going?

THE LADY: On an errand . . .

THE STRANGER: Are you religious?

THE LADY: No, I'm nothing at all.

THE STRANGER: Good! Then you can become something. Oh, how I wish I were your blind old father, whom you would lead about the streets while he sang for pennies. But the unfortunate thing is that I can't grow old. Same way with the elves' children. They don't grow up, they just grow a big head, and they cry and cry. . . . I wish I were somebody's dog. I could follow him around, never be alone. A scrap of food once in a while, a kick now and then, petted once a day, beaten twice —

THE LADY: Now I really have to go. Goodbye.

THE STRANGER (*absentmindedly*): Goodbye. (*He remains sitting on the bench. Takes off his hat and wipes his forehead. Then he begins to draw in the sand with his cane.*)

> *The Beggar enters. Very strange looking. He is grubbing about in the gutter.*

THE STRANGER: What do beggars hope to find in gutters?

THE BEGGAR: Is that any of your business? Besides, I'm not a beggar. Have I begged you for anything?

THE STRANGER: Sorry, I beg your pardon. Appearances can be so deceptive.

THE BEGGAR: I can assure you of that. For instance, can you guess who I am?

THE STRANGER: No, I neither can nor care to. I'm not interested.

THE BEGGAR: One doesn't know that in advance. Interest comes afterward, when it's too late. *Virtus post nummos!**

THE STRANGER: A bum speaking the language of the Romans! What next?

THE BEGGAR: You see! You are interested. *Omne tulit punctum qui miscuit utile dulce.*** My dear sir, you see before you a man who has succeeded in everything he's tried his hand at, for the very good reason that he hasn't ever done anything. I should call myself Polycrates—he of the golden ring. I've had everything I've wanted from life. However, since I never really wanted anything, it was all too easy, and bored by my success, I threw away the ring—. Now that I'm getting on in years, I regret my action and spend my time looking for it in the gutters. And since the search gets to be rather monotonous at times, I am not above picking up—in place of the golden ring, you understand—a few discarded cigar butts.

THE STRANGER: I can't make out whether you're ironic or incoherent.

THE BEGGAR: My problem, too.

THE STRANGER: Now do you know who I am?

---

* *Quaerenda pecunia primum, virtus post nommos.* First seek money; virtue or reputation is secondary.
** He who mixes entertainment with instruction wins complete approval. —Horace.

THE BEGGAR: Haven't the faintest idea. And I'm not interested.

THE STRANGER: Interest usually comes afterward –. How do you like that? You've got me mouthing your words. It's like picking up old butts. Disgusting!

THE BEGGAR (*tipping his hat*): And you wouldn't care to share a butt with me?

THE STRANGER: That scar on your forehead?! – How –?

THE BEGGAR: This? Oh, I got that from a close relative.

THE STRANGER: What are you trying to do? Scare me? Are you real? Let me touch you. (*He feels The Beggar's arm.*) Yes, you are. – Listen, would you be good enough to accept a small gift on condition that you look for Polycrates' ring in some other part of town? (*Hands him a coin.*) *Post nummos virtus.* – There I go again, chewing old –. Get out, get out!

THE BEGGAR: All right, I'm going. I'm going. Good sir! You've given me altogether too much. Here, let me give you back three-fourths of it. Then we can consider it a token of friendship.

THE STRANGER: Friendship! Who said we're friends?

THE BEGGAR: Well, at least I'm yours. And when you're *alone* in this world, you can't be too particular.

THE STRANGER: You're pushing your luck, old boy! Take my advice – Scram!

THE BEGGAR: Thank you, good sir! But the next time we see each other, I'll have some advice for you. See you around. (*Leaves.*)

THE STRANGER (*sits down and writes in the sand with his cane*): Sunday afternoon! Long, dull, gray, quiet Sunday afternoon. The families have eaten their sauerkraut and roast beef with boiled potatoes. The old ones are napping and the young men are playing chess and smoking cigarettes. The servants are off at vespers, and the stores are all closed. God, what a mortally dull afternoon, day of rest, when the soul itself nods off, when there's no more chance of seeing a familiar face than there is of getting a drink –.

The Lady returns. She now has a flower in her bosom.

THE STRANGER: Extraordinary! I can't say two words without having to eat them.

THE LADY: Still sitting here?

THE STRANGER: If I sit here writing in the sand or something else, seems to make no difference—as long as I write in the sand.

THE LADY: What are you writing? Let me see.

THE STRANGER: I believe it says: Eve, 1864. —No, don't step on it.

THE LADY: Why? What will happen?

THE STRANGER: Bad luck, for you—and for me.

THE LADY: You're sure?

THE STRANGER: Positive. Just as certain as I am that the Christmas rose you're wearing on your breast is a mandragora. It stands for evil and slander—as a symbol. As a medicine it is known as the hellebore and was formerly used to cure madness. Will you give it to me?

THE LADY (*hesitating*): As medicine—?

THE STRANGER: —Have you read my books?

THE LADY: You know I have. I can thank you for my independent spirit and my belief in justice and human dignity.

THE STRANGER: Then you haven't read my latest ones.

THE LADY: No. And if they're not like the first ones, I want nothing to do with them.

THE STRANGER: Good! Then you must swear, here and now, never to open another book of mine.

THE LADY: Let me think about it. . . . All right, I swear.

THE STRANGER: Don't forget now. And don't let me catch you breaking your promise. Remember what happened to Bluebeard's wife when curiosity tempted her to open the forbidden room.

THE LADY: You're behaving more and more like Bluebeard yourself. Or haven't you noticed? You're oblivious to the fact that I'm a married woman . . . that my husband is a doctor . . . that he admires your work so much that he would welcome you with open arms . . . if you were to come home with me.

THE STRANGER: I've done my best to forget all that. I've wiped it completely out of mind. It doesn't exist for me.

THE LADY: In that case, how about coming home with me this afternoon?

THE STRANGER: No. How about coming with me?

THE LADY: Where?

THE STRANGER: Out into the big wide world, no place in particular. Haven't got a home—live out of my suitcase. And as for money, I have some now and then, but not very often. It's the one thing that life obstinately refused to give me, perhaps because I haven't wished for it hard enough.

THE LADY: Hmmmm.

THE STRANGER: What are you thinking?

THE LADY: I'm astonished that I'm not insulted by your proposition. Are you joking?

THE STRANGER: Joking or serious, what's the difference? —Listen. . . . The organ's playing. Divine service is over. The bars will soon be open.

THE LADY: I'll bet you drink a lot, don't you?

THE STRANGER: Inordinately! Wine makes my soul shed its skin and soar out into space, to see things nobody ever imagined and hear things never heard before.

THE LADY: What about the morning after?

THE STRANGER: I suffer the exquisite pangs of conscience. All my tensions are relieved by feelings of guilt and remorse. I revel in my body's pain while my soul floats like a cloud around my head. It's like being suspended between life and death, when the soul tries out its wings and could fly away if it wanted to.

THE LADY: Come into the church with me. Only for a moment. No sermons, I promise you, only the beautiful music of vespers.

THE STRANGER: No, not into the church. Depresses me. Reminds me that I don't belong there, that I'm a lost soul, with about as much chance of getting in as I have of becoming a child again. And that happens only when you're in your dotage – or out of your mind.

THE LADY: You've already found that out, have you?

THE STRANGER: Oh, I've come a long ways. I can see myself lying chopped up in Medea's kettle, slowly boiling and bubbling away. Either I end up in the soap factory, or else I rise up rejuvenated from my own juices. It all depends on Medea's skill.

THE LADY: That sounds oracular. Shall we see if you can become a child again?

THE STRANGER: That would mean beginning at the cradle – and with the right one in it!

THE LADY: Exactly. – Now you wait for me right here while I go into St. Elizabeth's chapel. I'm glad the café isn't open. If it were, I'd beg you, "Please, pretty please, don't drink."

> *She leaves. The Stranger sits down again and writes in the sand. Six Pallbearers and some Mourners enter, dressed in brown. One of the Pallbearers is carrying a flag with the insignia of the carpenters' union on it, decorated with brown crepe. Another is carrying a huge broadax decorated with spruce branches. A third, a small cushion with a judge's gavel on it. They stop in front of the café and wait.*

THE STRANGER: Excuse me, whose funeral? (*Pointing to the ax.*) A lumberjack?

FIRST PALLBEARER (*points to the flag*): Close. A carpenter. (*He makes a sawing sound.*)

THE STRANGER (*imitates the sound*): A real carpenter or the insect?

SECOND PALLBEARER: The kind that bores into wood. (*He makes a ticking sound.*)

THE STRANGER: That's a beetle.

SECOND PALLBEARER: Yes. What do you call it?

THE STRANGER (*to himself*): Death-watch beetle. I won't say it. (*To the Second Pallbearer.*) Goldsmith beetle. Right?

SECOND PALLBEARER: No. The kind that bores into walls and sits there ticking when somebody's about to die. (*A ticking is heard, coming from nowhere.*)

THE STRANGER: What the hell's going on? Trying to scare me? Are the dead performing miracles? Won't work. I don't scare easily, and I don't believe in miracles. —All the same, I do find it eerie that you mourners are dressed in brown. Why not black, which is inexpensive, practical, and appropriate?

THIRD PALLBEARER: We are in black. So it seems to our simple minds. But if you, good sir, would have it brown, then so be it.

THE STRANGER: I find you all very peculiar, and that's a fact. I trust that my disquiet is part of my hangover. That Moselle wine! —Sir, that stuff on the ax—it looks like—. What is it?

FIRST PALLBEARER: The vine of the grape.

THE STRANGER: The grape, of course! I knew it couldn't be spruce. Looks exactly like spruce. —Ah, thank heavens, they're opening the bar! About time.

> *The Café Proprietor comes out to take orders. The Pallbearers and The Stranger sit down. During the following dialogue they give their orders and are served. The Stranger orders Moselle wine, and a bottle is brought to his table.*

THE STRANGER: He must have been a merry old soul, the man you buried. Here you are getting drunk immediately after the sobering occasion.

FIRST PALLBEARER: A good-for-nothing. Refused to take life seriously.

THE STRANGER: And probably drank too much?

SECOND PALLBEARER: Afraid so.

THIRD PALLBEARER: Didn't mind letting others care for his wife and children. A real bum.

THE STRANGER: Not very considerate of him, I'm sure. No doubt that accounts for the beautiful and moving funeral oration. —I say, would you mind not leaning on my table? You're spilling the wine.

FIRST PALLBEARER: Listen, mister, I paid just as much to drink here as you.

THE STRANGER: There is still a big difference between you and me.

> *The Pallbearers murmur ominously.*
>
> *The Beggar enters.*

THE STRANGER: Him again! Now he's cadging drinks.

THE BEGGAR (*sits down and strikes the table with his fist*): Waiter!

> *The Proprietor comes out. Looks disdainfully at The Beggar.*

THE BEGGAR: Bottle of wine. Moselle.

> *The Proprietor goes into the café and comes out with a poster in his hand.*

PROPRIETOR: I'm sorry but I'll have to ask you to leave. I can't serve you. You're wanted by the revenue service. For income tax evasion. Here's the wanted list—your name, age, and description.

THE BEGGAR: *Omnia serviliter pro dominatione.** I'm a man of

---

* "He played in every way the slave to secure the master's place." A reference to Otho's currying favor with the Roman soldiers in hope of becoming emperor. Tacitus, *Histories* I, 36.

independent means, with a Ph.D. I don't believe in paying taxes to a government I don't believe in. Now—if you don't mind—a bottle of Moselle!

THE PROPRIETOR: Moselle! That's very funny. You want something for nothing? You'll get a free ride to the police station and the workhouse.

THE STRANGER: Couldn't you settle this somewhere else? You're disturbing your customers.

THE PROPRIETOR: We'll settle this in a minute. And you can be a witness that I'm handling this fair and square.

THE STRANGER: I find this whole business extremely painful. Just because a man doesn't pay his taxes—(*Coughs self-consciously.*) —doesn't mean he hasn't a right to some of life's small pleasures.

THE PROPRIETOR: Listen to him! Friend of panhandlers and deadbeats! I got you pegged.

THE STRANGER: Now just a minute! I happen to be a respected and well-known—

The Proprietor and the Pallbearers laugh.

THE PROPRIETOR: Suspected, more likely!

More laughter.

Wait—wait. . . . This description—thirty-eight years old, brown hair, moustache, blue eyes—no occupation—no known source of income—married but has deserted his wife and abandoned his children—known for his subversive political views—gives the impression of not being in full possession of his faculties. —Well, I'll be—

THE STRANGER (*stands up, overwhelmed, his face ashen*): What's going on? What is this?

THE PROPRIETOR: Damned if it doesn't check out point for point.

THE BEGGAR: Could it be him and not me?

THE PROPRIETOR: Sure looks like it. That makes you two of a kind in my book, and you can trot out of here arm in arm.

THE BEGGAR (*to The Stranger*): Come on. We better move along.

THE STRANGER: We?! This is a frame-up!

> *The church bells begin to ring. The sun comes out and lights up the stained-glass rose window over the portal, which now opens to reveal the interior of the church. An organ is heard and a choir singing "Ave Maris Stella."*

THE LADY (*emerging from the church*): Where are you? What's the matter? Why did you call for me again? You're like a child on apron strings.

THE STRANGER: I'm scared, don't you see? Something's happening that I can't explain — something unnatural.

THE LADY: I thought you said you weren't afraid of anything, not even death.

THE STRANGER: I'm not — not of death — but this other thing — the unknown . . .

THE LADY: All right. There, there. Give me your hand like a good boy. You're sick. I'll take you to the doctor. My doctor. Come!

THE STRANGER: I just might take you up on that. — Tell me, is this carnival time or are they always dressed like that?

THE LADY: I don't see anything strange.

THE STRANGER: But that beggar — he's disgusting! Do I really look like him?

THE LADY: You will if you go on drinking. — Now you go in and pick up your letter at the post office, and then come on home with me.

THE STRANGER: No, no post office for me. Anyway there'll be nothing but court orders and legal papers in that letter.

THE LADY: But suppose there isn't — ?

THE STRANGER: There'll be some other kind of bad news.

THE LADY: All right, have it your way. But you can't escape destiny. Right now I feel as if some higher power were sitting in judgment over us, about to hand down a verdict.

THE STRANGER: You too! Just now I heard the gavel rap, the chairs being pushed back from the bench, the clerks sent out. . . . How agonizing. . . . No, I won't go with you.

THE LADY: What are you doing to me? . . . In the chapel I couldn't pray. The light went out on the altar and a cold wind blew across my face just when I heard you call for me.

THE STRANGER: I didn't call. I only longed for you . . .

THE LADY: You're not the helpless child you pretend to be. You're unbelievably strong. I'm afraid of you.

THE STRANGER: When I'm alone I'm like a paralytic. But as soon as I leech on to someone, strength comes flowing back into me. Right now I want to feel strong again. I'll go with you.

THE LADY: Good! You can be my hero and liberate me from the werewolf.

THE STRANGER: You've got a werewolf?

THE LADY: I've got a husband.

THE STRANGER: Great! I'm your man! Battling dragons, freeing princesses, slaying werewolves—that's living!

THE LADY: Well, then come, my liberator! (*She draws her veil down over her face, kisses him quickly on the mouth, and rushes out.*)

> *The Stranger stands for a moment stupefied.*
>
> *A high chord of women's voices, almost a shriek, is heard from within the church. The lighted rose window suddenly darkens. The tree over the bench trembles. The Pallbearers rise from their places and look upward at the sky as if they see something strange and terrifying.*
>
> *The Stranger hurries out after The Lady.*

* * *

At the Doctor's Home

A yard enclosed by the three wings of a one-story wooden house with a tiled roof. Rather small windows in all three wings. To the right, a veranda or porch enclosing the glass doors to the house. To the left, by the windows, a rambler rosebush, and some beehives on a stand. In the middle of the yard, a very high woodpile shaped like a gourd or an Oriental cupola. Beside it, a water pump. Above the middle wing rises the top of a huge walnut tree. In the right corner, a gate to the garden.

Near the pump is a big turtle.* To the right are steps down to a wine cellar. An icebox and a garbage can. Below the porch are a lawn table and some chairs.

The Doctor's Sister comes down from the porch with a telegram in her hand.

THE SISTER: Well, my dear brother, I think lightning is about to strike you.

THE DOCTOR: That's nothing new, my dear sister.

THE SISTER: This time it's different. It's Ingeborg. She's on her way home — and she's bringing someone with her. Guess who.

THE DOCTOR: Who? . . . I don't have to guess, I know. I've felt for a long time it was going to happen. Even wished for it. I've always admired him, learned a lot from his books, wanted to meet him. And now he's here. Well, well. Where on earth did Ingeborg dig him up?

THE SISTER: In the city, I'd guess. The literary salons.

THE DOCTOR: I've often wondered if he could possibly be one of my school chums who had that name. I hope not. There was something ominous about that young boy. And by this time all the fatal tendencies in him would have developed enormously.

---

* The Oriental shape of the woodpile and the presence of the turtle, living in a virtual state of Nirvana, are meant to suggest the peace and resignation of Buddhism.

THE SISTER: Don't let him come here. Go away. Say you have guests.

THE DOCTOR: No use. You can't escape fate.

THE SISTER: How odd. Nothing intimidates you, but you crawl on your belly before a chimera you call fate.

THE DOCTOR: Experience has taught me not to waste time and energy struggling against the inevitable.

THE SISTER: Why do you let your wife run around compromising herself and you?

THE DOCTOR: It all seems so simple to you. I let her do what she wants because after we'd been engaged I released her from all promises. I pictured to her a life of freedom in contrast to the virtual imprisonment she had known before. Besides, I couldn't love her if she only did what I told her. I didn't want a slave for a wife.

THE SISTER: So you invite your enemy into your home.

THE DOCTOR: All right, all right!

THE SISTER: You let her drag home the very man who'll destroy you. Oh, how I detest that man!

THE DOCTOR: I know. His last book is just as disgusting as the others. It also gives signs of mental disturbance.

THE SISTER: Then why don't they put him away?

THE DOCTOR: A lot of people think they should. But I can't find any evidence that he's actually gone over the edge.

THE SISTER: Naturally! You're half-crazy too. And you spend half your time with a wife who's completely out of her mind.

THE DOCTOR: I can't deny that maniacs have always attracted me. They're not boring. They've got originality (*A steamboat whistle is heard.*) —What's that? Someone's screaming!

THE SISTER: Your nerves *are* on edge. It's only a steamboat whistle. . . . Last warning: get away while you still have a chance.

THE DOCTOR: I might give it some thought if I weren't nailed to the spot. . . . From where I stand I can see his portrait in my study. . . . And the sunshine casts a shadow that distorts his face. He looks like – huh! My God, do you see what he looks like?

THE SISTER: He looks like the devil himself. – Run!

THE DOCTOR: I can't.

THE SISTER: You might at least defend yourself.

THE DOCTOR: That's what I used to do. But this time it's like a storm approaching. How many times haven't I wanted to stand my ground but couldn't. This time is different. The ground's a magnet and I'm a piece of metal. . . . If the worst comes, I can always say it wasn't my doing. . . . They're coming through the front door.

THE SISTER: I didn't hear anything.

THE DOCTOR: Yes, but I hear. I hear. And now I can see them, too. It is he, my childhood friend. . . . He got into trouble in school – some kind of prank. I got the blame and was punished. He got the nickname Caesar, I don't know why.

THE SISTER: And this man is –

THE DOCTOR: Yes. *C'est la vie.* . . . Caesar!

THE LADY (*entering*): Hello, my dear! I've brought someone with me. Very sweet and charming.

THE DOCTOR: So I hear. Bring him in. I'd like to meet him.

THE LADY: He's in the guest room freshening up.

THE DOCTOR: Are you pleased with your conquest?

THE LADY: I believe he's the most unhappy man I've ever met.

THE DOCTOR: That's extravagant.

THE LADY: Yes, I guess so. Everybody's unhappy nowadays.

THE DOCTOR: Isn't that the truth! (*To his Sister.*) Maybe you could show him the way.

The Sister leaves.

THE DOCTOR: Did you have an interesting trip?

THE LADY: Yes. I met an awful lot of strange people. . . .
Have you had many patients?

THE DOCTOR: No. This morning there was no one in the
waiting room. My practice seems to be going downhill.

THE LADY (*kindly*): You poor dear. . . . Shouldn't that wood
be taken inside pretty soon? It'll rot there.

THE DOCTOR (*without sounding reproachful*): Yes, of course it
should. And the bees should be killed and the fruit in the orchard
picked. But I just don't feel up to anything.

THE LADY: You're tired, my dear.

THE DOCTOR: Tired of everything.

THE LADY (*without bitterness*): And you've got a poor wife
who's no help to you.

THE DOCTOR (*gently*): You shouldn't say that. I'm not thinking it.

THE LADY (*facing the porch*): Now!

> *The Stranger, dressed more youthfully than in the first
> scene, enters from the porch, trying to appear confident
> and self-assured. He seems to recognize The Doctor, loses
> his composure momentarily, but regains it.*

THE DOCTOR: Hello. I hope you'll make yourself at home
here.

THE STRANGER: Thank you, Doctor.

THE DOCTOR: You've brought good weather with you. We
certainly need it here. It's been raining for six weeks.

THE STRANGER: Not seven? Rain on the Day of Seven Sleep-
ers* means seven weeks of rain. But now that I think of it, we
haven't come to that yet. Stupid of me . . .

* July 27.

THE DOCTOR: If you're accustomed to the pleasures of the city, I'm afraid our simple life here will seem rather tiresome.

THE STRANGER: Not at all . . . I'm as much at home in one place as another. . . . I don't have any reason for asking, but I can't help it. Haven't we met each other before—when we were boys?

THE DOCTOR: Never.

> *The Lady has sat down at the table and begun to crochet.*

THE STRANGER: Are you sure?

THE DOCTOR: Quite sure. I've followed your career from the beginning with the greatest interest, as my wife has no doubt told you. If we had met before, I would certainly have remembered it—your name, at least. . . . Well, now you see how a country doctor lives.

THE STRANGER: If you could imagine how a freedom-fighter—so-called—lives, you wouldn't envy him at all.

THE DOCTOR: I think I can guess. I know how people love their chains. Maybe things are supposed to be that way, since that's the way things are.

THE STRANGER (*listening to something offstage*): Strange. Who's playing the piano next door?

THE DOCTOR: Can't imagine. Do you know, Ingeborg?

THE LADY: No, I don't.

THE STRANGER: Mendelssohn's "Funeral March" still persecuting me. I don't know if it's something in my ear or . . .

THE DOCTOR: Have you had auditory hallucinations before?

THE STRANGER: Not hallucinations, but there are little recurring events, real ones, that seem to haunt me. . . . Don't you hear someone playing?

THE DOCTOR *and* THE LADY: Why, I think someone is—

THE LADY: And it is Mendelssohn.

THE DOCTOR: Mendelssohn *is* very popular nowadays.

THE STRANGER: I know that. But why do they have to play him just here, just now? (*He gets up.*)

THE DOCTOR: If it will make you feel any better, I'll ask my sister . . . (*He goes in by way of the porch.*)

THE STRANGER (*to The Lady*): I can't breathe here. I won't be able to sleep a night in this house. He actually looks like a werewolf. When he's around, you turn into a pillar of salt. This whole place reeks of murder, it's haunted. I'm getting out the first chance I get.

THE DOCTOR (*coming out*): Well, you were right. The girl who works at the post office was playing the piano.

THE STRANGER (*agitated and nervous*): Good. That explains that. . . . Rather a unique place you have here, Doctor. Everything is so—unusual. That woodpile, for instance—

THE DOCTOR: Yes, lightning has knocked it down twice.

THE STRANGER: How awful. And you still keep it there?

THE DOCTOR: For just that reason. That's why I built it two yards higher this summer. Tempting fate, you see. Also because it provides more shade that way. Like Jonah's gourd.* Looks like Jonah's gourd, doesn't it? Come autumn and away it goes into the woodshed.

THE STRANGER (*looking around*): And here you have Christmas roses. Where did you get them? And blooming in the summertime? . . . Everything is backward.

THE DOCTOR: Oh, those. Well, you see, I have a mental patient staying here—

THE STRANGER: Here in the house?

THE DOCTOR: Oh, he's harmless, quiet and tranquil. The only thing that gets him excited is the lack of plan and purpose in nature. He thinks it's stupid that the Christmas roses have to

* See Jonah 4:6.

freeze in the snow, so he brings them into the cellar and sets them out again in the spring.

THE STRANGER: A madman in the house. . . . How very disquieting.

THE DOCTOR: No need to worry. He's very peaceable, I assure you.

THE STRANGER: I wonder what drove him insane?

THE DOCTOR: Who can say? It's a mental disease; there's nothing physically wrong.

THE STRANGER: And is he . . . here . . . free and loose?

THE DOCTOR: The madman? Oh, he wanders about the garden, putting nature to rights. If his presence bothers you, I'll lock him up in the cellar.

THE STRANGER: Why not put the poor devils out of their misery?

THE DOCTOR: One never knows whether they are ripe and ready.

THE STRANGER: For what?

THE DOCTOR: For what comes next.

THE STRANGER: Nothing comes next.

    Pause

THE DOCTOR: Who knows?

THE STRANGER: I know it feels horrible here in this yard. Got any cadavers here?

THE DOCTOR (*at the icebox*): As a matter of fact, I do. I've got a few stumps on ice here, which I'm sending on to the medical school. (*Draws out a leg and an arm.*) Look at these.

THE STRANGER: My God, I must be in Bluebeard's castle.

THE DOCTOR (*sharply*): What's that supposed to mean?

(*Glances piercingly at his wife.*) Do you think I murder my wives? Hm?

THE STRANGER: Hardly. It's obvious you don't. —But you do have ghosts in the house, I'll bet.

THE DOCTOR: Do we! Talk to my wife. Ask her. (*He has withdrawn behind the woodpile so that he cannot be seen by The Lady and The Stranger.*)

THE LADY: You can speak up, if you want to. He's quite deaf. But watch it—he can read lips.

THE STRANGER: I know. . . . I've never spent a more painful half hour in all my life. We stand around talking like idiots because no one has the courage to say what's really on his mind. A moment ago I was in such agony I almost slit my wrists just to cool off a little. Right now I feel more like lighting a bomb under him and telling him the plain truth. Let's tell him right to his face that we're running off together, that we've had enough of his games.

THE LADY: I hate you when you talk like this. You can at least behave decently under all circumstances.

THE STRANGER: My, aren't you the proper little lady!

> *The Doctor reappears, visible to the two, who continue their conversation.*

THE STRANGER: Well, make up your mind. Are you coming with me now, before it gets dark?

THE LADY: I . . .

THE STRANGER: Why did you kiss me yesterday? Why?

THE LADY: Please . . .

THE STRANGER: Be funny if he's taking in every word of this. I wouldn't trust him.

THE DOCTOR: Now what should we do to amuse our guest?

THE LADY: I'm sure he doesn't expect much in the way of amusement. His life hasn't exactly been one long party.

The Doctor blows a whistle. The Madman appears in the garden. He is wearing a strange costume and has a laurel wreath on his head.

THE DOCTOR: Caesar! Come here!

THE STRANGER (*very uncomfortable*): Is his name Caesar?

THE DOCTOR: It's only a nickname I gave him in memory of an old school chum of mine . . .

THE STRANGER (*on edge*): What?

THE DOCTOR: Yes, a strange case. He framed me and I got all the blame.

THE LADY (*to The Stranger*): Can you imagine a child being so wicked?

The Stranger is in agony. The Madman approaches.

THE DOCTOR: Come in, Caesar, and make your bow to the great author.

THE MADMAN: Is he the great man?

THE LADY (*to The Doctor*): Why did you have to call him in here when you can see how it upsets our guest?

THE DOCTOR: Caesar will be on his best behavior, won't he? Otherwise he'll get a whipping.

THE MADMAN: He may be Caesar, but he isn't great. He doesn't know which came first, the chicken or the egg. But I do.

THE STRANGER (*to The Lady*): I'm going. I've had enough. You've lured me into an ambush. —Well, what am I supposed to think? Next minute he'll amuse me by releasing the beast.

THE LADY: You've got to have absolute faith in me, no matter how it looks. —And don't talk so loud.

THE STRANGER: I tell you, he won't leave us alone for a moment, that monster werewolf of yours—. Not for a second.

THE DOCTOR (*looking at his watch*): You must excuse me. I

have a call to make. Take about an hour. I hope you don't mind waiting.

THE STRANGER: I'm used to waiting—for what never comes.

THE DOCTOR (*to The Madman*): Caesar, you rascal, come here! I'm going to lock you in the cellar. (*He leaves with The Madman.*)

THE STRANGER (*to The Lady*): What's going on? Who's persecuting me? You tell me your husband is sympathetic toward me. I believe you, but he can't open his mouth without torturing me. Every word he spoke stabbed me like a needle. —God, there's that funeral march again! I can really hear it! . . . And there's the Christmas rose again. . . . Why does everything have to keep coming back again and again? Corpses and beggars and fools and madmen and whole lives and childhood memories. . . . You've got to get out of here, you've got to! It's sheer hell! Let me take you away from all this!

THE LADY: Why do you think I brought you here? You see, now no one can say you simply stole another man's wife. You're rescuing me. —But I have to know one thing: can I rely on you?

THE STRANGER: You mean how I feel about you?

THE LADY: Let's not talk about feelings. We took them for granted from the start. They'll last as long as they last.

THE STRANGER: You mean my finances? I've got a lot of money coming to me. All I have to do is write or send a wire—

THE LADY: That's good enough for me. —Well, that's it, then. (*She puts away her crocheting.*) Go out through the garden and follow the lilac bushes until you come to the wooden gate at the back. Open it and you'll be on the highway. I'll meet you in the next town.

THE STRANGER (*hesitates*): Slipping out through back doors isn't exactly to my taste. I'd rather have it out with him right here in the middle of the yard—

THE LADY (*with a gesture*): Hurry!

THE STRANGER: No. You come with me.

THE LADY: All right. . . . I will. I'll even go first. (*She turns around and throws a kiss in the direction of the porch.*) My poor little werewolf!

ACT II

In the Hotel Room

Enter The Stranger, The Porter, and The Lady.

THE STRANGER (*with an overnight bag in his hand*): You mean to say this is the only room available?

THE PORTER: Right.

THE STRANGER: But I can't stay in this one.

THE LADY: He says there isn't any other. And every hotel in town is filled.

THE STRANGER (*to The Porter*): That'll be all.

> *The Lady sinks down exhausted in a chair without taking off her hat or coat.*

THE STRANGER: Should I order something?

THE LADY: Yes: a cup of hemlock would do nicely.

THE STRANGER: I feel the same way. Kicked out of one hotel after another because we don't have a marriage license—wanted by the police for questioning because we don't have the right papers—and on top of all that we had to end up in this hotel of all hotels, the last one on earth for me. And in this room of all rooms—number eight. . . . Someone is setting me up. Someone.

THE LADY: Not number eight! I don't believe it.

THE STRANGER: You mean, you *too*? Here in this room!

THE LADY: Have you—?

THE STRANGER: Yes.

THE LADY: Let's get out of here. The street, the woods—anywhere.

THE STRANGER: I'd love to. But I'm just as tired as you are. Hounded from place to place — I feel I'm being hunted down by someone.* I knew we'd end up here, even though I fought against it and headed away from here. Who can fight against trains that are late, trains that break down, missed connections? We had to end up here, in this very room. The devil's behind it. But this isn't the last round between him and me.

THE LADY: I'm beginning to think we'll never have another moment of peace as long as we live.

THE STRANGER: Just look! Nothing's changed. There's that perpetually withering Christmas rose. And there, there's another. (*Pointing to a picture on the wall.*) And there hangs the Hotel Breuer in Montreux. I stayed there once, too.

THE LADY: Have you been to the post office?

THE STRANGER: I was waiting for that. As a matter of fact, I have. And in return for my five letters and three telegrams I got one telegram informing me that my publisher will be out of town for two weeks.

THE LADY: Then we're done for!

THE STRANGER: As good as.

THE LADY: In five minutes they'll be here to look at our passports. And then the manager will come and ask us to leave.

THE STRANGER: After that there's only one way out . . .

THE LADY: Two.

THE STRANGER: Forget it. The second one's impossible.

THE LADY: What's that?

THE STRANGER: Going to your parents.

THE LADY: You're already reading my mind.

THE STRANGER: We can't have any secrets from each other anymore.

---

* In the original the reference is to the Wild Hunt of Germanic folklore. Also at the end of Act II, p. 439.

THE LADY: The end of the honeymoon.

THE STRANGER: Maybe . . .

THE LADY: Send just one more telegram!

THE STRANGER: I know I should, but I can't budge from this spot. I no longer believe that anything I do can possibly have any effect whatsoever. —Someone has paralyzed me.

THE LADY: Me too. . . . We promised each other never to talk about the past, and all we do is drag it along just the same. Look at the wallpaper. He's lurking among the flowers.

THE STRANGER: Yes, I see him. Everywhere I look I see him. Repeated hundreds of times. . . . But I see someone else in the tablecloth pattern. . . . It's supernatural. It must be an illusion. . . . All I need now is to hear my funeral march and then everything will be just perfect. (*He listens.*) There it is!

THE LADY: I don't hear anything.

THE STRANGER: Really? I must be well on my way.

THE LADY: Shall we go home? My home?

THE STRANGER: The last and the worst possible way out. Coming home like tramps, like beggars. Anything but that.

THE LADY: But certainly it—. No, you're right. It's too much. Bringing shame and disgrace—and hurting my parents. We'd see each other humiliated. We'd never respect each other again.

THE STRANGER: I think I'd rather die. . . . Still I feel it's inevitable. I'm beginning to long for it. If it's got to happen, let's get it over with as soon as possible.

THE LADY (*takes out her crocheting*): Maybe so, but I have no desire to be humiliated in front of you. There must be some other way. . . . Suppose . . . suppose we got married. That could be managed quick enough. My marriage was annulled in the country where I got married. . . . All we have to do is take a little trip and get married by the same priest who married—. But I guess that would be humiliating for you.

THE STRANGER: It's right in style with everything else. This honeymoon is turning out to be a pilgrimage. Or running the gauntlet.

THE LADY: That's the truth. In five minutes the manager will be here to tell us to leave. There's only one way to put an end to all these humiliations. We've got to make up our minds to swallow the last bitter pill. Sh! I hear footsteps . . .

THE STRANGER: That's it then. But I'm ready this time—ready for anything. If I can't fight those I can't see, at least I can show them how much punishment I can take. —Pawn your jewels, and I'll redeem them as soon as my publisher gets back—that is, if he doesn't die in a train wreck or drown in his bathtub. —I've always wanted respect, so it's the first thing I have to sacrifice.

THE LADY: All right, we're agreed. Don't you think we better leave on our own before we get thrown out? My God, he *is* coming! The manager!

THE STRANGER: Off we go. Running the gauntlet between bellboys and waiters and doormen and room clerks. —Red with shame, white with rage. Wild animals can hide in their holes, but we're forced to parade our shame. —You might at least put down your veil.

THE LADY: Isn't it great?—the life of a liberated woman!

THE STRANGER: And here's the great liberator!

They leave.

* * *

By the Sea

A cabin on a cliff overlooking the seashore. Outside the cabin are a table and some chairs. The Stranger and The Lady, dressed in light-colored clothes, appear younger-looking than in the previous scene. The Lady is crocheting.

THE STRANGER: Three days of peace and happiness at the side of my wife—and now I feel uneasy again.

THE LADY: What are you afraid of?

THE STRANGER: That it won't last.

THE LADY: Why not?

THE STRANGER: I don't know. I just feel that it has to end—abruptly, terribly. There's something false in the very brightness of the sun and the stillness of the air. I just feel that happiness cannot be part of my life.

THE LADY: But it's all settled. My parents are resigned, my husband has been friendly and understanding in his letters—

THE STRANGER: What difference does all that make? Fate is spinning its web. Once again I can hear the gavel rap, the chairs being pushed back from the bench. Sentence has been pronounced. But I think it was pronounced even before I was born. Even in my childhood I began serving my sentence. . . . There isn't one single moment in my life I can look back on with joy.

THE LADY: Darling, you've had everything you wished for in life.

THE STRANGER: Everything I wished for, yes. Unfortunately, I forgot to wish for gold.

THE LADY: Back to that again.

THE STRANGER: Do you blame me?

THE LADY: Oh, be quiet.

THE STRANGER: What are you always crocheting? You sit there like one of the three Fates, drawing the threads between your fingers. . . . But I like it. The most beautiful sight I know of is a woman bent over her work or her child. What are you crocheting?

THE LADY: Nothing at all. Just crocheting . . .

THE STRANGER: It looks like a net of nerves and knots to catch your thoughts. I bet your brain looks like that inside.

THE LADY: If only I had half the thoughts you say I have! But I haven't any at all.

THE STRANGER: That's probably why I like to have you near me. It's why you're so good for me, so perfect I can't imagine life without you. . . . Now the clouds are gone and the sky is clear and the air is soft as baby's breath. Feel, feel! Now I'm filled with life. In moments like this I really live. I can feel myself swell up, thin out, and stretch out to infinity. I'm everywhere now, in the sea which is my blood, in the hills which are my bones, in the trees, in the flowers. My head reaches as high as the heavens and I look out over the whole universe, which is all me, and I feel all the strength and power of the creator in me, for he and I are one. I want to take it all in my hands and knead it into something more nearly perfect, more enduring, more beautiful. I want to see it all created anew and every created being happy—born without pain, living without sorrow, dying in silent contentment. Eve, come die with me now, Eve, this very instant, for in the next, all the pain will be back with us again.

THE LADY: No, I'm not ready to die yet.

THE STRANGER: Why not?

THE LADY: I keep thinking there's still something I have to do. Perhaps I haven't suffered enough yet . . .

THE STRANGER: Is that the reason for living?

THE LADY: It seems like it. —Let me ask you a favor.

THE STRANGER: Name it.

THE LADY: Please don't blaspheme against heaven the way you did just now. And don't compare yourself to the Creator. You remind me of Caesar back home.

THE STRANGER (*suddenly on edge*): Of Caesar! How can you know—? Tell me—

THE LADY: Did I say something wrong? I didn't mean to. It was stupid of me to say "back home." It just slipped out. Forgive me.

THE STRANGER: Why compare me to Caesar? Blaspheming —was that all?

THE LADY: Yes, of course, that's all.

THE STRANGER: I believe you. I know you don't want to hurt me. And yet you do hurt me, you like everyone else I come in contact with. Why, why?

THE LADY: Because you're too sensitive.

THE STRANGER: Now you're on that again. You mean I'm trying to hide something? You mean that makes me touchy?

THE LADY: God knows I didn't mean anything of the sort. —Here we go again, arguing, and suspecting each other. It's like an evil spirit between us. We've got to drive it out before it's too late.

THE STRANGER: Well, why accuse me of blasphemy? I'm simply quoting a very old saying, "Lo, we are gods!"

THE LADY: If that's true, why can't you get yourself out of this mess—get both of us out?

THE STRANGER: You think I can't? Give me time. You've only seen the beginning.

THE LADY: If the end is going to be anything like the beginning, heaven help us!

THE STRANGER: I know what you're afraid of. I had intended holding back my little surprise, but I won't torture you any longer. (*He pulls out a registered letter, unopened.*) Look what I've got!

THE LADY: The money!

THE STRANGER: Came this morning! "The smiting angel can do nought!"*

THE LADY: Don't! He can!

THE STRANGER: How?

THE LADY: "A haughty spirit goeth before a fall."

THE STRANGER: It isn't the haughtiness, it's the spirit the gods can't stand! (*Waving the letter.*) This was my Achilles' heel. I've been able to endure everything except this deadly poverty, which always hit me where it hurts.

THE LADY: If you don't mind my asking, just how much did you get?

* From Luther's "Ein' feste Burg." In the original Swedish, Strindberg paraphrases a line from a Swedish hymn.

THE STRANGER: I don't know. I haven't opened the letter yet. I have a pretty good idea how much I'm supposed to get. Let's take a look. (*Opens the letter.*) What's this? No money! It's a royalty statement showing I've got nothing coming. Something's wrong. It's crazy.

THE LADY: I'm beginning to think you're right.

THE STRANGER: That I'm damned and cursed, you mean? Didn't I tell you? So I take this little curse between my two fingers and throw it back at the magnanimous donor—(*He throws the letter up in the air.*)—followed by my curses.

THE LADY: Please! You scare me when you carry on like this.

THE STRANGER: Good! I'd rather see you scared than laughing at me. I won't be laughed at. —Now watch this! I've hurled the challenge. Now you're going to see a real wrestling match. A championship fight between giants! (*He bares his chest and throws a challenging glance upward.*) Come on out and fight. I'm ready and waiting! Strike me with thy lightning—if thou darest. Make me tremble with thy thunder—if thou canst!

THE LADY: No, no, don't!

THE STRANGER: Yes, yes! —Who are you who dare to wake me from my dream of love? To snatch the cup from my lips and the woman from my arms? What's the matter, are you jealous, you gods or devils? Little bourgeois gods, that's what you are— who parry the thrust of the sword with needle jabs from behind, who refuse to meet on the dueling ground but answer the challenge with an unpaid bill—the delivery boy's way of embarrassing the master before his servants. No lunge, no stoccado—just spit and whine. Well, you Powers, Principalities, Dominions, I spit on you!

THE LADY: May heaven never punish you.

THE STRANGER: Pooh! The heavens remain blue and still, the sea stays blue and silent. . . . Sh! an idea is beginning to ferment in my brain. I can hear a poem coming on. . . . The rhythm—that comes first. This time it's like hoofbeats, with spurs jangling and swords clanging. And there's a flapping sound

like sails being lashed by the wind. . . . No, they're flags . . .
flags . . .

THE LADY: It's the wind in the trees.

THE STRANGER: Shh. . . . They're riding over a bridge, a
wooden trestle over a dry river bed—flinty stones echoing the
hooves. . . . Wait . . . wait. . . . Now I hear voices saying
the rosary—men and women together. . . . The Hail Mary.
. . . But now I see—do you know where?—in your crocheting
—a huge kitchen—white—the walls are whitewashed. Three
small deep-niched windows with latticework, and flowers. In the
left corner, a stove. To the right, a table with pine benches. And
over the table in the corner, a black crucifix, and below it a lamp
burning. In the ceiling, soot-blackened beams. On the walls,
mistletoe hanging, dried mistletoe.

THE LADY (*frightened*): Where do you see this? Where?

THE STRANGER: In your crocheting.

THE LADY: Do you see any people?

THE STRANGER: I see an old man, a very old man, sitting at
the kitchen table . . . bent over a hunting bag . . . but his
hands are clasped together in prayer. . . . And an elderly
woman is kneeling on the floor. . . . And now I can hear—
coming from outside, from the porch, maybe—the Hail
Mary. . . . The two people inside look as if they were made of
wax. . . . And there's a veil over everything. . . . No, it's not
a poem, not my imagination. (*Awakens.*) —What was it?

THE LADY: It was real, all real. That was the kitchen in my
parents' home. And you've never seen it. The old man was my
grandfather—a forester. And the woman was my mother,
praying—for us. It's six o'clock now—that's when the workers are
in from the fields and saying their rosaries in the shade . . .

THE STRANGER: I don't know that I like this. Am I getting
to be clairvoyant, too? . . . But it was so restful there. A beautiful room, snow-white, with mistletoe and flowers. —Why were
they praying for us, I wonder?

THE LADY: Yes, I wonder, too. Have we done anything wrong?

THE STRANGER: Who knows what's wrong?

THE LADY: I've read that wrong simply doesn't exist, but still . . . I wonder. . . . I want so terribly much to be with my mother. Not my father. He abandoned me just as he deserted my mother.

THE STRANGER: Why did he leave your mother?

THE LADY: Who knows why people do things like that? The children least of all. —Please, please, let's go home. I want so much to go home.

THE STRANGER: One more lion's den, one more snake pit? Why not? For your sake I'll go home with you. But not like a prodigal son, no, you'll see me go through fire and water for your sake.

THE LADY: How do you know?

THE STRANGER: A hunch.

THE LADY: Then you must have guessed by now that it's a rough road. My parents live in the mountains. You can't even get a wagon up those trails.

THE STRANGER: It's like a fairy tale. It's like something I must have read or dreamed . . .

THE LADY: Maybe. Yet everything you'll see will be perfectly natural, though perhaps a little out of the ordinary—but then even the people aren't ordinary. . . . Are you ready to come with me?

THE STRANGER: Completely ready—come what may!

THE LADY (*kisses him on the forehead and makes the sign of the cross, simply, shyly*): Come.

*   *   *

On the Road

A landscape with rolling hills. On a bluff to the right stands a chapel. A road lined with fruit trees winds its

*way into the distance. Between the trees are shrines,
calvaries, and Alpine crosses marking the scenes of
accidents. In the foreground is a road sign with a notice:
"Vagrancy forbidden in this district."*

The Stranger and The Lady.

THE LADY: You poor man, you're exhausted.

THE STRANGER: Won't deny it. But to be hungry because
I've run out of money – that's humiliating. I never thought that
would happen to me.

THE LADY: I guess we had better be ready for anything and
everything. I think the gods are frowning on us. Look, my shoe
has split wide open. Oh, I could just cry when I think we have
to come home looking like tramps.

THE STRANGER (*pointing to the sign*): "Vagrancy forbidden in
this district." Why the devil does that sign have to be right there
in big, black letters?

THE LADY: It's always been there, as long as I can remember. . . . Just think, I haven't been here since I was a child. I
thought the road was so short then. Those hills weren't so high,
and the trees were smaller, and I could hear birds singing – or so
it seemed.

THE STRANGER: The birds sang for you all the year round
then. What a child you are. Now they sing only in the springtime
and it's already autumn. In those days you danced your way along
this endless calvary, picking flowers at the foot of the cross.

Far in the distance a hunting horn is heard.

What's that?

THE LADY: I know that sound. It's Grandfather's hunting
horn. He's coming in from the hills. . . . What a good, kind,
wonderful old man! Let's hurry. We can reach home before it
gets dark if we hurry.

THE STRANGER: How far do we have to go?

THE LADY: Not far. Only over the hill and across the river.

THE STRANGER: Is that the river I hear?

THE LADY: Yes. I was born and brought up near that big rushing river. I was eighteen before I crossed over to this side to find out what was shimmering on the horizon. . . . Now I know.

THE STRANGER: You're crying.

THE LADY: Good kind Grandfather. . . . When I was getting into the boat he said to me, "There lies the world, my child. When you've seen enough of it, come back to your hills. The hills will cover you and hide you." . . . Well, I've seen enough. . . . Enough.

THE STRANGER: We'd better move on. It's a long road, and night is falling.

> *They pick up their coats and move on.*

* * *

In the Ravine

> *The narrow entrance to a ravine between pine-covered cliffs.*
>
> *In the foreground, a shed. Leaning against the door is a broom with a goat's horn hanging from its handle.*
>
> *To the left, a blacksmith shop with the door open, emitting a red glow. To the right, a water mill.*
>
> *In the background, the ravine, with a millstream spanned by a footbridge. The jags in the cliffs form huge profiles.*
>
> *At the rise of the curtain The Blacksmith is standing in the doorway of his shop, and The Miller's Wife in the doorway of the mill. When The Lady enters, they gesture to each other and disappear through their respective doors. The clothes of The Lady and The Stranger are torn.*

The Lady enters and approaches the blacksmith shop.

THE STRANGER (*entering*): It looks like they're hiding from us.

THE LADY: I can't believe it.

THE STRANGER: What a strange landscape! Everything has been deliberately arranged to give me the willies. What's that broom doing there and that ointment horn? They've probably always been there, but I still can't help thinking of witches. . . . Why is the shop black and the mill white? Because one's covered with soot and the other with flour. Simple enough. All the same, when I saw that blacksmith standing in the red glow of his fire directly opposite that white miller girl, I couldn't help thinking of an old poem.* . . . Look at those giants up there. . . . It's insufferable! Look, you can see that werewolf of yours up there. I may have rescued you from him, but that's his profile up there all the same. . . . Look at it.

THE LADY: Yes, yes, I can see it. It's only the cliff.

THE STRANGER: I know it's only the cliff, but still it's *him*.

THE LADY: I don't have to tell you *why* we see him.

THE STRANGER: You're thinking of . . . conscience, which rears its ugly head when you're tired and hungry but goes away when you're full and rested. . . . Isn't it like being damned to have to make our way like beggars? —Look, even our clothes are ripped and torn after climbing the mountains and hiking through thorn bushes. . . . I tell you, someone's fighting against me.

THE LADY: Well, you challenged him!

THE STRANGER: I wanted a fair fight with clean weapons— not with unpaid bills and empty pockets. But if that's the way it's going to be, here's my last cent. Old Nix the water sprite is welcome to it—if he exists. (*He throws a coin into the stream.*)

* In the Icelandic poem *The Song of the Sun* (Sólarljóð), a product of a Christian visionary, the world mill stands at the entrance to the kingdom of the damned. The grain it grinds to powder are the giants.

THE LADY: Now look what you've done! We needed that to pay for the ferry across the river. Now as soon as we walk into the house, we'll have to talk about money.

THE STRANGER: What else do we ever talk about?

THE LADY: Maybe that's because you've never had anything but contempt for it.

THE STRANGER: As for everything else.

THE LADY: Everything isn't contemptible. Some things are good.

THE STRANGER: Name one!

THE LADY: You just come with me. You'll see . . .

THE STRANGER: All right, I'm coming—. (*He hesitates as he is about to pass by the blacksmith shop.*)

THE LADY (*who has gone ahead*): Are you afraid of the fire?

THE STRANGER: No, but—

> *The hunting horn is heard in the distance. He hurries past the shop after her.*

*   *   *

In the Kitchen

> *A large kitchen with whitewashed walls in a mountain cabin. Three windows in the right corner, two of them in the rear and one in the right wall. The windows are small and set in deep niches with flower pots. The beamed ceiling is black with soot. In the left corner, a built-in brick stove and oven with copper, bronze, iron, and pewter utensils, and wooden mugs and buckets. In the right corner, a crucifix with a votive candle. Beneath it, a rectangular table with benches along the wall.*
>
> *Mistletoe is hanging here and there. A door in the rear. Through it can be seen a poorhouse, and through the windows at the back, a church.*

Near the stove is bedding for the dogs and a table for the poor.

At the table under the crucifix sits The Old Man with his hands clasped and his hunting bag in front of him.

He is in his eighties, powerfully built, with white hair and a full beard, and dressed like a forester.

The Mother is kneeling in the center of the floor; gray-haired, going on fifty, dressed in black and white.

From outside the voices of men, women, and children can be heard clearly reciting the last words of the Hail Mary: "Holy Mary, Mother of God, pray for us sinners now and at the hour of our death. Amen."

THE OLD MAN *and* THE MOTHER: Amen.

THE MOTHER: You know what I heard today? They saw two vagrants down by the river. Their clothes were torn and dirty. Soaked to their skins from the water —. And when they were supposed to pay the ferryman, they didn't have a cent on them. Now they're sitting in the ferryhouse, drying out their clothes.

THE OLD MAN: Good! Let them sit there.

THE MOTHER: Be not forgetful to entertain beggars; they might be angels in disguise.

THE OLD MAN: True. —All right, let them come here.

THE MOTHER: I'll put some food out on the table for the poor folk, if that won't bother you.

THE OLD MAN: No, of course not.

THE MOTHER: Shall I set out some cider?

THE OLD MAN: Yes, let them have some cider. . . . You might also build a fire in the stove. They'll be cold and wet.

THE MOTHER: There isn't much time to get a fire going — but — well, if you wish it, Father.

THE OLD MAN (*looking out the window*): Yes, please.

THE MOTHER: What are you looking at?

THE OLD MAN: I'm looking at the rising river and wondering, as I've wondered for seventy-five years, when shall I ever reach the sea?

THE MOTHER: Feeling sad, Father?

THE OLD MAN: . . . *et introibo ad alterem Dei; ad Deum qui lactificat juventutem.** . . . Yes, I'm depressed. . . . *Deus, Deus meus; quare tristis es anima mea, et quare conturbas me?***

THE MOTHER: *Spera in Deo* – ***

> *A Maid enters, signals to The Mother, who goes over to her. They whisper. The Maid leaves.*

THE OLD MAN: I heard that. . . . My God, how much am I supposed to endure?

THE MOTHER: You don't have to meet them. You can go up to your room.

THE OLD MAN: No, I shall take it as a kind of penance. Why do they come here like tramps?

THE MOTHER: They must have got lost or run into some bad luck. . . . You don't suppose – ?

THE OLD MAN: But she's bringing her – her – lover with her. Shameless.

THE MOTHER: You know what a strange girl Ingeborg is. No matter what she does she gets away with it. Even makes it seem right and proper. Have you ever seen her blush because she did something indecent or look hurt because somebody rebuked her? I never have. It's not that she's impudent or shameless – quite the contrary. She's just innocent. Part of her charm.

---

* I will go unto the altar of God, to God, who giveth joy to my youth.
** O God, my God. Why art thou sad, O my soul, and why dost thou trouble me?
*** Hope in God. – This and the previous two Latin quotations are from Psalms 42 and 43.

THE OLD MAN: It's amazing how you can't get mad at her. She has no sense of responsibility. You can't insult her. It's as if she didn't have a self of her own—or as if she were two different persons, one doing bad all the time and the other always giving absolution. . . . But as for that man—! I've never detested anyone from afar as much as I detest him. He sees evil everywhere, yet there's no man I've heard more evil about than him.

THE MOTHER: True. Possibly Ingeborg has some role to play in that man's life—and he in hers. Maybe they're going to torment each other to redemption.

THE OLD MAN: Even if that were true, I have no desire to be an accomplice in an affair that seems shameless to me. . . . That man—under my roof! But I suppose I have to stand for it—like everything else. God knows, I've deserved it.

THE MOTHER: In God's name, then.

The Lady and The Stranger enter.

THE MOTHER: Come in. Welcome to you both.

THE LADY: Thank you, Mother.

She goes over to The Old Man. He rises and regards The Stranger carefully.

THE LADY: God bless you, Grandfather. . . . This is my husband. . . . Aren't you going to shake hands?

THE OLD MAN: Let me take a look at him first. (*He goes over to The Stranger, lays his hands on his shoulders, and looks him in the eye.*) Young man, what are your intentions in coming to this house?

THE STRANGER (*forthrightly*): None but to keep my wife company, and only because she insisted.

THE OLD MAN: If that's true, you're welcome here. I have a long and stormy life behind me, and I've finally found some peace and solitude. I beg you not to disturb it.

THE STRANGER: I didn't come to ask for any favors, and I'll leave without asking for any.

THE OLD MAN: I don't like that answer, young man. We all need each other. Perhaps even I need you. One never knows.

THE LADY: Grandfather, please!

THE OLD MAN: Yes, yes, my child. . . . Well, I won't wish you happiness – it doesn't exist. However, I will wish you the strength to bear your fate. . . . I'll leave you for a while with your mother. She'll take care of you. (*He leaves.*)

THE LADY (*to The Mother*): Have you set that table for us, Mother?

THE MOTHER: The table for the poor? Of course not. How could you think that? We thought you were somebody else.

THE LADY: I suppose we do look awful after getting lost in the mountains. And if Grandfather hadn't signaled with his hunting horn, I don't know what we'd –

THE MOTHER: Grandfather? Why, he gave up hunting long ago.

THE LADY: It must have been somebody else's horn. – But just look at me! I better go up to the Rose Room and get everything fixed up.

THE MOTHER: You just run along. I'll be up soon . . .

> The Lady wants to say something but cannot find the words. She leaves.

THE STRANGER (*to The Mother*): I've seen this room before.

THE MOTHER: And I've seen you before. In a way, I've been expecting you.

THE STRANGER: As one expects an accident?

THE MOTHER: Why do you say that?

THE STRANGER: I'm a walking catastrophe. Devastation wherever I go. But since I have to go somewhere, and since I can't change my fate, I feel no compunction . . .

THE MOTHER: Just like my daughter – no misgivings and no conscience.

THE STRANGER: Really? I'm surprised to hear you say that.

THE MOTHER: Why? You think I meant something bad? I don't go around saying bad things against my own child. I made the comparison only because I thought you knew what she was like.

THE STRANGER: I haven't noticed the characteristics you mention in Eve . . .

THE MOTHER: Why do you call Ingeborg Eve?

THE STRANGER: I gave her a name of my own choosing to make her mine. I intend to re-create her according to my tastes and desires —

THE MOTHER: In your image! (*She smiles.*) I've heard how the black magicians up in the hills carve a figure of the one they want to bewitch, and baptize it with the name of the person they want to destroy. That's how you're planning to use your self-made Eve to destroy her whole sex.

THE STRANGER (*stares astonished at The Mother*): I'll be damned! What a devil you are! Forgive me — you are my mother-in-law. You are also religious. How can you nourish such thoughts?

THE MOTHER: They are yours.

THE STRANGER: This is getting to be interesting. I thought I was going to enjoy an idyll of peace and quiet in the forest, and I end up in a witch's kitchen.

THE MOTHER: Not quite. However, you apparently forget, or perhaps didn't know, that I was shamefully disgraced by my husband who deserted me and that you're a man who ignominiously deserted his wife.

THE STRANGER: Frank enough. Now I know just where I stand.

THE MOTHER: Now I want to know where I stand. Can you support two families?

THE STRANGER: If everything goes well, yes.

THE MOTHER: Everything doesn't. Not in this world. And money can be lost.

THE STRANGER: My talent is my capital. I can't lose that.

THE MOTHER: Really? Don't tell me you haven't seen the greatest talents dry up . . . gradually over the years, or suddenly overnight?

THE STRANGER: I've never met anyone with such a knack for shaking a man's faith in himself.

THE MOTHER: You're bloated with over-confidence. That last book of yours must have knocked a few pounds off.

THE STRANGER: You read that too?

THE MOTHER: Yes. I know all your secrets. So don't play any games with me and we'll get along just fine. – One more thing – a trifle, but it casts an embarrassing shadow on this house: why didn't you pay the ferryman?*

THE STRANGER: Money is my Achilles' heel. I threw away my last cent. – Can't one talk of anything besides money in this house?

THE MOTHER: Yes. But in this house it's customary to think of one's obligations first and pleasures afterward. – You mean you came here on foot because you didn't have any money?

THE STRANGER: I'm afraid that's right.

THE MOTHER (*smiling*): And you have had nothing to eat?

THE STRANGER: No . . .

THE MOTHER: Why – you're just like a little boy, happy-go-lucky, careless –

THE STRANGER: I've had my share of rough times – never anything quite like this, though.

---

* Charon, who ferried the dead across the Acheron, demanded a fare of one obolus. The Acheron, river of woe, was one of several rivers in the realm of Hades.

THE MOTHER: I almost feel sorry for you. You look so miserable. I'd laugh if I didn't know you'd soon be crying – and others with you. . . . Now that you've won her be sure you hold on to her. She loves you. If you leave her, you'll never smile again, I promise you, or even remember what it was like to be happy.

THE STRANGER: A threat?

THE MOTHER: No, a warning. . . . Go and have your supper.

THE STRANGER (*indicating the table for the poor*): At that table?

THE MOTHER: A very poor joke, but it might come true. Wouldn't be the first time.

THE STRANGER: I'm sure. I'm ready to believe anything can happen. It can't get much worse.

THE MOTHER: That's what you think. Wait and see.

THE STRANGER (*depressed*): It wouldn't surprise me. (*Leaves.*)

> *The Mother is alone for a moment. Then The Old Man enters.*

THE OLD MAN: Well, that was no angel in disguise.

THE MOTHER: At least not an angel of light.

THE OLD MAN: Careful. The people around here are awfully superstitious. I heard them talking when I was down at the river. One fellow said that his horse shied at him. Another fellow said his dogs acted up so much he had to tie them up. The ferryman said he was certain the boat got lighter when he stepped on board. Superstitious nonsense, of course – but well –

THE MOTHER: Well what?

THE OLD MAN: Oh, nothing. . . . I saw a magpie fly through the window to their room, a closed window – right through the windowpane. I guess my eyes are failing me.

THE MOTHER: Probably that's it. But why do we sometimes see right and sometimes not . . . ?

THE OLD MAN: Just being in the same room with that atheist makes me sick. I get a pain, right here in my chest, if he so much as looks at me.

THE MOTHER: We've got to get him out of here. . . . You know, I don't think he's going to enjoy himself here.

THE OLD MAN: Exactly what I was thinking. He won't be around long. Did I tell you I got a letter tonight warning me about that man? The process servers are after him.

THE MOTHER: The process servers in this house!

THE OLD MAN: For his unpaid bills. —But we mustn't forget: he's our guest. The laws of hospitality have to be respected, even for tramps, even for our enemies. Leave him alone for a few days, let him catch his breath. He's being hunted down. You can see he's in the clutches of Providence now. He's going through the mill. First the grinder, then the sifter.*

THE MOTHER: I've already felt an irresistible call to act as the agent of Providence . . .

THE OLD MAN: Careful you don't get your revenge and your calling mixed up.

THE MOTHER: I won't—if it's possible.

THE OLD MAN: Good night . . .

THE MOTHER: Do you think Ingeborg has read his latest book?

THE OLD MAN: Have no idea. Probably not. How could she have become devoted to a man with ideas like that?

THE MOTHER: Exactly. She hasn't read it. But she will. . . . She will . . .

* The mills of the gods grind slowly, but they grind exceedingly fine. —Sextus Empiricus.

ACT III

In the Rose Room

A simply furnished, cozy room in the forester's lodge. The walls have been calcimined with a rose-red solution. The curtains are thin, rose-red muslin. Flowers are standing in the rather small lattice windows. To the right, a desk and a bookcase. To the left, a sofa, with rose-red drapes above it arranged to form a baldachin. Chairs and tables in Old German style.*

A door in the rear. Outside, a landscape and the poorhouse, a dark, dismal building, its black windows curtainless. The sun is shining brightly.

The Lady is sitting on the softa, crocheting. The Mother is standing, holding in her hand a book with red covers.

THE MOTHER: Don't tell me you won't read your own husband's books.

THE LADY: Not that one. I promised him I wouldn't.

THE MOTHER: I should think you'd want to find out everything you could about him. You're placing your whole future in his hands.

THE LADY: What good would that do? We're perfectly happy.

THE MOTHER: You don't ask much of life, do you?

THE LADY: Why should I? You don't get what you ask for anyway.

THE MOTHER: I don't know whether you were born with all the wisdom of the world or if you're as innocent as an idiot.

THE LADY: I don't know either.

* In *Inferno* Strindberg remarks that the old torture chamber in Stockholm was known as the Rose Chamber.

440

THE MOTHER: As long as the sun is shining and you've got something to eat, you're happy.

THE LADY: Yes. And if the sun isn't shining, I don't complain.

THE MOTHER: To change the subject—do you know the process servers are after your husband because of his debts?

THE LADY: Yes, I know. It's always that way with writers.

THE MOTHER: Honestly, can you tell me whether he's crazy or cunning or what?

THE LADY: No, don't you see—well, he's neither one nor the other. He's different, that's all. And what makes it boring sometimes is that there's nothing I can tell him that he hasn't heard before. So we don't talk very much. But he's happy when I'm around, and I'm happy when he's near.

THE MOTHER: I see. Well, that means you've already reached the still waters right above the falls. It won't be long now. —Maybe you'd have something to talk about if you read the things he's written.

THE LADY: Maybe. If you want to, you can leave it here. I don't care.

THE MOTHER: No, take it and hide it. Won't he be surprised when you start quoting from his masterpiece.

THE LADY (*hiding the book in her bag*): He's coming! I think he can feel from far off when somebody's been talking about him.

THE MOTHER: What a shame he can't feel when others suffer because of him—from far off. (*She leaves.*)

> *The Lady is alone for a moment. Reads at random in the book. Appears shocked. Hides the book in her bag.**

THE STRANGER (*entering*): I can tell your mother's been here. Naturally you talked about me. Her nasty words are still ricocheting from wall to wall—still slashing the air and blackening

---

* The book is *Le Plaidoyer d'un fou* (A Madman's Defense), Strindberg's frank and detailed account of his first marriage.

the sunbeams – I can even make out the impression her body left on the air in this room – and she left a little memento behind her, the fetid smell of a crushed snake.

THE LADY: My, you're really on edge today, aren't you?

THE STRANGER: I'm strung as tightly as a violin and someone's rasping out a duck call on my nerves with a horsehair bow. Onk! Onk! – You know what a duck call is, don't you? . . . There's someone here, someone stronger than I am – someone searching me out with huge searchlights wherever I go. – I wonder, do they practice witchcraft in these parts?

THE LADY: Don't turn your back to the sun. Look out at the countryside, and you'll calm down.

THE STRANGER: No, I can't bear to look at that poorhouse. It must have been built there just for me. And there's a crazy old woman always standing there, beckoning me.

THE LADY: What's the matter with you? Do you feel you're being treated badly here?

THE STRANGER: In one way, no. I'm stuffed with delicacies, as if I were being fattened for the kill. But nothing tastes good to me because I know they hate to give it to me. I can feel the hate here, like the cold blast from an ice cellar. I can feel a cold wind everywhere, even though it's deathly still and unbearably hot. And always I hear that damned mill grinding away . . .

THE LADY: It's not grinding now.

THE STRANGER: Oh, but it is. Grinding . . . grinding . . .

THE LADY: Now listen, darling, no one here hates you. Maybe they feel sorry for you, that's all.

THE STRANGER: And something else – why do the people cross themselves when they see me coming down the road?

THE LADY: Because they've just finished reciting their prayers to themselves – that's all. . . . . I hear you got a very unpleasant letter this morning.

THE STRANGER: Made my hair stand on end. I wanted to spit

fate right in the eye. Imagine, I've got money coming to me, but I can't put my hands on it, and now I'm being dragged into court—by my children's guardians, for not paying the alimony. Have you ever heard of such a humiliating situation? And I'm not to blame. I know what's right, I want to do the right thing, but I'm not allowed to. Is that my fault? No, but the shame is mine. The whole thing's unnatural. The devil's behind it.

THE LADY: But why?

THE STRANGER: Who the hell knows why? Why are we put here on earth poor ignorant creatures, ignorant of laws, customs, conventions, which in our ignorance we break and then get spanked for? Why do we grow up with our heads filled with noble dreams that we struggle to make come true? And why are we always forced down into all the filth we try to rise above? Why? Why?

> *The Lady has been reading in the book, unnoticed by The Stranger.*

THE LADY (*indifferently*): Must be some reason, even if we can't figure it out.

THE STRANGER: If the idea is to teach humility, as they say it is, then it's a damned poor way, because it only makes me more arrogant, more proud. . . . Eve—

THE LADY: Don't call me that!

THE STRANGER (*stung*): Why not?

THE LADY: I don't like it, any more than you like being called Caesar.

THE STRANGER: Back to that again.

THE LADY: Back to what again?

THE STRANGER: You had some ulterior motive for using that name. It didn't just—

THE LADY: Caesar? No, I didn't. But I see that I'm about to be enlightened.

THE STRANGER: Exactly. I want the honor of dying by my

own hand. — I am Caesar, the schoolboy who played a schoolboy trick for which someone else was punished. That someone was your husband — the werewolf. You see how fate amuses itself by weaving the strands together forever and ever. What a noble pastime!

> *The Lady is about to say something, but hesitates and remains silent.*

THE STRANGER: Well, say something.

THE LADY: I can't.

THE STRANGER: Come on. Can't you say he became a werewolf because of me — because I caused him to lose his faith in the justice of heaven when he was unfairly punished for what someone else had done? Say it, so I can tell you my conscience made me suffer ten times as much as he did, and that I came out of that religious crisis so cleansed in spirit that I never again did a thing like that.

THE LADY: It isn't that. It isn't that.

THE STRANGER: Then what is it? . . . I see. You no longer have any respect for me.

THE LADY: No, it isn't that either.

THE STRANGER: What then? You want me to writhe in shame in front of you? Then it really would be all over between us.

THE LADY: No. No.

THE STRANGER: Eve —

THE LADY: Don't call me that! You make me think awful things . . .

THE STRANGER: You've broken your promise. You've read my book.

THE LADY: Yes.

THE STRANGER: That was pretty mean.

THE LADY: My intentions were good. I thought that —

THE STRANGER: Good intentions! The road to hell. —Well, that does it. Blown to pieces! And I provided the powder myself. . . . It's great! Everything has to come back, repeat itself, everything—little schoolboy tricks and big manly crimes. That we reap as we sow, fair enough. But if only someday I could see a good deed get its reward. —Never get to see that. Shame on that angel who records every fault, big and small. There isn't a person living who would do that. And people forgive, but the gods never do.

THE LADY: Don't say that. Don't. Say you can forgive.

THE STRANGER: I'm not small-minded, you know that. But what have I to forgive you?

THE LADY: I don't know that I dare to tell you . . .

THE STRANGER: You might as well. Maybe that will make us even.

THE LADY: Well . . . he and I used to read the curse from Deuteronomy over you—the person who had ruined his life.

THE STRANGER: What sort of curse is that?

THE LADY: It's from the fifth book of Moses. The priests recite it in chorus when Lent begins.

THE STRANGER: I don't recall it. But what difference does it make?—one curse more or less.

THE LADY: It matters because in my family there's a tradition that whoever we curse will be struck down.

THE STRANGER: Well, I don't believe in it. —Although I haven't the slightest doubt that evil emanates from this house. May it redound on their heads! That's my prayer. . . . (*Reverting to earlier thoughts.*) According to the custom of the country, there's nothing for me to do now but blow my brains out—which I can't do since I still have some obligations to fulfill. How do you like that! I can't even be allowed to die—which means I've lost the last remnant of what I called my religion. That's really ingenious. I've heard that men can wrestle with God, and not without success, but even Job couldn't fight with Satan. . . . (*Pause.*) Maybe we should talk a little bit about you.

THE LADY: Not now, but perhaps soon. . . . After reading your terrible book—I've only glanced at it here and there, but that's enough—I feel as if I've eaten of the tree of knowledge. My eyes have been opened, and I know the difference between good and evil. I didn't before. Now I see what an evil man you really are, and I know why you wanted to call me Eve. But if she brought sin with her, another mother brought redemption. If the first brought corruption to life, the second brought life with a blessing. So you can't use me to destroy my whole sex. I think I may have an altogether different purpose in your life. We'll see.

THE STRANGER: So you've eaten of the fruit of the tree of knowledge, have you? —Goodbye.

THE LADY: Are you leaving?

THE STRANGER: Of course. You can't expect me to stay here.

THE LADY: Don't go!

THE STRANGER: I have to. I'm up to my neck in trouble. I have to clear it up. I'll go and say goodbye to the old folks and then come back to you. —I'll be back in a moment. (*He leaves.*)

THE LADY (*stands petrified for a moment. Then she goes to the door and looks out*): Oh, no! He's gone! He's gone! (*She sinks to her knees.*)

* * *

The Asylum

The refectory in an old cloister. It resembles a simple, whitewashed church with rounded Romanesque arches, but the walls are marked with damp stains forming strange figures.

A dining table with bowls on it. At the end of the table, a lectern. In the rear, a door to the chapel. Lighted candles on the table. On the left wall, a painting of Michael slaying the dragon.

At a long dining table to the left, The Stranger is sitting alone, dressed in a white hospital gown, with a bowl in front of him. At the table to the right are sitting the

Pallbearers in brown from the first act; The Beggar; a Woman in Mourning with Two Children; another Woman who resembles The Lady but is not she, and who is crocheting instead of eating; a Man who resembles The Doctor but is not he; The Madman's Double; Doubles of The Father and The Mother; The Brother's Double; The Parents of the "prodigal son," * and others. All are dressed in white but over their white gowns they are wearing gauze costumes in various colors. Their faces are waxen and deathly white. Their whole appearance and all their gestures are ghostlike.

As the curtain rises, all are finishing the Lord's Prayer, except The Stranger.

The Stranger gets up and goes over to The Abbess, who is standing at the serving table.

THE STRANGER: Mother, may I speak to you a moment?

THE ABBESS (*in the black-and-white habit of the Augustinians*): Yes, my son.

They go downstage.

THE STRANGER: First I want to know where I am.

THE ABBESS: In the cloister of "The Helping Hand." You were seen in the mountains above the ravine, with a cross you had torn down from a calvary, and you were using it to challenge someone you imagined you could see in the clouds. You had a fever, and you fell over the cliff. That's where you were found, uninjured but delirious, and then you were brought here to the hospital and put to bed. Since then you've been raving deliriously, and complaining of a pain in your thigh, although we haven't been able to find an injury.

THE STRANGER: What was I raving about?

---

* The parents of the "prodigal son" are The Old Man and The Mother, who had regarded The Stranger as their own son. Strindberg looked upon his wife's parents as his own.

THE ABBESS: You had the usual feverish dreams that sick people have. You reproached yourself with everything imaginable, and you kept seeing before you all your "victims," as you called them.

THE STRANGER: Anything else?

THE ABBESS: Your thoughts revolved mainly around money, and you kept insisting on paying for your treatment here in the hospital. I tried to calm you by assuring you that we don't accept payment here. This is a house of charity.

THE STRANGER: I don't want charity. I don't need charity.

THE ABBESS: It's true that it's more blessed to give than to receive, but it takes a certain nobility of soul to receive and be grateful.

THE STRANGER: I don't need to receive anything, and I ask for nothing. You can't force me to be grateful.

THE ABBESS: As you wish.

THE STRANGER: Can you tell me why none of these people will sit at the same table with me? They get up and move away . . .

THE ABBESS: Perhaps they're afraid of you.

THE STRANGER: Afraid? Why?

THE ABBESS: Well you do look rather . . .

THE STRANGER: I look! What about them? How do they look? Are they for real?

THE ABBESS: If you mean do they exist, yes, they are terribly real. If they appear strange to you, it may be because you still have the fever — or because of something else.

THE STRANGER: But I seem to recognize them, all of them. And I see them as if they were in a mirror. . . . They're only pretending to eat. Is this some kind of a charade? . . . That couple sitting over there, they look like my parents — fleetingly. . . . I've never been afraid of anything before, because life never meant anything to me. But now I'm growing more and more frightened.

THE ABBESS: If you don't believe that they are actual persons, we can call the confessor over and he can introduce them to us. (*She signals to The Confessor, who comes over.*)

THE CONFESSOR (*in a Dominican habit, black and white*): Yes, Sister?

THE ABBESS: Could you tell our patient here who those people are sitting at that table?

THE CONFESSOR: Of course. That's easily done.

THE STRANGER: Before you do that—haven't we met before?

THE CONFESSOR: Yes, I sat at your bedside while you were sick with fever, and, at your request, I heard your confession.

THE STRANGER: My confession!

THE CONFESSOR: Yes. I could not give you absolution, however, since I felt that your confession consisted of nothing but the ravings of a fevered mind.

THE STRANGER: What do you mean?

THE CONFESSOR: Why, there was scarcely a crime or a sin that you did not take upon yourself—and, moreover, deeds of such depravity that it is customary to submit to the strongest penance before asking for absolution. Since you have now regained your senses, I feel I should ask if there are any grounds for these self-accusations.

The Abbess withdraws.

THE STRANGER: What right do you have to ask that?

THE CONFESSOR: None at all, that's true. —But I forgot—you wanted to know about these people in whose company you find yourself. I believe it's fair to say that they are not the most fortunate of human beings. There, for example, we have a lunatic called Caesar.* He lost his mind reading the works of a certain

* At the end of 1888 Strindberg was corresponding with Nietzsche when the German philosopher went mad. Strindberg feared that the same fate might befall him. One of Nietzsche's letters was signed "Caesar."

author who was more notorious than praiseworthy. And then we have a beggar who won't admit he's a beggar because he's gone to the university, learned Latin, and doesn't believe in taxes. Next there's the doctor—or the werewolf, as he's called—whose story is too familiar to need repeating. And then a mother and a father who grieved themselves to death over a wicked and depraved son who raised his hand against them. That he did not follow his father's remains to the cemetery, and that he, while intoxicated, profaned his mother's grave, are deeds that need not concern us. And there sits his poor sister whom he drove out into the winter snow—with the best of intentions, or so he insisted. There sits a deserted wife with two uncared-for children, and there sits another wife, crocheting. All in all, nothing but old acquaintances. Go and say hello to them.

> *During the latter part of this speech, The Stranger has turned his back to the company. He now goes and sits at the table to the left, keeping his back to the others. When he lifts his head, he sees the picture of Michael and lowers his eyes.*

> *The Confessor goes forward and stands behind The Stranger. At the same time a Catholic requiem is heard from within the chapel. The Confessor speaks softly to The Stranger, while the music continues quietly.*

THE CONFESSOR:

> *Quantus tremor est futurus*
> *Quando judex est venturus*
> *Cuncta stricte discussurus,*
> *Tuba mirum spargens sonum*
> *Per sepulchra regionum*
> *Coget omnes ante thronum.*
> *Mors stupebit et natura,*
> *Cum resurget creatura*
> *Liber scriptus proferetur*
> *In quo totum continetur*
> *Unde mundus judicetur.*
> *Judex ergo cum sedebit*

Quidquid latet apparebit
*Nil inultum remanebit.**

He goes to the lectern at the table to the right. Opens the
breviary. The music ceases.

THE CONFESSOR: We shall now continue the lesson. "But if thou wilt not harken unto the voice of the Lord thy God, to observe all his commandments and his statutes, all these curses shall come upon thee, and overtake thee. Cursed shalt thou be in the city, and cursed shalt thou be in the field. Cursed shall be thy basket and thy store. Cursed shalt thou be when thou comes in, and cursed shalt thou be when thou goest out."

THE COMPANY (*with subdued voices*): Cursed shalt thou be!

THE CONFESSOR: "The Lord shall send upon thee curses, vexation, and rebuke, in all that thou settest thine hand for to do, until thou be destroyed, and until thou perish quickly; because of the wickedness of thy doings, whereby thou hast forsaken me."

THE COMPANY (*loud*): Cursed shalt thou be!

THE CONFESSOR: "The Lord shall cause thee to be smitten before thine enemies; thou shalt go out one way against them, and flee seven ways before them; and shalt be removed into all the kingdoms of the earth. And thy carcass shall be meat unto all the fowls of the air, and unto the beasts of the earth, and no man shall fray them away.

"The Lord will smite thee with the botch of Egypt, and with the

---

* From the *Dies Irae*, a *sequentia* peculiar to the requiem Mass, "What trembling there will be/ When the Judge comes/ To make stringent examination of all things./ The trumpet scattering awesome sound/ Through the tombs of the earth's regions/ Will herd all men before His throne./ Death and nature will stand aghast/ When creation rises again./ The written Book will be brought forth/ In which everything is contained/ From which the world will be judged./ Thus when the Judge is seated,/ There will emerge manifest anything that lies hidden;/ Nothing will be left unpunished."

scab and with the itch, and with a fever, and with an inflam-
mation, and with an extreme burning, and with madness and
blindness and astonishment of heart; and thou shalt grope at
noonday as the blind gropeth in darkness, and thou shalt not
prosper in thy ways: and thou shalt be only oppressed and spoiled
evermore, and no man shall save thee. Thou shalt betroth a
wife, and another man shall lie with her: thou shalt build an
house, and thou shalt not dwell therein: thou shalt plant a vineyard, and shalt not gather the grapes thereof. Thy sons and thy
daughters shall be given unto another people, and thine eyes
shall look, and fail with longing for them all the day long: and
there shall be no might in thine hand. And among these nations
shalt thou find no ease, neither shall the sole of thy foot have rest:
but the Lord shall give thee there a trembling heart, and failing
of eyes, and sorrow of mind. And thy life shall hang on a thread
before thee; and thou shalt fear day and night, and shalt have no
assurance of thy life. In the morning thou shalt say, Would God
it were even! and at even thou shalt say, Would God it were
morning! And because thou servedst not the Lord thy God in the
abundance of all things, therefore shalt thou serve Him in hunger
and in thirst, and in nakedness and in want of all things, which
the Lord shall send against thee. And he shall put a yoke of iron
upon thy neck, until he have destroyed thee."*

THE COMPANY: Amen!

> *The Confessor has read the curse fast and loud, without
> directing himself to The Stranger. The others, except for
> The Lady who is crocheting, have listened and joined in
> the curses, but without appearing to notice The*

---

* The curse is from Deuteronomy, Chapter 28. Though a Catholic version would be more appropriate to a reading in this
cloister, I have used the King James version because it follows
Strindberg's text more closely. However, I have had to make
some changes even in the King James version, most notably in
the last lines where it reads: "Therefore shalt thou serve thine
enemies. . . . " Strindberg himself did not reproduce the text of
any of the three or four Swedish Bibles that I have been able to
consult.

Stranger. Throughout the reading he has sat with his back to the others, lost in thought.

THE STRANGER: What was that?

THE CONFESSOR: That was the curse from Deuteronomy.

THE STRANGER: So that's what it was. But as I remember, it also offered a blessing.

THE CONFESSOR: Yes—to those who keep His commandments.

THE STRANGER: Ah, yes, of course. —I can't deny that for a moment I was quite shaken. The question is: am I being exposed to temptation that must be resisted or given warnings that must be obeyed? . . . Anyway, one thing is certain: I've still got my fever, and I'm going to see a real doctor.

THE CONFESSOR: Yes, but be sure he's the real one.

THE STRANGER: Of course, of course.

THE CONFESSOR: The one who cures those "exquisite pangs of conscience."

THE ABBESS: And if you should ever have need of charity, you know where you can find it, don't you?

THE STRANGER: No, I don't.

THE ABBESS (*softly*): Then let me tell you. In a rose-red room near a great rushing river.

THE STRANGER: In a rose-red room. . . . That's true. . . . How long have I been lying sick here?

THE ABBESS: Exactly three months today.

THE STRANGER: A fourth of a year! (*Sighs.*) Have I been asleep the whole time? Or where have I been (*Looks out the windows.*) Why, it's already fall. The trees are bare, and the clouds are blue with cold. . . . It's coming back to me. . . . Do you hear a millwheel turning? A hunting horn echoing in the hills? A forest murmuring . . . a river roaring . . . and a woman crying? Yes, you're right. That's the only place I'll find charity. —Goodbye. (*He leaves hastily.*)

THE CONFESSOR (*to The Abbess*): A mad fool! Mad fool!

*   *   *

The Rose Room

The curtains have been removed. The windows are like black holes gaping into the darkness outside. The furniture is covered with brown sheets and pushed together in the center of the room. The flowers are gone. A large black stove is lit. The Mother stands ironing white curtains by the light of a single lamp.

A knocking is heard at the door.

THE MOTHER: Come in.

THE STRANGER (*entering*): Hello. —Where's my wife?

THE MOTHER: So it's you. —Where have you been?

THE STRANGER: In hell—I think. . . . Where's my wife?

THE MOTHER: Which one?

THE STRANGER: That's good.

THE MOTHER: Don't you think the question has its point?

THE STRANGER: Absolutely. Everything has its point—except my existence.

THE MOTHER: There may be a reason for that. But the fact that you've noticed it is a point in your favor. —Now where have you been?

THE STRANGER: I don't know whether it was a poorhouse or a madhouse or just a plain ordinary hospital. I prefer to take it all as a bad feverish dream. I've been sick—lost my memory—I still can't believe that three months have gone by. . . . But where's my wife?

THE MOTHER: I should be asking you that. When you left her, she left here—to look for you. But whether or not she got tired of looking, I don't know.

THE STRANGER: It looks ghastly here. . . . Where's the old man?

THE MOTHER: Gone. And where he's gone he has no more sorrows.

THE STRANGER: Dead?

THE MOTHER: Yes, he's dead.

THE STRANGER: You say that as if you're trying to add him to the list of my "victims."

THE MOTHER: Would I be wrong?

THE STRANGER: He could take care of himself, and he was capable of nourishing a good healthy hatred.

THE MOTHER: You're wrong. He could only hate what was evil—in himself and others.

THE STRANGER: All right, I was wrong—as usual.

Pause.

THE MOTHER: What did you expect to find here?

THE STRANGER: Charity.

THE MOTHER: Really. —How was it at the hospital? Sit down and tell me about it.

THE STRANGER (*sitting down*): I don't care to recall it. Besides, I don't know if it actually was a hospital.

THE MOTHER: Strange. What happened after you left here?

THE STRANGER: I fell somewhere up in the mountains, hurt my thigh, and fainted. —None of your sarcasm now, or I won't tell you the rest.

THE MOTHER: I'll be sweet as sugar.

THE STRANGER: I wake up one day. I'm in a bed with steel rails, painted red. And three men are pulling on a rope that runs through two pulleys. And every time they pull, I feel myself grow two yards longer. And—

THE MOTHER: You were in traction, and they were trying to set your hip.

THE STRANGER: That could be. I never thought of that. But

later—oh . . . I lay there and saw—like a panorama—my whole life unroll before me, from childhood through youth and all the way up to . . . and when the roll ended, it began all over again. . . . And all the time I could hear a millwheel turning and the millstone grinding. . . . And I can still hear it . . . I can even hear it now.

THE MOTHER: Those couldn't have been very pretty pictures you saw.

THE STRANGER: No, they weren't. . . . I finally came to the conclusion that I was a louse.

THE MOTHER: Why use that expression?

THE STRANGER: You'd prefer me to call myself wicked, depraved, unprincipled, wouldn't you? But that sounds like bragging. Furthermore, it has the ring of certainty about it and I'm still not certain—about anything.

THE MOTHER: Still skeptical?

THE STRANGER: Afraid so, about a lot of things. One thing does seem clearer to me, however.

THE MOTHER: Yes?

THE STRANGER: That there are things . . . forces . . . powers . . . that I . . . didn't believe existed.

THE MOTHER: Haven't you also noticed that neither you nor anyone else has charge of your unusual destiny?

THE STRANGER: That's what I mean.

THE MOTHER: You're making progress.

THE STRANGER: That isn't all that's happened. I'm bankrupt. I can't write. And on top of that, I can't sleep at night.

THE MOTHER: Can't sleep?

THE STRANGER: Nightmares—I guess that's the word for them. . . . But last and worst is that I don't dare to die because I'm no longer certain that our misery ends when our end comes.

THE MOTHER: Oh?

THE STRANGER: That's not all. What's even worse is that I have become so disgusted with myself that I want to crawl out of my skin. I don't see much chance of that, however. If I were a Christian, I couldn't obey even the first Commandment—love thy neighbor as thyself—because that would mean hating my neighbor—which is exactly what I do. It really must be true that I'm a rotten heel. I've always suspected it, of course, but since I didn't want to be made a fool of, I kept a close eye on all the others. When I saw that they weren't any better than I, I became furious when they tried to act superior.

THE MOTHER: Don't you see that you've misunderstood everything by thinking of it as an affair just between you and the others, when it's really a matter between you and Him?

THE STRANGER: Who?

THE MOTHER: The Invisible One who has been working out your destiny.

THE STRANGER: I'd love to meet him face to face!

THE MOTHER: You'd die!

THE STRANGER: Oh, no, I wouldn't!

THE MOTHER: What is it that makes you so infernally rebellious? If you can't bend like the rest of us, you'll be snapped in half like a dry twig.

THE STRANGER: I don't know what it is that makes me as defiant as Satan himself. I can shake and tremble before an unpaid bill, but if I were to climb Mount Sinai and confront the Almighty Himself, I wouldn't even shield my eyes.

THE MOTHER: Holy Mary Mother of God! Talk like that, you must be the Devil's brood!

THE STRANGER: Seems to be the general opinion around here. I thought that those who were in league with Old Nick were showered with honors, goods, gold—especially gold. Now how can you suspect me?

THE MOTHER: Because you are a curse on my house.

THE STRANGER: Then I shall leave your house—

THE MOTHER: In the middle of the night? No. . . . Where do you intend to go?

THE STRANGER: I'm going to look for the only person I don't hate.

THE MOTHER: What makes you think she'll want to see you?

THE STRANGER: I'm certain she will.

THE MOTHER: I'm not!

THE STRANGER: Well, I am!

THE MOTHER: I'll change that. You'll see.

THE STRANGER: You can't do a thing about it.

THE MOTHER: Oh, yes, I can.

THE STRANGER: Like hell you can!

THE MOTHER: We seem to have used up the sugar. We'd better stop. . . . Do you mind sleeping in the attic?

THE STRANGER: Doesn't matter where, I won't sleep anyway.

THE MOTHER: All right. . . . Pleasant dreams—whether or not you think I mean it.

THE STRANGER: There aren't any rats in the attic, are there? I'm not afraid of ghosts, but I don't like rats.

THE MOTHER: Not afraid of ghosts? That's a relief. No one has ever slept through the night up there—whatever the reason may be.

THE STRANGER (*lingers a moment. Then says*): You know, you're the meanest person I've ever met in my life. Must be because you're religious.

THE MOTHER: Good night.

* * *

The Kitchen

It is dark, but the moon throws on the floor shifting shadows of the window lattices as storm clouds draw by.

*Under the crucifix in the corner to the right, where The
Old Man used to sit, a horn, a gun, and a hunting bag
are hanging on the wall. A stuffed hawk or similar bird
of prey stands on the table. The windows are open and
the curtains are fluttering, and the rags and cloths, the
aprons and towels that are hanging to dry on the line in
front of the stove are flapping in the wind. One can hear
the soughing of the wind, the roar of a distant waterfall,
and now and then the sound of pounding on a wooden
floor.*

THE STRANGER (*enters, half-dressed, a lamp in his hand*): Is
anyone here? . . . No one. (*Moves forward with the light, which
lessens somewhat the play of the shadows.*) What's that moving on
the floor? . . . Is anyone here? (*He goes toward the table, but
when he catches sight of the bird he stops, petrified.*) Jesus Christ!

THE MOTHER (*enters, dressed, a lamp in her hand*): You still
up?

THE STRANGER: Yes. I couldn't sleep.

THE MOTHER (*gently*): Why not, my son?

THE STRANGER: I heard footsteps over my room.

THE MOTHER: That's impossible. There's no attic above your
room.

THE STRANGER: I know. That's what bothered me. — What's
that crawling on the floor like snakes?

THE MOTHER: That's the moonlight.

THE STRANGER: Of course, the moonlight. And that's a
stuffed bird. And those are old rags. Everything is so simple and
natural — and that's exactly what bothers me. . . . Who was that
knocking in the middle of the night? Is somebody locked out?

THE MOTHER: No, it's a horse stamping in his stall.

THE STRANGER: I've never heard of a horse stamping like
that.

THE MOTHER: Some horses have nightmares.

THE STRANGER: Odd. What are nightmares?

THE MOTHER: Who knows?

THE STRANGER: Do you mind if I sit down for a moment?

THE MOTHER: Yes, sit down. Let's have a serious talk. I was mean and cruel to you last night. Please forgive me. You understand, it's just because I am so awfully mean that I make use of religion in the same way I'd make use of a hair shirt and a stone floor. . . . As for nightmares, not to offend you by asking, I'll give you my own opinion of what they are. They're my bad conscience. I don't know if it's myself or someone else who is punishing me, and I don't assume I have the right to find out. That's how I see it. . . . Now suppose you tell me what happened in your room.

THE STRANGER: I–I really don't know. I didn't actually see anything, but when I walked into the room, I felt there was someone there. Looked around with the lamp, but didn't see anyone. So I went to bed. Then it began–someone walking with heavy steps right over my head. . . . Do you believe in spooks and ghosts?

THE MOTHER: No, I don't. It's against my religion. But I do believe that our sense of right and wrong has the power to create its own form of punishment.

THE STRANGER: Yes. . . . Well, anyhow, after a short while, I felt an ice-cold current of air aimed at my chest – probing around until it found my heart – and then that grew cold – and I had to get out of bed . . .

THE MOTHER: And then?

THE STRANGER: Then I had to stand there in the middle of the room and watch the whole panorama of my life roll by – everything – everything. . . . There's nothing worse, nothing.

THE MOTHER: I know what it's like. I've been through it too. There's no name for that illness, and there's only one cure.

THE STRANGER: What's that?

THE MOTHER: You know what. You know what children have to do when they've been bad.

THE STRANGER: No, what do they have to do?

THE MOTHER: First, say they're sorry and ask to be forgiven —

THE STRANGER: And next?

THE MOTHER: Try to make things right.

THE STRANGER: Isn't it enough that you suffer as you deserve to suffer?

THE MOTHER: That's vengeance, that's all that is.

THE STRANGER: Of course, what else?

THE MOTHER: If you've ruined someone's life, can you make it good again? Can you undo a bad deed? Undo what's done?

THE STRANGER: No, that's true. —But I was forced to do what I did, forced to take, because nobody would acknowledge that I was right. Why blame me? Blame the one who forced me — and shame on him. —Ohh! (*His hand clutching his chest.*)* Ohh! He's here, here in this room — and he's tearing my heart from my chest. Ohh!

THE MOTHER: Bend down!

THE STRANGER: I cannot!

THE MOTHER: On your knees!

THE STRANGER: I will not!

THE MOTHER: Christ have mercy on you! The Lord have mercy on you! (*To The Stranger.*) On your knees before Him who was crucified! Only He can undo the past.

THE STRANGER: No, not before Him! No, not Him! And if I'm forced to, I'll take it back — later!

THE MOTHER: Kneel — kneel, my son!

THE STRANGER: I cannot kneel — I cannot. —Help me. Almighty God!

Pause.

---

* An attack of angina pectoris.

THE MOTHER (*quickly mumbles a prayer. Then says*): Is it better now?

THE STRANGER (*recovering*): Yes. . . . Do you know what that was? It wasn't death. It was annihilation.

THE MOTHER: Annihilation of the divine. What we call the death of the spirit.

THE STRANGER (*earnestly, without irony*): Is that what you're getting at? . . . I think I'm beginning to understand.

THE MOTHER: My son: you have left Jerusalem and you are on the way to Damascus. Go there. The same way you came here. And plant a cross at each station, but stop at the seventh. You don't have fourteen, as He had.

THE STRANGER: You're talking in riddles.

THE MOTHER: Let me put it this way. Travel. Look up those you have something to say to. And first of all, your wife.

THE STRANGER: Where?

THE MOTHER: Seek and ye shall find. And on your way don't forget one person in particular – the werewolf, as you call him.

THE STRANGER: Oh, no. Never!

THE MOTHER: I understand that's what you said when circumstances were forcing you this way. But, as I told you, I knew you would come. I was waiting for you.

THE STRANGER: Why?

THE MOTHER: No logical reason.

THE STRANGER: Just as I saw this kitchen in a – what shall I call it – a rapture of some sort . . .

THE MOTHER: That's why I regret having tried to separate you and Ingeborg. You were meant to meet each other. – Anyway, you better go and look for her. If you find her, good – if you don't, maybe that was meant to happen too. – The dawn is breaking. It's morning, and the night is over.

THE STRANGER: And what a night!

THE MOTHER: You won't forget it!

THE STRANGER: Not all of it, that's certain.

THE MOTHER (*looks out of the window. As if to herself*): Son of the morning, why art thou fallen from heaven?*

> *Pause.*

THE STRANGER: Have you noticed how — just before the sun goes up — a shiver runs through you? Are we children of darkness that we tremble before the light?

THE MOTHER: Don't you ever get tired of asking questions?

THE STRANGER: Never. I long for the light, you see.

THE MOTHER: Then go and look for it. And peace be with you.

---

* See Isaiah 14:12: "How art thou fallen from heaven, O Lucifer, son of the morning." Lucifer is the planet Venus when it appears as the morning star.

ACT IV

In the Ravine

Same landscape as before, but now it is autumn, and the trees are bare.

The mill is working, and there is hammering in the blacksmith shop.

The Blacksmith stands in his doorway at the left; The Miller's Wife in the doorway at the right.

The Lady is dressed in mourning, with a jacket and a patent leather hat (derby style).

The Stranger wears a Bavarian Alps outfit: lodenjoppe (shooting jacket), knickers, climbing shoes, alpenstock, and a green hat with a feather in it. Over this outfit he is wearing a brown ulster (Kaiser-mantel) with a hood.

THE LADY (*enters, in traveling clothes, tired and woebegone*): Did you by any chance see a man wearing a brown coat pass by here recently?

> *The Blacksmith and The Miller's Wife shake their heads.*

THE LADY: Could you put me up for the night?

> *The Blacksmith and The Miller's Wife shake their heads sternly.*

THE LADY (*to The Blacksmith*): Do you mind if I stand here in the doorway and warm myself for a moment?

> *The Blacksmith pushes her away.*

THE LADY: Thanks. God help you! (*She leaves and is seen on the footbridge before she disappears from sight.*)

THE STRANGER (*enters, in traveling clothes*): Did you by any chance see a lady wearing a jacket cross the stream here?

> *The Blacksmith and The Miller's Wife shake their heads.*

THE STRANGER: Could you let me have a loaf of bread? I've got money to pay for it.

> *The Miller's Wife spurns the money.*

THE STRANGER: No charity?

> *The echo in the distance mimics his voice, "Charity!" The Blacksmith and The Miller's Wife break out in long, loud laughter, which is picked up and repeated by the echo.*

THE STRANGER: This is more like it. Eye for eye, tooth for tooth! That always helped to relieve my conscience. (*He goes into the ravine.*)

* * *

On the Road

Same landscape as before, but now it is autumn.

*The Beggar is sitting at one of the shrines. Beside him are a lime twig and a birdcage with a starling in it.**

THE STRANGER (*enters, dressed as in the previous scene*): Did you see a lady wearing a jacket go by here? I suppose a beggar sees everybody who passes by.

THE BEGGAR: I've seen five hundred passers-by pass by. But

* The birdcage may be intended to associate The Beggar with the bird-catcher Papageno in Mozart's *The Magic Flute*. (Suggested by Barry Jacobs.)

would you mind not calling me a beggar? Seriously. I've got a job.

THE STRANGER: Oh, it's you. I didn't recognize you.

THE BEGGAR: *Ille ego qui quondam* —*

THE STRANGER: What kind of work do you do?

THE BEGGAR: I've got a bird here that whistles and talks.

THE STRANGER: I see: the bird does the work.

THE BEGGAR: Yes, I've got myself well set up.

THE STRANGER: Do you catch birds too?

THE BEGGAR: Oh, the lime twig? Not at all. That's only for appearance's sake.

THE STRANGER: You're only interested in appearances?

THE BEGGAR: Yes. What else is there to interest one? What's inside — nothing but muck.

THE STRANGER: And that's your philosophy in a nutshell?

THE BEGGAR: The whole of my metaphysical system. It may indeed appear to some to be antiquated; however —

THE STRANGER: Come now, let's have at least one serious word from you. Tell me something about your past.

THE BEGGAR: Usch! What good does it do to muck around in garbage? A waste of time. Push ahead, eyes front, keep moving. — Don't think I always feel like joking. Not on your life! It's only when I meet you. You're damned comical, you know.

THE STRANGER: How can you laugh? You've wasted your whole life.

THE BEGGAR: Now that's hitting home. — Listen, if you can't laugh at the whole mess, not even when it's someone else's, you'd

* I, the man who once —. From the *Aeneid*, the false opening. Aptly alluded to here because Virgil is speaking of his transformation from bucolic to martial poet. The Beggar is participating in The Stranger's transformation.

better cash in your chips. — Let me give you some advice. Follow these wheel tracks in the muck here; you'll come down to the sea; that's where the road ends. Sit down there and take a rest and you'll get a new slant on things. Up here there are too many bad omens, religious relics, unhappy memories, which keep your thoughts from flying off to the rose room. You just follow the trail, just follow the trail. And if it gets too dusty, lift up your wings and give a few flaps.

Talking about wings reminds me: a little bird once told me about Polycrates and his ring. Now he got all the good things in the world and didn't know what to do with them. So he spread the word in the east and in the west about the empty universe he had helped to create out of the universal void. I wouldn't insist it was you, except I'm so dead certain I'd take my dying oath on it. I once asked you if you knew who I was, and you said it didn't interest you. I offered you my friendship in return, which you refused with a curt little "Get out!" Fortunately I'm not one to take such things to heart. So I'm giving you a piece of good advice, something to ruminate on: follow the trail.

THE STRANGER (*avoiding him*): No, you're not going to trick me again.

THE BEGGAR: Good sir, you always think the worst, so you always end up with the worst. Just for once: why don't you try to think the best?

THE STRANGER: I want to. I do want to. But if I'm always tricked and cheated, I've got a right to —

THE BEGGAR: No. You've never got that right!

THE STRANGER (*as if to himself*): Who reads me like an open book? Turns my soul inside out? Who is persecuting me? Wherefore persecutest thou me?

THE BEGGAR: Wherefore persecutest thou me? Saul!

> *With a gesture of terror, The Stranger leaves. Chords from the funeral march are heard as before.*

THE LADY (*enters*): Has a man wearing a brown coat gone by here?

THE BEGGAR: Yes, just now. A poor devil limping on his way.

THE LADY: The man I'm looking for doesn't limp.

THE BEGGAR: Neither does this fellow, actually. But he seems to have contracted trouble in his thigh, which made him a little unsteady. Don't mind me: I'm just being mean. —Look in the dust of the road.

THE LADY: Where?

THE BEGGAR (*pointing*): There. You see the wheel tracks? And beside it the imprint of a thick shoe made by a heavy tread.

THE LADY (*looking carefully at the tracks*): That's him. Yes, they are heavy steps. . . . Do you think I can catch up with him?

THE BEGGAR: Follow the trail!

THE LADY (*takes his hand and kisses it*): Thank you, my friend. (*She goes.*)

* * *

By the Sea

The same landscape as before, but now it is winter. The sea is blue-black. Clouds like giant heads tower up on the horizon. In the distance are the three white, unrigged masts of a foundered ship, resembling three white crosses. The table and the bench under the tree are still there, but the chairs are gone.

Snow on the ground.

Now and then the clang of a bell buoy is heard.

The Stranger enters from the left. Stands for a moment looking out over the sea; then exits to the right, behind the cabin.

The Lady enters from the left and appears to be following the footprints of The Stranger in the snow. Goes out to the right in front of the cabin.

The Stranger reenters from the right, crosses left, discovers The Lady's footprints. Stands and looks back to the right.

The Lady reenters, runs into his arms, but suddenly falls back a step.

THE LADY: Are you pushing me away?

THE STRANGER: No. There seems to be something between us.

THE LADY: I suppose there is. What a reunion!

THE STRANGER: It's gotten very cold as you can see. Winter.

THE LADY: I can feel the cold streaming out from you.

THE STRANGER: I was caked in ice up in the mountains.

THE LADY: Will spring ever come again?

THE STRANGER: Not for us. We've been driven out of the Garden of Eden. All we can do is pick our way over the stones and thorns. And after we've cut our feet and pricked our hands, we'll pour salt in our wounds—each other's. And the mill will be grinding and grinding and never, never stop, for there's never a lack of water.

THE LADY: I'm afraid you're right . . .

THE STRANGER: But I refuse to submit to the inevitable. I won't have us lacerating ourselves. I'll carve myself up as an offering to the gods. I'll say I'm the one that's to blame. It was I who told you to break out of your prison, it was I who enticed you to come with me. You can lay all the blame on me for what we've done and for what came of it.

THE LADY: You couldn't bear it.

THE STRANGER: I think I could. There are moments when I feel that I bear within me all the sin and sorrow, all the scandal and shame of the whole world. There are moments when I think that we commit crimes and do wrong because the wrongdoing in and by itself is a punishment imposed on us. . . . Not so long ago, I lay sick with a fever. And among other things—so much happened – I dreamed I saw a crucifix without anyone crucified on it. And when I asked the Dominican – there was a Dominican there too – when I asked him what it meant he said, "You won't have Him suffering for you; consequently, you yourself must suffer." And that's why people have become so sensitive to their suffering – in a way they weren't in the old days.

THE LADY: And that's why our consciences crush us: there's no one to help carry them.

THE STRANGER: You've come around to that, eh?

THE LADY: Not quite – but I'm on my way.

THE STRANGER: Put your hand in mine and let's move on from here together.

THE LADY: Where to?

THE STRANGER: Back, the same way we came. Are you tired?

THE LADY: Not any longer.

THE STRANGER: I fell down exhausted time and again. But then I met a strange beggar – you probably remember him, the one they say looks like me. And he asked me, by way of an experiment, to believe that his intentions were good. So I believed – as an experiment – and . . .

THE LADY: And – ?

THE STRANGER: Everything went well for me! . . . And since then I've found the strength to push ahead.

THE LADY: Then let's push ahead!

THE STRANGER (*facing the sea*): All right, but it's getting dark and the clouds are piling up . . .

THE LADY: Don't look at the clouds . . .

THE STRANGER: Down below – what's that?

THE LADY: A shipwreck, that's all.

THE STRANGER (*whispers*): Three crosses. . . . What new Golgotha lies ahead of us?

THE LADY: They're white. That means something good.

THE STRANGER: Can anything good happen to us again?

THE LADY: Why not? Give it time.

THE STRANGER: Come on, let's go.

* * *

In the Hotel Room

Same as before. The Lady is sitting beside The Stranger, crocheting.

THE LADY: Say something.

THE STRANGER: What? Since we entered this room everything I say is dull and boring.

THE LADY: Why did you have to keep on going until we came to this awful room?

THE STRANGER: I don't know. It was what I wanted least of all. That's why I had this ache to come here—to be tormented.

THE LADY: And have you been tormented . . . ?

THE STRANGER: Yes. All the joy's gone out of life. I'm deaf to music and blind to beauty. All day long I hear that mill grinding and all I see is that great panorama of mine, only now it's expanded into a vast cosmorama. . . . And at night . . .

THE LADY: I heard you cry out in your sleep. What was it?

THE STRANGER: A dream I had . . .

THE LADY: A genuine dream—or—

THE STRANGER: Of terrifying reality. A dream with a curse on it. Because—because I have an irresistible urge to talk about it—and to you of all people. Which I mustn't, because that would be opening the door to the forbidden room.

THE LADY: The past?

THE STRANGER: Yes.

THE LADY (*without insinuation*): There's certain to be something crazy locked up in secret rooms . . .

THE STRANGER: Yes, isn't there.

Pause.

THE LADY: Well, tell me.

THE STRANGER: I'm afraid I can't stop myself. . . . Here goes: I dreamed I saw—your—former husband—married—to my former wife—so that my children now had him for a father . . .

THE LADY: Nobody but you could dream up a thing like that.

THE STRANGER: But suppose—suppose it's true. . . . And I saw him beat them—(*Rises.*)—and when, as a matter of course, I strangled him, I—. No, I can't go on with it. . . . All the same, I can't rest until I'm absolutely certain. And to be certain, I'll have to go to him in his own home.

THE LADY: So that's where we're heading!

THE STRANGER: To the edge of the abyss. And the guardrail is gone. I've got to take the plunge. I've got to see him.

THE LADY: But suppose he won't see you?

THE STRANGER: I'll apply as a patient. I'll tell him about my sickness.

THE LADY (*frightened*): I wouldn't do that if I were you.

THE STRANGER: I know what you're hinting. He'll find an excuse for locking me up. . . . I'm willing to risk it. I have a crazy desire to risk everything—freedom, life, comfort, happiness. What I need is an emotional blow so great it will shock me to the depths of my being, and what rises to the surface will be the real me. I need some torture that will redress the balance in our relationship. I don't want to be in debt any longer. So down into the snake pit, and the sooner the better.

THE LADY: Couldn't I go with you . . . ?

THE STRANGER: Why? My torments will do for both of us.

THE LADY: Then I can really call you my liberator, and the curse I pronounced over you would turn into a blessing. —Have you noticed that it's spring again?

THE STRANGER: I can tell by that Christmas rose. It's beginning to wither.

THE LADY: Don't you feel spring in the air?

THE STRANGER: Yes. I can feel the ice in my chest thawing . . .

THE LADY: Maybe the werewolf can cure you completely.

THE STRANGER: We shall see. We shall see. Perhaps he isn't so awful.

THE LADY: He's certainly not as cruel as you are.

THE STRANGER: Still—my dream. Suppose . . .

THE LADY: Suppose it was only a stupid dream. . . . Look, all my yarn is gone! That's the end of my silly crocheting. How terribly dirty it is!

THE STRANGER: You can always wash it.

THE LADY: Or dye it.

THE STRANGER: Rose-red.

THE LADY: Never.

THE STRANGER: It looks like a rolled manuscript.

THE LADY: With our story on it.

THE STRANGER: Written in blood and tears and the dust of the road.

THE LADY: Yes. End of story. Except for the last chapter. That's yours.

THE STRANGER: And we'll meet at the seventh station. Where we began.

ACT V

At the Doctor's

The set is very much as in Act I. The woodpile, however, is only half as big. Near the porch is a workbench with surgical instruments on it, scalpels, forceps, and so on.

The Doctor is polishing these instruments.

THE SISTER (*coming from the porch*): There's a patient to see you.

THE DOCTOR: Who is it?

THE SISTER: I didn't get to see him, but here's his card.

THE DOCTOR (*reading the card*): You know . . . this really beats everything.

THE SISTER: Is it he?

THE DOCTOR: It's he. Of all the brazen nerve. I don't despise courage but this direct approach smacks of contempt. It's like a challenge flung in my face. Well, show him in.

THE SISTER: Are you serious?

THE DOCTOR: Absolutely. However, if you feel like it, you can let him have a few of your blunt, well-chosen words.

THE SISTER: I'd already made up my mind to.

THE DOCTOR: Good for you. You rough him up a little and I'll polish him off.

THE SISTER: Don't worry. I'll tell him everything your soft heart keeps you from saying.

THE DOCTOR: Keep my heart out of it. —And get out of here before I lose my temper. —And close the door!

The Sister goes.

THE DOCTOR: Caesar, what are you doing over there by the garbage cans again?

The Madman enters.

Tell me, Caesar: if your worst enemy comes to you and puts his head in your lap, what do you do?

THE MADMAN: I cut off his head!

THE DOCTOR: Now, now, that's not what I taught you.

THE MADMAN: No, you said you should heap coals of fire on it. But I think that would be a pity.

THE DOCTOR: So do I. It's too cruel and cunning. . . . Don't you think it would be better to take just a little revenge so that he could stand up like a man and feel himself quits?

THE MADMAN: If you already know what to do, why ask me?

THE DOCTOR: Shut up, I'm not talking to you. . . . All right, we'll lop off his head and then – then we'll see!

THE MADMAN: Depending on how he behaves himself.

THE DOCTOR: Precisely. How he behaves himself. . . . Not a word out of you now. And get away from here.

THE STRANGER (*enters from the porch. He appears ill-at-ease and disturbed, but there is also an air of resignation about him*): Doctor, I . . .

THE DOCTOR: Yes?

THE STRANGER: I suppose you're surprised to see me here?

THE DOCTOR (*seriously*): I had long ago stopped being surprised by anything. I see I shall have to make a new beginning.

THE STRANGER: May I talk to you confidentially?

THE DOCTOR: Yes, about anything that may be considered proper between two civilized people. Are you ill?

THE STRANGER (*hesitating*): Yes.

THE DOCTOR: Why come to me?

THE STRANGER: You should be able to guess.

THE DOCTOR: I don't want to. . . . What's your trouble?

THE STRANGER (*faltering*): Insomnia.

THE DOCTOR: That's not an illness, that's a symptom. Have you been to see a doctor before?

THE STRANGER: I've been sick in bed . . . in an institution . . . with a fever. . . . But it was a most unusual fever.

THE DOCTOR: What was so unusual about it?

THE STRANGER: Let me ask you something. Is it possible to be up and about and still be delirious?

THE DOCTOR: Yes, if you're crazy — not otherwise.

The Stranger gets up and then sits down again.

THE DOCTOR: What was the name of the hospital?

THE STRANGER: It was called "The Helping Hand."

THE DOCTOR: There's no hospital with that name.

THE STRANGER: What is it — a cloister?

THE DOCTOR: It's a lunatic asylum.

The Stranger gets up, nervous.

THE DOCTOR (*gets up and calls*): Sister! Close the front door, will you? And the wooden gate in the back yard! (*To The Stranger.*) Please sit down, sit down. — I was just making certain the doors are closed. Too many tramps hanging around here.

THE STRANGER (*calming himself*): Doctor, tell me honestly: do you think I'm insane?

THE DOCTOR: As you know, it's not customary to give an honest answer to that question, and anyone who asks it usually doesn't believe what he's told. Therefore it doesn't make the slightest difference what my opinion is. On the other hand, if you yourself actually feel that your soul is sick, you'd better consult a spiritual healer.

THE STRANGER: Couldn't you take on that position just for a moment?

THE DOCTOR: No, I'm not qualified.

THE STRANGER: But if—

THE DOCTOR (*interrupting*): Besides, I haven't the time. We're preparing for a wedding here in the garden.

THE STRANGER: My dream . . .

THE DOCTOR: What's the matter? I thought it would ease your mind to hear that I had managed to console myself, as it's called. I thought it would make you happy, downright happy. That's usually the case. But instead you seem to feel even worse. . . . There's something beneath this. Let me probe around a bit. . . . Now why does it distress you so much if I marry a widow . . . ?

THE STRANGER: With two children?

THE DOCTOR: Ah, ha, let me see. . . . Ah! I understand. What a hell of an idea! Really worthy of you. You know, if there were a hell, you'd be commander-in-chief. Your ability to devise new tortures far surpasses my wildest creations. And yet they call me a werewolf.

THE STRANGER: It may be that—

THE DOCTOR (*interrupting*): For a long time I hated you, as you probably know, because an inexcusable act of yours furnished me with an undeserved reputation. But as I grew older and more understanding, I realized that although the punishment I received then was unjust, I had nevertheless deserved it for other pranks of mine that had never been discovered; and furthermore that you were a child with enough conscience to punish yourself. So that matter needn't bother you either. Is that what you came here to clear up?

THE STRANGER: Yes.

THE DOCTOR: Will you be satisfied if I say you are free to go?

The Stranger looks questioningly.

Or did you think I intended to lock you up? Or hack you to pieces with my instruments? Kill you, perhaps? "Why not kill the poor devils?"

The Stranger looks at his watch.

THE DOCTOR: You can still make the boat.

THE STRANGER: May I shake your hand?

THE DOCTOR: No, I can't shake hands with you. I can't bring myself to it. Besides, what good will it do for me to forgive you if you haven't the strength to forgive yourself? . . . There are some things that can be helped only by being undone. There's no help for this.

THE STRANGER: "The Helping Hand."

THE DOCTOR: Not so bad, after all, was it? —You challenged fate and you lost. No shame in a battle well fought. I did too, but as you can see, I've been dickering with my woodpile and got him to come down a bit. I want the thunder to stay out of my house, and I no longer play with lightning.

THE STRANGER: One station more—and then I'm home.

THE DOCTOR: Never home, my dear sir! —Goodbye.

THE STRANGER: Goodbye.

*   *   *

The Street Corner

Same as the first act. The Stranger is sitting on the bench under the tree, writing in the sand.

THE LADY (*entering*): What are you doing?

THE STRANGER: Writing in the sand. Still at it.

THE LADY: Same old song. Don't you hear any new ones?

THE STRANGER (*pointing to the church*): Yes, but from in there . . .

THE LADY: And there's still no music in your life?

THE STRANGER (*pointing to the church*): Yes, but it's coming from there. . . . There is someone I've wronged without knowing it.

THE LADY: And I thought our journey would be about over when we finally got back here.

THE STRANGER: Back where we began—on the street between the bar, the church—and the post office. The post office! P-O-S-T.* Wait a minute. Didn't I leave a registered letter there without bothering to claim it?

THE LADY: Yes, you said it was only bad news.

THE STRANGER: Or legal papers. (*Striking his forehead.*) Ooh, that's what it is.

THE LADY: Now, you go in there and tell yourself it's good news.

THE STRANGER (*ironically*): Good!

THE LADY: Pretend! Convince yourself!

THE STRANGER (*heading for the post office*): All right, I'll try.

> *The Lady waits, walking up and down the sidewalk. The Stranger comes out from the post office with a letter in his hand.*

THE LADY: Well?

THE STRANGER: Am I ashamed! It was the money. It was there the whole time.

THE LADY: You see! . . . All our trials and tribulations, all our tears—all in vain.

* The Stranger thinks of the Latin phrase *Post nummos virtus* from Act I, scene 1. (Suggested by Barry Jacobs.)

THE STRANGER: Not in vain! It may look like dirty playing, but it really isn't. I wronged someone, the Unseen One, when I suspected that—

THE LADY: Sh, sh. No more of that. No accusations.

THE STRANGER: Right. It was my own stupidity—or mean-ness. . . . I didn't want to be made a fool of by life—and so I was! . . . But what about those elves—?

THE LADY: They made the switch. . . . Let's go.

THE STRANGER: Yes, let's go and hide ourselves in the mountain where we can be alone with our misery.

THE LADY: Yes, the mountains hide and cover.* But first I have to light a candle for my good Saint Elizabeth.

The Stranger shakes his head.

THE LADY: Come. Please.

THE STRANGER: Oh, well, I can always pass through. But as for staying there—definitely not.

THE LADY: How do you know? . . . Come on. . . . You'll get to hear some new songs in there.**

THE STRANGER (*following her toward the church door*): Maybe. Maybe.

THE LADY: Come!

* See Revelation 6:16
** See Revelation 5:9 and 14:3; and frequently in Psalms.

Introduction

to

Crimes and Crimes

Strindberg had a hard time deciding what to call this play. *Intoxication* was one title; *Guilty?—Not Guilty?* another. The second is taken from an essay in Søren Kierkegaard's book *Stages on Life's Way*. There are three of these stages for Kierkegaard: the aesthetic, the ethical, and the religious; and Kierkegaard explains them by studying man's relation to woman in each of the three stages. For the aesthete, the relation is purely erotic; for the ethical man, the relation brings with it the obligations of marriage and of family; for the religious man, it means suffering and a questioning of God's purpose. Intoxicated by success, the hero of *Crimes and Crimes* slips from the ethical to the aesthetic stage, and then, accused of a crime he did not commit, comes to realize through his suffering that there is yet another stage that lies beyond his understanding.

Strindberg begins his play somberly in a Parisian cemetery to indicate the seriousness of his theme. After that, however, *Crimes and Crimes* becomes a play of sexual passion, adultery, and a mysterious death—the sort of play that would appeal to the average theatergoer. The characters are artists and lovers; the action moves from bohemian hangouts to glamorous restaurants; and the story has a great deal of suspense.

Strindberg knew the people he was writing about. He always associated with bohemians, even married them. In Berlin he was the center of a heavy-drinking group of poets and painters that included Edvard Munch. In Paris the still unappreciated Paul Gauguin was an acquaintance. A prominent member of the Berlin group was the Polish writer Stanislaw Przybyszewski, whose obsessions were sex and Nietzsche. Przybyszewski abandoned his common-law wife and two children to marry a Norwegian girl who was Munch's friend and model and, for a time, Strindberg's mistress. In 1896 the discarded wife killed herself and the children. Przybyszewski was detained by the police at first, suspected of having murdered them, and released after questioning. For the plot of *Crimes and Crimes*, Strindberg combined this actual event with an imaginary one. Alone in Paris, he had at times wished that his daughter Kerstin by his second wife might fall ill so that he would be summoned home to wife and child. Once he had thought it, he felt as guilty as if he had actually committed some crime. His first wife, Siri, had borne him a child with the same name, Kerstin, who had died in infancy shortly after he and Siri had hastily married to legitimize the baby's birth.* Was there in all this a complicated pattern drawn surreptitiously in the mind? Our consciences do punish us, not only for what we do but for what we think. There are crimes, and there are crimes. Some can be dealt with in the courts of law; some must be brought to a higher court, the court of individual conscience that has a place somewhere in Kierkegaard's third stage. Although Strindberg's hero never reaches those heights, he does come to understand that they exist, even if they are not for him.

Once again, as in *To Damascus*, Strindberg sought to give concrete dramatic form to intangible ideas. And once again he experimented with new techniques, even though he was presumably writing for the conventional theater. Parallel scenes make up the structure of the play, but Strindberg handles them like musical themes. *Crimes and Crimes* is a play in the form of a sonata. Scene by scene it corresponds to the structure of Beethoven's "Tempest" Sonata, opus 31, no. 2. A passage from that sonata, specified in the script, becomes a leading motif, the aural symbol of the hero's troubled conscience.

The musical shape of the play never constricts the dramatic flow. As a matter of fact, the repetition of scenes and themes lightens the tone, obvious patterns and repetitions being a characteristic of comedy. The atmosphere of the *belle époque* in Paris is as enchanting as an impressionist painting, and the emotionally overheated world of artists and writers has always been good theater. Offsetting these appealing qualities is the moralizing tendency of the play, which is likely to irritate those who find comedy and homily an unappealing mixture. Like Maurice in the play, they want the theater and the church to remain separate institutions, one for Saturday, one for Sunday.

* Gunnar Ollén, *Strindbergs dramatik*, 4th ed., Stockholm, 1982, p. 271.

Crimes and Crimes

or

Intoxication

(Brott och Brott)

A Comedy

CHARACTERS

MAURICE, playwright
JEANNE, his mistress
MARION, their five-year old daughter
ADOLPHE, artist
HENRIETTE, his mistress
EMILE, workingman, Jeanne's brother
MADAME CATHERINE
THE ABBÉ
MINOR CHARACTERS

SCENES

Cemetery

Crêmerie
Auberge des Adrets
Bois de Boulogne
Crêmerie
Auberge des Adrets
Luxembourg Gardens
Crêmerie

Paris. The 1890s

ACT I

Scene I

The upper allee of cypresses in the Montparnasse Cemetery in Paris. At the back can be seen burial chapels and stone crosses with the inscription "O Crux! Ave Spes Unica!"; also the ivy-covered ruin of a mill.

A Woman in Mourning, tastefully dressed in black, is kneeling and murmuring prayers at a grave covered with flowers.

Jeanne is walking up and down as if she were waiting for someone.

Marion is playing with withered flowers that she picks up from a heap of rubbish on the path.

The Abbe is walking far down the allee, reading his breviary.

THE CARETAKER (*enters. To Jeanne*): Look here, this ain't no playground!

JEANNE (*meekly*): I'm just waiting for someone. I'm sure he'll be here soon.

THE CARETAKER: Maybe so. But you can't touch the flowers.

JEANNE (*to Marion*): Throw the flowers away, darling.

THE ABBÉ (*approaches and is greeted by The Caretaker*): Can't the child play with flowers that have been thrown away?

THE CARETAKER: I'm sorry. We got orders. No touching the flowers. [They say there's a lot of arsenic in the ground here—

from all the bodies.]* Don't know if it's true, but I got my orders.

THE ABBÉ (*to Marion*): In that case there's nothing to do but follow orders. —What's your name, little girl?

MARION: Marion.

THE ABBÉ: And what is your daddy's name? (*Marion bites her finger and is silent.*) Forgive me, madam; I didn't mean to be inquisitive. I was just trying to calm the child.

    The Caretaker has left.

JEANNE: I know that, Father. I wish you could calm me, too. I'm all upset. I've walked and waited here for two whole hours.

THE ABBÉ: Two hours—for some man! How people torment each other! *"O Crux! Ave Spes Unica!"*

JEANNE: Yes, what does it mean? It's written all over here.

THE ABBÉ: It means: "Hail the cross! Our only hope!"

JEANNE: Is it the only one?

THE ABBÉ: Our only certain one.

JEANNE: Pretty soon I'll believe you're right, Father.

THE ABBÉ: May I ask why?

---

* The sentence within brackets is not in Strindberg's text. There was at this time concern about the prevalence of arsenic in burial grounds. The toxicologist M. J. B. Orfila had written about it, and Strindberg knew Orfila's chemical writings. In his poetic essay "In the Cemetery," Strindberg writes, "I had been warned that my frequent visits [to the cemetery] might be harmful because of the mephitic fumes that infused the air there. I had in fact noticed a certain taste of verdigris that remained in my mouth even two hours after my return home." The idea that the flowers in a cemetery might be dangerous was much more common in Strindberg's time than it is in ours. In one of his earlier works, *Old Stockholm* (1880–82), he quotes an old saying, "Children who pick flowers on graves will get maggots in their fingers."

JEANNE: You've already guessed. He has kept us waiting for two hours in a cemetery. That's the end of the affair, I suppose.

THE ABBÉ: And when he's left you once and for all, what then?

JEANNE: We'll throw ourselves into the river.

THE ABBÉ: Oh, no, no!

JEANNE: Oh, yes, yes.

MARION: I want to go home, Mama. I'm hungry.

JEANNE: Now, my dearest, just be patient a little while longer and we'll soon go.

THE ABBÉ: "Woe unto them that call evil good and good evil."

JEANNE: What is that woman doing over there at the grave?

THE ABBÉ: She seems to be communing with the dead.

JEANNE: But you can't, can you?

THE ABBÉ: She seems to be able to.

JEANNE: You mean that the misery doesn't end when the end comes?

THE ABBÉ: Don't you know that?

JEANNE: How can one know that?

THE ABBÉ: Hmm! . . . I see. . . . Well, my good woman, the next time you need to be enlightened on this point, look me up in the Chapel of Our Lady in Saint-Germain. —Ah, here comes the man I think you're waiting for.

JEANNE (embarrassed): No, that isn't him, but it's someone I know . . .

THE ABBÉ (to Marion): Goodbye, my little Marion! God bless you! (Kisses the child. Leaves.) Remember: in Saint-Germain-des-Pres!

EMILE: Hello, Sis! What are you doing here?

JEANNE: I'm waiting for Maurice.

EMILE: You'll have a long wait. I saw him on the Boul' Mich

having lunch with a bunch of his pals an hour ago. —Hello there, Marion! (*Kisses the child.*)

JEANNE: I suppose he was surrounded by women?

EMILE: Of course! Oh, that doesn't mean anything, Jeanne. After all, he's a playwright, with a new play opening tonight. They were probably some of the actresses.

JEANNE: Did he recognize you?

EMILE: No. He doesn't know me from Adam. No reason why he should. I'm an ordinary workingman—and I don't care to be treated condescendingly.

JEANNE: What if he leaves us without a penny?

EMILE: In that case I'll have to introduce myself to him. You don't expect that. He really loves you. And after all, he would never leave his little girl.

JEANNE: I don't know what to think. I just know that something's going to happen to me, something terrible!

EMILE: Hasn't he promised to marry you?

JEANNE: No, not promised, just acted like he would.

EMILE: Acted—! Oh, fine, fine! Remember what I told you in the beginning: don't get your hopes up; that kind doesn't marry our kind.

JEANNE: It has happened.

EMILE: Sure. —But face up to it: you wouldn't be happy in his world. You wouldn't even understand what they were talking about. Sometimes I eat at his restaurant—out in the back, of course—and I can't understand a single word they're saying.

JEANNE: You eat there?

EMILE: Yeah, in the kitchen.

JEANNE: Really? He's never invited me there.

EMILE: Well, you can give him credit for that. It means he's got some respect for the mother of his little Marion. A lot of very strange women there, I tell you.

JEANNE: Oh?

EMILE: Not that he ever bothers with them. No sir, he's all right!

JEANNE: I know. But if the right woman came along, she'd know how to drive him crazy.

EMILE (*smiling*): The things you say, Jeanne! —Listen, do you need some money?

JEANNE: No, not money.

EMILE: Things can't be too bad, then. —Look! Down there! There he comes. And here I go. Goodbye, Marion!

JEANNE: Is it really him? Yes, it is!

EMILE: Now don't you go driving him crazy, Jeanne—with your jealousy! (*Leaves.*)

JEANNE: Don't be silly!

Maurice enters.

MARION (*rushes to meet him and is swept up in his arms*): Papa! Papa!

MAURICE: Hello, hello, my darling little girl! (*Greets Jeanne.*) Jeanne! Can you ever forgive me for keeping you waiting so long? Can you?

JEANNE: Of course I can.

MAURICE: Well, say it as if you meant it!

Maurice goes up to her. Jeanne kisses him on the cheek.

MAURICE: Sorry, I couldn't hear.

Jeanne kisses him on the mouth.

Now I heard you! That's more like it! —Well, this is it. My fate hangs in the balance. Tonight is opening night. Either it's a big hit—or a huge flop. SRO or "Closes Saturday!"

JEANNE: I'll pray for you and it'll be a hit!

MAURICE: Good girl. Might help; it certainly can't hurt. —Look down there. See that haze? That's Paris! Today Paris doesn't know who Maurice is, but in twenty-four hours she will! That haze, which has wrapped me in obscurity for thirty years, will disperse. I'll blow it away, I'll suddenly appear, emerge like Aladdin's genie. I'll be somebody. My enemies—that means everybody who wishes they could do what I've done—will writhe with envy, and that will be my pleasure, seeing them suffer what I've had to suffer.

JEANNE: Please don't say such things! Please.

MAURICE: Why not? It's the simple truth.

JEANNE: Maybe, but don't say it anyway! —What about afterward?

MAURICE: Afterward we'll be in clover. You and Marion will bear the name of the great and famous playwright: Maurice Gérard!

JEANNE: Then you do love me?

MAURICE: Of course. I love you both, both just as much—but perhaps Marion just a little bit more.

JEANNE: I'm glad. You might get tired of me, but never of her! I know that.

MAURICE: Don't you have any faith in me?

JEANNE: I don't know. . . . I'm afraid of something, afraid that something terrible will happen . . .

MAURICE: You're just tired and depressed after waiting so long. Please forgive me, Jeanne. What is there to be afraid of?

JEANNE: The unexpected. Something you can feel, without having reasons . . .

MAURICE: I can't feel anything but success—and for very good reasons: the infallible instinct of the professional theater crowd, their knowledge of what the public wants—not to mention their intimate friendship with the critics! So now you just calm yourself and—

JEANNE: I can't. I just can't! You see, there was an abbé here just now who was very kind to us. I'd lost faith—in you—in everything—waiting so long for you. You'd sort of—well, not wiped it out exactly—but smeared it over, like you soap windows. But the old man rubbed the soap away and the light fell through the window, and I could see through it. —I'll pray for you tonight in the Chapel of Our Lady in Saint-Germain.

MAURICE: You're giving me the willies! Now I'm the one who's scared.

JEANNE: They say the fear of the Lord is the beginning of wisdom.

MAURICE: "God"? What's that? Who's he?

JEANNE: He gave you joy when you were a child and strength when you became a man. Now He will help us through the terrible times that lie ahead.

MAURICE: What lies ahead? You talk about the strangest things. Things I never even think about.

JEANNE: I don't know; I can't say. I haven't dreamed anything, haven't seen, haven't heard anything; but during the last two terrible hours I've suffered so much heartache I'm prepared for the worst.

MARION: I want to go home, Mama. I'm hungry.

MAURICE: Of course you shall go home, my darling child. (*Hugs her.*)

MARION (*whimpering*): Oh! You're hurting me, Papa.

JEANNE: We have to go home for dinner. Goodbye, Maurice. Good luck!

MAURICE (*to Marion*): Where did I hurt you, my sweetest, dearest little girl? You know that I only want to do good to you!

MARION: Then come home with us! Please! Please!

MAURICE (*to Jeanne*): You know, when I hear her say that, I feel I should do what she says. But then I hear the voice of reason calling me. I've got obligations. . . . Goodbye, my little girl! (*Kisses Marion, who puts her arms around his neck.*)

JEANNE: When do I see you again?

MAURICE: We'll meet tomorrow, darling! Never to part!

JEANNE (*embraces him*): Never, never, never to part! (*She makes the sign of the cross on his forehead.*) God go with you!

MAURICE (*moved in spite of himself*): My darling, dearest Jeanne!

> *Jeanne and Marion walk toward the right; Maurice toward the left. At the same moment they turn toward each other and throw kisses at each other.*

(*Coming back.*) Jeanne! I'm so ashamed! I'm always forgetting you, and you're the last person in the world to speak up. Here's the ticket for tonight.

JEANNE: Thanks, dear, but—you should be where you belong tonight, alone, and I should be where I belong—with Marion.

MAURICE: Dear Jeanne, who's as wise as she is good. I'll swear there's not another woman in the world who would give up a night on the town to do her guy a favor. It's my night to shine. Tonight I take on the world. The battlefield is no place for women and children. And you knew!

JEANNE: Maurice—don't make too much of a simple woman like me. I mean, I don't want to disappoint you, ever. —Oh, look! I'm just as forgetful as you are. I bought these for you—a tie and a pair of gloves. Maybe you could wear them tonight—for me. I'm so proud.

MAURICE (*kissing her hand*): Thank you, my darling girl!

JEANNE: Oh! And Maurice! Don't forget like you always do—to go to the barber. I want you to look so handsome. I want everybody to admire you—

MAURICE: You haven't a grain of jealousy in you, have you?

JEANNE: It's an ugly word.

MAURICE: You know, right now I could forget all about tonight's triumph—yes, it will be a triumph for me, I'm sure—

JEANNE: Sh! Sh! Don't—

MAURICE: —and come home with you!

JEANNE: Exactly what you mustn't do! —Go on now. Destiny calls.

MAURICE: All right. Goodbye. And let come what may!

JEANNE (*alone with Marion*): *O Crux! Ave Spes Unica!*

Scene 2

> *The Crêmerie, a small restaurant with regular customers.*
>
> *To the right, a buffet with a large goldfish bowl, vegetables, fruits, canned preserves, etc. Farther back right is the entrance door. At the rear the door to the kitchen, where the workingmen eat. Through the kitchen the back door to the garden can be seen. In the rear to the left is a raised counter and cupboard and shelves with all sorts of bottles. To the right, a long marble-topped table runs along the wall, and parallel to it in the middle of the floor stands another such table. Wicker chairs at the table. The walls are covered with oil paintings, given by artists in payment of their bills.*
>
> *Madame Catherine is sitting at the counter. Maurice is leaning against the counter, his hat on, smoking a cigarette.*

MADAME CATHERINE: Your big night, eh, Maurice?

MAURICE: That's right. In a few hours, it will all be over.

MADAME CATHERINE: Are you nervous?

MAURICE: Cool as a cucumber.

MADAME CATHERINE: I wish you the best of luck, anyway. You deserve it, Maurice, after the rough time you've had.

MAURICE: Thanks, Catherine. You've been very kind to me. Without your help I would have gone down the drain by this time.

MADAME CATHERINE: We won't talk about that now. I help anyone who isn't lazy and who's serious. I just don't like to be taken advantage of. Are you coming back here after the play is over and having a drink with your old friends? You won't forget us?

MAURICE: Forget you! Of course not. It was my idea, wasn't it?

> *Henriette enters from the right. Maurice turns about; tips his hat; stares at Henriette, who looks him over carefully.*

HENRIETTE (*to Madame Catherine*): Have you seen Adolphe?

MADAME CATHERINE: No, Madame! Expect he'll be here soon. Won't you sit down?

HENRIETTE: No thanks. I prefer to wait outside. (*She leaves.*)

MAURICE: Who in blue blazes was that?!

MADAME CATHERINE: That was Adolphe's—friend . . .

MAURICE: Ah, ha, so that's her!

MADAME CATHERINE: Haven't you seen her before?

MAURICE: No. He's been hiding her from me, afraid I'd steal her.

MADAME CATHERINE: Ha ha! —Good-looking, isn't she?

MAURICE: Good-looking? Let me see. . . . Funny, I can't tell you. I didn't even see her. It was as if she flew into my arms instantaneously; came so close to me that I couldn't focus my eyes on her. But she left her impression in the air. I can still see her as she stood there. (*He walks over to the door and makes a gesture as if he were putting his arm around someone's waist.*) Ow! (*Shakes his finger as if he'd been stuck with a needle.*) Why, she's got pins in the waist of her dress. A real stinger! Dangerous!

MADAME CATHERINE (*smiles*): You're crazy! You and your women!

MAURICE: Crazy, crazy! But you know what, Madame Catherine! I'm leaving before she comes again. Otherwise . . . well, who the hell knows? —Scary!

MADAME CATHERINE: Afraid?

MAURICE: Yes, not only for my sake—for others.

MADAME CATHERINE: Well, then, get out, get out!

MAURICE: You saw, didn't you? She didn't walk through the door: she vanished, and a little whirlwind sprang up which pulled me after her. —Go ahead and laugh! —But why is that palm tree on the sideboard still shaking? What a diabolic woman!

MADAME CATHERINE: Leave, man, leave, before you're really hooked.

MAURICE: I want to leave but I can't. . . . Do you believe in fate, Catherine?

MADAME CATHERINE: No, I don't. I believe in God and his goodness, and that He'll help us against the powers of darkness, that is, if we ask for His help in the right way.

MAURICE: Ah ha, you see? Powers of darkness! That's it! —And isn't that what I hear out in the hall right now?

MADAME CATHERINE: It certainly is. She's pacing back and forth, swishing her skirts. When you tear a sheet into rags, it sounds like that. Go! Get out! Out! Through the kitchen!

> *Maurice dashes for the kitchen door but bumps into Emile.*

EMILE: Beg your pardon! I'm sorry!

> *Emile withdraws to the kitchen. Adolphe enters, followed by Henriette.*

ADOLPHE: Why, if it isn't Maurice! Hello, how are you? Henriette, I want you to meet my oldest and dearest friend. Henriette—Maurice.

MAURICE (*stiffly formal*): How do you do?

HENRIETTE: We've met before.

ADOLPHE: Really? When? If I may ask.

MAURICE: Just a moment ago! Right in here.

ADOLPHE: Oh! — Well, you can't leave now. Not until we've had a little chat.

MAURICE (*after getting a warning signal from Madame Catherine*): I'd love to, but I don't have the time.

ADOLPHE: Take time! We won't stay long.

HENRIETTE: I won't bother you, if you men want to talk business. None of my affair.

MAURICE: Our sort of affairs have nothing to do with business! Won't do to talk about them.

HENRIETTE: Then we'll talk about something else! (*Takes his hat and hangs it up.*) Now why don't you be nice to me and give me a chance to get to know the great playwright!

> *Madame Catherine makes another warning gesture at Maurice, who takes no notice.*

ADOLPHE: That's right, Henriette; reel him in before he gets away!

> *They sit down at a table.*

HENRIETTE (*to Maurice*): You're lucky to have Adolphe for a friend, Maurice. He never talks of anybody but you. I feel I'm playing second fiddle.

ADOLPHE: Oh, cut it out! Look who's talking. She's never given me a moment's peace because of you, Maurice. She's read everything you've written. She wants to know who influenced you, what books you read. She's asked me how you looked, how old you were, what you like and what you don't like. I've had you for company morning, noon, and night. It's as if the three of us were living together.

MAURICE: Why, you dear sweet thing, why didn't you come here and take a look at the phenomenon for yourself? One look and your curiosity would have been satisfied.

HENRIETTE: Adolphe didn't want me to. (*Adolphe looks embarrassed.*) Not that he was jealous . . .

MAURICE: Why should he be jealous? He knows I've got a girl.

HENRIETTE: Maybe he felt he couldn't rely on your always having the same girl.

MAURICE: Can't imagine why. My heart is notorious for its constancy.

ADOLPHE: But that wasn't the reason—

HENRIETTE (*interrupting him*): Perhaps you haven't had to stand the acid test.

ADOLPHE: Now how do you—

HENRIETTE (*interrupting*): —There's never been a faithful man since this evil little world began.

MAURICE: Well, time there was one!

HENRIETTE: Where?

MAURICE: Here!

Henriette laughs.

ADOLPHE: You know, this sounds just like—

HENRIETTE (*interrupting again and continuing to talk directly to Maurice*): Do you think I'd trust my dear Adolphe for more than a season?

MAURICE: It's not for me to question your lack of faith in people, but I'd stake my life on Adolphe's faithfulness.

HENRIETTE: No need to. I was talking through my hat. I take it all back. Not because I'm trying to be as high-minded as you, mind you, but because Adolphe really *is* faithful. . . . It's become a habit with me—seeing only the bad side; I can't stop it, in spite of my best resolutions. But I'm sure if I were to see a lot more of you two, you'd bring out the best in me. Forgive me, Adolphe, will you? (*She puts her hand to his cheek.*)

ADOLPHE: You're always saying such bad things, and always doing the right thing. As for what's really going on in that head of yours—I haven't the faintest idea.

HENRIETTE: Who knows what goes on in our heads?

MAURICE: Yes, imagine being held responsible for our thoughts. Life would be impossible.

HENRIETTE: Don't tell me you have evil thoughts?

MAURICE: Of course I do. And in my dreams I commit the grimmest crimes . . .

HENRIETTE: In dreams, oh, well—! Do you know that I—no, I'm ashamed to talk about it—

MAURICE: Oh, come on! Come on!

HENRIETTE: Last night I dreamed that I was quite calmly dissecting the muscles in Adolphe's chest—sculptress that I am—and Adolphe, like the sweet man he is, didn't put up any resistance at all. He even helped me through some troublesome spots, since he knows more anatomy than I do.

MAURICE: Was he dead?

HENRIETTE: No, he was alive.

MAURICE: How disgusting! You must have waked up screaming.

HENRIETTE: No. That's what amazes me. I'm really quite sensitive to the suffering of others. Isn't that true, Adolphe?

ADOLPHE: Absolutely! I might even say extremely sensitive, especially to animals.

MAURICE: I'm just the opposite—quite insensitive to my own sufferings as well as to others' . . . !

ADOLPHE: Now he's telling lies against himself. Isn't he, Catherine?

MADAME CATHERINE: Maurice wouldn't say boo to a goose. He was on the verge of calling in the police because I didn't change the water for the goldfish often enough – the ones over there on the sideboard. . . . Look at the dears. It's as if they understood what I was saying . . .

MAURICE: Isn't this wonderful! Here we sit whitewashing ourselves to look like angels, and yet, by and large, each one of us is ready to stab someone discreetly in the back to win glory, gold, or a woman. . . . Did I hear you say you were a sculptor, Mademoiselle?

HENRIETTE: In a way. Good enough to make a bust. And as for making one of you, which I've long dreamed of doing, I think I'm more than good enough.

MAURICE: Help yourself! At least that's one dream that we can make come true. Want to start?

HENRIETTE: No. I don't want to begin to study you until after tonight, after you've become a success. You won't be the real you until that happens.

MAURICE: So sure of my success?

HENRIETTE: It's written all over you. You're going to be the conquering hero tonight. I'm sure you feel it yourself . . .

MAURICE: Why?

HENRIETTE: Because I feel it! This morning I was down in the dumps, now Henriette's herself again.

Adolphe looks somber, lost in thought.

MAURICE (*embarrassed*): Listen . . . I've got an extra ticket – but only one. Here, Adolphe, you can do what you want to with it.

ADOLPHE: Thanks, Maurice. I relinquish it to Henriette.

HENRIETTE: No, I can't let you do that.

ADOLPHE: Why not? Besides, I never go to the theater. Always too hot and stuffy there.

HENRIETTE: At least you'll come and take me home when the show's over?

ADOLPHE: If you insist. Otherwise there's Maurice. . . . He'll be coming back here. We'll be having a party for him.

MAURICE: Oh, come on, Adolphe, you can certainly take the trouble to come and meet us. I beg you! Look, I'm on my knees! All right. Don't wait outside the theater. Meet us at the Auberge des Adrets. You could wait for us there. How about it? Agreed?

ADOLPHE: Not so fast, not so fast! You're a genius at settling questions to your own advantage without giving a guy a chance to think about them.

MAURICE: What is there to think about? Are you going to pick up your girl or aren't you?

ADOLPHE: You don't seem to realize what insignificant little acts can lead to. But I've got my hunches.

HENRIETTE: Sh-sh-sh! Can't be spooky in broad daylight! Whether he comes or not, we can always find our way back.

ADOLPHE (*has gotten up from his chair*): I've really got to go— I've got a model coming. "Goodbye. —Best of luck to you, Maurice! Tomorrow you'll be in another world! Goodbye, Henriette!

HENRIETTE: Are you really going?

ADOLPHE: Have to!

MAURICE: All right. Goodbye. See you soon!

> *Adolphe leaves, nodding goodbye to Madame Catherine as he goes out.*

HENRIETTE: Well, we finally got to meet each other!

MAURICE: What's so extraordinary about that?

HENRIETTE: I guess it had to happen, since Adolphe did everything he could to prevent it.

MAURICE: Did he?

HENRIETTE: Don't tell me you didn't notice!

MAURICE: Yes, I noticed. Why do you have to mention it?

HENRIETTE: Just because.

MAURICE: But I don't have to mention that only a moment ago I was about to run off through the kitchen to avoid meeting you and that I was prevented by someone closing the door in my face.

HENRIETTE: Then why do you?

MAURICE: I don't know.

Madame Catherine knocks over some glasses and bottles.

Take it easy, Catherine. There's no danger.

HENRIETTE: Is that supposed to be a signal—or a warning?

MAURICE: Probably a bit of both.

HENRIETTE: What am I—a locomotive? Do I need signalmen to keep the track clear?

MAURICE: And switchmen! Switches are the dangerous places!

HENRIETTE: You can be nasty, can't you?

MADAME CATHERINE: Maurice isn't at all nasty. Up to now he's been as kind and loyal to those close to him as anyone could possibly be—especially those he's obligated to.

MAURICE: Oh, quiet, quiet!

HENRIETTE (*to Maurice*): The old cat is sharpening her claws . . .

MAURICE: We can walk down to the boulevard, if you want to.

HENRIETTE: Good idea! This is no place for me. I can feel her hatred clawing at me . . . (*Leaves.*)

MAURICE (*walking after her*): Goodbye, Catherine.

MADAME CATHERINE: Just a second! May I tell you something? Maurice!

MAURICE (*stopping reluctantly*): What is it?

MADAME CATHERINE: Don't do it! Don't do it!

MAURICE: Do what?

MADAME CATHERINE: Just don't do it!

MAURICE: Fear not! She's not my kind of girl. But I find her interesting in a way.

MADAME CATHERINE: You're too sure of yourself! That's bad.

MAURICE: No, that's good. —So long! (*Leaves.*)

ACT II

Scene 1

The Auberge des Adrets, on the Boulevard St. Martin, a café decorated in a flamboyantly theatrical, baroque style. Tables and armchairs here and there in nooks and corners. The walls are hung with weapons and armor; the wainscot shelves are lined with glasses and flagons, etc.

Maurice in tails and Henriette in evening gown are sitting at a table with a bottle of champagne and three filled champagne glasses. They are sitting facing each other, each with a glass. The third glass stands at the upstage side of the table, where a third empty armchair seems to be awaiting the missing third party.

MAURICE (*laying his watch on the table*): If he's not here in five minutes, he won't come at all. —In the meantime, what about drinking with his ghost? (*Clinking his glass against the third glass.*)

HENRIETTE (*doing the same*): Your health, Adolphe!

MAURICE: He won't come!

HENRIETTE: He will!

MAURICE: Won't!

HENRIETTE: Will!

MAURICE: What a night, what a wonderful day! I still can't believe it. A new life has begun for me! The producer thinks I'll make a hundred thousand francs out of this play. . . . You know how much that is? I'm buying a villa outside the city—and I'll still have eighty thousand left! I won't be able to take this all in until tomorrow, because right now I'm tired, tired, dead tired. (*Sinking down in his chair.*) Have you ever been really and truly happy?

HENRIETTE: Never! — How does it feel?

MAURICE: I can't begin to describe it! Can't find the words. I keep thinking how mortified and envious my enemies must be. . . . Awful, isn't it? But it's the truth.

HENRIETTE: Is that what success means — getting even?

MAURICE: Doesn't the conquering hero count bodies to measure the extent of his victory?

HENRIETTE: Are you that bloodthirsty?

MAURICE: Not really. But when you've been walked on year after year, it feels just great to get their heels off your chest and to breathe deeply again!

HENRIETTE: Don't you think it's strange that you're sitting here alone with me, an insignificant girl whom you don't know, on a night like this, when you should be showing yourself as the man of the hour before all the people on the boulevards, in all the night spots . . .

MAURICE: I suppose it is a little peculiar, but I like it here. Your company is all I need.

HENRIETTE: You're not happy, are you?

MAURICE: No, I feel rather sad. In fact, I feel like crying.

HENRIETTE: Why? What's the matter?

MAURICE: All this good luck. It all seems sour or on the verge of turning — into bad luck.

HENRIETTE: So sad, so melancholy! What more do you want?

MAURICE: The one thing that makes life worth living . . .

HENRIETTE: You don't love her any longer?

MAURICE: No, not in the way I think of love. She hasn't read my play, you know. Doesn't even want to. (*He sighs.*) Oh, she's good-hearted, self-sacrificing, sensitive, but to go out on the town with me, making a night of it like this — she'd think that was sinful. You know, I once treated her to a bottle of champagne.

Instead of enjoying it, she picked up the wine list to see how much it cost. And when she saw the price, she cried! She cried because little Marion needed new clothes! —Beautiful, isn't it? Even touching. But I don't get any fun out of it! And I want to get some fun out of life before it all disappears down the drain! All my life I've had to do without. But now, now—a new life begins for me!

The clock strikes twelve.

A new day. A whole new era.

HENRIETTE: Adolphe won't come.

MAURICE: No, now he won't. And now it's too late to go down to the Crêmerie.

HENRIETTE: They're waiting for you there.

MAURICE: Let them wait! They made me promise, and now I take back my promise. —Do you wish you were there?

HENRIETTE: No, not in the least!

MAURICE: Will you stay with me then?

HENRIETTE: With pleasure! If you can put up with me!

MAURICE: Would I ask you otherwise? —It's strange, but what good is the laurel crown of victory if you can't lay it at the feet of some woman. Everything is worthless if you don't have a woman . . .

HENRIETTE: Don't tell me you have to be without a woman! You?

MAURICE: Look at me!

HENRIETTE: Don't you know that a man at the peak of fame and fortune is irresistible?

MAURICE: How should I know? I haven't been in a position to find out.

HENRIETTE: You are strange! At this moment you're the most

envied man in Paris, and you sit here brooding, with a bad conscience, just because you ignored an invitation to drink a cup of chicory coffee with an old lady in that dump she runs . . .

MAURICE: Yes, my conscience does plague me. Even this far away I can tell they are hurt, can feel their righteous indignation, their animosity. They were my friends when I was nobody. Good old Catherine had first claim on my night of success. The party would have meant a lot to them. Cast a ray of hope over those who are still trying to make it. Now I've betrayed them. I can hear what they're saying. "He'll come. Good guy. Doesn't forget his friends. Doesn't go back on his word. He'll come, take my word." — Now they'll have to eat their words.

> *During this speech someone in the next room has begun to play Beethoven's Sonata No. 17 in D minor, Opus 31, No. 2 — the finale allegretto — at first very softly, then faster and faster, passionately, stormily, and finally with complete abandon.*

Who can be playing at this time of night?

HENRIETTE: Must be some night owl like us. . . . You know, you didn't present the case correctly. Remember that Adolphe promised to come and pick us up. We waited, and *he* didn't keep *his* promise. So you should have a clear conscience . . .

MAURICE: Do you really think so? . . . I believe you as long as you go on talking, but as soon as you stop, the millstones of my conscience begin to grind again. — What have you got in that package?

HENRIETTE: Oh, it's only a laurel wreath. I wanted to send it up to you on the stage, but I didn't get a chance. Let me give it to you now. If your head is hot, the laurel will cool it — so they say. (*She stands up and puts the laurel wreath on his head; kisses him on the forehead.*) Hail the conquering hero!

MAURICE: No, don't do that.

HENRIETTE (*on her knees*): Hail to the king!

MAURICE (*standing up*): No, please! It gives me the creeps!

HENRIETTE: You scaredy-cat! Maurice, the coward! Afraid of success! Who ran off with your self-confidence, little man?

MAURICE: Little man! Yes, you're right. I'm no giant hurling lightning bolts and rolling thunder balls. I'm the dwarf who guards the treasure, who forges his sword silently, deep within the mountain. So you think I shy from the victor's laurel? You think I fear that ghost there, staring at me with the green eyes of jealousy and monitoring my passions—passions of whose force you know nothing! —Vanish, ghost! (*He sweeps the third champagne glass to the floor.*) You have no place here! You stayed away and you lost your rights—if you ever had any! You stayed away from the battlefield because you knew you were beaten. As I crush this glass under my feet, so shall I grind into dust that image of yourself which you have built in a little temple that shall be yours no longer!

HENRIETTE: Bravo! That's more like it! Bravo!

MAURICE: There! I've sacrificed my best friend, my most devoted supporter, on your altar, Astarte! Are you satisfied?

HENRIETTE: Astarte! I love that! From now on I'm Astarte! —I think you really do love me, Maurice.

MAURICE: Of course I love you! —Ah, daughter of destruction, lady of pain! You like the smell of blood. You rouse my fighting spirit! Where did you come from? Where will you lead me? I must have loved you even before I saw you. When they talked about you, I trembled. When I glimpsed you in the doorway, I felt you physically. When you left, I still held you in my arms. I tried to get away from you, but someone stopped me. We were driven together, like wild game by the baying hounds. Who's guilty in all this? Your friend, my friend, our pander.

HENRIETTE: Guilty or not guilty—what's that got to do with it? And what's guilt? Adolphe is guilty, guilty of not having brought us together sooner. He committed the crime, robbing us—of two weeks of bliss that he had no right to. I'm jealous of him on your account. I hate him because he betrayed you with me. I want to wipe him from the living, erase even the thought of him, render him unborn, unmade, nonexistent.

MAURICE: Right! We'll drive his ghost into the wild woods,

bury our memories of him, and let the days we spend with each other pile up like rocks on top of him. (*Raising his glass.*) Our fate is sealed! Woe betide us! What's next, Astarte?

HENRIETTE: A new life! Remember? — What have you got in that package?

MAURICE: Package? I've forgotten.

HENRIETTE (*opens the package and takes out a tie and a pair of gloves*): My God, what an awful tie! Must have come from the five-and-dime!

MAURICE (*snatching the things from her*): Don't touch them!

HENRIETTE: From her?

MAURICE: Yes, from her.

HENRIETTE: Give them to me!

MAURICE: No! She's better than we are. Better than everyone!

HENRIETTE: No, not better. Just sillier and stingier! A ninny who cries because somebody drinks champagne . . .

MAURICE: Because her child didn't have enough clothes! She's good. Good.

HENRIETTE: My, aren't you the bourgeois one! I thought you were an artist. You're not — but I am and when I do your bust I'll carve MIDDLE CLASS on your brow — and skip the laurel crown! What's her name? Jeanne?

MAURICE: Yes. How did you know?

HENRIETTE: All housemaids are called Jeanne.

MAURICE: Henriette!

> *Henriette takes the tie and the gloves and throws them in the fireplace.*

(*Weakly.*) The Goddess Astarte! You want to see that woman sacrificed to you too? All right. You can have her. But if you demand an innocent child I'm through with you.

HENRIETTE: What draws you to me? Tell me.

MAURICE: If I knew, I could break the spell. I think it must be the bad qualities you possess and that I lack. I think it must be the evil in you, which attracts me with all the irresistible charm of the new and different . . .

HENRIETTE: Have you ever committed a crime?

MAURICE: No, not a real one. Have you?

HENRIETTE: Yes.

MAURICE: You have? What did it feel like?

HENRIETTE: Better than doing a good deed. That only makes you the same as the others. It felt greater than doing something heroic, because that only raises you above the crowd; they give you an award for that. But the crime I committed carried me away, transported me to the other side of life, beyond society, beyond my fellow human beings. Since that moment I've only lived a half life, a dream life, and that's why reality can never have any claim on me.

MAURICE: What did you do?

HENRIETTE: I won't tell you. Fraidy-cat!

MAURICE: Can't you ever be found out?

HENRIETTE: Never! But that doesn't prevent me from thinking about those five stones in the Place de Roquette where the guillotine used to stand. And I never cut cards, because I'm sure to turn up the five of diamonds . . . *

MAURICE: That kind of crime? Not –?

HENRIETTE: Yes, it was!

MAURICE: That's terrifying. –And fascinating! Doesn't your conscience bother you?

HENRIETTE: Never. Let's change the subject, if you don't mind.

* The guillotine was set up outside the Roquette prison in the center of five stones forming a design like that on the five of diamonds.

MAURICE: What shall we talk about? Love?

HENRIETTE: One doesn't talk about love until it's over!

MAURICE: Were you in love with Adolphe?

HENRIETTE: I don't know. His good heart had the same appeal as a beautiful, long-lost childhood memory. But when I looked at him carefully, there was so much about him I didn't like. I had to spend a lot of time changing, rubbing out and filling in, to make a decent picture of him. When I heard him talking, I couldn't help noticing how much he had learned from you, how he had misunderstood it and misapplied it. Now just imagine, when I got to see the original, how pitiful the copy seemed to be! —That was why he was afraid that you and I would meet. And when it happened, he understood immediately that his time was up.

MAURICE: Poor Adolphe!

HENRIETTE: I feel sorry for him too. I know how he suffers.

MAURICE: Quiet. . . . Someone's coming!

HENRIETTE: My God, suppose it's him!

MAURICE: That would be unbearable!

HENRIETTE: No, it isn't him. Suppose it had been. You're a playwright. Let's see you rehearse the scene.

MAURICE: All right. He'd be a little mad at you—at first— because he made a mistake about the café—looked for us in the wrong place—then his irritation would give way to pleasure at seeing us—seeing that *we* hadn't deceived him. And in the joy of discovering that he had unjustly suspected us, he would come to love and cherish us both. He would be delighted that we two had become such fast friends. It had always been his fondest dream—I can hear him making a long speech at this point—his fondest dream that we three might form a triumvirate to set the world a great example of a friendship that makes no demands. "Yes, I trust you, Maurice, not only because you are my friend, but because I know your heart lies elsewhere!"

HENRIETTE: Wonderful! Right on the nose! You must have

been in this situation before. You know, Adolphe is one of those men who believes that three's company and two's a crowd. He can never have any fun with his girl unless there's a friend along.

MAURICE: So I was called in to amuse you. —Sh! . . . There *is* somebody out there! —It's him!

HENRIETTE: No, it isn't. Don't you know this is the witching hour? That's when you hear things—and see things sometimes. Staying up all night has the same sort of magic as crime. Puts you over and above the laws of nature.

MAURICE: There's a horrifying punishment for that. . . . I've got goose pimples. I don't know whether I'm frozen or frightened.

HENRIETTE (*takes her long coat with the fur collar and wraps it around him*): Put something on. This will warm you.

MAURICE: Oh, that's wonderful! It's as if I had crawled inside your skin, as if my body, pulverized from lack of sleep, was being recast in your mold. I can actually feel how I'm being reshaped. I'm getting a new soul, new ideas. And here, where your breasts have formed a bulge, a new life begins to swell up.

> *During the whole of this scene, the pianist in the next room has been practicing the Beethoven Sonata, sometimes pianissimo, sometimes madly fortissimo. Occasionally there has been silence; occasionally only bars 96-107 of the finale have been heard.*

What a strange bird, practicing the piano in the middle of the night! . . . I've had enough! Do you know what? —We'll drive out to the Bois de Boulogne and have breakfast in the pavilion and watch the sun come up over the water.

HENRIETTE: Wonderful.

MAURICE: But first I have to send a message home to have the morning reviews sent out to the pavilion. —Henriette, what the hell! Let's invite Adolphe!

HENRIETTE: That's really crazy, but why not? Even an ass can help pull the triumphal chariot! Let him come!

They stand up.

MAURICE (*taking off the coat*): I'll go ring.

HENRIETTE: Wait a second! (*She throws herself into his arms.*)

Scene 2

A large, handsome room in a restaurant in the Bois de Boulogne. Carpets, mirrors, chaise longues, and divans. At the rear, French windows looking out on the lakes. In the foreground a table is spread with flower arrangements, bowls of fruit, decanters of wine, plates of oysters, varieties of wineglasses, and two lighted candelabra. To the right, a low table with newspapers and telegrams piled on it.

Maurice and Henriette are sitting at opposite sides of this table.

The sun is rising.

MAURICE: There isn't a shadow of a doubt. The newspapers say it's a hit; the telegrams congratulate me. A new life is beginning, and this is our wedding night because you were the only one to share my hopes and triumphs. You handed me the laurel crown of victory. I feel as if everything came to me from you!

HENRIETTE: What a wonderful night! Have we only dreamed it, or have we actually lived it?

MAURICE (*standing up*): And what a morning on top of such a night! It seems like the first day of creation, with the rising sun lighting up the newborn world. The earth is being created for the first time. Look! —It's breaking free of those clouds of placenta drifting off into space. There lies the Garden of Eden basking in the rosy light of a dawning day. And here stand the first two human beings. . . . You know, I'm so happy I feel like crying when I think that all of mankind is not just as happy as I am. . . . Do you hear that rustling and murmuring in the distance, like ocean waves washing stony beaches, like the soughing wind in the woods? Do you know what that is? That's Paris, Paris whispering my name! Do you see the columns of smoke rising to the sky, thousands upon thousands of them? That's from the fires on my altars—and if it isn't, it should be, because I want it to be. All the telegraph keys in Europe are tapping out my name at this very moment. The Orient Express is carrying the news to the Far East toward the rising sun, while ocean steamers are carrying it to the far, far West! —The world is mine, and that's why it's beautiful! Oh, how I wish I had wings for us both, to get away from here and fly far, far away, before someone spoils my happiness, before envy and jealousy wake me from my dream— because it probably is just a dream!

HENRIETTE (*offering her hand*): Feel! and you'll know you're not dreaming!

MAURICE: No, it isn't a dream, but once upon a time it was! You know, when I was a poor young man who walked down there in the woods and looked up to this pavilion, it seemed to me like a castle in a fairy tale, and I'd dream that being up in this room with its balcony and its thick curtains would be absolute bliss! And to sit here with the woman I love and watch the sun rise while the candelabra were still burning—that was the wildest dream of my youth. Now it's come true; I have nothing more to live for! —Do you want to die now, with me?

HENRIETTE: No! You crazy fool, now I want to begin to live!

MAURICE (*standing up*): To live? Living is suffering. —And now comes reality! I can hear him running up the steps, panting with anxiety, his heart pounding with the fear that he has lost his most precious possession. I'll bet you Adolphe is under this roof right now. And in one minute he'll be standing in the middle of this room.

HENRIETTE (*tense*): It was a stupid trick to invite him here. I'm sorry we did. —Anyhow, it will give us a chance to see how much you know about psychology—see how right you were.

MAURICE: When you're dealing with emotions, there's always room for error.

The Headwaiter enters to deliver a card to Maurice.

Show the gentleman in. (*To Henriette.*) We're going to regret this, I'm sure!

HENRIETTE: Bit late for that. —Quiet!

Adolphe enters, haggard, pale, and hollow-eyed.

MAURICE (*trying to appear casual*): Well, well, Adolphe! Where were you hiding out last night?

ADOLPHE: I looked for you at the Hôtel des Arrêts. I waited for an hour.

MAURICE: That was the wrong place. We waited for you at the Auberge des Adrets for two hours. And we're still waiting for you, as you can see.

ADOLPHE (*relieved*): Thank God.

HENRIETTE: Good morning! Adolphe, you must be jinxed! You've got to stop tormenting yourself for no good reason. I'll bet you're thinking that we tried to avoid you. You know we sent for you, but you still look as though you weren't wanted.

ADOLPHE: I'm sorry. Forgive me. I've had a horrible night.

They sit down. Embarrassed silence.

HENRIETTE (*to Adolphe*): Well, aren't you going to congratulate Maurice on his great success?

ADOLPHE: Oh, my God, of course! —The play is a great hit. Everyone says so—even those who envy you. The world is at your feet, Maurice. I feel such a nothing next to you.

MAURICE: Oh, nonsense! —Henriette, give Adolphe a glass of wine.

ADOLPHE: No thanks, not for me. Nothing at all, thank you.

HENRIETTE (*to Adolphe*): What's the matter with you? Are you sick?

ADOLPHE: No, but I think I'm coming down with something.

HENRIETTE: Your eyes . . .

ADOLPHE: What about them?

MAURICE: How did things go at the Crêmerie last night? I suppose they're mad at me?

ADOLPHE: No one's mad at you. But everyone was in such a gloom, I couldn't bear it. They're not mad at you, you understand, they're sympathetic and considerate. When you didn't show up, they understood. Madame Catherine herself defended you and proposed a toast to you. We all rejoiced in your success as if it had been our own.

HENRIETTE: Such good, kind people! Aren't you lucky to have such wonderful friends, Maurice!

MAURICE: Yes, better than I deserve.

HENRIETTE: Everybody has exactly the friends he deserves. Everybody likes you, Maurice. . . . Don't you feel how the air caresses you today? It's filled with the good wishes of a thousand souls . . .

Maurice stands up to conceal his emotion.

ADOLPHE: —a thousand souls thanking you for making them feel better. Everyone was writing such pessimistic stuff, saying people were bad, life hopeless, without meaning. Then you came along with your play. Made everybody feel good. Felt like lifting up their heads. Things aren't so bad, after all, they're thinking. And thinking like that actually makes them better, you know.

Henriette tries to hide her feelings.

ADOLPHE: I feel I'm intruding. I'll stay just a moment longer. I just want to warm myself in your sunshine, Maurice. Then I'll go.

MAURICE: Why do you want to go? You just got here.

ADOLPHE: Why? Because I've seen what I never really needed to see. I can tell what's going on. (*Silence.*) Sending for me was very considerate of you. Better, more straightforward than hiding it from me. Hurts less than being deceived. You see, I do think the best of people, Maurice. That's something you've taught me.

(*Silence.*) But there's something I think I should tell you, Maurice. Just a while ago I passed through the Church of Saint-Germain, and I saw a woman and a child there. I don't wish that you could have seen them—what's done can't be undone—but if you gave them a thought or a good word before you set them adrift in this big city, you might enjoy your success with complete peace of mind. That's all I wanted to say. Goodbye.

HENRIETTE: Why do you have to go?

ADOLPHE: You don't really want me to answer that!

HENRIETTE: No, I guess not.

ADOLPHE: Goodbye. (*Leaves.*)

MAURICE: "And lo, they knew that they were naked."

HENRIETTE: A bit different from the scene we were expecting, wasn't it? . . . He's too good for us.

MAURICE: I'm beginning to think everybody is.

HENRIETTE: Look. . . . The sun has gone behind the clouds, and the woods have lost their rosy hue.

MAURICE: So I see. And the blue water has turned black. Come on, let's leave. Let's fly south, where the skies are always blue and the trees are always green.

HENRIETTE: Yes, let's! —But without goodbyes to anyone!

MAURICE: No, *with* goodbyes!

HENRIETTE: You said we were going to fly. You offered me wings—but you've got lead weights on your feet. —I'm not jealous, but I know that if you go to say goodbye and find yourself with two pairs of arms around your neck, you'll never be able to break that stranglehold.

MAURICE: I'm sure you're right—except that it would take only *one* pair of arms to hold me fast.

HENRIETTE: The child? It's the child, not the woman. Right?

MAURICE: That's right. The child.

HENRIETTE: The child! Another woman's child! And for that

I have to suffer! Why does that child have to stand in my way when I want to get ahead, when I've got to get ahead?

MAURICE: Yes, why? Better if it had never existed!

HENRIETTE (*walking up and down in great agitation*): Absolutely! But it does exist! Like a rock in the road, an immovable rock that's bound to upset the wagon.

MAURICE: You mean the triumphal chariot! —You can drive the ass till it drops, but the rock remains. Damn it, damn it! (*Silence.*)

HENRIETTE: What are we going to do? Must be something.

MAURICE: There is! We'll get married. Then *our* child will make us forget the other child.

HENRIETTE: The one will kill the other!

MAURICE: Kill! What a word to use!

HENRIETTE (*suddenly soft, pleading*): Your child will kill our love!

MAURICE: Never! Don't you see, our love will kill everything that stands in its way, but it cannot be killed!

HENRIETTE (*cuts a deck of cards, which is lying on the mantelpiece*): You see! The five of diamonds! The guillotine! —Is it really possible that everything is all worked out in advance? That our thoughts are led like water through pipes, and that there's nothing we can do about it? No, I don't want it to end that way! I don't want to end there! . . . You know, it's the guillotine for me, if my crime is discovered.

MAURICE: Tell me about it. No better time than this.

HENRIETTE: No, I'd regret it later. And you'd loathe me. —No, no, no. . . . Have you ever heard that a person could be hated to death? No? Well, I tell you my father was seared with the hatred of my mother and my brothers and sisters, and he melted away like wax in the fire. (*Gesture of aversion.*) No, no. Let's talk about something else. —For God's sake, let's get away from here! The air is poisoned. Tomorrow the laurel will be withered, the triumph forgotten; within a week another conquering hero will be the public idol. We've got to get away! But first, Maurice, darling, you'll go and embrace your child and arrange for its immediate future. As for the mother of the girl, I don't see any reason why you should have to meet her.

MAURICE: Thank you, Henriette! You really have a good heart. You usually keep it under wraps. But I love you twice as much when you show it.

HENRIETTE: Afterward you'll go to the Crêmerie and say goodbye to the old lady and all your old friends! Be sure you settle all your affairs! Once we leave here, I don't want you brooding over what you should have done.

MAURICE: I'll clear up everything. And tonight we'll meet at the train station.

HENRIETTE: Right! We'll be on our way — south, toward the sea and the sun!

ACT III

Scene 1

The Crêmerie.

The gas lamps are lit. Madame Catherine is sitting at the buffet; Adolphe at one of the tables.

MADAME CATHERINE: My dear Adolphe, that's life! You young folks expect too much, and then you sit around and cry if you don't get it.

ADOLPHE: No, that's not how it is. I'm not reproaching anybody. I still like them both as much as ever. There's just one thing that really hurts me. You see, I felt so close to Maurice – so close that there was nothing I'd have denied him if it would have made him happy. But I've lost him. That's what hurts – more than the loss of her. I've lost them both. Makes me feel twice as lonesome. . . . There's still something else that bothers me. Can't put my finger on it.

MADAME CATHERINE: Don't sit there brooding. Get to work, amuse yourself. . . . Don't you ever go to church, Adolphe?

ADOLPHE: What on earth would I do there?

MADAME CATHERINE: There's a lot to look at – and there's the music. Be a change for you, anyway.

ADOLPHE: Perhaps. But this sheep doesn't belong to that fold: I'm not devout. And besides, Madame Catherine, you know that faith is a gift, and nobody's given it to me, not so far.

MADAME CATHERINE: All right, Adolphe, no use forcing things. – Now what's this I've been hearing today? I hear you sold a painting in London for a lot of money and got a medal for first prize? Is it true?

ADOLPHE: Yes, it's true.

MADAME CATHERINE: Well, of all the—! And you never said a word about it?

ADOLPHE: I'm afraid of success. —Besides, it doesn't mean a thing at this moment. It's like seeing a ghost. You know what they say: you mustn't tell anyone you've seen it because you're just asking for more trouble.

MADAME CATHERINE: Well, Adolphe, I've always said you were an odd duck!

ADOLPHE: You don't understand, Catherine. I've seen how bad luck goes hand in hand with the good. When things are going against you, you find out who your friends are. They stick by you. When things go well, everybody sticks by you. You don't know who your friends are. . . . You asked me if I ever went to church. I didn't give you a straight answer. You see, this morning, I did go into the Church of Saint-Germain—without really knowing why. I felt I was looking for someone whom I might thank for my good luck. But I didn't find anyone. . . . So instead I put a gold coin in the poor box—and that's all that came of my visit to the church. I don't call that much of a change.

MADAME CATHERINE: At least you did something—and it was good of you to think of the poor when luck came your way.

ADOLPHE: It was neither good nor bad; I did it because I couldn't help myself. —But something else happened to me in church. I saw Maurice's girlfriend Jeanne and their child there. Crushed beneath his triumphal chariot! They looked as if they'd lost everything in the world.

MADAME CATHERINE: I just don't understand how you kids have arranged things with your consciences. I can't figure it out! How could a good, conscientious, sensitive man like Maurice abandon his girl and his child without a moment's hesitation? Explain that, if you can.

ADOLPHE: I can't. I don't think he understands it himself. I met them this morning and everything seemed so perfectly natural to them. They couldn't imagine things could be any other way. They looked as if they'd just done their good deed for the day, or fulfilled a sacred duty. Catherine, there are some things we can't explain, so how can we judge them? Besides, you saw how the whole thing happened. Maurice felt the danger in the air; I sensed it. I tried to keep them from meeting; Maurice wanted to run away; but it was all no use. It was as if an invisible being had woven the plot and driven them into each other's arms. I suppose I should disqualify myself in this case, but I don't hesitate for a moment to pronounce the verdict: not guilty.

MADAME CATHERINE: Well, Adolphe, to be as forgiving as you are, that's true religion!

ADOLPHE: Goodness me! Catherine, you don't suppose I'm religious without knowing it!

MADAME CATHERINE: Still, letting oneself be driven to sin — or letting oneself be tempted — that's a sign of weakness — or corruption. If you feel you can't resist, you should pray for help, and then it comes. But he didn't. He was too stuck-up. — Who's this coming? Well, if it isn't the abbé!

ADOLPHE: What's he doing here?

The Abbé enters.

THE ABBÉ: Good evening, Madame. Good evening, young fellow.

MADAME CATHERINE: Can I be of any help, Father?

THE ABBÉ: I'm looking for Monsieur Gérard. Have you seen him today?

MADAME CATHERINE: No, I haven't. They're doing his play at one of the theaters; he's probably busy up there.

THE ABBÉ: I have some . . . some bad news for him — bad in more respects than one.

MADAME CATHERINE: May I ask what sort of news?

THE ABBÉ: Yes, of course; it's no secret. His daughter — the one born out of wedlock — to Jeanne — she's dead.

MADAME CATHERINE: Dead?

ADOLPHE: Marion dead!

THE ABBÉ: Yes. She passed away suddenly this morning without any apparent symptoms of earlier illness.

MADAME CATHERINE: Oh God! Mysterious are Thy ways.

THE ABBÉ: The mother's grief and distress make Maurice's presence imperative. We must try to find him. — Let me ask you one question — in strictest confidence, of course. Did Maurice love his child, or was he indifferent toward her?

MADAME CATHERINE: Love his little Marion! Father, all of us here know how dearly he loved her.

ADOLPHE: There's absolutely no doubt about that, Father.

THE ABBÉ: I'm certainly glad to hear that. Makes things clear in my mind, at least.

MADAME CATHERINE: Was there any doubt?

THE ABBÉ: Yes, unfortunately. There's an ugly rumor circulating in this part of town that he deserted his child and the mother to run away with another woman. Within the last few hours this rumor has turned into a direct accusation, and the people are furious. They're calling him a murderer. They are even threatening his life.

MADAME CATHERINE: My God, what on earth is going on? What is all this?

THE ABBÉ: Let me assure you. I am completely convinced that he is innocent. And the mother is just as certain as I am. But appearances are so much against him, I'm afraid he'll find it difficult to clear himself with the police.

ADOLPHE: Is this a police case?

THE ABBÉ: Yes, the police had to step in for his own good. To protect him against the anger of the people. The police inspector's probably on his way here right now.

MADAME CATHERINE (*to Adolphe*): Do you see what happens when you can't tell good from evil, and start flirting with sin? God punishes, that's what!

ADOLPHE: Then he's less merciful than people are.

THE ABBÉ: You seem to know a lot about this.

ADOLPHE: Not a lot, but I've got eyes.

THE ABBÉ: But do you understand what you see?

ADOLPHE: Perhaps not yet.

THE ABBÉ: Let's look at the matter more closely—. Oh, here's the inspector.

The Inspector enters.

THE INSPECTOR: Gentlemen, Madame Catherine. I'm sorry to disturb you. I have to ask you some questions concerning Monsieur Gérard, who, as I suppose you already know, is the victim of a hideous rumor, which, by the bye, I don't for a moment believe.

MADAME CATHERINE: No one here believes it either!

THE INSPECTOR: Good, that strengthens my opinion. Still, for his sake, I want to be certain he gets a proper hearing.

THE ABBÉ: Fair enough. I'm sure he'll get justice, even though it won't be easy.

THE INSPECTOR: Appearances are all against him; that's the trouble. I've seen innocent people die on the scaffold before they had a chance to prove they were innocent. Now here's the evidence against him. (*He consults his notebook.*) The little girl Marion, left alone by her mother, was secretly visited by her father, who seems to have gone to some trouble to find out exactly when the child would be alone. Just fifteen minutes after the father left, the mother came home and found the child dead. That looks bad for the accused man. On the other hand, the autopsy has revealed no signs of violence and no traces of poison. Good! But the doctors point out that there are some newly discovered poisons that do not leave any traces! Now, all this is circumstantial—and all quite likely due to coincidence. I'm accustomed to that in my business! Regrettably, there is more incriminating evidence. —Last night Maurice was seen at the

Auberge des Adrets with an unidentified lady. Their conversation, according to the waiter's testimony, dealt with crime. Words like Place de Roquette and guillotine were spoken—a rather strange subject for conversation between two lovers of good breeding and respectable position! . . . But let that pass. We all know that people who stay up all night drinking are quite likely to dig up some of the bad stuff that lies in the depths of their souls, however respectable they may be. —More damaging is the testimony of the headwaiter who served them a champagne breakfast in the Bois de Boulogne this morning. He testifies to having heard them wish for the death of a child. The man is reported to have said, "Better if it never existed." To which the woman replied, "Absolutely. But it does exist." And later in the conversation someone said, "The one will kill the other," to which the reply was: "Kill. That's no word to use," and "Our love will kill anything that stands in its way"! And also: "The five of diamonds" . . . "the guillotine" . . . "Place de Roquette." —Now as you can see, all this builds quite a case against the man. —As does one more final fact: the trip out of the country that the two of them have planned for tonight. There you have the hard facts.

MADAME CATHERINE: I never heard anything so horrible. I don't know what to believe.

THE ABBÉ: There's something unearthly about this. God help him!

ADOLPHE: Caught in a net of circumstances!

MADAME CATHERINE: He had no business there in the first place.

ADOLPHE: Are you beginning to lose faith in him?

MADAME CATHERINE: I don't know what to think. —People are angels one minute and devils the next.

THE INSPECTOR: It's all very odd. We'll just have to wait until we hear his explanation. We can't judge him unheard. Good evening, gentlemen—Madame Catherine. (*Exits.*)

THE ABBÉ: Something unearthly about this, truly!

ADOLPHE: I'd say it's demons at work, out to destroy man.

THE ABBÉ: No, it's either punishment for unknown transgressions—or it's a frightening testing of the soul.

Jeanne enters, in mourning.

JEANNE: Good evening. —Excuse me for asking, but has Maurice been here?

MADAME CATHERINE: No, Madame, but he might come at any moment. . . . I guess that means you haven't seen him since . . .

JEANNE: Not since yesterday morning . . .

MADAME CATHERINE: I can't tell you how sorry I am. You poor dear!

JEANNE: Thank you, Madame. (*To The Abbé.*) —Oh, Father?

THE ABBÉ: My child. I thought I might be of some help. And by a stroke of luck I had a chance to talk to the inspector here.

JEANNE: The inspector! I'm sure he suspects Maurice too, doesn't he?

THE ABBÉ: No, he doesn't. None of us does. It's just that appearances are against him—alarmingly, I must admit.

JEANNE: You mean the conversation the waiter overheard. That doesn't mean a thing. I've heard that sort of talk when Maurice has had a little to drink. He's always carrying on about crime and punishment. Besides, it seems to me that his woman friend said the worst things. Oh, how I'd like to meet her face to face and tell her what I think of her.

ADOLPHE: My dear Jeanne, that woman may have wronged you, but I know she never really meant to. She has no evil intentions, I assure you. Has no intentions at all, as a matter of fact. Just follows the inclinations of her heart. I know her. She's a good woman, and she's got nothing to be ashamed of.

JEANNE: All right, Adolphe. If you say so. That means that I have no one to blame for what happened except myself. I was a fool and that's why I'm being punished now. (*She's cries.*)

THE ABBÉ: Come now, don't be so hard on yourself. I know

you well enough, and I know how seriously you took the responsibilities of being a mother. The fact that there was no time to
give either religious or legal sanction to the birth of the child was
not your fault. No, there is more here than meets the eye.

ADOLPHE: What?

THE ABBÉ: I wish I knew.

Henriette enters, dressed for traveling.

ADOLPHE (*rises resolutely and approaches Henriette*): Henriette?

HENRIETTE: Hello, Adolphe. Where's Maurice?

ADOLPHE: Do you know what —. Or maybe you don't know?

HENRIETTE: I know the whole story. Forgive me, Madame
Catherine, but I'm going out of town, I just had to stop by for
a moment. (*To Adolphe, but indicating Jeanne.*) Who is that?
— Ah!

> *Henriette and Jeanne stare at each other. Emile can be
> seen in the kitchen doorway.*

HENRIETTE (*to Jeanne*): There must be something I can say,
without sounding crude or cynical. But if I simply tell you that
I sympathize as deeply with you in your great sorrow as anyone
closer to you does, you must believe me. . . . You must. I
deserve your pity even if not your forbearance. (*Holds out her
hand toward Jeanne.*)

JEANNE (*staring at her*): I believe you, at least for the moment.
(*She takes Henriette's hand.*)

HENRIETTE (*kissing Jeanne's hand*): Thank you!

JEANNE (*pulling her hand back*): Don't! I don't deserve it! I
don't!

THE ABBÉ: Excuse me, but since we are all together here and,
at least for the moment, in a conciliatory mood, I wonder if
Mademoiselle Henriette might not clear up some of the doubt
and confusion surrounding the main point of the accusation

against Maurice. Could you tell us, as between friends, what you meant when you spoke of killing, of crime, and of the Place de Roquette? We know truly that these words could have had absolutely nothing to do with the death of the little child, but it would relieve us to hear exactly what you were talking about. Won't you tell us?

HENRIETTE (*after a pause*): I can't! I can't tell you!

ADOLPHE: Henriette! What do you mean, you can't tell us? You can't leave us in the dark!

HENRIETTE: I can't tell you. Don't ask me to!

THE ABBÉ: Didn't I say there was something unearthly about this?

HENRIETTE: I knew all along this moment had to come. It had to! (*To Jeanne.*) I swear to you that I am without guilt in the death of your child. Isn't that enough?

JEANNE: Enough for us, perhaps. But what about justice?

HENRIETTE: Justice? If you only knew how right you are!

THE ABBÉ (*to Henriette*): And if you only understood the import of your words!

HENRIETTE: Do you understand them better than I?

THE ABBÉ: I think I do.

Henriette studies The Abbé.

Don't worry. Even if I guess your secret, I won't reveal it. Besides, legal justice is not my concern. But divine grace is.

Maurice, dressed for traveling, enters in a great hurry. Without noticing the rest of the people, who are in the foreground, Maurice goes directly to the counter where Madame Catherine is sitting.

MAURICE: Catherine, don't be mad at me because I didn't show up. Look, I've come here just to beg your forgiveness before I leave. I'm heading south tonight at eight o'clock.

Madame Catherine is stunned, silent.

You are mad at me! (*Looks around.*) What's going on? —Is this a dream, or isn't it? —I can see it's real, but you all look like figures in a wax museum. . . . Jeanne standing like a statue, dressed in black . . . and Henriette looking like a corpse. . . . What does it mean?

General silence.

No one answers—that means it's something terrible!

Silence.

MAURICE: Come on now, answer! —Adolphe, my friend, what is it? —And—(*Indicating Emile.*)—and there's a detective!

ADOLPHE (*coming forward*): Don't you know?

MAURICE: Know what? Tell me!

ADOLPHE: Marion is dead!

MAURICE: Marion . . . dead?!

ADOLPHE: Yes, this morning.

MAURICE (*to Jeanne*): That's why you're in black. Oh, Jeanne, Jeanne, who did this to us? Who?

JEANNE: God took her from us.

MAURICE: But I saw her in the pink of health this very morning! She couldn't just die! Somebody—somebody did this. (*Seeking out Henriette with his eyes.*)

ADOLPHE: Don't look for the guilty party here. No one here did it. But, unfortunately, the police have got leads pointing to the one person who should be above suspicion.

MAURICE: Meaning who?

ADOLPHE: Who do you suppose? Your careless talk last night —and this morning—puts you in a bad light, to say the least!

MAURICE: You mean they were listening to us? —Let me think . . . what were we talking about? . . . Oh! My God!

ADOLPHE: All you have to do is explain why you said those things. We'll believe you!

MAURICE: I can't! I won't! Go ahead and put me in jail, I don't care! Marion is dead . . . dead. . . . And I've killed her!

General commotion.

ADOLPHE: Think what you're saying, Maurice. Don't talk like that!

MAURICE: Like what?

ADOLPHE: You said you killed Marion.

MAURICE: Does anybody really believe that I'm a murderer? —That I could kill my own child? Catherine, you know me. Do you—?

MADAME CATHERINE: I don't know what to believe now. "Out of the abundance of the heart the mouth speaketh."

MAURICE: You don't believe me . . .

ADOLPHE: All you have to do is explain. —Explain what you meant when you said that your "love kills everything that stands in its way."

MAURICE: I see. You know that too! —Maybe Henriette will explain that?

HENRIETTE: You know I can't!

THE ABBÉ: Well, if you don't put your cards on the table, we can't help you. A moment ago I would have sworn you were innocent. Now I wonder.

MAURICE: Jeanne, what you have to say means more than all the rest put together.

JEANNE (*coldly*): Just answer me one thing: when you were having that orgy in that hotel, you swore you wanted someone dead. Who?

MAURICE: Did I? Well, maybe! Yes, yes, I know I'm guilty — but just as much not guilty! Let me out of here. I can never forgive myself.

HENRIETTE (*to Adolphe*): Go with him. He may do something stupid!

ADOLPHE: Why me?

HENRIETTE: Who else?

ADOLPHE (*without bitterness*): You're closer to him. —Wait, there's a carriage stopping outside.

MADAME CATHERINE: It's the inspector! —I've seen a lot in my time, but I've never seen fame and fortune vanish so quickly.

MAURICE (*to Henriette*): From the triumphal chariot to the police wagon!

JEANNE (*simply*): Pulled by an ass—who was that?

ADOLPHE: Me, of course.

The Inspector enters with a summons in his hand.

THE INSPECTOR: Summons to Police Headquarters—at once, tonight—for Maurice Gérard . . . and Henriette Mauclerc. . . . Are you both here?

MAURICE *and* HENRIETTE: Yes!

MAURICE: Are we being arrested?

THE INSPECTOR: No, not yet. You're just being called in for questioning.

MAURICE: And then what?

THE INSPECTOR: Who knows?

Maurice and Henriette go toward the door.

MAURICE: Goodbye, everybody.

Everyone is deeply moved. The Inspector, Maurice, and Henriette leave.

EMILE (*comes in and approaches Jeanne*): Come, Sis, I'll go home with you.

JEANNE: Emile, what do you think of all this?

EMILE: He's innocent!

THE ABBÉ: Too simple. As I see it, it's despicable to break one's promise—and unforgivable when a woman and a child are involved.

EMILE: I'd be inclined to feel the same way, since it's my own sister. But I can't throw any stones. I once made the same kind of mistake myself.

THE ABBÉ: Ah, yes. Well, that doesn't apply to me. Nevertheless, I won't cast the first stone. No need to, as I see it. Actions have a way of judging themselves: the consequences constitute the punishment.

JEANNE: Pray for him! For both of them!

THE ABBÉ: No, I'm not going to do that. It's impertinent to want to change God's mind. And, I tell you, there's certainly something unearthly about all this.

Scene 2

The Auberge des Adrets. Adolphe and Henriette are sitting at the same table at which Maurice and Henriette sat in Act II. Adolphe has a cup of coffee in front of him; Henriette, nothing.

ADOLPHE: You really think he'll come here?

HENRIETTE: I'm absolutely certain. The police released him this noon for lack of evidence. He didn't want to show himself on the streets until after dark.

ADOLPHE: I can imagine how he feels! —You know, since yesterday life has become a horrible nightmare for me, too.

HENRIETTE: What do you think it is for me? I'm afraid to live; I hardly dare to breathe; I'm even afraid to think. Spies everywhere, overhearing me. They even read my thoughts.

ADOLPHE: Yes. So it was here you were sitting that night I couldn't find you!

HENRIETTE: Oh, don't talk about it! I could die of shame when I think of it. Adolphe, you're made of different stuff than Maurice and me—better stuff. . . . (*Adolphe shushes her.*) But you are! What on earth induced me to stay with him? I was lazy, I was tired—he was drunk with success, he enraptured me—I don't know, I can't explain it. Yet, if you had come here, it would never have happened, I know that. —Anyway, today you're on top, and he's at the bottom. A nobody—worse! Yesterday he had one hundred thousand francs; today he doesn't have a sou to his name. They've closed his play. He'll never clear himself with the public after this scandal. Leaving the mother of his child—for another woman! He might just as well have murdered the child. They say he did, anyway. They've got it all figured out: the child died of sorrow, which, in their minds, makes Maurice responsible for her death.

ADOLPHE: Henriette, you know I'm on your side. But I want you above suspicion. Why can't you tell me what you were talking about? It was a party, a happy occasion—why talk about death and executions? It couldn't have been just chance.

HENRIETTE: No, chance had nothing to do with it. We couldn't help ourselves. I don't want to talk about it. Probably because I don't deserve to seem clean or above suspicion in your eyes. Because I'm not.

ADOLPHE: Above suspicion—or clean?

HENRIETTE: Oh, let's change the subject. —Don't you suppose that there are a lot of unpunished criminals walking around? Maybe our closest friends?

ADOLPHE (*fidgeting*): I don't know. What do you mean?

HENRIETTE: Don't you think that everyone at some point in his life has done something he could be punished for if the law knew about it?

ADOLPHE: I'm sure of it. But nothing goes unpunished; conscience takes care of it. (*Stands up and unbuttons his coat.*) And— something else—no one is truly good who hasn't made some bad mistakes. (*Breathes heavily.*) To be able to forgive, you've got to have felt the need to be forgiven. . . . I once had a friend, we called him "Wonder Man" because he never said a bad word about anybody, was ready to forgive everybody and everything, took every insult with a wonderful complacency. He baffled us. Finally, much later in life, he gave me his secret in a nutshell: "I'm full of remorse," he said, "I'm atoning." (*Sits down.*)

Henriette is silent. Looks at him wonderingly.

(*As if to himself.*) Some crimes you can't find in the lawbooks; they're the worst ones because we've got to punish them ourselves, and we're harder on ourselves than any judge or jury could be.

HENRIETTE (*after a pause*): What happened to your friend? Did he stop atoning?

ADOLPHE: He tormented himself for years. Eventually that gave him peace of mind. But life could never hold any joy for him. He could never take a compliment in the right spirit, never felt he was worthy of recognition, didn't dare accept awards. In a word, he could never forgive himself.

HENRIETTE: Never? What had he done?

ADOLPHE: He wanted his father dead. And when his father suddenly died, the son imagined he had murdered him. Such ideas were considered a sign of illness, of course, so they put him away — in an institution. And after a while he came out "sound as a bell" — as they put it. But the guilt feelings were still there, and he went right on punishing himself.

HENRIETTE: You said "imagined." Are you sure he didn't kill his father — by wishing him dead?

ADOLPHE: You mean in some mysterious way?

HENRIETTE: Maybe. Don't you believe that hate can kill? I'm certain that my mother and my family hated Father to death. He had an awful way of being systematically opposed to everything we wanted to do, every inclination we might have, every wish we cherished. And if it was more than just a wish — a desperate, heartfelt need we couldn't live without—he tried to cut it out of our systems. That only made the resistance against him grow. It collected in batteries generating hatred, and the current finally grew so strong he was blasted by it—shriveled—lost all interest—finally wished he were dead.

ADOLPHE: Your conscience never bothered you?

HENRIETTE: No! I don't know what conscience is.

ADOLPHE: Really? You'll soon find out. (*Silence.*) How do you suppose Maurice will look when he walks in here? What do you think he'll say?

HENRIETTE: That's funny. Yesterday morning when we were waiting for you, we tried to guess the same thing about you.

ADOLPHE: And—?

HENRIETTE: We got it all wrong.

ADOLPHE: Tell me, why did you send for me?

HENRIETTE: Wickedness. Arrogance. Sheer cruelty!

ADOLPHE: I don't understand. You confess your sins, but you don't regret them.

HENRIETTE: That's because I don't feel completely responsible for them. They're like dirt on things you handle every day. Some of it's bound to stick on you, but you wash it off at night. Do you really think people are as good as you say they are?

ADOLPHE: I think they're a little bit better than most people think—and a little worse.

HENRIETTE: You're being evasive.

ADOLPHE: No, I'm not. —Will you be evasive if I ask you something? Do you still love Maurice?

HENRIETTE: I won't know until I see him. Right now I don't feel any longing for him. I think I could survive without him.

ADOLPHE: That's probably true. But the fact is your life is now bound up with his. —Quiet!

HENRIETTE: Strange how everything comes again, everything

repeats itself. Exactly the same situation, the same words, as yesterday when we were waiting for you . . .

> *Maurice enters, white as a corpse, hollow-eyed, unshaven.*

MAURICE: Here I am, my friends – if it really is me. I've spent one night in jail, and now I don't know who I am. (*Looks carefully at Henriette and Adolphe.*)

ADOLPHE: Sit down and pull yourself together.

MAURICE (*to Henriette*): Maybe you don't want me around?

ADOLPHE: Cut it out. Why be bitter against us?

MAURICE: In these twenty-four hours I've grown so hateful and suspicious I can't stand to have anyone around. Besides, who wants to keep a murderer company!

HENRIETTE: But you've been cleared!

MAURICE (*producing a newspaper*): By the police, sure, but not by the public. Take a look at the murderer Maurice Gérard, former playwright, and his mistress Henriette Mauclerc, former –

HENRIETTE: They've got my picture! Oh, my God! When my mother sees this – and my family – oh, God!

MAURICE: I even look like a murderer. And they're dropping hints that my play is a plagiarism. What's left of the conquering hero of yesterday? Not one shred. And in my place in all the advertisements stands my enemy and rival Octave, raking in my hundred thousand francs. "Oh, Solon! Solon!"* There's justice for you! And success! Adolphe, you don't know how lucky you are that you haven't been lucky.

HENRIETTE: Evidently you don't know that Adolphe was a great success in London. He walked off with first prize. Got a gold medal for his painting.

---

* See the story of Croesus and Solon in Herodotus's *History* I, chap. 30.

MAURICE (*frowning*): No, I didn't know that. Is it true, Adolphe?

ADOLPHE: It's true enough. But the medal—I sent it back.

HENRIETTE (*pointing it up*): Sent it back! I didn't know that! Maybe you can't accept recognition either—like your friend?

ADOLPHE: My friend—? (*Embarrassed.*) Oh, yes; yes, of course.

MAURICE: Well, Adolphe, your success gladdens me—but it puts a lot of distance between us.

ADOLPHE: I understand. Good fortune or bad, doesn't make any difference. We'll each be alone. My success hurts your feelings. It's a great life!

MAURICE: You shouldn't complain! What about me! It's as if a black veil had been put over my eyes. Everything's there, but nothing's the same. I was in this very room, this very spot, yesterday, but now it's all different. I recognize you—and you—but you're wearing different faces. I sit here fumbling for the right words, and I can't find them. I ought to be defending myself, but I can't. I was better off in jail. At least there weren't any curiosity seekers staring at me. Look at Maurice the murderer! And his loving mistress! But you don't love me anymore, Henriette. And you don't mean a damn thing to me! Today you're ugly—coarse, empty, disgusting.

> *Two Plainclothes Men have quietly seated themselves at one of the rear tables.*

ADOLPHE: Take it easy, Maurice! You're free. You've been cleared of all suspicion. It will be in all the evening papers. There won't be any more accusations; your play will go on again. Listen, if worse comes to worse, you can write a new one. Get away from Paris for a year; let things die down. They loved you because you looked at the bright side. Said people were good and decent. They'll soon be saying the same about you.

MAURICE: Ha! People! Ha!

ADOLPHE: You don't really believe it, do you—that people are good?

MAURICE: Did I ever? It was only a passing mood, a new angle, a courtesy paid to the great beast, the people. I was admired, considered better than the average. And I'm rotten. Imagine what the others are like!

ADOLPHE: I'm going out to buy the evening papers. One of each. After you've read them, we'll see what you have to say.

MAURICE (*turning to the rear*): Two detectives! —You see, they let me go just to keep me under surveillance. They're waiting for me to spout off at the mouth and give myself away!

ADOLPHE: They're not detectives. You're imagining things! I know who they are. (*Starts to leave.*)

MAURICE: Don't leave us alone, Adolphe. I'm afraid Henriette and I might start letting down our hair.

ADOLPHE: Take it easy, Maurice. Don't think of the past, think of your future. Henriette, keep him calm and cool. Be back in a jiffy! (*Leaves.*)

HENRIETTE: Now what's your opinion—about being guilty —or not guilty?

MAURICE: Well, I haven't killed anyone, like some people I know. I was drunk and shooting off at the mouth. You're the one with a crime on your head. It's come back to haunt you, and you've tried to foist it off on me.

HENRIETTE: I like that! Of all the nerve! You cursed your own child—wished she didn't exist—and wanted to run away without saying goodbye. That was you! Who told you to go to Marion and to put in an appearance at Madame Catherine's? Me!

MAURICE: You're right, of course. I'm sorry. You were more thoughtful than I was. It's all my fault. Forgive me. —But still it isn't. I'm not to blame for what's happened. I feel I've been framed, set up. Guilty—not guilty. Not guilty—guilty? It's driving me crazy. —Look at them, sitting there, taking it all in. —And not even a waiter who wants to bother with us. I'm going out to tell them I want a cup of tea. Can I get you something?

HENRIETTE: Nothing, thanks.

Maurice goes out.

FIRST DETECTIVE (*coming over to Henriette*): Hey, Toots! Mind showing me your identification papers?

HENRIETTE: Who the hell do you think you're talking to?!

FIRST DETECTIVE: Watch your tongue, girlie! I'm talking to you!

HENRIETTE: What do you want?

FIRST DETECTIVE: I'm with the vice squad. Yesterday you were here with one guy and today you're here with another. That looks like soliciting to me, and that puts you under my jurisdiction. And they don't serve unescorted ladies here! So out you go. Come on!

HENRIETTE: My escort's coming right back . . .

FIRST DETECTIVE: What escort? He ain't even here.

HENRIETTE: Oh, God! Please—you don't understand. . . . My mother . . . my family! . . . I'm a respectable girl, I tell you.

FIRST DETECTIVE: That's what they all say. Listen, I know you from the papers. You got your picture in them. Now come on!

HENRIETTE: Where? Where are you taking me?

FIRST DETECTIVE: Where do you think? Down to headquarters. We'll give you a little card that authorizes you to get free and compulsory medical checkups!

HENRIETTE: Oh, my God! You're not serious! You can't be!

FIRST DETECTIVE (*grabbing Henriette by the arm*): Does this feel like I'm joking?

HENRIETTE: Oh, God, help me! (*On her knees.*) —Let me go! —Maurice! Help me!

FIRST DETECTIVE: Shut your damn mouth! What a crazy bitch!

Maurice comes in, followed by The Waiter.

THE WAITER: I'm telling you we don't want your sort in this place. Pay your check and get out! And take your floozy with you!

MAURICE (*completely crushed; looks through his billfold*): Henriette, pay for me and let's get out of here. I don't have a cent on me!

THE WAITER: What do you know! I ain't seen that before. The dame paying for her fancy-man.

HENRIETTE (*looking through her purse*): My God! I don't have any money either! Where's Adolphe? Why doesn't he come?

FIRST DETECTIVE: What a couple of crumbs! All right, start unloading. Find something you can leave as security. Tarts like her got lotsa rings on their fingers.

MAURICE: I can't believe this is happening! How could we —

HENRIETTE (*taking a ring off her finger and handing it to The Waiter*): The abbé was right; it's unearthly!

MAURICE: The devil's at work, if you ask me. — Look, if we go now, you know what Adolphe's going to think? — that we deceived him and ran off together.

HENRIETTE: That's right in style with everything else, isn't it? I'm ready to throw myself into the river. How about you?

MAURICE (*taking her by the hand and walking out with her*): End it all? Sure. Why not?

ACT IV

Scene 1

The Luxembourg Gardens. Near the statue of Adam and Eve. The wind is blowing in the trees and whipping up leaves, dried grass, and bits of paper on the ground.

Maurice and Henriette are sitting on a bench.

HENRIETTE: You don't want to die?

MAURICE: I'm not up to it. Can't face that cold grave. With just a sheet on top of me and a little sawdust under. No thanks! Besides, I've got some unfinished business this side of the grave — if I could figure out what it is.

HENRIETTE: I know what you're getting at.

MAURICE: What?

HENRIETTE: Revenge. It's obvious when you think about it. Jeanne and her brother deliberately sent those detectives to embarrass us. It was too perfect. Only a woman could think up that kind of revenge.

MAURICE: My thoughts exactly. — Only you don't go far enough. These past few days have given me some insight. That's what suffering does for you. Think about this: that waiter at the Auberge des Adrets and the *maître d'* at the Pavilion — why weren't they called to testify at the hearing?

HENRIETTE: My God! You're right! I never thought of that. They had no evidence to give because they never overheard anything!

MAURICE: But how could the inspector know exactly what we said?

HENRIETTE: He didn't. He guessed. Deduced it. He saw it was a case of sexual jealousy, and one case is like another.

MAURICE: No, I've got it! Our behavior gave it away. He saw it was a case of a woman and two men. He said we called Adolphe an ass. What else do you call the deceived man? Idiot, usually – right? But we had mentioned a wagon, the triumphal chariot, so it couldn't be "idiot"; it had to be "ass." Simple deduction.

HENRIETTE: What fools they made of us! And we let them get away with it!

MAURICE: That's what we get for blaming ourselves – thinking they're good and we're bad. No more of that! Take that inspector – there's a real bastard for you – there's somebody behind him. There has to be.

HENRIETTE: You mean the abbé, playing private detective.

MAURICE: Exactly! An abbé! He gets to hear confessions. It all fits in! Adolphe himself said he'd been to the Church of Saint-Germain in the morning. What was an atheist like him doing in church? He blabbed, of course, moaned about losing his girl. All the abbé had to do was make up a list of leading questions to give to the inspector.

HENRIETTE: You don't trust Adolphe?

MAURICE: I don't trust anybody, not anymore!

HENRIETTE: Not even Adolphe!

MAURICE: Least of all! How can I? I took his mistress from him.

HENRIETTE: Well, since you started this, I could tell you more. You heard him say that he refused the gold medal he won in London. You know why?

MAURICE: No.

HENRIETTE: Because he treats himself like dirt. Thinks he's unworthy. He once took a penitential vow never to accept any honors.

MAURICE: You're joking! I don't get it. What's he done that's so awful?

HENRIETTE: Some crime not punishable under the law. He virtually admitted it, pretending he was telling me about someone else.

MAURICE: Him too! "The Wonder Man!"—always so sweet and forgiving.

HENRIETTE: That's what I've been telling you. We're not worse than the others. But the devils are on our backs, riding us to hell. It's not fair!

MAURICE: Adolphe, too! I can't get over it. Makes you lose all faith in people. —Listen, if he was capable of one crime, why not others? Maybe he was the one who sicced the police on you yesterday. Come to think of it, didn't he slip away when he saw our pictures in the papers? And he lied when he said those guys weren't detectives! I tell you, a deceived lover is capable of anything—anything!

HENRIETTE: He couldn't be that low. It's impossible!

MAURICE: Why not? Face up to it—he's a bastard. . . . What did you talk about yesterday before I came?

HENRIETTE: He said only good things about you.

MAURICE: You're lying!

HENRIETTE (*controls herself; changes tone*): Listen . . . there's still somebody left whom you haven't cast your suspicions on, and I wonder why. Have you considered Madame Catherine? She's been very shifty—until finally she said straight out that she thought you were capable of anything.

MAURICE: She did, she did! Shows you what she's really like. Anybody who thinks somebody is a bastard for no good reason is a bastard himself! Take my word for it.

> *Henriette looks at him.*
>
> *Silence.*

HENRIETTE: Anybody who thinks somebody is a bastard is a bastard himself.

MAURICE: What are you getting at?

HENRIETTE: What I just said!

MAURICE: Are you implying that I—?

HENRIETTE: That's exactly what I'm implying! Tell me: did you meet anyone besides Marion that morning you went to say goodbye?

MAURICE: Why ask that?

HENRIETTE: One guess!

MAURICE: Well, since you seem to know, yes, I also met Jeanne.

HENRIETTE: Why did you lie to me?

MAURICE: I wanted to spare you.

HENRIETTE: You expect me to believe that, after you've lied to me! Oh, no, dear Maurice; now I believe you did do it. You killed her.

MAURICE: Wait a minute! Wait a minute! I've been blind. These thoughts—sneaking up on me, even though I fought against them. Now I see. It's remarkable that what lies right under your nose is the last thing you see. What you don't want to believe, you don't believe. —Tell me, where were you yesterday morning after we separated in the woods?

HENRIETTE (*uneasily*): I don't understand . . .

MAURICE: Either one of two places: either you were with Adolphe, which you couldn't have been because he was at his art class, or else you were—with Marion!

HENRIETTE: You did kill her, didn't you?

MAURICE: No, you did! You did. You were the only one who would gain anything if the child disappeared—if the rock was removed from the road, as you so aptly phrased it!

HENRIETTE: You said that; I didn't!

MAURICE: The one who stands to gain: that's the legal principle.

HENRIETTE: Oh, Maurice! We're running around in circles, like slaves on a treadmill whipping each other. Let's stop before we drive each other crazy.

MAURICE: You already are!

HENRIETTE: We can't go on like this, Maurice. Let's break it off, before we go insane.

MAURICE: All right. Let's.

HENRIETTE (*standing up*): Goodbye then.

> *Two Plainsclothes men can be seen at the rear. Henriette turns around and goes back to Maurice.*

Those two men again!

MAURICE: The dark angels who want to drive us out of the garden.

HENRIETTE: And who force us to come together – like metals being welded.

MAURICE: Welded, yes. Or do you mean wedded? Should we? Build a little nest; shut our doors on the world; find some kind of peace?

HENRIETTE: Lock ourselves in a torture chamber? The community property would be two skeletons in the closet. You'd torture me by bringing up Adolphe's name; I'd torture you by reminding you of Jeanne – and Marion.

MAURICE: Don't. Don't mention her. You know she's being buried today – perhaps at this very hour.

HENRIETTE: Why aren't you at the funeral?

MAURICE: Jeanne and the police both warned me off. My presence, they said, might inflame the crowd.

HENRIETTE: Besides everything else, you're a coward.

MAURICE: When it comes to failings, I lack for none. What did you ever see in me?

HENRIETTE: A couple of days ago you were a different person, worth loving.

MAURICE: And now I'm in the gutter.

HENRIETTE: No. But you're decking yourself with borrowed vices.

MAURICE: Borrowed? From whom? You?

HENRIETTE: You might say. Because when you appear to be getting worse, right away I feel a little bit better.

MAURICE: Like lovers transmitting diseases to each other.

HENRIETTE: On top of everything else you're coarse—vulgar.

MAURICE: You don't have to tell me. I don't feel I'm the same person since that night in jail. They locked up one guy and let out another—through the gates that separate us from society. Right now I feel like the enemy of all mankind. I'd like to set fire to the whole earth and dry up the seven seas. Nothing less than a *Götterdämmerung* can wipe out my shame.

HENRIETTE: I got a letter from my mother today. She's a widow. Father was a major. She had a proper upbringing, very genteel, and she's got old-fashioned ideas about honor and marriage and such things. Do you want to read it? —No, of course you don't. Do you know that I've become virtually an outcast? Nobody—I mean people with reputations—wants to be seen in my company. And if I walk around alone, the police will harass me. Don't you see? We have to get married.

MAURICE: We disgust each other, so we have to marry each other! Sounds like hell on earth. One thing, Henriette; if we're going to spend the rest of our lives together, you've got to tell me your secret—to even the odds and make a fair game of it.

HENRIETTE: All right. . . . I had a girlfriend, who got herself into trouble. You know, the usual story. I wanted to help her because her whole future was at stake. So. . . . But I bungled the job, and she . . . didn't survive.

MAURICE: You were foolish. You shouldn't have gotten involved. But you were trying to do the right thing; I can see that.

HENRIETTE: That's what you say now. But the next time you get mad at me, you'll use it against me.

MAURICE: No, I won't. The trouble is that it weakens my trust in you. And I'll be afraid to have you around. The girl's lover is still around, isn't he?—and knows what you did?

HENRIETTE: He went along with it!

MAURICE: That's what bothers me. Suppose his conscience should start gnawing at him? It happens, you know. Suppose he can't stand it and tells the whole story to the police.

HENRIETTE: You think I haven't thought about that? Those thoughts are always there, right behind me. That's why I live as fast as I can. I don't want to stop and let those thoughts catch up with me.

MAURICE: But you want to bring them into our marriage – as part of the community property. That's a bit much, isn't it?

HENRIETTE: It wasn't a bit much when I shared the shame and dishonor of Maurice the murderer!

MAURICE: For God's sake, let's get off this merry-go-round.

HENRIETTE: You're not getting off yet. Oh, no! Not until I've stripped you naked. You're not going to go around thinking yourself better than I am. Oh, no, you're not!

MAURICE: You want to fight. All right, if that's what you want!

HENRIETTE: A fight to the finish!

A roll of drums is heard in the distance.

MAURICE: They're closing the garden. . . . "Cursed is the ground for thy sake; . . . thorns and thistles shall it bring forth to thee."

HENRIETTE: "And the Lord said unto the woman . . . "

A CARETAKER (*in uniform. Politely*): Sorry, Madam, Monsieur; we have to close the garden.

Scene 2

The Crêmerie. Madame Catherine at the counter, making entries in her ledger. Adolphe and Henriette at a table.

ADOLPHE (*relaxed and friendly*): I swear to you for the last time: I did not sneak away from you. I thought you had gone off and deserted me. You've got to believe me.

HENRIETTE: But why did you tell us they weren't detectives?

ADOLPHE: I really didn't think they were. I was only trying to reassure you.

HENRIETTE: All right; if you say so, I believe you. But, then, you've got to believe me now. I've got these deep suspicions, and I can't harbor them any longer.

ADOLPHE: Very well.

HENRIETTE: And you mustn't tell me I'm seeing things or imagining them.

ADOLPHE: It sounds like you're afraid you are.

HENRIETTE: Nothing of the sort. But I know how skeptical you are. Anyway, you mustn't tell anybody. Promise?

ADOLPHE: Promise.

HENRIETTE: It's just too horrible! . . . I'm half certain that Maurice is guilty. Really. I've got evidence.

ADOLPHE: What!

HENRIETTE: Let me finish; then you can judge for yourself. —When Maurice said goodbye to me in the woods, he told me he wanted to see Marion alone, while her mother was out. But now we know that he met Marion's mother. In other words, he was lying to me!

ADOLPHE: Possibly. Maybe he had a good reason. Doesn't make him a murderer.

HENRIETTE: Don't you understand? Don't you see?

ADOLPHE: See what?

HENRIETTE: You don't want to see! —All right. There's nothing for me to do but tell the police. Then we'll see if he can come up with an alibi.

ADOLPHE: Henriette, you've got to listen to me. You've got to hear the truth, even if it hurts. You're pushing each other over the edge. I'm not joking. You both feel—to some extent—guilty. And that makes you—him and you both—suspect each other of anything and everything. . . . Tell me if I'm wrong: he suspects you of having killed Marion. Doesn't he?

HENRIETTE: He's that crazy, yes!

ADOLPHE: His suspicions are crazy but yours aren't?

HENRIETTE: Show me where I'm wrong. Prove my suspicions aren't justified.

ADOLPHE: That's easy. The coroner revised his report. They found that Marion died of some sort of disease—with an odd name I've forgotten.

HENRIETTE: Am I supposed to believe that?

ADOLPHE: It's in today's papers—the coroner's report.

HENRIETTE: I don't believe it! It could have been faked!

ADOLPHE: Cut it out, Henriette! Calm down. You're driving yourself crazy. And be careful about making reckless accusations. You might land in jail. Easy does it. (*He places his hand on her head.*) Do you hate Maurice?

HENRIETTE: Immeasurably!

ADOLPHE: If love can turn to hate, it must have been cankered to begin with.

HENRIETTE (*calming down*): What am I going to do? Tell me. You're the only one who understands me.

ADOLPHE: You don't want my sermons.

HENRIETTE: Is that all you've got to offer?

ADOLPHE: That's all. But they have helped me.

HENRIETTE: All right. Get up in your pulpit.

ADOLPHE: To start with, you've got to turn your hatred against yourself. Lance your own boils. And cut out the core.

HENRIETTE: You'll have to explain that.

ADOLPHE: First of all, leave Maurice. If you're apart from each other, you can't feed on each other's guilt. Give up your career as an artist. You only took it up because you wanted to get away from home—so you could lead a carefree existence. An artist's life! Well, you see how carefree it's been. Go home to your mother.

HENRIETTE: Never!

ADOLPHE: All right. Go somewhere else then.

HENRIETTE: You know a lot about these things, don't you? And I can guess why. I know why you refused to accept the gold medal.

ADOLPHE: You saw through that little story of mine?

HENRIETTE (*nods*): What did you do to find peace of mind?

ADOLPHE: Just what I told you to do. I admitted my guilt, took on the burden of it, felt remorse, decided to change my life, and settled down to a life of penance.

HENRIETTE: How can I feel remorse if I don't have a conscience? Is remorse a matter of grace, like faith?

ADOLPHE: Isn't everything? But it doesn't come unless you apply yourself. . . . So apply yourself.

Henriette is silent.

Don't wait too long. There's a time limit on applications. If you're late, you'll be turned out, and then there's no turning back.

HENRIETTE (*after a moment's silence*): Conscience—is it the fear of being punished?

ADOLPHE: No. It's the disgust our better half feels for the misdeeds of our worse half.

HENRIETTE: Then I must have a conscience, too?

ADOLPHE: Of course you have. But—

HENRIETTE: Tell me, Adolphe: are you what's called religious?

ADOLPHE: Not a bit.

HENRIETTE: It's all so strange. . . . What is religion, anyway?

ADOLPHE: I haven't the faintest idea. I don't think anyone has. Sometimes it strikes me that it's a punishment, because the only ones who get religion are the ones who suffer from a bad conscience.

HENRIETTE: A punishment. Yes. . . . Now I know what I have to do. —Goodbye, Adolphe.

ADOLPHE: You're leaving?

HENRIETTE: Yes, I'm leaving. Going where you said. —Goodbye, dear Adolphe. —Goodbye, Catherine.

MADAME CATHERINE: Are you off in such a hurry?

HENRIETTE: Yes.

ADOLPHE: Do you want me to go with you?

HENRIETTE: No. I want to go alone. That's the way I came in—one spring day—thinking I belonged where I didn't belong, and believing there was something called freedom, which doesn't exist! . . . Goodbye. (*Leaves.*)

MADAME CATHERINE: I hoped she'd never come here again. I wish she had never come here in the first place!

ADOLPHE: Who knows? Maybe she had some purpose to serve here. Anyway, she deserves sympathy, tons of it.

MADAME CATHERINE: Don't we all!

ADOLPHE: She's done less harm than we have, if you ask me.

MADAME CATHERINE: Possibly; but I doubt it.

ADOLPHE: You're always so hard and stern, Catherine. Why? Haven't you ever done anything wrong?

MADAME CATHERINE: Of course I have, I'm a poor sinner like everybody else. But if you've fallen through the ice once, you've got a right—I'd say a duty—to warn the others: "Danger!" Doesn't mean you're stern or heartless. Didn't I say to Maurice the instant that woman walked in here: danger, stay away! But he didn't listen. He went right ahead, like a stubborn, naughty child. And people who behave that way should get a spanking.

ADOLPHE: Hasn't he had his spanking?

MADAME CATHERINE: Apparently he didn't get spanked hard enough. He's still mad at the world.

ADOLPHE: A spanking! That's what most people think is the answer to a very involved matter.

MADAME CATHERINE: Bosh! You sit around cudgeling your brains, philosophizing about your wicked ways, and in the meantime, the police have solved the problem. Now leave me alone. I'm trying to add.

ADOLPHE: Here comes Maurice!

MADAME CATHERINE: Yes, God have mercy on him!

MAURICE (*comes in, flushed and excited; sits down with Adolphe*): Hello! Hello!

> *Madame Catherine nods and continues to add her accounts.*

ADOLPHE: Are you all right?

MAURICE: I am now. Because the pieces are beginning to fall into place!

ADOLPHE (*handing Maurice a newspaper, which he does not take*): So you've seen the paper?

MAURICE: No, I've had enough of papers – nothing but libels.

ADOLPHE: Better read it before you say anything more.

MAURICE: Forget it! Same old lies. I've got some real news for you! You want to know who committed the murder? I'll tell you who.

ADOLPHE: No one did. No one!

MAURICE: For fifteen minutes the child was left alone. And where was Henriette during that time? She was *there*! And she's the one who did it.

ADOLPHE: Oh, come off it, you're nuts.

MAURICE: Oh, no, I'm not! Henriette's nuts. She thinks I did it! She's threatened to turn me in to the police!

ADOLPHE: Henriette was just here and said exactly the same thing. You're both nuts! The doctors reexamined the evidence and found that Marion died from a well-known disease—only I can't remember the name of it.

MAURICE: I don't believe it!

ADOLPHE: That's what she said too. But the coroner's report is in the papers.

MAURICE: Coroner's report? . . . Ha! Probably faked to get somebody off the hook.

ADOLPHE: She said so, too. You're both sick. But at least I got through to her. She realized what was happening to her.

MAURICE: Where did she go?

ADOLPHE: To start over.

MAURICE (*hesitates; calms down*): Were you at the funeral?

ADOLPHE: Yes, I was there.

MAURICE: Well?

ADOLPHE: Jeanne has resigned herself to the situation. She has nothing against you.

MAURICE: She's a good woman.

ADOLPHE: Then why did you give her up?

MAURICE: I was in a crazy mood. Thought the world was my oyster. . . . And we were drinking champagne.

ADOLPHE: And Jeanne cried when you drank champagne.

MAURICE: Yes, now I see why. I've written to ask her to forgive me. . . . Do you think she will?

ADOLPHE: I believe so. She can't hate anyone.

MAURICE: Do you think she'll forgive me completely? Let me come back to her?

ADOLPHE: I don't know about that. After what you did to her, you can hardly expect her to trust herself with you again.

MAURICE: I still feel she keeps a corner of her heart for me. I know she'll come back.

ADOLPHE: That's pretty presumptuous. You suspected her and her decent, hardworking brother of taking revenge by sending the police to pick up Henriette as an unregistered prostitute! And now you think she'll take you back!

MAURICE: She wasn't taking revenge. She was only—. What I mean is—well, Emile's got a great sense of humor, I'll bet.

MADAME CATHERINE: You think he'd play a dirty trick like that? He may be only a workingman, but if only everyone was as decent and upstanding as he! He's a perfect gentleman: understanding, tactful—

EMILE (*entering*): Monsieur Gérard?

MAURICE: Yes, that's me.

EMILE: Pardon me, but I've got something to say to you in private.

MAURICE: You can say it here. We're all friends.

The Abbé enters and sits down.

EMILE (*glancing at The Abbé*): I still think it might be better if—

MAURICE: It doesn't matter. The abbé is also a friend of mine, even if we don't have the same views.

EMILE: I guess you know who I am. My sister has simply asked me to give you this package as her reply to your letter.

Maurice takes the package and opens it.

There's only one thing I've got to add. Since I seem to be my sister's guardian, and speaking for her and for myself, I acknowledge that Monsieur Gérard is freed from all obligations, now that the natural bond between you and her is no longer there.

MAURICE: No hard feelings?

EMILE: Why should there be hard feelings? On the other hand,

I'd very much like to hear you apologize, Monsieur Gérard, here in the presence of your friends, for believing that either I or my sister would be capable of such a low trick as sending the police to pick up Mademoiselle Henriette.

MAURICE: I withdraw those remarks. And I offer you my sincere apologies, if you'll be good enough to accept them.

EMILE: Accepted. Thanks. Good evening, everybody. (*Leaves.*)

ALL: Good evening.

MAURICE: The tie and the gloves that Jeanne gave me for the opening night of my play. I let Henriette throw them into the fire. . . . How did they get here? Everything is dug up again, everything comes back! . . . When she gave these to me at the cemetery, she said she wanted to see me looking my best. She wanted everyone to admire me. . . . But she stayed home alone. How it must have hurt her! How could it not? . . . I don't belong in the company of decent people. God! what have I done! Mocked the gift of a good heart, ridiculed the sacrifice made for my success. I threw this away. And for what! A laurel wreath that lies in a garbage can—a marble bust that belongs in the pillory. —Father, let me come to you.

THE ABBÉ: Welcome.

MAURICE: Give me comfort. Ease my heart.

THE ABBÉ: Do you expect me to contradict you and tell you that you have done nothing wrong?

MAURICE: Just say what is right.

THE ABBÉ: Since you ask, let me say I think your behavior has been every bit as disgusting as you've said it is.

MAURICE: What am I going to do? I can't go on like this.

THE ABBÉ: You know the answer to that as well as I do.

MAURICE: No. All I know is that I'm lost. My life is ruined; my career over before it got started; my honor and reputation forever destroyed.

THE ABBÉ: Ah! So that's why you turn your eyes to another and better world, which you now begin to believe in?

MAURICE: Yes, that's right.

THE ABBÉ: You've lived in the flesh, and now you want to live in the spirit. Are you quite certain that there is nothing in this world that can still tempt you?

MAURICE: Nothing! Fame is an illusion, gold is dry dust, and women are merely intoxicants. Let me hide myself behind your hallowed walls. Let me forget this terrible nightmare that lasted for two days and seemed like two eternities.

THE ABBÉ: Very well. But this is no place to arrange these matters. Let us meet in Saint-Germain tonight at nine o'clock. I happen to be preaching to the penitents of Saint-Lazare. This can be your first step on the long, hard road of penance.

MAURICE: Penance?

THE ABBÉ: Yes, I thought you wished to—

MAURICE: Oh, yes, yes . . . of course.

THE ABBÉ: There will be vigils from midnight until two.

MAURICE: That will be wonderful, glorious.

THE ABBÉ: Give me your hand. I don't want you looking back!

MAURICE (*standing up and offering his hand*): Here is my hand, and all my heart!

THE WAITRESS (*entering from the kitchen*): Telephone call for Monsieur Gérard!

MAURICE: From whom?

THE WAITRESS: From the theater.

> Maurice tries to break away from The Abbé, but The Abbé holds him fast by the hand.

THE ABBÉ (*to The Waitress*): Did you ask what it's about?

THE WAITRESS: Yes. They wanted to know if Monsieur Gérard would be at the play tonight.

THE ABBÉ (*to Maurice, who is trying to get away*): Oh, no, I shan't let go!

MAURICE: Play? What are you talking about?

ADOLPHE: Well, you wouldn't read the papers!

MADAME CATHERINE *and* THE ABBÉ: You haven't read the paper!

MAURICE: I've had enough of lies and slanders! (*To The Waitress.*) Tell them I can't go to the theater tonight. Tell them I'm busy. Tell them I'm going to church!

The Waitress goes out to the kitchen.

ADOLPHE: Since you won't read the papers, I guess I'll have to give you the news. Now that you've been cleared, the theater is putting on your play again. And your literary friends have arranged to give you an ovation on the stage – a tribute to a great new talent!

MAURICE: You're joking! It can't be true!

ALL: It is true! It's no joke.

MAURICE (*after some moments of silence*): I don't deserve it.

THE ABBÉ: Good.

ADOLPHE: That's not all, Maurice!

MAURICE (*his face hidden in his hands*): Not all?

MADAME CATHERINE: A hundred thousand francs, Maurice! You see, they've come back too! And the villa outside the city! Everything comes back – except Henriette!

THE ABBÉ (*smiling*): Madame Catherine should take this matter a little more seriously.

MADAME CATHERINE: I can't, I can't. I can't keep a straight face any longer. (*She explodes into laughter, covering her mouth with her handkerchief.*)

ADOLPHE: Hey, Maurice! Eight o'clock at the theater!

THE ABBÉ: Nine o'clock at the church!

ADOLPHE: Maurice!

MADAME CATHERINE: Well, playwright? How are you going to end this?

Maurice puts his head on the table and wraps his arms over his head.

ADOLPHE: Release him from his pledge, Father!

THE ABBÉ: No, indeed I shan't. It's not up to me to release him or bind him.

MAURICE (*standing up*): Very well. I'll go with you, Father.

THE ABBÉ: No, young man. I have nothing to give you except a good scolding and you can give yourself that. And you have other obligations—to yourself and to your public. The fact that you've learned your lesson so fast indicates to me that you have suffered as much as if it had lasted an eternity. And if Providence has given you absolution, what more can I do?

MAURICE: But why was I punished so severely? I was innocent.

THE ABBÉ: Severely? Two days! And you weren't innocent. We're also accountable for our words, our thoughts, our desires. And you murdered in your thoughts when some demon in you wished that your child were not alive.

MAURICE: You're right, of course. —But I stick to my decision. Tonight I meet you at the church to settle accounts with myself. Tomorrow—I go to the theater.

MADAME CATHERINE: Maurice, I think you've got it!

ADOLPHE: I know he's got it!

THE ABBÉ: Why, I believe he has!

Introduction

to

The Dance of Death

Ambrose Bierce defined marriage as "a community consisting of a master, a mistress, and two slaves—making, in all, two." *The Dance of Death* is often interpreted to be about such a community, another version of the marital hell that Strindberg had depicted in *The Father*. It isn't. The sexual conflict is not fundamental in this play, and the strongest scenes do not reveal any bedroom secrets. Rather, the life of the senses is pitted against the life of the spirit. The title alludes to the medieval dance that pictured the omnipresence of death and reminded mortals that at any moment death might seize them and bring them to judgment.

Nor does *The Dance of Death* describe Strindberg's own marriage. The wife and husband in the play were modeled after Strindberg's sister Anna and her husband, Hugo Philp. Anna was musically gifted, but, like Alice in the play, her career and her love of music suffered because of her marriage to a man who had no artistic interests or inclinations. Hugo was a hardened materialist, unchanged in his outlook since his youth when he and Strindberg had been close friends. After Strindberg was blinded by the light on the road to Damascus and renounced the law of materialism, he put a great distance between himself and Hugo. He described his brother-in-law as "a black-hearted man, a despairing, anguished man, who believed in nothing but muscle power and malevolence—a cartload of topsoil, as he referred to himself" (*En blå bok*). Strindberg wrote *The Dance of Death* (Part One) in 1900, some months after Hugo, ill with diabetes, had suffered a heart attack. Like Curt in the play, Strindberg had stayed with him overnight on that occasion.

Written two years after *To Damascus, The Dance of Death* is another symbolic drama about a spiritual conversion. The round room, the setting sun, the churning sea, the pacing sentry, the telegraph apparatus, the grotesque dances, first Edgar's and later Alice's, are all elements in a spiritual drama in which Edgar comes so close to the line that divides the living from the dead, the body from the soul, that he catches a glimmering of what the life of the spirit is all about. Put more prosaically, his close brush with death makes him realize that he is more than a cartload of fertilizer in a Darwinian world and causes him to look at his fellow creatures with a more tolerant eye.

The five scenes of the play (Strindberg objected to act divisions, but costume and makeup changes made an intermission necessary) image a descent into a Swedenborgian hell, which is not a place but a state of mind in which physical needs and desires are dominant, and self-interest governs. After Edgar suffers a heart attack and learns that his wife is going to betray him, there occurs an influx of spirit, brought about by his anguish, and represented on stage in a remarkable actor's scene that is all pantomime.

The Dance of Death contains two magnificent roles: Edgar, a full-length portrait of domestic egomania, a parlor Napoleon; and Alice, his wife, the aborted actress, her career cut short by her marriage, who turns her home into a stage for her scenes of flamboyant rage, and who scarcely knows herself when she is acting and when she is not. Actors can, if they have the right temperaments, make comic mayhem of some of the scenes, and quite properly. Hell, not heaven, as the great poets have known is a place of laughter.

The Dance of Death is definitely not a tragedy. Although Strindberg is usually thought of as a gloomy writer, there is much more optimism in his work than in Beckett's, for instance. *Waiting for Godot*, a fashionably pessimistic play, has the same cyclical structure as Strindberg's play, the end linking up with the beginning. In *Godot*, nothing changes; everything will go on in the same ineffably boring way. In *The Dance of Death*, Edgar acquires a new outlook. He is wiser and more understanding than he was at the beginning.

Rilke understood. After seeing *The Dance of Death*, he said that "at first it seems so hopelessly obstinate to present humanity's disconsolation as its absolute condition, but when someone like this has power over even the most disconsolate, there hovers above the whole, unspoken, a concept of illimitable human greatness. And a desperate love."

The Dance of Death

(Dödsdansen)

Part One

CHARACTERS

EDGAR, captain in the Coast Artillery Corps
ALICE, his wife, formerly an actress
CURT, superintendent of the quarantine station
JENNY, a maid
AN OLD WOMAN
SENTRY

Scene: A military installation on an island in the Baltic Sea off the coast of Sweden.

Time: About 1900.

Scene: A round room, the interior of a fortress tower built of granite and situated on an island off the coast. At the rear, a wide, arched doorway with glass doors like French windows, through which can be seen an artillery emplacement, a large gun, the parapet, the shoreline, and the sea itself.

On each side of this doorway are windows with deep sills holding flowerpots and a birdcage. To the right of the doorway, an upright piano. Downstage of it, a small drop-leaf worktable with two armchairs on each side. Left of stage center is a flattop desk with telegraph apparatus on it. Farther downstage is a whatnot or étagère displaying portrait photographs. Near it, a chaise lounge. Against the wall, a sideboard.

A lamp hangs from the ceiling. Fastened to the wall near the piano are two large laurel wreaths with ribbons attached to them, and between the wreaths hangs the picture of a woman in theatrical costume.

By the doorway, a hat tree. Hanging on it, a military uniform, a sword, a belt, a helmet. Next to it, a secretary-bookcase with a hinged front. On its ledge, a candelabrum with six branches. Candlesticks on the desk, piano, and elsewhere.

On the wall to the left of the door, a mercury barometer.

[1]

It is a warm evening. The glass doors are wide open, and one can see the Sentry on duty guarding the artillery battery, pacing back and forth on the platform outside the doorway. He is wearing a helmet with crest. Now and then his saber, which he carries at a slant to his shoulder, glitters as it catches the red rays of the setting sun. The sea is dark and quiet.

Edgar is sitting in the armchair to the left of the work-table, thumbing and twirling the butt of a burned-out cigar. He is in fatigue dress, rather threadbare, and has on riding boots with spurs. He looks tired and bored.

Alice is sitting in the chair to the right, doing nothing. She looks tired but watchful.

EDGAR: How about playing something for me?

ALICE (*indifferently, not sharply*): Such as?

EDGAR: Something *you* like, my sweet.

ALICE: My repertoire is not to your taste.

EDGAR: Nor mine to yours.

ALICE (*avoiding a confrontation*): You want the doors left open?

EDGAR: Whatever you wish, my pet.

ALICE: All right, we'll leave them open. (*Pause.*) You're not smoking. Why not?

EDGAR: They don't seem to agree with me. Too strong.

ALICE (*almost kindly*): Get some milder ones. It's your only joy—so you say.

EDGAR: Joy? Where have I heard that word?

ALICE: Why ask me? It's as strange to me as it is to you. . . . Time for your whiskey, isn't it?

EDGAR: I'm going to hold off for a little while. . . . What's for supper?

ALICE: How should I know? Ask Christine.

EDGAR: About time for the mackerel to be running. It's autumn.

ALICE: Yes; autumn.

EDGAR: Autumn outside, autumn inside. However, even

though the autumn does bring with it the cold – outside and inside – a grilled mackerel, served with a slice of lemon, a glass of white Burgundy on the side, has something to be said for it.

ALICE: Food does make you eloquent.

EDGAR: Do we have any Burgundy left in the wine cellar?

ALICE: As I recall, we haven't for the last five years had a wine cellar.

EDGAR: You're so disorganized, Alice. Always have been. Well, we've got to stock up on provisions, for our silver wedding anniversary.

ALICE: You don't really intend to celebrate that!

EDGAR: Naturally!

ALICE: It would be more natural if we hid our misery – twenty-five years of it.

EDGAR: Dear, sweet Alice: miserable they may have been, but we've had our fun – now and then. Time is short and we've got to make the best of it. Time has an end.

ALICE: An end? If only there might be.

EDGAR: There is. An end. Period. Then you take what's left, put it in a wheelbarrow, and use it to fertilize the garden.

ALICE: There must be a simpler way to fertilize a garden.

EDGAR: That's the way it is. I didn't arrange it.

ALICE: Much ado about nothing. (*Pause.*) Has the mail come?

EDGAR: Yes.

ALICE: Did the butcher's bill come?

EDGAR: Yes.

ALICE: How much was it?

> *Edgar takes a sheet of paper from his pocket, puts his spectacles on his nose, and makes a stab at reading the bill. Then takes off his glasses.*

EDGAR: Read it yourself. I can't see anymore.

ALICE: What's the matter with your eyes?

EDGAR: Don't know.

ALICE: Age.

EDGAR: Nonsense! Me?

ALICE: Not me, certainly.

Edgar mutters.

ALICE (*looking at the bill*): Can you pay this?

EDGAR: Of course. (*Spitefully.*) But not today. Later.

ALICE: Later? —When you're placed on the retired list with a small pension? No good. Later, when you get sick again?

EDGAR: Sick? I've never been sick in my life. A little under the weather, maybe—once. I'll be around for another twenty years.

ALICE: Doctor doesn't think so.

EDGAR: That sawbones!

ALICE: He's a doctor. Who else knows about sickness?

EDGAR: I'm not sick. I've never had any sickness. And I'm not going to have any. I'm going to drop down dead—bam!—like a soldier in the field.

ALICE: Speaking of the doctor—you know he's giving a party tonight?

EDGAR (*riled*): What of it? . . . We're not invited because we don't associate with the doctor and his wife. And we don't associate with the doctor and his wife because we don't want to, and we don't want to because I despise them both! Scum!

ALICE: You call everybody scum.

EDGAR: Because everybody is scum.

ALICE: Except you.

EDGAR: Yes. Because I have conducted myself like a respectable human being no matter what happened. That's why I'm not scum. (*Pause.*)

ALICE: How about a game of cards?

EDGAR: Fire away.

ALICE (*takes a deck of cards from a drawer in the worktable and shuffles them*): You know the doctor gets the regimental band to play at his private parties.

EDGAR (*furious*): Because he pals around in town with the colonel. Playing footsie – that's all it takes!

ALICE (*dealing and turning up trumps*): Gerda was my good friend once. False friend, I found out.

EDGAR: You should have known better; you can't trust anybody. – What's trump?

ALICE: Put your glasses on.

EDGAR: Doesn't help. (*Impatiently.*) Well? – well?

ALICE: Spades is trump.

EDGAR (*disgruntled*): Spades?

ALICE (*leading a card*): Be that as it may, the fact is the wives of the new officers have blackballed us.

EDGAR (*playing a card and taking the trick*): So what! Who's going to notice? We never give any parties. I can be alone. Always have been.

ALICE: So can I. But what about the children? They're growing up without any friends.

EDGAR: They can make their own friends in town. – That one's mine. Do you have any trumps left?

ALICE: One. This one's mine.

EDGAR: Six and eight make fifteen.

ALICE: Fourteen. Fourteen.

EDGAR: Six and eight gives me fourteen. I've even forgotten how to add. And two makes sixteen. (*Yawns.*) Your deal.

ALICE: You're tired.

EDGAR (*dealing*): Not a bit.

ALICE (*listening to sounds in the distance*): You can hear the music all the way out here. (*Pause.*) You think Curt was invited?

EDGAR: Probably; he arrived this morning. Would have had all day to unpack his tuxedo. Even though he hasn't found time to call on us!

ALICE: Superintendent of the quarantine station. What do you know? Are they really going to have a quarantine station here?

EDGAR: Yes. Yes.

ALICE: Well, he's my cousin, in any case. He and I once bore the same name—

EDGAR: Hardly an honor—

ALICE: Listen, Edgar—(*Sharply.*) Leave my family alone, and I'll leave yours alone. Otherwise—

EDGAR: All right, all right! Don't let's start that again!

ALICE: Doesn't a superintendent of quarantine have to be a doctor?

EDGAR: No. It's only a civil service job—administration, book-keeping. Anybody can do it. How do you think he got the job? He never amounted to anything.

ALICE: Poor Curt . . .

EDGAR: Poor! He cost me plenty. And leaving his wife and children like that! Disgraceful!

ALICE: Easy does it, Edgar.

EDGAR: I say disgraceful! . . . What the hell was he up to in America anyway? What? . . . I can't honestly say I long to see him. . . . But he was a decent chap, I'll give him that. At least you could have an intelligent argument with him.

ALICE: You mean he always gave in to you.

EDGAR (*haughtily*): Whether he gave in or not, he was still a person you could talk to. . . . On this island there isn't one damn person, not one, who understands what I'm talking about. It's a community of idiots.

ALICE: Odd, how Curt should come here just in time for our silver anniversary—whether or not we celebrate it.

EDGAR: What's so odd about that? —Oh, I see what you mean. Curt brought us together, didn't he? Or gave you away, as they say.

ALICE: Yes, he did.

EDGAR: Did he not! Just an idea he had. Hitching you and me together. Brilliant—wouldn't you say?

ALICE: Just popped into his head.

EDGAR: Yes, but we had to pay for it—not him.

ALICE: I might still be in the theater. All my old friends are stars now.

EDGAR (*standing up*): You see what I mean. . . . Now it's time for my whiskey. (*He goes to the cupboard and mixes himself a whiskey and water, which he drinks standing.*) What we need here is a footrail—to rest one's foot on. You could imagine yourself in Copenhagen, the American Bar.

ALICE: If all it takes to recall Copenhagen is a footrail, let's install one. Our happiest times, weren't they?

EDGAR (*pouring his drink down*): Yes. Remember Nimbs Restaurant? The *navarin aux pommes*? (*Smacks his lips.*)

ALICE: No, I remember the orchestra concerts at Tivoli.

EDGAR: That's what I like about you, Alice. All that culture.

ALICE: You ought to be happy that someone around here has some taste—

EDGAR: Oh, I am, I am.

ALICE: Everybody needs something to brag about—even you.

EDGAR (*drinking*): They must be dancing at the doctor's. I can hear the tubas. Oompah, oompah. Three-quarter time. Oompah, oompah.

ALICE: I can hear the melody. The "Alcazar Waltz." God, when was the last time I went waltzing?

EDGAR. You think you can still dance, Twinkle Toes?

ALICE: Ha!

EDGAR: Come off it! Your dancing days are over—like mine.

ALICE: I'm ten years younger than you.

EDGAR: That makes us exactly the same age. The lady is supposed to be ten years younger to even things up.

ALICE: How can you say that with a straight face? You're an old man. And I'm in the prime of life.

EDGAR: Of course you are. And you're so charming and gracious, sweet Alice—toward others. And how you lay it on.

ALICE: Should we light the lamp now?

EDGAR: Good idea!

ALICE: Then ring for Jenny.

> *Edgar goes slowly and stiffly to the desk and rings a bell. Jenny enters from the right.*

EDGAR: Jenny, be a good girl and light the lamp for us. Hm?

ALICE (*sharply*): Light the lamp, he said. The ceiling lamp!

JENNY (*saucily*): Yes, ma'am! (*She lights the ceiling lamp, while Edgar watches her attentively. Then she starts to clean the lamp on the desk.*)

ALICE (*cuttingly*): Is that what you call wiping the chimney?

JENNY: Yes, I think so.

ALICE: Think so! What kind of answer is that?

EDGAR: Now, now. She's doing her best.

ALICE (*to Jenny*): Go! Get out! I'll light the lamp myself. I have to do everything around here.

JENNY: Yes, you may have to . . . (*She starts to leave.*)

ALICE (*standing up*): Go! Get out!

JENNY (*turning at the door*): I just wonder what you would say, ma'am, if I really did go.

> *Alice is silent. Jenny exits. Edgar crosses over and lights the lamp.*

ALICE (*uneasily*): You don't really think she'll give notice?

EDGAR: Wouldn't surprise me. We'd really be up the creek.

ALICE: It's all your fault. You spoil them.

EDGAR: That's not so. You can see for yourself they're always polite to me.

ALICE: Because you bow and scrape to them. You always do. You bow and scrape to everybody who's under you. You're a bully with the soul of a slave.

EDGAR: Is that so?

ALICE: Yes! You grovel before your own soldiers and your NCOs, but you think you're better than your equals and your superiors.

EDGAR: Ha!

ALICE: Typical tyrant! . . . Do you think she'll leave?

EDGAR: Unless you go out and apologize to her.

ALICE: Me?!

EDGAR: Well, not me. You'd say I was flirting with her.

ALICE: Oh, God! Suppose she goes! I'd have to do everything myself—all the cleaning—like the last time—and ruin my hands.

EDGAR: That wouldn't be the worst of it. If Jenny moves out, Christine will leave too, and we'd never get another servant to come out to this godforsaken island. You know how the pilot on the steamer deliberately warns off anybody who comes here looking for a job. And if he doesn't, my NCOs scare them off.

ALICE: Those damned NCOs—don't I know! I have to feed

them in my own kitchen because you haven't the guts to tell them to get out.

EDGAR: That's right. If I kicked them out of the kitchen, they wouldn't re-up for another hitch. And that, my pet, would be the end of the whole shebang. They'd put Long Tom in mothballs and close up the whole hardware shop.

ALICE: It would be the end. What would become of us?

EDGAR: Exactly. That's why the officers are thinking about petitioning the crown for commutation of rations.

ALICE: What?

EDGAR: Per diem payment instead of rations.

ALICE: For the officers?

EDGAR: No, for the noncoms of course.

ALICE (*laughs*): You've really lost your marbles!

EDGAR: That's more like it! That's what we need here—a good laugh.

ALICE: I've almost forgotten how to laugh.

EDGAR (*lighting a cigar*): Don't! Never forget how to laugh. Life's so tiresome.

ALICE: Fun it isn't, that's for sure. . . . Want to play another hand?

EDGAR: No, I've had enough.

> *Pause.*

ALICE: You know, it gets my dander up, when I think about it, that my cousin, now that he's superintendent of the quarantine station, calls on our enemies first.

EDGAR: Who cares? Not worth talking about.

ALICE: Didn't you notice that in the list of arrivals in the newspaper he gave his occupation as "investor"? He must have inherited some money.

EDGAR: No kidding! A relative with money. That's a first in this family.

ALICE: In your family, maybe. Not in mine. We have a lot of rich relations.

EDGAR: If he's come into money, won't he be high-and-mighty! Need cutting down to size. Which means playing my cards very close to my chest.

The telegraph sounder begins to click.

ALICE: Who can that be?

EDGAR (*standing still*): Please, I'm trying to listen.

ALICE: Well, walk over to it.

EDGAR: Sh! I can hear . . . what they're saying. . . . It's the kids. (*He goes over to the telegraph apparatus and taps out a reply. Then the telegraph sounder sends a signal, and Edgar sends an answer.*)

ALICE: Well?

EDGAR: Hold your horses! (*Signs off.*) It was the kids. They called from the guardhouse in town. Judith wasn't feeling good and is staying home from school.

ALICE: Again! What else did they say?

EDGAR: Asked for money, of course.

ALICE: Why is Judith in such a hurry to get through school? If she graduated next year, it would be soon enough.

EDGAR: Try telling her that.

ALICE: She won't listen.

EDGAR: How often haven't I told her! But you know as well as I do that children do what they feel like.

ALICE: At least in this house.

Edgar yawns.

ALICE: Fine husband! Yawning in your wife's face.

EDGAR: What am I supposed to do? — Haven't you noticed that
we say the same things to each other every day? Just now when
you made your routine comment: "At least in this house," I
would have given my routine reply: "It's not just *my* house." But
since I've gone through that routine five hundred times, I decided
to liven things up—to yawn instead. Which can be interpreted as
meaning I'm too lazy to answer. Or it might mean: "Right you
are, my pet." Or: "I've had enough."

ALICE: Aren't you in a lovely mood tonight!

EDGAR: Isn't it time for dinner?

ALICE: I suppose you know the doctor's supper party is being
catered by the Grand Hotel.

EDGAR: No, I didn't. The Grand Hotel. At this time of year
they've got woodcock on the menu. Makes my mouth water.
Woodcock is the finest game bird of all—did you know that? But
some people ruin the dear thing—they roast it in bacon fat. Barbarians!

ALICE: Disgusting! —Must you talk about food?

EDGAR: How about wine? I wonder what those barbarians are
drinking with the woodcock.

ALICE: Should I play something for you?

EDGAR (*sitting at the desk*): The last resource! Sure, why not.
—But please skip the funeral marches and your sad songs. I don't
like propaganda with my music. I can always make out the message. "Listen to my sad song. I'm so unhappy." Miaow, miaow!
"Listen to what a horrible husband I have." Baroom, baroom,
baroom! "Oh, wouldn't it be lovely if he were dead!" Drum roll.
Fanfare. And end with the "Alcazar Waltz." Da-da-da-da-dum-da-
dum. And the Champagne Gallop." Darup, darup, darup!
—Apropos champagne: there are two bottles left, if memory
serves. Let's bring them up and pretend we have company.
Hmm?

ALICE: No, let's *not* bring them up. They're mine. They were
a present to *me*.

EDGAR: You're always so economical.

ALICE: And you're always so stingy. At least with your wife.

EDGAR: Well, it was only an idea. Now I don't know what to suggest. Maybe I should dance for you.

ALICE: No thanks. Your dancing days are over.

EDGAR: What you need is a woman in the house – someone you can talk to.

ALICE: Thank you. You need a man in the house.

EDGAR: Thank you. It's been tried, and to the mutual dissatisfaction of both parties. But it was fascinating to observe – like an experiment. – As soon as a stranger came into our house, we were happy. At the beginning.

ALICE: But not at the end.

EDGAR: Don't even think about it.

A knock is heard on the door at left.

ALICE: Who can be knocking this late in the day?

EDGAR: Jenny doesn't usually knock.

ALICE: Go and open the door. Don't stand shouting "Come in!" like you usually do. This isn't GHQ, you know.

EDGAR (*going to the door*): What have you got against GHQ?

Another knock.

ALICE: What are you waiting for? Open it.

Edgar opens the door and is handed a visiting card.

EDGAR: It's Christine. – Has Jenny gone?

Christine's answer cannot be heard.

(*To Alice.*) Jenny has gone.

ALICE: That makes me a housemaid again.

EDGAR: And me a hired hand.

ALICE: Can't you take one of the enlisted men and have him help out in the kitchen?

EDGAR: On permanent KP? These are not the good old days, Alice.

ALICE: The visiting card! Jenny wouldn't leave a visiting card when she's leaving. Whose is it?

EDGAR (*looks at the card through his spectacles, then hands it to Alice*): Read it. I can't see.

ALICE (*reading the card*): Curt! It's Curt! Hurry! Go out and fetch him in. Don't let him stand out there.

EDGAR (*as he goes out to the left*): Curt! Well, that's more like it!

Alice, perking up noticeably, arranges her hair.

* * *

Edgar enters from the left, with Curt.

EDGAR: Well, here he is: the man who abandons his friends! It's good to see you, you old son-of-a-gun! (*Embraces him.*)

ALICE (*going up to Curt*): Thank you. . . . It's been a long time.

EDGAR: Yes. Must be—let's see—fifteen years. And we've grown old.

ALICE: Oh, no. Curt hasn't changed. Still the same.

EDGAR: Sit down, sit down. —Now, first things first. What's on your roster? Are you invited out tonight?

CURT: Yes. I'm invited to the doctor's house not far from here. But I didn't promise I'd go.

ALICE: Good, then you can stay here where you belong—with your relations.

CURT: That does seem the most natural thing; but the doctor is my superior, and he might take it amiss.

EDGAR: Stuff and nonsense! I've never been afraid of my superiors.

CURT: It's not a question of being afraid; it's a question of tact —making things as pleasant as possible.

EDGAR: On this island, I'm the big shot. Stick with me, and no one will bother you.

ALICE: Oh, be quiet, Edgar. (*She takes Curt's hand.*) Big shots and superiors all aside, you're going to stay here with us. Why, it's only fit and proper, as they say.

CURT: All right, why not? You do make me feel welcome.

EDGAR: And why shouldn't you? We don't have any bones to pick . . . with each other . . .

> *Curt looks away, a little hurt.*

EDGAR: What's that supposed to mean? So you were a little careless. But you were young, and I've forgotten the whole thing. I'm not one to harbor grudges.

> *This turn of conversation has made Alice uneasy. All three seat themselves around the worktable.*

ALICE: So you've been out in the wide world?

CURT: Yes; and landed back here with you two.

EDGAR: Who you brought together in marriage twenty-five years ago.

CURT: It wasn't exactly like that, but never mind. It's great to see that you've stuck together for twenty-five years.

EDGAR: Oh, we've managed one way or another. Sometimes it's been touch and go, but, as you can see, we're still together. And Alice hasn't any cause to complain. Everything she could want; money pouring in. You didn't know I'm a famous author, now did you? Textbooks.

CURT: Yes, I remember when we went our separate ways you had written a book on firearms. Is it still used in the military schools?

EDGAR: Still used. Still number one—though they've tried to replace it with a poorer one. They use that one in *some* schools. Piece of junk!

Painful silence, broken by Curt.

CURT: I hear you've done some traveling, too. Gone abroad.

ALICE: Copenhagen. We've been there five times. Can you imagine?

EDGAR: Right. You see, when I took Alice out of the theater—

ALICE: *Took* me?!

EDGAR: Took, yes. A man takes a wife, and I took you!

ALICE: Brave, strong man, isn't he?

EDGAR: I never stopped hearing how I had cut short her brilliant career—hm, hm, hm—so to make it up to her, I had to promise to take her to Copenhagen. And I've kept my promise—faithfully. *Five* times we've gone there! Five. (*He holds up the five fingers of his left hand.*) Have you ever been to Copenhagen?

CURT (*smiles*): No; I've spent most of my time in America.

EDGAR: America? Must be an awful place. Nothing but bums and bushwhackers, I hear.

CURT (*frowning*): Well, it's not Copenhagen, admittedly.

ALICE (*trying to ease the tension*): Tell me—. Have you . . . ? Do you ever hear from your children?

CURT: No.

ALICE: You're a dear old friend, Curt, and I hope you won't mind my saying this, but wasn't it ill-considered to leave them like that?

CURT: I didn't leave them. The court took them from me and put them in the care of their mother.

EDGAR: Let's not talk about that now! It seems to me you are well out of that mess anyway.

CURT (*to Alice*): How are your children?

ALICE: Fine, thanks. They're attending school in the city. Nearly full-grown now.

EDGAR: A couple of able kids. The boy's got a brilliant mind. Brilliant! He'll be going to General Staff College.

ALICE: *If* they accept him.

EDGAR: Accept him? He's got the stuff the big brass is made of!

CURT: If I might change the subject: — the quarantine station that's being set up here for cholera, plague, what-have-you — the doctor will be my boss, as you know. Do you know him? What sort of man is he?

EDGAR: Man? He's no man. He's a dim-witted scoundrel, who'll stab you in the back.

CURT (*to Alice*): Doesn't sound too good, does it?

ALICE: Oh, it's not as bad as Edgar makes it sound. Although I have to admit we don't exactly get along.

EDGAR: A scoundrel, I tell you! That's what they all are: the customs inspector, the postmaster, the telephone operator, the druggist, the ship's pilot, the—the—what the hell do you call him?—the alderman—scoundrels one and all. And that's why I don't associate with them.

CURT: Have you locked horns with all of them?

EDGAR: Each and every one!

ALICE: Edgar's right, you know. It's impossible to associate with them.

EDGAR: This is the Devil's Island for tyrants and bullies. They were all shipped here.

ALICE (*sarcastically*): Didn't miss nary a one.

EDGAR (*taking it in stride*): Hm, hm, hm. That's supposed to be a dig at me. But I'm no tyrant. At least, not in my own house.

ALICE: Watch it, Edgar.

EDGAR (*to Curt*): Don't listen to her. I'm a very congenial husband. And the old lady is the best wife in the world.

ALICE: Curt, how about something to drink?

CURT: No, thanks, not now.

EDGAR: You're not on the wagon?

CURT: No, just not overdoing it.

EDGAR: Like the Americans, eh? The average, the common denominator?

CURT: Maybe.

EDGAR: Not my style. I want to go all the way; otherwise, forget it. A man should be able to hold his liquor.

CURT: To get back to your neighbors here on the island. My position is going to put me in contact with all of them. It won't be easy to steer clear of them. I mean, even if you don't want to get mixed up in other people's affairs, you can't help it.

ALICE: Don't fret, Curt. Mix with them if you have to. You'll always come back to us. This is where you have your real friends.

CURT: Isn't it awful to sit here surrounded by people you hate?

ALICE: It isn't fun, that's for sure.

EDGAR: It isn't at all awful. My whole life I've had nothing but enemies. I've thrived on them. As a matter of fact, they've helped me more than they've hurt me. And when I die I'll have the satisfaction of knowing I don't owe anybody a goddamn thing. Nobody ever gave me anything. Everything I own I had to fight for.

ALICE: True. Edgar's path hasn't been strewn with roses.

EDGAR: No. With thorns, with stones – sharp stones! And I did it with my own strength! Do you know what I mean?

CURT (*quietly, unassumingly*): Oh, yes. I know what you mean. And I came to see, ten years ago, how insufficient one's own strength is.

EDGAR: Ha! Then I feel sorry for you.

ALICE (*remonstrating*): Edgar!

EDGAR: No, I mean it! I really feel sorry for him – for anyone who doesn't rely on his own strength. Listen, it's perfectly true that when the machine breaks down, there's nothing left but what you can put in a wheelbarrow and haul out to manure the garden. But as long as the gears are turning, you've got to use them, use your hands and feet, keep slugging and kicking as long as the parts hold out! That's my philosophy.

CURT (*smiling*): I've always enjoyed hearing you talk, Edgar.

EDGAR: But you don't believe it's true.

CURT: No, I don't believe it's true.

EDGAR: Well, it is true, whether you like it or not.

> *During the last few minutes the wind has come up, and now one of the doors at the back swings open with a bang.*

EDGAR (*getting to his feet*): The wind's come up. I could feel it blowing up. (*He goes to shut the door. Taps the barometer.*)

ALICE (*to Curt*): You're staying for supper, aren't you?

CURT: Yes, if it's not a bother.

ALICE: No bother. It'll be something simple, I'm afraid. Our cook has moved.

CURT: That will be fine, I'm sure.

ALICE: Dear Curt; so easy to please. That's what I like about you.

EDGAR (*studying the barometer*): Fantastic how the barometer is falling. Look at it. I could feel it.

ALICE (*to Curt, softly*): Bad case of nerves. Worse tonight.

EDGAR: Shouldn't we be eating soon?

ALICE (*standing up*): I'm just about to take care of it. You two sit down and carry on with your philosophizing. (*To Curt, quietly.*) Don't contradict him; puts him in a bad mood. And for God's sake, don't ask why he never got to be a major.

>   *Curt nods understandingly. Alice crosses to the right. Edgar sits down with Curt at the worktable.*

EDGAR: Whip up something special for us, honeybunch.

ALICE: Give me money, and you'll get something special, lambykins.

EDGAR: Money, always money.

>   *Alice exits.*

* * *

EDGAR (*to Curt*): Money, money, money! I spend so much time doling out money, I'm beginning to think I'm a wallet with legs. Ever had that feeling?

CURT: I sure have. I thought I was a checkbook.

EDGAR (*laughing*): Oh, yes, you've been through the mill. Women, women! And, by God you latched on to a good one!

CURT (*patiently*): And that's water over the dam; let's forget it!

EDGAR: She was a pearl, wasn't she? Ha, a real gem! —Well, now, in my case, I can say that—in spite of everything—I got myself a good woman. She's solid, reliable—in spite of everything.

CURT (*smiles*): In spite of everything!

EDGAR: What's so funny?

CURT (*smiling*): In spite of everything! That's funny.

EDGAR: She's been a faithful wife, a fine mother—extraordinary. —But—(*He glances toward the door at right.*) she's got the temper of a she-devil. You know, there are moments when I've cursed you for hanging that albatross around my neck.

CURT (*amicably*): Don't blame me for that, Edgar, I never—

EDGAR: Yeah, yeah, yeah. A lot of talk. But you forget what's unpleasant to remember. Don't get your dander up. I'm used to giving orders and sounding off. You know what I'm like, you son-of-a-gun.

CURT: Yes; but the point is I did not foist Alice on you. Quite the contrary.

EDGAR (*not letting his flow of thought be interrupted*): Life is strange, don't you think?

CURT: You can say that again!

EDGAR: Getting to be old, I mean. Not much fun, but it's damned fascinating. Oh, I'm not saying I'm old; it's just that I'm *beginning* to get the feel of it. All one's friends die off. It gets lonesome.

CURT: You're lucky to have a wife to keep you company when you get older.

EDGAR: Lucky? Yes, I guess so. Even the children leave. . . . You know, you shouldn't have left yours.

CURT: But I tell you I didn't leave them. They were taken from me.

EDGAR: Now don't get sore just because I tell you—

CURT: But I keep telling you it wasn't like that.

EDGAR: Well, however it was, it's over and forgotten. Fact is, you're alone.

CURT: One gets used to everything, Edgar.

EDGAR: I wonder. Can you—I mean, can one get used to— being completely alone?

CURT: Look at me.

EDGAR: Yes. . . . What have you been doing these past fifteen years?

CURT: What a question! These fifteen years!

EDGAR: I hear you struck it rich.

CURT: I'm not rolling in the stuff.

EDGAR: Don't worry, I'm not putting the touch on you.

CURT: Edgar, if you need a loan . . .

EDGAR: Thank you very much, but I've got money in the bank — my own checking account. Listen — (*Casting a glance at the door at right.*) in this house we don't lack for anything. Can't. If I went broke, she'd pack up and leave.

CURT: I don't believe that.

EDGAR: It's a fact. You know what her SOP is? She doesn't ask for money any old day. She waits — waits until she knows I haven't got any, so she can yell at me, saying I can't support a family. She loves that!

CURT: I thought you said money was pouring in.

EDGAR: Of course. It just doesn't go very far.

CURT: Then it's not pouring in — not in the ordinary sense.

EDGAR: It's strange. Life. And so are we. Right?

The telegraph receiver has begun to click.

CURT: What's that?

EDGAR: Only a time check.

CURT: Don't you have a telephone here?

EDGAR: It's out in the kitchen. We use the telegraph so the telephone girls can't stick their nose in our business.

CURT: You must have a hell of a social life out here on the coast.

EDGAR: Stinks. But, then, life itself stinks. And you believe it goes on! Tell me, since you believe in a life after death, will there be peace in the life to come?

CURT: I'm sure there'll be storms and struggles even there.

EDGAR: Even there! If there is any *there*. I'd prefer annihilation.

CURT: What makes you think that annihilation occurs without pain and suffering?

EDGAR: Not for me. I'm going to drop down dead – bam! No pain, no suffering.

CURT: How do you know that?

EDGAR: I know what I know.

CURT: Sounds like you're not too happy with your life.

EDGAR (*sighs*): Happy? The day I die, I'll be happy.

CURT: That's something you don't know. (*Standing up.*) What on earth is going on in this house? What's happening? The place smells poisonous, like old peeling wallpaper. Just coming in here makes you sick. I'd walk out this instant if I hadn't promised Alice I'd stay. There must be corpses rotting under the floorboards. The air is so full of hate it's suffocating.

> *While Curt has been talking, Edgar has fallen into a semiconscious state, eyes open and staring.*

CURT: What's the matter with you? Edgar!

> *Edgar does not move. Curt shakes him by the shoulder.*

CURT: Edgar!

EDGAR (*coming to*): What did you say? (*Looking around.*) I thought it was Alice. . . . Oh, it's you. – Listen, I – (*He falls into a stupor again.*)

CURT: This is terrible! (*Curt goes to the door at right, opens it, and calls.*) Alice!

* * *

ALICE (*enters, wearing an apron*): What's the matter?

CURT: I don't know. Look at him!

ALICE (*calmly*): Oh, he gets those spells every once in a while. He just fades out. I'll play; that will make him come to.

CURT: No, don't do that! Don't –. Let me take care of this. . . . Can he hear? Can he see?

ALICE: Right now he can't hear, can't see.

CURT: You say that as if nothing has happened! Alice, what's going on here?

ALICE: Ask that one!

CURT: "That one?" God, Alice, that's your husband.

ALICE: A stranger to me, just as much a stranger as he was twenty-five years ago. I don't know anything about that man — except that —

CURT: Shhh! He can hear you.

ALICE: When he's like that, he can't hear a thing.

> *A bugle call is heard. Edgar starts, leaps to his feet, crosses to the hat tree, and puts on his saber and military cap.*

EDGAR: Excuse me! Got to check the guard posts. (*Exits through the rear doors.*)

*   *   *

CURT: Is he ill?

ALICE: I don't know.

CURT: Is he out of his mind?

ALICE: I don't know.

CURT: Has he been drinking?

ALICE: He talks liquor more than he drinks it.

CURT: Alice, now you sit down and you tell me what's going on. Calmly and truthfully.

ALICE (*sitting down*): You want the story of my life? How I've been sitting in this round tower for a lifetime, like a prisoner, guarded by a man I've always hated. A man I now hate so much that the day he dies I'll burst out laughing with joy.

CURT: Why haven't you left him?

ALICE: A good question. We separated twice while we were engaged, and since then we've thought of separating every day that passes. But we're welded together, I guess, and we can't free ourselves. Once we were separated—that is, we went our separate ways in the same house—for five years. Now nothing but death can separate us. And we know it. So we await death as a deliverance.

CURT: Why are you so alone, so isolated?

ALICE: Because he isolated me. Cut me off. Made my relatives leave the house. He *weeded* them out—that's what he called it. "Weeded" out my friends, everybody.

CURT: What about *his* relations? Did you "weed" them out?

ALICE: My God! I had to! They would have been the death of me. They took away my reputation, my self-respect. Would have taken my life, too. Finally I was reduced to keeping contact with people by means of that telegraph. The telephone was no good—those girls always listening in. I've taught myself how to use the telegraph, and he doesn't know it. —For God's sake, don't say a word about it, he'd kill me if he knew.

CURT: How awful, awful! —But why does he blame me for your marriage? You know how it was. Edgar was my friend when we were young. When he saw you, it was love at first sight. He came to me and asked me to be go-between. Right away I said no. My dear Alice, I can be honest with you. I knew how strong-willed you were, knew you had a cruel streak in you; I warned him. But when he became more insistent, I sent him around to your brother to let him plead his case.

ALICE: I'm sure that's how it was. Not that it makes any difference. He's told himself another story for so many years you can never make him believe anything else.

CURT: All right, let him blame me for everything, if that makes him feel any better.

ALICE: That's asking too much.

CURT: I'm used to it. What irks me is when he accuses me of abandoning my children. That's unfair.

ALICE: He's like that. He says whatever comes into his head; and what he says he believes. But he really likes you—you don't contradict him. Please try to bear with us. Maybe you came to us at this moment because you were meant to. . . . Sometimes I think we're the unhappiest couple on the face of the earth. (*She cries.*)

CURT: I've seen *one* marriage at close quarters. That was bad enough. But this is almost worse.

ALICE: You think so?

CURT: I do.

ALICE: Whose fault is it?

CURT: Alice, the moment you stop trying to find whose fault it is you'll feel a whole lot better. Try to accept it as a fact of life, or as a test.

ALICE: I can't. It's asking too much. (*Standing up.*) It's hopeless.

CURT: You poor fool. —Why do you hate each other like this? Do you know?

ALICE: No. It's a hate beyond reason. Without cause, without point or purpose. And also without end. It's crazy. You know why he's afraid to die? Because he's afraid I'd marry again.

CURT: Then he must love you.

ALICE: Probably. That doesn't prevent him from hating me.

CURT (*as if to himself*): That's love-hate, and it comes from the pit of hell. —Does he like it when you play for him?

ALICE: Oh, yes, but only ugly tunes. The uglier the better. Like that awful "Entrance of the Boyars," for instance. When he hears it, he becomes possessed and wants to dance.

CURT: He—dance?

ALICE: Oh, he can be a real card at times.

CURT: Maybe I shouldn't ask, but I can't help it. Your children—where are they?

ALICE: Two died. I guess you didn't know.

CURT: I'm sorry. You've had to bear that, too.

ALICE: What haven't I had to bear?

CURT: And the other two?

ALICE: Living in town. We couldn't have them here with us. He turned them against me.

CURT: And you, against him.

ALICE: Naturally. We formed factions, held caucuses, solicited votes, offered bribes. So, in order not to destroy them utterly, we sent them away. Children! They're supposed to make a marriage; they broke ours. The blessing became a curse. Sometimes I think we belong to a family with a curse on it.

CURT: Yes, after the Fall—it's true.

ALICE (*giving him a withering look; sharply*): Which fall?

CURT: The first. Adam and Eve.

ALICE: Oh. I thought you meant—something else.

> *Embarrassed silence.*

ALICE (*clasping her hands together*): Curt, we're cousins, and you're my oldest friend. I know I haven't always behaved toward you as I should have, but, Lord knows, I've been punished. You've had your revenge.

CURT: What revenge? Nothing of the sort. Now just forget it!

ALICE: Do you remember that Sunday after you had gotten engaged? I had invited the two of you to dinner.

CURT: I say forget it!

ALICE: I have to say this—so you'll forgive me. When you arrived, we had gone and you had to go back.

CURT: So you had been invited out yourselves. There's nothing to talk about. Why are you so upset?

ALICE: There's more, Curt. Just now when I invited you to stay for supper, I thought there was something to eat in the kitchen. (*She hides her face in her hands.*) There isn't a scrap, not even a dry crust of bread. (*She sobs.*)

CURT: You poor darling! It's nothing to get upset about.

ALICE: Oh, no? Wait till he comes back, expecting dinner, and there's nothing. He'll explode. You've never seen him when he gets mad. Oh, God, the humiliation –!

CURT: Now you just let me take care of this. I'll go out and buy something.

ALICE: Buy? There's no place to buy anything on this island.

CURT: It makes no difference to me, you understand. But for his sake, and yours – there must be something. . . . We could –. We'll make a joke of the whole business when he comes in. Laugh about it. I'll say it's time for a drink, and I'll think of something while we're drinking. . . . You put him in a good mood, humor him, play something for him, some silly tune. Come here. Be sitting at the piano when he arrives.

ALICE: Look at my hands! Who can play the piano with hands like these? I have to scrub the pots and pans, wash the glasses, lay the fire, dust and mop –

CURT: I thought you had two servants.

ALICE: On paper an officer gets two servants. But they're always leaving us. Sometimes there's nobody. Nobody. Most of the time. – Oh, Curt, what am I going to do? – I mean, about supper? I wish the whole damn place would burn down.

CURT: Now, now, Alice.

ALICE: I wish the sea would rise and wash us all away.

CURT: Now, now. I won't hear such talk, Alice.

ALICE: What will he say? What will he do? – Curt, please, Curt, don't leave me!

CURT: No, Alice, I'm not going anyplace. I promise I won't leave.

ALICE: But you'll have to leave – sometime. . . . And then –!

CURT: Has he ever struck you?

ALICE: Me?! Course not! He knows I'd walk out on him. I've got some pride left.

> *From outside on the platform can be heard the Sentry's voice challenging someone: "Halt! Who goes there?" And Edgar's voice replying, "Friend."*

CURT (*standing up*): Is that him?

ALICE (*frightened*): Yes, it's him.

> *Pause.*

CURT: Now what do we do? What on earth do we do?

ALICE: I don't know. I don't know.

*   *   *

> *Edgar enters through the rear doors, in high spirits.*

EDGAR: There! That's tended to. Made the rounds. Now I'm free. —Well, has she poured out her heart to you? Unburdened her soul? Isn't she the poor, unhappy one? Eh? Eh?

CURT: How's the weather out there?

EDGAR: Blowing up a storm. (*He opens one of the rear doors a trifle. Joshingly.*) Bluebeard and the maiden in the tower. And out there, the sentry, with saber unsheathed, guards the beautiful maiden. Then along come her brothers to rescue her. But the sentry is there, pacing. Look at him! Keeping time. A good sentry. Look at him. (*He hums and beats out a march rhythm in time with the sentry*.) Meli-tam-tam-ta, meli-talia-lie. Should we dance the sword dance? That will be something for Curt to see!

CURT: How about "The Entrance of the Boyars" instead?

EDGAR: Oh, ho, you know that, do you? —Alice, pretty Alice in her little apron, come and play for us. —Come, I said!

> *Alice goes reluctantly to the piano. As she passes Edgar, he pinches her arm.*

EDGAR: And what little slanders have you been spreading about me?

ALICE: Me?

Curt averts his eyes.

*Alice plays "The Entrance of the Boyars." Edgar impro-
vises a kind of Hungarian dance in the area behind the
writing desk, clanging his spurs as he dances. Suddenly
he falls to the floor, unnoticed by Curt and Alice. Alice
plays the piece to its end.*

ALICE (*without turning around*): Once more?

Silence.

*Alice turns and sees Edgar lying unconscious, hidden
from the audience by the desk.*

ALICE: God in heaven! (*She stands with her arms crossed over her
breasts and sighs deeply, a sign of gratitude and release.*)

CURT (*turning around and hurrying to Edgar*): What is it? What's
happened?

ALICE (*in the greatest possible suspense*): Is – he – dead?

CURT: I don't know! Help me!

ALICE (*not moving*): I can't. I can't touch him. . . . Is he dead?

CURT: No. He's still alive.

*Alice sighs. Curt helps Edgar, who gets to his feet and
is supported to a chair.*

EDGAR: What was that?

Silence.

What was that?

CURT: You fell. Don't you know?

EDGAR: Fell?

CURT: Fell to the floor. How do you feel now?

EDGAR: Me? Feel? Nothing's the matter. Don't know what
you're talking about. What are you gaping at?

CURT: You're ill.

EDGAR: Nonsense! Come, Alice, play–. Oh, it's coming again! (*His hand goes to his head.*)

ALICE: You see! You're sick.

EDGAR: Stop yelling! It's only a dizzy spell.

CURT: We've got to get a doctor. I'll telephone–

EDGAR: No, I don't want any doctor.

CURT: You have to have a doctor. If not for your sake, then for ours. We'll be held responsible.

EDGAR: I'll drive him out if he comes. I'll shoot him down! –Oh, it's coming again! (*Grabs his head.*)

Curt crosses to the door at right.

CURT: I'm telephoning! (*He exits.*)

* * *

Alice takes off her apron.

EDGAR: Will you get me a glass of water?

ALICE: I suppose I have to. (*She gives him a glass of water.*)

EDGAR: Aren't you a dear!

ALICE: Are you sick?

EDGAR: Forgive me for not being well.

ALICE: Can you take care of yourself?

EDGAR: It's obvious you won't.

ALICE: You can be sure of that.

EDGAR: This is it, Alice. The moment you've been waiting for, for so long.

ALICE: Yes. The moment you thought would never come.

EDGAR: Don't get mad at me.

* * *

Curt enters from the right.

CURT: Dreadful.

ALICE: What did he say?

CURT: He hung up. Just like that!

ALICE (*to Edgar*): You always treated him like dirt—you and your arrogance! What did you expect?

EDGAR: I'm feeling worse. Could you get a doctor from town?

ALICE: I'll have to use the telegraph. (*She goes to the telegraph apparatus on the desk.*)

EDGAR (*half-rising in astonishment*): Can—you—telegraph?

ALICE (*tapping out a message on the telegraph key*): Yes! Yes, I can telegraph.

EDGAR: You really can. All right: get to it. —What a deceitful woman! (*To Curt.*) Come and sit next to me.

Curt seats himself next to Edgar.

EDGAR: Hold my hand. . . . I'm sitting—and yet I'm falling. Can you imagine? Falling down something. . . . It's strange.

CURT: Have you had these attacks before?

EDGAR: Never.

CURT: While we're waiting for an answer from town, I'll walk over to the doctor's house and speak to him. He's attended you before, hasn't he?

EDGAR: Yes, he has.

CURT: He should know your medical history, then. (*He crosses left.*)

ALICE: We'll get an answer soon. —You're very kind, Curt. Come back as soon as you can.

CURT: As soon as I can. (*He leaves.*)

*   *   *

EDGAR: He's very kind—Curt. And so changed.

ALICE: And all for the better. I'm sorry for his sake that he should come to us right now, in all our misery.

EDGAR: Come to congratulate us! . . . I wonder how things really are with him. Did you notice that he didn't want to talk about himself?

ALICE: I noticed—but did anybody ask him?

EDGAR: His life. . . . Strange. . . . Our life. . . . I wonder if everybody's life is like this.

ALICE: Perhaps. The difference is that they don't talk about it.

EDGAR: Sometimes I've had this idea that misery seeks its own kind. I mean, those who are happy avoid those who are unhappy. That's why we never get to see anything but misery.

ALICE: Who do you know who's happy?

EDGAR: Let me think. . . . No. —Yes! The Edmarks.

ALICE: The Edmarks?! She was operated on last year. Still sick.

EDGAR: That's right. —Well, then I can't think of anybody. . . . What about the Krafts?

ALICE: Perfect example. Have you forgotten? The whole family lived in a paradise. Rich, respected, nice children, good marriages—everything perfect till the Krafts got to be fifty. Then their cousin killed a man, went to prison, dragged their name into all the papers. That was the end of paradise. The Kraft name in all the headlines. The Kraft murder case, remember? The old respected Krafts couldn't even show themselves in public. The children had to be taken out of school. My God, such happiness!

EDGAR: I wonder what sort of sickness I've got.

ALICE: What do you think it is?

EDGAR: Something to do with the heart. Or the head. It's as if my soul wanted to fly out and dissolve itself in a cloud of smoke.

ALICE: Do you feel like eating?

EDGAR: Yes, I could eat something. What are you cooking for supper?

ALICE (*agitated, she crosses the floor*): I'll ask Jenny.

EDGAR: Jenny? She left us.

ALICE: Yes, I know, I know. I forgot.

EDGAR: Ring for Christine. I want a fresh glass of water, anyway.

> *Alice rings.*

ALICE: God, you don't suppose—? (*Rings again.*) She doesn't hear.

EDGAR: Go and look for her. If she's left too—God!

> *Alice goes to the door at left and opens it.*

ALICE: Look. She's packed her suitcase. It's standing here in the hall.

EDGAR: Then she's left.

ALICE: What a hell! What a hell! (*She falls, sobbing, to her knees, and puts her head on a stool. Starts to sniffle.*)

EDGAR: Everything all at once. Even Curt had to show up to see us in this stinking mess. The only humiliation left is for Curt to walk in right now and see you like that and me like this.

ALICE: Don't worry, he won't. He's left us, too. You can bet on it. He won't be back.

EDGAR: Just like him!

ALICE: We're cursed, damned!

EDGAR: What's that supposed to mean?

ALICE: Don't you see how everybody avoids us? What's the matter with you!

EDGAR: Let them! I don't give a damn!

The telegraph sounder begins clicking.

EDGAR: There's the reply. —Shh! let me listen. . . . Everyone's busy. . . . Excuses. —Scum!

ALICE: You see! You didn't give a damn about doctors and now they don't give a damn about you. Didn't even pay their bills!

EDGAR: That's not true.

ALICE: Even when you could have, you didn't. You despised the doctors' work, just as you despise my work—everybody's work. They don't want to come. And the telephone is shut off because you despised that, too! Nothing means anything to you except your guns and cannons!

EDGAR: Don't stand there shooting your mouth off.

ALICE: You're getting yours, Edgar. Everything comes back. The big and the small.

EDGAR: Silly superstition! You talk like an old woman.

ALICE: You wait, you'll see. —Do you know we owe Christine six months' wages?

EDGAR: So what! She's stolen more than that from us.

ALICE: But I've had to borrow cash from her!

EDGAR: That's just like you!

ALICE: You ought to thank me! You know very well I had to borrow the money to pay for the children's travel home.

EDGAR: Didn't Curt time things perfectly! Scamp! And a coward to boot. Didn't have the guts to say he had had enough of us. Saw he was going to get a lousy meal here and skipped off to the doctor's party! Miserable wretch. They're all alike!

* * *

Curt enters hurriedly through the door at left.

CURT: Well, Edgar, old fellow, this is how it is. The doctor knows what the trouble is. It's your heart.

EDGAR: Heart?

CURT: For a long time now you've been suffering from arterio-sclerosis and calcification around the heart.

EDGAR: Stony heart?

CURT: And—

EDGAR: Is it serious?

CURT: Well, it can be.

EDGAR: So it is serious.

CURT: Yes.

EDGAR: Fatal?

CURT: You simply have to be very careful. First, no cigars.

Edgar tosses his cigar away.

CURT: Second: no whiskey. . . . And next: off to bed.

EDGAR (*fear in his voice*): No. Not that. Not to bed. That's the end. Once in bed, you never get up again. I'll sleep on the sofa tonight. —What else did he say?

CURT: He was very kind and helpful, really. He'll come here right away, if you call for him.

EDGAR: Kind? Helpful? That hypocrite! I don't want to see his face! . . . Am I allowed to eat?

CURT: Not tonight. And for the next few days—only milk.

EDGAR: Milk! I can't stomach the stuff.

CURT: You'll have to learn.

EDGAR: No, I'm too old to learn. (*He clasps his hands to his head.*) Oh, it's coming again! (*He sits and stares unseeingly.*)

ALICE (*to Curt*): What *did* the doctor say?

CURT: That he *might* die.

ALICE: Hallelujah!

CURT: Take care, Alice. Take care. —Could you get a pillow and a blanket? I'll tuck him in on the sofa. I'll sit here on the chair and spend the night with him.

ALICE: What about me?

CURT: You go to bed. Your presence only seems to make his condition worse.

ALICE: All right. You're in charge. I know you mean the best for both of us. (*She crosses to the left.*)

CURT: "Both of you" —mind. I'm not going to get involved in your battles.

> *He takes the water carafe and goes out to the right, while Alice exits left.*

*   *   *

> *The sound of the wind outside is heard, louder. The doors at the rear blow open, and an Old Woman, sleazily dressed and unpleasant looking, peeps in.*

> *Edgar wakes up, pulls himself up, and looks around.*

EDGAR: They've left me —the bastards! (*He catches sight of the Old Woman and is suddenly frightened.*) Who are you? What do you want?

OLD WOMAN: I just wanted to close the door, mister.

EDGAR: Why? Why?

OLD WOMAN: Because it blew open, just as I was passing by.

EDGAR: You were going to rob us!

OLD WOMAN: Not much worth taking, is there? That's what Christine says.

EDGAR: Christine!

OLD WOMAN: Good night, sir. Sleep well. (*She closes the door and leaves.*)

*   *   *

Alice enters from the left, carrying pillows and a blanket.

EDGAR: Who was that at the door just now? There was someone, wasn't there?

ALICE: That was only Maia, from the old folks' home, on her way back.

EDGAR: Are you certain?

ALICE: Are you scared?

EDGAR: Scared? Never.

ALICE: Since you won't go to bed, you're going to sleep out here.

EDGAR (*goes to the chaise lounge and lies down*): This is where I want to lie. (*He attempts to take Alice's hand, but she pulls her hand away from him.*)

Curt enters with a carafe of water.

EDGAR: Curt, don't leave me!

CURT: I'm going to sit here with you the whole night, Edgar. Alice is going to say good night to you and go to bed.

EDGAR: Good night, Alice.

ALICE (*to Curt*): Good night, Curt.

CURT: Good night.

*   *   *

Curt takes a chair and places himself close to Edgar.

CURT: Don't you want to take off your boots?

EDGAR: No. A soldier wants to be armed and ready, always.

CURT: Are you expecting a battle?

EDGAR: Maybe. (*Raising himself up.*) Curt! You are the only person I've bared myself to. Promise me one thing. . . . If I die tonight . . . take care of my children.

CURT: Don't worry. I will.

EDGAR: Thank you, Curt. I know I can count on you.

CURT: Why is that? Why can you count on me?

EDGAR: We've never been friends, Curt; I don't believe in friendship. And our two families were born enemies, always fighting.

CURT: Yet you say you can count on me.

EDGAR: Yes. And I don't know why.

Silence.

Do you think I'm going to die?

CURT: Yes, you like everyone else. They're not going to make an exception of you.

EDGAR: So bitter, Curt?

CURT: Yes. — So afraid of dying, Edgar? The wheelbarrow, the manure for the garden?

EDGAR: What if — what if that wasn't the end?

CURT: Many people think it isn't.

EDGAR: And what comes after?

CURT: One surprise after another, I suppose.

EDGAR: But nothing is known for sure.

CURT: Exactly. That's the point. That's why one has to be ready for anything.

EDGAR: You're still not such a child, Curt, that you believe in hell?

CURT: And you don't believe in it? You're in the midst of it.

EDGAR: That's only a way of speaking, a metaphor.

CURT: You've described your hell so realistically that there's no way it can be a metaphor, poetic or otherwise.

Silence.

EDGAR: If you only knew the pain I'm suffering.

CURT: Physical?

EDGAR: No, not physical.

CURT: Then it must be spiritual. There's no third alternative.

Silence.

EDGAR (*raising himself up on his elbows*): I don't want to die!

CURT: A short while ago you wanted annihilation.

EDGAR: On condition it was painless.

CURT: But you see it isn't.

EDGAR: This? Is this annihilation?

CURT: The beginning of it.

EDGAR: Good night, Curt.

CURT: Good night, Edgar.

[2]

Same set, but the ceiling lamp is on the verge of going out. Gray morning light and an overcast sky is visible through the windows and the doors at the rear. Heavy seas. The Sentry is on duty as before. Edgar is lying on the chaise lounge, asleep. Curt is sitting in the chair next to him, pale and exhausted.

Alice enters from the left.

ALICE: Is he asleep?

CURT: Yes. Has been ever since the sun was supposed to rise.

ALICE: A bad night?

CURT: He slept off and on. Mostly he talked.

ALICE: About what?

CURT: He argued about religion like a high-school kid and presumed to think that he had solved all the great mysteries of life.

Finally, long about morning, he made a great discovery: the immortality of the soul.

ALICE: For his own everlasting glory!

CURT: Absolutely. I have never in my life met anyone with such a high opinion of himself. "*I* exist; therefore there is a god."

ALICE: Now you see the real Edgar. —Those boots! He would have trampled the earth flat, if he had had his way. With those boots he stomped through life, stepping on everybody's toes and walking all over me. Well, buster, there was a bullet with your number on it.

CURT: He'd be comical if he weren't so tragic. You know, there's a streak of greatness in all that pettiness and small-mindedness. I'll bet you could find something good to say about him if you tried.

ALICE (*sitting down*): Yes, if I were certain he couldn't hear me. He's so stuck on himself; encourage him and he'll never come unglued.

CURT: He can't hear; he's been given morphine.

ALICE: He came from a poor family, you know. Lots of children, and he had to support them, when he was still young, by giving lessons. His father was a louse—a good-for-nothing. So Edgar was denied all the pleasures of a normal adolescence. Had to slave for a bunch of ungrateful kids whom he never put on this earth. I was only a small girl when I first saw him. He was just a young guy who had to go without an overcoat even when it was ten below zero because he couldn't afford one. But his little sisters had duffel coats. I couldn't help but admire him. Even though he was so ugly he made one cringe. Have you ever seen anybody so ugly?

CURT: I don't think so. It can be horrifying at times. Every time I quarreled and broke off with him, I noticed his ugliness. When he wasn't around, the image of him took over, grew into a giant ogre. He literally haunted me.

ALICE: Imagine what it's been like for me! . . . Anyway, his career in the army when he was training as an officer was sheer torture for him. But some rich people helped him financially.

He'll never admit it, though. Everything he's been able to get his hands on he takes as his due. Not a word of thanks.

CURT: I thought we were going to say something nice about him.

ALICE: It can wait until he's dead! —Anyhow, that's all I remember.

CURT: Has he been mean to you? Spiteful?

ALICE: Oh, God! What do you think? . . . Funny. Sometimes he's been so kind and sensitive. —It's when he turns against you, that's when he's absolutely terrifying.

CURT: Why didn't he ever get to be major?

ALICE: Obvious, isn't it? Listen, if he thinks he's Caesar when he's only a captain, who'd be dumb enough to make him a major? —But don't even bring up that subject. He says he never wanted to be top brass. —Did he talk about the children?

CURT: Yes. He longed to see Judith.

ALICE: I thought so. Judith. Do you know Judith? Judith is his second self. He's trained her to bait and badger me. My own daughter . . . and she hit me.

CURT: No! How could she?

ALICE: Quiet! He's stirring. —My God! Suppose he heard me. He's sly; oh, God, he's sly!

CURT: I think he really is waking up.

ALICE: Like a troll, isn't he? Makes me shiver.

> *Silence.*
>
> *Edgar stirs, wakes up, raises himself on his elbows, and looks around.*

EDGAR: So it's morning. Finally.

CURT: How do you feel now?

EDGAR: Not so hot.

CURT: Do you want the doctor?

EDGAR: No. I want to see Judith. My Judith.

CURT: Don't you think you should be settling your affairs? I mean, before—or in case—anything happens.

EDGAR: What do you mean? What's going to happen?

CURT: I mean what happens to everyone.

EDGAR: Crap! I don't die easy, so get that out of your mind. Don't count your chickens, Alice.

CURT: You should give a thought to your children. And you should make a will so your wife at least will hold on to the furniture.

EDGAR: How can she inherit while I'm still alive?

CURT: It's not a case of that. But if something does happen, she shouldn't end up in the street. This furniture—she's cleaned and dusted and polished this furniture for twenty-five years; she's got a right to hold on to it. Do you want me to call the lawyer in regimental headquarters?

EDGAR: No.

CURT: You're a hard man, Edgar, harder than I thought.

EDGAR: It's coming again! (*He falls back on the chaise lounge, senseless.*)

ALICE (*crossing right*): Somebody's in the kitchen. I have to see—

CURT: Go on. There's not much that can be done here.

> *Alice exits.*

> * * *

> *Edgar comes to.*

EDGAR: Well, Curt, how do you plan to set up the quarantine station?

CURT: I'll manage—somehow.

EDGAR: Maybe. But I'm in command on this island, and you'll have to deal with me. Don't you forget it.

CURT: Have you ever seen a quarantine station?

EDGAR: Are you kidding? I knew about them before you were born. A bit of advice: don't put the disinfecting ovens too near the shore.

CURT: I thought the idea was to place them as near the water as possible.

EDGAR: Ha! A lot you know about it. Bacilli thrive on water; it's their element.

CURT: But you need the saltwater and lots of it to wash away the wastes.

EDGAR: Idiot! . . . Anyway, when you get settled in and have a place for yourself, you should bring your children to live with you.

CURT: You don't really think my wife will let them come?

EDGAR: I said "bring." Are you a man or aren't you? It will make a good impression here if people see that you are a caring father and fulfill your responsibilities as head—

CURT: I've never neglected my responsibilities as father!

EDGAR (*raising his voice*): —as head of the family, which you never were!

CURT: I've told you time and again—!

EDGAR (*plunging ahead*): Because the head of the family doesn't leave his children the way you did!

CURT: Charrrge!!

EDGAR: . . . I think of you as a relative, Curt. I'm like an uncle to you, and that makes me feel I have to tell you the truth, even if it hurts. Now don't misunderstand me; it's—

CURT: Aren't you hungry?

EDGAR: As a matter of fact, I am.

CURT: You want something light?

EDGAR: No, something strong.

CURT: That would finish you.

EDGAR: I'm sick; am I supposed to starve, too?

CURT: That's the way it is.

EDGAR: Can't drink; can't smoke. A high price to pay for a little life.

CURT: Death demands its sacrifices; otherwise it doesn't wait.

* * *

> *Alice enters, carrying some bouquets of flowers and several telegrams and letters.*

ALICE: These are for you. (*She throws the flowers on the desk.*)

EDGAR (*flattered; enjoying himself*): For me! . . . Let's see what we've got here!

ALICE: They're only from the sergeants, the corporals, and the regimental band.

EDGAR: Jealousy! Tut, tut, Alice.

ALICE: Don't be ridiculous! Now, if they sent you a prize or a medal—or a laurel wreath—. (*She gestures toward the laurel wreath on the wall.*) —But why talk of things that can never be!

EDGAR: Ha-ha. —Ah, a telegram from the colonel himself—from the Big Brass himself, Alice! Read it, will you, Curt? The colonel is a real gentleman, you know. Even if he is a bit of an idiot. —What's this one? From—? Can't read it. Ah, it's from Judith. . . . Do me a favor and telegraph her and ask her to come with the next boat. —Here's . . . well, well, it's good to have friends who appreciate you. Good people who don't forget a sick man, a man passed over in the promotions; a deserving man, without fear above censure.

ALICE: I don't get it. Are all these nice people congratulating you for being sick?

EDGAR: Bitch!

ALICE (*to Curt*): We once gave a wonderful going-away party here for a doctor. Everybody hated him. So he got his going-away party after he had gone.

EDGAR: Put the bouquets in vases, will you? . . . I'm certainly not credulous, and people – they're just scum. But believe me, this little show of affection is really sincere. By God, it is. No other way of taking it.

ALICE: What an ass!

CURT (*reading one of the telegrams*): Judith says she can't come. The steamship has been delayed because of the storm.

EDGAR: Is that all she says?

CURT: No-o. There's more.

EDGAR: Out with it.

CURT: She says her daddy ought not to drink so much.

EDGAR: Shame on her! One's own child! My dear, sweet daughter. My Judith. My image of heaven.

ALICE: Image of yourself, you mean.

EDGAR: That's life for you. And the best it offers. To hell with it!

ALICE: You're just reaping what you sowed. You taught her to go against me; now she's turned against you. It's enough to make one believe in God!

EDGAR (*to Curt*): What does the colonel have to say?

CURT: He has approved a leave of absence for you, to take effect immediately.

EDGAR: Leave of absence? I never asked for one.

ALICE: I did.

EDGAR: I won't accept it!

ALICE: It's all been arranged and approved.

EDGAR: Not by me, it hasn't!

ALICE: Look at him, Curt! For him regulations don't apply; rules don't exist; directives are not to be obeyed. He's above everything, everybody. The universe was created for his personal enjoyment. The sun and the moon travel the heavens just to carry his praises to the farthest stars. Look at him! A stinking wretch of a captain who never got to be major. A scarecrow who thinks his men are trembling in their boots when they're shaking with laughter. A sniveling coward who is afraid of the dark and believes in barometers. And why all the hullabaloo over this man? For the grand finale when this bag of wind turns into a sack of shit to fertilize the garden! And second-rate shit at that!!

> *Edgar has been vaingloriously fanning himself with a bouquet of flowers, blithely indifferent to Alice's tirade.*

EDGAR: Have you asked Curt to stay for breakfast?

ALICE: No.

EDGAR: All right. Broil two steaks. Chateaubriands will do very nicely. Two of the best.

ALICE: Two?

EDGAR: I'm thinking of having one myself.

ALICE: There are three of us.

EDGAR: You mean, you–? Oh, very well. Three, then.

ALICE: And where am I supposed to get them? Yesterday you invited Curt to supper when there wasn't a crust of bread in the house. He's had to sit up all night, on an empty stomach, without so much as a cup of coffee, because we haven't got any food, and can't buy any because we can't get any more credit!

EDGAR: Oh, dear, she's mad at me because I didn't die–last night.

ALICE: No, I'm mad because you didn't die twenty-five years ago–because you didn't die before I was ever born.

EDGAR (*to Curt*): Listen to her carry on! –This is what happens when you make the marriages, Curt. Wasn't made in heaven, that's certain.

> *Alice and Curt exchange glances.*

EDGAR (*rising and going toward the door*): Enough of this. You can talk all you want. I have my duties to perform. (*Puts on an old-fashioned helmet with crest, buckles his sword around his waist, and puts his army coat on.*)

Alice and Curt try to stop him from going.

EDGAR: Out of my way! (*He leaves.*)

ALICE: Yes, walk out! You always leave when you see you're losing. You turn your back and run away and let your wife cover your retreat. You bigmouth, blowhard bully! All the courage you've ever had came from a bottle of booze. I spit on you!

*   *   *

CURT: We just sink lower and lower, don't we?

ALICE: You haven't seen anything yet!

CURT: There's worse?

ALICE: Much worse, only I'm ashamed to . . .

CURT: Where is he going now? Where does he find the strength?

ALICE: How the hell do I know?! He's going down to the barracks to thank the NCOs for the flowers. He'll sit down and eat and drink with them. Regale them with gossip about the officers. They've threatened to discharge him for doing that. The officers felt sorry for me and the children. That's all that saved him. And he thinks he stays on because they're afraid of him. The officers' wives, who went out of their way to help us—he hates them and tells lies about them.

CURT: It's funny. I took this job because I thought I might find some peace and quiet by the sea. I didn't know how things were with you.

ALICE: Poor, dear Curt. . . . What am I going to feed you?

CURT: Don't worry about me. I can drop in on the doctor. What about you? Let me do something about it.

ALICE: But don't let him know. He'd kill me.

A memo from Strindberg to the director of *The Dance of Death* showing the correct type of old-fashioned helmet worn in the Swedish artillery (upper left). From August Falck, *Fem år med Strindberg [Five Years with Strindberg]* (Stockholm: Wahlström and Widstrand, 1935).

CURT (*looking out the window*): Look at him! He's standing on the platform—right in the wind.

ALICE: I feel sorry for him—for being the way he is.

CURT: I feel sorry for both of you. —What's to be done?

ALICE: I don't know. . . . And we got another big pile of bills. He didn't notice.

CURT: Sometimes it's a blessing not to see.

ALICE (*at the window*): He's opened his coat. He's letting the wind strike his chest. He wants to die.

CURT: I don't believe that. Only a little while ago, when he felt his life slipping away, he clung to me, began to dig into my personal affairs, as if he wanted to creep into my skin and live my life.

ALICE: Of course. He's a vampire. Meddling in other people's business, sucking around others, worming his way into their lives because his own life is an empty shell. And I warn you, Curt, don't ever let him into your private affairs. Never let him get to know your friends. He'll take them from you and make them his. . . . It's like witchcraft. . . . If he got to know your children, they'd soon be calling him uncle. They'd be listening to everything he said, and he'd teach them everything you're dead set against.

CURT: Tell me Alice: at the time of my divorce wasn't he the one who saw to it that my children were taken from me and given to my wife?

ALICE: I guess there's no harm in telling you—now that it's all over. Yes, it was Edgar.

CURT: I always suspected something like that. So it was Edgar.

ALICE: You trusted him and sent him to your wife to patch up things between you and her. Instead he flirted with her and advised her what to do if she wanted to hold on to the children.

CURT: God! . . . God in heaven!

ALICE: Man of a thousand faces, isn't he?

Silence.

CURT: It's strange. Last night—when he thought he might die—he made me promise—that I'd look after his children.

ALICE: You're not thinking of taking your revenge out on my children?

CURT: By keeping my promise? Yes, I'll look after his children.

ALICE: Marvelous! That's the worst revenge you could take. There's nothing he detests so much as magnanimity.

CURT: I would have my revenge. Without taking revenge.

ALICE: I believe in revenge—that's real justice. Nothing pleases me more than seeing a bad man get his punishment.

CURT: Is that all life has taught you?

ALICE: It's the ultimate lesson. If I ever forgave my enemy or loved him, I'd hate myself for being a hypocrite.

CURT: Alice, sometimes it's best to bite your tongue or look the other way. It's called making allowances. We all need it.

ALICE: I don't. I've got nothing to hide, and I've always played fair and square.

CURT: That's a large claim.

ALICE: Not large enough. You don't know what I've suffered undeservedly for the sake of this man, whom I've never loved—

CURT: Why did you marry him?

ALICE: Who knows? . . . Because he took me. Because he seduced me. I don't know. . . . I wanted some sort of social position.

CURT: So you left the theater.

ALICE: The theater—ha!—too bohemian. I wanted respectability. But he cheated me. He pictured a good life for me, a lovely home. What did I get? A pile of unpaid bills. The only gold I saw was the braid on his uniform. And that wasn't gold either. He cheated me.

CURT: Come on, Alice! It's only natural for a young man to have high hopes for the future. If things didn't work out the way he dreamed, you can't blame him. I've disappointed people in the same way, but I don't think of myself as a cheat. —What are you looking at out there?

ALICE: Looking to see if he has fallen in.

CURT: He hasn't?!

ALICE: No, unfortunately. You see: cheated again!

CURT: I'm going to the doctor and the lawyer.

Alice sits down by the window.

ALICE: You do that, Curt. I'll sit here and wait. God knows, I'm good at that.

INTERMISSION

[3]

Same set. Daylight. The Sentry is on duty outside, as before, pacing back and forth. Alice is now seated in the armchair to the right. Her hair is gray.

Curt knocks and enters from the left.

CURT: Hello, Alice.

ALICE: Hello, dear Curt. Sit down.

Curt sits in the armchair to the left.

CURT: The steamer is at the dock now.

ALICE: I know what that means if *he's* on board.

CURT: He is. I could see his helmet shining. . . . What's he been up to in town?

ALICE: That's easy to figure out. He wore his dress uniform. That means he called on the colonel. He put on his white gloves. That means he's been paying social calls.

CURT: Didn't you notice yesterday how quiet he had become? Since he stopped drinking, he's become another person—calm, reserved, considerate.

ALICE: Don't be taken in by that. Sober, he would have been a holy terror. It's lucky for the human race that he took to the bottle. Whiskey made him ridiculous and harmless.

CURT: That's a new one. I hadn't realized that bottled spirits could be moral spirits. Surely you've seen the change in him. After that brush with death he's acquired a kind of dignity. He seems elevated somehow, uplifted. Maybe when he began to have thoughts about immortality, he got a new slant on life, too.

ALICE: Don't kid yourself. He's up to no good. And don't you believe a word he says. He lies like the devil, cooks up plots behind your back—

CURT (*staring at her*): Alice. You look so different. These two nights have made your hair turn gray.

ALICE: No, dear boy. I've been gray a long time. But there's no point in dyeing my hair when my husband is half dead. . . . Twenty-five years in a fortress! —Do you know that these rooms used to be the prison in the old times?

CURT: Prison? Yes, you can almost tell by the walls.

ALICE: And by my skin. Even the children got prison pallor here.

CURT: It's hard to imagine small children laughing and playing within these walls.

ALICE: There wasn't much laughter. And the two that died—they didn't get enough sun.

CURT: What's next, do you suppose?

ALICE: The crucial battle between him and the two of us. I recognized that baleful glance, that flash in his eye, when you read him the telegram from Judith. Of course the lightning was intended to strike her, but, as you know, she lives in a charmed circle. So the lightning struck you.

CURT: And just what does he intend to do with me?

ALICE: Hard to say. He has a genius for nosing out other people's secrets. Didn't you see how all day yesterday he kept worming his way into your quarantine business, leeched on to your life, gobbled up your children. He's a cannibal, a blood-sucker. I know him for what he is. There's nothing left of his own life.

CURT: I see what you mean. He's already crossed over to the other side. His face is phosphorescent, as if he were dissolving. His eyes glimmer like will-o'-wisps over swamps and graves. —I can hear him; he's coming. —Did it ever occur to you that he might be jealous?

ALICE: Forget it! He's too conceited. "Show me the man I should be jealous of!" His very words.

CURT: He's marvelous! Even his failings have merit. —Should I rise and greet him or just sit here?

ALICE: Be rude—otherwise he'll think you're putting on an act. And when he starts telling his stories, go along with him, pretend to believe him. I can translate his lies into the truth. I've got this little dictionary up here. . . . God, something awful is about to happen. I don't know what. —And, Curt! don't lose control. The only advantage I've had over him in all my battles was that I was always cold sober and never lost my head. He always lost his in booze. Ready?

*   *   *

> *Edgar enters from the left, wearing his dress uniform, helmet, overcoat, white gloves. He is calm and dignified but looks pale and hollow-eyed. He walks unsteadily across the room, keeping his helmet and coat on, and sits down at the right, far from Curt and Alice. During the following dialogue he keeps his officer's sword between his knees.*

EDGAR: Good day! Forgive me for sitting down like this. I'm a little tired.

CURT and ALICE (at the same time): Hello, Edgar! —Welcome back!

ALICE: How are you feeling?

EDGAR: Fine, fine. A little tired, that's all.

ALICE: What news from the big city?

EDGAR: Not much. It's short but sweet. Stopped in to see the doctor, and he tells me it's nothing serious. I can live for twenty years more, if I take care of myself.

ALICE (*to Curt, sotto voce*): He made that up. (*To Edgar.*) How wonderful, darling!

EDGAR: Yes, isn't it.

> *Silence, during which Edgar looks at Alice and Curt as if begging them to speak.*
>
> *Curt is about to say something, but Alice stops him.*

ALICE (*To Curt, sotto voce*): Don't say anything! Let him be the first. He'll show his hand.

EDGAR (*to Alice*): I'm sorry; I didn't hear.

ALICE: I didn't say anything.

EDGAR (*speaking slowly*): Ahem, Curt . . . you know I . . .

ALICE (*to Curt*): You see! He's playing his first card.

EDGAR: . . . you know . . . that I was in town. Yes, of course you know.

> *Curt nods.*

EDGAR: Yes, in town. And I met a few people. Talked a bit. One was a young cadet – new recruit – (*Drawing it out.*) in . . . the . . . artillery.

> *Pause. Curt senses trouble.*

And since we don't have many cadets – out here, I mean – I struck a bargain with the colonel and . . . arranged that he – the cadet . . . should . . . be transferred out here. This should come as very good news – especially to you, since the lad in question is – I am happy to inform you – your son!

ALICE (*to Curt*): What did I tell you! A vampire!

CURT: Under ordinary circumstances a father might be pleased by this news of his son. But in my situation I find it extremely painful.

EDGAR: You're upset! I don't understand.

CURT: There's nothing to understand! Just forget about my son!

EDGAR: Well, well, you're serious. How very awkward! You see, the young man has already been ordered to report here, and as of this moment he is under my command.

CURT: Then I shall make him ask for a transfer to another outfit.

EDGAR: You can't. You have no rights over him.

CURT: No rights? I'm his father!

EDGAR: Yes. But the court assigned the rights over him to his mother!

CURT: Then his mother will tell him what to do! And I'll tell her!

EDGAR: That really won't be necessary.

CURT: Good!

EDGAR: Because I've already spoken to her. —It's all settled, you see. (*He smacks his lips contentedly.*)

Curt starts to rise from his chair but falls back.

ALICE (*to Curt*): Does that man deserve to live?

CURT: He *is* a cannibal!

EDGAR: Well, we can put paid to that. (*Peering at Alice and Curt.*) Did you say something?

ALICE: No! Are you hard of hearing?

EDGAR: A little. Why don't you move over here, Alice, so that I can talk just to you?

ALICE: That isn't necessary. Having a witness might be good for both parties.

EDGAR: You may be right. A witness always comes in handy. —Now, have you prepared the will?

Alice hands him a document.

ALICE: It's the standard form. The judge advocate himself drew it up.

EDGAR: With your best interests in mind. (*He reads here and there in the document.*) Good. . . . Good. . . . Good. (*He carefully and deliberately tears it into long strips, which he throws on the floor.*) So much for that! Another matter settled. (*He smacks his lips contentedly.*)

ALICE (*to Curt*): Do you believe this?

CURT: He isn't human!

EDGAR: I have something else to say to you, Alice.

ALICE (*on edge*): Go ahead.

EDGAR (*still speaking calmly*): By reason of your frequently expressed wish to put an end to this unhappy marriage, and by reason of the lack of love you have shown toward your husband and children—and by reason of the debts you have incurred through careless management of the household, I have—only now while I was in the city—applied to the court baron for a divorce.

ALICE: Really? And your reasons?

EDGAR (*still speaking slowly and deliberately*): I just gave them. Apart from those, there are personal ones. Having recently learned that I might live for another twenty years, I have considered the desirability of dissolving this unhappy union and forming a better one. With that in mind, I intend to take as my wife a woman who knows that her husband is to be treated with respect and who will bring with her into the home youth, charm, and—what shall I say?—a little beauty.

Alice takes off her wedding ring and throws it at Edgar.

ALICE: Take it!

Edgar picks up the ring and puts it in his vest pocket.

EDGAR: She threw away her wedding ring. Curt, you're the witness. Please take note.

ALICE (*rising, barely able to control her voice*): And you intend to toss me out and bring another woman into my house?

Edgar smacks his lips and nods.

ALICE: All right! No holds barred. Curt, I'm telling you, as my cousin, that this man is guilty of having attempted to murder me!

CURT: Murder you!

ALICE: Yes! He pushed me into the ocean.

EDGAR: No witnesses!

ALICE: You lie! Judith saw the whole thing!

EDGAR: So what!

ALICE: She can testify to what I said.

EDGAR: No, she cannot! Because she will say that she didn't see anything!

ALICE: You've taught that poor child to lie!

EDGAR: Why would I waste my time? You had already taught her.

ALICE: You've spoken to Judith?

Edgar smacks his lips, and nods.

ALICE: Oh, my God, my God!

EDGAR: The fortress surrenders, the enemy capitulates. The victor grants the vanquished freedom to withdraw and gives them ten minutes notice. (*He puts his watch on the table.*) Ten minutes. According to the timepiece on the table. (*As he stands by the table, he clutches at his heart.*)

ALICE (*moving to his side and holding his arm*): What is it?

EDGAR: I don't know.

ALICE: Can I get you something? Something to drink?

EDGAR: Whiskey? No, I don't want to die. You—! (*He straightens up and shrugs off Alice's hand.*) Don't touch me! —Ten minutes! Or I level the fortress. (*He draws his sword from its scabbard.*) Ten minutes! (*He exits at the rear, holding his sword high.*)

* * *

CURT: I don't believe he's human.

ALICE: He isn't. He's a demon.

CURT: What does he want with my boy?

ALICE: He wants to hold him hostage so he can control you. He wants to isolate you, cut you off from the officers, the doctor, everybody important. . . . Do you know what the people around here call this island? "Little Hell."

CURT: It fits. . . . You know, Alice, you're the first woman I ever felt sorry for. All the others I felt got what they deserved.

ALICE: Don't leave me now, Curt. Don't abandon me. He'll hit me. . . . He's hit me for twenty-five years. Sometimes in the presence of the children. . . . He pushed me into the ocean.

CURT: Yes, hearing that turned me absolutely against him. I came here without any malice in my heart, having put out of my mind all his humiliating treatment of me, his spite. I even forgave him when I learned from you that he had helped my wife get the children. After all, he was sick, dying. But now, when he wants to take my son from me, he's got to go. It's either him or me.

ALICE: Good! No surrender! Blow the fortress sky high. Blow him to smithereens!—even if we go up with it. I've got the dynamite that will do the job.

CURT: I had no evil thoughts when I came here. At first I wanted to run away when I felt how your hatred for him was infecting me. But now I feel called upon to hate this man as I hate evil itself. . . . What do you suggest?

ALICE: I've learned the strategy from the master himself. First, drum up all his enemies; form a league against him.

CURT: I can't get over it! He tracked down my wife just for this. Why didn't the two of them meet thirty years ago? What a pair they would have made. Put the two of them in the ring together and the earth would shake.

ALICE: Well, now they have met – the two soulmates! And now they must be parted. I think I know how to get at him; I've had my suspicions.

CURT: Who is his most dedicated enemy on this island?

ALICE: The supply officer.

CURT: A man to be trusted?

ALICE: Absolutely. And he knows what I –. Well, we both know. . . . He knows what the staff sergeant and Edgar have been up to.

CURT: Up to? Up to what?

ALICE: Lining their own pockets.

CURT: Embezzlement? Oh, no. Leave me out of that. I want nothing to do with it.

ALICE (*laughs sarcastically*): What's the matter? Can't strike the enemy?

CURT: I could at one time. Not now.

ALICE: Why not?

CURT: Because I found out . . . that justice is done – eventually.

ALICE: Have fun while you wait! Wait while your son is taken from you. Wait like I've had to wait. Look at my gray hair. . . . Go ahead, feel it. At least it's thick. . . . He's going to get married again, and I'll be free – to do the same. I'm free. Free! And in ten minutes he'll be sitting down there in a prison cell, down there in the clink – (*She stamps on the floor.*) – down there in the pokey – and I'll dance on his head. I'll dance the Boyar dance. (*Starts to dance, hands on hips, and laughs wildly.*) And hallelujah! I'll play the piano! And God! will he hear it! (*Hammers the piano keys.*) Ho, ho! The prison tower will open wide its gates and the guard with his drawn sword will no longer guard me but him! But him! But him! But'im, but'im, but'im!! (*She imitates the Sentry and makes the sound of a marching band.*) Barum, barum, barum-barum, barum! But him! But him! But'im, but'im, but'im!!

Curt has been staring at her, fascinated and aroused.

CURT: Alice, Alice! You devil!

Alice climbs on a chair and takes down the laurel wreaths.

ALICE: These go with me as my army withdraws. The laurel wreaths of victory! (*Straightening the ribbons on the wreaths.*) And streamers in the air! A little dusty, but forever green. Like me! —I'm not old, am I, Curt?

CURT (*passionately, his eyes flashing*): You *are* a devil!

ALICE: Of course! This is "Little Hell!" —I'm going to fix my hair—(*She undoes her hair and lets it fall about her shoulders.*)— change my dress—in two minutes—we go to the supply officer— two minutes—and then—Bang!—the fortress blows sky high!

CURT (*aroused*): A devil! A devil!

ALICE: You always said so, even when we were children. Remember when we were kids, and we played at getting married? Ha-ha! You were so shy—

CURT (*reproachfully*): Alice!

ALICE: Oh, but you were. It made you irresistible. Bold women like bashful men, that's what they say. And shy men like coarse women. You sure liked me a little then. Didn't you?

CURT: My head's spinning. I don't know where I am.

ALICE: Here, with an actress. An actress. No inhibitions, no prejudices—but a woman all the same—all woman. . . . And now I'm free, free, free! —Turn around. I'm going to change my blouse.

> *She unbuttons her blouse. Curt rushes to her, embraces her, lifts her high. Kisses her on her neck until she screams. Then he casts her down onto the chaise lounge and runs out the door at left.*

[4]

> *Same set. Evening. Through the windows and glass doors at the rear the Sentry can still be seen, pacing back and forth as before. The laurel wreaths are draped over the arm of one of the chairs. The ceiling lamp is lit.*

> *Soft music covers the break between scenes, continues after the rise of the curtain until Alice's entrance.*

> *Edgar, dressed in his worn fatigue uniform, wearing his riding boots, looking pale and hollow-eyed, his hair streaked with gray, is sitting at the writing desk, playing solitaire. He has his glasses on.*

> *As he moves and shifts the cards, he occasionally gives a slight start, looks up, and listens anxiously.*

> *The solitaire apparently defeats him; he becomes impatient and gathers the cards together. Goes to the window at left, opens it, and throws out the deck of cards. The window remains open, shaking on its hinges.*

> *He goes to the cupboard, opens it, and is frightened by the noise of the window. Looks round to see what is causing it. Takes from the cupboard three dark, square-shaped whiskey decanters. Gives them a long, steady look—and throws them out the window. Takes out several boxes of cigars, sticks his nose in one of them—and throws them all out the window.*

> *Next he removes his glasses, wipes them, and tries looking through them. Throws them out the window. Stumbles his way back through the furniture as if he had trouble seeing, goes to the secretary, and lights the six*

candles in the candelabrum. Catches sight of the laurel wreaths; picks them up and heads for the window. Changes his mind and goes to the piano. Takes the runner from the top of the piano and carefully wraps the wreaths in the runner. Using common pins he finds on the desk, he fastens the corners of the runner, and places the wreaths on a chair. Walks to the piano and strikes the keys with his fist. Closes the cover, locks it with the little key, and throws the key out the window. Then he lights the candles on the piano. Goes to the étagère, picks up the portrait photo of Alice, studies it, tears it to pieces, and throws the pieces on the floor. Again the window suddenly shakes on its hinges, frightening Edgar.

After he has calmed himself, he takes the pictures of his son and daughter, kisses them quickly, and puts them in his breast pocket. The other pictures he sweeps off the étagère with a stroke of his arm, and kicks them into a pile with his boots.

He goes to the writing table, slumps down in a chair, and clutches his chest. Lights the candles on the desk. Sighs and stares ahead as if seeing unpleasant visions.

He stands up and walks to the secretary, opens the leaf, and takes from one of the compartments a packet of letters tied with a blue ribbon. Throws the packet into the fire in the tile stove. Closes the secretary.

The telegraph sounder clicks once—once only—and is silent. Edgar is deathly frightened. Stands immobile, hand at heart, listening. When there is no further sound from the telegraph, he listens in the direction of the door at the left. Walks over to it, opens it, steps out, and returns a moment later with a cat in his arms. He strokes its back, crosses the room, and exits by the door at the right.

The soft music ceases.

[5]

Alice enters through the glass doors at the rear. She is dressed in outdoor clothes, hat, gloves. Her hair is dark again. Seeing all the candles lit, she stops and looks around in amazement.

Curt enters from the left, tense and nervous.

ALICE: It looks like Christmas Eve.

CURT: Now what?

Alice stretches out her hand for Curt to kiss.

ALICE: Time to thank me.

Curt reluctantly kisses her hand.

ALICE: Six witnesses. Four of them absolutely unshakable. They've made their depositions, and we'll get the news here on the telegraph—smack in the middle of the fortress.

CURT: Really?

ALICE: "Really?" Is that all you can say? You might thank me.

CURT: Why has he lit all these candles?

ALICE: Because he's afraid of the dark, I told you. —Look at that telegraph key. Looks like the handle of a coffee grinder. I'll grind, I'll grind, and the beans will crack like broken teeth being pulled.

CURT: What's he been doing? Look at the room!

ALICE: I'll bet he was thinking about moving. He'll move, all right. Downstairs! (*Taps the floor with her foot.*)

CURT: Steady, Alice! I think the whole thing stinks. We were friends when we were young, and he was often good to me when I was having a rough time of it. I feel sorry for him.

ALICE: And not for me? I never hurt anybody, but for the sake of that monster I had to sacrifice my career!

CURT: What career? When were you a blazing star?

ALICE (*furious*): What the hell are you saying? Do you know who I am? What I've been?

CURT: Easy, take it easy.

ALICE: Just like him—already!

CURT: Already?

> *Alice runs to Curt, hangs on his neck, and kisses him. He takes her arms, pulls them back, and bites her throat. She cries out.*

ALICE: You're biting me!

CURT (*beside himself*): Yes, I want to bite your neck, suck your blood like a panther! There's a wild animal in me and you've let him loose. For years I tried to slay it by living like a monk. I came here thinking I was a bit better than you and Edgar. I'm not. Now I'm the worst. The moment I saw you, really saw you, naked and terrible, I changed. I felt the power of what's evil. What's ugly became beautiful, and what's good grew soft and weak. Come here, Alice. I'm going to suffocate you with my lips and mouth.

> *He kisses her long and passionately. When they separate, she holds out her left hand for him to see.*

ALICE: There's the mark left by the chain that you broke. I was a slave and now I'm free.

CURT: But I'm going to capture you and tie you up.

ALICE: You?

CURT: Yes, me!

ALICE: For a while there I thought you were . . .

CURT: A saint?

ALICE: Well, you spoke about the Fall.

CURT: Did I?

ALICE: I thought you were going to give me a sermon.

CURT: A sermon! We'll be in town within an hour—in our hotel room. I'll give you a sermon!

ALICE: I want to go to the theater tonight. I want to be seen in public. Edgar is the one who suffers the humiliation if I walk out on him, don't you see?

CURT: I see, all right. Prison isn't enough: you want more.

ALICE: That's right! It's not enough. There's got to be shame and humiliation also.

CURT: Crazy world! You're the one who behaves shamefully, and he's the one who has to bear the shame.

ALICE: It is a stupid world, but I didn't make it.

CURT: These prison walls must have absorbed all the crimes of the world. They reek of them. All you have to do is breathe and you get them in your system. Look at you: all you're thinking about is the theater and supper afterward, while I was thinking about my son.

ALICE (*flicking her glove at his mouth*): You fake! Don't give me that crap!

> *Curt raises his hand, about to slap her face. Alice shies back.*

ALICE: Down, boy, down!

CURT: I'm sorry.

ALICE: On your knees!

> *Curt kneels.*

On your face!

> *Curt puts his forehead to the floor.*

Kiss my foot.

> *Curt kisses her shoe.*

And don't you ever dare do that again! —Rise!

> *Curt stands up.*

CURT: God, what's happened to me? Where the hell am I?

ALICE: You know where you are!

CURT (*looking around in horror*): I almost believe that . . . I am in hell!

* * *

Edgar enters from the right, looking wretched, supporting himself with a cane.

EDGAR: Could I talk to Curt? —Alone.

ALICE: What about? Surrendering the fortress?

EDGAR (*sitting down at the worktable*): Curt, would you mind sitting down with me for a minute? Alice, maybe you could give us a few moments—in peace.

ALICE: Now what are you up to? Changing your strategy? (*To Curt.*) Go ahead; sit down.

Curt sits down, reluctantly.

ALICE: Out of the mouths of babes—and old men! —If a telegraph message comes through, give a call.

Alice exits to the left.

* * *

EDGAR (*after a pause, speaks in a very serious tone of voice*): Does it make any sense? An existence like mine—like ours?

CURT: No, no more than mine does.

EDGAR: Then what's the meaning of the whole mess?

CURT: In my better moments I came to believe that the meaning was not to know the meaning, and, while not knowing, going along with it, bending with it.

EDGAR: Bend? Without a fixed point outside myself to hold on to, I can't bend. I'd fall.

CURT: Quite right. But you use mathematics when you aim

your guns. You should be able to find the unknown point when you have several knowns.

EDGAR: I have sought, but—I haven't found.

CURT: You've miscalculated. Try again.

EDGAR: I shall. —Tell me, Curt: where did you acquire your fund of patience and resignation?

CURT: Whatever I had, it's all used up by now. Don't overestimate me.

EDGAR: I suppose you have noticed that for me the art of living has consisted in canceling out what's happened. I mean, crossing out and moving on. Long ago I got myself a big sack. I kept stuffing all my humiliations and frustrations in it, one after the other, and when it was full, I threw it into the sea. . . . I don't believe anybody has suffered so many humiliations as I have. But when I crossed them out and moved past them, they ceased to exist.

CURT: Yes, I have noticed how you make your own world.

EDGAR: How do you think I could have gone on living? How could I have borne it? (*He clutches at his heart.*)

CURT: Are you all right?

EDGAR: No, I'm poorly, poorly. (*Pause.*) The trouble is—there comes a moment when the ability to make my own world, as you put it, vanishes. And in place of that world is reality—naked, ugly reality. Awful! (*His face sags, and he talks like an old man, half-sobbing.*) You see, Curt, my dearest friend—. (*Gets control of himself and speaks in his normal voice.*) Forgive me. Just now when I was in town and saw my doctor—(*With tears in his voice again.*) he said I was a broken man—(*With his normal voice.*) and that I didn't have long to live.

CURT: Is *that* what he said?

EDGAR: That's what he said.

CURT: Then it wasn't true!

EDGAR: What wasn't? —Oh! —No, it wasn't true.

Pause.

CURT: And the rest of it? Wasn't that true either?

EDGAR: What, my dear friend, wasn't true?

CURT: That my son was ordered to report here as cadet.

EDGAR: I never heard that.

CURT: You know, Edgar, your talent for crossing out what you've done is fantastic!

EDGAR: Curt, dear fellow, I don't know what you're talking about.

CURT: You're hopeless, Edgar.

EDGAR: Yes, I guess there isn't much hope left for me.

CURT: Come to think of it, perhaps you haven't tried to shame your dear wife publicly—by applying for a divorce, for instance?

EDGAR: Divorce! Where did you hear that?

CURT (*standing up*): All right, Edgar. Admit it: you've been lying.

EDGAR: Such harsh words—and from my best friend. We all need to make allowances.

CURT: You've come to realize that, have you?

EDGAR (*firmly, with a strong voice*): Yes, I've come to realize that. . . . That's why I ask your forgiveness, Curt. For everything.

CURT: Well, that's frank enough, and straightforward. But there's nothing for me to forgive, Edgar. And I'm not the man you think I am. Not anymore. Certainly not the man to hear your confessions.

EDGAR (*firmly, without whining*): Life played such awful tricks on me. Always setting me back, ever since childhood. And when people were cruel, I got to be cruel also.

> *Curt paces the floor and glances at the telegraph apparatus.*

EDGAR: What are you looking at?

CURT: Can you shut that thing off?

EDGAR: No, not very likely.

CURT (*more and more anxious*): What sort of fellow is this staff sergeant of yours? This Eastberg?

EDGAR: Oh, a good, decent fellow. A little too much interested in money, of course.

CURT: And what about the supply officer?

EDGAR: He and I are sworn enemies; but I can't honestly say he's a bad sort.

> *Curt is looking out the window. In the distance a lantern can be seen, moving and swinging.*

CURT: What are they doing with a lantern out there near the gun battery?

EDGAR: A lantern?

CURT: And some soldiers moving around.

EDGAR: Must be the "bloodhounds." That's what we call them.

CURT: "Bloodhounds"?

EDGAR: The military police. Somebody's got himself in trouble, and they've come to put him in the brig.

CURT: Oh?!

> *Pause.*

EDGAR: Tell me, Curt, now that you've gotten to know her better—what do you think of Alice?

CURT: Hard to say. . . . I guess I really don't understand people at all. She's as much a mystery to me as you are—or as I am, for that matter. I've reached that point in life when my wisdom has crystallized and I can say: I don't know anything; I don't understand anything. . . . However, when something happens, I'm still curious to know why it happened. . . . Why did you push her into the ocean?

EDGAR: I don't know. It just seemed like the thing to do. She was standing on the dock, and it struck me she had to go in.

CURT: No regrets?

EDGAR: None.

CURT: Strange.

EDGAR: Yes, it is. So strange that I don't actually believe I ever did such a thing.

CURT: You must have known that she would get her revenge, sooner or later.

EDGAR: That she has, with a lot left over. For her, that was the thing to do.

CURT: Talk about resignation! What has happened to make you, all of a sudden, so cynical, so resigned?

EDGAR: Since I saw death face-to-face, I've had a different slant on life. . . . Tell me, Curt, if you had to judge between Alice and me, who would you say was right?

CURT: Neither. I have infinite sympathy for both of you. —Maybe a little more for you.

EDGAR: Give me your hand, Curt.

> *Curt extends his right hand and puts his left hand on Edgar's shoulder.*

CURT: Old friend!

* * *

> *Alice enters from the left, carrying a parasol.*

ALICE: Well, well! The old, trusty friends. Isn't that touching? —Did the telegram arrive?

CURT (*coldly*): No.

ALICE: I don't like delays. They make me impatient, and when I get impatient, I give things a push. —Watch this, Curt! I'm going to give him the *coup de grâce*. I'm going to finish him off.

Watch him fall! —First I load the rifle, like this. —I know the manual by heart—that famous manual on hand weapons that didn't even sell five thousand copies. Then I take aim. . . . (*She aims the parasol at Edgar.*) Fire!! (*She pops open the umbrella.*) How's the new wife, Edgar? The young, the beautiful, the non-existent wife. —You don't know how she feels? What a pity! But I know how my lover feels.

> *She puts her arms around Curt's neck and kisses him.*
> *He shoves her away.*

ALICE: Oh, he feels so good. He's just a little shy—still! —You stupid wretch! I never loved you! You were too proud to be jealous. Too blind. You never saw how I pulled the wool over your eyes.

> *Edgar unsheathes his sword and goes after her, swinging his sword but hitting only the furniture.*

ALICE: Help! Help!!

> *Curt does not move.*
> *Edgar falls to the floor, sword in hand.*

EDGAR: Judith! Avenge me, Judith!!

ALICE: Hurray, he's dead! He's dead!

> *Curt sidles up to the rear doors.*
> *Edgar gets to his feet.*

EDGAR: Not—quite—yet! (*He sheathes his sword and goes to sit in the armchair near the worktable.*) Judith! Judith!

> *Alice moves up to Curt.*

ALICE: I'm leaving! With you.

> *Curt repulses her with such force that she falls to her knees.*

CURT: Go to hell! Go back to the abyss you came from! —God! I hope I never see you again! (*He is at the door.*)

EDGAR: Don't leave me, Curt! She'll kill me!

ALICE: Curt, don't abandon me like this! Don't abandon us!

CURT: Goodbye. (*He leaves.*)

* * *

ALICE (*doing a complete about-face*): That sneaky bastard! You call that a friend?!

EDGAR (*gently*): Forgive me, Alice. And come over here. Come quickly!

ALICE (*going to him*): The biggest ninny and worst hypocrite I ever did see! You know, Edgar, at least you're a man.

EDGAR: Alice, listen to me now. . . . I haven't long to live.

ALICE: Oh?

EDGAR: The doctor told me.

ALICE: You mean—everything else was a lie too?

EDGAR: Yes.

ALICE (*frantic*): God! What have I done?

EDGAR: No matter. Whatever it was, it can be put right.

ALICE: Not this! It can never be put right!

EDGAR: Yes, everything can. Just cross it out and move on.

ALICE: No. The telegram! The telegram!

EDGAR: What telegram?

ALICE (*on her knees before Edgar*): We must be damned! Why did this have to happen? I've blown myself sky-high—blown *us* to bits. —Why did you make up those stories? Why did Curt have to come and tempt me? We're lost! —Oh, Edgar, you're a great-souled, generous man. You can forgive, even what's unforgivable.

EDGAR: What's this that can't be forgiven? What haven't I forgiven you?

ALICE: Oh, you're right, Edgar, you're right. But this can never be put right.

EDGAR: I can't even guess what it might be—and I know how fiendish you can be.

ALICE: Oh, if I ever get out of this! If I ever get out of this, Edgar, how I'll care for you, and love you. Oh, Edgar, I'd love you so much!

EDGAR: My ears must be deceiving me. What's going on?

ALICE: No one can help us, can they? No one.

EDGAR: Who do you have in mind?

ALICE (*looking him in the eyes*): I don't know. . . . What will happen to the children?

EDGAR: Have you brought shame and disgrace on them?

ALICE: I can't have! Not me! . . . They'll have to drop out of school. . . . And when they go out into the world, they'll be as lonely as we are, and just as mean. —You never did run into Judith, it's obvious.

EDGAR: No. Cross it out!

> *The telegraph ticker begins clicking. Alice jumps up.*

ALICE (*crying out*): That's it! The end! It's all over. (*To Edgar.*) Don't listen to it!

EDGAR (*calmly*): I won't listen, my darling. Calm yourself.

> *Alice is by the telegraph apparatus. She stands on tiptoe to look out the window.*

ALICE: Don't listen! Don't listen!

EDGAR (*putting his hands over his ears*): I'm not listening, Lisa. Lisa, my little angel, I'm not listening.

Alice kneels with upstretched arms.

ALICE: Oh, God, help us! The "bloodhounds," the hounds of heaven. (*Sobbing violently.*) God in heaven!

> *Her lips move in a silent prayer. The telegraph recorder goes on rapping for a while longer, and a long ticker tape emerges from it. Then all is quiet.*
>
> *Alice gets up, tears off the paper ribbon, and reads it to herself. Then she casts a glance upwards, sighs, and walks over to Edgar. She kisses him on the forehead.*

ALICE: It's over. . . . It was nothing. (*She sits down in the other armchair and cries unrestrainedly into her handkerchief.*)

EDGAR: What are you hiding?

ALICE: Don't ask. Anyway, it's over now.

EDGAR: As you wish, sweetheart.

ALICE: You wouldn't have talked to me like that three days ago. What's come over you?

EDGAR: A change, my darling. When I fell the first time, I went a bit over the other side of the grave. What I saw there I've forgotten, but it left an indelible impression.

ALICE: Of what?

EDGAR: Of hope. The hope of something better.

ALICE: Better?

EDGAR: Yes. That this life was real, was life itself—I've never really believed that. This life is death. Or something even worse.

ALICE: And we are—

EDGAR: We must have been given the job of torturers—torturing each other. So it seems.

ALICE: Have we tortured each other enough?

EDGAR: Yes. I'm inclined to think so. Maybe overdid it a bit: look at the place! (*He looks around the room.*) Isn't it time we tidied things up? And cleaned up this mess?

ALICE (*getting up*): If you think it's possible.

EDGAR (*walks around the room, surveying the damage*): Well, not in one day. Not a chance.

ALICE: Two days, perhaps? Or many days.

EDGAR: Let's hope so. (*Pause. Edgar sits down again.*) So—you didn't get away, did you? Not this time. And you didn't catch me, did you?

> *Alice stands aghast.*

Yes, yes, I know you tried to get me locked up. But—I cross it out! —Well, it's not the worst thing you've tried to do.

> *Alice is still speechless.*

Furthermore, I was never involved in any embezzlement!

ALICE: And so now I'm supposed to be your nurse?

EDGAR: If you want.

ALICE: What else should I do with myself?

EDGAR: I don't know.

ALICE (*sits down apathetically. Looks crushed*): This must be the everlasting fire. Is there no end?

EDGAR: There is, if we have patience. Maybe when death comes, life begins.

ALICE: Would it were so!

> *Pause.*

EDGAR: So you think Curt was a fake and a hypocrite?

ALICE: Of course I do.

EDGAR: I don't believe it. The trouble is that anyone who comes near us becomes like us. Then off they go. Curt was weak, and we were too strong for him. (*Pause.*) Still, it's all so boring nowadays. There was a time when men fought with their bare fists; now they only shake them at each other. . . . Tell you what I do believe, though. In three months I'm pretty certain that you and I will be giving a party. Our silver anniversary. With cousin Curt giving you away — again, like he did twenty-five years ago. And the supply officer will be toastmaster, making pretty speeches, and my staff sergeant will lead the singing: "For they are jolly good fellows. . . . " And if I know my man, the colonel will pop up too. — Uninvited.

> *Alice laughs.*

You think that's funny? What about Adolf's silver anniversary? You know, Adolf in the rangers. His bride of twenty-five years had to wear her wedding ring on this finger — (*He points to his right hand.*) — because Adolf in one of his tender moments had chopped off her left ring finger with his machete.

> *Alice puts her handkerchief to her mouth to suppress a giggle.*

EDGAR: I know. It's enough to make you cry. — Ah, ha, you're laughing. Well, my precious, sometimes we laugh, sometimes we cry. I don't know which is right. . . . I read in the paper the other day about a man. Been divorced seven times. Consequently married seven times. Finally ran away — ninety-eight years old — and remarried his first wife! If that isn't love, what is? . . . Whether life is a serious business or a big joke is something I've never been able to figure out. As jokes go, it's rather sick. Better to take it seriously. Makes it more peaceful and pleasant. . . . However, just when you've made up your mind to be serious, along comes somebody who puts you on. Like Curt. . . . Well, what do you say? A party for our silver anniversary?

Alice is silent.

Oh, come on! Say yes. Sure, they'll laugh at us, but what the hell! We'll laugh with them. Or be very solemn. Whatever we feel like.

ALICE: All right. Why not?

EDGAR (*seriously*): Right. A silver wedding anniversary. (*He stands up.*) Cross out and move on. So—let's move on.

Introduction
to
A Dream Play

The film critic for a leading American newspaper recently said of *A Dream Play* that "it has a cast of fifty, requires sets that are virtually unrealizable, has no coherent story line, and is obsessed with the spectacle of human suffering during the dream that is Life."*

This "unrealizable" play is one of Strindberg's more frequently produced works in Sweden and has had a number of important productions in other European countries. It has been given Reinhardtian treatment with elaborate sets and performed as Grotowskian "poor theatre." It has been staged with projections incorporated in the design, and it has been done with no sets at all—on the radio. Strindberg's own preference was for simple staging. He wanted to "de-materialize" the stage.** In a dream nothing should seem substantial; the sets should be made out of baseless fabric and the characters of the stuff that dreams are made on.

As for actors, *A Dream Play* has been performed with both small casts and huge casts. Significantly, Strindberg did not provide a list of characters. In his preliminary note, he speaks of the characters as dissolving and coalescing, as they do in dreams. The doubling of parts is not an economic desideratum in this play; it is essential to its method. In the ideal production, there would be not fifty actors but two: one man, one woman, who would fragment themselves.

The basis of the critic's mistaken notions about *A Dream Play* is, I suppose, the lack of a "coherent story line." Drama has

* Vincent Canby, *The New York Times*, 21 June 1984.
** See *Strindberg och teater*, ed. August Falck (Stockholm, 1918). German translation of relevant sections in *August Strindberg über Drama und Theater*, ed. Marianne Kesting and Verner Arpe. See also G. M. Bergman, "Strindberg and the Intima Teatern" in *Theatre Research/Recherches Théâtrales*, vol. 9, no. 1 (1967), 14–47.

always meant story and plot. Plot was the most important element in Aristotle's formulation, and character the second most
important. In *A Dream Play*, there is no plot to speak of and no
characters in the conventional sense, since the figures dissolve
into one another.

How can one bring dramatic order and coherence to a plotless
and characterless series of incidents and images? One cannot—
unless one reexamines the basic nature of dramatic art itself. This
is what Strindberg did from 1898 through 1903, his most creative
period, when he wrote over twenty-two plays. Those years that
saw the birth of a new century also saw the origin of a new form
of dramatic art. In seeking to picture the new cosmos that was
taking shape in his mind, Strindberg had to create new forms.
Similarly, the art of the novel and of painting were to be revolu-
tionized in the first decades of the century. The great innovation
in painting followed the realization that in essence a painting was
not a representation or imitation of objects but an arrangement
of shapes and colors on a canvas. "Remember," said Maurice
Denis in 1890, "that a picture—before being a battle horse or a
nude woman or some anecdote—is essentially a flat surface
covered over with colors in a certain order." Cubism and abstract
painting disavowed what was formerly thought absolutely necessary: a recognizable object in a setting of some sort, temporal or
spatial. In classic drama the essential elements were plot and
character. In *A Dream Play*, Strindberg replaced plot and character with theme and motif. He used the theater as painters like
Kandinsky and Pollock were later to use canvas. What *Oedipus
Rex* is to Aristotelian drama, and what *Hamlet* is to the drama of
character, *A Dream Play* is to the drama of pure form.

Strindberg certainly did not consciously set out to revolu-
tionize dramatic art when he wrote *A Dream Play* in 1901. It
grew out of the profound sense of loss that he experienced when
his third wife left him. It had a slow genesis, evolving out of a
cluster of germinal ideas that Strindberg succeeded in bringing
together by treating them as a musician handles motifs and
themes. In his preliminary note, Strindberg comments on the
musical structure.

To the casual reader, *A Dream Play* may appear to be improvised, a paratactic arrangement of episodes. Actually, like great
music, it is worked out with extraordinary skill. It is complex in
its details, simple in its themes. There are two principal themes

that are varied and repeated: (1) for human beings to live, they must inevitably hurt other human beings; (2) one cannot help feeling sorry for them. Out of this rather banal material, Strindberg created his most compassionate drama, and his most comprehensive. Like a piece of music or a nonrepresentational painting, it allows for all kinds of responses. "Its power of suggestion," writes Maurice Valency in *The Flower and the Castle*, "is enormous, and this is to a considerable degree the result of the intricate scheme of correspondences by means of which the action and its symbols are laced together." In the welter of images and incidents only a few points are fixed and definite. Earthly existence is a dream, a Platonic nonreality; reality exists in the life of the spirit; and the artist who creates dreams is closest to the source of all being.

A Dream Play

(Ett drömspell)

A Note from the Author

Following the example of my previous dream play *To Damascus*, I have in this present dream play sought to imitate the incoherent but ostensibly logical form of our dreams. Anything can happen; everything is possible and probable. Time and space do not exist. Working with some insignificant real events as a background, the imagination spins out its threads of thoughts and weaves them into new patterns—a mixture of memories, experiences, spontaneous ideas, impossibilities, and improvisations.

The characters split, double, multiply, dissolve, condense, float apart, coalesce. But one mind stands over and above them all, the mind of the dreamer; and for him there are no secrets, no inconsistencies, no scruples, no laws. He does not condemn, does not acquit; he only narrates the story. And since the dream is more often painful than cheerful, a tone of melancholy and of sympathy with all living creatures runs through the pitching and swaying narrative. Sleep, which should free the dreamer, often plagues and tortures him instead. But when the pain is most excruciating, the moment of waking comes and reconciles the dreamer to reality, which, however agonizing it may be, is a joy and a pleasure at that moment compared with the painful dream.

The idea that life is a dream* seemed to us in the past to be no more than a poetic dream of Calderon's. But when Shakespeare in *The Tempest* has Prospero say that "we are such stuff as dreams are made on," and when elsewhere this wise Briton, speaking through Macbeth, talks about life as "a tale told by an idiot," we should probably give the matter some more thought.

Whoever during these brief hours follows the sleepwalking author on his wanderings may find a certain similarity between the apparent jumble of a dream and the disordered and mottled

---

* This paragraph and the ones following were written in 1907 in connection with the first staging of the play. They were inserted in the director's copy of the play but not printed at that time. —Trans.

cloth of life, woven by the great World Weaver, who winds the warp of human destinies and then fills the woof using our conflicting aims and changeable passions. Anyone who notes the similarity is surely entitled to think that there may be some substance to it.

As far as the loose, disconnected shape of the play is concerned, that too is only apparent. On closer examination, the composition is seen to be quite firm and solid—a symphony, polyphonic, now and then like a fugue with a constantly recurring main theme, which is repeated in all registers and varied by the more than thirty voices. There are no solos with accompaniments, that is, no big parts, no characters—or rather, no caricatures; no intrigue; no strong curtains demanding applause. The voice parts are subjected to strict musical treatment; and in the sacrificial scene of the finale, all that has happened passes in review, with the themes once again repeated, just as a man's life with all its incidents is said to do at the moment of death. Yet another similarity!

Now it is time to see the play itself—and to hear it. With a little goodwill on your part, the battle is half-won. That is all we ask of you.

Curtain going up!

PROLOGUE*

The backdrop represents banks of clouds resembling shattered slate cliffs with ruins of castles and fortresses.

The constellations Leo, Virgo, and Libra can be seen; in their midst the planet Jupiter is shining brightly.**

Indra's Daughter is standing on the highest cloud.

THE VOICE OF INDRA
(*from above*):
Where are you, my daughter? Where?

INDRA'S DAUGHTER
Here, Father! Here!

THE VOICE OF INDRA
You've gone astray, my child. Be careful;
you're drifting down.
How did you get there?

INDRA'S DAUGHTER
I followed a flash of lightning from the empyrean,
riding on a cloud. But the cloud
sank beneath me, and now I'm drifting down.
Tell me, Indra, my father, what place is this
that I have come to? Why is it so stifling,
so hard to breathe?

THE VOICE OF INDRA
You've left the second world and gone into the third.

---

*This prologue is a later addition to the play. It was written in 1906, in anticipation of the first production of the work, which took place in Stockholm on 17 April 1907.
**Leo, the Lion, is associated with Hercules and stands for man; Virgo, the Virgin, represents woman; Libra is the balance; and Jupiter is God.

You've left Sukra,* the morning star, far behind,
and now you've entered the atmosphere of earth.
Regard, my child, the seventh house of the zodiac,
Libra, the Scales, in which the daystar stands
as the year tips toward autumn
and day balances night.

INDRA'S DAUGHTER

The earth, you said? This dark and heavy world
that is lit by the light of the moon?

THE VOICE OF INDRA

Earth is the heaviest, the most leaden
of all the orbs that roam the void.

INDRA'S DAUGHTER

Tell me, doesn't the sun shine there?

THE VOICE OF INDRA

Of course the sun shines there; only not all the time.

INDRA'S DAUGHTER

There's a rift in the cloud. I can see all that's below.

THE VOICE OF INDRA

And what do you see, my child?

INDRA'S DAUGHTER

I see . . . how beautiful it is. . . . Green woods,
blue waters, white peaks, golden fields.

THE VOICE OF INDRA

Yes, beautiful like all Brahma's creations.
But it was still more beautiful once
at the dawning of time. Something happened,
a warping of its orbit—or was it something else?
A revolt, and in its wake
crimes that had to be quelled.

INDRA'S DAUGHTER

Now I can hear sounds from there. . . .
What sort of beings are they who dwell below?

*Venus, in Sanskrit.

THE VOICE OF INDRA

Go down and see for yourself.
Far be it from me to malign
the Creator's creatures, but that sound you hear
is the language they speak.

INDRA'S DAUGHTER

It sounds like—. Well, to my ears
it doesn't ring with joy.

THE VOICE OF INDRA

I can well imagine. All their tongues can speak
is the language of complaint. Indeed
those earthly beings are a bickering, badgering,
ungrateful race.

INDRA'S DAUGHTER

Don't say that. I can hear cries of joy,
and shots and roars; see flares bursting.
Bells are ringing, fires blazing,
and voices, thousands upon thousands,
singing the praises of heaven.

Pause.

You judge them too harshly, Father.

THE VOICE OF INDRA

Go down and see. Listen to them.
Then come back up here and tell me
if there is any reason, any grounds
for all their wailing and complaining.

INDRA'S DAUGHTER

Very well. I will go down there.
But you come with me, Father.

THE VOICE OF INDRA

No, I cannot breathe in those depths.

INDRA'S DAUGHTER

The cloud is sinking. The air's so heavy,
I'm suffocating. It isn't air, it's smoke and water.
So heavy, heavy, it's dragging me down, down.

Now I can see it clearly, wobbling and careening. . . .
No, the third world is not the best of worlds.

THE VOICE OF INDRA

The best? Of course not. Neither is it the worst.
Dust they call it, and it rolls round like the others.
That's why those creatures of dust are always dizzy,
lurching between folly and madness.
Don't be afraid, my child. It's only a test.

INDRA'S DAUGHTER

(*on her knees, as the cloud descends*):
I'm sinking.

[1]

The backdrop represents a forest of giant hollyhocks in full bloom — white, pink, purple, violet, sulphur-yellow — and over the top of them can be seen the top of a castle crowned with a dome that resembles a flower bud. Beneath the footings of the castle are scattered stacks of straw covering the manure and litter from the stables. The wings and tormentors, which remain unchanged throughout the play, are stylized wall paintings suggesting rooms, buildings, and landscapes simultaneously.

The Glazier, an elderly man, and Indra's Daughter enter.

DAUGHTER: The castle is still growing up out of the earth — you see how much it's grown since last year.

GLAZIER (*to himself*): I've never seen that castle before in my life — never heard of a castle growing. Oh, well — . (*To the Daughter, with complete conviction.*) Yes, indeed, it's grown two yards. That's because they've manured it good. And if you'll notice, another wing is beginning to sprout over there on the sunny side.

DAUGHTER: It's going to bloom soon, isn't it? It's past midsummer.

GLAZIER: Don't you see that flower bud up there?

DAUGHTER: Oh, yes, yes, I do! (*Claps her hands in joy.*) I wonder, why do flowers grow up from dirt?

GLAZIER (*gently, piously*): They don't like to be in the dirt, so they hurry up into the light as fast as they can — to bloom and die.

DAUGHTER: Who lives in that castle? Do you know?

GLAZIER: I used to know. Can't seem to remember now.

DAUGHTER: I think there's a man imprisoned there. . . . And I'm sure he's waiting for me to come and rescue him.

GLAZIER: Careful. You both might get more than you bargain for.

DAUGHTER: One doesn't haggle over what has to be done! Come on, let's go in!

GLAZIER: All right, all right, let's go.

[2]

They approach the backdrop, which slowly opens up toward the sides.

The stage is now a simple, bare room with a table and a few chairs. An Officer in a very unusual modern uniform is sitting in a chair. He is rocking back and forth and striking the table with his saber.

The Daughter goes over to the Officer and carefully and gently takes the saber from his hands.

DAUGHTER (*as if to a child*): Mustn't do, mustn't do!

OFFICER: Oh, please be nice to me, Agnes; let me keep my saber.

DAUGHTER: No, no! You're chopping the table to pieces! (*To the Glazier.*) You can go down to the harness room and put in the windowpane. I'll meet you later.

The Glazier leaves.

*   *   *

DAUGHTER: You are a prisoner in your own rooms. I have come to rescue you!

OFFICER: I think I've been expecting this, but I couldn't be sure you'd want to help.

DAUGHTER: It's a strong castle — it's got seven walls — but — well, we'll think of something. . . . Well, do you want to or don't you?

OFFICER: To be perfectly frank, I really don't know. Either way I'll be in trouble. You have to pay for every joy in life with twice its price in sorrow. I hate to sit imprisoned here, but if I bought myself some joy and freedom, I'd pay for it three times over in pain and suffering. — Agnes, I'd just as soon put up with it, as long as I can look at you.

DAUGHTER: What do you see in me?

OFFICER: Beauty personified, the harmony of the universe. There are curves and lines in your form and features that can't be found anywhere else except in the orbits of the planets, in the strings that vibrate with music, in the trembling pulsations of the light. . . . You've come from heaven.

DAUGHTER: So have you.

OFFICER: Then why do I have to take care of horses? Be a stableboy and carry out manure?

DAUGHTER: So that you'll want to get away from it.

OFFICER: I do want to, I do! I want to rise above it. But it's so difficult, so hard.

DAUGHTER: But, don't you see, it's your duty to find your way to the light.

OFFICER: Duty? Doesn't life owe me something?

DAUGHTER: You think life's been unfair to you? Is that what you think?

OFFICER: Yes! Unfair, unjust . . .

*   *   *

One can now hear voices from behind a partition, which is promptly drawn aside. The Officer and the Daughter look in that direction and then freeze in position, their gestures and expressions frozen, too.

The Mother, looking very ill, is sitting at a table. In front of her is a lighted tallow candle, which she trims and crops now and again with candle snuffers. On the table are piles of new-made shirts and linen, which she is marking with ink and a quill pen. To the left stands a brown wardrobe or clothespress.

The Father hands her a silk shawl.

FATHER (*gently*): You mean you don't want it?

MOTHER: A silk shawl—for me? Oh, dearest, what use can I have for a silk shawl? I'm not long for this world.

FATHER: Do you believe what the doctor says?

MOTHER: Not only what he says. Most of all I believe the voice I hear inside me.

FATHER (*gloomily*): Then it's really serious? . . . And here you are thinking only of the children—first, last, and always.

MOTHER: They were my whole life, my reason for living . . . my joy . . . and my sorrow.

FATHER: Forgive me, Christine. . . . For everything.

MOTHER: For what? You must forgive me, my darling. We've been hard on each other. And why? We don't know. We couldn't help ourselves. . . . Anyway, here are new shirts and linen for the children. You must see to it that they change twice a week. Wednesdays and Sundays. And be sure Louisa gives them their baths, and washes them—all over, you understand. . . . Are you going out?

FATHER: I have to be up at the school—eleven o'clock.

MOTHER: Would you ask Alfred to come in before you leave?

FATHER (*pointing at the Officer*): But, dearest, he's standing right here.

MOTHER: Can you imagine, I'm beginning to lose my sight, too. . . . Yes, yes, it's getting dark. (*She trims the candlewick.*) Alfred, come here.

* * *

The Father goes out straight through the wall, nodding goodbye.

* * *

The Officer goes over to his Mother.

MOTHER: Who is that girl?

OFFICER (*whispering*): Why, that's Agnes.

MOTHER: Oh, really, is that Agnes? Do you know what they're saying? That she's the daughter of the god Indra, and that she asked to come down here on earth to find out what life is really like. —Shh! Not a word!

OFFICER: Yes, indeed, she is a child of the gods.

MOTHER (*aloud*): My dearest Alfred, soon I'll have to leave you and the rest of my children. There's something I want to tell you, something I want you to remember all through life.

OFFICER (*dark and gloomy*): Yes, Mother.

MOTHER: Just one word of advice: don't ever quarrel with God.

OFFICER: I don't understand you, Mother.

MOTHER: You mustn't go around thinking that life has treated you unfairly.

OFFICER: Not even when it has, when I know I've been unjustly accused?

MOTHER: I know, I know. You're thinking of the time you were punished because they said you stole a coin and later it turned up.

OFFICER: That's right. It was unjust. It got me started through life on the wrong foot. Things were never the same.

MOTHER: I see. Now you just go over to that wardrobe and—

OFFICER (*blushing in shame*): You mean you know? You know? That's where—

MOTHER: *The Swiss Family Robinson.* . . . And your—

OFFICER: Please! Don't say any more!

MOTHER: —your brother got punished for having torn it up. But it was *you* who tore it up and hid it.

OFFICER: It's strange. That wardrobe is still standing there after twenty years. We've moved so many times since then, and Mother died ten years ago.

MOTHER: Now, what's that got to do with it? There you go— always asking questions. That's how you destroy the best things in life for yourself. . . . Oh, here's Lina!

* * *

LINA (*entering*): Oh, missis, it's awfully kind of you, and I want to thank you, but I can't go to the christening.

MOTHER: But why not, my child?

LINA: I haven't a thing to wear.

MOTHER: Why, I'll lend you my shawl! —This one.

LINA: Oh, dearest me, I can't take *that*! It wouldn't be right.

MOTHER: I don't understand you. Don't you see, I'll never be going to parties again.

* * *

OFFICER: What will Papa say? He gave it to you. It was a gift.

MOTHER: Oh, what small minds!

* * *

FATHER (*sticking his head in*): Don't tell me you're going to lend my present to a scrubwoman?

MOTHER: Don't say that. . . . I was once a maid, too—remember? . . . Why do you have to hurt the feelings of an innocent girl?

FATHER: Why hurt *my* feelings? I'm your husband.

MOTHER: Oh, I give up! If you're nice to somebody, you're mean to someone else. Help one, hurt another. What a life!

> *She trims and crops the candle until it dies. The stage grows dark, and the partition is drawn back in and conceals the scene.*

* * *

DAUGHTER: Yes, what a life. Poor souls, I feel sorry for them.

OFFICER: Do you really?

DAUGHTER: Yes, life is hard. But love—love conquers everything. You'll see! Come.

> *They move toward the rear of the stage.*

[3]

> *The backdrop is drawn up, and a new backdrop is seen, representing a dirty, brick or stone, peeling party wall. In the middle of the wall is a gate opening onto an alleyway that leads out to a bright green area, in the center of which stands a colossal plant—a blue monkshood (Aconitum). The gate functions as a stage door entrance and to the left of it sits the Stage-Door Keeper—a woman wearing a shawl over her head and shoulders. She is working on a huge bedspread with a pattern of stars. To the right is a billboard, and the Billposter is washing it. Leaning against the wall next to him is a dip net with a green handle. Farther to the right is a door with an air hole in the shape of a cloverleaf. Left of the gate stands a small linden tree with a pitch-black trunk and a few pale green leaves. Next to it is a small, round, cellar window.*

DAUGHTER (*approaching the Stage-Door Keeper*): Haven't you finished that star quilt yet?

STAGE-DOOR KEEPER: of course not, deary! Twenty-six years is no time at all for a job as big as this.

DAUGHTER: Your fiancé never came back?

STAGE-DOOR KEEPER: No. Wasn't his fault, my dear girl. He *had* to leave, *had* to . . . the poor man. Thirty years it's been.

DAUGHTER (*to the Billposter*): She was with the ballet, wasn't she? Here in the opera house?

BILLPOSTER: She was prima ballerina. But when *he* up and left *her*, he took all her dances with him, you might say. . . . She never got any parts after that . . .

DAUGHTER: All they do is complain. At least with their eyes — and their tone of voice . . .

BILLPOSTER: Oh, I don't. Not like I used to — not since I got my dip net and my green fish pot.

DAUGHTER: That makes you happy?

BILLPOSTER: Yes. So happy, I — I — . It was what I dreamed of when I was a boy, and now it's come true. Of course, I'm fifty years old, but —

DAUGHTER: Fifty years for a dip net and a fish pot . . .

BILLPOSTER: Not any fish pot! A *green* one. Green! . . .

* * *

DAUGHTER (*to the Stage-Door Keeper*): Let me have the shawl. I'll sit here for a while and watch the passing parade. You stand behind me and let me know what's going on. (*She puts on the shawl and sits down at the gate.*)

STAGE-DOOR KEEPER: This is the last day of the opera before it's closed for the season. This is when they find out if they got renewed for next year.

DAUGHTER: And those who don't get a place — what about them?

STAGE-DOOR KEEPER: God, I can't bear to see them! I have to cover my face with the shawl, I really do.

DAUGHTER: Those poor people. How awful.

STAGE-DOOR KEEPER: Look, there's one of the girls coming now! . . . She's not one of the lucky ones. Look at her cry.

*   *   *

A Singer enters from the right and hurries through the gate. She is holding her handkerchief to her eyes. She stands for a moment in the passageway outside the gate, and leans her head against the wall. Then rushes out.

DAUGHTER: Poor souls, I feel so sorry for them.

*   *   *

STAGE-DOOR KEEPER: Ah, but look at him! Want to see a really happy man? There he is!

*   *   *

The Officer comes down the alleyway and through the gate. He is wearing a high hat and tails and carrying a bouquet of roses. He is beaming with happiness.

STAGE-DOOR KEEPER: He's going to marry Miss Victoria!

OFFICER (*coming downstage, looks upward, and sings out*): Victoria!

STAGE-DOOR KEEPER: Miss Victoria will be down in just a moment.

OFFICER: Good, good! The carriage is waiting, the table is spread, the champagne's on ice—oh, let me kiss you, ladies! (*He embraces the Daughter and the Stage-Door Keeper. Sings out.*) Victoria!

A WOMAN'S VOICE (*from above, singing out liltingly*): Here I am!

OFFICER (*beginning to wander up and down*): All right, I'll be waiting!

* * *

DAUGHTER: Don't you recognize me?

OFFICER: No, for me there's only one woman in the whole world—Victoria! —For seven years I've walked up and down here, waiting for her. In the morning when the sun reached the chimney tops, and in the evening as night began to fall. . . . Look here in the asphalt; you can see the path worn by true love. Hurrah, hurrah! She's mine, she's all mine! (*Calls out.*) Victoria!

No answer.

Hm, I guess she must be getting dressed. . . . (*To the Billposter.*) I see you've got a dip net. Everybody at the opera is crazy about dip nets—or should I say, about fish. You know why? No voices, that's why. No competition. —How much does a thing like that cost?

BILLPOSTER: Pretty expensive.

OFFICER (*singing out*): Victoria! . . . (*Shakes the linden tree.*) It's blooming again! Look! For the eighth time. . . . (*Singing out.*) Victoria! . . . Now she's combing her bangs. . . . (*To the Daughter.*) Oh, come on now, my good woman, let me go up and fetch my bride!

STAGE-DOOR KEEPER: Sorry, no one's allowed backstage.

OFFICER: Seven years I've been walking and waiting! Seven years! Seven times three hundred and sixty-five makes two thousand five hundred and fifty-five. (*Stops and pokes with his cane at the door with the cloverleaf air hole.*) And I've looked at this door two thousand five hundred and fifty-five times without ever finding out where it leads to. And that cloverleaf hole to let in light—who's in there who needs to have light? Is there anyone in there? Someone live there?

STAGE-DOOR KEEPER: I don't know. I've never seen anyone open that door.

OFFICER: It looks like a door to a pantry I saw when I was four years old and nanny took me out one Sunday afternoon to visit her friends. Out—other families, other maids—but I never got farther than the kitchen—had to sit there and wait between the water barrel and the salt tub—I've seen so many kitchens in my time—and the pantry was always out next to the porch—with round holes bored through it and a cloverleaf. . . . But an opera house can't have a pantry—there's no kitchen! (*Singing out.*) Victoria! . . . Say, she couldn't possibly leave the theater by some other door, could she?

STAGE-DOOR KEEPER: Oh, no, dearie, there's no other way out.

OFFICER: Good, then I can't miss her!

> *The Actors and Dancers come pouring out. The Officer looks them all over.*

* * *

OFFICER: She's got to come along pretty soon. . . . Madame —that blue flower out there—that monkshood. I remember it from the time I was a child. Can't be the same one, can it? . . . It was at the parsonage, I remember, the minister's house—the garden. I was seven years old. . . . Fold back the top petals— the pistil and stamen look like two doves. We used to do that as children. . . . But this time a bee came—went into the flower. "Got you!" I said. And I pinched the flower together. And the bee stung me. . . . And I cried. . . . Then the minister's wife came and put mud on my finger. . . . Later we had strawberries and cream for dessert at supper. . . . I do believe it's getting dark already. —Where are you off to?

BILLPOSTER: Home. Time for my supper.

OFFICER (*rubbing his eyes*): Supper?! At this time of day? —Say, wait a minute! Do you mind if I make a phone call to "the growing castle"? Take just a minute.

DAUGHTER: Why, what do you have to do?

OFFICER: I have to tell the glazier to put in the storm windows. Winter's almost here, and I'm freezing to death. (*He goes into the Stage-Door Keeper's office.*)

* * *

DAUGHTER: Who is this Victoria he keeps calling for?

STAGE-DOOR KEEPER: His sweetheart. The dearest person in the world to him.

DAUGHTER: I understand. What she may be to us or to anyone else doesn't concern him at all. Whatever he sees in her, that's what she really is.

It grows dark very suddenly.

STAGE-DOOR KEEPER (*lights a lamp*): It's getting dark so early today.

DAUGHTER: For the gods in heaven a year is only a minute.

STAGE-DOOR KEEPER: And for us here on earth a minute can seem like a year . . .

* * *

The Officer returns. He looks rather dusty and dirty. The roses have withered.

OFFICER: Hasn't she come down yet?

STAGE-DOOR KEEPER: No.

OFFICER: She will, she will. I know *she'll* come! (*Walks up and down.*) But it's true, the sensible thing for me to do, I suppose, is to cancel the dinner reservation anyway—since it's already nighttime. . . . Yes—yes, that's what I'll do. (*Goes in to telephone.*)

* * *

STAGE-DOOR KEEPER (*to the Daughter*): I guess I'd better take my shawl back now.

DAUGHTER: No, no this is your time off. I'll do your work for you. . . . I want to learn all about people and this life on earth—I want to find out if it is as hard as they say it is.

STAGE-DOOR KEEPER: You know you can't sleep at this post, don't you? Can't ever sleep—neither day nor night.

DAUGHTER: Not sleep at night?

STAGE-DOOR KEEPER: Well, you can try—with a string from the doorbell tied to your arm. You see, they've got watchmen on duty backstage, and they spell each other every three hours.

DAUGHTER: Forced to stay awake—sounds like torture!

STAGE-DOOR KEEPER: You think so? I know a lot of people who would be glad to have my job. You don't know how they envy me!

DAUGHTER: Envy you! Envy someone who's being tortured?

STAGE-DOOR KEEPER: Well, they do. . . . Darling, I haven't told you the worst part. The worst part isn't slaving all day and staying awake all night, or sitting in the draft, getting cold and damp—it's to have to listen, like I have to, to all their sad stories. All the actors, all the dancers, they all come to me and pour their hearts out. Why do they come to me? I guess it's these wrinkles. What I've suffered is scrawled all over my face, and that's what makes them confide in me. . . . In this shawl, dearie, there's thirty years of suffering, my own and others', all tucked away.

DAUGHTER: It's so heavy—and it stings like nettles . . .

STAGE-DOOR KEEPER: Wear it if you want to, dearie. If it gets too heavy, give a call, and I'll come and relieve you.

DAUGHTER: You run along. If you can bear it, I certainly should be able to.

STAGE-DOOR KEEPER: You be kind to my friends now. Don't let their complaining get you down. (*She disappears down the passageway.*)

> *Complete blackout while the scene changes. The linden tree is stripped bare of all its leaves. The monkshood is virtually dead and withered. And when it grows light again, the green patch seen through the perspective of the alleyway has turned autumn-brown.*
>
> *The Officer enters when the lights come up. Now his hair*

and beard are gray. His clothes are shabby and thread-bare. His detachable shirt collar is badly soiled and limp as a rag. The roses have fallen from his bouquet so that nothing is left but a bunch of twigs. He wanders up and down.

OFFICER: No doubt about it. Everything points to the fact that summer is over and autumn is on its way. I can tell from the linden tree—and the monkshood. (*Wanders up and down.*) So what! Autumn is spring for me! That's when the theater opens again. And then she's got to come! —My dear lady, would you mind if I sat down on that chair a few minutes?

DAUGHTER: No, of course not. I can stand for a while.

OFFICER (*sitting down*): If I could grab forty winks, I'd feel better. . . . (*He falls asleep for a moment, then wakes up with a start and begins to pace up and down. Stops in front of the cloverleaf door and pokes at it.*) That door . . . can't get it out of my mind. . . . What's behind it? There's got to be something behind it.

> *From above one can hear the soft strains of ballet music.*

Ah ha! The rehearsals have begun!

> *The stage is lit up in flashes as if by the revolving lamp in a lighthouse.*

What's going on? (*In time with the flashes.*) Light and dark—light and dark!

DAUGHTER: Day and night—day and night! . . . A merciful providence wants to shorten the time you have to wait. The days are flying by, chasing the nights.

> *The flashes die away, and the light becomes constant. The Billposter enters with his dip net and his paste bucket, paste brush, and the rest of his equipment.*

OFFICER: The billposter, with his net. —Make a good catch?

BILLPOSTER: Sure did! It was a hot summer and it dragged on a bit. . . . The net was all right, I guess, but it wasn't exactly what I'd imagined.

OFFICER (*stressing the words*): "Not exactly what I'd imagined." Perfectly put! Nothing is as I imagined it to be. You see, the thought is greater than the deed, finer than the thing itself . . . (*Paces up and down and slaps the rose bouquet against the wall so that the last few petals fall off.*)

BILLPOSTER: You mean to say she hasn't come down yet?

OFFICER: No, not yet. She's on her way, on her way. . . . Say, you don't happen to know what's behind that door, do you?

BILLPOSTER: No, can't say as I do. Never saw that door open.

OFFICER: Well, I think it's about time. I'm going to phone for a locksmith to come and open it. (*Goes in to telephone.*)

> *The Billposter pastes up a poster and moves out to the right.*

DAUGHTER: What was the matter with the dip net?

BILLPOSTER: Matter? Nothing. There wasn't anything really the matter—it just wasn't exactly like I imagined it would be. So the pleasure wasn't all *that* great.

DAUGHTER: How had you imagined it would be?

BILLPOSTER: How had I—? Well, it's hard to say . . .

DAUGHTER: Let me say it. You had imagined it *different* from what it was. It was supposed to be green, but not *that* green!

BILLPOSTER: That's right. It just wasn't the same. You know what it's like, don't you? You really do—and that's why everybody comes to you with their troubles. . . . Maybe you'd listen to me too . . . sometime?

DAUGHTER: Of course I will. . . . Come in here and pour out your heart . . . (*She goes into the Stage-Door Keeper's cage.*)

> *The Billposter stands outside and talks to her through the window.*

* * *

Complete blackout again. When the lights come up, the linden tree is leafy, the monkshood is in full bloom, and the sun is shining on the green place at the end of the alleyway.

The Officer comes in. He is old and completely gray-haired. Clothes ragged and torn, shoes full of holes. Carries the bare twigs of what was once the bouquet of roses. Walks up and down—slowly, like an old man. He studies the poster.

* * *

A Ballet Girl enters from the right.

OFFICER: Has Victoria left?

BALLET GIRL: No, she's still here.

OFFICER: Good, I'll wait. You think she'll be leaving soon?

BALLET GIRL (*earnestly*): I'm sure she will.

OFFICER: Don't run off now or you won't get to see what's behind this door. I've sent for a locksmith.

BALLET GIRL: How exciting! I'd love to see that door opened. That door gets me—and that growing castle. —Do you know the growing castle?

OFFICER: Do I? Who do you think was imprisoned there?

BALLET GIRL: No! Was that you?! —Tell me, why did they have so many horses there?

OFFICER: Because they had all those stalls—why do you think?

BALLET GIRL (*hurt; almost crying*): Oh, I'm so dumb! Why didn't I think of that?

* * *

A Singer from the Chorus enters from the right.

OFFICER: Has Miss Victoria left?

SINGER (*earnestly*): Of course she hasn't left. She never leaves.

OFFICER: That's because she loves me! —Don't go away before the locksmith gets here. He's going to open this door.

SINGER: Really? The door's going to be opened? Hey, that's great! —Excuse me, I want to ask the doorkeeper something.

* * *

The Prompter enters from the right.

OFFICER: Has Miss Victoria left?

PROMPTER: Not as far as I know.

OFFICER: You see! What did I tell you, didn't I say she was waiting for me? —Don't go, don't go, the door's going to be opened.

PROMPTER: What door?

OFFICER: What door? Is there more than one door?

PROMPTER: Oh, that one! The door with the cloverleaf! Don't worry, of course I'll stay for that. —Just have to say a few words to the doorkeeper.

* * *

The Ballet Girl, the Chorus Singer, and the Prompter group themselves beside the Billposter outside the window to the Stage-Door Keeper's cage, and they all take turns talking to the Daughter.

The Glazier enters through the gate.

OFFICER: Are you the locksmith?

GLAZIER: No, he couldn't come; he had company. I'm a glazier and I can handle it just as well.

OFFICER: Of course . . . of course. . . . But do you have your diamond with you?

GLAZIER: Naturally! A glazier without his diamond! What do you take me for?

OFFICER: Never mind, never mind. —All right, let us proceed! (*Claps his hands.*)

> *Everyone gathers in a circle around the door. Singers from the Chorus in "Die Meistersinger" and Ballet Dancers and Extras from "Aida," both groups in costume, pour onstage from the right.*

* * *

OFFICER: Locksmith—or glazier, or whatever you are: do your duty!

> *The Glazier comes forward with his diamond.*

OFFICER: Moments like this recur very seldom in one's life, my good friends, and therefore I urge you strongly to—to—consider carefully what—

* * *

> *Policemen come forward.*

POLICEMAN: In the name of the law I forbid the opening of this door!

OFFICER: Oh, my God, what a lot of fuss and feathers whenever you want to do something new and great! . . . All right, we'll take it to court! We'll get a lawyer. We'll see what the law has to say! They can't stop us! To the lawyer!

[4]

> *In full view of the audience, the set is changed to the Lawyer's office in the following way. The gate remains standing but now functions as the gate in the office railing, which runs straight across the stage. The Stage-Door Keeper's office or cage remains as the Lawyer's small inner office with his desk, but the opening of the*

office now faces downstage. The linden tree, stripped of its leaves, serves as a hat tree. The billboard is now a bulletin board covered with government decrees and court decisions. The cloverleaf door now belongs to a filing cabinet.

The Lawyer, dressed in white tie and tails, is sitting at a high desk, completely covered with papers and documents, just to the left inside the gate. His appearance suggests he has experienced indescribable suffering in his life. His face is white as chalk and scarred with deep wrinkles, and the hollows of his face are filled with purple shadows.

He looks hideous, his face reflecting all the crimes and sins his profession has brought him in contact with.

He has two Clerks, one of whom has only one eye, the other only one arm.

The crowd that had gathered for the opening of the door remain in their places, but now they seem to be clients waiting to see the Lawyer, and they appear to have been standing there always.

The Daughter, wearing the shawl, and the Officer are far downstage.

LAWYER (*goes down to the Daughter*): Excuse me, Sister Agnes, but may I have that shawl? I'll hang it in my office until I get a fire going in the stove. Then I'll burn it, and send all the sorrows it contains up in smoke.

DAUGHTER: Not just yet, Brother Axel. First I want to fill it to bursting. Above all, I want to gather up all your pains, all the confessions you've had to take to your heart, of crimes and vices, false arrests, libels, slanders . . .

LAWYER: My dear friend, your shawl wouldn't be nearly large enough. Look at these walls — black with the soot of sin. Look at these legal briefs: one miscarriage of justice after another. Look at *me*! No one comes to me with a smile on his face. They glare at me, bare their teeth, shake their fists. They spew their venom at me, their malice, their envy, their suspicions. Look at my hands—black, and I can never wash them clean. Cracked and bleeding. My clothes have to be cleaned almost every day, they smell so of crime. Sometimes I fumigate the office with sulphur, but it doesn't help. I sleep on a couch in the next room, and all I dream about is crime. Right now I've got a murder case on my hands. That's all right; I can get through that. What's much worse—the worst of all—is divorce. A divorce case is like a cry from the center of the earth, a shriek heard in heaven. Because it goes against nature itself, against the source of all good, against love. And what's the cause of it all? When both parties have filled reams of paper with mutual accusations and finally some dear soul grabs one of them, looks him—or her—straight in the eye, and gently asks, "Come now, what have you really got against your husband—or wife?"—that person will stand there tongue-tied, unable to offer one good explanation. One time—yes, one time all the trouble started over a vegetable salad. Another time, a single wrong word. Most times, nothing at all. But the anguish, the pain! It all falls on me. Look at my face! Look at me. No woman could love me; I look like the worst sort of criminal. Do you think anyone wants me as a friend? No; I'm the man who makes them pay up—either for their debts or their sins. I tell you it's a wretched business. Living, I mean.

DAUGHTER: Poor souls. I feel so sorry for them.

LAWYER: Well you might! What do they live on? They get married on an income of ten thousand a year when they know they need twenty thousand. They borrow, of course, everybody borrows. They scrimp and scrape—live on credit—until the day they die. Who finally pays? Can you tell me that?

DAUGHTER: What of the birds of the air and the lilies of the field? Someone has his eye on them.

LAWYER: Yes. Perhaps He should take His eye off them, come down to earth and take a look at human beings. Then He might have pity for them.

DAUGHTER: Poor souls. I do feel sorry for them.

LAWYER: Who wouldn't? (*To the Officer.*) What can I do for you?

* * *

OFFICER: I just wanted to find out if Miss Victoria has left.

LAWYER: No, she hasn't, I assure you. You can put your mind at ease about that. —Why are you poking at my filing cabinet?

OFFICER: This cloverleaf—it's just like—

LAWYER: Oh, no, no. Oh no.

> *Church bells begin to ring.*

*   *   *

OFFICER: Is there a funeral today?

LAWYER: No, commencement exercises at the university! I'm just about to receive my degree: Doctor of Laws. —Say, maybe you might like to come along, get a degree and wear a mortarboard.

OFFICER: Yes, why not? Might help to break up the day a bit.

LAWYER: Excellent! Time to get ready to march in the procession. —Hurry and change your clothes!

[5]

> *The Officer exits. Blackout onstage while the following changes are made. The office railing remains standing, but it now serves as the railing to the choir in a cathedral. The bulletin board becomes a hymn board with numbers of the psalms to be sung. The linden tree/hat tree becomes a candelabrum. The Lawyer's high desk in its niche becomes the dais and lectern for the Dean conferring the degrees. The cloverleaf door now leads to the sacristy of the cathedral.*

> *The Singers from "Die Meistersinger" become Heralds with staffs, and the Extras in "Aida" carry the laurel crowns that are to be given to the degree candidates. The rest of the company are spectators.*

> *The backdrop is pulled up, and the new drop represents immensely high organ pipes; at bottom, the console and the organist's mirror.*

Music is heard. The faculties of philosophy, theology, medicine, and law are grouped at the sides of the stage. The rest of the stage is empty for a moment.

The Heralds enter from the right. Following them come the Extras from "Aida," carrying the laurel crowns on their outstretched arms.

Three Doctoral Candidates enter one after the other from the left, are invested, crowned with laurel wreaths, and go out to the right.

The Lawyer comes forward to receive his laurel crown. The Extras turn their backs on him, refusing to give him one. They leave. The Lawyer, shattered, leans against a pillar. Everyone leaves. The Lawyer is left alone.

*   *   *

The Daughter enters. She is wearing a white veil over her head and shoulders.

DAUGHTER: Do you see? I've washed the shawl. —Why are you standing here? Didn't you get the laurel crown?

LAWYER: No, I wasn't worthy of it.

DAUGHTER: Why on earth not? Because you spoke up for the poor, put in a good word for the criminal, lightened the burden of the guilty, sought to pardon the condemned? . . . What wretched people! They're not angels, are they? Still, I feel sorry for them.

LAWYER: Don't say anything bad about human beings. I'm going to take their case.

DAUGHTER (*leaning against the organ*): Why do they spit in the face of anyone who tries to help them?

LAWYER: Because they don't know any better.

DAUGHTER: Can't we teach them? Will you help? You and I together!

LAWYER: They don't want to be taught. . . . Oh, if only our grievances could be heard by the gods in heaven—!

DAUGHTER: They shall be heard, they shall reach the highest throne! (*Standing before the organ.*) Do you know what I see in that mirror? — The world — right way round. Because in reality it's backwards.

LAWYER: How did it get turned around?

DAUGHTER: When the copy was made —

LAWYER: How right you are! A copy . . . I'd always suspected it was a bad copy. And when I began to recollect the original image, everything was a disappointment to me. People said I did nothing but complain and that I had bits of the devil's mirror in my eyes* — and so on . . .

DAUGHTER: It's a mad world. Just look at the four faculties of the university. The conservative government pays the salaries of all four of them. Theology, the study of God, which is always being attacked and ridiculed by philosophy, which sets itself up to be the essence of wisdom. And medicine, which is always challenging philosophy and dismissing religion from the learned disciplines and calling it superstition. And yet they all sit together on the University Council which is supposed to teach the youth of the land respect — for the university. It's a madhouse. Heaven help him who first comes to his senses.

LAWYER: The first ones to do so are the theologians. As undergraduates they study philosophy, which teaches them that theology is nonsense. Then they go on to study theology, where they learn that philosophy is nonsense. Fools, aren't they?

DAUGHTER: And the law! Serving everyone — everyone who can afford to have servants!

LAWYER: And the poor judges! — when they try to execute justice, they end up executing people. Justice — so often unjust.

DAUGHTER: What a mess you children of God have made of your earthly lives. Children, little children! . . . Come here. I shall give you a crown — one that becomes you better. (*She places a crown of thorns on his head.*) And I shall play for you! (*She seats herself at the organ and plays a Kyrie. But instead of organ notes human voices well up.*)

* See H. C. Andersen's fairy tale *The Snow Queen.*

VOICES OF CHILDREN: Lord Almighty! Lord Almighty! (*The last note is held.*)

VOICES OF WOMEN: Have mercy on us! (*The last note is held.*)

VOICES OF MEN: Show us thy mercy and deliver us! (*The last note is held.*)

VOICES OF MEN (*basses*): Spare us, oh Lord! Be not angry with your children.

* * *

EVERYONE: Have mercy on us! Listen to our voices! Pity us mortals! . . . Oh, Almighty One, why art thou so far away? . . . From the depths we call to you: mercy, oh Almighty One! Lay not too heavy a burden on thy children! Hear our voices! Hear!

[6]

The stage grows dark. The Daughter rises and approaches the Lawyer. By means of lighting, the organ is transformed into Fingal's Cave. The waves of the sea wash in under the basalt pillars, producing a choir of wind and waves.

LAWYER: Where are we, Agnes?

DAUGHTER: Don't you hear – ?

LAWYER: I hear . . . drops . . . falling.

DAUGHTER: Those are tears. . . . People are crying. What else do you hear?

LAWYER: Sighing . . . wailing . . . moaning . . .

DAUGHTER: The complaints of mortals. They reach this far and no farther. Why are they always complaining? Are there no joys in life at all?

LAWYER: Yes, yes! The sweetest thing in life. And the most bitter! Love. A wife and a home. The best of life and the worst.

DAUGHTER: I want to know it. I want to know everything, try everything.

LAWYER: With me?

DAUGHTER: With you. You know where the dangerous corners are, the stumbling blocks. We can avoid them.

LAWYER: I'm a poor man. Haven't a penny.

DAUGHTER: What does that matter, as long as we have each other? A little joy and beauty doesn't cost anything.

LAWYER: What if we don't like the same things? You like what I dislike?

DAUGHTER: We'll have to learn to get along with each other.

LAWYER: Suppose we get bored with each other?

DAUGHTER: A baby will come. We'll be too busy to be bored.

LAWYER: You really want to marry me? Me—a poor and ugly man, cast out, despised by all?

DAUGHTER: Yes. Let us unite our destinies.

LAWYER: If you wish. So be it.

[7]

A very plain and simple room adjacent to the Lawyer's office. To the right, a large four-poster double bed with tester and hangings. A window near it. To the left, a kitchen stove with pots and pans on it. Christine is busy sealing up the inner window of the double window, using strips of paper as weather stripping. In the rear the door to the office stands open; through it can be seen a group of poor clients waiting to see the Lawyer.

CHRISTINE: I'm pasting and sealing. I'm pasting and sealing!

DAUGHTER (*pale and haggard, is sitting at the stove*): You're shutting out all the air. I'm suffocating.

CHRISTINE: Just one little crack left.

DAUGHTER: I've got to have air! Air! I can't breathe.

CHRISTINE: I'm pasting and sealing. I'm pasting and sealing!

LAWYER: That's right, Christine. You're doing fine. Heat's expensive.

DAUGHTER: Oh, I feel as if you were sealing up my mouth.

LAWYER (*standing in the doorway to his office with papers in his hand*): Is the baby asleep?

DAUGHTER: Yes—finally!

LAWYER (*gently*): I'm sorry. It's just that his bawling frightens away my clients.

DAUGHTER (*without harshness*): I don't know what we can do about it, do you?

LAWYER: Nothing.

DAUGHTER: We'll have to get a larger apartment.

LAWYER: With what?

DAUGHTER: Do you mind if I open the window? This stale air is suffocating me.

LAWYER: You'll let all the heat out. You want to sit here and freeze to death?

DAUGHTER: I don't know. It's awful. . . . Maybe at least we could scrub the floor out there?

LAWYER: You're not up to scrubbing any floors now. I'm not either. And Christine's got to go on pasting. She's got to seal up the whole house—every crack—in the ceiling, in the floor, in the walls.

DAUGHTER: I expected to be poor, but I didn't expect to be dirty.

LAWYER: The poor are always relatively dirty.

DAUGHTER: It's worse than I ever dreamed it could be.

LAWYER: We don't have it the worst. There's still food in the pot.

DAUGHTER: Do you call that food?

LAWYER: What's wrong with cabbage? It's cheap—nourishing—tastes good—

DAUGHTER: —If you happen to like cabbage! It makes me sick.

LAWYER: Well, why didn't you say so?

DAUGHTER: Because I want you to be happy. I don't mind giving up something I like for you.

LAWYER: All right, then I have to give up something I like: cabbage. The sacrifices have to be mutual.

DAUGHTER: Then what will we eat? Fish? You hate fish.

LAWYER: It is also expensive.

DAUGHTER: I never imagined it would be like this.

LAWYER (*making a joke of it*): You don't have to imagine any longer – you can see for yourself. . . . What about the baby? It was supposed to be a blessing. It's going to be the death of us.

DAUGHTER: Darling . . . dearest. . . . I'll die in this air, in this room, with nothing to look at but a backyard – with the baby crying for hours on end and never a moment's sleep – with all those people out there, always complaining, quarreling, accusing one another. I can't stand it any longer. I'll die in here.

LAWYER: My poor beautiful flower – without sun, without air . . .

DAUGHTER: And you say some people have got it even worse!

LAWYER: In this part of town I'm envied.

DAUGHTER: I think I could stand anything, if only I could have some beauty in my home.

LAWYER: I know, I know. A flower – a heliotrope – that's what you want! But it costs as much as six quarts of milk or half a bushel of potatoes.

DAUGHTER: I wouldn't mind starving if I could have flowers to look at.

LAWYER: Well, now that you mention it, there is one kind of beauty that doesn't cost anything. And a man with a sense of beauty misses it more than anything else when he can't find it in his home.

DAUGHTER: What's that?

LAWYER: No, you'll get mad.

DAUGHTER: No, I won't! We've agreed not to get mad.

LAWYER: So we have. We can say whatever's on our minds – as long as we don't snap at each other. So far we haven't.

DAUGHTER: And never will.

LAWYER: Never, as far as I'm concerned.

DAUGHTER: All right, now tell me what you were going to say.

LAWYER: All right. When I come into somebody's house, the first thing I look at is the curtains, to see if they're hanging straight. (*He goes over to the window and straightens the curtain.*) If they hang like strings or old rags, I leave—right away. The next thing I look at is the chairs. If they're grouped properly, I stay. (*He adjusts the position of a chair against the wall.*) And then I look at the candles in the candlesticks. If they're crooked, it's a sign the whole house needs straightening. (*He straightens a candle on the chest of drawers.*) There, you see! Now that, my friend, is the kind of beauty that doesn't cost a cent!

DAUGHTER (*lowering her head to her bosom*): You're being snappish!

LAWYER: I am not being snappish!

DAUGHTER: Yes, you are!

LAWYER: Oh, for Christ's sake—!!

DAUGHTER: You see?! Listen to you!

LAWYER: I'm sorry, Agnes . . . but I've suffered just as much from your untidiness as you have from the dirt. And I haven't dared to tidy up things myself, because then you'd think I was reproaching you and you'd get mad. —Oh, what's the use! We'll stop right now. Not a word more. All right?

DAUGHTER: It's awfully hard to be married. It's the hardest thing of all. I guess you have to be an angel.

LAWYER: I guess so.

DAUGHTER: I think I'll begin to hate you after this.

LAWYER: Heaven help us! . . . I tell you what: let's forestall the hate before it comes! I promise I'll never make any more remarks about your housekeeping . . . although it is sheer torture to me.

DAUGHTER: And I'll eat cabbage—although it makes me sick.

LAWYER: Fine! We'll live together and make each other sick. Your pleasure—my pain; and vice versa.

DAUGHTER: We poor souls. I feel sorry for us.

LAWYER: You've come to realize that, have you?

DAUGHTER: Yes. But in the name of God, let's avoid the dangerous corners, since we know exactly where they are.

LAWYER: Let's! After all, we're humane, reasonable, enlightened people. We should be able to make allowances, forget and forgive —

DAUGHTER: —Laugh at the small things —

LAWYER: That's right. If anyone can, we can! . . . You know, I read in *The Times* this morning that — by the way, where is the paper?

DAUGHTER (*abashed*): Which paper?

LAWYER (*snappishly*): Do I get more than one?

DAUGHTER: Smile! And don't bark at me. —I used the paper to start the fire.

LAWYER (*sharply*): Oh, for Christ's sake!

DAUGHTER: Come on now, smile. —I hate that paper. It makes fun of everything that I love and respect.

LAWYER: And that I hate and detest! —Ohhh! (*Throws up his arms, unable to contain himself.*) All right, I'll smile. Grin and bear it. I'll be humane, reasonable, and keep my opinions to myself, and say yes to everything, and be sneaky and hypocritical! . . . So you burned up my paper. . . . How about that! . . . (*He adjusts the bed hangings.*) Look at me! Here I am tidying up again and making you mad. . . . Agnes, the whole thing's impossible.

DAUGHTER: It certainly is.

LAWYER: But we still have to go on with it. Not because of the promises we swore to each other, but because of the child.

DAUGHTER: That's true. For the sake of the child. (*Sighing deeply.*) We have to go on with it . . .

LAWYER: And I've got to go to work. My clients are waiting for me. Listen to them. Growling with impatience to get at one

another's throats, tear each other to pieces, force each other to
pay penalties and go to jail. . . . Cursed creatures . . .

DAUGHTER: Poor, wretched people. . . . And this pasting,
pasting . . . (*She bows her head in silent despair.*)

CHRISTINE: I'm pasting and sealing. I'm pasting and sealing!

> *The Lawyer stands at the door, nervously twisting the
> doorknob.*

DAUGHTER: Oh, how that doorknob squeals. It's as if you
were squeezing my heart . . .

LAWYER: I squeeze, I squeeze . . .

DAUGHTER: Don't! Don't!

LAWYER: I squee–ee–ze . . .

DAUGHTER: No, no!

LAWYER: I–

*   *   *

OFFICER (*from inside the office, grabbing the doorknob from the
other side*): May I come in?

LAWYER (*letting go of the doorknob*): Help yourself! You're a big
shot! You've got your doctor's degree!

OFFICER: That's right. The world is at my feet. I can go where
I want, do what I want. I've climbed Parnassus, won the laurel
crown. Honor, fame, immortality, it's all mine!

LAWYER: And what are you going to live on?

OFFICER: Live on?

LAWYER: Yes. Clothing, housing, food?

OFFICER: Oh, you can always make out, as long as there is
someone who loves you and wants you to be happy.

LAWYER: Oh, sure! Sure! . . . Paste away, Christine! Paste
until they suffocate! (*He is moving out backward, nodding his
head.*)

CHRISTINE: I'm pasting and sealing. I'm pasting and sealing! Until they suffocate!

* * *

OFFICER: Well, are you coming along?

DAUGHTER: Right away! Where are we going?

OFFICER: To Fair Haven! It's summer there, the sun is shining. There's youth and happiness, children and flowers, singing and dancing, picnics and parties!

DAUGHTER: That's where I want to go!

OFFICER: Well, come on!

* * *

LAWYER (*reenters*): Now I shall go back to my first hell. This here was the second hell—and the greatest. The most beautiful was the greatest hell of all. . . . Look, she's been dropping hairpins on the floor again . . . (*He is picking them off the floor.*)

OFFICER: Good Lord! He's found out about the hairpins too.

LAWYER: Too? Of course! There are two prongs, but one hairpin. Two making one. If I straighten it out, it's one single piece. If I bend it, it's two, without ceasing to be one. This means the two are one. But if I break one off—like this—then the two are two. (*He breaks the hairpin and throws away the pieces.*)

OFFICER: Marvelous! He's understood the whole thing! —But before you can break it, the prongs must diverge. If they converge, they stay together.

LAWYER: And if they're parallel, they never meet. It neither breaks nor holds.

OFFICER: The hairpin is absolutely the most nearly perfect of all created things. A straight line that is the same as two parallel lines!

LAWYER: A lock that holds when it's open.

OFFICER: Holds a free band of hair that remains free when it closes.

LAWYER: Like this door! When I close it, I open the way—for you, Agnes! (*He withdraws and closes the door.*)

* * *

DAUGHTER: And now what?

[8]

Scene change. The four-poster with its tester and hangings is transformed into a tent. The stove remains where it was. The backdrop is drawn up. In the foreground to the right are charred hills covered with the red brush and black and white tree stumps remaining after a forest fire; also red pigsties and privies. At the foot of this is an open-air gymnasium for invalids and convalescents where the patients exercise on mechanical contraptions and machines that resemble instruments of tortue. To the left in the foreground are some of the open sheds of the quarantine station, housing the boilers, piping systems, and furnaces used in the disinfecting processes. Beyond the foreground is a strait of water. The backdrop represents a beautiful wooded shore lined with docks decorated with flags. White boats, some with sails hoisted, others not, are moored alongside. Between the trees one can catch glimpses of small Italian-style villas, with pavilions, belvederes, and marble statues.

Dressed up like a Moor, the Medical Inspector of the quarantine station is walking along the shore. The Officer goes over and shakes his hand.

OFFICER: Well, I'll be darned, if it isn't old Gabby himself! So this is where you disappeared to!

MEDICAL INSPECTOR: That's right. Here I am!

OFFICER: Is this Fair Haven or isn't it?

MEDICAL INSPECTOR: No, Fair Haven is on the opposite shore. You're in Foul Strand.

OFFICER: Oops! We've come the wrong way.

MEDICAL INSPECTOR: We? —Ah, yes! Aren't you going to introduce me?

OFFICER: Can't. Just wouldn't do. (*Sotto voce.*) She's the daughter of Indra himself!

MEDICAL INSPECTOR: Indra? Don't you mean Varuna himself? —Well, what do you say? Aren't you surprised my face is black?

OFFICER: Dear boy, I'm fifty years old. At that age nothing surprises you. I guessed right away that you were going to a masquerade tonight.

MEDICAL INSPECTOR: Right on the head! Why don't you come along? How about it?

OFFICER: Great idea! This place isn't—. Can't say it attracts me. . . . What sort of people live here, anyway?

MEDICAL INSPECTOR: The sick ones here, the healthy ones over on the other side.

OFFICER: You mean these are all poor people here?

MEDICAL INSPECTOR: Don't be ridiculous! The rich ones here. Look at the fellow on the rack. He's eaten too much *pâté de foie gras*, and drunk so much Burgundy he's got knotted feet.

OFFICER: Knotted?

MEDICAL INSPECTOR: That's right; feet like knotted wood. . . . And that fellow over there lying on the guillotine— he's drunk so much cognac, we've got to straighten out his spine by putting him through the mangle.

OFFICER: Don't like the sound of that!

MEDICAL INSPECTOR: Fact is, on this side everyone's got some sort of problem he wants to hide. Look at the one who's coming now. A real dilly!

> *An elderly Dandy enters in a wheelchair, pushed by an Attendant. Accompanying him is a scrawny, ugly, sixty-year-old Coquette, dressed in the height of fashion. She in turn is accompanied by the "Friend," a man in his early forties.*

OFFICER: Why, there's the Major himself! Went to school with us, didn't he?

MEDICAL INSPECTOR: Yes, that's him: Don Juan! Look at him—he's still in love with that skinny spook at his side. He can't see that she's grown old—that she's ugly, faithless, cruel!

OFFICER: That's real love for you. I never thought that old playboy could ever be so deeply in love, so seriously in love.

MEDICAL INSPECTOR: You do see the bright side of things, I must say.

OFFICER: Well, you see, I've been in love myself. Victoria. . . . Yes, yes, I'm still walking up and down in that corridor waiting for her.

MEDICAL INSPECTOR: Don't tell me you're the stage-door Johnny waiting in the corridor!

OFFICER: That's me.

MEDICAL INSPECTOR: Well, well. Have you got the door open yet?

OFFICER: No, the case is still pending in the courts. The lawyers are fighting it out. . . . Trouble is that the billposter is out fishing with his net, as you might have known, so he's not available to give evidence. . . . And in the meantime, the glazier has put the windowpanes in the castle, which has grown half a story. . . . It's really been a very good year this year. . . . Very warm and humid.

MEDICAL INSPECTOR: You don't know what heat is. I've got heat like nobody else!

OFFICER: How hot does it get in those ovens anyway?

MEDICAL INSPECTOR: When we're disinfecting cholera carriers, we get it up to one hundred forty degrees.

OFFICER: Not another cholera epidemic?

MEDICAL INSPECTOR: Yes, didn't you know?

OFFICER: Of course I knew. My trouble is I keep forgetting what I know.

MEDICAL INSPECTOR: I wish I could forget—at least forget myself. That's why I dress up, go to masquerades, Halloween parties, play charades.

OFFICER: What have you been up to anyway?

MEDICAL INSPECTOR: If I tell you, you'll say I'm bragging. If I don't, you'll call me a hypocrite.

OFFICER: I get it. That's why you painted your face black!

MEDICAL INSPECTOR: That's right. A little blacker than I really am!

OFFICER: Who's that coming this way?

MEDICAL INSPECTOR: That, my friend, is a real live poet. On his way to his mud bath.

> *The Poet comes in. He is walking with his eyes fixed on the heavens, and he is carrying a bucket of mud.*

OFFICER: Mud? Damnation! He should be bathing himself in light and air!

MEDICAL INSPECTOR: Oh, no. He's got his head in the clouds so much of the time, he gets homesick for the mud. Wallowing in the mud makes his skin tough—same as with pigs. After that he doesn't feel the gadflies stinging.

OFFICER: What a strange world! All contradictions!

* * *

POET (*ecstatically*): Out of clay the god Ptah created man on a potter's wheel, a turning lathe—(*Skeptically.*) or what the hell was it? (*Ecstatically.*) Out of clay the sculptor creates his more or less imperishable masterpieces—(*Skeptically.*) or are they only junk? (*Ecstatically.*) Out of clay are created for the world's kitchens and pantries those indispensable vessels known under the generic name of pots, plates, and—(*Skeptically.*) actually, I really don't care what they're called. (*Ecstatically.*) I say to you: lo, here is clay! In its liquid state, it's called mud. —And that's where I come in. (*Calls out.*) Lina!

* * *

Lina enters with a bucket.

POET: Lina, come here and let Agnes have a look at you. She knew you ten years ago, when you were young, happy, and – let's say – pretty. . . . Look at her now! Five kids – and a husband who beats her! Scrimping, slaving, starving! All her beauty faded, all her joy withered, while she was being a good mother and wife – which should have given her an inner satisfaction, a sense of fulfillment that should have found expression in a radiant smile on her face and the glow of contentment in her eyes –

MEDICAL INSPECTOR (*puts his hand over the Poet's mouth*): Shut up, you fool! Shut up!

POET: That's what they all say! And if you shut up, they say, "Speak out, man, speak out!" Crazy people. No rhyme or reason

* * *

DAUGHTER (*moves over to Lina*): What's the matter? I want to know.

LINA: No, I don't dare. They'll punish me. Make things worse for me.

DAUGHTER: Who would be that cruel?

LINA: I don't dare tell you. They'll beat me!

POET: That's the truth! But I can talk – even if this big Moor here knocks my teeth out. – Let me tell you, Agnes, daughter of the gods, about injustice. Do you hear music and dancing up there on the hill? You know who that's for? That's for Lina's sister. She's just come home from the big city. When she was in the big city, she wasn't exactly a good girl, if you know what I mean. But now they've slaughtered the fatted calf for her. And Lina, who stayed at home, has to carry the buckets to feed the pigs!

DAUGHTER: Don't you see? They're happy because the girl was going astray and she found her way back, not because she's come home. What's wrong with that?

POET: Then why not give a party every night for the blameless working girl who never went dancing down the primrose path?

Why not? Where's Lina's party? When she quits work, she has to go to a prayer meeting and be preached at for not being perfect. Is that fair?

DAUGHTER: I don't know. It's hard to say because—because there are always unforeseen circumstances.

POET: That's what the famous caliph realized, too: Harun al-Rashid, Harun the Just sat quietly on his throne, and from up there he could never see how the others had to live way down here. But finally some complaints floated up to his sublime ear. Then one fine day he climbed down from his throne, disguised himself, and took his place with the crowds in the street to learn all about justice in this world.

DAUGHTER: You surely don't take me for Harun the Just, do you?

OFFICER: Let's change the subject. —Look at the new arrivals.

> *Gliding into the strait from the left comes a white boat shaped like a dragon, with a pale blue, silken sail hoist on a golden arm and a rose-colored pennant flying from a golden masthead. Sitting at the helm with their arms around each other are He and She.*

OFFICER: Now just look at that, will you? Look at that! There's real happiness, boundless bliss, the ecstasy of young love!

> *The stage grows bright.*

* * *

HE (*stands up in the boat and sings*):

> Hail to thee, my beautiful bay,
> Where in my green seasons
> I dreamed my golden dreams.
> I've come back to you,
> Not alone as I was then.
> Blue water, blue skies,
> Sparkling bays, shady bowers,

Greet the girl of my dreams—
My love, my bride,
My sunshine, my life!

*The flags on the docks at Fair Haven dip in salute.
White handkerchiefs can be seen waving from the villas
and from the shore. An arpeggio of harps and violins
ripples across the water.*

POET: See how the world is lit up by love. Listen to the music ringing across the water! —Eros!

OFFICER: Why, that's Victoria!

MEDICAL INSPECTOR: Now you've had it!

OFFICER: That's *his* Victoria. I've got my own all to myself. And my Victoria—nobody can see her! She's mine! . . . All right, time to hoist the quarantine flag, and I'll haul in our catch.

*The Medical Inspector waves a yellow flag. The Officer
tugs on a line that makes the boat head in toward Foul
Strand.*

OFFICER: Put in! Put in! Come ashore! Come ashore!

*He and She suddenly notice the hideous landscape and
utter cries of fear and loathing.*

MEDICAL INSPECTOR: Yes, I know, it's pretty tough on you, but everyone who comes from infected places has got to go through this station. You've got to be inspected and fumigated.

POET: How can you talk that way, how can you act this way?! They're two people deeply in love. Leave them alone. Let the lovers be. Meddling with true love is a capital crime. . . . Why does everything beautiful have to be dragged down, dragged through the mud?

Ashamed and downcast, He and She come ashore.

HE: What do you want with us? What have we done?

MEDICAL INSPECTOR: Who says you've done anything? You needn't have done anything to have to suffer the little vexations of life.

SIIE: Happiness never lasts.

HE: How long do we have to stay here?

MEDICAL INSPECTOR: Forty days and nights.

SHE: I'd rather end it all!

HE: Yes. Live here among charred hills and pigsties? Not a chance!

POET: Wait! Love conquers everything—including sulphur fumes and carbolic acid!

* * *

MEDICAL INSPECTOR (*lights the stove. Blue sulphur fumes rise up*): I'm getting the sulphur going. Now, if you don't mind, please step in.

SHE: But this blue dress will lose its color!

MEDICAL INSPECTOR: And turn white! And those red roses will turn white!

HE: And your cheeks, too. Forty days! Forty nights!

SHE (*to the Officer*): I hope you're satisfied! This is just what you wanted!

OFFICER: No, not at all! —It's true that your happiness was the source of my unhappiness, but—well, it doesn't matter anymore. I've got my degree from the university, and I've got a very good position right across there. . . . Ho, ho, yes, yes, I'm doing all right! . . . And this fall I'll be teaching in a school. . . . Teaching class to the little boys, the same lessons I read all the time I was a child . . . all my youth. . . . And now I'll have to read the same old assignments, the same old lessons over and over again while I pass through middle age. . . . And then through old age . . . the same old assignments. How much is two times two? How many times does two go into four? . . . Until they retire me. . . . Nothing to do but wait for the next meal and the morning paper and the evening paper.

. . . Until by and by I'm hauled out to the crematory and burned to ashes. . . . Don't you have any retired people out here? That's the worst thing, you know—after two times two is four—to start in grade school again after you've been through the university—to ask the same questions over and over again until you die . . .

> *A Middle-aged Man walks by with his hands clasped behind his back.*

There goes a retired man, living on his pension, and waiting for his life to trickle out. Probably an army captain who never got to be major. Or a CPA who never quite made it to office manager. Many are called but few are chosen. . . . Walking and waiting for his breakfast—

MIDDLE-AGED MAN: No! For my paper. My morning paper!

OFFICER: And he's only fifty-four. He can go on for another twenty years like that, waiting for his meals and his papers. . . . It's enough to make you sick.

MIDDLE-AGED MAN: What is there in life that doesn't make you sick? Tell me that, will you? Tell me that.

OFFICER: I wish someone could. . . . Now I've got to go and study with little boys—two times two is four—how many times does two go into four? (*He grabs his head in desperation.*) —Oh, Victoria, Victoria! I loved her and wanted her to be the happiest girl in the world. Now she is happy, as happy as she can be. And that makes my heart ache—ache—ache!

* * *

SHE: Do you really think I can be happy when I see how you suffer? How can you think that? Maybe your heart won't ache so much when you see me sitting here like a prisoner for forty days and nights? Maybe you won't suffer so much?

OFFICER: Maybe yes, maybe no. It can't make me happy to see you suffer. Ohhh . . .

HE: How do you think I feel? How can I build a happy life out of your agony?

OFFICER: We are poor lost souls—all of us!

EVERYONE (*stretching their arms toward heaven and giving out a cry or shriek like a dissonant chord*): Ohhhh—!

DAUGHTER: Almighty One, listen to them! Life is cruel! Poor lost souls! Take pity on them!

EVERYONE (*as before*): Ohhh—!

[9]

> *Blackout for a moment while all those onstage either leave or change places. When the lights come up again the shoreline of Foul Strand is in the back and lying in shadow. The strait lies between it and Fair Haven, which is now in the foreground. Both Fair Haven and the strait are brightly lit. To the right, one corner of a ballroom, its windows wide open, can be seen. Couples are dancing within. Standing on an empty box outside the ballroom are three Young Girls, holding one another around the waist and looking in at the dance. On the terrace steps to the casino is a bench on which Ugly Edith is sitting, bareheaded, melancholy-looking, with her hair like a wild mop. In front of her is a grand piano with its lid raised. To the left, a yellow frame house. Outside it two Children, in summer clothes, are playing catch.*
>
> *Back of the foreground is a pier with white boats tied up and with flags flying from flagpoles. Lying at anchor out in the strait is a white ship of war, square-rigged, gunports open.*
>
> *But the landscape as a whole suggests winter, with snow on the ground and on the bare trees.*
>
> *The Daughter and the Officer enter.*

DAUGHTER: How wonderful! This is vacation land! Everybody's resting and happy! No work for anybody—parties every day—everybody's dressed in their finest clothes—music and dancing even before lunch! (*To the three Young Girls.*) Why aren't you girls in there dancing?

YOUNG GIRLS: Us?

OFFICER: Don't you see they're chambermaids?

DAUGHTER: Oh, of course! . . . But why is Edith sitting out here? Why isn't she dancing?

Edith hides her face in her hands.

OFFICER: Don't embarrass her! She's been sitting there for three hours and nobody's asked her to dance. (*He goes into the yellow house at the left.*)

DAUGHTER: What a cruel game!

* * *

MOTHER (*in a low-cut dress, comes out and goes over to Edith*): What are you doing out here? Why don't you go in and dance like I told you?

EDITH: Please, Mother! . . . I can't be forward like the other girls, I can't. I know I'm ugly, I know that no one wants to dance with me. Why do you have to remind me of it all the time? (*She begins to play on the piano Johann Sebastian Bach's "Toccata con Fuga," in D Minor, BWV 913.*)

From within the ballroom the waltz can be heard softly at first, then growing louder, as if it were competing with Bach's Toccata. But Edith outplays it, and reduces the waltz to silence. The guests at the ball can be seen in the doorway listening to her play. Everyone on the stage stands entranced by her playing.

Then a Navy Lieutenant grabs Alice, one of the guests at the ball, around the waist, and rushes off with her down to the pier.

NAVY LIEUTENANT: Come on, let's get out of here!

Edith breaks off playing, rises and follows them with her eyes, her face registering her heartache. She remains standing as if turned to stone.

* * *

Now a wall of the yellow frame house is lifted away and we see the interior of a small schoolhouse and three benches with small boys sitting on them. Among them is the Officer, looking troubled and ill at ease. Standing in front of them is the Teacher, wearing glasses, a piece of chalk in one hand and a ruler in the other. He handles the ruler as if threatening punishment.

TEACHER (*to the Officer*): Now, boy, tell me: how much is two times two?

The Officer remains sitting. Searches desperately for the answer.

TEACHER: Stand up when I ask you a question!

OFFICER (*in torment, gets to his feet*): Two . . . times two . . . is—let me see now, it's . . . it's two—two!

TEACHER: I see. I see. You haven't learned your lesson.

OFFICER (*ashamed*): Yes, I have, it's just that . . . well, I know how to do it, but I—I just can't tell you.

TEACHER: Don't try to wiggle out of it! —So you know what it is, but you just can't say it. Well, now, maybe I can help you. (*He grabs the Officer by the hair and shakes him.*) Maybe that will shake it out of you!

OFFICER: My God, this is disgraceful! Disgraceful!

TEACHER: It's disgraceful to see a big boy like you turning into a lazy—

OFFICER (*hurt and stung*): A *big* boy?! Yes, I am big, much bigger than these boys. I've finished school—(*As if waking up.*) I've got my doctor's degree. What am I doing sitting here? Don't I have my doctorate?

TEACHER: Certainly you do. But you've got to sit here and mature. You've got to mature. —Don't you think that's right?

OFFICER (*his hand on his forehead*): Yes, of course. That's right; you've got to mature. . . . Yes. . . . Two times two—. Two times two—is two! Yes! I shall prove it by means of analogy, the highest form of proof. Follow carefully. One times one is one; therefore two times two is two. What applies to one applies to the other.

TEACHER: Your proof is completely in accord with the laws of logic. But the answer is wrong!

OFFICER: Whatever is in accord with the laws of logic can't be wrong. Let's test it. One goes into one once; therefore two goes into two twice!

TEACHER: Absolutely right according to analogy. But now tell me how much is one times three?

OFFICER: Three!

TEACHER: It therefore follows that two times three is also three!

OFFICER (*pondering*): No, that can't be right. . . . It can't be. . . . Or maybe . . . (*Sits down, looking lost and hopeless.*) I guess I'm not mature yet.

TEACHER: You're not nearly mature enough! Not nearly!

OFFICER: How long will I have to sit here?

TEACHER: How long here? Do you think time and space exist? Suppose time exists. Then you should be able to tell me what time is. All right, what is time?

OFFICER: Time. . . . (*Thinking.*) I can't exactly tell you, but

I know what it is. Ergo, I can know how much two times two is without being able to tell you! Can Teacher tell us what time is?

TEACHER: Of course I can!

ALL THE BOYS: Tell us! Tell us!

TEACHER: Time . . . ? Let me think. (*Stands motionless with his finger alongside his nose.*) While we're talking, time is flying. Therefore time is something that flies while I'm talking!

ONE OF THE BOYS (*stands up*): Teacher, now you're talking, and while Teacher is talking, I'm going to fly from here. Therefore I am time! (*He flees from the classroom.*)

TEACHER: Absolutely correct according to the laws of logic!

OFFICER: Then the laws of logic are crazy. Johnny who flew away can't be time!

TEACHER: That, too, is absolutely correct according to the laws of logic, even though it's crazy.

OFFICER: Then logic is crazy!

TEACHER: It does seem so, doesn't it? But if logic is crazy, then the whole world's crazy. And I'll be damned if I'll sit here and teach these boys how to act crazy! What do you say? If someone will treat me to a drink, we'll go for a swim!

OFFICER: That's a *posterus prius* or the world upside down! You're supposed to take a swim first and a drink after. Stupid old fool!

TEACHER: Don't get arrogant with me, Doctor!

OFFICER: Colonel, if you don't mind! I'm an army officer. And I don't understand why I have to sit here and be scolded and insulted and treated like a schoolboy.

TEACHER (*raising his finger*): We have to mature!

* * *

MEDICAL INSPECTOR (*enters*): We're all under quarantine as of now!

OFFICER: Ah, there you are! Where have you been? Do you

realize this fellow here has been making me sit on this bench with the other boys—and I've got a Ph.D.

MEDICAL INSPECTOR: Really? Why don't you just get up and leave?

OFFICER: Leave! That's a good one! . . . Easier said than done!

TEACHER: You know it, boy! Just you try to leave!

OFFICER (*to the Medical Inspector*): Save me! Hide me from his eyes!

MEDICAL INSPECTOR: Well, come on, never mind! Come and help us dance and make merry. Dance before the plague breaks out! We've got to dance!

OFFICER: Will the warship sail then?

MEDICAL INSPECTOR: That's the first thing! The ship will sail away. What a lot of sobbing and crying there'll be.

OFFICER: Always crying. When the ship comes in and when it puts to sea. . . . Well, let's go!

> *They leave the schoolhouse. The Teacher continues teaching silently.*

* * *

> *The three Young Girls, who were watching the dance through the window, move sadly down to the pier. Edith, who has been standing as if turned to stone at the piano, follows them slowly.*

DAUGHTER (*to the Officer*): You mean there isn't a single happy person in this paradise?

OFFICER: Yes, there is. Two of them. A newlywed couple. Listen to them.

> *The Newlywed Couple enters.*

HUSBAND (*to his Wife*): I'm so happy I want to die.

WIFE: Die because you're happy?

HUSBAND: Yes. "There lives within the very flame of love a kind of wick or snuff that will abate it."* And knowing what's to come turns my love to ashes when it burns most brightly.

WIFE: Then let's die together. Now, before it's too late.

HUSBAND: Die? Why not? I'm afraid of happiness. A mirage, made to lure us on.

They go down toward the sea.

* * *

DAUGHTER (*to the Officer*): What a cruel world! And the poor souls who live in it!

OFFICER: You think so? Look at this man who's coming now. Of all the mortals in this place he's the most envied.

A Blind Man is led in.

He owns every one of these hundred villas. The bays and harbors, the beaches and woods are all his, including the fish in the water, the birds in the air, and the beasts in the woods. All these thousands of people are nothing more than his tenants. The sun rises on his waters and sets on his lands—

DAUGHTER: So? Does he have something to complain about, too?

OFFICER: Yes, and with good reason: he can't see.

MEDICAL INSPECTOR: He's totally blind.

DAUGHTER: The most envied of them all!

OFFICER: He's come to see the warship sail. His son is on board.

* * *

* Strindberg does not quote this passage from *Hamlet* (IV, 7) but seems to echo it.

BLIND MAN: I can't see it, but I can hear it. I can hear the claws of the anchor tearing at the mud at the bottom of the sea. Sounds like the hook when it's pulled out of the fish and the heart is ripped out through the throat. . . . My son, my one and only child, is leaving me to travel far from home, to sail the seven seas; and all I can do is follow him in my thoughts. . . . I can hear the anchor chain clanking and scraping. . . . And there's something flapping and snapping like wet sheets on the line whipped by the wind . . . handkerchiefs wet with tears, hm? . . . And I can hear sighing and sobbing and sniffling, like people crying . . . maybe little waves lapping against the hull, maybe the girls on the shore . . . the girls that get left behind . . . with nothing to console them. . . . I once asked a little boy why the sea was salt, and the boy, whose father was away on a long journey, said right away, "The sea is salt because the sailors cry so much." "But why do the sailors cry so much?" I asked. "Because," he said, "they always have to go away from home—and that's why they're always drying their handkerchiefs up on the masthead!" And then I asked him, "But why do people cry when they're sad?" And he said, "That's because they have to wash the glasses of their eyes so they can see better."

> *The warship has gotten under sail and glides away. The Girls on the shore are alternately waving goodbye with their handkerchiefs and drying their tears with them. Suddenly, a signal flag with red, white, and blue stripes* signifying "Yes" is hoisted on a halyard to the yardarm of the foremast. Alice jubilantly waves her answer back with her handkerchief.*

DAUGHTER (*to the Officer*): What does the flag mean?

OFFICER: It means "Yes." It's the lieutenant's way of writing "yes" with the red blood of his heart on the blue cloth of heaven.

DAUGHTER: What does "No" look like?

* In the original, a red ball on a white field, which most people today would take for the Japanese flag.

OFFICER: A blue and white checkerboard—tainted blood and anemia.* —Look at Alice! Have you ever seen anyone look so happy?

DAUGHTER: Look at Edith! Have you ever seen anyone look so sad?

BLIND MAN: Coming and going—meeting each other and leaving each other—that's life. I met his mother one day—and then she left me. But at least I had my son with me. Now he's gone!

DAUGHTER: But he'll surely come again!

BLIND MAN: Who are you? I've heard your voice before . . . in my dreams . . . in my youth . . . when summer vacation began . . . when I was a newlywed . . . when my child was born. . . . Every time life smiled on me, I heard that voice, like a softly stirring south wind, like harps from heaven, like the songs I imagine the angels sang the first Christmas . . .

* * *

The Lawyer enters, goes over to the Blind Man, and whispers in his ear.

BLIND MAN: Is that so!

LAWYER: The honest truth! (*He approaches the Daughter.*) You've seen just about everything there is to see, but you haven't experienced the worst thing we've got to live through.

DAUGHTER: The worst! What can that be?

LAWYER: Repeating everything . . . going through it again! Going back to the beginning! . . . Having to learn your lesson all over again! —Come on!

DAUGHTER: Where?

LAWYER: Back to your duties!

* A blue flag in the original. The translator has followed the modern International Code of Signals.

DAUGHTER: Duties? What are my duties?

LAWYER: Everything you shy away from. Everything you hate to do and have to do! It means doing without, giving up, denying yourself. It means everything unpleasant, disgusting, and painful.

DAUGHTER: You mean there aren't any pleasant duties?

LAWYER: Yes. After you've done them, they're pleasant.

DAUGHTER: You mean when they don't exist. If duty is everything that's unpleasant, then what's pleasure?

LAWYER: What's pleasant is sin.

DAUGHTER: Sin?

LAWYER: That's right. And sin is something to be punished for. If I have a good time, the next day I have a bad conscience and suffer the torments of hell.

DAUGHTER: Strange!

LAWYER: But true. I wake up in the morning with a headache, and then I have to go through the whole thing again, repeat everything, but in a perverted way. So that all the beauty, fun, and wit of the night before appears, in the light of the morning after, to be ugly, disgusting, and stupid. The good times turn sour; the laughter rings hollow. It's the same with success. Success just sets you up to be knocked down. All the successes I had were the death of me. Because people instinctively hate to see someone get lucky. They think it's unfair that fate should favor any one person, so they try to make things even by switching the dice or changing the rules. Take talent, for instance. A real handicap. If you've got a real gift, you can easily starve to death. —Why are we talking? You've got to go back to your duties! Or else I'll take you to court—county, state, federal, and Supreme Court, if necessary.

DAUGHTER: Go back! To the kitchen stove, with the cabbage stinking up the place, the diapers in the sink—

LAWYER: That's right, my dear! We've got a big wash today—all the handkerchiefs!

DAUGHTER: Oh, no, I can't go through it again!

LAWYER: That's what life is—going through it again and again. —Look at the teacher in there. He got his doctor's degree yesterday, was crowned with the laurel, honored with a ten-gun salute, climbed Parnassus, and got a medal from the king. And today he begins school all over again, asking how much two times two is, and he'll keep on asking until the day he dies. . . . That's how it is. Now come back with me, back to your chores.

DAUGHTER: I'd rather die!

LAWYER: You mean kill yourself? You can't. The game isn't played that way. Suicide is a disgrace—in the first place—so much so that one's corpse is defiled. And in the second place—you'll send yourself to perdition; it's a mortal sin.

DAUGHTER: It isn't easy to be a human being, is it?

* * *

EVERYONE: Bravo! Hear, hear!

* * *

DAUGHTER: I won't go back with you. I won't sink back and be treated like dirt. I want to rise. I want to rise to the place I first came from. . . . But before I go, I want the door to be opened so that I shall know the secret. I want the door to be opened!

LAWYER: Then you'll have to double back on your tracks, go back the same way you came, and suffer through all the horrors of a trial and lawsuit, the hearings and rehearings, the repetitions and transcriptions, the recapitulations and summations!

DAUGHTER: If that's the way it has to be, very well. But first I want to be alone. I want to go out into the wilderness where I can find myself. We'll see each other soon. (*To the Poet.*) Come along with me.

Distant cries, wails, and moans are heard from the rear.

DAUGHTER: What is that?

LAWYER: The lost souls of Foul Strand.

DAUGHTER: Why are they complaining more than ever now?

LAWYER: Because the sun is shining *here*, because there's music *here*, and dancing *here*, and youth and life *here*. That's why they feel their misery so much more deeply.

DAUGHTER: We must set them free!

LAWYER: Go ahead. Try! Someone once came to set them free. They hanged him on a cross.

DAUGHTER: Who did?

LAWYER: *They* did. All the right-minded, well-meaning people.

DAUGHTER: Who are *they*?

LAWYER: You mean you don't know the right-minded, well-meaning people? You soon will!

DAUGHTER: Were they the ones who turned against you at the university?

LAWYER: Yes.

DAUGHTER: I know them!

[10]

The Riviera.* In the foreground to the left stands a white wall, over the top of which the fruit-laden branches of an orange tree can be seen. In the rear are villas and a casino. On the terrace of the casino are tables with parasols. To the right is a huge pile of coal, and near it two wheelbarrows. In the rear to the right one can catch a glimpse of the blue ocean.

Two Coal Haulers, naked to the waist, their faces, hands, and bodies blackened with coal soot, are sitting, hunched in tired despair, on the wheelbarrows.

The Daughter and the Lawyer enter at the rear.

DAUGHTER: Oh! This is paradise!

FIRST COAL HAULER: This is hell.

---

* In Strindberg's manuscript the Riviera scene has been added as an afterthought.

SECOND COAL HAULER: Hundred twenty in the shade.

FIRST COAL HAULER: Let's go for a swim.

SECOND COAL HAULER: Can't. Police will stop you. No swimming allowed.

FIRST COAL HAULER: What about picking an orange?

SECOND COAL HAULER: Can't. Police will come.

FIRST COAL HAULER: But I can't work in this heat. I've had it! I'm getting out of here.

SECOND COAL HAULER: Can't. Police will stop you. (*Pause.*) Besides, you'd starve to death.

FIRST COAL HAULER: Starve to death? We do most of the work and we get the least to eat. And the rich who don't do nothing get the most. . . . Wouldn't it be fair to say — without being too blunt about it — something's wrong somewhere? Daughter of the gods, what do you say?

* * *

DAUGHTER: I have no answer. . . . But tell me, what have you done? Why are you so black? Why do you have to work so hard?

FIRST COAL HAULER: What have we done? We picked the wrong parents — poor and disreputable. . . . And maybe we got arrested and sentenced a couple of times.

DAUGHTER: Sentenced?

FIRST COAL HAULER: Sure. Some get away with it and some don't. Those who get away with it are sitting up there in the casino eating eight-course dinners — with wine.

DAUGHTER (*to the Lawyer*): Can that be true?

LAWYER: Generally speaking, yes.

DAUGHTER: You mean that everybody at one time or another broke some law and could have been sent to prison?

LAWYER: Yes.

DAUGHTER: Even you?

LAWYER: Even I.

*   *   *

DAUGHTER: Is it true that the poor folk can't go swimming here?

LAWYER: That's right—not even with their clothes on. Only those who try to drown themselves get away without paying. But don't worry, they have to settle up in court.

DAUGHTER: Why can't they go outside the town, out in the country for a swim?

LAWYER: There isn't any open country; it's all fenced in.

DAUGHTER: I mean way out, where there aren't any fences, where the land is free.

LAWYER: There isn't any free land. It's all owned and occupied.

DAUGHTER: The ocean, the wide-open sea—

LAWYER: Everything! You can't even take a boat out or come ashore without signing a piece of paper and paying money. Neat, isn't it?

DAUGHTER: This is no paradise.

LAWYER: I can promise you that!

DAUGHTER: Why don't the people do something to change things?

LAWYER: They do. But all who want to make the world better end up in prison or in the madhouse.

DAUGHTER: Who puts them in prison?

LAWYER: All the right-thinking, fair-minded—

DAUGHTER: But not the madhouse?

LAWYER: Their own despair puts them there when they realize how hopeless it all is.

DAUGHTER: Hasn't it occurred to anyone that there might be a good reason why things are the way they are?

LAWYER: Yes, as a matter of fact. Everyone who is well-off believes that.

DAUGHTER: Believes that things are best as they are?

* * *

FIRST COAL HAULER: You see in us the foundation of society. If we didn't carry the coal, the kitchen stoves would go out, the rooms you live in would grow cold, the factories would close down. The lights in your streets, your stores, your homes would die. Darkness and cold would fall upon you. Yet we sweat like the damned in hell to carry the black coal. . . . What wilt thou do for us?

LAWYER (*to the Daughter*): Do something for them. . . . (*Pause.*) I realize that complete equality is impossible, but why, why must there be such great inequality?

* * *

A Man and his Wife cross the stage.

WIFE: Are you going to join us for a game of cards?

MAN: No, I've got to take my constitutional. Got to work up an appetite.

* * *

FIRST COAL HAULER: Work up an appetite!!

SECOND COAL HAULER: Work up—!

* * *

Some Children come running in. When they see the coal-blackened workers, they cry and scream in terror.

FIRST COAL HAULER: One look at us and they scream! They scream . . . !

SECOND COAL HAULER: God damn it! It's a sick society. I say it's time to operate on it—with the guillotine!

FIRST COAL HAULER: Damn right! (*He spits in disgust.*)

* * *

LAWYER (*to the Daughter*): Something's wrong. Anyone can see that. People aren't so bad. It's just that—

DAUGHTER: Just what?

LAWYER: The system. The organization.

DAUGHTER (*hides her face and leaves*): It's no paradise!

BOTH COAL HAULERS: No. It's hell.

[11]

Fingal's Cave. Long green waves roll gently into the cavern. In the foreground a red whistling buoy rocks on the waves, but the bell does not sound except when indicated.

The music of the winds. The music of the waves.

The Daughter and the Poet onstage.

POET: Where have you brought me?

DAUGHTER: Far from the murmuring and moaning of human beings – to the outermost edge of the world and the sea – to this grotto we call Indra's Ear. For it is said that here the god of the skies and sovereign of the heavens listens to the pleas and petitions of mortals.

POET: Listens? How?

DAUGHTER: Don't you see that this grotto is built like a seashell? You see it is. Don't you know that your ear is shaped like a seashell? You know it is, but you never thought about it before. (*She picks up a shell from the shore.*) When you were a child, did you never hold a shell to your ear and listen? Listen to the singing of your blood, to the swirling of the thoughts in your brain, to the thousands of tiny little explosions as the wornout threads in the fabric of your body snap and break? . . . If you can hear all that in such a little shell, imagine what you can hear in this great big one!

POET (*listening*): I don't hear anything, except the sighing of the wind . . .

DAUGHTER: Let me help you. I'll be the interpreter. Listen. . . . The lament of the winds. (*Recitative to the accompaniment of soft music.*)

Born in the clouds,
chased by Indra's lightning,
we fled to clayey earth.
The mulch in the fields
sullied our feet.
The dust of the road,
the smoke of the city
we had to endure—
foul smell of crowds,
stale beer, sour wine.
Out to the open sea we swept
to breathe clean air,
to flutter our wings,
to bathe our feet.
Indra, ruler of heaven,
listen to us.
Hear our sighs.
The earth is not clean,
life is not kind.
Man is not evil,
nor is he good.
People live as best they can,
one day at a time.
Living in ashes and dust,
they breed and die:
ashes to ashes, dust to dust.
Feet for plodding
were they given,
not wings for flying.
So the dust covers them.
Is the fault theirs
or yours?

*   *   *

POET: Once long ago I heard the same—

DAUGHTER: Shhh! The winds are still singing. (*Recitative to the accompaniment of soft music.*)

We are the winds.
It is we who carry

man's complaints.
On autumn nights you heard us
whistling in chimneys,
howling in the stove,
as the autumn rain
cried on the roof.
On winter nights you heard us
whisper in the snow-laden trees.
Out on the storm-swept sea
you heard our whining
in the ropes and sails.
You heard us,
creatures of air,
who learned our songs
in passing through
the lungs of men.
The hospital, the battlefield
taught us what to sing.
Most we learned in the nursery
where the newborn cry,
mewl, and scream
with the pain of coming alive.
We are the winds,
howling, whining,
whistling, wailing.

* * *

POET: I believe that once before —

DAUGHTER: Shh! Now the waves are singing. (*Recitative to the accompaniment of soft music.*)

We are the waves.
We cradle the winds
and lull the winds
to sleep.
Green cradles, wet and salt,
shaped like flames,
flames of water,
slaking, burning,
cleansing, bathing,

spuming, spawning.
We are the waves.
We cradle the winds
and lull the winds
to sleep.

* * *

DAUGHTER: False and faithless waves! Everything on earth that doesn't get burned up gets drowned—in the waves. —Do you see what I mean? Look. (*She points to a scrap heap.*) Look at what the sea has pillaged and plundered and destroyed. . . . All that's left of the sunken ships are these figureheads—and their names. The good ships *Justice, Friendship, The Golden Peace, Hope*—here's all that's left of *Hope*—deceptive *Hope* . . . lee-boards, oarlocks, bailing buckets . . . ! And there's the life buoy. It saved itself and let the souls in distress go down.

POET (*poking around in the scrap heap*): Here's the nameplate of the *Justice*. It must be the same one that sailed from Fair Haven with the Blind Man's son. It must have gone down. And on board was Alice's fiancé, too, the lieutenant Edith loves so hopelessly.

DAUGHTER: Blind Man? Fair Haven? I must have dreamed all that. And Alice's lieutenant, ugly Edith, Foul Strand and the quarantine, sulphur and phenol. Graduation exercises in the cathedral, the lawyer's office, the corridor and Victoria, the growing castle and the officer—it's all a dream I've dreamed.

POET: It's all in a poem I once wrote.

DAUGHTER: Then you know what poetry is.

POET: I know what dreams are. What is poetry?

DAUGHTER: Not reality. Something more than reality. Not dreams, but wide-awake dreams.

POET: And people, innocent earthlings, believe that we poets merely play and pretend and make it all up.

DAUGHTER: And a good thing, too, my friend. Else no one would believe there was any point to living and working, and the world would go to rack and ruin. Everyone would lie on his back and look at the sky. No one would lift a hand to use a plow or rake, pick or shovel.

POET: You admit that, do you? You the daughter of Indra, whose home is the heavens?

DAUGHTER: You're right to reproach me. I've been down here on earth too long and taken too many of your mud baths. My thoughts refuse to take wing. My wings are laden with clay, my feet are heavy with dirt and earth. . . . And, as for myself—(*She lifts her arms up high.*) I'm sinking, sinking. . . . Help me, Father, God of heaven, help me! (*Silence.*) I can no longer hear him. The ether cannot carry the sound of his voice from his lips to the sounding shell of my ear. The silver cord is broken. . . . I am earthbound . . . earthbound.

POET: Do you intend to rise from earth soon?

DAUGHTER: As soon as I have burned away the ashes and dust that cling to me, for not all the water in the world can wash me clean. Why do you ask?

POET: Because I—I have a prayer and a plea—

DAUGHTER: What sort of plea?

POET: A petition on behalf of humanity, addressed to the ruler of the world, and drawn up by a dreamer.

DAUGHTER: And to be conveyed and presented by—?

POET: By Indra's daughter.

DAUGHTER: Can you say the words of your poem?

POET: I can.

DAUGHTER: Then say them.

POET: Better if you did.

DAUGHTER: Where are they?

POET: In my thoughts. And here. (*He hands her a scroll.*)

DAUGHTER: Very well, I shall say them. (*She takes the scroll but recites without looking at it.*)

* * *

DAUGHTER:

> "Why are we born in pain,
> we human beings? Why
> do we hurt our mothers
> when we should be giving them
> the greatest of joys?
> Why do we come crying hither,
> why do we greet the light,
> wailing in pain and wrath?
> Why do we not laugh and smile?
> The gift of life should be full of joy.
> Why are we, the progeny of angels,
> the image of God, born like beasts?
> Our souls would have a vesture
> other than this of blood and filth.
> Must the paragon of created beings
> cut his eyeteeth and descend into the flesh?"

You presume too much! The work should praise its creator.* No one has yet solved the riddle of life and being.

> "Now the passage through life begins,
> over thorns, thistles, sharp stones.
> If you find a smooth, well-worn path,
> there will soon be detours through the rough.
> If flowers will make your journey lighter,
> they will cost you more than you can pay.
> To make your way you'll have to fight
> the crowd and step on someone's toes.
> No matter: soon the others will step
> on yours to keep the race a close one.
> Every joy that comes to you will leave

* The Daughter alludes to a saying, "The work praises the master," not uncommon in Swedish, from Ecclesiasticus, an apocryphal book of the Bible. The standard version in English is ineffective: "For the hand of the artificer the work shall be commended."

some poor soul depressed and sadder.
But sorrow breeds no happiness;
all goes one way: from joy to pain,
and the world's cup fills up with sorrow.
So shall it be even when you're dead:
your grave will be the digger's bread."

Is this how you hope to approach
the throne of the Almighty?

POET:

How can a man of earth like me
find words bright enough, pure enough,
light enough to fly from earth?
Child of the gods, will you
render our lament in the tongue
the immortals best comprehend?

DAUGHTER: I will.

POET (*indicating the whistling buoy*): What is that floating there?
A buoy?

DAUGHTER: Yes.

POET: It looks like a human lung with the larynx attached.

DAUGHTER: It's the watchman of the sea. When danger lurks,
it sings.

POET: I think the sea is rising now. The waves are turning
white.

DAUGHTER: I believe you are right!

POET: There's trouble ahead. Do you see what I see? A ship —
out beyond the reef.

DAUGHTER: What ship can that be?

POET: It looks to me like the ghost ship.

DAUGHTER: The ghost ship?

POET: *The Flying Dutchman.*

DAUGHTER: Is that the *Dutchman*? . . . Why was he punished so harshly? And why does he never put in to land?

POET: Because he had seven unfaithful wives.

DAUGHTER: Why should he be punished for that?

POET: All the right-thinking people condemned him.

DAUGHTER: Strange world! . . . How can he be freed from his curse?

POET: Freed? Best beware setting anyone free—

DAUGHTER: Why?

POET: Because that—. No, it isn't the *Dutchman*, after all. It's an ordinary ship in distress! —Why doesn't the buoy sound off and warn them? Before it's too late! —Look, the sea is rising, the waves are mounting higher. In a minute we'll be trapped in this cave! —The ship's bells are ringing! Abandon ship! —Won't be long before we can add another figurehead to the pile! —Cry out, buoy! Come on! Do your duty, sentinel of the sea!

> *The whistling buoy sings out with a four-tone chord of a fifth and sixth, the sound resembling foghorns.*

POET: The crew is waving to us for help—but we ourselves are drowning!

DAUGHTER: I thought you wanted to be set free!

POET: Yes, of course I do. But not now! And not in water!

* * *

THE CREW (*singing in four-part harmony*): *Christ Kyrie!*

POET: Now they're calling. And the sea is calling. But no one hears.

THE CREW (*as before*): *Christ Kyrie!*

DAUGHTER: Who is that out there coming toward us?

POET: Walking on water? There's only one who walks on water—certainly not Peter "the rock"; he sank like a stone.

A white glow appears out on the water.

THE CREW: *Christ Kyrie!*

DAUGHTER: Is that he?

POET: Yes, that is He, the Crucified One . . .

DAUGHTER: Why—tell me now, why was he crucified?

POET: Because He wanted to set all men free . . .

DAUGHTER: And who—I have forgotten—who wanted to crucify Him?

POET: All the right-thinking ones.

DAUGHTER: It is a strange world!

POET: The sea is rising. Darkness is falling. The storm rages.

* * *

The Crew screams.

POET: The sailors scream in terror when they see their Saviour. . . . And now . . . they're jumping overboard—afraid of their Redeemer!

The Crew screams again.

POET: Now they're screaming because they're about to die. They scream when they're born and they scream when they die!

The rising waves threaten to drown them in the cave.

DAUGHTER: If I could only be certain that it is a ship—

POET: I see what you mean—I don't think it is. It's a two-story house, with trees around it—and—a telephone communication tower—a tower reaching up to the skies. It's a modern Tower of Babel, sending its wires upward—to let those up there know—

DAUGHTER: You know better than that. Thoughts do not need metal threads to move from place to place. Devout prayers can force their way through all the world. I say it's definitely not a Tower of Babel. If you want to storm the walls of heaven, besiege it with your prayers.

POET: No, it's not a house . . . not a telephone tower. . . . You see what it is?

DAUGHTER: No, what do you see?

POET: I see a plain covered with snow—a drill field. . . . The winter sun is shining behind a church on a hill, and the church tower casts a long shadow on the snow . . . a platoon of soldiers is marching across the field—marching across the tower—up the spire—now they're on the cross—I have a feeling that the first one who steps on the weathercock at the top must die—they're getting closer—the corporal's leading the way. —Ha! a cloud is sweeping over the plain, blotting out the sun, naturally—it's all disappeared—the wet cloud put out the sun's fire. The light of the sun created the dark tower, but the cloud's dark shadow smothered the tower's dark shadow . . .

[12]

While the Poet has been speaking, the set has changed back to the theater corridor.

DAUGHTER (*to the Stage-Door Keeper*): Has the president of the university arrived yet?

STAGE-DOOR KEEPER: No, he hasn't.

DAUGHTER: The deans of the colleges and faculties?

STAGE-DOOR KEEPER: No.

DAUGHTER: Well then, you'd better call them. Right away! Because the door is going to be opened.

STAGE-DOOR KEEPER: Is it really so urgent?

DAUGHTER: Yes, very urgent. A lot of people have come to suspect that the key to the mystery of the universe is kept there. So if you don't mind, call the president and the deans at once.

> *The Stage-Door Keeper pulls out a whistle and blows on it.*

DAUGHTER: And don't forget the glazier and his diamond. Without him there can be no opening of the door.

*   *   *

> *The Actors and Dancers come in from the left, as at the beginning of the play.*

*   *   *

OFFICER (*enters from the rear, wearing top hat and tails, carrying a bouquet of roses, radiantly happy*): Victoria!

STAGE-DOOR KEEPER: Miss Victoria will be down in just a moment.

OFFICER: Good, good! The carriage is waiting, the table is spread, the champagne's on ice. Oh, let me kiss you, madame! (*He embraces the Stage-Door Keeper.*) Victoria!

*   *   *

A WOMAN'S VOICE (*from above, singing out liltingly*): Here I am!

OFFICER (*beginning to pace back and forth*): Very good. I'll be waiting!

*   *   *

POET: I have a strange feeling I've been through this before.

DAUGHTER: Me too.

POET: Maybe I dreamed it . . . ?

DAUGHTER: Or wrote it in a poem, maybe?

POET: Or wrote it in a poem.

DAUGHTER: Then you know what poetry is.

POET: Then I know what dreams are.

DAUGHTER: And I have the strange feeling that we once stood somewhere else and said these same words.

POET: Then it shouldn't take you long to figure out what reality is.

DAUGHTER: Or dreams!

POET: Or poetry!

* * *

Enter the President of the University, the Dean of the Theological Seminary, the Dean of the Faculty of Philosophy, the Dean of the School of Medicine, and the Dean of the School of Law.

PRESIDENT: You all know what brings us here: the opening of the door. Let me call first upon the Dean of the Theological Seminary. What is your view of the matter?

DEAN OF THEOLOGY: I don't have any views; I believe! — *Credo* —

DEAN OF PHILOSOPHY: I postulate —

DEAN OF MEDICINE: I know —

DEAN OF LAW: I object — until I've seen the evidence and heard the witnesses.

PRESIDENT: Here we go! Quarreling already! . . . Let me begin again. What does the Dean of Theology *believe*?

DEAN OF THEOLOGY: I believe that this door should not be opened. It obviously conceals dangerous truths.

DEAN OF PHILOSOPHY: The truth is never dangerous!

DEAN OF MEDICINE: What is truth?

DEAN OF LAW: Whatever two witnesses testify to.

DEAN OF THEOLOGY: With two false witnesses anything can be proved — by a shyster!

DEAN OF PHILOSOPHY: Truth is wisdom; and wisdom and knowledge constitute philosophy itself. Philosophy is the science of sciences, the knowledge of knowledge; and all other branches of learning are its servants.

DEAN OF MEDICINE: The only science is natural science. Philosophy is not science; it's only empty speculation.

DEAN OF THEOLOGY: Bravo!

DEAN OF PHILOSOPHY (*to Dean of Theology*): Bravo, you say! What do you think you are? You're the archenemy of all knowledge. You're the very antithesis of science. You're ignorance and obscurantism itself—!

DEAN OF MEDICINE: Bravo!

DEAN OF THEOLOGY (*to Dean of Medicine*): Bravo, you say! You of all people! Who can't see farther than the end of your nose in a magnifying glass—you, who don't believe in anything but what your deceptive senses tell you—what your eyes tell you, for example, even though you may be far-sighted or near-sighted; cross-eyed, wall-eyed, or one-eyed; color blind, red-blind, green-blind.

DEAN OF MEDICINE: You blithering idiot!

DEAN OF THEOLOGY: Jackass!

They start fighting.

PRESIDENT: Stop that! Let's not have you birds pecking each other's eyes out.

DEAN OF PHILOSOPHY: Well, if I had to choose between those two—theology and medicine—I would choose—neither!

DEAN OF LAW: And if I sat on the bench and you three were brought before me, I'd sentence—all three of you! You can't agree on a single point, and you never could. . . . Let's get back to business. Mr. President, what is your own view on the opening of this door?

PRESIDENT: My view? I don't have any views. I have simply been appointed by the state to see to it that during our executive meetings you don't tear one another to pieces—while you're educating our youth. Views? Ah, no, indeed, I'm very careful not to have any views. There was a time when I had a few, but they were quickly refuted. Views are always quickly refuted—by those with the opposite views, you understand. . . . And now, perhaps we might proceed to the opening of the door, even at the risk of revealing some dangerous truths?

DEAN OF LAW: What is truth? What is *the* truth?

DEAN OF THEOLOGY: I am the truth, the way, and the life—

DEAN OF PHILOSOPHY: I am knowledge of knowledge—

DEAN OF MEDICINE: I am exact knowledge—

DEAN OF LAW: I object!

They all start to fight.

* * *

DAUGHTER: Aren't you ashamed? You, the teacher of our youth!

DEAN OF LAW: Mr. President! As the representative of the government and as the head of the faculty, you must bring charges against this woman for her remarks. She said we ought to be ashamed. Now that's an insult. And when she referred to us as the teacher of the young, her ironic tone of voice implied that we were incapable. Now that's slander!

DAUGHTER: Heaven help the students!

DEAN OF LAW: Do you hear? She's excusing the students! —That's the same as accusing us. Mr. President, I insist that you prosecute her!

DAUGHTER: Yes, that's right! I accuse you, you as a group, of sowing doubt and breeding skepticism in the minds of our youth.

DEAN OF LAW: Listen to her! There she stands telling the students to have no respect for our authority, and yet she has the gall to accuse us of breeding skepticism! If that isn't a criminal act, what is? I put it to you, all you good, right-thinking people.

* * *

ALL THE RIGHT-THINKING PEOPLE: Yes, yes, absolutely criminal!

DEAN OF LAW: There! All the right-thinking people have condemned you! —Now go in peace and be content with thy gain. Otherwise—!

DAUGHTER: My gain? —Otherwise! Otherwise what??

DEAN OF LAW: Otherwise thou shall be stoned.

POET: Or crucified.

DAUGHTER: Very well, I'll go. —Come with me and I'll give you the answer to the riddle.

POET: What riddle?

DAUGHTER: What did he mean by "my gain"?*

POET: Probably nothing. Just a lot of hot air, as we say. Talking through his hat.

DAUGHTER: But nothing could have hurt me more.

POET: I suppose that's why he said it. That's how people are.

* * *

ALL THE RIGHT-THINKING PEOPLE: Hooray! The door is open!

* * *

PRESIDENT: What lay hidden behind the door?

GLAZIER: I can't see anything.

PRESIDENT: You can't see anything? Well, I can't say I'm surprised—. Learned deans, what lay hidden behind the door?

DEAN OF THEOLOGY: Nothing. That is the key to the riddle of the world. In the beginning God created heaven and earth out of nothing.

* The exchange between the Dean of Law and the Daughter evidently reflects the words of Paul, I Timothy 6:1-6, with the Dean turning Paul's admonition against the Daughter.

DEAN OF PHILOSOPHY: Nothing comes of nothing.

DEAN OF MEDICINE: Bosh! Nothing. Period.

DEAN OF LAW: I object to the whole thing. It's a clear case of fraud. I appeal to all the right-thinking people!

DAUGHTER (*to the Poet*): What are the right-thinking people?

POET: I wish I knew. They usually turn out to be a party of one. Today it's me and my side – tomorrow it's you and your side. . . . You get appointed – or rather, you're self-appointed.

* * *

ALL THE RIGHT-THINKING PEOPLE: We've been swindled! Tricked!

PRESIDENT: And who has swindled you?

ALL THE RIGHT-THINKING PEOPLE: She did! The Daughter!

PRESIDENT (*to the Daughter*): Would you be so good as to tell us what you had in mind with this door-opening?

DAUGHTER: No, good people, I won't. "If I tell you, ye will not believe."

DEAN OF MEDICINE: But there's nothing – nothing at all.

DAUGHTER: You say right. But you understand not.

DEAN OF MEDICINE: She's talking nonsense!

EVERYONE: Nonsense! Boo!

DAUGHTER (*to the Poet*): Poor lost souls. I feel sorry for them.

POET: You serious?

DAUGHTER: Always serious.

POET: Do you also feel sorry for the right-thinking people?

DAUGHTER: Perhaps most of all for them.

POET: And what about the four learned faculties?

DAUGHTER: Them too, no less than the others. Four heads on one body, four minds! Who created the monster?

EVERYONE: She's not answering us!

PRESIDENT: Down with her!

DAUGHTER: But I have answered you!

PRESIDENT: Don't you talk back to me!

EVERYONE: Listen to her! She's talking back!

DAUGHTER: Answer or not answer, I can't win. . . . Come with me, you poet and seer, and I shall tell you – somewhere far from here – the answer to the riddle. Somewhere, out in the desert, where no one can hear us, no one see us. Because –

* * *

LAWYER (*coming forward and grabbing the Daughter by the arm*): Have you forgotten your responsibilities?

DAUGHTER: God knows I haven't. But I have more important responsibilities.

LAWYER: What about your child?

DAUGHTER: My child – oh yes! What about her?

LAWYER: Your child is crying for you.

DAUGHTER: My child! How that child ties me down! I feel chained to the earth. . . . And I have this pain in my breast, this feeling of anguish. What is it?

LAWYER: Don't you know?

DAUGHTER: No.

LAWYER: The pangs of conscience.

DAUGHTER: Is that what it is? The pangs of conscience?

LAWYER: That's right. They show up after every duty you neglect, after every pleasure you enjoy, however innocent – if there are any innocent pleasures (which I doubt), and after every harm you do your friends and neighbors.

DAUGHTER: And there's no cure for these pangs, I suppose?

LAWYER: Oh, yes; but only one. You must discharge your duty without a moment's hesitation.

DAUGHTER: You know, you look just like a demon when you say that word "duty." —But what am I supposed to do if I have two duties to discharge?

LAWYER: Simple! First you discharge one, and then the other.

DAUGHTER: The most important one first. —So I leave my child in your care, while I go to discharge my first duty.

LAWYER: But the child needs you; you'll break its heart. Can you bear to know that someone is suffering on account of you?

DAUGHTER: You're turning me against myself. You've broken my heart in two and it's pulling me both ways.

LAWYER: Life is full of little conflicts like that.

DAUGHTER: Oh, how my heart is torn. I don't know which way to turn.

*   *   *

POET: If you knew how much sorrow and misery I caused by discharging the obligations I owed to my calling in life—notice: my calling, the most important duty of all—you would shun me.

DAUGHTER: Why? What did you do?

POET: My father placed all his hopes in me. I was his only son and he dreamed about how I would carry on the business he had built up. I ran away from business school and my father never got over it. My mother wanted me to study religion, but I didn't have the heart for it. So she disowned me. I had a friend who gave me a helping hand when I was down and out. But my friend had different political views, fought against the causes I spoke for and fought for. I had to cut down my best friend and benefactor in order to be true to myself. Since then I've never known any peace. They call me disloyal, a stinker. And a fat lot of good it does me to hear my conscience tell me, "You did right," because the next moment it's telling me how wrong I was. And that's life for you.

*   *   *

DAUGHTER: Come with me out into the desert.

LAWYER: Your child! Your child!

DAUGHTER (*indicating all those present*): Here are my children! Taken one by one, they're good and gentle. But put them together and they fight with one another and turn into demons. . . . Goodbye . . .

[13]

Outside the castle. Same set as in the first scene of the first act. Only now the ground below the footings is covered with flowers (blue monkshood or aconite). At the very top of the castle, surmounting its tower and lantern, is a chrysanthemum bud ready to burst into bloom. The windows have candles burning in them.

The Daughter and the Poet are onstage.

DAUGHTER: The time has nearly come when with the help of the fire I shall rise and return to the empyrean. This is what you call death, what you approach with fear in your hearts.

POET: Fear of the unknown.

DAUGHTER: Which you really know.

POET: Who knows?

DAUGHTER: Everyone! Why do you not believe your prophets?

POET: Prophets have never been believed. I wonder why? — "If God has spoken, why will men not believe?" His power to persuade must surely be irresistible!

DAUGHTER: Have you always been a skeptic?

POET: No. Many a time I've had absolute faith and certitude, but it always faded away after a while, like a dream upon awakening.

DAUGHTER: It isn't easy to be a human being. I know that.

POET: You have come to realize that, have you, and admit it?

DAUGHTER: Yes.

POET: Tell me something. Was it not Indra who once sent his son here to earth to hear the complaints of mankind?

DAUGHTER: Yes, it was. And how did the people receive him?

POET: What did he do to accomplish his mission?—to answer with a question.

DAUGHTER: To answer with another question: was not the condition of mankind improved as a result of his visit to earth? Tell me truly.

POET: Improved? Yes, a little. Very little! —Now, instead of asking questions, will you solve the riddle?

DAUGHTER: I could. But what good would it do? You wouldn't believe the answer.

POET: You, I will believe. I know who you are.

DAUGHTER: Very well, I shall tell you. . . . At the dawn of time before the sun shone, Brahma, the divine primal potency, went forth and let himself be seduced by Maya, the creative mother of the world, so that he might propagate himself. The divine element thus joined with earthly matter. This was the fall of heaven. Consequently, the world and its inhabitants and life itself are nothing more than phantoms, mirages, images in a dream—

POET: My dream!

DAUGHTER: A dream come true. Now, to free themselves from earthly matter the progeny of Brahma seek deprivation and suffering. There you have suffering as the redeemer. But this yearning for suffering comes into conflict with the craving for pleasure. Which is love. Now do you understand what love is, offering the most sublime joys along with the most profound suffering, sweetest when it is most bitter? Do you understand what woman is? Woman, through whom sin and death entered into life?

POET: I do understand. And the upshot?

DAUGHTER: I don't have to tell you. Constant strife between the anguish of joy and the pleasure of suffering, the torments of remorse and the delights of sensuality.

POET: Strife—is that all we can hope for?

DAUGHTER: The conflict between opposites produces energy, just as fire and water generate steam power.

POET: And peace? And rest?

DAUGHTER: I've said enough. You mustn't ask any more, and I mustn't answer. . . . The altar is decked for the sacrifice. . . . The flowers keep watch, the lights are lit. . . . The funeral wreaths hang in the windows and doors.*

POET: You say that as calmly and coolly as if you didn't know what it means to suffer.

DAUGHTER: Not know? I have suffered all that mortal man suffers but felt it a hundred times more, because my senses are keener.

POET: Tell me what you suffered.

DAUGHTER: You're a poet, but could even you tell me your troubles in words that said it all? Was there ever a time when your words and your thoughts were in perfect harmony? A time when your words soared to the level of your thoughts?

POET: No, you're right. Before my own thoughts I stood deaf and dumb. And when the crowd listened in admiration to my song, it sounded like bawling to me. I guess that's why I always blushed when I heard my praises sung.

DAUGHTER: And yet you expect me to—? Look me in the eye!

POET: I can't. Your gaze is too intense.

DAUGHTER: And so would my words be if I spoke in my own tongue.

POET: At least tell me—before you go—what was the hardest thing to endure—down here?

DAUGHTER: Being, just being. Feeling my sight clouded by these eyes, my hearing muffled by these ears, and my thoughts,

---

* In place of the funeral wreaths, the original has "white sheets in the windows, pine cuttings on the walk"—once customary features at Swedish funerals.

my bright, airy thoughts trapped in the labyrinth of coiled fat. You know what a brain looks like—what crooked ways, what secret pasages!

POET: I know. I suppose that's why all the right-thinking people think crooked.

DAUGHTER: Always ready with sarcasm. That's how you all are.

POET: What do you expect?

DAUGHTER: Now I'm going to shake the dust off my feet first—the earth, the clay.) *She takes off her shoes and lays them on the fire.*)

* * *

STAGE-DOOR KEEPER (*enters and lays her shawl on the fire*): Maybe you wouldn't mind if I added my shawl to the fire, would you, deary? (*Exits.*)

OFFICER (*enters*): And I my roses? Nothing left but thorns. (*Exits.*)

BILLPOSTER (*enters*): The posters can go. But my dip net, never! (*Exits.*)

GLAZIER (*enters*): The diamond glass cutter that opened the door! Goodbye! (*Exits.*)

LAWYER (*enters*): The minutes of the great lawsuit concerning the pope's beard or the diminishing water supply in the sources of the Ganges River. (*Exits.*)

MEDICAL INSPECTOR (*enters*): Only a small contribution: the black mask that made me black against my will. (*Exits.*)

VICTORIA (*enters*): My beauty—my sorrow! (*Exits.*)

EDITH (*enters*): My ugliness—my sorrow! (*Exits.*)

BLIND MAN (*enters, sticks his hand into the fire*): I give my hand in place of my eye! (*Exits.*)

> *The old Don Juan enters in his wheelchair, accompanied by the Coquette and the "Friend."*

DON JUAN: Hurry up! Hurry up! Life is short! (*Exits with the others.*)

* * *

POET: I once read that when life nears its end, everything in it comes rushing past in single file. Is this the end?

DAUGHTER: It is for me. Goodbye.

POET: Not even a few parting words?

DAUGHTER: There's nothing I can say. Do you still believe that your words can express our thoughts?

* * *

DEAN OF THEOLOGY (*enters, raging mad*): I've been repudiated by my God, I'm persecuted by the people, disowned by the administration, ridiculed by my colleagues! How can I have faith, how can I believe, when no one else does? How can I fight for a God who does not fight for his own? Junk! That's what it is—junk! (*He throws a book on the fire and leaves.*)

* * *

POET (*snatching the book from the fire*): You know what it is? A martyrology. It lists a martyr for each day of the year.

DAUGHTER: Martyr?

POET: Yes—someone who was tortured and put to death for his beliefs. And why? —Do you think that everyone who is tortured suffers, and that everyone who is put to death feels pain? Doesn't suffering melt our chains and doesn't death set us free?

* * *

CHRISTINE (*enters with her strips of paper and weatherstripping*): I'm going to paste and seal and paste and seal until there's nothing more to paste and seal!

POET: And if heaven itself split wide open, you'd try to paste and seal that too! Go away!

CHRISTINE: Aren't there any inner windows in the castle for me to seal up?

POET: No, there certainly aren't! Not there!

CHRISTINE (*leaving*): Well, then I'm leaving.

*   *   *

DAUGHTER:

> It's time! Give me your hand, my friend,
> Farewell, you human being, you dreamer,
> you poet, who knows best how to live,
> soaring on wings above the earth,
> swooping down when you feel like it,
> to graze the dust, not to drown in it.
>
> Now when I must leave, how hard it is
> to say goodbye, to bid farewell.
> One longs for all that one has loved,
> regrets all that one has offended.
> Now, now I know what it means to live;
> I feel the pain of being human.
> You miss what you never wanted;
> regret even misdeeds never done.
> You want to leave, you want to stay;
> your heart's drawn and quartered, torn apart
> by conflicting wishes, indecision, doubt.
>
> Goodbye, my friend! Tell your fellow men
> that where I'm going I shall think of them
> and that in your name I shall convey
> their plaints and protests to the throne on high.
> Farewell!

> > *She enters the castle. Music. The rear of the stage is lit up by the burning castle and reveals a wall of human faces, questioning, sorrowful, despairing.*
> >
> > *As the castle burns, the flower bud at the top bursts and blossoms into a huge chrysanthemum.*

Introduction

to

The Ghost Sonata

1906 and 1907 saw a remarkable improvement in Strindberg's theatrical fortunes. *Miss Julie* was performed in Stockholm for the first time, and *A Dream Play* was also staged there for the first time anywhere. Both productions received generally good reviews, and Strindberg followed up these successes by establishing his own theater and writing four plays for it. The man who brought *Miss Julie* to Stockholm was a young actor, August Falck, whose venturesome spirit attracted Strindberg. The two of them determined to open an intimate theater in Stockholm that would be devoted to highbrow drama, classic and modern. The theater they finally got was a small one, seating 161, and with a stage that measured only eighteen by twelve feet. The size of the theater and its lack of technical resources did not dampen Strindberg's spirits. To the theatrical vanguard, heavily realistic stage sets were passé, and theoreticians like Georg Fuchs with his book *Die Schaubühne der Zukunft* and artists like Gordon Craig with his *The Art of the Theatre*, both published in 1905, were opening the way to a simplified symbolic stage that suited Strindberg's artistic purposes. "Retheatricalize the theater" was Fuchs's motto; "dematerialize the stage" was Strindberg's.

The ninety-minute plays (the now successful *Miss Julie* was a ninety-minute play) that Strindberg wrote for his Intimate Theatre were called chamber plays, a term suggesting intimacy, exclusiveness, and a musical treatment. "If you were to ask me," he wrote,

> what the aim of an intimate theater is and what is meant by a chamber play, I would say that in this kind of drama we single out the significant and over-riding theme, but within limits. In handling it we avoid all ostentation — all the calculated effects, the bravura roles, the solo numbers for the stars, and the cues for applause. The author rejects all predetermined forms because the theme determines the form.

> Hence complete freedom to treat the theme as he
> will, limited only by the harmony of ideas and a sense
> of style. [*Öppna brev till Intima teatern.*]

The Ghost Sonata, the third of the chamber plays, is one of
Strindberg's most original and startling creations, along with *To
Damascus* and *A Dream Play*. Containing many of the forces,
impulses, and ideas of the experimental theater of the twentieth
century, it defies classification. Ingmar Bergman, who has
directed it three times, ranks it among the ten greatest plays of
all time.

In saying that theme determines form, Strindberg is not telling us what makes *The Ghost Sonata* such a special play. Theme
determines the form of *A Dream Play*, too, but there the freedom
with which he handled the theme seems natural because anything
can happen in a dream. In *The Ghost Sonata* Strindberg makes
theatrical poetry out of everyday reality by magnifying it, x-
raying it, so that the familiar and the trivial seem strange, significant, and frightening.

"The earlier dream plays," explains Swedish theater historian
Agne Beijer,

> had been set in a visionary, unreal world, where no
> one expected the same logic and the same scale of
> values to apply as in everyday life. The chamber
> plays seek out this everyday world directly and depict
> it with a naturalism that does not shun the coarsest
> vulgarities but that simultaneously shatters all the
> ordinary conceptions of them by distorting the
> standards by which we measure such things, over-
> stressing the insignificant and italicizing the trivial in
> order thereby to give them a new import, in other
> words, to bring the material world we live and work
> in to the point at which it splits so that through the
> cracks we can catch glimpses of another world.

In *The Ghost Sonata*, this other world is the world of the spirit,
and the action takes place when the spirit is being separated from
the physical body. For the visionary Swedenborg, whose theory
of correspondences exercised an enormous influence on Strind-

berg, the physical world was like a mask on the face of the spirit. Remove the mask, remove all that places one in a particular society, all the attributes that go with one's position, and the true person will be revealed. Strindberg provides a vivid demonstration of this unmasking and undressing in the second scene of the play.

At death, of course, the spirit is finally separated from the body. *The Ghost Sonata* represents a journey, signaled by the bells at the beginning, that transports us to the Isle of the Dead and that parallels the emergence of the soul from its physical husk. Visionaries need not take the actual journey. They look at the "real" everyday scene. It breaks up as they look at it and see what lies behind. This mystical, visionary experience constitutes the action of *The Ghost Sonata*.

To elevate the play above the physical, to dematerialize the stage, Strindberg constructs the play along musical lines, as its title intimates. What happens to the characters is less important than what happens to the principal themes, which are announced in the first few moments and developed and varied from episode to episode. Then at the very end, a new kind of music is heard and an even newer kind of theater is created, as Strindberg assembles a montage – before the term had been coined – a collision of elements, of sights and sounds, that together form an artistic unity encompassing the contradictions of life and resolving them in a higher unity.

The Ghost Sonata

Opus Three
of
The Chamber Plays

CHARACTERS

THE OLD MAN, Mr. Hummel
THE STUDENT, Arkenholz
THE MILKMAID, an apparition
THE SUPERINTENDENT's WIFE
THE SUPERINTENDENT
THE DEAD MAN, formerly a consul
THE WOMAN IN BLACK, daughter of The Dead Man and
The Superintendent's Wife
THE COLONEL
THE MUMMY, The Colonel's wife
THE YOUNG LADY, The Colonel's daughter, actually The
Old Man's daughter
BARON SKANSKORG, engaged to The Woman in Black
JOHANSSON, Hummel's servant
BENGTSSON, The Colonel's manservant
THE FIANCÉE, Hummel's former fiancée, now a white-haired
old woman
[THE COOK*]
BEGGARS
A HOUSEMAID

Scene: Stockholm

* Not included in Strindberg's list of characters.

The first two floors of a facade of a new house on a city square. Only the corner of the house is visible, the ground floor terminating in a round room, the second floor in a balcony with a flagpole.

When the curtains are drawn and the windows opened in the round room, one can see a white marble statue of a young woman surrounded by palms and bathed in sunlight. On the windowsill farthest to the left are pots of hyacinths—blue, white, pink.

Hanging on the railing of the balcony on the second story are a blue silk bedspread and two white bed pillows. The windows to the left are covered with white sheets signifying a death in the house. It is a bright Sunday morning.

A green park bench is downstage toward the left.

Downstage right is a drinking fountain with a long-handled drinking cup hanging at its side. To the left a kiosk, plastered with advertisements. A telephone booth is also onstage.

The main entrance to the house is at the left. Through the door can be seen the hall and the staircase with marble steps and balustrade of mahogany and brass. On the sidewalk on both sides of the entryway are tubs with small laurels.

The corner of the house with the round room also faces a side street that runs upstage.

On the first floor to the left of the entryway is a window with a special mirror, quite common in Sweden around the turn of the century, which enables those inside to

*view the passing scene without sticking their heads out
the window.*

*At the rise of the curtain, the bells of several churches
can be heard ringing in the distance.*

*The double doors in the entryway are wide open. The
Woman in Black stands motionless in the doorway.*

*The Superintendent's Wife is sweeping the vestibule.
Having finished that, she polishes the brass on the door
and then waters the laurels.*

*Sitting in a wheelchair near the kiosk is The Old Man,
reading a newspaper. He has white hair and beard and
is wearing glasses.*

*The Milkmaid comes in from around the corner,
carrying a wire basket filled with bottles. She is wearing
a summer dress, with brown shoes, black stockings, and
white cap. She takes off her cap and hangs it on the
drinking fountain; wipes the sweat from her brow; takes
a drink from the cup; washes her hands; arranges her
hair, using the water in the fountain as a mirror.*

*The ringing of a steamship bell is heard, and now and
then the silence is broken by the deep notes of the organs
in the nearby churches.*

*After a few moments of silence, and after The Milkmaid
has finished arranging her hair, The Student enters from
the left. He is unshaven and looks haggard from lack of
sleep. He goes directly to the drinking fountain.*

Pause.

THE STUDENT: Could I borrow the cup, please?

The Milkmaid hugs the cup to herself.

Aren't you through using it?

The Milkmaid stares at him in terror.

THE OLD MAN (*to himself*): Who on earth is he talking to? —I don't see anyone! —Is he crazy? (*He continues to stare at them in amazement.*)

THE STUDENT: What are you looking at? Do I look so awful? —Well, I haven't slept a wink all night. I suppose you think that I've been out doing the town . . .

> *The Milkmaid still stares at him in terror.*

Think I've been drinking, don't you? —Do I smell like it?

> *The Milkmaid as before.*

I haven't had a chance to shave. . . . Come on, let me have a drink of water. After last night, I think I've earned it. (*Pause.*) Must I tell you the whole story? I've spent the night caring for the injured. I've bound up their wounds. You see, I was there when the house collapsed last night. I was there. . . . Well, that's it.

> *The Milkmaid rinses the cup and offers him a drink of water.*

Thanks!

> *The Milkmaid does not move.*

(*The Student continues, slowly*): I wonder if you would do me a great favor? (*Pause.*) The thing is, my eyes are inflamed, as you can see—but I've had my hands on wounds and on corpses—so I don't want to risk using my hands to wash my eyes. . . . Would you take this clean handkerchief, dip it in that fresh water, and bathe my sore eyes with it? —Would you do that? —Will you be my Good Samaritan?

> *The Milkmaid hesitates for a moment before doing as asked.*

That's very kind of you. And here's something for your trouble—

(*He has taken his wallet out and is about to offer her some money. The Milkmaid makes a gesture of refusal.*) I'm sorry. Forgive me. I'm still in a daze . . .

* * *

THE OLD MAN (*to The Student*): Forgive my speaking to you, but I could not help hearing you say you were in on that terrible accident yesterday evening. I was just sitting here reading about it in the paper.

THE STUDENT: Is it already in the paper?

THE OLD MAN: The whole story! And they've got a picture of you too. But they regret they were unable to obtain the name of the courageous young student . . .

THE STUDENT (*looking at the paper*): So that's me! What do you know!

THE OLD MAN: Who . . . who was that you were talking to just now?

THE STUDENT: Didn't you see?

Pause

THE OLD MAN: I suppose I'm being nosey, but would you do me the honor of giving me your name?

THE STUDENT: Why do you want to know that? I don't care for publicity. First they build you up, then they tear you down. The insult now ranks among the fine arts—and the ranker the finer. Besides I'm not looking for any reward.

THE OLD MAN: Rich, I suppose?

THE STUDENT: Not at all! I haven't got a dime to my name.

THE OLD MAN: It's strange . . . but I can't help thinking that I've heard your voice before. . . . When I was a young man I had a friend who couldn't pronounce window, he always said winder. I've only met one person who said that, and that was him. The other is you, of course. Is it possible that you are related to Arkenholz, the wholesale dealer?

THE STUDENT: He was my father.

THE OLD MAN: Isn't fate strange? Then I saw you when you were a child—under very trying circumstances.

THE STUDENT: I suppose so. I understand I came into the world right in the middle of bankruptcy proceedings.

THE OLD MAN: Exactly!

THE STUDENT: May I ask what your name is?

THE OLD MAN: My name is Hummel.

THE STUDENT: Hummel? Then you're—. Yes, I remember . . .

THE OLD MAN: You've heard my name mentioned in your family?

THE STUDENT: Yes.

THE OLD MAN: And mentioned, perhaps, with a certain antipathy?

> *The Student remains silent.*

I can well imagine! . . . No doubt you heard that I was the man who ruined your father? . . . Everyone who is ruined by stupid speculations comes to realize sooner or later that he was actually ruined by someone he couldn't fool. (*Pause.*) The truth of the matter is that your father fleeced me of seventeen thousand crowns, every cent I had saved up at the time.

THE STUDENT: It's remarkable how the same story can be told in two exactly opposite ways.

THE OLD MAN: Surely you don't think I'm being untruthful?

THE STUDENT: What do you think? My father didn't lie.

THE OLD MAN: That's true, a father never lies. . . . But I too am a father, and consequently . . .

THE STUDENT: What're you getting at?

THE OLD MAN: I saved your father from the worst possible

misery, and he repaid me with all the terrible hatred of a man who feels obliged to be grateful. He taught his family to speak ill of me.

THE STUDENT: Maybe you made him ungrateful. The help you gave him was probably poisoned with unnecessary humiliations.

THE OLD MAN: My dear young man, all help is humiliating.

THE STUDENT: What do you want of me?

THE OLD MAN: Don't worry, I'm not asking for the money back. But if you would render me a few small services, I would consider myself well repaid. You see that I'm a cripple — some say it's my own fault — others blame my parents — personally I blame it all on life itself, with all its traps — in avoiding one you fall right into the next one. Anyway, I can't run up and down stairs — can't even pull bell cords. And so I ask you: help me!

THE STUDENT: What can I do?

THE OLD MAN: Well, first of all you might give my chair a push so that I can read the posters. I want to see what's playing tonight.

THE STUDENT (*pushing the wheelchair*): Don't you have a man who takes care of you?

THE OLD MAN: He's off on an errand. . . . Be right back. . . . Are you a medical student?

THE STUDENT: No, I'm studying languages. But I really don't know what I want to be.

THE OLD MAN: Ah ha! — How are you at mathematics?

THE STUDENT: Fairly good.

THE OLD MAN: Good! Good! — Would you possibly be interested in a job?

THE STUDENT: Sure, why not?

THE OLD MAN: Splendid! (*Reading the posters.*) They're giving *Die Walküre* at the matinee. . . . That means that the colonel will be there with his daughter. And since he always sits on the aisle in the sixth row, I'll put you next to him. . . . You go into that telephone booth over there and order a ticket for seat number eighty-two in the sixth row.

THE STUDENT: An afternoon at the opera!

THE OLD MAN: That's right! Just do as I tell you and you won't regret it. I want to see you happy—rich, respected. Your debut last night as the courageous rescuer is the beginning of your fame. From now on your name is your fortune.

THE STUDENT (*going toward the telephone booth*): All right! Sounds like fun. Let's see what happens.

THE OLD MAN: You're a good sport, aren't you?

THE STUDENT: Suppose so. That's my misfortune.

THE OLD MAN: No more. This will make your fortune.

> *He picks up his newspaper and starts to read. In the meantime The Lady in Black has come out on the sidewalk and is talking with The Superintendent's Wife. The Old Man listens furtively, but the audience hears nothing. The Student returns.*

All set?

THE STUDENT: It's all taken care of.

THE OLD MAN: Take a look at that house.

THE STUDENT: I have already looked at it—very carefully. . . . I went by here yesterday, when the sun was glittering on the panes—and dreaming of all the beauty and luxury there must be in that house, I said to my friend, "Imagine having an apartment there, four flights up, and a beautiful wife, and two pretty kids, and twenty thousand crowns in dividends every year."

THE OLD MAN: Did you now? Did you say that? Well, well! I too am very fond of that house . . .

THE STUDENT: Do you speculate in houses?

THE OLD MAN: Mmm—yes! But not in the way you think . . .

THE STUDENT: Do you know the people who live there?

THE OLD MAN: Every single one. At my age you know everyone, including their fathers and their grandfathers—and you always find you're related to them somehow. I've just turned eighty. . . . But no one knows me, not really. . . . I take a great interest in human destinies . . .

> *The curtains in the round room are drawn up. The Colonel is seen inside, dressed in civilian clothes. After having looked at the thermometer, he moves away from the window and stands in front of the marble statue.*

Look, there's the colonel! You'll sit next to him this afternoon.

THE STUDENT: Is that him—the colonel? I don't understand anything that's going on. It's like a fairy tale.

THE OLD MAN: My whole life, my dear young man, is like a book of fairy tales. But although the stories are different, one thread ties them all together and the same leitmotif recurs constantly.

THE STUDENT: Who is that marble statue in there?

THE OLD MAN: That's his wife, naturally . . .

THE STUDENT: Was she so wonderful? Did he love her so much?

THE OLD MAN: Hmm yes . . . yes, of course . . .

THE STUDENT: Well, tell me!

THE OLD MAN: Come now, you know we can't judge other people. . . . Suppose I were to tell you that she left him, that he beat her, that she came back again and married him again, and that she is sitting in there right now like a mummy, worshiping her own statue. You would think I was crazy.

THE STUDENT: I can't understand it!

THE OLD MAN: That doesn't surprise me! —And over there

we have the hyacinth window. That's where his daughter lives. She's out horseback riding, but she'll be home soon . . .

THE STUDENT: Who's the lady in black talking to the caretaker?

THE OLD MAN: Well, that's a little complicated. But it's connected with the dead man upstairs, there where you see the white sheets.

THE STUDENT: And who was he?

THE OLD MAN: A human being, like the rest of us. The most conspicuous thing about him was his vanity. . . . Now if you were a Sunday child, you would soon see him come out of that very door just to look at the consulate flag at half-mast for himself. Yes, you see, he was a consul. Liked nothing better than coronets and lions, plumed hats and colored ribbons.

THE STUDENT: Sunday child, did you say? I was actually born on a Sunday, so I'm told.

THE OLD MAN: Really! Are you—! I should have guessed it. I could tell by the color of your eyes. . . . But—then you can see . . . what others can't see, haven't you noticed that?

THE STUDENT: I don't know what others see. But sometimes—. Well, there are some things you don't talk about!

THE OLD MAN: I knew it, I knew it! But you can talk to me about it. I understand—things like that . . .

THE STUDENT: Yesterday, for example. . . . I was drawn to that little side street where the house collapsed afterward. . . . I walked down the street and stopped in front of a house that I had never seen before. . . . Then I noticed a crack in the wall. I could hear the floor beams snapping in two. I leaped forward and grabbed up a child that was walking under the wall. . . . The next moment the house collapsed. . . . I escaped—but in my arms—where I thought I had the child—there wasn't anything . . .

THE OLD MAN: Remarkable. Remarkable. . . . I always knew that. . . . But tell me something: why were you making all those gestures just now at the fountain? And why were you talking to yourself?

THE STUDENT: Didn't you see the milkmaid I was talking to?

THE OLD MAN (*in horror*): Milkmaid?!

THE STUDENT: Yes, of course. She handed me the cup.

THE OLD MAN: Indeed? . . . So that's the way it is? . . . Very well, I may not have second sight, but I have other powers . . .

> *A white-haired woman sits down at the window with the mirror.*

Look at the old lady in the window! Do you see her? . . . Good, good! That was my fiancée — once upon a time — sixty years ago. . . . I was twenty. Don't be afraid, she doesn't recognize me. We see each other every day, but it doesn't mean a thing to me — although we once vowed to love each other forever. Forever!

THE STUDENT: How foolish you were in those days! Nowadays we don't tell girls things like that.

THE OLD MAN: Forgive us, young man. We didn't know any better! . . . But can you see that that old woman was once young and beautiful?

THE STUDENT: No, I can't. . . . Well, maybe. I like the way she tilts her head. . . . I can't see her eyes.

> *The Superintendent's Wife comes out carrying a basket of spruce greens, which she strews on the sidewalk, in accordance with Swedish custom at funerals.*

THE OLD MAN: Ah ha, the wife of the superintendent! The lady in black is her daughter by the dead man upstairs. That's why her husband got the job as superintendent. . . . But the lady in black has a lover — very aristocratic and waiting to inherit a fortune. Right now he's in the process of getting a divorce — from his present wife, who is giving him a town house just to get rid of him. The aristocratic lover is the son-in-law of the dead man, and you see his bedclothes being aired on the balcony up there. — Complicated, wouldn't you say?

THE STUDENT: It's damned complicated!

THE OLD MAN: Yes, indeed it is, both on the inside and the outside, although it all looks so simple.

THE STUDENT: But then who is the dead man?

THE OLD MAN: You just asked me and I told you. If you could look around the corner where the service entrance is, you'd see a pack of poor people whom he used to help – when he felt like it.

THE STUDENT: Then I suppose he was a kind and charitable man?

THE OLD MAN: Oh, yes – sometimes.

THE STUDENT: Not always?

THE OLD MAN: No, that's how people are! – Listen, will you give me a little push over there into the sun? I'm so terribly cold. When you never get to move around, the blood congeals. I'm going to die soon, I know that. But before I do, there are a few things I want to take care of. – Feel my hand, just feel how cold I am.

THE STUDENT: My god! It's unbelievable! (*He tries to free his hand, but The Old Man holds on to it.*)

THE OLD MAN: Don't leave me, I beg you – I'm tired, I'm lonely – but it hasn't always been this way, I tell you. – I have an infinitely long life behind me – infinitely long – I've made people unhappy and people have made me unhappy, the one cancels out the other. But before I die, I want to make you happy. . . . Our destinies are tangled together through your father – and other things.

THE STUDENT: Let go, let go of my hand – you are drawing all my strength from me – you're turning my blood to ice – what do you want of me?

THE OLD MAN: Patience. You'll soon see and understand. . . . There she comes –

THE STUDENT: The colonel's daughter?

THE OLD MAN: Yes! *His* daughter! Just look at her! – Have you ever seen such a masterpiece?

THE STUDENT: She looks like the marble statue in there.

THE OLD MAN: She should. That's her mother!

THE STUDENT: Incredibly beautiful! "Thou art fairer than the evening air, clad in the beauty of a thousand stars."

THE OLD MAN: Yes, indeed. "And happy he who on her lips shall press the bridegroom's greeting." —I see you appreciate her beauty. Not everyone recognizes it. . . . Well, then, it is ordained!

* * *

> *The Young Lady enters from the left dressed in a riding habit like a modern English horsewoman, and, without taking notice of anyone, crosses slowly over to the door of the house. Before entering, she stops and says a few words to The Superintendent's Wife. The Student covers his eyes with his hands.*

Are you crying?

THE STUDENT: When I see how far beyond my reach my happiness is, what can I feel but despair?

THE OLD MAN: But I can open doors—and hearts—if only I can find an arm to do my will. Serve me, and you shall be a lord of creation!

THE STUDENT: A devil's bargain? You want me to sell my soul?

THE OLD MAN: Sell nothing! —Don't you understand, all my life I have *taken, taken*! Now I crave to give, to give! But nobody will take what I have to offer. I'm a rich man, very rich—and without any heirs. —Oh, yes, I have a good-for-nothing son who torments the life out of me. . . . You could become my son, become my heir while I'm still alive, enjoy life while I'm here to see it—at least from a distance.

THE STUDENT: What do you want me to do?

THE OLD MAN: First: go an hear *Die Walküre*!

THE STUDENT: That's already been taken care of. What else?

THE OLD MAN: This evening you shall be sitting in there—in the round room!

THE STUDENT: How do you expect me to get in?

THE OLD MAN: By way of *Die Walküre!*

THE STUDENT: Why did you pick me for your—your medium? Did you know me before?

THE OLD MAN: Of course, of course! I've had my eye on you for a long time. . . . Ah! Look up there, on the balcony, where the maid is raising the flag to half-mast for the consul—and now she's turning over the bedclothes. . . . Do you see that blue quilt? It was made for two to sleep under, and now it covers only one . . .

> *The Young Lady, in a change of clothes, appears at the window to water the hyacinths.*

There's my dear little girl. Look at her, just look at her! . . . She's talking to the flowers now. Isn't she just like a blue hyacinth herself? She gives them water to drink, the purest water, and they transform the water into color and perfume. --Here comes the colonel with a newspaper. . . . Now he's pointing to your picture! She's reading about your heroic deed. --It's starting to cloud over. Suppose it starts to rain? I'll be in a pretty mess if Johansson doesn't come back soon.

> *It grows cloudy and dark. The Old Woman at the window mirror closes her window.*

I see my fiancée is closing up shop. . . . Seventy-nine years. . . . That window mirror is the only mirror she ever uses. That's because she can't see herself in it, only the outside world and from two direction at once. But the world can see her. She doesn't realize that. . . . All the same, not bad-looking for an old woman.

> *The Dead Man, wrapped in a winding sheet, is seen coming out of the main door.*

THE STUDENT: Oh my god, what—?

THE OLD MAN: What do you see?

THE STUDENT: Don't *you* see? Don't you see, in the doorway, the dead man?

THE OLD MAN: No, I don't see anything. But I'm not surprised. Tell me exactly what—

THE STUDENT: He's stepping out into the street. . . . (*Pauses.*) Now he's turning his head and looking up at the flag.

THE OLD MAN: What did I tell you? Watch, he will count every wreath and read every calling card. I pity whoever is missing!

THE STUDENT: Now he's turning the corner . . .

THE OLD MAN: He's gone to count the poor people at the service entrance. The poor add such a nice touch to an obituary: "Received the blessings of the populace!" Yes, but he won't receive my blessing! —Just between us, he was a big scoundrel.

THE STUDENT: But benevolent.

THE OLD MAN: A benevolent scoundrel. Always thinking of his own magnificent funeral. . . . When he could feel his end was near, he embezzled fifty thousand crowns from the state. . . . Now his daughter is running around with another woman's husband and wondering about the will. . . . The scoundrel can hear every word we're saying. I hope he gets an earful! —Here's Johansson.

> *Johansson enters from the left.*

Report!

> *Johannson speaks to The Old Man, but the audience cannot hear what he says.*

What do you mean, not at home? You're an ass! —What about the telegram? —Not a word! . . . Go on, go on! . . . Six o'clock this evening? That's good! —An extra edition? —With all

the details about him? . . . Arkenholz, student . . . born
. . . his parents. . . . Splendid! . . . It's beginning to rain, I
think. . . . And what did he say? . . . Really, really! —He
didn't *want* to? Well, he's going to have to! —Here comes the
baron, or whatever he is! —Push me around the corner, Johansson. I want to hear what the poor people are saying. —And
Arkenholz! Don't go away. Do you understand? —Well, come on,
come on, what are you waiting for!

> *Johansson pushes the wheelchair around the corner.*

* * *

> *The Student has turned to look at The Young Lady,
> who is loosening the earth in hyacinth pots.*

* * *

> *Dressed in mourning, Baron Skanskorg enters and
> speaks to The Lady in Black, who has been walking up
> and down the sidewalk.*

BARON SKANSKORG: What can we do about it? We simply
have to wait.

LADY IN BLACK (*intensely*): But I can't wait, don't you understand?

BARON SKANSKORG: Well, if that's the way it is, you'll have
to go to the country.

LADY IN BLACK: I don't want to do that!

BARON SKANSKORG: Come over here. Otherwise they'll
hear what we're saying.

> *They move over toward the kiosk and continue their con-
> versation unheard by the audience.*

* * *

> *Johansson enters from the right.*

JOHANSSON (*to The Student*): My master asks you not to forget that other matter . . .

THE STUDENT (*warily*): Just a minute—I want to know something first. Tell me, exactly who is Hummel? What is he?

JOHANSSON: What can I say? He's so many things, and he's been everything.

THE STUDENT: Is he in his right mind?

JOHANSSON: Who is? All his life he's been looking for a Sunday child. That's what he says—but he might be making it up . . .

THE STUDENT: What's he after? Money?

JOHANSSON: Power. —All day long he rides around in his chariot like the great god Thor. . . . He keeps his eye on houses, tears them down, opens up streets, builds up city squares. But he also breaks into houses, sneaks in through the windows, ravages human lives, kills his enemies, and forgives nothing and nobody. . . . Can you imagine that that little cripple was once a Don Juan? But no woman would ever stick with him.

THE STUDENT: Sounds inconsistent.

JOHANSSON: Oh, no. You see, he was so sly that he knew how to get the women to leave when he got bored with them. But that was a long time ago. Now he's more like a horse thief at a slave market. He steals people—in more ways than one. . . . He literally stole me out of the hands of the law. I made a little mistake— that's all—and he was the only one who knew about it. But instead of putting me in jail, he made me his slave. I slave for him just for my food—which isn't the best in the world.

THE STUDENT: What's he got up his sleeve? What's he want to do in this house?

JOHANSSON: I wouldn't want to say! I wouldn't even know where to begin!

THE STUDENT: I think I'd better get out while the getting is good.

JOHANSSON: Look at the young lady! She's dropped her bracelet out of the window.

> *The bracelet has fallen off The Young Lady's arm and through the open window. The Student crosses over slowly, picks up the bracelet, and hands it to The Young Lady, who thanks him stiffly. The Student goes back to Johansson.*

I thought you said you were leaving. It isn't as easy as you think once *he* has slipped his net over your head. . . . And he's afraid of nothing between heaven and earth – yes, one thing – or rather one person.

THE STUDENT: I bet I know.

JOHANSSON: How can you know?

THE STUDENT: Just guessing! Could it be . . . he's afraid of a little milkmaid?

JOHANSSON: He turns his head away whenever he sees a milk wagon. . . . Sometimes he talks in his sleep. He must have been in Hamburg once . . .

THE STUDENT: Can I depend on him?

JOHANSSON: You can depend on him – to do anything and everything!

THE STUDENT: What's he up to around the corner?

JOHANSSON: Eavesdropping on the poor. . . . Planting a word here and there, chipping away at one stone at a time – until the whole house falls – metaphorically speaking. Oh yes, I've had an education. And I used to be a bookseller. . . . Are you leaving or staying?

THE STUDENT: I don't like to be ungrateful. This man once saved my father, and all he's asking for now is a little favor in return.

JOHANSSON: What's that?

THE STUDENT: He wants me to go and see *Die Walküre*.

JOHANSSON: That's beyond me. . . . He's always got something up his sleeve. . . . Look at him, he's talking to the policeman. He's always in with the police. He makes use of them, gets them involved in his business, ties them hand and foot with false promises of future possibilities. And all the while, he's pumping them, pumping them. — Mark my words, before the night is over he'll be received in the round room.

THE STUDENT: What does he want in there? What's he got to do with the colonel?

JOHANSSON: I'm not sure, but I've got my ideas. You'll be able to see for yourself when you go there!

THE STUDENT: I'll never get in there . . .

JOHANSSON: That depends on you! Go to *Die Walküre.*

THE STUDENT: Is that the way?

JOHANSSON: If he said so, it is! —Look at him, just look at him! Riding his war chariot, drawn in triumph by the beggars, who don't get a cent for it, just a hint that something might come their way at his funeral!

> *The Old Man enters, standing in his wheelchair, drawn by one of the Beggars and followed by the others.*

THE OLD MAN: Let us hail the noble youth, who risked his own life to save so many in yesterday's disaster! Hail Arkenholz!

> *The Beggars bare their heads but do not cheer. The Young Lady, standing in the window, waves her handkerchief. The Colonel looks at the scene from his window. The Fiancée stands up at her window. The Housemaid on the balcony raises the flag to the top.*

Hail the hero, my fellow citizens! I know indeed it is Sunday, but the ass in the pit and the ears of corn in the field absolve us. And though I may not be a Sunday child, I can see into the future and I can heal the sick. I have even brought a drowned soul back to life. . . . That happened in Hamburg, yes, on a Sunday morning, just like this—

* * *

The Milkmaid enters, seen only by The Student and The Old Man. She stretches her arms above her head like a drowning person and stares fixedly at The Old Man.

* * *

The Old Man sits down and shrivels up in terror.

Get me out of here, Johansson! Quick! —Arkenholz, don't you forget *Die Walküre!*

THE STUDENT: What is all this?

JOHANSSON: We shall see! We shall see!

[2]

In the round room. At the back of the stage a stove of white glazed porcelain, its mantel decorated with a mirror, a pendulum clock, and candelabra. At the right side of the stage a hallway can be seen and through it a view of a green room with mahogany furniture. At the left of the stage stands the statue in the shadow of the palm trees, and with a curtain that can be drawn to conceal it. In the rear wall to the left of the stove is the door to the hyacinth room, where The Young Lady is seen reading. The Colonel's back can be seen in the green room, where he is writing at his desk.

The Colonel's valet, Bengtsson, wearing livery, enters from the hall, accompanied by Johansson, wearing the formal attire of a waiter.

BENGTSSON: Now, Johansson, you'll have to wait on the table while I take care of the coats. Have you done this before?

JOHANSSON: During the day I push that war chariot, as you know, but in the evenings I work as a waiter at receptions. It's always been my dream to get into this house. . . . They're peculiar people, aren't they?

BENGTSSON: Well, yes, I think one might say that they're a little strange.

JOHANSSON: Are we going to have a musicale this evening? Or what is the occasion?

BENGTSSON: Just the ordinary ghost supper, as we call it. They drink tea, without saying a word, or else the colonel talks all by himself. And they chomp their biscuits and crackers all at once and all in unison. They sound like a pack of rats in an attic.

JOHANSSON: Why do you call it the ghost supper?

BENGTSSON: They all look like ghosts. . . . This has been going on for twenty years—always the same people, always saying the same things. Or else keeping silent to avoid being embarrassed.

JOHANSSON: Where's the lady of the house? Isn't she around?

BENGTSSON: Oh, yes. But she's crazy. She keeps herself shut up in a closet because her eyes can't stand the light. She's sitting in there right now. (*He points to a wallpapered door.*)

JOHANSSON: In there?

BENGTSSON: I told you they were a little peculiar.

JOHANSSON: What on earth does she look like?

BENGTSSON: Like a mummy. Do you want to see her? (*He opens the papered door.*) There she sits!

JOHANSSON: Je-sus!

* * *

THE MUMMY (*babbling*): Why do you open the door? Didn't I tell you to keep it closed?

BENGTSSON (*as if talking to a baby*): Ta, ta, ta, ta, ta! —Is little chickadee going to be nice to me? Then little chickadee will get something good! —Pretty Polly!

THE MUMMY (*like a parrot*): Pretty Polly! Are you there, Jacob? Jacob? Cluck, cluck!

BENGTSSON: She thinks she's a parrot—and maybe she is. (*To The Mummy*.) Come on, Polly, whistle for us!

The Mummy whistles.

JOHANSSON: I thought I had seen everything, but this tops it all.

BENGTSSON: Well, when a house grows old, it turns moldy and rotten, and when people are together too much and torment each other too long, they go crazy. Take the lady in this house— shut up, Polly! —This mummy has been sitting here for forty years—the same husband, same furniture, same relatives, same friends. . . . (*Closing the door on The Mummy*.) And imagine what's gone on in this house! Even I don't know the whole story. . . . Look at this statue. That's the lady of the house as a young girl!

JOHANSSON: Oh my god! —Is that the mummy?

BENGTSSON: Yes. It's enough to make one cry! But this lady— carried away by her imagination or something—has acquired certain peculiarities, as babbling parrots do. She can't stand cripples, for instance—or sick people. She can't even stand the sight of her own daughter because she's sick.

JOHANSSON: Is that young girl sick?

BENGTSSON: Yes. Didn't you know?

JOHANSSON: No. . . . What about the colonel? Who is he?

BENGTSSON: Wait awhile and you'll see!

JOHANSSON (*looking at the statue*): It's terrifying to realize that—. How old is the lady now?

BENGTSSON: Who knows? But I've heard it said that when she was thirty-five she looked like she was nineteen. —And she convinced the colonel that she was . . . here in this house. . . . Do you know what that black Japanese screen by the couch is for? It's called a death screen, and when somebody's going to die, it's placed around them, same as in a hospital.

JOHANSSON: What a horrible house. . . . That poor student thought that when he entered this house he would be entering paradise.

BENGTSSON: Which student? Oh, yes, of course! The one that's coming here tonight. The colonel and his daughter met him at the opera and were captivated by him. . . . Hm. . . . But let me ask you a couple of questions. Who's your master? The financier in the wheelchair?

JOHANSSON (*nodding*): Yes, that's right. —Is he coming here too?

BENGTSSON: He's not invited.

JOHANSSON: He'll come uninvited—if he has to.

> The Old Man appears in the hallway dressed in frock coat and high hat. He creeps silently forward on his crutches and eavesdrops on the servants.

BENGTSSON: I'll bet he's a real mean old one.

JOHANSSON: A perfect specimen!

BENGTSSON: He looks like the devil incarnate!

JOHANSSON: And he's a black magician, I tell you. He can go through locked doors—

*   *   *

THE OLD MAN (*coming forward and grabbing Johansson by the ear*): Fool! Hold your tongue! (*To Bengtsson.*) Announce me to the colonel.

BENGTSSON: But we're expecting company here.

THE OLD MAN: I know you are! My visit is not unexpected— although undesired.

BENGTSSON: I see. What was the name? Mr. Hummel?

THE OLD MAN: That's right! Precisely!

> Bengtsson goes down the hall into the green room and closes the door.

*   *   *

THE OLD MAN (*to Johansson*): Disappear!

Johansson hesitates.

Vanish!

Johansson vanishes down the hall.

*   *   *

The Old Man inspects the room. Stops in front of the statue. Much amazed.

THE OLD MAN: Amelia! . . . It is she! . . . Amelia! (*He roams about the room fingering objects. Stops in front of the mirror to adjust his wig. Returns to the statue.*)

THE MUMMY (*from within the closet*): Pretty Polly!

THE OLD MAN (*startled*): What on earth? Sounded like a parrot in the room. But I don't see any.

THE MUMMY: You there, Jacob?

THE OLD MAN: Place is haunted.

THE MUMMY: Jacob!

THE OLD MAN: It's enough to frighten one! . . . So that's the kind of secrets they keep in this house. (*With his back to the closet, he studies a portrait on the wall.*) There he is! —The old colonel himself!

*   *   *

THE MUMMY (*coming out of the closet, goes up to The Old Man from behind and gives his wig a pull*): Coo, coo, coo! Cuckoo, cuckoo!

THE OLD MAN (*frightened out of his skin*): Oh my God in heaven! —Who are you?

THE MUMMY (*speaking in her normal voice*): Is that you, Jacob?

THE OLD MAN: Yes. My name is Jacob.

THE MUMMY (*movingly*): And my name is Amelia!

THE OLD MAN: Oh no. . . . No, no. . . . Oh my God!

THE MUMMY: Yes, this is how I look! —And that's how I did look once upon a time. Life gives one a great education. Most of my life I've spent in the closet, so that I won't have to see—or be seen. . . . But you, Jacob, what are you looking for here?

THE OLD MAN: My child! Our child!

THE MUMMY: She's sitting in there.

THE OLD MAN: Where?

THE MUMMY: In there, in the hyacinth room.

THE OLD MAN (*looking at The Young Lady*): Yes, there she is! (*Pause.*) And what does her father think of her—I mean, the colonel—your husband?

THE MUMMY: I had a quarrel with him once, and told him everything . . .

THE OLD MAN: And . . . ?

THE MUMMY: He didn't believe me. He said, "That's what all women say when they want to murder their husbands." . . . All the same it was a terrible crime. His whole life has been falsified, including his family tree. When I look at his family record in the peerage, I say to myself she's no better than a runaway servant girl with a false birth certificate, and girls like that are sent to the reformatory.

THE OLD MAN: A lot of people forge their birth certificates. I seem to remember that even you falsified the date of your birth.

THE MUMMY: It was my mother who put me up to it. I'm not to blame for that! . . . And furthermore, you played the biggest part in our crime.

THE OLD MAN: Not true! Your husband started it all when he stole my fiancée from me! I was born unable to forgive until I have punished. I've always looked upon it as an imperative duty. And I still do!

THE MUMMY: What do you expect to find in this house? What do you want here? And how did you get in? — Does your business concern my daughter? Keep your hands off her, I warn you, or you'll die!

THE OLD MAN: I wish her nothing but the best!

THE MUMMY: And you must have consideration for her father, too!

THE OLD MAN: Never!

THE MUMMY: Then you must die. In this room. Behind that screen.

THE OLD MAN: Be that as it may. But I'm a bulldog. I never let go.

THE MUMMY: You want to marry her to that student. Why? He has nothing; he is nothing.

THE OLD MAN: He'll be a rich man, thanks to me.

THE MUMMY: Are you one of the invited guests tonight?

THE OLD MAN: No. I've decided to invite myself to this ghost supper!

THE MUMMY: Do you know who'll be here?

THE OLD MAN: Not entirely.

THE MUMMY: The baron — who lives upstairs, and whose father-in-law was buried this afternoon —

THE OLD MAN: Yes, the baron — who is getting a divorce in order to marry the daughter of the superintendent's wife. The baron — who was once — your lover!

THE MUMMY: And then there'll be your former fiancée — whom my husband seduced . . .

THE OLD MAN: A very select gathering . . .

THE MUMMY: Oh God, why can't we die? If only we could die!

THE OLD MAN: Then why do you keep seeing one another?

THE MUMMY: Our crimes and our secrets and our guilt bind us together! We have split up and gone our separate ways an infinite number of times. But we're always drawn back together again . . .

THE OLD MAN: I believe the colonel is coming.

THE MUMMY: Then I'll go in to Adele. . . . (*Pause.*) Jacob, don't do anything foolish! Be considerate toward him . . .

> *A pause. She leaves.*

> * * *

THE COLONEL (*enters, cold and reserved*): Please sit down.

> *The Old Man takes his time seating himself. A pause. The Colonel stares at him.*

Did you write this letter?

THE OLD MAN: I did.

THE COLONEL: And your name is Hummel?

THE OLD MAN: It is.

> *Pause.*

THE COLONEL: Since it's clear that you have bought up all my outstanding promissory notes, it follows that I'm completely at your mercy. Now what do you want?

THE OLD MAN: I want to be paid—in one way or another.

THE COLONEL: In what way?

THE OLD MAN: A very simple way. Don't let's talk about money. Allow me to come and go in your house—as a guest.

THE COLONEL: If that's all it takes to satisfy you—

THE OLD MAN: Thank you!

THE COLONEL: And what else?

THE OLD MAN: Dismiss Bengtsson!

THE COLONEL: Why? Bengtsson is my devoted servant. He's been with me during my whole career. The army awarded him a medal for faithful service. Why should I dismiss him?

THE OLD MAN: I have no doubt he's a very fine man in your eyes. But he's not the man he seems to be!

THE COLONEL: Who is?

THE OLD MAN (*taken aback*): True! — But Bengtsson must go!

THE COLONEL: Are you going to give orders in my house?

THE OLD MAN: Yes! Since I own everything that you can lay your eyes on — furniture, curtains, dinner service, linen . . . and other things . . .

THE COLONEL: What other things?

THE OLD MAN: Everything. I own it all. Everything that you see here is mine!

THE COLONEL: I can't dispute that. But my family honor, my coat of arms, and my good name are things you cannot take from me!

THE OLD MAN: Yes, I can. They don't belong to you. (*Pause.*) You are not a nobleman.

THE COLONEL: I shall give you the opportunity of withdrawing those words!

THE OLD MAN (*producing a piece of paper*): If you will take the trouble to read this extract from the standard book of genealogy, you will see that the family whose name you have assumed has been extinct for over a century.

THE COLONEL (*reading*): Of course I've heard rumors like this before. But it was my father's name before it was mine (*Reading on.*) I can't deny it. You are quite right. . . . I am not a nobleman! Not even that. . . . Therefore I shall take this signet ring off my hand. — Oh, but of course, excuse me: it belongs to you. There you are.

THE OLD MAN (*putting the ring in his pocket*): Let us continue. — You are not a colonel either!

THE COLONEL: Am I not?

THE OLD MAN: No! You held a temporary commission as a colonel in the American Volunteers, but at the end of the Spanish-American War and the reorganization of the army, all such titles were abolished.

THE COLONEL: Is that true?

THE OLD MAN (*reaching into his pocket*): Do you want to see for yourself?

THE COLONEL: No, it won't be necessary. . . . Who are you? What gives you the right to sit there and strip me naked in this way?

THE OLD MAN: Patience, my good man! And as far as stripping is concerned—do you really want to know who you are?

THE COLONEL: Have you no decency?

THE OLD MAN: Take off that wig of yours and have a look at yourself in the mirror. And while you're at it, take out those false teeth and shave off that moustache and let Bengtsson unlace your metal corset, and then we shall see if a certain valet who shall be nameless won't recognize himself—the cupboard lover who flirted with the maids so he could scrounge in the kitchen.

> *The Colonel reaches for the bell on the table. The Old Man stops him, saying:*

I wouldn't touch that if I were you. If you call Bengtsson I'll order him arrested. . . . I believe your guests are arriving. Now let us be calm and go on playing our old roles for a while longer.

THE COLONEL: Who are you? I've seen your eyes and heard your voice before.

THE OLD MAN: Never mind that. Be silent and do as you're told!

* * *

THE STUDENT (*enters and bows to The Colonel*): How do you do, sir!

THE COLONEL: Welcome to my house, young man! Your heroism at that terrible accident has brought your name to everybody's lips. I deem it an honor to receive you in my house.

THE STUDENT: You're very kind, sir. It's a great honor for me, sir. I've never expected—well, my humble birth—and your illustrious name and your noble birth . . .

THE COLONEL: Mr. Hummel, may I introduce Mr. Arkenholz, who is a student at the university. The ladies are in there, Mr. Arkenholz—if you care to join them. I have a few more things I want to say to Mr. Hummel.

The Colonel shows The Student into the hyacinth room, where he remains visible to the audience, engaged in shy conversation with The Young Lady.

* * *

THE COLONEL: An excellent young man—musical, sings, writes poetry. . . . If it weren't for his birth and social position I certainly wouldn't have anything against—my . . .

THE OLD MAN: Against what?

THE COLONEL: Having my daughter—

THE OLD MAN: *Your* daughter! . . . Apropos of her, why does she always sit in that room?

THE COLONEL: She feels she has to sit in the hyacinth room whenever she's in the house. A peculiarity of hers. . . . Here comes Miss Beatrice von Holsteinkrona. Charming woman. —Very distinguished family, but hasn't a cent to her name. All she's got goes to the nursing home.

THE OLD MAN (*to himself*): My fiancée!

* * *

The Fiancée enters, white-haired and giving every appearance of being crazy.

THE COLONEL: Miss Holsteinkrona—Mr. Hummel.

The Fiancée curtsies and takes a seat.

* * *

Baron Skanskorg enters next—dressed in mourning and with a strange look on his face—and sits down.

THE COLONEL: Baron Skanskorg—

THE OLD MAN (*in an aside, without rising*): A jewel thief, if ever I saw one. (*To The Colonel.*) Now let the mummy in, and the party can begin.

THE COLONEL (*in the doorway to the hyacinth room*): Polly!

* * *

THE MUMMY (*enters*): Coo, coo! Cuckoo, cuckoo!

THE COLONEL: Shall we invite the young people, too?

THE OLD MAN: No! Not the young people! They shall be spared.

They seat themselves in a circle. Silence.

* * *

THE COLONEL: Shall I ring for tea?

THE OLD MAN: Why bother? No one cares for tea. Why play games?

Pause.

THE COLONEL: Then perhaps we should start a conversation?

THE OLD MAN (*slowly, deliberately, and with frequent pauses*): About the weather? Which we know. Ask one another how we're feeling? Which we also know. I prefer silence . . . in which one can hear thoughts and see the past. Silence cannot hide any-thing—which is more than you can say for words. I read the other day that the differences in languages originated among the primi-tive savages, who sought to keep their secrets from other tribes. Languages are therefore codes, and he who finds the key can understand all the languages of the world. But that doesn't mean that secrets cannot be discovered without a key. Especially in those cases where paternity must be proved. Legal proof is of course a different matter. Two false witnesses provide complete proof of whatever they agree to say. But in the kind of escapades I have in mind, one doesn't take witnesses along. Nature herself has planted in man a blushing sense of shame, which seeks to hide what should be hidden. But we slip into certain situations without intending to, and chance confronts us with moments of revelation, when the deepest secrets are revealed, the mask is ripped from the imposter and the villain stands exposed . . .

Pause. All look at one another in silence.

Extraordinary, how silent you all are! (*Long silence.*) Take this house, for example. In this estimable house, in this elegant house, where beauty, wealth, and culture are united. . . . (*Long silence.*) All of us sitting here, we know who we are, don't we? . . . I don't have to tell you. . . . And you know me, although you pretend ignorance. . . . Sitting in that room is my daughter, yes mine, you know that too. . . . She had lost all desire to live, without knowing why. . . . She was withering away because of the air in this house, which reeks of crime, deception, and lies of every kind. . . . That is why I had to find a friend for her, a friend from whose very presence she would apprehend the warmth and light radiated by a noble deed. . . . (*Long silence.*) That was my mission in this house. To pull up the weeds, to expose the crimes, to settle the accounts, so that these young people might make a new beginning in this home, which is my gift to them! (*Long silence.*) Listen to the ticking of the clock, like a deathwatch beetle in the wall! Listen to what it's saying: "time's-up, time's-up! . . . " When it strikes—in just a few moments—your time is up. Then you may go—not before.

The clock can be heard preparing to strike the hour.

Hear! The hammer draws back, the wheels whir. It's warning you: "clocks can strike!" —And I can strike too! (*He strikes the table with his crutch.*) Do you understand?

Silence.

* * *

THE MUMMY (*goes over to the clock and stops its pendulum. In her normal voice, speaking purposefully*): But I can stop time in its course. I can wipe out the past, and undo what is done. Not with bribes, not with threats—but through suffering and repentance. (*Approaching The Old Man.*) We are poor miserable creatures, we know that. We have erred, we have transgressed, we, like all the rest. We are not what we seem to be. At bottom we are better than ourselves, since we abhor and detest our misdeeds. But when you, Jacob Hummel, with your false name, come here to sit in judgment over us, that proves that you are more contemptible than we! And you are not the one you seem to be! You are a slave trader, a stealer of souls! You once stole me with false promises. You murdered the consul who was buried today; you strangled him with debts. You have stolen the student and shackled him with an imaginary debt of his father's, who never owed you a penny . . .

> *The Old Man has tried to rise and speak but has collapsed in his chair and shriveled up, and, like a dying insect, he shrivels up more and more during the following dialogue.*

But there is one dark spot in your life, which I'm not sure about—although I have my suspicions. . . . I think that Bengtsson might help us. (*She rings the bell on the table.*)

THE OLD MAN: No! Not Bengtsson! Not him!

THE MUMMY: Then it is true? He does know! (*She rings again.*)

> *The Milkmaid appears in the door to the hall, unseen by all except The Old Man, who shies in terror. The Milkmaid disappears when Bengtsson enters.*

Bengtsson, do you know this man?

BENGTSSON: Yes, I know him, and he knows me. Life has its ups and downs, as we all know, and I have been in his service, and once he was in mine. To be exact, he was a sponger in my kitchen for two whole years. Since he had to be out of the house by three o'clock, dinner had to be ready at two, and those in the house had to eat the warmed-up food left by that ox. Even worse, he drank up the pure soup stock and the gravy, which then had to be diluted with water. He sat there like a vampire, sucking all the marrow out of the house, and turned us all into skeletons. And he nearly succeeded in putting us into prison, when we accused the cook of being a thief. . . . Later I met this man in Hamburg under another name. He had become a usurer or bloodsucker. And it was there that he was accused of having lured a young girl out onto the ice in order to drown her, for she was the only witness to a crime that he was afraid would come to light . . .

THE MUMMY (*passes her hand over The Old Man's face*): That is the real you! Now empty your pockets of the notes and the will!

> *Johansson appears in the door to the hall and watches The Old Man intently, knowing that his slavery is coming to an end. The Old Man produces a bundle of papers, which he throws on the table.*
>
> *The Mummy strokes The Old Man's back.*

> Little Polly Parrot
> Sat in the garret,
> Eating toast and tea.

THE OLD MAN (*like a parrot*):

> Polly put the kettle on,
> Polly put the kettle on,
> We'll all have tea.
> Jack and Jill, Jack and Jill!

THE MUMMY: Can—clocks—strike?

THE OLD MAN (*making clucking sounds*): Clocks can strike! (*He imitates a cuckoo clock.*) Coo-coo! Coo-coo! Coo-coo!

THE MUMMY (*opening the jib door to the closet*): Now the clock has struck! Stand up and enter the closet where I have sat for twenty years, crying over our misdeeds. You'll find a rope in there. It can stand for the one you strangled the consul with—for the one you intended to strangle your benefactor with. . . . Go in!

> *The Old Man goes into the closet. The Mummy closes the door.*

THE MUMMY: Bengtsson! Put up the screen. The death screen.

> *Bengtsson places the screen in front of the door.*

It is finished. —May God have mercy on his soul!

ALL: Amen!

> *Long silence.*

* * *

> *In the hyacinth room, The Young Lady can be seen sitting at a harp on which she accompanies The Student. After a prelude played by The Young Lady, The Student recites.*

THE STUDENT:

> I saw the sun
> And from its blaze
> There burst on me
> The deepest truth:
>
> Man reaps as he sows;
> Blessed is he
> Who sows the good.
>
> For deeds done in anger
> Kindness alone
> Can make amends.
>
> Bring cheer to those
> Whom you have hurt,

And kindness reaps
Its own rewards.

The pure in heart
Have none to fear.
The harmless are happy.
The guileless are good.

[3]

A room decorated in a bizarre style, predominantly
oriental. A profusion of hyacinths in all colors fills the
room. On the porcelain tile stove sits a large Buddha
with a bulb of a shallot (allium ascalonicum) *in its lap.*
The stem of the shallot rises from the bulb and bursts
into a spherical cluster of white, starlike flowers. In the
rear to the right, a door leads to the round room. The
Colonel and The Mummy can be seen in there sitting
motionless and silent. A part of the death screen is also
visible. To the left in the rear, a door to the pantry and
the kitchen. The Student and The Young Lady (Adele)
are near a table, she seated at her harp, he standing
beside her.

THE YOUNG LADY: Now you must sing a song to my flowers!

THE STUDENT: Is this the flower of your soul?

THE YOUNG LADY: The one and only! Don't you love the
hyacinth?

THE STUDENT: I love it above all other flowers — its stem
rising straight and slender, like a young maiden, from the round
bulb, which floats on water and sends its white rare roots down
into clear, colorless nothingness. I love it for its colors: the snow-
white, innocent and pure — the golden yellow, sweet as honey —
the shy pink, the ripe red — but above all the blue ones — blue as
morning mist, deep-eyed blue, ever-faithful blue. I love them
all — more than gold and pearls. Have loved them ever since I was
a child, have worshiped them because they possess all the virtues
I lack. . . . But still —

THE YOUNG LADY: What?

THE STUDENT: My love is not returned. These beautiful blossoms hate and detest me.

THE YOUNG LADY: How?

THE STUDENT: Their fragrance—as strong and clear as the first winds of spring, sweeping down from the fields of melting snow—confuses my senses—they deafen me, blind me, drive me out of my mind—impale me with their poisonous arrows that stab my heart and set my head afire! . . . Don't you know the story behind that flower?

THE YOUNG LADY: No. Tell me.

THE STUDENT: First you have to interpret it. The bulb is the earth, whether floating on water or buried deep in black humus. Here the stalk shoots up, straight as the axis of the world, and here at its upper end are gathered together the six-pointed star flowers.

THE YOUNG LADY: Above the earth, the stars! How sublime! How did you know that? Where did you discover that?

THE STUDENT: I don't know. Let me think. —In your eyes! . . . So you see, it's an image of the whole cosmos. That's why Buddha sits there with the bulb of the earth in his lap, watching it constantly to see it shoot up and burst forth and be transformed into a heaven. This poor earth shall become a heaven! That is what Buddha is waiting for!

THE YOUNG LADY: Of course! I see that now! —And don't the snowflakes have six points like the hyacinth?

THE STUDENT: Exactly! Then snowflakes are falling stars—

THE YOUNG LADY: And the snowdrop is a snow-star—growing out of the snow.

THE STUDENT: And Sirius, the largest and most beautiful of all the stars in the firmament, golden-red Sirius is the narcissus with its golden-red chalice and its six white rays—

THE YOUNG LADY: Have you seen the shallot burst into bloom?

THE STUDENT: Yes, of course I have! It hides its blossoms

in a ball—a globe just like the celestial globe, strewn with white stars.

THE YOUNG LADY: How heavenly! Wonderful! Whose idea was it?

THE STUDENT: Yours!

THE YOUNG LADY: Yours!

THE STUDENT: Ours. We have given birth to something together. We are wedded . . .

THE YOUNG LADY: No, not yet . . .

THE STUDENT: Why not? What else?

THE YOUNG LADY: Time—testing—patience.

THE STUDENT: Very well! Put me to the test! (*Pause.*) So silent? . . . Why do your parents sit in there, silent, without saying a single word?

THE YOUNG LADY: Because they have nothing to say to each other, since they don't believe what the other says. My father explains it this way: he says, "What good does talking do, we can't pull the wool over our eyes."

THE STUDENT: It makes me sick to hear things like that . . .

THE YOUNG LADY: The cook is coming this way . . . Look at her, how big and fat she is . . .

THE STUDENT: What does she want?

THE YOUNG LADY: She wants to ask me about dinner. I've been managing the house during my mother's illness.

THE STUDENT: What have we got to do with the kitchen?

THE YOUNG LADY: We have to eat, don't we? . . . Look at her, look at her. I can't bear to . . .

THE STUDENT: Who is that bloated monster?

THE YOUNG LADY: She belongs to the Hummel family of vampires. She's eating us up . . .

THE STUDENT: Why don't you fire her?

THE YOUNG LADY: She won't leave! We can't control her. We got her because of our sins. . . . Don't you see that we're wasting away, withering?

THE STUDENT: Don't you get enough food to eat?

THE YOUNG LADY: We get course after course, but all the strength is gone from the food. She boils the beef until there's nothing left of it and serves us the sinews swimming in water while she herself drinks the stock. And when we have a roast, she cooks all the juice out of it and drinks it and eats the gravy. Everything she touches loses its flavor. It's as if she sucked it up with her very eyes. We get the grounds when she has finished her coffee. She drinks the wine and fills up the bottles with water.

THE STUDENT: Get rid of her!

THE YOUNG LADY: We can't!

THE STUDENT: Why not?

THE YOUNG LADY: We don't know! She won't leave! No one can control her. . . . She has taken all our strength from us.

THE STUDENT: Let me get rid of her for you.

THE YOUNG LADY: Oh, no! I guess this is how it's supposed to be. . . . Here she is! She'll ask me what we're having for dinner—I'll tell her this and that—she'll make objections—and finally we'll have what she says.

THE STUDENT: Then let her decide in the first place!

THE YOUNG LADY: She won't do that.

THE STUDENT: What a strange house! It's haunted, isn't it?

THE YOUNG LADY: Yes. —She's turning back now. She saw you!

* * *

THE COOK (*in the doorway*): Ha, that ain't why! (*Grinning so that all her teeth show.*)

THE STUDENT: Get out!

THE COOK: When I feel like it I will! (*Pause.*) Now I feel like it!

She vanishes.

THE YOUNG LADY: Don't lose your temper. Learn to be patient. She's part of the trials and tribulations we have to go through in this home. And we've got a housemaid, too! Whom we have to clean up after!

THE STUDENT: I can feel myself sinking into the earth! – *Cor in aethere!* – Let's have music!

THE YOUNG LADY: Wait!

THE STUDENT: No! Music now!

THE YOUNG LADY: Patience! – This room is called the testing room. It's beautiful to look at, but it's full of imperfections.

THE STUDENT: I don't believe it. But if it's true, we'll just have to ignore them. It's beautiful, but a little cold. Why don't you start the fire?

THE YOUNG LADY: Because it smokes up the room.

THE STUDENT: Can't you have the chimney cleaned?

THE YOUNG LADY: It doesn't help! . . . Do you see that writing table?

THE STUDENT: What an extraordinarily handsome piece!

THE YOUNG LADY: But it wobbles. Every day I lay a piece of cork under that foot, but the housemaid takes it away when she sweeps, and I have to cut a new piece. The penholder is covered with ink every morning, and so is the inkstand, and I have to clean them up after her, as regularly as the sun goes up. (*Pause.*) What do you hate most to do?

THE STUDENT: To sort the week's wash! (*Grimaces in disgust.*)

THE YOUNG LADY: That's what I have to do! (*Grimacing in disgust.*)

THE STUDENT: What else?

THE YOUNG LADY: To be awakened in the middle of the night, to have to get up and close the banging window – which the housemaid forgot to close.

THE STUDENT: Go on.

THE YOUNG LADY: To climb up on a ladder and fix the damper on the stovepipe after the maid broke off the cord.

THE STUDENT: Go on.

THE YOUNG LADY: To sweep up after her, to dust after her, and to start the fire in the stove after her – all she does is bring in the wood! To adjust the damper, to dry the glasses, to set the table *over* and *over* again, to pull the corks out of the bottles, to open the windows and air the rooms, to make and remake my bed, to rinse the water bottle when it's green with sediment, to buy matches and soap, which we're always out of, to wipe the chimneys and trim the wicks to keep the lamps from smoking – and to keep the lamps from going out, I have to fill them myself when we have company . . .

THE STUDENT: Let's have music!

THE YOUNG LADY: You have to wait! – First comes the drudgery, the drudgery of keeping oneself above the dirt of life.

THE STUDENT: But you're well off. You've got two servants.

THE YOUNG LADY: Doesn't make any difference! Even if we had three! Living is such a nuisance, and I get so tired at times. . . . Imagine, if on top of it all one had a nursery and a baby crib.

THE STUDENT: The dearest of joys!

THE YOUNG LADY: The dearest in more ways than one. . . . Is life really worth so much trouble?

THE STUDENT: I suppose that depends on the reward you expect for all your troubles. . . . There's nothing I wouldn't do to win your hand.

THE YOUNG LADY: Don't say that! You can never have me!

THE STUDENT: Why not?

THE YOUNG LADY: You mustn't ask.

Pause.

THE STUDENT: You dropped your bracelet out the window . . .

THE YOUNG LADY: Because my hand has grown so thin.

> *Pause. The Cook appears with a Japanese bottle in her hand.*

She's the one who's eating me—and all the rest of us.

THE STUDENT: What is she holding in her hand?

THE YOUNG LADY: It's a bottle of coloring matter. It's got letters on it that look like scorpions. It's filled with soy sauce— which takes the place of gravy, which is transformed into soup, which serves as stock for cooking cabbage in, which is used to make mock turtle soup . . .

THE STUDENT: Get out!

THE COOK: You suck the sap from us and we from you. We take the blood and give you back water—with coloring added. This is the coloring! —I'm leaving now, but you won't ever be rid of me.

> *She leaves.*

THE STUDENT: Why was Bengtsson given a medal?

THE YOUNG LADY: Because of his great merits.

THE STUDENT: Has he no faults?

THE YOUNG LADY: Yes, many great ones. But you don't get medals for them.

> *They smile at each other.*

* * *

THE STUDENT: You have a great many secrets in this house.

THE YOUNG LADY: As in all houses. Permit us to keep ours.

Pause.

THE STUDENT: Do you admire frankness?

THE YOUNG LADY: Yes, within moderation.

THE STUDENT: Sometimes there comes over me a crazy desire to say everything I'm thinking. But I know the world would collapse completely if we were completely honest. (*Pause.*) I went to a funeral the other day. . . . In church. . . . Very solemn, very beautiful.

THE YOUNG LADY: Mr. Hummel's funeral?

THE STUDENT: Yes, my false benefactor's. At the head of the coffin stood an old friend of the deceased. He carried the mace. The priest impressed me especially, his dignified manner and his moving words. I cried. We all cried. And afterward we went to a restaurant. . . . And there I learned that the macebearer had been in love with the dead man's son.

The Young Lady looks at him to catch his meaning.

Yes. And the dead man had borrowed money from his son's lover. . . . (*Pause.*) The day after that, they arrest the priest for embezzling church funds! It's a pretty story isn't it?

The Young Lady turns her head away in disgust. Pause.

Do you know what I think of you now?

THE YOUNG LADY: You must not tell me or I'll die!

THE STUDENT: But I must or I'll die!

THE YOUNG LADY: In an asylum they say whatever they feel like.

THE STUDENT: Exactly right! That's where my father ended up—in a madhouse.

THE YOUNG LADY: Was he ill?

THE STUDENT: No, he was quite healthy. But he was crazy! It just came over him. Let me tell you how it happened. . . . Like all of us, he had his circle of acquaintances, whom for convenience' sake he called his friends. Of course they were a pretty sorry bunch of good-for-nothings – like most people. But he had to have some acquaintances, he couldn't just sit alone. Now one doesn't tell a person what one really thinks of him, not in ordinary conversation anyway – and my father didn't either. He knew how false they were. He saw through their deceitfulness right to the bottom of their souls. But he was an intelligent man, brought up to behave properly, and so he was always polite. But one day he gave a big party. It was evening, he was tired after a day's work, and under the strain of forcing himself to hold his tongue half the time and of bullshitting with his guests the other half . . .

The Young Lady glances at him reproachfully.

Well, whatever the reason, at the dinner table he rapped for silence, raised his glass, and began to make a speech. . . . Then something loosed the trigger, and in a long oration he stripped naked every single person there, one after another. Told them of all their deceits. And at the end, exhausted, he sat down right in the middle of the table and told them all to go straight to hell!

The Young Lady moans.

I was there and heard it all. I'll never forget what happened afterward. . . . Father and Mother began to fight, the guests rushed for the door – and my father was taken off to the madhouse, where he died! (*Pause.*) If you keep silent too long, things begin to rot. Stagnant, stinking pools begin to form. That's what's happening in this house. Something's rotting here. And I thought it was paradise when I saw you come in here for the first time. . . . It was a Sunday morning, and I stood looking into these rooms. I saw a colonel who wasn't a colonel. I had a magnanimous benefactor who turned out to be a bandit and had to hang himself. I saw a mummy who wasn't one, and a maiden who – speaking of which, where can one find virginity? Where is beauty to be found? In nature, and in my mind when it's all dressed up in its

Sunday clothes. Where do honor and faith exist? In fairy tales and plays for children. Where can you find anything that fulfills its promise? Only in one's imagination! . . . Now your flowers have poisoned me, and I have passed the poison back. I begged you to become my wife in my home. We played and we sang. We created poetry together. And then came the cook. . . . *Sursum corda!* Try just once again to pluck fire and brightness from the golden harp! Please try! I beg you, I implore you on my knees! . . . Very well. Then I shall do it myself. (*He takes the harp, but no sound comes from the strings.*) It is silent and deaf. Tell me, why are beautiful flowers so poisonous, and the most beautiful the most deadly? Why? The whole creation, all of life, is cursed and damned. . . . Why would you not become my bride? Because you are sick, infected at the very core of life. . . . Now I can feel that vampire in the kitchen beginning to suck the blood from me. She must be one of those lamias that suck the blood of suckling babes. It's always in the kitchen that the children are nipped in the bud. And if not there, then in the bedroom. . . . There are poisons that seal the eyes and poisons that open them. I must have been born with the latter kind in my veins, because I cannot see what is ugly as beautiful and I cannot call what is evil good. I cannot. They say that Christ harrowed hell. What they really meant was that He descended to earth, to this madhouse, jail-house, charnel house. And the inmates crucified Him when He tried to free them. But the robber they let go. Robbers always win sympathy. . . . Woe! Woe to all of us! Saviour of the World, save us! We are perishing!

> *The Young Lady has collapsed during this speech. She is obviously dying. She rings the bell. Bengtsson enters.*

THE YOUNG LADY: Bring the screen. Quickly! I'm dying.

> *Bengtsson returns with the screen, opens it, and places it in front of The Young Lady.*

THE STUDENT: Your redeemer is coming! Welcome, pale and gentle one. . . . And you, my darling, you beautiful, innocent, lost soul who suffers for no fault of your own, sleep, sleep a dreamless sleep. And when you wake again . . . may you be greeted by a sun that doesn't scorch, in a home without dust, by friends without faults, and by a love without flaw. . . . Buddha, wise and gentle Buddha, sitting there waiting for a heaven to grow out of the earth, grant us the purity of will and the patience to endure our tribulations that hope will not come to shame.

> *The harp strings begin to move and hum. Pure white light pours into the room.*

I saw the sun
And from its blaze
There burst on me
The deepest truth:

Man reaps as he sows;
Blessed is he
Who sows the good.

For deeds done in anger
Kindness alone
Can make amends.

Bring cheer to those
Whom you have hurt,
And kindness reaps
Its own rewards.

The pure in heart
Have none to fear.
The harmless are happy.
The guileless are good.

> *A moaning is heard from behind the screen.*

You poor little child! Child of this world of illusion and guilt and suffering and death—this world of eternal change and disappointment and never-ending pain! May the Lord of Heaven have mercy on you as you journey forth . . .

> *The room vanishes. In the distance Boecklin's* The Island of the Dead *appears. Music—soft, pleasant, and melancholy—is heard coming from the island.*

CURTAIN

Introduction

to

The Pelican

"Life is such a web of lies, errors, misunderstandings, of debts due and owing, that a closing of the books is impossible" [*En blå bok*].

That was how Strindberg summed up the human condition when he was in a forgiving and compassionate mood. Because our lives are intricately ensnarled and entangled with one anothers', everyone is guilty of some cruelty or offense. This state of affairs is represented in the first scene of *The Ghost Sonata*. All too often, however, Strindberg was quick to sit in judgment on individuals who did not measure up to his standards and to presume that he could separate the strands in the web of guilt. In *The Dance of Death*, he had condemned his brother-in-law for his materialistic beliefs, castigated him for his self-centeredness, and monumentalized his conceit and intellectual arrogance. When Hugo Philp died in 1906, Strindberg regretted what he had done. In *The Pelican*, the fourth of the chamber plays, Strindberg tried to set the record straight by showing the other side of the man. The dead man haunts the play just as he haunted Strindberg's conscience.

But that is only the starting point for another moral inquiry and only incidental to a drama in which Strindberg once again studies the web of guilt. At the center of the web, he finds the vampire cook of *The Ghost Sonata*. She is seen to be the mother, the terrible mother who deprives her children of spiritual nourishment, who gives them mustard instead of milk. Then, as the picture becomes clearer, the mother in her turn is seen to be a somnambulist, like the hyacinth girl. In Swedenborg's metapsychology, somnambulists were those people, perhaps the majority of humankind, who live the lives of beasts, acting from the will, the senses, the instincts, "while the understanding sleeps." Strindberg's first title for this play was "The Sleepwalkers." Unintentionally and unconsciously, the sleepwalking mother has ruined the lives of her children. But there were sleepwalkers in her life, too, which was warped and twisted when she was a child. Is she more to be blamed than her children?

Unlike *The Ghost Sonata*, with its quietly magical ending, a musical invocation to death the liberator, *The Pelican* ends with an explosion of destructive energy. Death comes not so much as a release from daily tribulations and unavoidable guilt, or as a diminishment of spiritual energy in accordance with some principle of moral entropy, but as a violent stab at justice, a willful act of annihilation, both absurd and necessary, that blots out the heavens and causes the moral universe to collapse into a primeval state of innocence.

The Pelican

Opus Four
of
The Chamber Plays

CHARACTERS

THE MOTHER, Elise, a widow
THE SON, Frederick, a law student
THE DAUGHTER, Gerda
THE SON-IN-LAW, Axel, married to Gerda
MARGARET, the cook

[1]

A living room. A door in the rear wall to the dining room. To the right, at an angle, a door to the balcony. A secretary-bookcase; a writing table; a chaise longue with a woolen purple-red lap rug; a rocking chair. The Mother enters, dressed in mourning; sits listlessly in an armchair. Listens agitatedly. Beyond the room Chopin's "Fantaisie Impromptu," Oeuvre Posthume, opus 66, *is being played. Margaret, the cook, enters from the rear.*

THE MOTHER: Would you mind closing the door?

MARGARET: Are you sitting here alone?

THE MOTHER: Would you mind closing the door? — Who's playing the piano?

MARGARET: Such awful weather tonight, windy and rainy . . .

THE MOTHER: Would you mind closing the door? I can't stand the smell of flowers and disinfectants.

MARGARET: Don't blame me. I told you to have him taken to the cemetery as quickly as possible.

THE MOTHER: It was the children who wanted the funeral at home, not I.

MARGARET: Well, why on earth do you stay in this place? Why don't you all move?

THE MOTHER: The landlord won't let us move. We're all stuck here. (*Pause.*) Why did you take the slipcover off the red chaise longue?

MARGARET: I had to have it cleaned. (*Pause.*) I know you can't help being reminded that your husband drew his last breath on that sofa, but all you have to do is take away the sofa—

THE MOTHER: I'm not allowed to touch a thing until the inventory has been taken. I sit here like a prisoner. . . . And I can't endure being in the other rooms.

MARGARET: Now what's the matter with them?

THE MOTHER: Memories—all unpleasant. —And that horrible smell. . . . Is that my son playing?

MARGARET: Yes. He doesn't like it in here, I can tell you. Can't sit still. And he's always hungry. Says he's never had a full stomach in his life.

THE MOTHER: He was weak from the day he was born.

MARGARET: A bottle baby needs rich, good food after it's been weaned.

THE MOTHER (*sharply*): Really! Didn't I give him everything he wanted?

MARGARET: Not exactly: You always shopped for the cheapest and poorest food. Sending a child off to school on a cup of chicory coffee and a slice of bread—imagine!

THE MOTHER: The children have never complained.

MARGARET: Not to you, oh, no, they wouldn't dare. But when they grew up, how often didn't they come out to me in the kitchen—

THE MOTHER: We've always had limited means—

MARGARET: Come now! I read in the paper how your husband some years paid taxes on twenty thousand crowns.

THE MOTHER: It all went, I don't know where.

MARGARET: Yes, yes, of course. But look at the children. Look at Miss Gerda—twenty years old and she hasn't filled out yet.

THE MOTHER: What are you trying to say?

MARGARET: All right, never mind. (*Pause.*) Don't you want me to put some logs in the stove? It's cold in here.

THE MOTHER: No, thank you. We can't afford to burn up our money.

MARGARET: But Frederick is frozen to his bones. He has to go outside to get warm — or else play the piano.

THE MOTHER: He's always been cold.

MARGARET: I wonder why?

THE MOTHER: That's enough, Margaret! . . . (*Pause.*) Do you hear someone walking out there?

MARGARET: No, there's no one.

THE MOTHER: I suppose you think I'm afraid of ghosts?

MARGARET: I'm sure I wouldn't know. . . . But one thing I do know: I'm not staying here any longer than I can help it. I first came to this house as if I had been condemned to watch over the children. I wanted to get away when I saw how the servants were mistreated, but I couldn't — or I wasn't allowed to — I don't know which. But now that Miss Gerda is married, I feel that I've done my duty, and soon the doors will open for me and I'll be free. But not quite yet . . .

THE MOTHER: I don't understand a word you're saying. The whole world knows how much I have sacrificed for my children, how I have taken care of this house and never neglected my duties. You're the only one who accuses me. But don't think that bothers me for a moment. You're free to leave whenever you want to. When my daughter and her husband move into this apartment, I don't intend to keep any servants.

MARGARET: I wish you the best of luck. Children aren't grateful by nature. They don't care to see their mothers-in-law moving in unless they bring money with them.

THE MOTHER: Don't you worry yourself about me, Margaret. I'll pay for my keep, and help about the house too. Besides, my son-in-law isn't like other sons-in-law.

MARGARET: That one! Ha!

THE MOTHER: He isn't! He doesn't treat me like a mother-in-law. He treats me like a sister, like a friend . . .

>   *Margaret grimaces.*

What are you smirking about? Oh, I know what you're thinking. But I happen to like my son-in-law; there's no law against that, and he's very likeable. . . . Of course, my husband didn't like him. He was envious, I might even say jealous. (*Laughs quietly.*) Flattering, don't you think, even if I'm not so young anymore. —What did you say?

MARGARET: Nothing. I thought I heard someone. . . . It must have been Frederick. He's the only one who coughs. Let me light the fire.

THE MOTHER: No, it isn't necessary!

MARGARET: Listen to me. I have been frozen to the marrow of my bones in this house; I've starved; and I haven't complained. But at least you can give me a bed, a decent bed. I'm old and I'm tired—

THE MOTHER: Fine time to ask, when you're all set to leave!

MARGARET: That's true, I almost forgot. But for the sake of your own self-respect, burn up my bedclothes where people have lain and died, so you won't have to be ashamed when the next maid comes—if any ever will.

THE MOTHER: Don't worry. No one will.

MARGARET: But if anyone should, I can tell you she won't stay. I've seen fifty maids come and go.

THE MOTHER: Because they were unreliable and disreputable. That's what you all are.

MARGARET: Thank you! How kind of you! . . . But your time is coming. Just wait. Everyone gets his turn. Soon it will be yours.

THE MOTHER: Don't you ever stop? I'll soon have had enough of you.

MARGARET: Yes, soon. Very soon. Sooner than you think!

She leaves.

* * *

The Son enters with a book in his hand, coughing. He has a slight stammer.

THE MOTHER: Would you mind closing the door?

THE SON: Give me one good reason.

THE MOTHER: Is that any way to answer me? — What do you want?

THE SON: Do you mind if I sit in here and read? It's too cold in my room.

THE MOTHER: Oh, you're always cold, you are.

THE SON: When you sit still, you feel it more, if it is cold. (*Pause. He pretends to read at first.*) Is the inventory finished yet?

THE MOTHER: Why do you ask that? Can't you wait until after the mourning is over? Or perhaps you don't mourn the loss of your father?

THE SON: Yes — but — well, he's better off. And I envy him the peace he found, the peace he finally found. But that doesn't prevent me from being concerned and worried about my own position. I have to know whether I can get through my exams without having to borrow money.

THE MOTHER: Your father didn't leave anything, you know that — except debts, I suppose.

THE SON: But the business must be worth something?

THE MOTHER: There isn't any business if there isn't any stock or goods. Can't you understand that?

THE SON (*pondering a moment*): But the company, the name, the clientele — ?

THE MOTHER: You can't sell a clientele.

A pause.

THE SON: I've heard you can!

THE MOTHER: Have you been to see a lawyer? (*Pause.*) So that's the way you mourn your father?

THE SON: No, it isn't. —But one thing at a time, you know. . . . Where's my sister and my new brother-in-law?

THE MOTHER: They got back from their honeymoon this morning—. Got themselves a room in a boardinghouse.

THE SON: Where they can at least eat their fill!

THE MOTHER: Always harping on that! Anything wrong with the food you get here?

THE SON: Oh no, Mother! Of course not.

THE MOTHER: Tell me something. Recently, when I had to live separated from him for a time, you and your father were alone here—didn't he ever talk about his business?

THE SON (*engrossed in his book*): No, I can't remember anything special.

THE MOTHER: Then how do you explain why he didn't leave anything behind him when he was making twenty thousand crowns the last few years?

THE SON: I don't know anything about Father's business. He said the house cost a lot. And then he bought all this new furniture recently.

THE MOTHER: Is that what he told you? Do you think he was in debt?

THE SON: I don't know. He had been, but he got out.

THE MOTHER: Then where did the money disappear to? Didn't he make a will? He hated me, that's it. More than once he said he'd cut me off without a cent. I wonder if he could have hidden his savings somewhere? (*Pause.*) Is someone out there?

THE SON: I don't hear anything.

THE MOTHER: All this business about the funeral and the money has made me a little nervous the last couple of days. . . . By the way, you know you'll have to see about getting a room in town before Gerda and her husband move in here.

THE SON: Yes, I know.

THE MOTHER: You don't like him, do you?

THE SON: We don't have much in common.

THE MOTHER: Well, he's a fine boy and very capable. You should force yourself to like him. Might do you good.

THE SON: He doesn't like me. And besides, he was very unkind to Father.

THE MOTHER: And whose fault was that?

THE SON: Father wasn't unkind —

THE MOTHER: Oh, no?

THE SON: I think you're right, there is someone out there!

THE MOTHER: Turn on a couple of lights. But only a couple!

The Son turns on the electric lights. A pause.

Why don't you take your father's portrait into your room? That one on the wall.

THE SON: Why do you want me to?

THE MOTHER: I don't like it. The eyes look so evil.

THE SON: I don't think so.

THE MOTHER: Then take it. If you like it so much, you can have it.

THE SON (*taking the portrait down*): Yes, I just might do that.

A pause.

THE MOTHER: I'm expecting Axel and Gerda at any moment. Do you want to meet them?

THE SON: No, thanks. I'm going to my room. —But I could use a little fire in the stove.

THE MOTHER: We can't afford to burn up our money.

THE SON: I've heard that for twenty years. But we've always been able to afford idiotic trips abroad so you could brag about them. And to eat in restaurants where the check came to a hundred crowns, which is just about the price of four cords of birchwood. Four cords of wood for one lunch!

THE MOTHER: Nonsense!

THE SON: There have been a lot of crazy things going on here, but it's all over now. Except for a final settling of accounts—

THE MOTHER: What do you mean?

THE SON: I mean the inventory, and other things . . .

THE MOTHER: What other things?

THE SON: The debts, the unfinished business . . .

THE MOTHER: Oh.

THE SON: In the meantime, I hope you don't mind if I buy myself some warm clothes?

THE MOTHER: How can you ask that now? It's about time you began thinking about earning something for yourself.

THE SON: When I pass my exams, I—

THE MOTHER: Until you do, you'll have to borrow as everyone else does.

THE SON: Who would lend me anything?

THE MOTHER: Your father's friends.

THE SON: He didn't have any friends. A man who thinks for himself can't afford to have friends—because having friends means belonging to a mutual admiration society.

THE MOTHER: Aren't you the wise one! You must have learned that from your father.

THE SON: He wasn't stupid—although he did some foolish things once in a while.

THE MOTHER: Not really! . . . Tell me, when are you going to get married?

THE SON: Never. Running an escort service for bachelors— being a legalized pimp for some tramp—handing yourself over on a silver platter to be carved up by your best friend—I mean your worst enemy—I'm not that stupid!

THE MOTHER: What *are* you saying? —Oh, go to your room. I've had enough of you for today. You must have been drinking.

THE SON: I have to—a little—all the time. To stop coughing, and to feel a little less hungry.

THE MOTHER: Complaining about the food again?

THE SON: Oh, no, no complaints. Only it's so light, it tastes like air!

THE MOTHER (*stung*): Get out!

THE SON: Or else it's got so much salt and pepper in it, eating it only makes you hungrier. It's like spiced air.

THE MOTHER: You are drunk! Get out of here!

THE SON: Yes, I'm going. . . . There was something I was going to say. . . . But it can wait. . . . Yes. (*He leaves.*)

* * *

The Mother, restless, paces the floor. Looks through the drawers in the table.

* * *

The Son-in-Law enters hastily.

THE MOTHER (*greeting him warmly*): At last! You're really here, Axel! I've been longing to see you. But where's Gerda?

THE SON-IN-LAW: She's coming. Well, how are you? Tell me all about yourself.

THE MOTHER: No, you sit down and let me ask the questions first. I haven't seen you since the wedding. — What are you doing back home so soon? You were going to be gone for eight days, and it's only three days since you left.

THE SON-IN-LAW: Oh, it got to be tiresome, you know, after we had talked ourselves out. Being alone together got to be oppressive. And we were so used to having you around, we missed you very much.

THE MOTHER: That's kind of you, Axel. Well, I suppose we three have stuck together through thick and thin, and I believe I can say I have been of some use, don't you think?

THE SON-IN-LAW: Gerda's only a child. She doesn't know how to live. She's prejudiced, and stubborn — like a fanatic sometimes.

THE MOTHER: I know, I know. But tell me, what did you think of the wedding?

THE SON-IN-LAW: It was perfect, absolutely perfect! And my poems, how did you like my poems?

THE MOTHER: The ones you wrote to me, you mean? I don't suppose a mother-in-law ever got such poems on her daughter's wedding day. . . . You recall the one about the pelican that gives its own blood to its young ones? You know, I cried, I really —

THE SON-IN-LAW: Not for long, you didn't. You danced with me, remember? Our dance. Gerda was almost jealous of you.

THE MOTHER: It wouldn't be the first time. She wanted me to come dressed in black — for proper mourning, she said. But I didn't pay any attention to her. Why should I obey my own children?

THE SON-IN-LAW: Don't pay any attention to Gerda. She's crazy sometimes. I only have to look at a woman —

THE MOTHER: What's this? Doesn't she keep you happy?

THE SON-IN-LAW: Happy? How do you mean?

THE MOTHER: It sounds as if you've been quarreling already.

THE SON-IN-LAW: Already? We haven't done anything else since we were engaged. . . . And now I had to tell her I'll have to leave her for a while, since I'm a reserve officer. —You know, it's funny, but I think she likes me less in civvies.

THE MOTHER: Then why not wear your uniform? I have to admit, I hardly recognize you as a civilian. You're a completely different person.

THE SON-IN-LAW: I'm not supposed to wear my uniform except on duty and on parade days.

THE MOTHER: Why not?

THE SON-IN-LAW: Regulations.

THE MOTHER: It's a shame about Gerda in any case. She got engaged to a lieutenant, and she married a bookkeeper.

THE SON-IN-LAW: What do you expect me to do? I have to live. And speaking of that, what have you found out about the business?

THE MOTHER: Quite honestly, nothing much. But I'm beginning to wonder about Frederick.

THE SON-IN-LAW: Wonder what?

THE MOTHER: He talked so strangely just now.

THE SON-IN-LAW: That sheepshead!

THE MOTHER: I've heard that sheep are rather crafty. And I just wonder if there might not be a will or some savings lying around somewhere—

THE SON-IN-LAW: Have you looked?

THE MOTHER: I've searched all his things.

THE SON-IN-LAW: The boy's?

THE MOTHER: Yes, of course. And I look through his waste-paper basket all the time. He writes letters which he tears up—

THE SON-IN-LAW: You're wasting your time. Haven't you looked through the old man's desk?

THE MOTHER: Well, naturally!

THE SON-IN-LAW: I mean carefully. All the drawers?

THE MOTHER: Every one.

THE SON-IN-LAW: But there are always secret drawers in secretaries.

THE MOTHER: I hadn't thought of that.

THE SON-IN-LAW: Then let's take a good look at it.

THE MOTHER: No, you mustn't touch it! It's been sealed by the inventory people.

THE SON-IN-LAW: Can't you get around the seal?

THE MOTHER: No! I don't see how you can.

THE SON-IN-LAW: Yes, you can, if you loosen the boards in the back. Secret drawers are always in the back.

THE MOTHER: You would have to have tools for that.

THE SON-IN-LAW: Not necessarily; it could be managed without.

THE MOTHER: But Gerda mustn't know anything —

THE SON-IN-LAW: Of course not. She'd only go and squeal to her dear brother.

THE MOTHER (*closing the doors*): Let me close the doors just to be safe.

THE SON-IN-LAW (*examining the back of the secretary*): Look, someone has already been in here — the whole back is loose — I can put my whole hand in —

THE MOTHER: It's the boy, he's done it. I told you — I suspected him —. . . . Hurry, someone's coming.

THE SON-IN-LAW: I can feel some papers in there —

THE MOTHER: Hurry, I can hear someone coming.

THE SON-IN-LAW: A big envelope —

THE MOTHER: Gerda's coming! Give me the papers — quick!

THE SON-IN-LAW (*giving The Mother a large envelope, which she hides*): Take it! Hide it!

* * *

Someone tries to open the door; then there is knocking.

THE SON-IN-LAW: You stupid—! You locked the door. We're caught!

THE MOTHER: Quiet!

THE SON-IN-LAW: You idiot! —Open it! —Or else I will! —Get out of the way! (*He opens the door.*)

THE DAUGHTER (*enters, looking out of sorts*): Why did you lock yourselves in?

THE MOTHER: Aren't you even going to say hello first, my dear child? I haven't seen you since the wedding. Did you have a nice trip? Now tell me all about it. And don't look so gloomy.

THE DAUGHTER (*sits down in a chair, looking dejected*): Why did you lock the door?

THE MOTHER: Because it keeps opening by itself, and I get so tired of nagging at everybody to close it. . . . Now we've got to think about the furniture for your apartment. You're going to live here, aren't you?

THE DAUGHTER: I guess we have to. It doesn't make much difference to me. What do you say, Axel?

THE SON-IN-LAW: I think this will be fine. And your mother won't have it bad at all, since we all get along so well . . .

THE DAUGHTER: Why, where is Mother going to stay?

THE MOTHER: Right here. I'll only have to move in a bed.

THE SON-IN-LAW: Come now, dear, you don't plan on having a bed in the living room?

THE DAUGHTER (*thinking she is being spoken to*): Are you asking me?

THE SON-IN-LAW: No, I – was – asking your mother. . . .
But we can arrange that later. We have to help one another out
now, and we can live on what Mother will be paying us.

THE DAUGHTER (*brightening*): And she can help me with the
housekeeping –

THE MOTHER: Of course, dear child. Only don't ask me to
wash the dishes. You know how I hate that.

THE DAUGHTER: Don't be silly! Everything will be all right,
as long as I can have my husband to myself. I don't want anybody
so much as looking at him. That's what they were doing at that
hotel. So we cut the honeymoon short. If anybody tried to take
him from me, I'd kill her! I mean it.

THE MOTHER: I think we had better start rearranging the
furniture.

THE SON-IN-LAW (*holding The Mother's eyes with his*): Good
idea! And Gerda, you can begin in here –

THE DAUGHTER: Why me? I don't like to be left alone in
here. I won't feel right until we've moved in completely.

THE SON-IN-LAW: All right, if you're afraid of the dark, then
let's all go together.

> *All three leave.*

> * * *

> *The stage remains empty for a while. The wind is blow-
> ing outside. One can hear it rattling the windows and
> howling in the stove. Papers from the writing table fly
> around the room; a potted palm on the console trembles
> crazily; a photograph falls from the wall. The voice of
> The Son is heard:* "Mama!" *Shortly thereafter:* "Close
> the window!" *A pause. The rocking chair begins to
> rock. The Mother enters, wild with rage, reading a paper
> that she holds in her hand.*

THE MOTHER (*sees the rocking chair*): What – ! The rocking
chair – it's moving!

THE SON-IN-LAW (*coming in after her*): What is it? What does it say? For God's sake, let me read it! Is it the will?

THE MOTHER: Close the door before we're blown away! I have to open a window, I can't stand this smell. No, it wasn't the will. It was a letter to the boy, filled with lies about me—and you!

THE SON-IN-LAW: Give it to me!

THE MOTHER: No, it would only poison your mind. I'm going to tear it up. Thank heavens it didn't fall into the boy's hands! (*She tears up the letter and throws it into the stove.*) He rises from his grave and you can't shut him up. He's not dead! I tell you I could never stay here. He wrote that I murdered him. I didn't! He died of a stroke; the doctor certified it. But that isn't all he wrote. Lies, all of it lies! He says I ruined him! —Listen to me, Axel! You must see to it that we leave this apartment at once. I can't stand it here. Promise me! —Look at the chair rocking!

THE SON-IN-LAW: It's the draft from the hall.

THE MOTHER: We have to get away from here! Promise me!

THE SON-IN-LAW: I can't promise that. I've been counting on the inheritance. You hinted at something like that, otherwise I wouldn't have gotten married. Now we have to take things as they are. You can consider me from now on as a swindled son-in-law—and bankrupt! We have to stick together now in order to live. We'll have to pinch pennies, and you'll have to help us.

THE MOTHER: Are you suggesting I'm to be employed as a maid in my own house? Oh, no. Oh, no, you don't!

THE SON-IN-LAW: Necessity knows no—

THE MOTHER: You're contemptible!

THE SON-IN-LAW: Listen, you old—

THE MOTHER: Be a maid to you!

THE SON-IN-LAW: It'll give you a chance to see how your maids have had it, freezing and starving. At least you won't have to do that.

THE MOTHER: I have my annuity—

THE SON-IN-LAW: That wouldn't get you a spare room in an attic! But here it will take care of the rent *if* we take it easy and don't live it up. And if you don't take it easy, I'm leaving.

THE MOTHER: Leave Gerda! You have never loved her—

THE SON-IN-LAW: You know better than I. You tore her out of my heart and my mind, pushed her aside everywhere—except in the bedroom; that was hers at least. And if a baby comes, you'll take that away from her, too. She doesn't know anything yet, doesn't understand anything. But she's going to stop walking in her sleep pretty soon. And when she opens her eyes, watch out!

THE MOTHER: Axel, you know we have to stick together! We mustn't part. I could never live alone. I'll go along with whatever you say. But not the chaise longue—

THE SON-IN-LAW: The chaise longue stays! I don't want to spoil the place by having a bedroom in here. That's final.

THE MOTHER: But let me have another one then—

THE SON-IN-LAW: We can't afford it. That one's pretty enough.

THE MOTHER: My God, it looks like a gory butcher's block!

THE SON-IN-LAW: Oh, shut up. Listen, if you don't want it this way, there's always a lonely room in some attic, and handouts from the church, and the nursing home.

THE MOTHER: All right, you win.

THE SON-IN-LAW: Now you're being sensible.

> *A pause.*

THE MOTHER: But can you imagine that he wrote to his son that he was murdered?

THE SON-IN-LAW: There's more than one way of committing murder. And your way has the advantage of not coming under the law.

THE MOTHER: You mean *our* way. You were in it as deep as me. You teased and tormented him and drove him to despair.

THE SON-IN-LAW: He was getting in my way. What did you expect me to do?

THE MOTHER: The only thing I reproach you with is that you lured me away from home. I'll never forget that evening, the first evening in your home, when we sat at that beautiful dinner table, and we could hear those horrible cries from the garden below. They sounded as if they came from the prison or from the mad-house. Do you remember? It was him walking in the garden in the darkness and the rain, crying out in anguish for his lost wife and children.

THE SON-IN-LAW: Why talk about that now? You don't even know if it was him.

THE MOTHER: It said so in his letter!

THE SON-IN-LAW: What does that have to do with us? He was no angel.

THE MOTHER: No, he wasn't. But he had some human feel-ings, sometimes. More than you, I might say—

THE SON-IN-LAW: Changing sides, are you?

THE MOTHER: Now don't get mad. We have to learn to get along with each other.

THE SON-IN-LAW: Yes, we have to. Like cell mates in a prison.

Hoarse cries from within.

THE MOTHER: What's that? Do you hear? It must be him . . .

THE SON-IN-LAW (*brutally*): Which him?

The Mother listens.

Who is it? . . . The boy! He's been drinking again.

THE MOTHER: Frederick? Oh, yes, of course. But for a moment it sounded just like—like *him*. I thought—. I can't stand much more of this. What's the matter with him?

THE SON-IN-LAW: Go and see! He's probably stinking drunk!

THE MOTHER: That's no way to talk! He's my son in any case.

THE SON-IN-LAW: In every case, yours! (*Taking out his watch.*)

THE MOTHER: Why are you looking at your watch? Aren't you going to stay for supper?

THE SON-IN-LAW: No, thanks. I don't like weak tea and I never touch rancid fish—or pudding. Besides, I have to go to a meeting.

THE MOTHER: What kind of a meeting?

THE SON-IN-LAW: Business that doesn't concern you. Don't tell me you intend to start behaving like a mother-in-law?

THE MOTHER: And do you intend to leave your wife the first night you move into your new home?

THE SON-IN-LAW: Now that's another thing that doesn't concern you.

THE MOTHER: I begin to see what lies ahead for me—and my children. The masks are coming off, aren't they?

THE SON-IN-LAW: That's right. They're coming off.

[2]

Same set. The "Berceuse" from Godard's Jocelyn *is being played within. The Daughter is sitting at the desk.*

A long pause.

THE SON (*enters*): Are you alone?

THE DAUGHTER: Yes. Mama is in the kitchen.

THE SON: Well, where's Axel?

THE DAUGHTER: Oh, he's at some kind of meeting. . . . Sit down and talk to me, Frederick. Keep me company.

THE SON (*sits down*): I don't think we've really spoken to each other before. We always avoided each other. Never had anything in common.

THE DAUGHTER: You were always on Father's side, and I was always on Mother's.

THE SON: Maybe that will change now. Did you really know Father?

THE DAUGHTER: What a strange question. But it's true I only saw him through Mother's eyes.

THE SON: But couldn't you see how fond he was of you?

THE DAUGHTER: Then why did he want me to break off my engagement?

THE SON: Because he saw that your fiancé would never give you the kind of support you need in life.

THE DAUGHTER: And that's what he was punished for— when Mama went away and left him.

THE SON: Wasn't it your boyfriend who talked her into leaving?

THE DAUGHTER: Yes, he and I together! I wanted Father to know how it feels to be separated from the one you love, as he tried to separate me.

THE SON: So you simply shortened his life, you know that. Believe me, he only wanted you to be happy.

THE DAUGHTER: You were with him. —What did he say? How did he take it?

THE SON: I wouldn't know the words to describe his misery.

THE DAUGHTER: What did he say about Mama?

THE SON: Nothing. . . . But after all that I've seen, I'm never going to marry! (*Pause.*) Are *you* happy, Gerda?

THE DAUGHTER: Oh, yes! When you catch the man you've had your eye on, you're happy.

THE SON: Why did he leave you tonight—your first night at home?

THE DAUGHTER: Business. He had to go to a meeting.

THE SON: At a restaurant?

THE DAUGHTER: What do you mean? How do you know?

THE SON: I thought you knew!

THE DAUGHTER (*crying into her handkerchief*): Oh, my God! My God!

THE SON: I'm sorry, I didn't mean to hurt you.

THE DAUGHTER: But you did! So deeply! Oh, I wish I could die!

THE SON: Why did you come back from your honeymoon so soon?

THE DAUGHTER: He was worried about his business. He wanted to see Mama. He hates to be away from her—

> *They look at each other.*

THE SON: I see. (*Pause.*) How was your trip otherwise? Pleasant?

THE DAUGHTER: Oh, yes!

THE SON: My poor Gerda!

THE DAUGHTER: What do you mean?

THE SON: Well, you know Mother's curiosity. She can use a telephone like nobody else.

THE DAUGHTER: I don't understand. Has she been spying?

THE SON: Hasn't she always? She's probably behind one of those doors right now listening to us.

THE DAUGHTER: You always think the worst of Mama.

THE SON: And you always think the best! Why is that? You know what she's like —

THE DAUGHTER: No, I don't! And I don't want to.

THE SON: That's something else — you don't want to know. You probably have your reasons.

THE DAUGHTER: Sh! I know I'm walking in my sleep, I know I am. But I don't want anyone to wake me up. I couldn't live if they did.

THE SON: Don't you think we're all walking in our sleep? Listen, I study law, as you know, and I'm always reading the transcripts of famous trials, cases involving great criminals. And, you know, they can't explain how it happened. They thought they were doing the right thing right up to the moment they got caught. Then they woke up. If they weren't dreaming, at least they must have been sleeping.

THE DAUGHTER: Let me sleep. I know I shall have to wake up sometime, but please let it be a long time from now. Oh how many things there are I don't exactly know but have an inkling of! Do you remember as a child — ? They called you evil if you spoke the plain truth. "You're so evil-minded," they always said to me when I told them that something ugly was ugly. So I learned to hold my tongue. Then they began to tell me what a pleasant disposition I had. So then I learned to say things I didn't mean at all. And then I was ready to make my debut.

THE SON: It's best to overlook your neighbor's faults and weaknesses, no doubt of that. But the first thing you know you're flattering and fawning and playing up to people. It's hard to know what to do. But sometimes it's your duty to speak out.

THE DAUGHTER: No, please!

THE SON: All right. I'll be quiet.

Pause.

THE DAUGHTER: No, I'd rather have you talking. But not about what you're thinking! I can hear your thoughts in the silence. When people get together they talk, talk, talk, all the

time, just to hide their thoughts. To forget, to benumb themselves. They want to hear all the latest, of course, about the
others. But their own affairs they keep concealed.

THE SON: Poor little Gerda!

THE DAUGHTER: Do you know what hurts more than anything in the world? (*Pause.*) To find that everything you've
dreamed of really amounts to nothing.

THE SON: That's the truth.

THE DAUGHTER: I'm freezing. Can't we have a little fire?

THE SON: Are you cold, too?

THE DAUGHTER: I've always been cold and hungry.

THE SON: You too! What a strange house! But if I went out and
got some wood, what a scene there would be! She wouldn't get
over it for a week.

THE DAUGHTER: Maybe a fire has already been laid. Mama
sometimes used to lay a fire just to make fools of us.

THE SON (*goes over to the tile stove and opens it*): Well! There
actually are a few sticks laid here. (*Pause.*) What on earth is this?
A letter, all torn up. Good for starting the fire —

THE DAUGHTER: Frederick, don't light the fire. It would
only start a quarrel that would go on forever. Come and sit down,
and let's talk some more. Please!

> *The Son crosses over and sits down, putting the torn
> letter on the table next to him. A pause.*

Do you know why Father hated my husband as he did?

THE SON: Yes. Your Axel came and took away his daughter and
his wife and left him sitting all alone. And then the old man
noticed that the rest of you were eating better food than he was.
You shut yourselves up in the parlor, played music, read
books — and always the kind that he didn't like. He was shut out
and eaten out of his own home. And so finally he took to hanging
around the bars.

THE DAUGHTER: We didn't know what we were doing.
. . . Poor Father! It's good to have parents whom everybody
respects, with reputations above reproach. I guess we have a lot
to be thankful for. . . . Do you remember their silver wedding
anniversary? And the wonderful speeches everybody made?

THE SON: I remember. And I thought what a cheap sideshow
it was, with everybody celebrating the happy couple who had
lived together like cat and dog.

THE DAUGHTER: Frederick!

THE SON: I can't help it. You know as well as I how they lived.
Don't you remember the time Mama wanted to jump out the
window and we had to hold her back?

THE DAUGHTER: Please, Frederick!

THE SON: I'm sure there were reasons that we don't know
about. . . . And when they were separated and I had to watch
over the old man, he seemed to want to say something, many
times, but the words never got past his lips. . . . I still dream
of him sometimes . . .

THE DAUGHTER: I do too. And when I see him in my
dreams, he's thirty years old. He looks at me in a friendly way,
hinting at something. I don't know quite what. Sometimes Mama
is along. But he's not angry with her. Because he always held her
dear. Even up to the last, in spite of everything. You remember
how beautifully he spoke to her on their silver anniversary,
thanking her *in spite of everything.*

THE SON: In spite of everything! That's saying a lot, and yet
not enough.

THE DAUGHTER: But it was beautiful! And she did have
many merits. She was a good housekeeper.

THE SON: Ah, but was she? That's the question!

THE DAUGHTER: What do you mean?

THE SON: Now look how they stick together! Just so much as
mention housekeeping and you're on the same team. What is it?
A secret lodge, the Mafia? Even if I ask my dear old friend

Margaret anything about the household finances – if I ask her for instance why you can never get a full meal here, then she, who is always willing to talk your ears off, she shuts up! Shuts up and gets mad! Can you explain that?

THE DAUGHTER (*curtly*): No.

THE SON: It isn't hard to see that you belong to the secret lodge too!

THE DAUGHTER: What on earth do you mean? I don't understand.

THE SON: Sometimes I believe that Father must have fallen a victim to the Mafia, which he probably uncovered.

THE DAUGHTER: Sometimes you talk just like an idiot.

THE SON: I remember Father sometimes used to mention the Mafia as a joke, but toward the end he kept silent.

THE DAUGHTER: It's awful how cold it is here, cold as a tomb.

THE SON: Then let's light the fire, whatever the consequences. (*He picks up the torn letter, absentmindedly. Something catches his eye and he begins to read.*) What is this? (*Pause.*) "To my son!" In Father's handwriting! (*Pause.*) It's to me! (*He reads. He half falls into a chair and continues reading to himself.*)

THE DAUGHTER: What are you reading? What is it?

THE SON: It's awful! (*Pause.*) I can't believe it!

THE DAUGHTER: Tell me, what is it?

A pause.

THE SON: No, it's too much. . . . (*To The Daughter.*) It's a letter from my dead father, written to me. (*Reading on.*) Now I'm beginning to wake up.

> *He throws himself on the chaise longue and writhes in agony. Puts the letter in his pocket. The Daughter kneels beside him.*

THE DAUGHTER: What is it, Frederick? Tell me what it is. Frederick, Frederick. Are you ill? Say something, Frederick! Speak to me!

THE SON (*sitting up*): I don't want to live any longer.

THE DAUGHTER: Tell me what it is, Frederick.

THE SON: It's unbelievable. (*He recovers himself and stands up.*)

THE DAUGHTER: Perhaps it's not true.

THE SON (*bristling*): Oh, yes it is! He wouldn't spread lies from his grave.

THE DAUGHTER: He let his imagination get the better of him. He was sick. He didn't know what he was saying.

THE SON: The Mafia! Well, let me tell you! You just listen!

THE DAUGHTER: I think I know it all already. But I won't believe it anyway!

THE SON: I know you don't want to! But here's how it is, all the same. The dear mother who gave us life was nothing but a thief!

THE DAUGHTER: No!

THE SON: She stole from the housekeeping money, she forged bills, she bought the poorest stuff for the highest prices, she had her meals in the kitchen in the morning and let us have what was left over, thinned out and warmed up, she skimmed the cream off the milk—that's why we're poor, miserable children, always sick and hungry. She stole the money for the wood and let us freeze. And when Father found out about her, he warned her, and she promised to be better. But she went right back to her old tricks and even came up with two new ones—Worcestershire sauce and cayenne pepper!

THE DAUGHTER: I don't believe a word of it!

THE SON: The Mafia! —But that isn't the worst, Gerda! Oh, no! That contemptible person who is now your dear husband has never loved you, Gerda. He loves your mother!

THE DAUGHTER: No! No!

THE SON: When Father found out, and when your boyfriend borrowed money from your mother – our mother – he tried to pull a fast one by proposing marriage to you! That's the general idea, you can fill in the details for yourself.

The Daughter cries into her handkerchief.

THE DAUGHTER: I knew this all along – but I didn't want to. I closed my mind to it because it was too awful.

THE SON: What are you going to do now to salvage what's left of your pride?

THE DAUGHTER: Go away.

THE SON: Where?

THE DAUGHTER: I don't know.

THE SON: So you'll stay and see how things develop.

THE DAUGHTER: You can't raise your hand against your own mother. She's like something sacred.

THE SON: Like hell she is!

THE DAUGHTER: Don't talk like that!

THE SON: She's as sly as a fox, but so much in love with herself she can't see farther than her nose.

THE DAUGHTER: Let's run away.

THE SON: Where to? No, we'll stay right here until her darling boy drives her out of the house. – Shh! I think lover-boy is coming home. – Listen, Gerda! Now we two are going to form a secret order of our own. I'll give you the word, our password: "He struck you on your wedding night."

THE DAUGHTER: Yes, remind me of that often, Frederick! Otherwise I'll forget. I want so much to forget.

THE SON: It's all over for us Gerda. No one to believe in, nothing to have faith in. . . . Impossible to forget. . . . Let's live to redeem ourselves, and the memory of Father.

THE DAUGHTER: And see justice done!

THE SON: Justice? You mean revenge!

*   *   *

The Son-in-Law enters.

THE DAUGHTER (*feigning*): Why, good evening, Axel! Did you have a good time at your meeting? Did they give you anything good?

THE SON-IN-LAW: It was put off.

THE DAUGHTER: You were put out, did you say?

THE SON-IN-LAW: It was put off, I said!

THE DAUGHTER: Oh. — Tell me, are you going to take care of things around the house tonight?

THE SON-IN-LAW: You're in such a good mood tonight, Gerda. Frederick must be delightful company.

THE DAUGHER: Oh, he is. We've been playing secret societies.

THE SON-IN-LAW: You shouldn't play such games. They're dangerous.

THE SON: Then we can play Mafia instead! Or vendetta!

THE SON-IN-LAW (*uneasily*): What are you talking about? What's been going on here? Are you keeping secrets?

THE DAUGHTER: You're not going to tell us your secrets, are you? Maybe you don't have any secrets?

THE SON-IN-LAW: What happened here tonight? Has someone been here?

THE SON: Gerda and I were holding a séance, and we were visited by a departed spirit.

THE SON-IN-LAW: All right, cut the games! You're too cute, the two of you. — But I must say it is very becoming, Gerda, to see you smiling. You're usually so sullen. (*He starts to pat her cheek, but she pulls away.*) Are you afraid of me?

THE DAUGHTER (*stops acting*): Not at all. I may look afraid, but you're wrong. Some gestures speak more plainly than looks do. And if neither the way I act nor the way I look tell you what I'm really feeling, what I say won't tell you anything either.

> *Astonished, The Son-in-Law fumbles at a bookshelf. The Son rises from the rocking chair, which continues to rock until The Mother enters.*

THE SON: Here comes Mother with her oatmeal.

THE SON-IN-LAW: Is it –?

*   *   *

> *The Mother enters, sees the chair rocking, starts back in fear, but controls herself.*

THE MOTHER: I've made something for supper. Anyone interested?

THE SON-IN-LAW: No thanks. What is it? Oatmeal? Give it to the dogs. Bran meal? Put it on your boils.

THE MOTHER: I can't help it. We have to economize.

THE SON-IN-LAW: Not with twenty thousand a year you don't.

THE SON: You do if you lend it to those who don't pay it back!

THE SON-IN-LAW: What are you talking about? Are you nuts?

THE SON: Maybe I have been.

THE MOTHER: Are you coming or not?

THE DAUGHTER: Come, let's go and eat! Don't look so glum. Come with me and you shall have steaks, sandwiches, whatever your hearts desire.

THE MOTHER: Where will they get them? From you?

THE DAUGHTER: Yes, from me! It's my house!

THE MOTHER: Listen to her! Found your tongue, have you?

THE DAUGHTER (*gesturing toward the door*): Gentlemen, if you please!

THE SON-IN-LAW (*to The Mother*): What the hell's going on?

THE MOTHER: I think I smell a rat!

THE SON-IN-LAW: I think you're right!

THE DAUGHTER: Come, gentlemen!

They all start to leave.

THE MOTHER (*to The Son-in-Law*): Didn't you see the chair rocking? *His* chair rocking?

THE SON-IN-LAW: No, I didn't. I saw something else!

[3]

Same set. A waltz, "Il me disait" by Ferrari, is being played on the piano offstage. The Daughter is sitting, reading a book.

THE MOTHER (*coming in*): Do you recognize it?

THE DAUGHTER: The waltz? Of course.

THE MOTHER: Your wedding waltz. I danced it all night long.

THE DAUGHTER: You? —Where is Axel?

THE MOTHER: How should I know?

THE DAUGHTER: It's like that, is it? Have you quarreled already?

A pause. They exchange glances.

THE MOTHER: What are you reading, my child?

THE DAUGHTER: The cookbook. Can you tell me why it doesn't say how long you're supposed to cook anything?

THE MOTHER (*evasively*): It varies so much, you see. It's a matter of taste. Some like it one way, some another.

THE DAUGHTER: I don't understand that. Food should be served freshly cooked; otherwise it's only warmed-up food, which means spoiled. Yesterday, for example, you roasted a small game bird for three hours. The first hour the whole apartment was filled with a wonderful gamey smell. Then it became quiet in the kitchen. And when the food was finally served all the aroma was gone and it tasted like air. How do you explain that?

THE MOTHER (*embarrassed*): I don't understand at all.

THE DAUGHTER: Then tell me what happened to the sauce and the gravy. Where did that disappear to? Who ate that up?

THE MOTHER: I have no idea what you're talking about.

THE DAUGHTER: I've been asking myself some questions lately, and now I know a lot about a great many things.

THE MOTHER (*turning on her sharply*): I know you do. But you can't teach me anything I don't already know. I could show you a thing or two about housekeeping—

THE DAUGHTER: Like using Worcestershire sauce and cayenne pepper? —I know that one already. And preparing for friends dishes you know they don't like so there will be plenty left over for the next day. And inviting people in when you see the pantry is filled with leftovers—oh, I know all those tricks, so from now on I'm going to be in charge here!

THE MOTHER (*furious*): You mean I'm going to be your maid?

THE DAUGHTER: I, yours; and you, mine. We'll help each other. —Here comes Axel.

* * *

THE SON-IN-LAW (*enters with a heavy cane in his hand*): Well, how do you like the chaise longue?

THE MOTHER: All right, I guess.

THE SON-IN-LAW (*threateningly*): You mean you don't like it? What's the matter with it?

THE MOTHER: I think I understand.

THE SON-IN-LAW: Good for you! And while I think of it,

since Gerda and I never get enough to eat in this house, we intend to eat by ourselves from now on.

THE MOTHER: And what about me?

THE SON-IN-LAW: Why, you're as big as a barrel. You don't need much. In fact, you should reduce a little bit for your health's sake, as we've had to do. —And listen, while I'm thinking of it, you go out for a moment, Gerda; and in the meantime, Mother can start a big warm fire in the stove for us.

THE MOTHER (*trembling with rage*): There's wood there—

THE SON-IN-LAW: Oh, but just a few sticks. Now I want you to go out and get some more. Fill up the whole stove.

THE MOTHER (*hesitating*): Do you want to burn up money?

THE SON-IN-LAW: No, but wood doesn't do us any good unless we do burn it, now does it? Get going! March!

The Mother hesitates.

One. Two . . . three! (*Strikes the table with his cane.*)

THE MOTHER: I don't think there's any wood left.

THE SON-IN-LAW: Either you're lying or you've stolen the money. A whole cord was ordered the day before yesterday!

THE MOTHER: Now I see what you're really like.

THE SON-IN-LAW (*sitting in the rocking chair*): You would have seen that long ago, if your age and experience hadn't taken advantage of my youth and innocence. Snap to it! The wood—or—else—(*Raises his cane.*)

The Mother goes out. Returns shortly with the wood.

Now let's have a real fire. Nothing halfway. One, two, three!

THE MOTHER: How much you're like the old man now, sitting in his rocking chair!

THE SON-IN-LAW: Light it!

THE MOTHER (*controlling her rage*): I will, I will.

THE SON-IN-LAW: Now you stay here and keep your eye on the fire, while we go into the dining room and eat.

THE MOTHER: And what am I supposed to eat?

THE SON-IN-LAW: The oatmeal Gerda put out for you in the kitchen.

THE MOTHER: With blue skim milk?

THE SON-IN-LAW: Why not? You devoured all the cream. It's only fitting. And just!

THE MOTHER (*hollowly, dully*): I'm leaving here. I'm getting out.

THE SON-IN-LAW: You can't. I'll lock you in.

THE MOTHER (*whispering*): Then I'll throw myself out the window!

THE SON-IN-LAW: As you wish! You should have done that long ago. You would have spared the lives of four people. —Now light it. Blow on it! That's better. Now you sit right there until we come back.

> *He leaves.*

* * *

> *A pause. The Mother stops the chair from rocking; listens at the door; and then she takes some of the wood from the stove and hides it under the chaise longue. The Son enters, somewhat drunk. The Mother is startled.*

THE MOTHER: Is it you?

THE SON (*sitting in the rocking chair*): Yes, just me.

THE MOTHER: How do you feel?

THE SON: Terrible. I won't last much longer.

THE MOTHER: That's just your imagination. —Don't rock like that! —Look at me, I've reached a certain —well, respectable age—although I've worked and slaved and done my duty to my children and my home. Now haven't I?

THE SON: Ha! Like the pelican, which does not give its heart's blood. The zoology books say it's all a lie.

THE MOTHER: If you've anything to complain about, out with it!

THE SON: Listen, Mother, if I were sober, I couldn't answer you honestly because I wouldn't have the nerve. But now I'm going to tell you that I have read Father's letter, the one you stole and threw into the stove.

THE MOTHER: Letter? What do you mean, what letter?

THE SON: Always lying! I remember when you first taught me how to lie. I was hardly old enough to talk. Remember?

THE MOTHER: No, I don't remember anything of the kind! —Stop rocking!

THE SON: Not remember the first time you told lies about me? When I was little? I had hidden myself under the piano, when one of my aunts came to call on you. You sat and lied to her for three hours straight, and I had to listen to it all.

THE MOTHER: That's a lie!

THE SON: Do you want to know why I'm so utterly worthless? Because I was never breast-fed. All I got was a nursemaid with a glass bottle. And when I was a little older, she took me along with her to her sister, who was a prostitute. And there I got to see all the most secret, most intimate scenes, the kind that children are ordinarily treated to only by dog owners on the street in the spring and fall. When I told you about it—I was only four years old—when I told you what I had seen in that house of sin, you said it was a lie, and you struck me for lying, but I was telling the truth. This encouraged the nursemaid—she thought you approved—so she initiated me—at the age of five—into all the secrets. Five years old. (*He starts to cry.*) And then I began to get cold and hungry, like Father and the rest of us. I never knew until today that you stole the housekeeping money and the wood money. —Look at me, pelican. Look at Gerda, with her flat chest.

How you murdered my father you know as well as I do – how you dragged him down to the depths of despair, a crime that isn't punishable by law. And how you murdered my sister you know better than anyone. But now she knows it too!

THE MOTHER: Stop rocking, will you! – What does she know?

THE SON: What you know and what I can't bring myself to say. (*Sobbing.*) It's terrible that I've said what I have. But I had to. When I sober up, I'll kill myself. I can feel it. That's why I keep on drinking. I don't dare sober up.

THE MOTHER: Tell me some more lies.

THE SON: Father once said in anger that you were the greatest fraud ever perpetrated by nature. He said that you didn't learn to talk like other children; you learned to lie from the first word. He said that you always shirked your duties. Parties came first: I remember when Gerda was virtually dying, you went off that evening to see an operetta. I remember your very words: "Life is sad enough without making it any sadder." And that summer, for three whole months, when you were in Paris with Father, going to parties while the family was going into debt, Gerda and I had to live shut up with two maids in this apartment. And in our parents' bedroom a fireman made himself at home with the housemaid, and the marriage bed rocked to their lovemaking.

THE MOTHER: Why haven't you told me this before?

THE SON: You have forgotten that I did tell you, just as you have forgotten that I was whipped for tattling – or lying, to use your other word for it. As soon as you heard an honest word, you called it a lie.

THE MOTHER (*paces the room like a caged tiger*): I've never heard a son say such things to his own mother!

THE SON: Yes, isn't it strange? Entirely contrary to nature. Don't tell me. But it had to come out sometime. You went about as if you were asleep. And no one could wake you up, so you couldn't change your ways. Father said that even if they stretched you on the rack, no one could make you admit a simple fault or confess you ever told a lie.

THE MOTHER: Father! Father! Do you think he was so perfect?

THE SON: He had great failings, but not in his relations with his wife and children. —And there are other secrets in your marriage that I have guessed, suspected, but never wanted to admit even to myself. Secrets that Father took with him to his grave—partly!

THE MOTHER: Have you said all you're going to say?

THE SON: Yes. I'm going out for a drink. . . . I could never pass my exams. I could never be a lawyer. I don't believe in the legal system. The laws must have been passed by thieves and murderers for the benefit of criminals. One truthful witness proves nothing, but two false witnesses is proof positive. At noon I've got a clear-cut case; at twelve-thirty I've lost it. One slip of the pen, one missing marginal comment, can put a blameless man behind bars. If I take pity on some scamp, he sues *me* for defamation of character. I tell you my contempt for life, humanity, society, and myself is so boundless, I wouldn't raise my little finger to go on living. (*Goes toward the door.*)

THE MOTHER: Don't go!

THE SON: Afraid of the dark?

THE MOTHER: I'm a little nervous.

THE SON: That follows.

THE MOTHER: That chair drives me insane. It always sounded like two knives being whetted when he rocked in it . . . and hacked at my heart.

THE SON: Don't tell me you have one!

THE MOTHER: Don't go! I can't stay here. Axel is so cruel!

THE SON: I thought so too until recently. Now I believe he's only the victim of your vicious tendencies—the young man who was seduced.

THE MOTHER: You must keep very bad company!

THE SON: Bad company? What other kind have I ever kept!

THE MOTHER: Please don't go!

THE SON: What good can I do here? I would only torture you to death with my talk.

THE MOTHER: Please don't go!

THE SON: Are you waking up?

THE MOTHER: Yes, I'm waking up. As if out of a deep, deep sleep. It's terrifying! Why couldn't someone wake me before?

THE SON: Since no one could, I guess it was impossible. And if it was impossible, then you weren't responsible.

THE MOTHER: Yes, that's true! That's true!

THE SON: I suppose it couldn't possibly be any other way.

THE MOTHER (*kissing his hand servilely*): Yes, yes. Tell me more!

THE SON: I can't, I can't. —Yes, one thing more: I beg you, don't stay here. You would only make the bad worse.

THE MOTHER: You are right. I shall go—away from here!

THE SON: Poor Mother!

THE MOTHER: Do you take pity on me?

THE SON (*crying*): Yes, of course I do! How many times haven't I said of you, "Her heart is so black, I feel sorry for her!"

THE MOTHER: Thank you, Frederick, thank you. —Go now.

THE SON: It's hopeless, isn't it?

THE MOTHER: Yes, there's no hope at all.

THE SON: That's right. . . . No hope at all! (*He leaves.*)

* * *

A pause. The Mother alone. Stands with her arms crossed over her bosom a long time. Then she goes to the window, opens it, and looks down. Moves back into the room and prepares to leap out the window. But changes her mind when she hears three knocks on the door at the rear.

THE MOTHER: Who is it? What was that? (*She closes the window.*) Come in.

> *The rear door opens.*

Is someone there?

> *The Son can be heard bawling within the apartment.*

It's him — in the garden! Isn't he dead? What shall I do? Where can I go?

> *She hides behind the secretary. The wind begins to blow as before; the papers fly around.*

Close the window, Frederick!

> *A flowerpot is blown down.*

Close the window! I'm freezing to death and the fire is dying in the stove!

> *She lights all the electric lights and closes the door, which is immediately blown open again. The chair rocks in the wind. She goes around and around the room, finally throwing herself headlong on the chaise longue, burying her face in the pillows.*
>
> * * *
>
> "Il me disait" *is played within. The Mother lies as before on the chaise longue, her face hidden. The Daughter enters, with the oatmeal on a tray. She sets it down. She turns off all the electric lights except one.*

THE MOTHER (*awakens and sits up*): Don't turn off the lights!

THE DAUGHTER: We have to economize.

THE MOTHER: You came back soon.

THE DAUGHTER: Yes, he didn't think it very amusing when you weren't around.

THE MOTHER: Well, thank you!

THE DAUGHTER: Here's your supper.

THE MOTHER: I'm not hungry.

THE DAUGHTER: Oh, but you are hungry, you just won't eat oatmeal.

THE MOTHER: Yes, I do—sometimes.

THE DAUGHTER: No, never! But I don't care about that. This is for every time you smirked and smiled as you tortured us with your oatmeal. You reveled in our suffering. You cooked the same slop for the dogs in the backyard.

THE MOTHER: I can't eat blue milk. It gives me chills.

THE DAUGHTER: You always skimmed the cream for your morning coffee! Now help yourself! (*She serves the oatmeal on a small table.*) Eat! I want to watch you!

THE MOTHER: I cannot!

THE DAUGHTER (*bends down and takes some of the wood from under the chaise longue*): If you don't eat, I'll show Axel you've been stealing wood.

THE MOTHER: Axel loves my company—he won't hurt me. Do you remember how he danced with me? *"Il me disait!"* There it is! (*She hums the second refrain, which is now being played.*)

THE DAUGHTER: How can you have the nerve to remind me of that outrage!

THE MOTHER: He sent me a bouquet of flowers, with a card.

THE DAUGHTER: That's enough!

THE MOTHER: Shall I tell you what the card said? I know it by heart. . . . "In Ginnistan. Ginnistan is the Persian Garden of Paradise, where the fairest peris live on fragrances. And peris are genii or spirits, so created that the longer they live, the younger they grow . . . "

THE DAUGHTER: Oh, my God, do you think you're a peri?!

THE MOTHER: Yes. He said I was. And your Uncle Victor has proposed to me. What would you say if I got married again?

THE DAUGHTER: Poor Mother! You're still asleep, as we all were. But will you never wake up? Don't you see how everybody laughs at you? Don't you understand it when Axel insults you?

THE MOTHER: Insults me? I have always found him to be more polite to me than to you.

THE DAUGHTER: Even when he raised his cane against you?

THE MOTHER: Against me? That was against you, my dear child!

THE DAUGHTER: Mama, Mama, have you gone out of your mind?

THE MOTHER: He missed me this evening. We have so much to talk about. He's the only one who understands me. And you're only a child, after all . . .

THE DAUGHTER (*taking The Mother by the shoulders and shaking her*): For God's sake, wake up!

THE MOTHER: You're not full-grown yet, not mature. But I'm your mother, I've nourished you with my life's blood.

THE DAUGHTER: No, you gave me a bottle and stuck a rubber in my mouth. I had to go to the cupboard and steal. But there was nothing there except stale rye bread, which I ate with mustard. And when that burned my throat, I cooled it with vinegar. The vinegar bottle and the bread box—that was the pantry for me!

THE MOTHER: You see! Even as a child you were stealing! Oh, how nice! And you're not even ashamed to tell me about it! What kind of children have I sacrificed myself for?

THE DAUGHTER (*crying*): I could forgive you for everything but not for taking my life from me, never. Yes, he was my life, because with him I first began to live.

THE MOTHER: Can I help it if he preferred me? He probably found me—how shall I say?—more amiable. He had much better taste than your father, who didn't appreciate me until he had rivals, and then—

There are three knocks on the door.

Who is that knocking?

THE DAUGHTER: Don't you dare say anything unkind about Father! I don't think my life will be long enough for me to make up for what I did to him. But you shall have to pay for it—for setting me up against him. Do you remember when I was still a very small child how you taught me to say ugly, insinuating things to him that I didn't understand? He had sense enough not to punish me for rubbing salt into his wounds because he knew who had put him up to it. Do you remember how you taught me to lie to him? I would tell him I needed money for schoolbooks, and when we had wormed the money out of him, we split it. How can I ever forget all the lies in the past? Isn't there some drug that wipes out memories without snuffing out life? If only I had the strength to escape. But I'm like Frederick. We're weak, helpless sacrifices—your sacrifices. You with your heart of stone, you couldn't suffer for your own sins!

THE MOTHER: And what do you suppose my childhood was like? Have you any idea what an ugly home I had, what evil things I learned there? It's all inherited—. From whom? From generation to generation. From the first parents, it says in children's books, and that seems to make sense. So don't blame me, and I won't blame my parents, who won't blame theirs, and so on and on. Besides, it's just as horrible in all families, except that outsiders don't get to see it.

THE DAUGHTER: If that's true, I don't care to live. And if I'm forced to, I'd prefer to walk deaf and blind through this miserable existence, hoping for a better life to come . . .

THE MOTHER: You're too sensitive, too delicate, my dear child. When you have a baby, there will be other things to think about.

THE DAUGHTER: I'll never have any children.

THE MOTHER: How do you know?

THE DAUGHTER: The doctor has told me.

THE MOTHER: He's mistaken.

THE DAUGHTER: There you go making up lies again! —I'm sterile, stunted. Don't you understand? I, like Frederick! —I don't want to go on living.

THE MOTHER: Oh, how you talk!

THE DAUGHTER: If I could only do the cruel things I want to do, you—you wouldn't exist anymore! Why should it be so difficult to be cruel? When I lift my hand against you, I only hurt myself!

> *The music stops suddenly. The Son is heard bawling within.*

THE MOTHER: He's been drinking again!

THE DAUGHTER: What else can he do? Poor Frederick!

*   *   *

THE SON (*enters, noticeably drunker*): There's . . . smoke . . . I think . . . coming from—the kitchen . . .

THE MOTHER: What? . . . Smoke?

THE SON: I—think—I think there's—a fire!

THE MOTHER: A fire? What are you saying?

THE SON: I—I think—I think it's all on fire! The whole house!

THE MOTHER (*rushes to the rear of the stage and opens the door. The bright red glow of fire confronts her*): Fire! —How can we get out?! —I don't want to burn! —I don't want to burn! (*She rushes around in distraction.*)

THE DAUGHTER (*taking her brother in her arms*): Frederick! Run, the fire is on top of us! Run!

THE SON: I haven't the strength.

THE DAUGHTER: Escape, Frederick! You must!

THE SON: Where to? . . . No, I don't care to.

THE MOTHER: I'd rather go through the window! (*She opens the balcony door and throws herself out.*)

THE DAUGHTER: Oh, God in heaven, help us!

THE SON: It was the only way!

THE DAUGHTER: You did this!

THE SON: Yes, what could I do? – There was no other way. – Was there any other? Was there?

THE DAUGHTER: No. Everything had to burn up, otherwise we could never get out of here. Hold me in your arms, Frederick, hold me tight, dear brother! I'm happier than I've ever been before. It's getting light, poor Mama, who was so mean, so mean . . .

THE SON: Dear sister, poor Mama, do you feel how warm it is, how wonderful, I'm no longer cold, listen to it crackling out there, everything old is burning up, everything old and mean and evil and ugly . . .

THE DAUGHTER: Hold me close, dear brother, we're going to be burned, we'll smother in smoke, doesn't it smell good? That's the palm plants burning and Papa's laurel wreath from the university – now the linen closet is burning, smell the lavender, and now, now the roses! Dear little brother! Don't be afraid, it's soon over, dearest, dearest, don't fall, poor Mama! who was so mean! Hold me tighter, squeeze me, as Papa used to say! It's like Christmas, when we got to eat in the kitchen, dipping into all the pots, the only day we got to eat our fill, as Papa used to say. Smell, oh, smell, it's perfume, it's the cupboard burning, with the tea and the coffee, and all the spices, and the cinnamon, and the cloves . . .

THE SON (*in ecstasy*): Is it summer? The clover's in bloom, summer vacation is beginning. Remember when we ran down to the steamboats and clapped their sides, fresh with paint and waiting for us, how happy Papa was then, this is really living, he said, and we threw away our schoolbooks! This is how it should always be, he said. It was he who was the pelican, he picked himself clean for us, he always had baggy pants and dirty collars, while we went around like little aristocrats. . . . Gerda, hurry up! Come on, will you, the boat bells are ringing, and Mama's sitting in the salon, no she's not here, poor Mama! She's not with us, did we leave her on the shore? Where is she? I don't see her anywhere. It's no fun without Mama. There she comes! —Now it's summer again!

> *A pause. The door at the rear opens. The glow is a strong, vivid red. The Son and The Daughter sink to the floor.*

CURTAIN

Strindberg's Plays

Strindberg's Plays

Fritänkaren (The Freethinker), 1869*
Hermione, 1869–70
I Rom (In Rome), 1870
Den fredlöse (The Outlaw), 1871
Mäster Olof (Master Olof), prose version, summer 1872
Mäster Olof, in verse, 1875–76. Epilogue probably written
   1877
Anno fyrtioåtta (1848), 1876–77
Gillets hemlighet (The Secret of the Guild), 1879–80
Lycko-Pers resa (The Travels of Lucky Peter), 1882
Herr Bengts hustru (Sir Bengt's Wife), summer 1882
Marodörer (Marauders), 1886. Revised in collaboration with
   Axel Lundegård as *Kamraterna (Comrades)*, 1887
Fadren (The Father), January–February 1887
Fröken Julie (Miss Julie), summer 1888
Fordringsägare (Creditors), summer 1888
Den starkare (The Stronger), December 1888–January 1889
Paria (Pariah), January 1889
Hemsöborna (The People of Hemsö), January–February 1889.
   Adapted by Strindberg from his novel of the same name.
Samum (Simoom), February–March 1889
Himmelrikets nycklar (Keys to the Kingdom of Heaven), autumn
   1891–February 1892
Första varningen (The First Warning), February–March 1892
Debet och kredit (Debit and Credit), February–March 1892
Inför döden (Facing Death), March–April 1892
Moderskärlek (A Mother's Love), April–May 1892
Leka med elden (Playing with Fire), August–September, 1892
Bandet (The Bond), August–September 1892
Till Damaskus, Part I *(To Damascus)*, January–March 1898
Till Damaskus, Part II, summer 1898
Advent, November–December 1898
Brott och brott (Crimes and Crimes), January–February 1899

*Dates correspond to year of composition.

Folkungasagan (Saga of the Folkungs), January–April 1899
Gustav Vasa, April–June 1899
Erik XIV, summer 1899
Gustav Adolf, September 1899–March 1900
Midsommar (Midsummer), summer 1900
Kaspers fet-tisdag (Punch's Shrove Tuesday), September 1900
Påsk (Easter), autumn 1900
Dödsdansen, Part I *(The Dance of Death)*, October 1900
Dödsdansen, Part II, December 1900
Kronbruden (The Bridal Crown), August 1900–January 1901
Svanevit (Swanwhite), February–March 1901
Karl XII (Charles XII), spring 1901
Till Damaskus, Part III, February–September 1901
Engelbrekt, August–September 1901
Kristina (Queen Christina), September 1901
Ett drömspel (A Dream Play), September–November 1901
Gustav III, February–March 1902
Holländarn (The Flying Dutchman), not completed, July 1902
Näktergalen i Wittenberg (The Nightingale in Wittenberg),
  August–September 1903
*Genom öknar till arvland, eller Moses (Through the Wilderness
  to the Land of Their Fathers, or Moses)*, September 1903
Hellas, eller Sokrates (Hellas, or Socrates), October 1903
*Lammet och vilddjuret, eller Kristus (The Lion and the Lamb,
  or Christ)*, October–November 1903
Oväder (Storm Weather), January–February 1907
Brända tomten (The Burned House), February 1907
Spöksonaten (The Ghost Sonata), February–March 1907
Toten-Insel (The Isle of the Dead), a fragment, April 1907
Pelikanen (The Pelican), May–June 1907
Siste riddaren (The Last Knight), August 1908
Abu Cassems tofflor (Abu Cassem's Slippers), August–September
  1908
Riksföreståndaren (The Regent), September 1908
Bjälbo-Jarlen (The Earl of Bjälbo), autumn 1908
Svarta handsken (The Black Glove), November–December 1908
Stora landsvägen (The Highway), spring 1909

Selected Readings

Selected Readings

SURVEYS OF THE LIFE AND WORKS

Campbell, G. A. *Strindberg*. London, 1933.

Gustafson, Alrik. *A History of Swedish Literature*. Minneapolis, 1961.

Johnson, Walter. *August Strindberg*. Boston, 1978.

Lagercrantz, Olof. *August Strindberg*. Translated by Anselm Hollo. New York, 1984.

Lamm, Martin. *August Strindberg*. Translated and edited by Harry G. Carlson. New York, 1971.

Lind-af-Hageby, L. *August Strindberg*. London, n.d.

McGill, V. J. *August Strindberg, the Bedeviled Viking*. New York, 1930.

Meyer, Michael. *Strindberg*. New York, 1985.

Mortensen, Brita M. E. and Downs, Brian W. *Strindberg: An Introduction*. Cambridge, 1949.

Ollén, Gunnar. *August Strindberg*. Translated by Peter Tirner. New York, 1972.

Sprigge, Elizabeth. *The Strange Life of August Strindberg*. New York, 1949.

Steene, Birgitta. *August Strindberg: An Introduction to His Major Works*. Atlantic Highlands, N.J., 1982. (A revised edition of *The Greatest Fire: A Study of August Strindberg*. Carbondale, 1973.)

Uddgren, Gustaf. *Strindberg the Man*. Translated by Axel Johan Uppvall. Boston, 1920.

ON STRINDBERG'S DRAMATIC WORKS

Bentley, Eric. *The Playwright as Thinker*. New York, 1946. Paperback edition, revised: New York, 1955.

Blackwell, Marilyn Johns, editor. *Structures of Influence: A Comparative Approach to August Strindberg*. Chapel Hill, 1981.

Brustein, Robert. *The Theatre of Revolt*. Boston, 1964.

Carlson, Harry G. *Strindberg and the Poetry of Myth*. Berkeley, 1982.

Huneker, James. *Iconoclasts: A Book of Dramatists*. New York, 1905.

Reinert, Otto, editor. *Strindberg: A Collection of Critical Essays*. Englewood Cliffs, N.J., 1971.

Smedmark, Carl Reinhold, editor. *Essays on Strindberg*. Stockholm, 1966.

Sprinchorn, Evert. *Strindberg as Dramatist*. New Haven, 1982.

Törnqvist, Egil. *Strindbergian Drama*. Atlantic Highlands, N.J., 1982.

Valency, Maurice. *The Flower and the Castle*. New York, 1963.

Ward, John. *The Social and Religious Plays of Strindberg*. London, 1980.

Williams, Raymond. *The Drama from Ibsen to Eliot*. London, 1953.

SPECIALIZED STUDIES

Andersson, Hans. *Strindberg's Master Olof and Shakespeare*. Uppsala, 1952.

Bergman, G. M. "Strindberg and the Intima Teatern," *Theatre Research/Recherches Théâtrales*, vol. 9, no. 1 (1967), pp. 14–47.

Berman, Greta. "Strindberg: Painter, Critic, Modernist," *Gazette des Beaux-Arts*, vol. 86 (1975), pp. 113–22.

Borland, Harold H. *Nietzsche's Influence on Swedish Literature with Special Reference to Strindberg, Ola Hansson, Heidenstam and Fröding*. Göteborg, 1956.

Brandell, Gunnar. *Strindberg in Inferno*. Translated by Barry Jacobs. Cambridge, Mass., 1974.

Bulman, Joan. *Strindberg and Shakespeare*. London, 1933.

Dahlström, Carl Enoch William Leonard. *Strindberg's Dramatic Expressionism*. Ann Arbor, 1930.

Dittmar, Reidar. *Eros and Psyche: Strindberg and Munch in the 1890s*. Ann Arbor, 1982.

Johannesson, Eric O. *The Novels of August Strindberg*. Berkeley, 1968.

Johnson, Walter. *Strindberg and the Historical Drama*. Seattle, 1963.

Kauffman, George B. "August Strindberg's Chemical and Alchemical Studies," *Journal of Chemical Education*, vol. 60, no. 7 (July 1983), pp. 584–90.

Madsen, Børge Gedsø. *Strindberg's Naturalistic Theatre: Its Relation to French Naturalism*. Seattle, 1962.

Marker, Frederick J. and Marker, Lise-Lone. *The Scandinavian Theatre*. Oxford, 1975.

Meidal, Björn. *Från profet till folktribun. Strindberg och Strindbergsfejden 1910–12*. Stockholm, 1982. (English summary, pp. 390–403). On Strindberg's last years.

Palmblad, Harry V. E. *Strindberg's Conception of History*. New York, 1927.

Sprinchorn, Evert. "Strindberg and the Psychiatrists," *Literature and Psychology*, vol. 14, nos. 3–4 (1964), pp. 128–37. (Comment and reply by Theodore Lidz and Harry Bergholz in the following issue.)

Sprinchorn, Evert. Introduction to Strindberg, *Inferno, Alone, and Other Writings*. New York, 1968.

Stockenström, Göran. *Ismael i öknen. Strindberg som mystiker*. Uppsala, 1972. (English summary pp. 451–82.) On the religious and mystical thought in the post-Inferno works.

Uhl, Frida. *Marriage with Genius*. London, 1937. On Strindberg's second marriage.

FURTHER READING

Bryer, Jackson R. "Strindberg 1951–1962: A Bibliography," *Modern Drama*, vol. 5, no. 3 (December 1962), pp. 269–75.

Gustafson, Alrik. Bibliographical guide in his *History of Swedish Literature*, pp. 601–9.

Lindström, Göran. "Strindberg Studies 1915–1962," *Scandinavica*, vol. 2, no. 1 (May 1963), pp. 27–50.

Steene, Birgitta. "August Strindberg in America, 1963–1979: A Bibliographical Assessment," in *Structures of Influence. A Comparative Approach to August Strindberg*, edited by Marilyn Johns Blackwell, pp. 256–75.

Evert Sprinchorn, professor of drama at Vassar College, is the author of *Strindberg as Dramatist*, editor and co-translator of Strindberg's *Chamber Plays* (revised edition, Minnesota, 1981), and translator of several of the dramatist's autobiographical works. He has also edited Ibsen's letters and Wagner's writings on music and drama.